BODYLINE AUTOPSY

The full story of the most sensational
Test cricket series: AUSTRALIA v ENGLAND 1932-33

DAVID FRITH

AURUM PRESS

First published in Great Britain
2002 by Aurum Press Ltd
25 Bedford Avenue, London WC1B 3AT

First published in Australia 2002 by ABC Books for the
Australian Broadcasting Corporation

First published October 2002

A catalogue record for this book is available from the British Library.

ISBN 1 85410 896 4

3 5 7 9 10 8 6 4
2004 2006 2005 2003

Design Reno Design / Graham Rendoth
Set in 10/15pt Palatino with Eagle Book
Colour separations Colorwize, Adelaide
Printed and bound in Great Britain by MPG Books Ltd, Bodmin, Cornwall

BODYLINE AUTOPSY

OTHER BOOKS BY DAVID FRITH

RUNS IN THE FAMILY [WITH JOHN EDRICH]

'MY DEAR VICTORIOUS STOD': A BIOGRAPHY OF A.E.STODDART

THE ARCHIE JACKSON STORY

THE FAST MEN: A 200-YEAR CAVALCADE OF SPEED BOWLERS

CRICKET GALLERY: 50 PROFILES OF FAMOUS PLAYERS FROM THE CRICKETER [ED.]

GREAT MOMENTS IN CRICKET [AS 'ANDREW THOMAS', WITH NORMAN HARRIS]

AUSTRALIA VERSUS ENGLAND: A PICTORIAL HISTORY OF THE TEST MATCHES SINCE 1877

THE ASHES '77 [WITH GREG CHAPPELL]

THE GOLDEN AGE OF CRICKET 1890–1914

THE ILLUSTRATED HISTORY OF TEST CRICKET [ED. WITH MARTIN TYLER]

THE ASHES '79

THOMMO [WITH JEFF THOMSON]

ROTHMANS PRESENTS 100 YEARS ENGLAND V AUSTRALIA
[ED. WITH DOUG IBBOTSON & RALPH DELLOR]

THE SLOW MEN

CRICKET'S GOLDEN SUMMER: PAINTINGS IN A GARDEN [WITH GERRY WRIGHT]

ENGLAND v AUSTRALIA TEST MATCH RECORDS 1877–1985 [ED.]

PAGEANT OF CRICKET

GUILDFORD JUBILEE 1938–1988

BY HIS OWN HAND

STODDY'S MISSION: THE FIRST GREAT TEST SERIES 1894–95

TEST MATCH YEAR 1996–97 [ED.]

CAUGHT ENGLAND, BOWLED AUSTRALIA [AUTOBIOGRAPHY]

THE TRAILBLAZERS: THE FIRST ENGLISH CRICKET TOUR OF AUSTRALIA 1861–62

SILENCE OF THE HEART: CRICKET SUICIDES

CONTENTS

	Preface	7
1	ORIGINS	18
2	THE TARGET — THE SNIPERS	35
3	SOUTHWARD HO	51
4	THE MAN IN THE HARLEQUIN CAP	67
5	ACROSS THE WIDE BROWN LAND	74
6	THE MAGIC OF McCABE	109
7	DON'S ODD DOUBLE	138
8	ADELAIDE EARTHQUAKE	168
9	CABLES AND LABELS	216
10	SILENT MANOEUVRES	241
11	FROM A HOSPITAL BED	260
12	THE FINAL SHOOT-OUT	304
13	SACKCLOTH AND ASHES	332
14	CONSEQUENCES	378
15	THE CORPSE TWITCHES	398
16	GATHERING OF THE GHOSTS	418
	Endnotes	451
	Acknowledgments	463
	Index	467

PREFACE

The day has come. With the death of Sir Donald Bradman on February 25, 2001 all the 1932–33 Test cricketers and umpires and newspaper-men, and almost all of the spectators too, have now departed this life. No more argument. No more first-person recollections. The chronicle is complete.

Or is it? Indeed, will it ever be?

Even though there have been over 1300 Test matches in the 70 years since "Bodyline", it remains the most dramatic Test series of them all. It incorporated the Wild West shoot-out between the smart young sheriff (Don Bradman from Bowral, New South Wales) and the narrow-eyed gunslinger (Harold Larwood from Nuncargate, Nottinghamshire). In London and in the cash-strapped dominion of Australia it sparked cloak-and-dagger activity in the cloisters of power — governmental as well as cricketing. With the unrepentant and emotionally repressed Douglas Jardine bestriding the tumult, tempers rocketed. Cricket enthusiasts were shaken by what was going on out on the field of play and off it. Relations between England and Australia were severely damaged.

Although repair work was urgently undertaken in the wake of the Bodyline tour, there have been sinister echoes whenever England and Australia have fought over the hallowed little Ashes urn ever since. By its divisive nature, and because of the vast mass of conflicting views and claims springing from it, no other Test series even remotely compares with it. Each of the major players was distinctly either hero or villain. Bodyline polarised two nations, though not quite in total terms, since there are and were Australians who accepted it and Englishmen who deplored it.

By 1982 Bodyline seemed to be receding slowly into history. Then all kinds of 50th anniversary celebrations and commemoratives materialised. Passions were rekindled. Australian republicans pointed afresh at Albion's cricketing perfidy and asked what further proof could possibly be needed that the constitutional break was both desirable and necessary. English cricket-lovers, currently bowing before fast bowling, sought comfort in the long-ago triumph wrought by Harold Larwood and his team-mates under their extraordinary captain. As for Larwood, now 78 years old and happily settled in the land of his old adversaries, a new intake of hate mail came his way.

The 1982 revival of interest has been strongly sustained. To the original batch of contemporary books on Bodyline came important additional volumes, together with a definitive television documentary by the BBC and an entertaining Australian drama-documentary which added to the excitement while being seriously flawed. Since then, the images and texts from the stormy days of 1932–33 have continued to hang over cricket and wider society, sometimes being utilised to further an argument, or to justify strategy, to condemn, to gloat, to berate.

My personal stance is as an Anglo-Australian who cares deeply about these two nations and the bonds between them, and about the cricket relationship in particular. One of the benefits this hybrid condition affords is that one can stand back and consider the foibles of both countries with even-handed amusement.

It is, I plead, both understandable and excusable that my feelings about Bodyline have vacillated over the years. As a London-born boy growing up in Sydney in the 1950s, I was moved to write a fan letter to Harold Larwood. It remained unacknowledged, but years later I was extremely happy to get to know him. Later, the more I read about Bodyline and the harm it did to Anglo-Australian relations the more reservation I felt about the English campaign. Caught up in the Bradman legend, like most people, and later in a personal friendship with him, I saw the broader implications of the desperate attempt to cut him down to size after 1930. "No — the subject won't ever die," he wrote in a 1983 letter to me, "the reason being that publishers and editors (like you) appreciate the news value of the subject. It creates interesting reading matter and the only people who suffer (or should I say the main person who suffers) is me, because I am the focal point. Larwood doesn't suffer because he adopts a pious, innocent stance."

Bodyline bowling was worrying on two levels. Physically, it was aimed at Australian throats. Figuratively, the "mother country" seemed to be hitting below the belt. Two estimable umpires were distressed at some of the things they witnessed from close quarters, but they did not intervene, for the brutal English bowling was not against the Laws of Cricket as they then stood. But it was thought by the majority to be against the spirit of the game. Ethics had been firetorched. (As recently as January 2002, Dave Richardson, the International Cricket Council's newly appointed cricket guardian, reaffirmed that "it's a man's game and I'm all for that, but the players also need to decide for themselves if they want to play it as a gentleman's game", a tenet that stretches back to Regency days.)

I began to dislike D.R. Jardine intensely. The supercilious, aloof, beaky-nosed, tight-mouthed, ruthless, austere, Aus-hating England captain was, I decided, the source of a major stain on the game that I cherished. The image of the haughty "Iron Duke" served my native land poorly in the eyes of my adopted countrymen. So I joined them in their heated disapproval of Jardine, and saw him as even more stigmatic after discovering certain chilling remarks attributed to him.

But over the years I learned of other people's admiration and affection for the man, particularly in his later life, long after he had bitterly turned his back on cricket, his patriotic mission complete. His committee-room collaborators had turned on him, leaving him isolated but impenitent. His better qualities were now more freely displayed. John Arlott told me of his warmth and gentle humour at the dinner table. We were to read of his war service. As a family man in his 40th year, as his daughter recently pointed out, he need not have gone to war. Australian batsmen had similar thoughts in 1932–33!

In a newsreel clip after England's victory in the opening Test of '32–33, Douglas Jardine seems gentle and — laugh not, ye Jardine haters — almost apologetic: "I'm naturally very pleased and proud to have won the first Test match, and I'm naturally particularly proud of my side. But we shall not suffer from over-confidence because we won the first round of what I'm sure will be a magnificent series." In monochrome close-up the thin lips past which the clipped, slightly strangulated upper-class vowels were enunciated were surmounted by eyes that, if not warm, were certainly neither icy nor dismissive.

This was the man who, in a speech made when his team had moved on to New Zealand, was to quote lyrically a definition of cricket as: "That beautiful, beautiful game that is battle and service and sport and art."

As years passed, and the beautiful game underwent more change (and at a more hectic pace than any previous generation had had to endure), I talked with players who took part in the Bodyline series, and came to know well eight of the English team (Sir George "Gubby" Allen, Les Ames, Bill Bowes, Freddie Brown, Harold Larwood, Eddie Paynter, Herbert Sutcliffe, Bob Wyatt), five of the Australians (Sir Donald Bradman, Jack Fingleton, Leo O'Brien, Bert Oldfield, Bill O'Reilly), as well as two of the contemporary journalists (Ray Robinson and Gilbert Mant) and several others, such as R.S. Whitington, who played in the State matches, and Bill Brown, who scored 69 and 25 against the Englishmen for New South Wales but played in no Tests ("A good series to miss," he mused in 2002, by which time he had become Australia's oldest surviving Test cricketer). Treasured friendships they have been. I also had passing acquaintance with nine of the other players (Harry Alexander, Len Darling, Clarrie Grimmett, Alan Kippax, Stan McCabe, Bill Ponsford, Tim Wall, Tommy Mitchell, Bill Voce), and met both umpires, the courteous George Borwick, at the 1977 Centenary Test in Melbourne, and George Hele in 1971. None of them ever forsook the slightest dignity in discussing that red-hot, long-ago Bodyline Test series, though their convictions, one way or the other, remained strong.

In the late 1970s there came upon Test cricket a brand of bowling that put Bodyline into perspective. Compared with what was now being laid before us, the 1932–33 attack began to seem mild by virtue of its restricted and intermittent usage. Four West Indies fast bowlers habitually bowled bouncers all day long, dragging their overs out — usually 10 overs per hour, about half the rate recorded when Larwood and Voce were in action. None of them ever tired and there was never a let-up, for the battery was conveniently rotated all day. Over a 15-year period, around 40 opposing batsmen were taken to hospital casualty wards after blows to ribs, arms, hands (usually in the process of protecting the face) and heads. Since 1978, batsmen's heads have been almost universally sheathed in helmets; but still there have been injuries. Don Bradman again, on helmets: "Much as I hate the sight of them and think they rob a batsman of personality, I would have worn one had they been invented in my day. It is a wonder more people have not been seriously injured — especially in pre-helmet days — and especially in 1932–33. Perhaps a tribute to man's evasiveness."[1]

At Caribbean venues these excesses, permitted by timid umpires, went on unabated year after year, lapped up with delirious joy by the home spectators, who never tired of the day-long diet of vicious bouncers. The bowling tactics were occasionally condemned by writers and commentators, who were often then subjected to sour, muddle-headed and desperate accusations of racism by "academics" and boring, paranoid windbags whose understanding of the game of cricket was impoverished.

There was no inconsistency on my part in a flow of magazine editorials. I had already tut-tutted in print at Dennis Lillee's tasteless statements in his 1974 book *Back to the Mark*, wherein he asserted that he wanted his bouncers to "hit a batsman in the rib-cage" and "I want it to hurt so much that the batsman doesn't want to face me any more." He generously conceded that he didn't want to hit a batsman on the head "because I appreciate what damage that can do". But the effect that all this might have on young, aspiring fast bowlers was worrying.

I have no idea whether he wrote to all writers who hammered Lillee's remarks, but Marylebone Cricket Club (MCC) secretary Jack Bailey dropped me a line of support. By the beard of Grace! The secretary of the same organisation that backed Jardine in his nefarious venture to Australia so long ago commending me for condemning a bloodthirsty fast bowler! And there was more to come, for the near-unknown Jeff Thomson, who joined Australia's fast attack in 1974–75, now put *his* blood-curdling philosophy down on paper in an Australian magazine. The ferocious Lillee–Thomson bombardment was overseen by a captain, Ian Chappell, who happened to be a grandson of one of Bodyline's battered, Victor Richardson. The going-over experienced by the West Indians in Australia in 1975–76 was then trotted out as justification for their adoption of the four-prong smash attack.

West Indies dominated Test cricket for many years, the splendour of their batting overshadowed by the brutality on show while they were in the field. Batsmen certainly hadn't a full Bodyline field to contend with. The massing of fielders on the leg side, close in to catch the desperate parries and in the distance to catch lobbed hooks, has been reduced by legislation. But there were still enough vultures around the bat — themselves protected by helmets, boxes and shinpads — to catch the desperate jabs and fend against the relentless day-long barrage of short balls. It was not as if the West Indian fast bowlers were lacking in skill and control. Quite the opposite, for

Michael Holding, Malcolm Marshall, Andy Roberts, Joel Garner, Courtney Walsh and Curtly Ambrose stand in the fast bowlers' all-time Hall of Fame for their speed and inherent know-how.

It was a lamentable fact that throughout an entire innings front-foot batsmanship was all but impossible against West Indies sides captained by Clive Lloyd and, later, Vivian Richards. Scarcely a ball was pitched further than three-fifths of the way down the track. Spin bowling was apparently obsolete. And so marked had been the change in society's temperament and attitude since Bodyline — on the other side of a terrifying global war in the time-line — that nobody seems to have been inclined to jump over the fence to express personal outrage at what was on show — apart from one cheesed-off young man who did leap the Adelaide Oval pickets one afternoon in 1993 and run out to the middle to express his disapproval and despair at the interminable short stuff sent down by Ambrose, Bishop, Walsh and Kenny Benjamin. Yet back in 1933 a squadron of mounted troopers had come within a shout of being summoned to quell a riot at the normally tranquil Adelaide Oval after Australia's wicketkeeper had been sent reeling after edging a ball from Larwood onto his skull, their captain having been badly hurt two days previously.

In February 1933, at the height of the furore, the magazine *The Australian Cricketer* offered an unwittingly accurate prediction that was so many years later to fit the West Indian terror squad: had Australia retaliated, perhaps forcing England to desist from bowling Bodyline, "the argument would have been postponed until another day, perhaps when a captain would field several really fast bowlers who would bowl nothing else, and, by sheer frightfulness, win matches. Then cricket would become a war, and Marylebone would move in the matter ... The only other alternative is the transformation of the game into a battle of armoured men ... This would mean goodbye to cricket as it has been known to the present generation." It was almost as if the writer had somehow foreseen the Black Bodyline which would blot out its opponents' sun half a century later.

One of Australia's punching-bags in the Bodyline series of 1932–33 was Leo O'Brien, as tough a sportsman as they come, his array of achievements including a spell as a lightweight boxer who won 29 of his 30 fights. Towards the end of his long life he expressed an opinion on the West Indian approach: "Fifty overs against this attack would test the *courage* and *technique* of most teams. I don't think many would like to play a five-day

Test with this attack at your throat every minute. 12th man the ideal job. Just as well there is a limit on the leg side. Wacko."[2] (In an earlier letter, contemplating the general rise in aggression, he said of helmets that "I think you are wise to wear one, as a matter of fact Ned Kelly's armour would be ideal.") When O'Brien, silver hair parted in the middle in the style of the 1930s, unearthed the bat he used in his two Bodyline Tests — he went in ahead of Bradman in the first of them — he was dismayed to find that borers had got into it. He later gave me one of his insubstantial rubber-nippled batting-gloves from that series. Like so many of his team-mates, his only other protection apart from pads and box was a sock or hand-towel stuffed into his leading pocket.

With such fast-bowling riches at their disposal from 1976 to 1991, West Indies, by their peculiar obsession with the short-pitcher, squandered a golden chance of becoming not only the premier cricket team in the world but one to be universally admired and feted by posterity. Even in 1995, Lord Deedes, journalist/editor, former cabinet minister, and cricket-lover, was moved to write, after watching the West Indies fast bowlers in action in the Old Trafford Test that year, that some of the bowling on view had been "far more intimidatory than any of the old bodyline stuff bowled by Larwood and Voce".[3] Bill Deedes, who once graphically described Bodyline as "cricket's Hiroshima", went on to pen a consoling thought: "Our chaps took it on the chin, whereas the Australians [in 1933] screamed 'murder!'" Then a philosophical "Rest in peace, Larwood", for England's Bodyline hero had just died.

Jack Fingleton's view was more authoritative than most, since he had weathered Bodyline from the batting end. In *Batting From Memory*, his final book, he wrote of Colin Croft's indifference after he had struck Geoff Boycott's helmeted head. "I thought the two English umpires were very lax; he should have been warned at least. Also I didn't think much of those of the television commentators who wouldn't speak out and condemn the tactics." (Might this have had something to do with the fact that since the Packer Revolution of the late 1970s there seems to have been a conscious need for cricket on TV to be more "entertaining" in the interest of ratings, and therefore the more physical risk and high drama portrayed the better? The warped drama–documentary series on Bodyline drew very high audience figures. Were the true-life series, by some magic of time distortion, to be played today, the dreaded commercial slots would sell for astronomical rates.)

Fingleton went on to remark: "Richie Benaud got near to it when he said he felt a warning to the bowler was imminent but Jim Laker was the most outspoken when he said near-murder was going on on the field. I didn't pull any punches in the *Sunday Times*. I saw the tactics for what they were, sheer intimidation, and I further offered the opinion that the West Indians, in the field, were the most boring team I had seen, with their super-abundance of fast bowlers who bowled so many bouncers (and therefore unplayable balls), their slow over rates with their incomprehensively long run-ups."

This was indeed England's Bodyline set into accurate perspective by one who was *there*.

Nor was it a case of Test cricket alone being cheapened during the 1980s by the violent tactics. Weeds always spread faster, and throughout first-class cricket the pattern was clear. On June 26, 1985 the *Daily Telegraph* published a letter from a reader in London, a Mr Hastings, who wrote in support of E.W. Swanton's recent questioning of the "complete silence on the matter of the plainly intimidatory bowling of the West Indians". He had been to a Kent v Gloucestershire match at Tunbridge Wells, and had witnessed David Lawrence, Courtney Walsh and Kevin Curran bowling two or three short-pitched balls every over throughout the day. It was not until 6.44 pm that one of the umpires at last issued a reprimand. No spin bowling and hardly any batting strokes were seen all day, and the fielding was largely limited to two men in close waiting to catch rebounds from gloves or face. Batting points then were awarded during the first 100 overs, but this surfeit of bouncers rendered about 40 overs unplayable. "As with the last West Indies series this match became a farce," wrote Mr Hastings, "with all the fine pleasures of our great game banished." He concluded by writing that umpires were mostly incompetent and lacking in courage.

All things pass. Blessed was the day when not only was there a resurgence of spin bowling, inspired primarily by Shane Warne, but the West Indians resorted to more conventional methods, though the transition was enforced by circumstances. The Caribbean supply-line of fast men stuttered and came nearly to a halt, and legislation at last resulted in a worldwide reduction in bouncers, to a chorus of squeals from fast bowlers everywhere, even though almost 200 lifters — still far too many, in my view — may still be bowled in a day's play if so desired. Now bowlers have taken to bleating about the number of no-balls counted against them, as if somebody else is responsible for their plonking their front feet beyond the popping crease.

This longstanding gripe against the sickening hostility that overtook the game can be signed off through someone whose words are immune to cheap charges of racism, the saintly Conrad Hunte, the greatly respected and zealous Christian who made many runs for West Indies in an earlier era. Mike Coward, in his book *Calypso Summer*, wrote of Hunte that "he said publicly [in 1991] that he feared the excesses of competitiveness and professionalism in the modern game had tarnished the good name of West Indies cricket. At the time there was widespread criticism of the mentality and methodology employed by the West Indies to maintain their supremacy in world cricket." And the late, lamented Hunte is quoted: "It does sadden me that some of our top players are beginning to break the spirit of the game. It takes a strong mind and spirit to be able to absorb such high glory that sportsmen and film stars have. There is no point in winning matches and losing the respect of the people."

As the game has become more global and as more money has been showered upon it (mainly from television) so the cricketers of most countries have laid themselves open to Hunte's politely worded charge. It all seems inescapable, given the old truism that cricket inevitably reflects the world outside.

England's 1932–33 strategy also differed in another significant detail. Before the Packer Era it was more than a fast bowler's pride was worth to bowl at the throat of a tailend batsman. The less scrupulous fast bowlers of the modern age, all rationality lost, rather than employing fast, swinging yorkers or skilful changes of pace, have sought primarily to frighten out clueless numbers 9, 10 and 11 batsmen. Great fast men such as Fred Trueman, Brian Statham, Ray Lindwall, Graham McKenzie, and Wes Hall, another exceptional West Indian, or, in the old days of chivalry, the likes of Tom Richardson — who formed, with Bill Lockwood, also of Surrey and England, the first great fast-bowling partnership — would not stoop to this. The headhunters of today have deluded themselves into believing that helmets will always save a batsman from death or serious injury.

A photographic image that would serve as a caution for bowlers everywhere as they pass through the dressing-room door is of fast bowler Peter Lever, down on his knees and sobbing, as Ewen Chatfield, the New Zealander he had just struck on the temple, lay apparently dead in the Auckland Test of 1975.

In recent years, although no Test batsman would mortgage his pride by complaining, there have been thousands more bouncers bowled (early in his fruitful career South Africa's Shaun Pollock was thought to have "crusted" — i.e. struck on the helmet — just on 30 batsmen already, a statistic that shades his hostile Springbok predecessors Peter Heine and Neil Adcock). There has been far more nastiness than in any earlier era, including the summer of Bodyline. Robin Smith, fighting for England in Antigua on a typical day of very speedy bouncing balls, once had to deal with 15 consecutive bouncers coming at his face. The umpire did nothing about it. The batsman, who had managed to get the occasional pull shot away, heroically insisted that it had been exhilarating, as did Mike Atherton after Allan Donald's very personalised assault one evening in 1998 as he stirred the ghosts at Trent Bridge. This much can be said about it at least: it was only an *isolated* burst of dangerous cricket. Smith's disclaimer, by contrast, was not in keeping with his pallor and the haunted look in his eyes which the close-up camera revealed during that disgraceful passage of play. "Well, Judge," was all I could think to say to Smith, the smiling hero, "you're lucky you didn't have to sit there watching it all."

Bodyline, which was employed not on a day-long basis but for an hour or so at a time, continues to fascinate partly because of the *unprecedented* nature of England's tactics and partly because of the world-rocking outcry it triggered. The tactics were surprising to the degree that old Joe Darling, Australia's tough captain in the Trumper era at the start of the 20th century, was so shocked by what he pictured as Jardine's leg-side field setting, as described in the wireless commentary while he sat in an armchair in his Tasmanian home, that he leapt up, exclaiming through his drooping moustache, "My God, they're going to bowl at our batsmen's body!"

He seemed momentarily to have forgotten that his key fast bowler, Ernie Jones, who would have looked at home in any Klondike saloon, used to bounce the tripe out of his opponents, one of whom, Dr W.G. Grace, spluttered a high-pitched protest when one ball sizzled through his beard. "Sorry, Doc. She slipped," was the time-honoured reaction from the bowler. Then came Tibby Cotter, the slinger from Sydney, who could not decide which he liked more: splitting stumps like matchwood or leaving indentations on batsmen's torsos. He was roundly hooted at Trent

Bridge when he sent fusillades of bouncers down at A.C. MacLaren and J.T. Tyldesley in the 1905 Test match. Crucially, of course, there had been no intensity of leg-side fieldsmen to complicate the batsman's difficulties.

It is quite entertaining to reflect on how very slowly the realisation of what England were up to dawned firstly across Australia and then England in 1932–33. This very slowness, of course, was the impediment to swift resolution of the problem. If it had been possible then to beam into living-rooms and committee-rooms around the world instantaneous pictures via satellite television, in full-colour close-up, with frenzied comment from the gaggle of former players in the commentary booth, Bodyline might have lasted no more than a day or two.

But we cannot be certain. *Would* it have ceased? Or had it been sanctioned and directed by a higher authority than the body (Marylebone Cricket Club) which ran English cricket at that time, powerful outsiders who were unaccustomed to backing down but who were collectively blind and perhaps indifferent to the outrage it was to cause?

Here and there a considerable amount of material has appeared in recent years, some of it speculative, some of it enlightening and surprising. Pungent letters have been uncovered. Obscure items from newspapers and unpublished sources have broadened the picture. No other Test cricket series has spawned so many dramatic incidents or produced so many anecdotes, quotes and clichés.

A cartoon was published at the end of the 1932–33 series, showing a coffin behind which walked a weeping Jardine and Larwood. "Alas, poor Yorick!" It represented Bodyline's demise. Bodyline laid to rest? Not a bit of it. The time is ripe for a fresh investigation into the most eventful Test cricket series of them all, for it might just be true, as Nigel Nicolson recently suggested, that "historians, who have access to all the records, know much more about a battle than the participants".[4]

CHAPTER ONE

ORIGINS

"**B**odyline" is a word that D.R. Jardine, its architect, deplored and refused to recognise. He regarded the term as a vulgar and inappropriate Australian invention. To him and to his two principal applicators, Harold Larwood and Bill Voce, it was "leg theory".

Leg theory in the pure sense had been a far from uncommon form of bowling. It was based on a heavy leg-side field setting and was devoid of serious physical threat. Batsmen certainly knew it when a ball from Yorkshire's George Hirst clanged their metal protective box at a brisk pace and crashed into the insubstantial leg-guards of the period; but he was strictly aiming to knock out the leg stump with late inswing or to induce a catch at short leg. So was F.R. Foster, the oddball who captained Warwickshire to their first County Championship title in 1911 and, with the mighty S.F. Barnes, took Australia by storm that winter, rendering raw pink the inside of the left thighs of Victor Trumper and others as he bent the ball sharply in. Trumper was annoyed and complained to Bob Crockett, but apologised and was satisfield when that highly respected umpire assured him that the ball was swinging and Foster was not deliberately trying to hit him. Not one of Foster's 62 tour wickets came through an lbw, though he bowled many of his victims with his sharp, late swing. We are left to guess just how many more batsmen would have fallen to the likes of Foster and Hirst after the 1935 broadening of the lbw law. (Hirst, incidentally, threatened to land one on Foster with his bat if he kept on smacking *him* on the thighs and body.) As Alan Kippax pointed out in his protest book on Bodyline, English batsmen had been "packing-up" (using their pads to anything pitching off the line of the stumps) ever since Arthur Shrewsbury in the 1880s. Shrewsbury had shown Tom Hayward, another maker of huge aggregates, and in the 1920s, batsmen such as J.W. Hearne and Wilfred Rhodes specialised in it. Bowlers became extremely frustrated.

Foster it was whom Jardine consulted about field settings, visiting the eccentric at his flat in London's Belgravia during the summer of 1932 — a year after Foster had been questioned over a bounced cheque he had given to a woman who had been murdered shortly afterwards. (The police were satisfied as to his innocence on the latter count, but this once-brilliant cricketer, whose career was ended by a car accident before his 30th birthday, was to come to grief finally in 1950 when, found guilty of passing dud cheques, he was committed to a hospital for the insane. He died in May 1958, ironically only a few weeks before Jardine.)

FRANK FOSTER, THE ONCE-TALENTED BOWLER WHO UNWITTINGLY HELPED CONSTRUCT BODYLINE.

Foster protested after the tour that he had had no conception of Jardine's sinister intentions, and would have had nothing to do with him had he known. His open apology appeared in *Smith's Weekly*, an Australian periodical, on March 18, 1933 ("Douglas Jardine, I am ashamed of England's win. I will face you on your return with these words on my lips..."). He also cut a gramophone record, expounding his grievance.[1] Through the fuzz inflicted by almost 70 years of survival, a pleasant voice emerges, slightly flat, clipped of phrase, with the faintest touch of Edgbaston about it:

I contend that no fast right-hand bowler, especially Larwood, whose pace off the wicket has been estimated at 90 miles per hour, should ever attempt to bowl leg theory. Again, no left-arm fast bowler should ever bowl to a leg-side field when bowling over the wicket. Both are extremely dangerous because the man wielding the bat has not time, particularly in the case of Larwood, to circumvent the short-pitched ball on a fast wicket. In the case of a fast left-arm bowler bowling over the wicket, it is practically impossible for the bowler to see all three stumps … Would any parent willingly allow their boys to go in to bat against a bodyline bowler bowling at a speed of 90 miles per hour [145 km/h] off the wicket and willingly run the risk of that boy being hit on the head by a hard cricket ball when the blow might either put him into a mental home or kill the boy outright? As an old cricketer of 25 years' standing, it is my firm conviction that Larwood is the fastest bowler either England or Australia have had for the past 30 years … There is a definite danger in bodyline bowling. There is a very great difference between bodyline bowling and leg-theory bowling. To my mind there is only one kind of fast bowling permissible to a leg-side field and that is a left-arm bowler bowling round the wicket. Twenty-two years ago I played Test cricket myself, and some people say that I originated leg-theory bowling in Australia in 1911–12. That may be so or it may not, but I refer my listeners to understand that never once did I bowl over the wicket …when I was termed a fast left-arm bowler. [*He then mentioned having captained Warwickshire from 1911 to 1914 and played in 11 Test matches in nine months.*] To think of this I am very sad.

It surely cannot have taken very long for Foster to explain his 1911–12 field placing to Jardine. With three fielders on the off, there was a deepish mid-on, a long leg, and the rest — George Gunn, Frank Woolley, Bill Hitch, and Wilfred Rhodes — in the "death trap", as Foster termed the short-leg ring. In his autobiography, *Cricketing Memories*, published in 1930, Foster strongly refuted any suggestion that he bowled to hit the batsman. "My objective was always the leg trap." He took 32 wickets in the series, at 21.63 apiece. Barnes, bowling medium-fast spin and swerve, took 34 at 22.88 and England won that 1911–12 rubber 4–1. The captain (although ill-health kept him from the field almost throughout) happened to be Pelham Francis Warner, who was to find himself agonisingly trying to steer Jardine's tour 21 years later as manager. Plum Warner had first led England in Australia in 1903–04, when Hirst had employed a leg-theory field to match his sharp inswing, a method that was comparable to Foster's there eight years later.

Warner now, in Foster's book, testified that Foster was pleasant on tour, loyal, affectionate, generous, kind, and especially nice to children. These fast bowlers are without doubt a deceptive lot, for Foster, in his book, raised the temperature of Anglo-Australian relations by writing that "the Aussie thinks, and informs you, that Australia is God's own country. Let him think so, it will harm no-one."

On the reverse side of the fragile 10-inch (25-cm) record is Harold Larwood's response to the criticism of his type of bowling. He delivered the words in a light Nottinghamshire voice, obviously reading from a script:

I am nervous about making this record. [*It was his first experience and was indeed a rare thing for anybody in those distant days.*] I have never in my life bowled at any batsman. [*He then describes how "my friend Jack Hobbs" had written in condemnation of Larwood's tactics while overlooking the countless times he had beaten the bat only for the batsman to use his pad to save his wicket, as was then permitted under an lbw law that gave immunity to a batsman so long as a ball had pitched outside the line of the stumps.*] Does Jack really think that an action which robs the bowler of a wicket to be fair cricket? I know it is not against the laws of cricket, but neither is my fast leg-theory bowling. [*He — or whoever was his scriptwriter — then accuses batsmen of indulging in "too much paddling and not battling".*] Actually it was pad play that was partly responsible for the leg-side attack. So if the latter's not cricket, those who use their pads too much must shoulder at least some of the blame for it. [*Modestly, if somewhat ill-informedly, he continues.*] I'm afraid my friend Frank Foster flatters me when he estimates that I bowl at 90 miles per hour [145 km/h]. Is it possible for anyone to bowl so fast? [*Today we can answer that with an assured affirmative. As for Larwood's speed, Sandy Bell, in a letter to an admirer in 1982, recalled that Larwood was "electrically timed by Percy Fender and his White City greyhound boffins in 1929" at over 100 mph [160 km/h]. Vic Richardson believed that Larwood was once timed electronically at Aldershot at 92 mph [148 km/h], while George Hele, an umpire in the Bodyline series, said in a 1975 ABC radio interview, "I'm not exaggerating when I say it was 97 miles per hour [156 km/h]!" During the Ashes Test at Headingley in 2001, a ball was timed as leaving Brett Lee's hand 0.48 seconds before it struck Andy Caddick's forearm, while a ball from Jason Gillespie took a bit longer — 0.54 seconds — to reach Mark Ramprakash's wrist. Both Australians were known to be regularly in the 90 mph zone.*] In my opinion the whole matter of danger in fast bowling has been greatly exaggerated. I hope the parents addressed by Mr Foster will let their boys play against as much fast bowling as they can. Believe me that it is not first-class cricket unless you have some really fast bowling in it. [*He concludes by suggesting that some England batsmen were now getting nervous: what would happen if Australia brought two bowlers over in the summer of 1934 who were as fast as or faster than himself? Would the Englishmen refuse to play against them?*] Would that be cricket? No! Cricket is our national game. Let us zealously guard its traditions. [*And he asks for the "struggle that surrounds us at the moment" to be resolved in the interests of a game that should be "the greatest, finest, and more British than ever before".*]

In the 19th century it was not uncommon for a bowler to apologise if he delivered a ball on or outside leg stump, and gentlemen batsmen blushed appropriately should they inadvertently have hit to leg. It had been a strictly off-side game until such bounders as George Parr of Notts and E.M. Grace, eldest of the Gloucestershire brotherhood, began smashing everything to the leg boundary. Cricket reached maturity as a 360-degree game at last when it became acceptable for bowlers to aim wherever they wished and for batsmen to play strokes to all parts, with the late 20th century addition to the textbook of the reverse sweep.

Concentration on and outside the leg stump, with a crowded leg-side field, would never draw crowds, but it brought success to bowlers of the early years of the 20th century, such as Basil Melle, from South Africa, whose inswingers, with three short legs catching, helped Western Province to the Currie Cup in 1908–09 and Oxford University to victory over Cambridge at Lord's in 1913. W.T. Greswell bowled slow-to-medium inswingers to a leg field and reaped hundreds of wickets for school, for county and in matches in Ceylon (now Sri Lanka), where he spent most of his working life (he played for Somerset when home on leave). He unwrapped his teasing dippers in four Gentlemen v Players matches.

Arthur Jaques took 112 Championship wickets (18.26) for Hampshire in the 1914 season, a year before being killed at Loos in the uniform of major in the 12th West Yorkshires in the Great War, when he was 26. A gangling 6 ft 3 in (190 cm), long-nosed amateur cricketer, Jaques bored many a batsman out with inswing and occasional offcut going down the leg side, with almost all the fieldsmen poised in that half of the field, waiting for the imperfect glance or pull. Twice in his best summer he took 14 wickets in a match, against Derbyshire at Basingstoke, and for a mere 54 against Somerset at Bath. Inswing bowling to a field of several short legs was a recurring spectacle around the counties, and had the European bloodbath not interrupted cricket, Jaques's success might have inspired many more imitators.

As it was, Fred Root, most renowned of the leg-theory specialists of the period, who played either side of that war, won three caps for England against Australia in the rainy 1926 season, when he was 36. At Lord's (it was Larwood's maiden Test), operating with five men between fine leg and mid-on, Root took four wickets and was economical, but failed to worry either Warren Bardsley, the 43-year-old left-hander, who carried his bat for 193, or Charlie Macartney, still brilliant at 40, who picked Root off with ease through the leg side during a second-innings century. At Old Trafford, where Hobbs became captain when Arthur Carr went down with tonsillitis, Root's field when bowling to Bill Woodfull and Charlie Macartney was astonishing: three fine legs two yards (metres) apart, square leg three yards away, a silly (short) leg, wide mid-on and deep square leg. Only a mid-off and cover patrolled the off side while Root trotted in and bowled his accurate, negative induckers. He finished with 4 for 84 off 52 overs, of which over half (27) were maidens. It was his last Test.

In his book *A Cricket Pro's Lot*, Root identified his own influence on Larwood in the Tests of 1926. The young Notts miner "bowled like a hero, only to see the batsmen refuse to play at ball after ball pitched just outside the off stump. I have seen him shyly relaxing in a corner of the dressing-room at night, disconsolately wondering why his wholehearted efforts have been rewarded with such figuratively poor analyses in return for magnificent fast bowling ... When Billie Woodfull had been more than usually careful not to play at anything with the slightest suspicion of a slip catch suggested, Bert Strudwick [England's wicketkeeper] said to Larwood, 'Lol, after tea we will go on the middle on our own. It seems a waste of time for the other nine to leave the comfort of the dressing-room!' The point of this remark lies in the fact that for nearly an hour Larwood and Strudwick had been the only players to handle the ball when Lol was bowling from the Nursery end."

Root's analysis extended to Larwood's change of direction a few years later: now abandoning the off theory, "when a batsman missed a ball, it either bowled him out, or hit him, he sustaining bruises the wicketkeeper had previously suffered". No longer could a batsman pad away with impunity anything not pitched between wicket and wicket, the umpire's powers of vision remaining his sole worry apart from tender flesh after half an hour of padding away Larwood's lightning offcutters.

As one who knew him well in his heyday, Root, who became a newspaper columnist, believed that nothing upset Larwood more than hitting a batsman. "To suggest that he deliberately placed his leg-side field to enable him the better to bowl at the batsman is a slander beyond forgiveness. He used his brains, he used his skill, he used his pace, never with the slightest suggestion of the bully, always with scrupulous fairness to all opponents, whether Australians or English; and the tragedy of his life was brought about by narrow-minded, ignorant critics and chicken-hearted, inept batsmen who not only ran away, 'ducked', and dodged, but squealed even when they had reached the safe security of the pavilion."

A strong defence, but not altogether watertight. When shown film of Indian tailender Captain Joginder Singh being unceremoniously carried off with a large bump protruding from his forehead after he had been hit in the 1932 tourists' match against Notts, I was told by Frank Woodhead, a Notts player in the 1930s, that Larwood and Voce had had a bet — a pint of beer or packet of fags — on who would be the first to ping Joginder's turban. Larwood won that bet. And when Bill Andrews of Somerset went to bat against the fearsome Notts duo with a chest-protector under his shirt, Larwood tapped it playfully and called across to Voce, "Look at that, Bill, let's both try and see if we can hit it."[2] In another match, Voce was peppering a No. 11 batsman when umpire E.J. "Tiger" Smith, who was no pansy himself, pulled the bowler up and suggested he try instead to knock the wicket over, which Voce promptly did.

What stands out among Root's remarks concerning Larwood is the phrase "never with the slightest suggestion of the bully". How many fast bowlers in recent years, from all parts of the world, have defiled the game with their melodramatic antics, blitzing a batsman then glaring like horror-film monsters and mouthing obscenities? A schoolboy who tried this would be sent from the field in shame by any decent coach. The Test player usually gets away with it, oblivious or uncaring as to how much this back-alley behaviour tarnishes his image. By contrast, when Larwood was being heckled and hooted during the '32–33 Australian tour, this sometime poultry farmer, rather than adopt the theatrical glare, would often softly mimic the sound of his roosters, "Bodyline'll do!"

As for Root's own strangling leg theory at medium-fast pace, when D.R. Jardine encountered it in a Surrey v Worcestershire match he glared at the squad of short-leg fielders and warned them: "If I offer, I shall offer hard!"[3]

SURREY'S NEW CAPTAIN, D.R. JARDINE, WEARING HIS BELOVED HARLEQUIN CAP, PLAYS AN INSWINGER FROM FRED ROOT INTO THE LEG TRAP DURING HIS INNINGS OF 164 AGAINST WORCESTERSHIRE IN 1932. "I SHALL OFFER HARD," HE WARNED.

It was not enough to "offer hard" when the lumbering, tight-lipped giant Warwick Armstrong bowled his accurate legspinners to a negative pattern for Australia. Batsmen such as the regal Archie MacLaren would kick the ball away in disgust, though the nimble J.T. Tyldesley skipped to leg and cut and drove through an open off side. This became Bradman's strategy, though the ball from Larwood was coming down very much faster. When the towering Hugh Trumble bowled medium-pace leg theory to MacLaren at Melbourne in 1901–02, the disdainful batsman simply milked him for ones and twos. In England, however, Trumble did tie C.B. Fry down. The batsman was greatly irritated, but there were no protests. Nor were there any at Headingley in the Australians' match against Yorkshire on that 1902 tour, when Hirst bowled his nifty late inswingers with a crowded leg-side field and bemused Clem Hill. "He's worrying you, Kruger. Leave him to me for a while," said Trumper. With glorious footwork, Trumper hit boundaries all around the field, leaving the broad-shouldered Yorkshireman to scratch his head.

On the 1905 tour of England, during which Armstrong amazingly amassed 1902 runs and 122 wickets, Surrey were chasing victory against Joe Darling's side at The Oval when Armstrong dropped into his wide-of-leg mode, with everybody on the leg side. With eight wickets in hand the Browncaps needed only 41 in 45 minutes, but one by one the frustrated batsmen panicked and got themselves out. Six perished trying to score off Armstrong, and there were run-outs, one victim being Jack Hobbs, who was in his first season with Surrey. He seemed to be shaking his head still in disbelief at this collapse over a quarter-century later.

When, late in 2001, England left-armer Ashley Giles bowled negatively at the pads of a frustrated Sachin Tendulkar at Bangalore, with wicketkeeper James Foster crouching a foot (30 cm) outside leg stump, Sunil Gavaskar's strictures echoed Sydney Pardon's branding (in *Wisden*) of Armstrong's leg theory "a confession of weakness" after daily Press condemnation during that 1905 tour. Might not MCC step in to stop it? Well, murmured Australians, have Len Braund's similar tactics on recent MCC/England tours of Australia been so soon forgotten?

Thus the transfer of culpability has gone persistently on, not just through periods of a couple of years, but from generation to generation. When England's heavyweight Andrew Flintoff bowled short to Tendulkar on a leg-stump line from around the wicket at Bangalore early in 2002, Craig White having briefly tried something similar at Ahmedabad, the cerebral former England captain Mike Brearley wrote: "This was Bodyline bowling, though nowhere near as ruthless as Jardine's to defeat Bradman. Rule changes have reduced its power."[4] He commented further that Nasser Hussain had "a tough streak in his make-up and, dare one say it, a slice of that British steel most notably displayed by Douglas Jardine — also, suggestively, born in India." When Australian crowds gave Brearley a bad time on his second tour, in 1979–80, he grew a beard in order to look tougher and less like the toff figure that Australians enjoy mocking. The beard, however, merely led to cries of "Ayatollah!" Jardine's ghost will have smiled. Perhaps.

Retribution has often been pious, sometimes virulent, in respect of intimidatory bowling. Negative leg theory at medium pace was certainly unattractive to batsmen and spectators, as was the stultifying offspin to packed leg fields in the 1950s. But passions have become quite blinding at times as batsmen of one era have been seriously injured and frightened, only for their successors to enjoy the benefit of an express bowler or two of their own to apply the payback and feeling themselves to be in possession of a historical credit-note to do so. If, as was recently suggested, aggressive Australian fast bowlers Jack Gregory and Ted McDonald were sent to punish England soon after Gallipoli in 1915, when British leaders were held to account for Australian deaths, and if Ray Lindwall and Keith Miller were dishing out retribution for British negligence that led to the fall of Singapore to the Japanese in 1942, and if the bombardment by Dennis Lillee and Jeff Thomson was actually an expression of Australian indignation at the United Kingdom's advances into the European Common Market in preference to nurturing Commonwealth links — to say nothing of the post-colonial attitudes of cricketing regions such as the West Indies and the subcontinent — then the payback theory is persuasively endorsed.

Then again, latter-day Australian bouncer attacks will have satisfied people who felt that England had much to answer for after the Bodyline assault of 1932–33. In 1948, when Keith Miller seemed to be after the heads, literally, of Len Hutton and Denis Compton, the hooting and hollering at Trent Bridge, where spectators were still seething at the treatment dealt out 15 years earlier to their heroes, Larwood and Voce, was quite understandable. Miller, who had fought a real war, on the seat of his pants as a Mosquito pilot, grinned broadly. And even in the 1970s, as Mike Denness's England XI were torn apart in Australia, Larwood's name was evoked from time to time.

Retribution? "Men regard it as their right to return evil for evil — and, if they cannot, feel they have lost their liberty." So pronounced the learned Aristotle, who lobbed his slow teasers in Greece over 2300 years ago.

There were clear instances of leg theory in Australia during the 1920s — indeed, E.E. Bean logged the first sighting as having been much earlier, in February 1882, when Tom Horan employed it during W.L. Murdoch's marathon and then-record score of 321 for New South Wales against Victoria at Sydney. Some of it has been not only negative but hostile; consider that dispensed by Harold Larwood on the first of his two tours, in 1928–29. Having astounded opponents and spectators alike with his velocity in earlier matches, he found himself shouldering a heavy work-load on a good pitch in the Adelaide Test, with 19-year-old Archie Jackson stroking 164 on debut for Australia. At one point Larwood bowled a spell of medium-fast off only a few paces, and then for a time he bowled with five or six fieldsmen on the leg side to Jackson and Bradman without attracting undue attention, for his length was a little fuller than it was to be on this very ground four years later.

Earlier still, however, and also on Adelaide's attractive cricket ground, a young man in his first match for South Australia caused a sensation by bowling the nearest thing to Bodyline almost eight years before English Bodyline itself exploded into reality. In a Sheffield Shield match against New South Wales in January 1925, 21-year-old Lance Gun, described years later as a "deep thinker about the game",[5] was called in at the last minute, scored 136 not out, batting fifth wicket down, and when put on to bowl by his skipper, Vic Richardson, proceeded to hurl down fast, short balls with a thickly populated leg field.[6] Next day the Adelaide *Advertiser* featured a sketch of the field — seven men on the leg side, five of them behind square — their reporter calling it "diagonal bowling" and asserting that it was "something new in big cricket". Gun took 2 for 38 (he bowled Test batsman Tommy Andrews) in his 11 overs and was called for one wide. He was to play for South Australia in a further seven matches, setting a first-wicket record with 313 (Gun made 129, and Arthur Richardson, himself an exponent of slow–medium leg theory around the wicket — for the State and against Hobbs and Sutcliffe for Australia in the famous 1926 Oval Test — made 227) against Western Australia later that same year, but Gun was never entrusted with the ball again for his State. Vic Richardson, later a central figure in the Bodyline series, disappointingly, makes no reference to Gun in his 1967 autobiography.

One of the New South Wales players in that 1925 match was Jack Scott, a tearaway, bone-crunching fast bowler not noted for self-discipline, and then approaching his 37th birthday. This chunky fellow, who had once leapt over the boundary fence while playing grade cricket for Marrickville to get at a spectator who had barracked him, was to become a Test umpire in 1936–37, and many were the suppressed smiles when, in November 1937 and now wearing a white hat and coat, he entered the Adelaide dressing-rooms and read the riot act to the fast bowlers —"No bumpers!" — before the Grimmett–Richardson testimonial match.

Back in 1908 Scott had scored the first try ever in Australian Rugby League, and in 1911–12, for his State against the MCC tourists, he let go a burst of "very fast bumping deliveries" at Jack Hobbs, Wilfred Rhodes and Gunn (George, of Notts). Scott had been hit painfully on the thigh three times by Frank Foster in that match, which inflamed him somewhat. However, little attention was paid at the time to this conspicuous piece of ugliness. The nearest thing to a scandal that season stemmed instead from the accusations directed at bowlers suspected of using resin on their fingers. England's stand-in captain, Johnny Douglas, quietly pointed at Australians "Ranji" Hordern and Charlie Kelleway during the Adelaide Test, only for some of the Australians to say that Douglas's habit of frequently shaking hands with his wicketkeeper, who used to smear his gauntlets with resin, had not gone unnoticed.

Whether influenced by Lance Gun's manic spell of bowling in 1925 or not, Jack Scott gave something similar a try at Sydney against the luckless Victorians a few days later and took five wickets (but not that of Australia's future Bodyline captain, Bill Woodfull, who scored 81) for 149 off 33.1 eight-ball overs, which included 13 no-balls.

Scott was at it again four years later when the 1928–29 Englishmen encountered him, now aged 41 and in South Australia's colours. Only Bradman and Wally Hammond were more successful that summer than Douglas Jardine, but Scott got Jardine for 8, and in the second innings, when Scott raced in with seven men placed on the leg side, Sutcliffe, a canny hooker, mistimed the shot and was caught. Ernest Tyldesley soon followed. Hobbs and Jardine then made centuries, and the MCC batsmen had no further concerns. But Larwood, not playing in this match, was probably watching Scott with special interest for, having himself got Kippax out hooking during a mini-spell of leg theory (but with only three men protecting the leg side) in the Melbourne Test, it was only a week later that Larwood employed brisk leg theory in the Adelaide Test match, though not with quite the same venom — yet.

Jardine, on the first of his two Australian tours, was doubtless storing all this up in his acute brain, even though the thinly populated leg side meant he had to do a lot of running around. Surely more fieldsmen were needed there?

Other fast bowlers who instilled terror in opposition ranks in the years before the 1932–33 Bodyline series? The cavalcade is long: the gentle giant Alfred Mynn, who couldn't help himself; another roundarm bowler, Walter Marcon, a minister of the church, who broke a batsman's leg; John "Foghorn" Jackson and George "Tear'em" Tarrant, who both showed Australia what fast bowling was about on the early tours; George Howitt, who plunged the ball in short, getting it up at the ribs, aiming for catches by the earliest of short-leg fieldsmen (W.G. Grace was very concerned about him and fell to him for a "pair" at Neath in 1868); George Freeman, rated by the supreme WG as the best of his time ("When the ball hit you, you felt as if you had been cut with a knife"); Jack Crossland and Arthur Mold, who were later deemed to be chuckers; the early Fred Spofforth,

Australia's "Demon" of the 1870s and '80s; Tom Richardson and Bill Lockwood, England's first great fast-bowling pair, and Charles Kortright of Essex, who never managed to play in a Test and yet was spoken of for years afterwards as the fastest who ever drew breath; from the colonies there were Ernie Jones and Albert "Tibby" Cotter of Australia and J.J. "Kodgee" Kotze of South Africa. And the muscular Gilbert Jessop, hallowed as perhaps the greatest hitter among batsmen but also, for a time, a wild and diabolical proposition as a bowler who loved to bang the ball in short. Joe Darling never forgot the going-over Jessop gave his Australians one season, stating that he bowled deliberately at the batsmen on a fiery pitch.[7] Ernie Jones retaliated and laid out one local batsman, who was confined to bed for a fortnight afterwards. Jessop, who later strongly disapproved of Bodyline, said he never bowled at a man, but in the 1896 Varsity match at Lord's he unleashed a chain of bumpers from around the wicket at the hapless Oxford batsmen, injuring a few, breaking a stump, and knocking out his own wicketkeeper.

ERNEST TYLDESLEY REELS AWAY AFTER BEING STRUCK IN THE FACE BY A BALL FROM JACK GREGORY. THE BALL REBOUNDED INTO THE STUMPS.

Soon after the First World War, the bounding Jack Gregory (in particular) and the smooth Ted McDonald scythed through the English ranks during the 1921 tour by Armstrong's Australians. Ernest Tyldesley's grisly fate in being bowled off his jaw and knocked senseless in the Trent Bridge Test was the most notorious flash of horror, but there were many other instances, and a war hero was among those seen to be shaking with fear before taking his turn at the wicket. In the second Test, at Melbourne, in the Ashes series of 1920–21, England wicketkeeper Herbert Strudwick, who was not a very capable batsman, took painful thumps around the heart from three consecutive balls from Gregory. On his second Test tour of England, in 1926, Gregory's bowling (and his left-hand batting too, for that matter) was still based on ferocity of purpose. In a match at Scarborough he bounced the first five balls of the innings over R.E.S. Wyatt's head.

It was from the swift and stealthy hand of McDonald that Jardine first withstood what he perceived as leg theory. McDonald settled in England and played for Lancashire, causing havoc in many a county match, including one against Yorkshire at Old Trafford in 1927 in which he bowled with four in the leg trap and no slips. The cool Herbert Sutcliffe, who fell to him twice, for 0 and 38, wrote that he was "happy to deal with him", and in the return match, when he scored 95 and 135, doubtless he was. Sutcliffe also reckoned that for several seasons before Bodyline, whenever Yorkshire played Notts they had to face fast leg theory. Nobody, he said, was permitted to back away, and with practice he was able to place the ball safely, although sometimes holing out with his otherwise profitable hook shot.

The charismatic West Indian Learie (later Lord) Constantine recalled that when an MCC team toured the Caribbean in 1911, George John, a high-class Trinidad fast bowler, indulged in what would later have been called Bodyline. Young Middlesex batsman Jack Hearne complained, but Constantine had no time for that, for he had faced it too — some balls he hit, some hit him, and he found the whole thing "very exciting". Not so some of England's premier batsmen when spurts of West Indian short stuff came their way in the 1928 Old Trafford Test match. Hobbs told Constantine he wasn't young any more and had no intention of being hit, and the West Indian claimed that Hammond *and Jardine* also complained. (In this match, Jardine trod on his wicket, but, as Constantine recalled, as umpire Morton was about to raise his finger the batsman told him he had completed his stroke. "Not out.")[8]

The 1928 tourists had a dose of Larwood at his fastest that they would never forget. In the Lord's Test, West Indies' first ever, he "tried to take our noses off". And when England toured the West Indies just over a year later, Bill Voce had a leg field and sent the ball fizzing through head-high. There were groans when a young batsman named Inniss was knocked out by a ball from Voce, but Clifford Roach hooked him hard, and when Constantine bowled outside leg to Andy Sandham (then, in his 40th year, scorer of the first Test triple-century, in the Kingston Test), the mild little Surrey man shifted his guard outside leg, still got hit, and showed his anger. The MCC manager suggested Constantine stopped bowling in this fashion, and he duly complied, while the captain, the Honourable Freddie Calthorpe, stated openly that he felt Constantine's tactics were "not cricket".

On the previous MCC tour of the West Indies, Wally Hammond, who was about to contract a nasty anti-social disease that almost cost him his life, made very plain his dislike of Constantine's bouncers. But his skipper, the Honourable Lionel Tennyson, who had once scored 99 runs in a Test match batting one-handed against Gregory and McDonald, told Hammond to shut up and bat.[9]

When Constantine, the electric-heeled cricketer with the big grin, bounced four in a Test match over at Bill Ponsford during West Indies' first tour of Australia, in 1930–31, his captain, G.C. "Jack" Grant, a white man, removed him from the attack. Years later, reflecting on the implications of all this, Constantine wrote that Bodyline was something new in fast bowling — it was always latent in the old, but had never been allowed to emerge fully until Jardine came along. Putting all those fielders on the leg side, he felt, was a "farce",[10] the logical outcome of the win-at-all-costs policy.

After the 1932–33 series R.H. Campbell produced a booklet for the Australian Broadcasting Commission entitled *Cricket Casualties*, in which he undertook to log every instance of batsmen struck painfully and possibly injured in the 129 Tests to date between Australia and England. While doubt lingers as to how inclusive Campbell's figures were, he calculated that there had been 203 blows, 118 sustained by Australians and 85 by Englishmen. The severity ranged from Grace and Will Scotton being rapped on the hands by Spofforth to Ranjitsinhji's ear being split by Ernie Jones, Bill Storer remonstrating with Jones for bowling at his body and J.W.H.T. Douglas taking heavy blows from McDonald "without flinching", as might be expected of an Olympic boxing champion. Not all the injuries listed were inflicted by fast bowlers. Harry Makepeace was hit in the chest while trying to sweep Arthur Mailey, as was Joe Darling when facing slow left-armer Colin Blythe. Some made it an occupational pastime: "R.B. Minnett was struck by a ball from Foster, and later by a rising ball from Barnes, and again Foster struck him in the groin."

For December 1928, at Melbourne, there is a notable entry: "D.G. Bradman was struck on the body by a fast ball from Larwood"; followed by August 1930, at The Oval: "Bradman, when 175, was struck under the heart by a fast rising ball from Larwood. He appeared to be in great pain, and the game was held up for five minutes." Not only did Bradman make it his business throughout his career to score more runs than had ever been scored before, but he prided himself in avoiding injury, or even being hit. This was a passionate aim of his during Bodyline, and he almost succeeded.

The prizes — and by clear margins — on Campbell's summary tables go to Sutcliffe for absorbing most hits (18) in Ashes Tests for England, and Woodfull (11) for Australia. The arch villains, judged on these statistics, were Jack Gregory, who hit 20 batsmen while bowling for Australia, and for England, Harold Larwood with 34 (a figure Larwood challenged in his autobiography: he thought the figure on the low side). Chronicled from the five Test matches of 1932–33 are 35 hits of varying severity by England's bowlers, Larwood (around two-thirds of them), Voce, Allen and Bowes.

An update on Campbell's list is long overdue, although logging the widespread human damage and misery inflicted in the Test matches of the past 70 years would be a truly formidable task. A partial update appeared in 1994 when Simon Wilde researched injuries inflicted in Test matches over the preceding 20 years. He found that 89 batsmen had retired hurt: almost half (40) against West Indies fast bowlers, 16 against Australia, 11 against England, 9 against New Zealand, 8 against Pakistan, 3 against India, 2 against Sri Lanka.[11]

And what of the perils faced by batsmen ever since the game began? As *Wisden*'s editor in 1922 reminded readers, the old Middlesex champion batsman R.D. Walker's glib dictum was that the batsman who could not take care of himself ought not to play cricket.

The fast and furious W.B. Burns of Worcestershire, whose action was dubious but whose pace was undeniable, was another of the earliest exponents of something resembling Bodyline. He tried it against Middlesex at Lord's in 1910, but was taken off after a few overs following a protest from the opposing captain, none other than P.F. Warner, who was to squirm his way through the 1932–33 tour as manager. Billy Burns, a fine "gentleman" batsman who became an officer in the Worcestershire Regiment, was killed in France six years later.

It was while trying to cope with Burns and Surrey express bowler Neville Knox in Edwardian days that the slender Middlesex batsman Cyril Foley devised a theory about avoiding short-pitched balls which may well embody a timeless truth. He was convinced that the increased popularity of the squarer batting stance caused the bowler to bowl *at* the batsman "for the very good reason that there is nothing else for him to bowl at. If the bowler happens to bowl short and fast the batsman says it is dangerous. So it is — damnably. But whose fault is that?" Frank Foster's belief, tabled earlier, that a left-armer, for this very reason, should never bowl over the wicket makes interesting collateral reading.

"The wicket was rough," Foley continued in his article in *The Field*, recalling his joust with Neville Knox and Burns not without a tinge of hilarity, "and I do believe that had I adopted the two-eyed stance I should have been killed twice and permanently injured four times, if you follow me. Balls grazing my eyebrows would have hit me in the eye; balls that hit me on the shoulder would have hit me on the heart ... In my humble opinion bowling at the batsman *in order to get him out* is a justifiable and unavoidable challenge to the two-eyed stance."

So there we have the opinion of an English gentleman who played this complex game over a century ago, took part in the Jameson Raid, fought in the Boer War and the First World War, and also searched for the Ark in the Holy Land. If only Bradman, Ponsford and Woodfull had had access to his wisdom before undertaking their task of handling Harold Larwood during that inferno of a summer 70 years ago.

CHAPTER TWO

THE TARGET — THE SNIPERS

"Who invented the name I do not know, nor do I care. It was merely a name coined to designate a certain type of bowling which was different from anything used before, and it will probably remain for want of a better term."[1] Don Bradman's dismissive summary was written some years before it became widely known who coined the expression. To that person should go here some sort of proper acknowledgment.

There were numerous possible alternative appellations. Joe Darling said it should have been called simply The Bradman Theory. Arthur Mailey, the cartoonist, writer, humorist and former Australian legspinner, referred to it seriously as The Shock Attack. English journalist Bruce Harris cleverly suggested The Larboard Attack. *The Australian Cricketer* referred to Header Bowling. The former England captain Archie MacLaren had described something similar years previously as Body Bowling. Australian players (and victims) Vic Richardson and Bill O'Reilly respectively dubbed it Headline Bowling and The Scone (pronounced 'scon') Theory. (O'Reilly was a champion at creating vivid nomenclature: modern one-day cricket, which he despised, should be referred to, he said, as Crackit.) Learie Constantine, the West Indies fast bowler, called it the Jardinian Theory. The old English cricketer E.H.D. Sewell felt that Torso Bowling was most apt. Larwood's Nottinghamshire captain Arthur Carr, some time later, came up with the characteristically lavish Bumping Bombs. MCC and *Wisden* were to refer to Direct Attack. The one-time Australian wicketkeeper Jim Kelly spoke of

Body Theory. Ranjitsinhji, the magical little batsman of the turn of the century, whose life ended soon after the series closed, preferred the cumbersome Meretricious Bashing Attack. Ray Robinson, then a young journalist on the *Herald*, Melbourne's afternoon daily paper, toyed with Blitzcrick. The aggressive Australian journalist Frank Browne imaginatively thought of it as Murder Incorporated, "founded on terror, plus cold efficiency", while from elsewhere came the faintly humorous Human Skittles.

But the germ of the word that was to stick — seen as a pejorative of the worst kind by MCC and Jardine and unused by them in written or oral communications — originated in the copy of John Worrall, formerly an Australian Test batsman and top Aussie Rules footballer, and now a writer on the weekly *Australasian*. During the Englishmen's early match against an Australian XI at the MCG, Worrall referred to Voce's "half-pitched slingers on the body line". Worrall first used the word "bodyline" in print on December 10, 1932, just after the opening Test had ended.

R.W.E. Wilmot had had similar thoughts in one of his *Argus* reports, using the phrase "on the line of the body". Ray Robinson, then with the Melbourne *Herald*, had seen virtue in these expressions and created "body-line" as an adjective and the unhyphenated version as a noun. It would have featured in a headline earlier than it did, but a conservative editor, Syd Deamer, ruled against it.[2]

The consensus of credit for the decisive promotion of the word — possibly appropriated rather than invented by him — finally rests with Hugh Buggy, then aged 36, who was writing for the Melbourne *Herald*. The word "bodyline" appeared in his story on the opening day of the opening Test match.

Among the colourful Buggy's talents was an alleged ability to recall accurately every innings total in Australia v England Tests. A career newspaper reporter and author, he spent many years covering the crime world and was General MacArthur's chief operational censor during the Second World War, having numbered the fatal Squizzy Taylor shoot-out and the Pyjama Girl murder among his many big stories and ghosted a book on the historic pan-Pacific flight in *Southern Cross* by Charles Kingsford Smith and Charles Ulm. The prolific Buggy, who was to leave 300 scrapbooks of his newspaper cuttings when he died in 1974, was forever looking for the clever angle, the colourful phrase, and he spoke tersely, between pauses, out of the corner of his mouth, putting many in mind of a Damon Runyon character.[3]

"Buggy here," he once growled down the telephone wire to a Melbourne bureaucrat, as Jack Fingleton recalled. The stunned recipient of the call, the latest in a long line who failed to comprehend precisely what this legendary reporter had mumbled, retorted: "And bugger you, too!"

HUGH BUGGY (1896–1974), THE MAN WHO PUT THE WORD "BODYLINE" INTO PRINT.
(COURTESY OF THE HERALD & WEEKLY TIMES PHOTOGRAPHIC COLLECTION)

Bodyline's principal target was Don Bradman, a 24-year-old who was to live a very long life, by the end of which he had been exalted to little short of sainthood. In 1932 his stocks could hardly have been higher. "I was in Canada when the English team was announced," he recalled in an ABC interview in 1975, "and I promptly forecast that we would see an avalanche of bumpers because the team was loaded with fast bowlers. But what I did not foresee was the use of them in association with a packed leg-side field. The two combined made it a clearly preconceived plan of action, and as such I believe it was extremely detrimental to the game of cricket."[4]

He conceded that, as a young man with good eyesight who could hook and pull, he did not face as great a problem against Bodyline as did the older Australian batsmen. What was it like to be out there with Larwood bowling fast bouncers to the leg field? "It was not funny at all," he went on. "The risk of injury was extremely great ... a great many others escaped injury by sheer luck and that's all." He conceded that England didn't bowl it at the lower-order Australians, but pointed to a wider danger than the damage it caused to Test cricket: it had been instantly adopted in district and junior cricket around Australia, mostly on high-bouncing concrete pitches. He was far from being alone in his alarm. His broadest concession was an acknowledgment that Bodyline led to a beneficial amendment to the laws, whereby bowlers could at last get their due by winning leg-before decisions to balls coming in, having pitched outside off stump.[5]

Bradman, of course, was Australia's darling, its star of stars, bareheaded, boyish and brazen at the batting crease against all comers. Bowlers found his confidence intimidating. He grinned a lot. He knew his God-given ability, incomparably strong mind and unique appetite for runs had brought him — and would, with luck, continue to bring him — success such as no batsman in the long history of cricket had ever imagined, let alone achieved. He convinced himself throughout that he was a better batsman than this chap was a bowler. "Surely defence should be secondary. Batsmen should be ready to attack and only defend when forced to. They should force the bowler to defend."[6] If only it were so straightforward for the mere mortals.

DON BRADMAN: HIS STUPENDOUS RUN AGGREGATES CREATED
DEEP CONCERN IN ENGLISH CRICKET.

To comprehend England's deep anxiety as they prepared to send a team to Australia at the end of the 1932 season, one needs to look no further than Bradman's principal scores since his name first appeared in the newspapers: 118 on first-class debut in December 1927; twin centuries against Queensland a year later, and 87 and 132 not out the following week against MCC in his first international match; 79 and 112 against England at Melbourne in his second Test match; 340 not out against Victoria; 123 at the MCG as Australia at last beat the conquering 1928–29 England combination; 1586 runs (113.29) in the following season, including 124 and 225 in the trial match for the 1930 tour of England and the world record innings of 452 not out at Sydney for New South Wales against Queensland.

All well and good on Australia's favourable pitches, some said, but his keenness to unleash his crisp pull shot against anything even only a touch short of a length was bound to make life difficult for him on England's slower and often less reliable wickets.

Well, in England in 1930 Bradman's name, beyond argument, came once and for all to overshadow those of his towering contemporaries Walter Hammond, the elderly Jack Hobbs and Bill Ponsford (George Headley, the West Indian, was of a similar class but was not playing quite the volume of cricket to register with the average cricket-follower). Bradman came to within 40 of recording 3000 runs on that first tour of England. He made 10 centuries, six of them multiples, and averaged 98.67. His scores in the Tests have become something of a psalm for cricket worshippers: Trent Bridge 8 and 131, Lord's 254 and 1, Headingley 334, Old Trafford 14, The Oval 232. This aggregate, 974, remains the highest for any Test rubber (and there have been series consisting of *six* Tests in modern times). Together with the resultant average of 139.14, this was what sent shivers through the very souls of English bowlers and administrators as they looked towards the next venture to Australia. What might Bradman do on his home pitches and in Test matches with no time limit? A score of 500 seemed worth betting on — or perhaps he'd do that twice? Maybe 600?

He averaged a mere 79 in 1930–31, but there were three double-centuries, one of them in the Brisbane Test match against West Indies, a series which ended with his first Test duck, bowled by Herman Griffith. This was stunning news at the time. In 1931–32 he tormented the South Africans, racking up 1190 runs in matches against Jock Cameron's team, the climax being a poignant 299 not out in the Adelaide Test, followed by the anticlimax of not being fit to bat in the final Test after catching his sprigs in the coir matting in the MCG dressing-room and twisting an ankle. Jack Fingleton, 12th man at Adelaide, observed that Sandy Bell, South Africa's biggest and fastest bowler, close to desperation late in Bradman's extraordinary knock, decided to bounce a few at him.[7] And he was clearly ruffled. Fingleton stops just short of accusing Bradman of feigning injury at Melbourne, where rain turned the pitch into a horror strip and it was all over in less than six hours of play: South Africa 36 and 45 (Bert Ironmonger 11 for 24), Australia 153 (Kippax 42, Fingleton 40, Bradman dnb).

This last season before Larwood and company came to spoil it all had begun with a shock for Bradman at the Gabba, when Eddie Gilbert, an Aborigine, bowled the fastest few balls he, by his own estimation, was ever to face. He toppled onto his backside, his cap-peak was knocked askew, for the only time in his career the bat was knocked from his hands, and after swinging at and missing the next two balls he got a touch and was caught by the keeper. It was the hottest and most humiliating of his ducks —"the luckiest duck I ever made"— and the reports of it would have been studied in England.

Clacking away with his typewriter, to the annoyance of other Press-box occupants, Percy Fender, who led Surrey throughout the 1920s, an innovative, thinking cricketer with a record 35-minute century to his name, abandoned his earlier doubts over Bradman's skill after watching his astonishing performances in England in 1930 — not least the 252 not out pointedly carved from the Surrey attack while its helpless captain — Fender himself — bowled and changed his field in vain. (Jardine was another helpless fieldsman.) "I feel convinced that something new will have to be introduced to curb Bradman," Fender wrote in *The Observer*, "and that the best way of selecting that something new is to seek it along the lines of theory." Were these desperate words, or did he have something specific in mind? His successor as Surrey captain was to be D.R. Jardine.

While having written in 1920 that bowling outside leg stump with six or seven fielders on the leg side was "unsportsmanlike" (now *there* was a word to reverberate a dozen years later) "and quite contrary to the spirit and traditions of the game", P.F. Warner, as one of the principal nabobs of

English cricket, was another who felt that something had to be devised urgently to contain Bradman.[8] "It is a disturbing thought that he is only a boy," he wrote in the *Morning Post* after The Don's 334 at Headingley in 1930. "England must evolve a new type of bowler and develop fresh ideas and strange tactics to curb his almost uncanny skill." *Strange?* Not Bodyline, though. While he was to be exposed as inconsistent and even insincere at times, Warner deserves the benefit of any doubt here. He was horrified at W.B. Burns's startling assault at Lord's in 1910: "My objection to it, therefore, goes back to a period when Jardine was a boy of ten at a preparatory school."[9] Maybe the "strange" strategy he envisaged was a real-life version of Arthur Conan Doyle's creation, "Spedegue's dropper"— a ball tossed way, way into the sky before descending pinpoint onto the bails? There have been plenty of instances of it in county cricket. It resulted in wickets falling, too. Long ago, W.G. Grace's brother Teddy used it frequently — to choruses of booing and hissing. Yet Don Bradman would probably have had an answer even to that kind of bowling.

He had unquestionably had an answer to England's premier fast bowler to this point. In the 17 innings over two seasons in which Larwood had bowled to Bradman, he had got him out only once, after Bradman had scored 232 in the 1930 Oval Test, and even then the ball, said Bradman years later, had touched his shirt-sleeve and not his bat. In those 17 innings the Boy from Bowral (born in Cootamundra, actually, on August 27, 1908) had made 1564 runs at an average of 111. And it seemed that the 1931 enlargement of the wicket's width to nine inches (23 cm) and height to a maximum of 28 inches (71 cm), while adding an appreciable percentage to that target area, would elevate bowlers' prospects against Bradman to no significant degree.

The notion of aggressive fast leg theory was to come not from Plum Warner but from elsewhere: Nottingham, not then so much the county of Robin Hood but of the colliery. Sturdy ex-miners Harold Larwood and Bill Voce, under A.W. Carr's belligerent county captaincy, had been refining this kind of bowling over recent seasons, laying out a few county batsmen in the process and causing great discontent around the shires. In 1930 Voce pounded inswingers at the bodies of the Australians in the Nottinghamshire match, with a few leg-side catchers in position. Alan Kippax waddled his runs, catching the eye with his abundant padding, which was tested time and again. Bradman was being rested — protected, in fact, for the nature of the Notts attack was now widely recognised. Having just scored 254 at Lord's in the Test match, he went to the tennis at Wimbledon, wandered around London, and then drove in a baby Singer motor-car up to Leeds to score 334 in the next Test. Larwood, returning from injury, was not at full pace in that Notts game against the Australians in July, and left-armer Voce was hammered pointedly by Stan McCabe and Vic Richardson (50 in 35 minutes: "Somebody's got to crack this fellow"). They were both bruised but, the Australians were pleased to hear, the England selectors decided not to pick Voce for the Tests, though he went with the MCC team to South Africa that winter and took 23 wickets in the five Tests, employing leg theory at times — and drawing ironic cheers from the members at Kingsmead, Durban.

Batting of a lesser order by Somerset in their match against Notts at Taunton in June had seen George Hunt, fed up with taking so many blows to the heart region, desperately switching over to left-handed batting, and poor C.C.C. "Box" Case was so befuddled after Voce sent him collapsing into his wicket that he departed, dazed, with a stump in his hand instead of his bat. Frank Lee, a Somerset stalwart and later a Test umpire, was knocked out some years later by a Voce bouncer, and was taken away for observation. When he turned up next day, he was greeted with a remark from the bowler which was perhaps more in keeping with the sphere of prizefights: "Hello, Frank, I didn't expect to see you. I heard you'd died in the night."[10]

The signal moment of the 1930 summer came late on the fourth day of the final Test. The matchwinning stand of 243 between Bradman and Archie Jackson had been interrupted halfway through by the weather on the previous afternoon, and there was general surprise when the umpires ordered a resumption at 6.25 pm, allowing 13 more balls to be bowled. This interlude and the next day's play found Bradman displaying uncharacteristic discomfort as the ball kicked off the wet turf. He and Jackson (who sustained many painful body blows but never gave an inch) were severely inconvenienced by balls which leapt off a length, not only from Larwood, who struck Bradman hard on the chest, but from Hammond too. England's wicketkeeper, George Duckworth, made sure everybody was alerted to the sudden change in flavour. Bradman was stepping back, and of course Larwood, who had noticed Bradman's flinching, was set thinking.

The slowness in runmaking during this tense time was sporadically hooted by ignorant onlookers.

The seeds of England's 1932–33 campaign, it has repeatedly been claimed, were sown here (though Bill O'Reilly wouldn't have a bar of it: "No batsman was really worth a damn when the ball was rising at varying heights"). And although Douglas Jardine, who played little cricket in 1930, preferring to pursue his business interests, was not at the Test match, his Surrey friends, including Percy Fender, soon appraised him of what they had seen. Indeed, during the Notts v Surrey match at The Oval at the beginning of August, Fender told Arthur Carr that Jardine would like to know more. This led to the celebrated gathering in a discreet corner of the grill-room in the Piccadilly Hotel, where, over a few drinks and a plate of food, Carr, Jardine, Larwood and Voce had a momentous exchange of intelligence that led to plans which gave shape to England's 1932–33 strategy in Australia, notwithstanding the many claims that it "just evolved". In *The Larwood Story*, first published in 1965, Harold Larwood confirms that Jardine asked if he could bowl leg stump and make the ball "come up into the body" to force Bradman to make all his shots to leg. "Yes, I think that can be done," said the bowler. "It's better to rely on speed and accuracy than anything else when bowling to Bradman because he murders any loose stuff."

HAROLD LARWOOD: TOUCHED AS A FAST BOWLER WITH THE SAME KIND
OF GENIUS THAT IMBUED BRADMAN AS BATSMAN.

There is much detail in an undated (probably post-war) but seemingly well-informed article by Wally Hammond in *The People*, in which he visualises Carr positioning bread rolls and pepperpots and silver coins on the white tablecloth, showing the leg-side field perfected for his two firebrand bowlers. This was the way to get Bradman, Woodfull, Ponsford, Kippax and company. Jardine queried the open off-side field. Carr said Larwood was so accurate that there need be no concern. "When the four shook hands," wrote Hammond, "the line of attack for Britain's 'Commando bowlers' had been settled." As the group broke up, Carr is said to have taken Jardine to one side and said quietly, "If any of them are hard to move, tell Lol that they have been saying he is not so fast as he used to be. Then he'll show them what pace on the leg stick really is."

In his uninhibited 1935 autobiography, Carr claimed that Lancashire's Ernest Tyldesley and George Duckworth (contradictorily) believed that fast leg theory would not be successful in Australia.[11] (He further wrote that Larwood regarded Bradman as conceited.) Carr, originally concerned about Larwood's slight stature, had fed him beer. He also painted a fascinating picture of his prized fast bowler on his first visit to London. The young ex-miner was sitting with team-mates in the vestibule of a West End hotel, idly watching the passing pageant. Eventually he turned to one of the others and asked, in wide-eyed innocence: "Are *all* these women for hire?"

ARTHUR CARR, WHO PERFECTED BODYLINE WITH LARWOOD AND VOCE AT COUNTY LEVEL, PREPARES FOR A NET, WITH BEN LILLEY, THE NOTTS WICKETKEEPER, AND HAROLD LARWOOD (IN CIVVIES). IT WAS JUNE 1934, AND TENSION AT TRENT BRIDGE WAS STILL HIGH.

Beyond Carr's influence was the telling technical input from Notts coach Jim Iremonger. The old pros usually commanded enormous respect from the players. Even after the Bodyline tour, Iremonger wielded power over them. When Larwood and Voce indulged in some wild horseplay in the showers Iremonger shouted: "'Arold, Bill, coom 'ere at once!" Tom Reddick recalled how "England's two fast bowlers made their appearance before Iremonger as naked as the day they were born. 'I was under the impression that you two lads play cricket for England,' said Jim looking very fierce. 'That's quite right, Jim,' said Bill staring at his bare feet rather ashamedly. 'That's very interesting,' came the reply. 'I hope I'm not asking too mooch then if I ask you both to bloody well behave like England cricketers.'"[12]

In Notts' final Championship match of 1932, to the frowning resentment of Lancastrian spectators, Larwood and Voce again bowled plenty of "fast, rising balls" as was sometimes the genteel description. Ernest Tyldesley, a polished batsman, was among those who suffered, one ball from Larwood striking him in the face. Left-hander Eddie Paynter sampled the experimental Bodyline too, though very briefly. Larwood bowled him for a duck.

Throughout 1932 the Notts fast bowlers continued to refine their fearsome methods, and many a match finished in two days. Having been county champions in 1929, they continued to finish in the higher reaches of the table for several seasons subsequently. As for visual evidence, two films shot by a Mr Stevens at Trent Bridge in 1932 — Notts beat Derbyshire and then Hampshire by innings margins — happen to show Larwood and Voce operating to orthodox fields, sometimes with a couple of short-leg fieldsmen and with discernible backward steps by batsmen facing Larwood's shorter balls. The frustrating pushing of pads outside off stump is seen time and again. The terror pair still finished with 28 wickets between them in these two matches, Larwood ending the season with 141 Championship wickets (11.62), Voce 106 (16.79).

In the closing days of the 1932 season, there was enough "leg theory" on view for the perceptive to have realised that Larwood and Voce — and Bill Bowes too — must surely be planning to turn it on in Australia. At Leyton, during the first week of August, immediately following the tactical dinner at the Piccadilly Hotel, Larwood and Voce blitzed Essex for a few overs. In the first innings Jack O'Connor retired hurt, Dudley Pope was on his backside as he watched himself being caught, and tailender G.R.R. Brown sustained several bruises. In the second innings it was not long before Arthur Carr altered the field for further "leg theory". John Arlott was there, with a pal. "Is Larwood going to bowl offspinners?" "No, the wicketkeeper is standing back." Arlott (horrified): "He's going to bowl at his head."[13] The damage was limited in that match because the pitch lacked life, and Essex drew the match with ease.

D.F. POPE (ESSEX) LOSES HIS COMPOSURE AND HIS WICKET AT LARWOOD'S HANDS AT LEYTON.

Towards the end of that month young Arlott went to Wales and found himself watching a further Bodyline rehearsal as Glamorgan played Notts. One of the Welsh heroes in that match, Dai Davies, left a colourful account: "Maurice Turnbull and I came together and clouted the bowling all over the farm. Turnbull got 205 and I made 106. So much for bodyline bowling! ... I got most of my runs by shovelling the ball over the wicket-keeper's head, but Turnbull played a beautiful innings, and it was a pleasure to watch him."[14] Again the pitch was too slow for Larwood and Voce's liking, and after the Notts players had sunk a fair quantity of beer with the opposition that evening they went out to the centre and "watered" the pitch to show what they thought of it. The groundsman, tipped off, was out there at six next morning making good and fobbing off inquisitive reporters.

Should there be any doubts about Larwood's pace, Davies told of an ailment known as "Larwooditis" which unaccountably forced batsmen into the lavatory. And Frank Lee remembered his first encounter. He was on a pair: "As I commenced my bat uplift, 'something' hit it; that 'something' turned out to be the ball which flew between the many slips and gulleys down to third man! Breathing a silent prayer of thanks I ran a single ... to be greeted by Jim Street the umpire, with the remark, 'A nice lad, Harold, he bowled you a slower one.'"[15]

Lee also recalled George Brown's experience. There has never been a more fearless cricketer than the Hampshire batsman, whose gaunt, sunburnt cheeks gave him the appearance of a Cherokee. He deliberately let two bouncers from Larwood hit him on the chest, then called down the pitch: "When are you going to bowl really fast, Harold?" But as Larwood prepared to bowl again, Brown was seen to sag at the knees and stagger away, rather as the Herculean Brian Close did at Old Trafford in 1976 after one blow too many from the West Indians. Brown was all right. It was just that the ball-punches over the heart had forced him to take a short breather.

When Larwood laid out the Middlesex amateur Dick Twining at Lord's in 1927, the barely conscious batsman heard the doctor say, as he walked away across the dressing-room, having worked desperately to bring him round, "I've done all I can for him." Hammond said of Larwood's "red cannonballs" that you could sometimes *hear* them whistling down. Batsmen such as South Africa's Jock Cameron and Middlesex and England's Patsy Hendren may not have heard or seen much at all as Larwood knocked them senseless in 1929 and 1931 respectively. They were both taken to hospital and some worrying hours ensued. Even in 1934 Larwood was capable of knockout blows, though we are asked to accept his constant assertions that he never relished them. Reg Sinfield, having batted for Gloucestershire for four hours, was unconscious for an hour after a ball crashed into his skull. The gutsy former sailor came back and batted for another four hours in the second innings and gallantly wrote a column devoted to praising and excusing the bowler.

While Turnbull and Davies were reducing Notts to beers at Cardiff in the summer of 1932, down at Dean Park, Bournemouth, the venerable Honourable Lionel Tennyson was taking a fairly dreadful pounding from Yorkshire's Bill Bowes. Eleven years earlier the rumbustious Tennyson, a survivor of the hell of the Western Front, had made gallant runs against Australia's fiery Gregory and McDonald with only one good hand, and had been severely hurt by McDonald when struck near the heart. Now he was being subjected to Bowes's ferocity, to which his typical response was a series of defiant and ostentatious strolls down the pitch to smack the divots.[16] Tennyson still became a staunch supporter of Jardine's Bodyline tactics that winter, believing it fair that past bombardments from the Australians should be paid back, with interest.

A fortnight later, during a fixture at Folkestone between the MCC team about to embark for Australia and a Rest of England XI, Larwood and Voce gave Bodyline one final airing before the voyage. They sprayed bouncers at the towering and legendary left-hander Frank Woolley, who was now 45 years of age, and at his young partner Bryan Valentine during their 70-minute stand of 108. Not renowned for tolerance, Woolley at one point looked Larwood in the eye and questioned him: "Are you trying to hurt me, Harold?" The bowler looked slightly sheepish.

The finest South African batsman to date, Herby Taylor, then 43, was guesting for the Rest of England XI, and probably in deference to his hallowed standing as much as his age, he was spared the nasty stuff. The consequence was obvious. His partners preferred to leave him on strike. Jack Fingleton speculated that Taylor, who spent that summer in England, may well have made mention "in high places" about Bradman's discomfort against Sandy Bell in the Adelaide Test a few months earlier.[17]

England's 1932 captain, D.R. Jardine, had demonstrated his acute tactical awareness as well as ruthlessness in the Test match against India — their first ever — at Lord's in late June. With the difficult background of the pavilion (there was no sightscreen) and the glare off the white seats at the Nursery end in mind, he ordered his fast bowlers, Voce and Bowes, to send down one full toss each over, which the batsman was sure to misjudge, as had several of England's batsmen. Voce quietly said to Bowes that he'd prefer to bowl yorkers. After England had won, the skipper sent for his fast men. "Jardine told us that if we played under him we would do as he said and not as we thought," recalled Bowes in his autobiography *Express Deliveries*. (The author has Jardine's copy, which is inscribed: *To my friend and greatest of captains — D.R.J. May you recapture a few of your triumphs in these pages. "Bill" Bowes.*) In the MCC v All India match before the Test Bowes had cracked Wazir Ali on the head, causing his retirement from the match. The thoughtful Bowes was heavily built and had a shuffling approach, and the massing of his weight from a back-foot-*behind*-front-foot leg movement as he swung into the delivery stride (as in the case also of the equally tall and big-framed Bill Voce) made him a daunting proposition, especially when there was give in the pitch.

There had even been unpleasant scenes in the traditional and usually

JACK HOBBS, THE OLD MASTER, HAS A FEW FRIENDLY WORDS WITH THE YORKSHIREMEN
AFTER BOWES'S FUSILLADE OF BUMPERS.

rarefied setting of the Varsity match at Lord's early in July, when the young Essex giant Ken Farnes hit a few Oxford batsmen, none more painfully than fellow giant Pieter van der Bijl, whose "bull-like bellows" echoed around Lord's and could still be heard by E.W. Swanton — who had been in the Press box — some 45 years later.[18] Farnes, a sensitive young man who was to die at the controls of a Wellington bomber during the war, had a rougher time a few weeks after the Varsity match, when his barrage of leg-theory bumpers was carted by Yorkshire's Sutcliffe and Leyland for 75 runs in *four overs* in the Championship match at Scarborough. Sutcliffe's 194 gave him 507 runs in his two innings against Essex that summer, and this little episode may have played Farnes out of the running as England assembled the deadly fast-bowling platoon for the Australia tour.

Yet of all the altercations in 1932, that English summer of destiny, in terms of irony none compares with the spat between Bill Bowes and the revered 50-year-old Jack Hobbs at The Oval (while, incidentally, several Worcestershire batsmen were being injured up at Trent Bridge). During his innings of 90 for Surrey, Hobbs was at his impregnable best, so Bowes bounced him, as he had been bouncing all season. The old maestro walked far down the pitch and patted the spot, which enraged Bowes. Another bumper cleared Hobbs's head, and as the Ovalites noisily vented their anger Hobbs was seen in meaningful conversation with several of the Yorkshiremen. The match proceeded, and George Macaulay later flung two beamers in the direction of Surrey's captain, Jardine (in the course of a three-hour innings for 35), who coolly ducked. The newspapers next day seized upon these incidents, the greatest dissent coming from the pen of Plum Warner, who had been seated not in the Press box but among Surrey members in the pavilion. His criticism of Yorkshire, and Bowes in particular, in the *Morning Post* and later in *The Cricketer*, which he edited, was to be thrown in his face time and again in the months to come.

Not everybody took exception to the antics in the middle. Ranjitsinhji laughed when he heard that Hobbs had complained. The Indian prince, whose enchanting batsmanship for Sussex and England had illuminated earlier seasons, felt that bouncers were all right in measured quantity. His captain at Cambridge, the Honourable F.S. Jackson (who was now a leading MCC figure), once told him he knew how to get him out: bowl at his leading elbow, with many fielders on the leg side. That, Ranji felt, was going a little too far: "Yes, you would get me out, Jacker, but it would not be cricket." Anywhere one cares to look in the bulky annals of hostile bowling and opinions on it, it will be found to be all a matter of degree. The Hobbs who was now lodging a protest at Bowes's excessive short-pitching was the same Hobbs who — as Alan Kippax mused in his 1933 book *Anti Body-line* — had felt hundreds of express deliveries whizzing past his ears and over his head from the likes of Cotter, Gregory, Walter Brearley, Kotze and Larwood. He was not the sort of man to complain without good cause.

In the middle of this formative summer of 1932, it is slightly amusing to contemplate the fact that the greatest figures — to this day — ever returned by a bowler in first-class cricket were registered at Headingley early in July. Hedley Verity's analysis was 19.4 overs 16 maidens 10 wickets for 10 runs. He was bowling for Yorkshire, who became champions yet again, and the opposition were none other than Notts. And, amidst all the bouncers and bruises of that summer, Verity was, of course, a slow left-arm bowler.

As for the true genesis of Bodyline, the key moment had come some time earlier, when D.R. Jardine, having watched film of the 1930 Oval Test match in the company of a gathering of MCC committeemen at Lord's, spotted Don Bradman's discomfort on the damp pitch, and suddenly ejaculated: "I've got it! He's yellow!"[19]

CHAPTER THREE

SOUTHWARD HO

England's battalion to fight for the Ashes in Australia in 1932–33 was assembled piecemeal. And there was, after all, some uncertainly surrounding the captaincy. Douglas Jardine was invited to lead, but had last-minute reservations which were overcome only after his father had a word with him following pleas from P.F. Warner. It was an outstanding example of the Old Boy network at play. Warner had made Jardine captain of England in the first place in 1931. Both were Oxford University men, and had the lurid Harlequin caps in their bags. H.D.G. "Shrimp" Leveson Gower, another power at Lord's, was also an Oxonian, and happened to have been educated at Jardine's old school, Winchester College, Hampshire. Jardine's father, Malcolm, who spent much of his career in India and became Advocate-General of Bombay, was a friend and contemporary of both Warner and Leveson Gower.

It was all so cosy — though not always for R.E.S. Wyatt, who was not a university man. Bob Wyatt, having captained England in that 1930 Oval Test after A.P.F. Chapman had been dumped, took it like a man when Chapman was restored for the tour of South Africa that winter and when Jardine was installed as captain in 1931. Bob Wyatt's turn would come again when the dust and smoke of Bodyline had cleared. Meanwhile, he was pleased to serve — and with unwavering loyalty — as Jardine's vice-captain in Australia.

Neville Cardus, cricket's incomparable word-composer, told readers of *The Observer* that "absurd stories are going around that Jardine is a combination of a Prussian junker and schoolmaster Dr Switchem with his cane. But if the Australians are to be tackled, give me a captain who smiles only when the enemy are being rubbed into the dust." Jardine's reputation was unshiftable, and even 50 years after the tour he remained a grim figure, to be lampooned whenever possible, as in a cartoon showing one man telling the other that "I have it on good authority that during the '32 tour Jardine throttled a koala."

After Jardine's appointment Warner was announced as manager. (Lord Hawke asked him; he was "fond" of Australia, so agreed. Harold Larwood, in retirement, saw it slightly differently: he believed that "P.F. Warner, who was very much of a dictator in those days at Lord's, he decided he was going himself.") Joint manager, with special responsibility for the finances, was to be R.C.N. Palairet, brother of elegant Golden Age batsman Lionel and, until recently, Surrey's secretary. H.A. Brown and R.V. Ryder, secretaries of Notts and Warwickshire respectively, both had cause to believe they were in the running, but it was probably a foregone conclusion. Some eyebrows were raised at the thought that P.F. Warner had had a hand in selection, was also a journalist, and now took on the role of tour manager. What was not widely known was that he also had ambitions to broadcast during the tour. He hadn't the voice for it — too lugubrious — but he secured permission from MCC to do three broadcasts, all for no fee: from Perth at the start, then Sydney, and from New Zealand at the end. A further request, to do one from Adelaide, was turned down.[1]

On July 15, the names of K.S. Duleepsinhji, Walter Hammond, Herbert Sutcliffe, Leslie Ames and George Duckworth were released (the latter two were wicketkeepers), and 22 players were selected for a trial match at Cardiff, a spectacle ruined by rain, but not before Duleepsinhji, Ranji's brilliant nephew, had made a charming 92 not out.

At the beginning of August the selectors, Lord Hawke (chairman of MCC's cricket committee), Percy "Pete" Perrin (formerly a high-scoring Essex amateur batsman), Tom Higson (a Manchester businessman and lawyer), Warner and Jardine, built the MCC team up to 13, adding the amateurs Gubby Allen, Freddie Brown, the Nawab of Pataudi, R.W.V. Robins and Bob Wyatt, and professionals Larwood and Voce.

Larwood had felt himself by no means a certainty for selection. He had half-expected to spend the winter with wife Lois and their four-year-old girl (four more daughters were to follow; when news of June's birth reached him during a county match in 1928 he took three wickets in four balls:

"Bloody good job it wasn't twins," someone murmured). This coming winter might well have been spent tending to his chicken farm and probably returning to the grim filth and darkness of the coal-face, where he had begun work as a tiny, shy pit-boy at 14 years of age, walking the three miles (4.9 km) between home and the mine.

After lengthy cogitation by the selection panel, three more names were announced a fortnight later: Maurice Leyland, Maurice Tate and Hedley Verity. When Robins withdrew for business reasons (he was to tour Australia four years later), the Derbyshire legspinner Tommy Mitchell was enlisted.

Then, when thoughts were on tidying up commitments and packing, Duleepsinhji collapsed in the pavilion during Sussex's match at Taunton. He was to spend the winter in the Swiss Alps, to continue his fight against pulmonary tuberculosis — and to exorcise the death-threat letter he had received after his selection for the Australian tour: "You two [Pataudi as well] may go to Australia but you will never come back. At least *not alive*."[2] Duleep was a charming and modest man with an enchanting style at the crease. In 1930 he scored 173 against Australia at Lord's on his Test debut, and made twin centuries for the Gentlemen against a Players attack which included Larwood. His 333 was the highest score ever made for Sussex, and now he had captained the county to runners-up position in the Championship. But this 90 at Taunton was to be his final innings. His Test average was a proud 58.52. P.F. Warner thoughtfully wrote to him during the '32–33 tour, telling him of Jardine's "obsessive hatred of Australians" and that England's bowling was "conceived in hate", remarks that were hardly likely to improve the health of this gentle person. Duleep, having toured with the non-Test-playing MCC side in Australia in 1929–30, did make it back there — 18 years later, as India's High Commissioner. As for Eddie Paynter, who took Duleep's place, immortality in Brisbane was to be his reward.

There remained one further manoeuvre in this untidy assembly of England's most famous or notorious team. Tate, now 37 but lion-hearted as ever, fifth in the national bowling averages this season and a popular hero even among Australians on his two previous highly successful tours, was summoned to Lord's, and there, in an office "cold as the Old Bailey", he was insultingly told that he was lucky to be chosen, for there was no certainty that he had been bowling flat-out recently. He passed his medical, but on the way home to Brighton he began to wonder if he really ought to tour.

Perhaps he had been overworked. He certainly felt a bit seedy. And while packing, he collapsed, as much a victim of nervous as physical breakdown. His pregnant wife Kath tended him for several days before falling ill herself.[3] Tate phoned Lord's, pulling out of the tour.

This distressed the loyal and loving Kath, who wrote to Billy Findlay, MCC's secretary, urging him to disregard her husband's phone call. When nothing happened she wrote again, the English team having sailed by now. MCC's doctor examined the huge Sussex bowler, and while the club considered its verdict, Maurice Tate walked pensively over the Downs. An eminent nerve specialist pronounced him fit, and two days later he was on his way overland to Marseilles to catch the P&O steamer *Strathnaver*. As the ship passed Stromboli, the little Mediterranean island, the wireless operator informed Tate that his twin girls and young son had a new brother. He was not to see and hold little Michael until the team returned 30 weeks later.

RUSHING TO PACK AND FINALISE MATTERS: BILL BOWES WITH ESME, HIS FIANCÉE.

The doubts over Tate had prompted the selectors belatedly to add Bill Bowes to the team. The lofty, lumbering Yorkshireman had finished fourth in the averages, with 190 wickets at 15.14, and his selection — probably clinched by his 7 for 65 at The Oval for Yorkshire (county champions once more) against The Rest on September 12 — made it four fast bowlers plus a few medium-pacers, highly unusual for that period. It triggered a few early alarm bells. Don Bradman, far away, must have pursed his lips thoughtfully (Bill O'Reilly reckoned he heard him say the Tests looked like being turned into shooting galleries), and the respected J.C. Davis ("Not Out") wrote in Sydney's *The Referee*, alertly, or was it with undue panic: "If the battery achieves success it may be done by contravening the spirit of cricket."

MCC TOURING PARTY 1932–33

Full name and county	Nickname	Born	Died	* denotes amateur
Douglas Robert JARDINE* (Surrey)	Skipper	Bombay, India, Oct 23, 1900	Montreux, Switzerland, June 18, 1958	
Robert Elliott Storey WYATT* (Warwickshire)	Bob	Milford, Surrey, May 2, 1901	Cornwall, April 20, 1995	
George Oswald Browning ALLEN* (Middlesex)	Gubby	Bellevue Hill, Sydney, July 31, 1902	St John's Wood, London, Nov 29, 1989	
Leslie Ethelbert George AMES (Kent)	Les	Elham, Kent, Dec 3, 1905	Canterbury, Kent, Feb 26, 1990	
William Eric BOWES (Yorkshire)	Bill	Elland, Yorkshire, July 25, 1908	Leeds, Yorkshire, Sept 5, 1987	
Frederick Richard BROWN* (Surrey)	Freddie, Ginger	Lima, Peru, Dec 16, 1910	Ramsbury, Wiltshire, July 24, 1991	
George DUCKWORTH (Lancashire)	Duckie	Warrington, Lancashire, May 9, 1901	Warrington, Lancashire, Jan 5, 1966	
Walter Reginald HAMMOND (Gloucestershire)	Wally	Dover, Kent, June 19, 1903	Durban, South Africa, July 1, 1965	
Harold LARWOOD (Nottinghamshire)	Lol	Nuncargate, Nottinghamshire, Nov 14, 1904	Sydney, New South Wales, July 22, 1995	
Morris LEYLAND (Yorkshire)	Maurice	Harrogate, Yorkshire, July 20, 1900	Harrogate, Yorkshire, Jan 1, 1967	
Thomas Bignall MITCHELL (Derbyshire)	Tommy	Creswell, Derbyshire, Sept 4, 1902	Doncaster, Yorkshire, Jan 27, 1996	
Nawab of PATAUDI* (Sussex)	Pat	Pataudi, India, March 16, 1910	New Delhi, India, Jan 5, 1952	
Edward PAYNTER (Lancashire)	Eddie	Oswaldtwistle, Lancashire, Nov 5, 1901	Keighley, Yorkshire, Feb 5, 1979	
Herbert SUTCLIFFE (Yorkshire)	Herbe, Suttie	Summer Bridge, Harrogate, Yorkshire, Nov 24, 1894	Crosshills, Yorkshire, Jan 22, 1978	
Maurice William TATE (Sussex)	Chub	Brighton, Sussex, May 30, 1895	Wadhurst, Sussex, May 18, 1956	
Hedley VERITY (Yorkshire)	Hedley	Headingley, Leeds, Yorkshire, May 18, 1905	Caserta, Italy, July 31, 1943	
William VOCE (Nottinghamshire)	Bill, Tangy	Annesley Woodhouse, Nottingham, Aug 8, 1909	Nottingham, June 6, 1984	
Co-Managers				
Pelham Francis WARNER	Plum	Port-of-Spain, Trinidad, Oct 2, 1873	West Lavington, Sussex, Jan 30, 1963	
Richard Cameron North PALAIRET	Dick	Broughton East, Lancashire, June 25, 1871	Knowle, Devon, Feb 11, 1955	
Scorer & Baggagemaster				
William Henry FERGUSON	Fergie	Dunedin, New Zealand, June 6, 1880	Bath, Somerset, Sept 22, 1957	

Bowes was taken out of the final match at The Oval and sent home to deal with such pressing matters as his medical examination, his passport application, and to be fitted out with blazer (extra large), cap and so on, and to deal with hundreds of wellwishers and photographers. He had three days in which to sort all this out. It also meant postponing the wedding planned for that winter.[4] He then joined fellow Yorkies Sutcliffe, Leyland and his bosom pal Verity at Leeds station, and they made the rail trip by Pullman to London for the MCC farewell dinner.

Having obeyed the captain's edict that they should all have dental check-ups (Larwood had to have much work done on his teeth), the team were now all together at last, apart from Pataudi, who was in India, and Tate. Their contracts stipulated, among other things, no communication with the Press and no air travel. The 12 professionals were to receive £400 each, plus post-tour bonuses which were to be awarded according to performance and ranged from £175 (Hammond, Larwood, Sutcliffe) down to £75 (Bowes, Mitchell, Tate) for what was in effect a seven-month world tour.[5] The co-managers were paid £500 each plus expenses and the five amateur cricketers were on allowances of £150. All hotel accommodation was covered, of course, and MCC later decided that there should be money for souvenirs for the amateurs (£100 each) and mementos for everyone (£50 each) after their return. It may be helpful to note that £1 sterling was then worth £1.25 Australian (A$2.50), and in the interests of reality, these 1932–33 figures should be converted into something perhaps 40–50 times larger to equate with today's currency.

The tour selection committee would be Jardine, Hammond, Wyatt, Sutcliffe and Warner. But there were other — less obvious — selections, and they were in the newspaper ranks. These had impact on the fashion in which forthcoming sensations were to be handled. For Reuters news agency, Gilbert Mant, an experienced and urbane 30-year-old Australian (born 11 days before Gubby Allen and in the same fashionable neighbourhood in Sydney), was appointed in preference to Sydney Southerton, 58, who was soon to become the (short-lived) editor of *Wisden*. Mant always believed that Southerton would have been a better choice for the tour, for as a senior figure he might well have been both keen and able to speak out against England's unpalatable (to the majority) bowling at the time.[6] As it was, Jardine refused to speak to Mant throughout the tour. Having politely introduced himself when he spotted the captain reading in a deckchair early on the voyage to Australia, Mant was made to wait for perhaps 10 seconds before Jardine looked up briefly to say only, "I see." He then returned his gaze to his book. Feeling himself obliged to write nothing beyond a strictly factual, non-judgmental day-by-day account of the tour, the erudite Mant, for the rest of his long life, had to endure a troubled conscience for not having written more strongly about the cricket the English played in 1932–33.

Percy Fender's hopes of touring for the *Star* were dashed, the paper preferring to send Jack Hobbs, with his ghost-writer Jack Ingham (who also wrote for the *News Chronicle*). Disappointed too was the 25-year-old E.W. "Jim" Swanton, who was then writing for London's *Evening Standard*. Midsummer 1932 found him covering the Essex v Yorkshire match, and at the instant that Herbert Sutcliffe and Percy Holmes broke the world record with a first-wicket stand of 555 there was a stampede by the four reporters covering the match to the one public telephone at the Leyton ground.[7] Swanton was not even a bronze medal-winner, and missed the edition. He had already been assured that he was being sent to cover the tour of Australia, but the sports editor now changed his mind, believing that if his man failed to get the story in promptly from the East End of London, what chance from Melbourne or Sydney? The *Standard* sent Bruce Harris instead, an experienced newspaperman who specialised in tennis but had little understanding of cricket, though, like many a tabloid scribbler, he was skilful at concealing his ignorance. Jardine took him under his wing and he was no trouble. Harris's book on the tour declared his viewpoint by its very title: *Jardine Justified: the Truth About the Ashes*. Young Swanton, on the other hand, had he covered the tour, might just have rocked the boat by instantly condemning what he saw in Australia, establishing for himself that much sooner what was to become a weighty reputation during numerous post-war cricket tours. Forty years later he gently dismissed Harris's stuff as having been given "an importance out of all proportion to the intrinsic worth of his opinions".[8]

None of the nationals or provincials sent reporters. The cost would have been unjustifiable. How were they to know what lay ahead? The upshot of this narrow direct journalistic feed to English readers was that Warwick Armstrong alone (in the London *Evening News*) condemned Bodyline, and then in relatively mild terms. The reaction in England was that, well, he would, wouldn't he? On the eve of the first Test his speculative use of the word "unsportsmanlike" — a term that was shortly to come close to slashing the bonds between Britain and Australia — attracted no undue attention.

Jack Hobbs, loved and admired in both countries, was simply unwilling to be critical of either his country or his own county captain. Frank Browne, known as the last of the "wild men of Sydney", mobster, commando in Spain and Rhodesia, jailed in 1955 for trying to intimidate a Member of Parliament, harshly judged that the tone of Hobbs's writing during the tour "provided additional evidence in support of a belief held by people as widely separated by distance, color and tradition as the Irish and the Indians. That is that the English have two sets of rules. One for themselves and one for other people."[9] But it is not that Hobbs was incurably bland. He had strong opinions, but discretion and good manners were uppermost among his qualities. His apparent dullness disappeared in private conversation — or in letters, such as the one in which he dismissed the all-powerful Lord Harris as "an old bore" who thought about nothing but Kent, and another, written to a friend in May 1933: "As for 'His Lordship' [Lord Hawke], he is a silly old fool and he never has had a kind thing to say about me. My crime with him is that I am not a Yorkshireman."[10] The opinion Jack Hobbs had, when he was in his late seventies, of Don Bradman is just as compelling: "Young O'Neill has got off to a fine start and although I wish him well I do hope he will not, repeat not, turn out to be another Bradman. He was too good!"[11]

On Saturday, September 17, 1932 the English (MCC) team gathered on the deck of the Orient Line steamship *Orontes* to be introduced to the captain by their captain, D.R. Jardine, who, the newsreel shows, was impeccably dressed in dark hat, suit and waistcoat and was carrying an umbrella. Paynter, the bespectacled Mitchell, Leyland, Larwood, Hammond, Bowes, Duckworth … one by one they self-consciously step forward to shake Captain O'Sullevan's hand. Jardine thanks those who have come to see them off and expresses the hope that his team will bring back the Ashes. (Of course, the little urn remained in its glass case at Lord's no matter who won the last series.) The urgent scream of whistles drowns Jardine's voice, and the 31-day voyage gets under way.

MINUTES FROM DEPARTURE: JARDINE, IN HAT, WITH THE SHIP'S CAPTAIN, HAVING INTRODUCED HIS PLAYERS. SEEN HERE ARE ALLEN, BROWN, BOWES, DUCKWORTH (HOLDING HAT), LARWOOD, LEYLAND, MITCHELL, PAYNTER, SUTCLIFFE, VERITY AND VOCE.

A vast gathering of cricket-lovers had gone to Tilbury to see them off, and yet the cheers, tears and waving had started all over England a good deal earlier. The four Yorkshiremen — Bowes, Leyland, Sutcliffe and Verity — had been seen off by around 5000 excited admirers at Leeds Central railway station, including old Bobby Peel, the canny slow left-armer who had toured Australia four times late last century. He presented each player with a white rose.[12] Verity had had a visit from the wily veteran Wilfred Rhodes, who gave him advice and encouragement as a fellow slow left-arm bowler. One of the earliest entries in Verity's tour diary read: "It will be a wonderful holiday and education apart from the cricket."[13]

The nation's enthusiasm was so intense that players were cheered at railway stations along the way, and there were cheering crowds awaiting the arrival at St Pancras of managers, players and the busy perennial scorer-baggageman Bill Ferguson, whose runs diagrams from past Tests Jardine studied closely during the voyage. "Fergie" was to make 41 tours in all before his death in 1957.

George Duckworth almost missed the connection for the short train haul to Tilbury. He was so busy talking on the platform that, according to Hammond, "someone got him by the ear and scrambled him inside". Eddie Paynter and some of the other Northerners made their way to the station from the Palace Hotel in Bloomsbury, his nervousness under control even though his previous maritime experience was limited to a ferry ride from Fleetwood to Knott End-on-Sea across the River Wyre, a journey which Paynter said you could almost make on foot at low tide.[14]

Some great names from cricket's past and several of the departing Indian team were there to see them off, and two young girls presented Warner with sprigs of heather for each player and a little can of ashes: "To be returned intact".[15] The players—amateurs and professionals alike—found themselves in cabins scattered around the first-class section of the 20,000-ton vessel.

THE HISTORIC JOURNEY BEGINS: SS *ORONTES* EASES AWAY FROM TILBURY.

They had Harry Hopman and two other Australian Davis Cup tennis players on board with them, and also Arthur Mailey, now covering the Ashes tour, having just finished an unusual Australian junket in North America — Bradman's honeymoon tour, where he scored 3777 runs (102.08), with 18 centuries at venues as unfamiliar as Guelph, New York, Moose Jaw and San Francisco, met Babe Ruth, and sailed home with Jessie somewhat worn out.

"Shrimp" Leveson Gower and Lionel Tennyson were the Englishmen's fellow passengers as far as Gibraltar, but even before they had got that far the rough seas in the Bay of Biscay rendered many seasick. "We have three in bed," wrote Verity, "Larwood, Paynter and Mitchell." Jardine, occasional pipe-smoker, spotted reading Chaucer from time to time, issued an edict that autographs were not to be given on tour, and kept himself much to himself, though Verity appreciated being summoned to his skipper's cabin 10 days out for a tactical discussion, mainly about the need for him to *contain* the Australians between the fast bowlers' spells. Verity found his skipper "a well-read and intelligent man".

After Gibraltar, where they were feted and provided with cars by the Governor, they berthed briefly at Toulon, where Jack Hobbs boarded (having travelled across France; he was a woeful sailor) and somebody ruined lunch by remarking "Not a bad piece of horsemeat!" The studious Bowes and Verity took a bus to Marseilles for a brief survey.

Next came Naples, where the Yorkshiremen were stunned by the street con-men, and a trip to Pompeii, with wisps of smoke drifting threateningly out of the mouth of Mount Vesuvius. Australian journalist Reg Wilmot ("Old Boy" of the *Argus* and *Australasian*, sometimes known as "Bun", and father of Chester, the journalist and wartime ABC broadcaster, who was killed in the 1954 Comet airliner crash) noted that the English cricketers "were just a happy band of tourists, entering into the sightseeing like schoolboys, thoroughly enjoying everything, and making themselves very popular with the other passengers".[16]

From there they steamed down through the narrow Straits of Messina, where, almost 11 years later, with terrible chest and shoulder wounds, brave and gallant Captain Hedley Verity of the Green Howards would be conveyed in an open railway truck across that same stretch of water to Reggio on the Italian mainland, thence to Naples and a military hospital in Caserta. There he was still able to whisper and to show an English corporal a photograph of his wife and two boys, but after an operation he very soon lost his fight for life.[17] His great Yorkshire pal Bill Bowes, captured at Tobruk, was completely numbed when he received the news from a Canadian airman who was a fellow prisoner-of-war in the camp at Chieti.

Verity, Bowes and the rest of the cricketers sailed on through the wondrous Suez Canal in late September 1932 after a further stop at Port Said, a couple of British soldiers calling out, "Bring back the Ashes!" Then down the Red Sea they forged. It was swelteringly hot. Bob Wyatt had what he later said was the only disagreement ever with Jardine when he baulked at visiting the pyramids, afraid they might miss the ship. Jardine thoughtfully ensured that Duckworth, the Lancashire lad, enjoyed this rare opportunity. At Port Said, Bowes and Verity sat sipping lager on a hotel verandah, the latter bartering with a gillygilly man and getting a pair of bangles for 15 shillings. Bowes, later buying a topee (pith helmet) for himself at the famous Simon Artz store, gleefully spotted the same bangles for 3/6d. Back at the ship, there was pleasure in seeing an obstinate Wyatt finally outwitted by another gillygilly man and losing his two shillings.

NORTHERN PROS STICKING TOGETHER: THE WELL-DRESSED SEAFARERS LARWOOD, VOCE, MITCHELL
AND LEYLAND USE UP SOME MORE TIME WITH A CHALLENGE AT THE DARTBOARD.

The ship's crew were now wearing their tropical whites, and the heat dictated afternoon siestas for the passengers. There were a gymnasium and a cinema, dances and race meetings, with wooden horses and real bookmakers. There were fitness sessions on deck, and a choir, with Leyland as chairman and Voce conducting, which sang for hours in the evenings in the smoking-room. One night Tommy Mitchell, the life and soul of the party, suggested they sang hymns, and they embarked on such soul-stirring fare as *Abide with Me* and *Onward, Christian Soldiers*, performances that — coupled with Father O'Hannan's speech on playing the game on and off the field — the outraged spectators on Australian cricket grounds some weeks later would scarcely have credited possible. Eventually the cricketers had to be shepherded out at midnight by the nightwatchman, who called,

"Eight bells, gentlemen; good night!" So they all stood and sang *Auld Lang Syne* and the national anthem, and retired to their cabins.[18]

Eddie Paynter, already aged 30, was so carried away by the delights of the fancy-dress party that he succumbed to temptation when Larwood and Voce urged him to drink a shandy, the first alcohol ever to pass his lips. But when Freddie Brown, a fine dancer and the baby of the team at 21, overdid it at one of the parties the skipper sent for him next day and ordered him to drink nothing stronger than orange juice. "But he was wasting his time," said Brown years later, "because I arranged with George Duckworth to lace all my orange drinks with gin." He remembered his Surrey colleague Jardine as a "lonely man, changeable, moody, asking at breakfast what quarter might the moon be in" (and thus inviting comparison with another original thinker among later England captains, Ted Dexter). Brown was destined to return to Australia 18 years later as an extremely popular England captain, if not necessarily through the eyes of one of his young players, Brian Close, whose golf clubs Brown confiscated when concerned about Close's form at the crease — just as Jardine had confiscated his (Brown's) in Perth in 1932.

There was already friction between Jardine and Warner. "One early disagreement," Wyatt recalled, "ended in a first-class row in which Jardine was extremely rude to the Manager, and from that moment their relationship was profoundly unhappy ... When he took against anyone Douglas Jardine could be insufferably offensive, adopting an air of cold disdain which upset Warner just as much as blatant rudeness."[19] Gubby Allen claimed that Warner was so upset that he went more than once to Allen's cabin to "cry on my shoulder". Which picture raises a pretty point.

Was Plum Warner Gubby Allen's real father? Rumours arose during the 1980s, and when I put the matter to Bob Wyatt he replied with some gusto: "Oh, we all knew that in the Thirties!" The notion may have been put about out of sheer mischief by some person or persons with an axe to grind, but circumstantially the speculation is not lacking in possibilities: Warner looked upon young Gubby (whom he often referred to as "Obby") with marked interest through his schooldays at Eton and then while at Cambridge and when he began playing for Middlesex, Warner's county, at 19. He was ushered into the England captaincy by Warner in 1936. From the earliest opportunity Allen was closely associated with MCC, and in time he succeeded Warner (who had followed Lords Harris and Hawke) as the dominant influence at Lord's.

Born in Darling Point, Sydney on July 31, 1902 (two years before Plum Warner married his Agnes), Allen certainly bore more of a facial resemblance to Warner than to Sir Walter Allen. Sir Walter, a distinguished lawyer whose brother played for Australia in a Test at Sydney in 1887, and Gubby's mother Pearl were both half-Australian, half-English. Pearl's father was once Queensland's Minister of Lands. In E.W. Swanton's doting 1985 biography of Gubby Allen he inserts the intriguing remarks that Pearl "kept at a discreet distance a string of admirers, of whom Plum was not the least" and that on the morning of Gubby's first match for Middlesex, in 1921, "he had the encouraging word which he then most valued, from Plum Warner". From Gerald Howat's 1987 biography of Plum Warner comes the cautious conjecture: "Warner, as a carefree young bachelor, may have admired Pearl, a young married woman, when he visited Australia very briefly with Hawke's 1902–03 side on the way home from New Zealand ... Whether that early meeting between Warner and Pearl ever took place or not, Agnes Warner was a little jealous of Pearl Allen in the earlier years of the family friendship though always very kind to Pearl's children, Patricia, Geoffrey and Gubby." He later writes: "it was openly accepted that Warner was very fond of Allen, regarded him almost as a member of the family"; and in 1938, "for a spell relations between Warner and Allen were cool and it may be suggested that the favoured son had shown rather too much of a rebellious spirit".

Returning to the 1932 journey to Australia: Jardine so cared for his men that he ordered no undue exposure to the sun: "No more than 20 minutes!" When Leyland did get burned, his skipper, perhaps aware of the Yorkshireman's carelessness, slapped him heartily on the back and then rested his hand heavily on his shoulder as he talked tactics, Leyland gritting his teeth in suppressed agony.[20]

Alert to considerations of both comfort and security, Jardine forbade his players to go ashore at Aden. Up went the cricket nets on deck as they steamed across the Arabian Sea. Hammond wasn't interested, but Mitchell spun viciously off the timber deck, Warner, celebrating his 59th birthday on October 2, played an impressive straight bat, and Mailey's legspin range was confusing. Then Voce twisted his ankle as the ship lurched and the programme was abandoned. Fitness remained important, and the players ran regularly and threw themselves into deck games. Duckworth had fallen behind with his mixed-doubles deck quoits, and Wyatt, as chairman of the sports committee, told him to contact his partner, "if you know who she is". "Aye," came the reply, "I know her by sight. She's Ploom's tart." The dignified lady, it turned out, was an old friend of Warner's.[21]

They reached Ceylon on October 8. MCC were to show the flag in a one-day match against All Ceylon, captained by Dr C.H. Gunasekera, who had played for Middlesex. On a turf pitch at the Sinhalese Sports Club, Colombo, play was watched by almost the entire English colonial population, parasols aloft, and close to 10,000 excited, noisy, white-clad Sinhalese, many females among them and many perched on the branches of surrounding trees. Rain delayed the start and eventually forced a premature finish when it came down with monsoon heaviness, and the humidity was so oppressive that some of the less worldly Englishmen could hardly believe it. But the travellers were glad to stretch their legs on firm land at last, even if the solar topees on their heads were uncomfortable. Paynter's chin was marked for days afterwards by the chafing from the strap. Nor could he get over the size of the bull-ants in the outfield as he trooped off after being bowled for 4. The wide-eyed little chap from Oswaldtwistle was taking in a daily education.

His Highness the Nawab of Pataudi (family motto: The Help of God, and a Quick Victory) joined the team here, having travelled from his 150-room palace in the Punjab state over which he ruled, which was about the size of Rutlandshire and with 25,000 inhabitants. Over land and water for four days and nights he had travelled, to receive a full-scale official welcome in Colombo. Wilmot was fascinated by the rather shy 22-year-old Indian with the infectious giggle: "a highly-strung young man, with most wonderful eyes, which seemed unfathomable in their depth, but from their corners lurked a merry twinkle". On the drying and difficult pitch "Pat" batted for three hours for his 62, Wyatt's 54 coming in 75 minutes, and Freddie Brown's 24 including two sixes out of the ground. Earlier, the English bowlers looked rusty as W.T. Brindley, a Buckinghamshire player now with Ceylon Police, scored 82 not out, having an opening stand of 79 with Charles Clover-Brown, also of Bucks, who had captained Harrow in 1927.

SINHALESE SPORTS CLUB, COLOMBO, OCTOBER 8, 1932

ALL CEYLON 125 for 3 dec (W.T. Brindley 82 not out); MCC 186 for 7 (Nawab of Pataudi 62, R.E.S. Wyatt 54, G.O.B. Allen 23, F.R. Brown 24). DRAWN.

(Full scores are given in the tour books by Hobbs and Wilmot.)

There was a banquet that evening at the Galle Face Hotel in the presence of the Governor, Sir Graeme Thompson. Plum Warner gave one of the Empire-rousing speeches at which he was so adept. It was extremely relaxing, especially for team manager (finance) R.C.N. Palairet. When Wyatt rounded up the stragglers, Dick, who had drunk more than a fair share, pointed at a clock without hands and told him he was talking nonsense. He was bundled into a car, threw one of his two umbrellas out of the window and almost fell out of the launch carrying them across the harbour to *Orontes*. Bill Voce saved him and also helped him up the swinging ship's ladder, acts which bonded the old Somerset amateur and the mighty Notts pro and softened relations all round within the team.[22]

In driving rain the ship left Colombo harbour and headed south-east, next stop Australia. The cricketers' holiday was almost over. The Equator was crossed, with the usual ceremonial nonsense on deck, and as they passed the Cocos (Keeling) Islands they slowed down for a better view of the rainbow spray from the beautiful reefs and passengers oohed and aahed at the glorious hues of the Blue Lagoon.

Then, on the morning of October 18, they saw the thin outline of the western coastline of Australia, and soon *Orontes* was nuzzling into Fremantle harbour. Looking back on the voyage, Wilmot believed that Jardine had not seen much of his team: "He has the military idea that the general must hold aloof, and he considers that any undue mixing with his rank and file is not conducive to discipline." He observed too that team spirit had developed and a resolve for strong endeavour had been born.

He may not have been aware that England's captain, despite later denials by others, had discussed leg theory with Larwood and other bowlers, and also perhaps Sutcliffe and Hammond.[23] And according to some, he had been instructing his team to *hate* the opposition who lay in wait (a sentiment unremarkable in today's abrasive, cut-throat sporting world, but one that would have shocked most cricketers in the 1930s), and even to refer to Australia's diminutive, indescribably popular champion never as "Don" or "Bradman" but as "the little bastard".[24]

CHAPTER FOUR

THE MAN IN THE HARLEQUIN CAP

It was a scene which, if reflected to a wider Australia a few weeks later, would have drawn scornful groans. As *Orontes* headed slowly towards tying up at Victoria Quay, the sailors aboard HMAS *Canberra* stood at attention on deck.[1] A marine band struck up *See the Conquering Hero Comes*, a rousing piece which had greeted visiting English cricket teams to Australia as far back as the first, in 1861–62. There was sustained cheering upon the appearance of that English sportsman and gentleman, MCC's cricket ambassador, D.R. Jardine, Esquire, and even more as the players were conveyed in beribboned cars into Perth, through Peppermint Grove and King's Park, where they placed a wreath on the war memorial. There was an official welcome at the magnificently appointed Palace Hotel (which boasted the most elegant dining-room in Australia), then came practice in the afternoon and a "Flagship dance" in the evening.

Next day saw the first of many civic receptions, followed after lunch by a matinee cabaret at the Ambassadors' Theatre (where Bradman would soon be speaking to audiences over two nights about his recent trip to Hollywood). Eddie Paynter had an unexpected visit from his long-lost cousin Albert, who had emigrated from Oswaldtwistle 10 years ago and now spoke with an Australian accent. There were visits to wool stores and a factory, to the races in the small country town of York just over 50 miles (80 km) away (in company with the players of the Combined Australian XI). There the four Yorkshire cricketers were made a special fuss of, Warner made the first of his pious but earnest speeches, and Jardine adjudged as a draw a contest between two young racecard vendors who had boxed keenly for the privilege of selling him a card. Fingleton observed years later that "it was the only known diplomatic move he made in Australia".

To the small gathering of Australian Pressmen Warner intoned: "The very word 'cricket' has become a synonym for all that is true and honest. To say 'that is not cricket' implies something underhand, something not in keeping with the best ideals. There is no game which calls forth so many fine attributes, which makes so many demands on its votaries, and, that being so, all who love it as players, as officials or spectators must be careful lest anything they do should do it harm. An incautious attitude or gesture in the field, a lack of consideration in the committee-room and a failure to see the other side's point of view, a hasty judgment by an onlooker and a misconstruction of an incident may cause trouble and misunderstanding which could and should be avoided. This is the aim of the Marylebone Cricket Club, of which I am a humble if devoted servant, in sending teams to all parts of the world to spread the gospel of British fair play as developed in its national sport."[2] Fingleton detected a "vein of apprehension, a foreboding of something evil in the scheme of things" running through Warner's words.

And so the cavalcade began. The Englishmen were filmed at the nets at the WACA ground, Jardine wearing his MCC cap and batting in the pimpled gloves of the day, smiling co-operatively for the camera and playing a flashing drive for its benefit. The team gathered for a group shot, all smiling happily, the skipper looking cool in a white neckerchief.

In an age when media liaison officials were unheard of, Jardine had methodically prepared a message for publication ahead of the team's arrival. It was released in Colombo: "While our statesmen have drawn closer than ever before, at Ottawa, may the friendly rivalry on the cricket field, our joint national pastime, add its quota of cement to the foundation laid in the past and at Ottawa."[3] He was referring to the recent Imperial Economic Conference, during which countries within the British Empire agreed reciprocal preferences among themselves for the goods they produced, a move warmly welcomed by Australia's Prime Minister, Joe Lyons, who presided over one of the most troubled economies in the world during this period of the Great Depression. Britain was allowing favourable entry to most of Australia's principal exports.

The first sour note of the cricket tour was soon struck. Because of the pressing deadlines on Australia's east coast (as far away from Perth as Moscow is from London), Claude Corbett, of Sydney's *Sun* newspaper, asked Jardine for his selected team for the opening match in Perth and was told, after a prolonged frown, "What damned rot! We didn't come here to provide scoops for yours or any other bally paper."[4] An associated version of the scene has a journalist pleading that Sydney and Melbourne were waiting (being some hours ahead of Perth); to which the captain piped: "Tell Sydney and Melbourne they can bloody well wait." He thus broke the first rule in the manual for touring captains: Keeping Sweet with the Press.

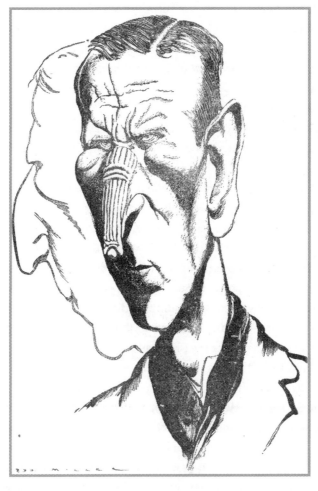

AS THE TOUR PROGRESSED, NO COMMENT ABOUT OR CARICATURE OF THE ENGLAND CAPTAIN WAS DEEMED TOO HARSH BY AUSTRALIANS. HERE IS SYD MILLER'S VIEW IN *SMITH'S WEEKLY*.

Wally Hammond believed that Jardine was the right man to lead if the Ashes were to be regained, but he knew also that Australians had unhappy memories of the man from his previous tour, in 1928–29, and perceived in his superior posture somebody who was "giving them the Colonial" — nothing got — or still gets — Australian backs up faster than this.[5] What they may not have realised was that Jardine treated everybody in exactly the same way: "his own team, distinguished patrons of the game and autograph-hunters".

The whimsical Rockley Wilson, one of the masters when Jardine was at Winchester, got as close to the young man as anybody was ever likely to, and the affection was mutual, as evidenced by Jardine's later tributes to this man, who had bowled legspin for Yorkshire and England and been cruelly jeered in Australia in 1920–21 for throwing in underhand, for writing articles mildly critical of the umpiring and the jeering, and for being old — 41. Wilson's remark when he heard of Jardine's appointment as captain for the '32–33 tour has entered folklore: "We shall win the Ashes ... but we may very well lose a Dominion."

With typical perversity, Jardine was to choose as his favourite from all the cricket matches he played in the one in which he scored 89 to help Winchester beat Eton in 1919, their first victory over the old foe for 12 years.[6] Two years later he played a slow, studious innings of 96 not out for Oxford University in the Australians' eighth tour match, the highest score played against them to date on that tour. Some have marked this as the point where his martial attitude towards Australians was born, but although it is feasible that Armstrong may have grunted something sarcastic at him while he built his innings, the tourists had to bowl with a greasy ball, and *Wisden* remarked that "with a little more energy Jardine might have had the satisfaction of getting his 100". Generously, Syd Smith, the Australians' manager, wrote: "We were all sorry he did not get his century."[7]

When Jardine first toured Australia, in 1928–29, he met with exceptional success at the crease, making hundreds with measured strokeplay in his first three innings (against Western Australia, Victoria, and New South Wales), 214 against Tasmania, and further centuries against South Australia and Victoria to finish second to the sublime Hammond with 1168 tour runs at 64.89. In the Tests he averaged 42.63, with a highest score of 98 at Adelaide (caught by Woodfull at silly mid-off) ... and he had a close first sighting of Bradman. So it has to be said that at least Jardine liked Australian pitches and bowlers, even if he was less keen on what lurked on the other side of the pickets. Nor did he think much of his tour captain, the rosy-cheeked swashbuckler Percy Chapman, whose gung-ho approach and love of booze led to Jardine's claim to Wyatt that if there had been a revolver available he would willingly have shot him.

During the first of Jardine's centuries against Victoria on the '28–29 tour, wearing his colourful Harlequin cap (maroon, buff and dark blue segments) he played all the strokes but was barracked noisily during a slower period. Passing him at the end of the over, the even taller Hunter "Stork" Hendry offered sympathy, but Jardine gave him a short homily he was never to forget: "All Australians are uneducated, and an unruly mob." Hendry blinked, then retorted: "Well, if that's what you think you can go to buggery!"[8] Seven weeks later, as Hendry, his score 96, joined the Englishmen during a drinks break in the Sydney Test match (oddly enough, in the wake of some leg theory from Tate, Geary and Larwood), Patsy Hendren quietly warned him that his glass had been spiked with whisky. Jardine, it seems, was the culprit. Hendry defiantly swallowed it anyway and was soon banging Hammond to the fence to post his only Test century.

Hendren, in contrast to Jardine, was keen to win Australian barrackers over, and knew how to: he simply acknowledged their presence, laughed with them, and quipped back. They loved it. Ben Travers, the playwright, travelled with the Englishmen on that 1928–29 tour, and recalled the insults hurled at Jardine, Harlequin cap and all, during his century at Sydney: "The word must have got round that Jardine was a stiff-necked, high-nosed type of cove, as indeed he was." Then, he recalled, Hendren said: "They don't seem to like you very much over here, Mr Jardine." DRJ replied: "It's ******* mutual."[9]

Travers, creator of the Aldwych Farces — humorous stage productions — might have written one around the Test match at Sydney that season, for during his glorious innings of 251 Hammond would pass the lunch interval with Travers's binoculars to his eyes, perusing non-stop the glamour on display in the Ladies' Stand. And Travers noticed that when England were in the field the Hill crowd were giving Jardine, the third-man fieldsman, a hard time of it. Jardine took not the slightest notice of the personal abuse until he vacated the position for the last time. Then "he half-turned his head, spat on the ground and moved off".[10]

While batting with Hammond in the Adelaide Test, Jardine appeared to obstruct Clarrie Grimmett as he went for a return catch, and umpire George Hele, who was to stand in all the Bodyline Tests four years later, told the bowler that if he had appealed he would have given Hammond out on the grounds of Jardine's obstruction.[11] That would have hardened DRJ's heart even more.

Sutcliffe, the senior professional on the '32–33 tour, and fiercely loyal to the cause, admired Jardine's resolute batsmanship enormously but had thought him a "queer devil" on the earlier tour, saying how difficult — impossible — it was to get to know him.[12] He later came to consider Jardine one of the greatest men he had met, "a stern master but every inch a man and as straight as they make 'em. Jardine had the courage of his convictions … He planned for us, he cared for us, he fought for us on that tour."

The captain was certainly keen to show his appreciation of his men, even sending gifts and cards to their womenfolk. Out of admiration, Verity named his second son Douglas. It seems all the Yorkshiremen found DRJ's grittiness a feature to be especially admired. After all, it was an outstanding quality in Captain James Cook, who first claimed the southern continent for his King.

Even in the bitter immediate wake of Bodyline, some Australians could still pay him a compliment of sorts. *The Australian Cricketer* told of a bold young local player who had given the Englishman cause to turn round when Jardine broke a long spell of runlessness with a single: "Well hit, Jardine," he chirped; to which the batsman replied, "Mister Jardine, to you."

Alan McGilvray, the former New South Wales cricketer and in-comparable commentator, looking back from 60 years on, and perhaps with encouragement from his ghost-writer, identified Douglas Jardine as the most notorious Englishman since Jack the Ripper. No slavish fan of Bradman's, McGilvray, who watched both Sydney Tests of '32–33, still heaped great blame upon Jardine for driving a wedge between the two countries. He deplored the "imperious and insensitive manner in which Jardine latched on to the throat of Australian cricket and dug in like a famished bulldog".[13]

Nonetheless, grass-roots Australian cricket-lovers were prepared to give the supercilious Jardine of the earlier tour the benefit of any doubt as he arrived back as captain of his country, while Arthur Mailey actually nurtured enormous admiration for the England captain, and later chose him in his mythical World XI to play against Mars. Mailey's belief was that "he wasn't really tough or relentless at heart". Although not facially so,

Jardine "resembles an oyster": the brittle exterior got tougher as opposition mounted. It is an irrefutable fact that later in life his friends discovered less cynicism and greater humour.[14]

During his first voyage to Australia, Jardine revealed some sensitivity in writing the following in the autograph-book of a young girl:[15]

> *When you are old and grey and lacking dreams*
> *What will you think when you take down this book?*
> *Of fancy dresses? Double ice creams?*
> *Wedding cake? Or cannibals' dreams?*
> *Or will you have no use for such?*

DOUGLAS R. JARDINE

Given that it was not in his nature to utter bland — let alone false — remarks, it is worth noting that whatever impression of Australia and Australians he had acquired on his first tour, when faced with the newsreel camera soon after arrival in Perth on the second tour he declared: "It's four years since we were in Australia. It's nice to be here again."

What do we make of him then, this man who ended the succession of good chaps, "social captains", who took England teams to Australia? Neither admired nor hated *universally*, the enigma that was Jardine lends itself to a range of interpretations. New Zealand-born Australian columnist Frank Devine wrote of Jardine's school, Winchester, that during the First World War, when Jardine was a pupil, "it was at its ghastliest, hurrying students through so they could make it to the Western Front and such places. Dreadful food and plumbing, discipline verging on sadism and an attitude of superiority to non-Wykehamists were among the school's hideous aspects. A Winchester variation on rugby football involved players standing still while an opponent booted the ball at them from point blank range. To flinch was to bear the shame of it for life. It was a bit different from the summer afternoons spent in Bowral by Don Bradman, wheedling his mother, 'Come on, Mum. Give us a bowl.'"[16]

Devine asserted that England has had to bear the shame of Bodyline, leaving Australians to ask themselves, "Do we really want to be like them?"

CHAPTER FIVE

ACROSS THE
WIDE BROWN LAND

As Herbert Sutcliffe took his guard before facing the first ball of the tour, at the unsophisticated WACA ground in Perth, what was the state of the nation which the Englishmen were about to traverse over the next five months? In a word: depressed. The years of economic depression following the Wall Street crash of October 1929 had brought hysteria and grievous deprivation. Across the Pacific, Australia's very soul was suffering torture. Government funds were belatedly and inadequately channelled into public works programmes and relief projects, but the dole queues went on lengthening. Australia's lingering grief over the heavy losses of men, mostly young, in the First World War was still tangible, while fresh, ominous rumblings from Europe were being heard. The one vital commodity which is essential for peace of mind — beyond food, shelter and good health — is hope, and that was in desperately short supply.

Australian politics, state and federal, were in disarray following the economic collapse. Life-and-death coalitions had become the necessity of the hour. As the worrying months ran into years, one emergency measure followed another as the unemployment figures swelled and trade figures, especially for primary industries, rapidly declined. Wages were cut, taxes increased. Allowances and pensions were reduced, sometimes withdrawn. Migration to Australia was severely cut back (an intake of 13,000 in 1929 — almost all British — shrank to a mere 275 in 1931).

A few days after Don Bradman had completed his mammoth runmaking in the 1930 Tests in England, Australia's state premiers had met in Melbourne for a key conference on the economic crisis. They were addressed by Sir Otto Niemeyer, a former official at the British Treasury and now adviser to the Bank of England, and Sir Robert Gibson, of the Common-wealth Bank. Niemeyer strongly advocated a heavy programme of deflation if Australia were to weather the storm. The premiers' deliberations resulted in an agreement to take severe measures to balance the budgets and to avoid entering into any further loans from overseas. Labor people naturally saw this as a form of debt-collecting on behalf of British bond-holders.

Australian batsman Jack Fingleton, whose father had been a tram-driver and State Labor MP, later colourfully wrote that Niemeyer "delivered to Australians a depressing lecture on how to run their country — a lecture dictating financial belt-tightening in a land of primary abundance".[1]

Just over a year later the British government passed a statute which unshackled the Australian Parliament from Imperial legislation in a number of ways. The convention that the UK would not legislate for the Dominions unless requested was now also written into the preamble of the Statute of Westminster.

Australia, however, remained not only strongly linked culturally but deeply beholden to Britain because of enormous loans which it simply could not for the moment contemplate repaying. And it was implicitly under-stood in Canberra that there were many key figures in London who wanted to continue to control events and conduct in Australia. There was great displeasure, from the Throne downwards, at the appointment of Sir Isaac Isaacs as Governor-General early in 1931 — he was the first Australian-born person to hold this position. An Australian Citizens' League held its first meeting in Melbourne to debate Australia's poor image in Britain.

A central figure amidst the chaos was the thundering, square-jawed New South Wales Premier Jack Lang, "The Big Fella", worshipped by the working classes, and for good reason. His government, apart from improving workers' compensation, had been the first in the world to introduce child endowment and widows' pensions. Now he told Canberra that the State would not be meeting interest payments due to London owners of government bonds. New South Wales needed the money, he roared, "more than those bowler-hatted bastards in Britain". The Federal government honoured the debt, then tried to get the money back from Lang. Having seen to it that £1 million was physically removed from two

Sydney banks under police escort and deposited in the New South Wales Treasury, he refused. So the Governor, Air Vice-Marshal Sir Philip Game, a slight, rather nervous Englishman with a piping upper-class accent, a DSO and five Mentioned-in-Dispatches, sent for Lang on May 13, 1932 — two months after Lang had opened the Sydney Harbour Bridge — and dismissed him.

On December 19, 1931 the Scullin Federal government had fallen, and Joseph Aloysius Lyons, a Tasmanian and leader of the United Australia Party, became Prime Minister. Having moved away from extreme left-wingism because class hatred conflicted with the Christian love that he and Enid taught their 11 children, "Honest Joe" also left his earlier republican inclinations behind and became a monarchist. He assured the electorate that by turning their backs on Labor and J.H. Scullin — as he had done — they had averted a financial and economic disaster. (James Scullin it was who spoke to British Prime Minister Ramsay MacDonald when the radio-telephone link between London and Canberra was opened. For 20 minutes they talked of many things, including Test cricket. Among the benefits ushered in by the new link was a perceptible improvement in newspaper content — there was greater coverage of overseas news.)

But there was no instant remedy for the catastrophic condition of the country. Bankruptcies proliferated. Men, women and children still knocked on doors for assistance or begged in the streets, and lived in hessian tents in the parks, on racecourses and sand dunes and on scrubland, sheltering even in the caves by the Domain in Sydney. They sought small handouts as they offered for sale collar-studs and soap and mothballs and holy pictures, or by singing or even by just standing there. For most of the men there remained a need to maintain a respectable appearance. Trilby hats and jackets and ties were worn. Many were ex-Servicemen. An Anti-Starvation Crusade was started in Melbourne, aimed at stopping landlords from throwing penniless tenants out into the street and seizing their furniture. "Susso" (weekly dole payments) could be as little as 1/6d (about $6.75 in today's money) a week.

There was violence amidst the despair, none worse than on Bloody Friday in March 1931 in Newtown, Sydney, where thousands watched as police evicted 18 Communists in a frightening encounter in which rocks and iron bars were used, the baton-wielding police employing barbed wire and sandbags. Even in sedate Adelaide there was fighting in the streets between police and unemployed men.

Australia's population in 1932 was 6.6 million, of which 337,000 workers were without jobs. Turning their backs on their problems for a while, so long as they had the necessary pennies, people went to the cinema for an escape to another world, if only for a short time: Garbo, Barrymore, *Tarzan*, Gable and Harlow, and the locally made talkies *On Our Selection* and *The Sentimental Bloke*, of which they were so proud, together with the new Cinesound newsreels. Some will have seen the first talking feature of Australian cricketers on screen as Bill Woodfull introduced some of his players in *That's Cricket*, out of which Bradman's young voice crackled confidently across the auditorium.

Sydney's Grand Opera House was defiantly reopened as the New Tivoli, with comedians Mo and Sid Beck top of the bill, three shillings (about $13.50) top ticket price. And it cost nothing to gaze at the marvellous Sydney Harbour Bridge, opened in March 1932 after eight years' work and the loss of 16 workers' lives. The ceremony was turned into a fiasco as Captain de Groot of the right-wing New Guard rode his horse through Premier Jack Lang's official party and, after obstruction, slashed the ribbon with his sabre, declaring the bridge open "on behalf of decent and loyal citizens of New South Wales" before being carted off to a psychiatric centre.

The Jolly Bridge in Brisbane was opened to road traffic about the same time, though without quite the massive public excitement, but any mild euphoria was soon dampened across the nation by news from America of the mysterious death of Phar Lap, deemed by Australians then — and many still today — as the greatest racehorse of them all. Just over a year previously another iconic figure, Dame Nellie Melba, had died, aged 69, in the same hospital, St Vincent's in Sydney, in which Victor Trumper had breathed his last in 1915. Melba possessed "the most glorious voice ever put into the throat of a woman", drooled an eminent admirer in London, a tribute qualified by Australian critic Max Harris, who described her as "demanding, dictatorial, ruthless, appallingly snobbish, imperious, vain, capricious, inconsiderate, tight-fisted … ungrateful, pathologically jealous, publicity-hungry and supremely egotistical". She would surely have been much at home in today's "celebrity" world.

As commercial air routes were developed there were continuing aviation feats to thrill, such as C.W.A. Scott's new England-to-Australia record of just under nine days, set in 1932, which Queenslander Bert Hinkler now intended to challenge; in September 1932, Lores Bonney, in her wood-and-fabric

77

biplane *My Little Ship*, became the first woman to fly around Australia (in 1933 she was to make the first flight by a woman from Australia to England, reversing Amy Johnson's first in 1930); and Charles Kingsford Smith, the greatest air hero of them all (and possessed of a physical stature and countenance not dissimilar to Bradman's), continued to set records from pillar to post — in between violent bouts of airsickness. There was distressing news in March 1931, however, when *Southern Cloud*, from his ANA (Australian National Airlines) fleet, crashed in the Snowy Mountains, killing eight, including Harry Shortridge, the experienced pilot who had flown Don Bradman from Adelaide to Goulburn a few months earlier, on his way home from the tour of England. The wreckage was not discovered until 1958.

Late in 1932, just outside Gundagai, Prime Minister Lyons unveiled the dog-on-the-tuckerbox memorial to the pioneers, affording a timely reminder of the fortitude of the men and women, some renowned, most of them anonymous, who had developed Australia to this point in its history.

In sport, Australia was pleased with three gold medals (for single sculls, cycling and women's breaststroke) at the 1932 Olympics in Los Angeles — Babe Didrikson's Games — where Britain won four. Walter Lindrum had a record billiards break of 4137 against England's Joe Davis; but Australia's Rugby League side lost 1–2 to Great Britain that winter, and the Rugby Union side fared just as badly against New Zealand.

Towering above it all — all 5 ft 7 in (170 cm) of him — was the man in Jack O'Hagan's stirring, bouncy song: *Our Don Bradman*, which sold tens of thousands of copies in sheet-music form. For a few pennies more you could have bought the 1930 gramophone record of his piano-playing and advice to cricketers, or Jack Lumsdaine's *Every Day Is a Rainbow Day for Me*, for which Bradman wrote the music. Then, when the skies turned dark for Australia in the Tests, out came Neil McBeath's *Keep Your Tail Up Kangaroo*.

Bradman's matchless and everlasting fame, of course, came from making runs in abundance; his appetite and method were truly incomparable in the annals of a lavishly chronicled game. He meant so much to Australians, even to those for whom cricket was a remote phenomenon. He drew them closer to it. He inhabited their minds and souls. In these terrible times he represented hope and defiance and indestructibility. People could turn their backs on the dreadfulness of the moment and find some sort of succour in the triumphs of The Don. It came close to religious devotion and dependence. Woe to the man or force that sought to harm him.

From his bush beginnings he had risen with great rapidity and determination to his pinnacle. He married his childhood sweetheart, Jessie, in an Anglican church in Burwood, Sydney, on April 30, 1932, and a delayed honeymoon came in the form of the American tour. Now he was back, sailing through the Heads on September 23. He and his wife set up home at Lower Bayview Street, McMahon's Point, renting half of a two-storey house on the north shore of the harbour, practically in the sunrise shadows cast by the Bridge. The problems they were now contemplating were how to preserve their privacy, settling a secure future as far as employment went (for nobody in Australia made a living from cricket), and something which was more readily if painfully attended to: extensive dental treatment for the world's greatest batsman.

Sutcliffe faced the first ball of the tour. It was bowled by Western Australia's Ron Halcombe, who had previously been called for throwing. The WACA pitch had been gingered up by rain, but the reliable Yorkshireman batted as calmly as usual for two hours, and the slender, elegant Pataudi, in at the fall of the first wicket (Leyland 15), compiled a handsome 166 in 4¼ hours, giving only one chance. When the Saturday was washed out, even though the pitch-ends were covered, having celebrated his 32nd birthday on the Sunday with a quiet party, Jardine declared first thing on Monday morning, gave his bowlers a few overs each as the State subsided for 135, and heard the first of the barracking that was to nauseate him throughout the coming weeks. When Bowes struck Bert Drew, Western Australia's No. 3 batsman, on the shoulder sections of the crowd of 3000 became "caustic". Nor were officials amused when the England captain turned up late for a pitch inspection. They registered a formal complaint with the Australian Cricket Board. (*Note*: the Board was then known as the Australian Board of Control for International Cricket, but for convenience will be referred to here as the Board or the ACB, its modern title.)

A batsman by the name of Curtin had faced the first ball when the State batted (and was bowled sixth ball by Larwood for 0), a symbolic coincidence of sorts, since that same name 10 years later would plant itself momentously into Anglo-Australian history at the height of the Second World War crisis: in the desperate days of the Japanese thrusts southwards, a man bearing that surname became the first Australian Prime Minister to look away from Britain and towards the USA. It so happened that at the time of this cricket match in Perth there were strong elements in favour of that State's secession from the Australian Federation. Their cricketers, like their politicians, often felt themselves to be the Cinderellas of the nation.

Clem Hill's nephew, left-hander Wyndie Hill-Smith, who many years later rejoiced as generous host to the entire travelling cricket fraternity at his Yalumba winery during Adelaide Test matches, opened the innings with Curtin and scored 26, and Western Australia's captain, Dick Bryant, top-scored with 35 as the home side narrowly escaped the follow-on. Brown's legspin and Larwood's pace and accuracy were forbidding, and Larwood also hit the first six of the tour. MCC batted out the match, keen for practice in the middle, Brown's 28 owing everything to five dropped catches, four off Teddy Martin, a googly bowler.

Eyes were already turning towards the really big event, the match starting three days later against a Combined XI for whom a contingent of big names, including D.G. Bradman, had come many miles to play. The Association, having lost money on this opening fixture, were hoping for better weather and attendances for the second game. They still took the precaution of insuring against rain interruption this time.

WACA GROUND, PERTH, OCTOBER 21, 22 (NO PLAY), 24, 1932

MCC 334 for 8 dec (H. Sutcliffe 54, Nawab of Pataudi 166, D.R. Jardine 38, R.A. Halcombe 3 for 48, E.J. Martin 3 for 115) and 152 for 5 (M. Leyland 69, E.J.Martin 3 for 50); **WESTERN AUSTRALIA** 135 (R.J. Bryant 35, F.R. Brown 3 for 29). **DRAWN**

A postscript to the opening fixture concerns Ron Halcombe. Apart from the doubts about the legality of his bowling action, batsmen on the whole preferred not to be exposed to his ferocity. That is why, as the season progressed, there were cries, especially from the West, for his inclusion in the Australian Test team, which relied almost exclusively on Tim Wall for pace. The hopes and visions of Halcombe ripping through Jardine's men intensified when, after he had taken 12 for 39 for Central Province against Port Province, the opposing captain, Mervyn Inverarity (father of as-yet-unborn Test batsman John), protested vigorously to the umpire and then to the WACA: "Halcombe has been deliberately bowling at the batsmen of my team." Hostile deliveries with a concentrated leg-side field had reduced the game to a farce. Besides that there was the matter of a "distinct jerk" in Halcombe's elbow. Inverarity threatened to retire from the game if something wasn't done.[2] Halcombe, who later became an ABC cricket commentator, was never brought in by the Test selectors. And not until 1947–48 did Western Australia enter the Sheffield Shield competition, from which point its players vied with the rest on equal terms for Test selection.

Now the Combined Australian XI faced Jardine's MCC side. The match attracted record crowds: over 10,000 on each of the first two days and an uncomfortable crush of just on 20,000 on the Saturday. It seems reasonable to assume that the presence of Don Bradman brought a high percentage of them through the gates.

The rail journey for Bradman, Fingleton and McCabe from Sydney to Perth lasted five tedious days and nights. Vic Richardson and Roy Lonergan joined up with them at Adelaide. Bradman and McCabe had played Test cricket and toured England but Fingleton was still a bit wide-eyed about it all, having scored 40 in his only Test to date, at Melbourne against South Africa earlier that year, when Bradman was unfit to bat. Now he was about to tread the same cricket field as Hammond and Sutcliffe, Larwood and Jardine. Disillusionment lurked only a month away.

They rumbled and rattled their way across the breadth of Australia, tucked into their sleeping bunks by night, playing cards to break the boredom by day. In Melbourne they were taken to lunch by the ACB chairman, Dr Allen Robertson, and two other members. Fingleton was taken aback by Robertson's pessimism: "Cricket is doomed in Australia."[3] Those words must have surprised cricket's greatest drawcard, Bradman, even more.

As the train chugged westwards across the long, straight link over the Nullarbor Desert, people who had somehow found out that the cricketers — one in particular — were in transit and within reach of them came from far and wide for a glimpse of them, moving frantically along the platform or through the carriages, demanding The Don's acknowledgment of their adulation. At sleepy little Quorn the mayor laid on a civic reception for them in the shade of some peppercorn trees, and at Kalgoorlie the bearded 6 ft 6 in (198 cm) Mayor Leslie, a veteran of the gold rush 40 years before and sporting a sombrero, threw another reception. Then came Coolgardie, and little short of a stampede by flocks of miners keen to see and touch the nation's hero. When Bradman locked himself in his cabin they began to ransack the train, and the driver deemed it wise to pull out slightly ahead of schedule. When the dust-laden locomotive finally reached Perth a posse of police was needed to escort the cricketers to the comfort of their rooms at the Palace Hotel.[4] Australia's champion might already have been harbouring regrets at having accepted the invitation to play. Within a few days he most certainly did.

On top of his tiredness from the North America tour and the marathon train trip, he was in dispute with the ACB over their ongoing ban on players' newspaper writing — he had a contract (part of a triple employment deal which saved him from having to earn a living by playing league cricket in England) with the *Sun*, the Sydney daily, which he intended to honour — and he was still smarting at the Board's £50 fine for allowing extracts from his 1930 book to be serialised in a newspaper. Tempting him from London, just to add to the pressures, came a very lucrative offer or two to write on the forthcoming Tests.

It was not that Bradman was short of runs, however. Before he strapped on his pads in Perth, onto the phenomenal output of the American jaunt he had tacked two fast centuries for St George in grade cricket and 145 in 1¾ hours against good bowling in a State trial match.[5] Now, to the roars of the keen Western Australian ranks, he fielded and threw like a god and unexpectedly bowled his leg-breaks for over after over, for Dick Bryant, the captain, had to withdraw with a leg strain. Bradman got through 19 overs and took two wickets for 106 (a rare century *against* his name): Gubby Allen leg-before for 16, and — this will have given the part-time bowler quiet joy in retrospect — Jardine for 98, caught by McCabe at mid-on.

As far as local preferences were concerned, the Englishmen batted too slowly and too long. After Leyland's departure, lbw to McCabe for 2, Sutcliffe and Pataudi had a sedate stand of 283, full of good strokes, though the Indian, collecting 295 runs in his first two innings in Australia, batted more slowly the longer he was in. Sutcliffe's innings ended with a stupendous boot-high catch at third man by substitute fielder Inverarity. Neither side had much strength in bowling, even Vic Richardson having a few overs, and if the Combined XI had had first use of a decent pitch they would probably have made about as many as MCC. As it was, Jardine was thought to have batted on much too long before he declared, not far short of 600 late on the second day. Hammond had looked in the sort of shape that brought him 905 Test runs in Australia four years ago and Paynter's breezy knock brightened the closing stages. Richardson and Fingleton posted a very quick 50 that evening.

ALWAYS A TOP-FLIGHT SLIPS FIELDER, HAMMOND MAKES SURE OF THIS CHANCE FROM
BRADMAN'S REVERED BAT IN PERTH. SUTCLIFFE AT FIRST SLIP, WICKETKEEPER DUCKWORTH,
MITCHELL SILLY MID-ON.

Overnight rain altered the mood. It was a struggle for the Combined XI batsmen even though Larwood and Voce were not playing. Verity's shrewd slow left-arm flourished in conditions that must have reminded him of a damp Headingley. McCabe, unexpectedly bowled by Paynter, was the only batsman to pass 30 in the dismal total of 159, and grief and abject disappointment were felt all around the ground at Bradman's dismissal for 3, brilliantly caught one-handed wide at slip by Hammond at full stretch off Verity (dubbed "Variety" by the wits in the crowd). There was a deep collective sigh from all round as The Don trotted from the field. And that was not all. In the follow-on, Allen, having flashed a ball through Richardson's defence, leaving the stump stuck in the ground a few yards back (much to Duckworth's relief), shortly afterwards had Bradman caught at short leg for 10. It was the only time in his first-class career that he was out twice in one day.[6] Hobbs wrote that "some of us thought Bradman did not care a lot for the fast bowling of Allen", and years later Fingleton claimed that during his short second innings, Bradman said to him in mid-pitch, "I think they're going to have a pop at me", and requested him to take Allen's bowling.[7]

Unreality surrounded the rest of the day, Jardine giving three-quarters of the bowling to Leyland, Paynter, Ames, Sutcliffe and himself. And the awful news about Bradman's twin failures was mercifully delayed several hours before reaching the rest of Australia, for high winds had brought down telegraph wires.

Only recently a 1932 letter written by Bradman to two young fans came to light in a story in the *Broome Advertiser*. On a Palace Hotel letterhead he wrote: "So you are both very keen little cricketers — what a pity you could not come to Perth to see these famous Englishmen in action. Never mind, when you get a little older I'm sure mother will let you make the trip — perhaps in 1936." The boys lived in Broome, over 1000 miles (1609 km) north of Perth as the West Australian crow flies.

Another latterday glimpse of the two big matches in Perth came unexpectedly in 2001, when Teddy Martin, the legspinner, was discovered by John Townsend of the *West Australian*. At 98, Martin was thought to be Australia's oldest surviving first-class cricketer. He played in both these matches, taking six wickets for the State but 0 for 126 for the Combined XI. In the first match, when he batted at No. 9, he recalled that "Bowes gave me a couple of whacks", and pointed to where he wore his inadequate box: he got a bruise "an inch and a half down there". His skipper, Dick Bryant, was so badly bruised that it appeared he had been hit with a hammer.

In the bigger match, Martin recalled that of his five imported team-mates, Vic Richardson was the only one who talked: "He thought he was an important man but he wasn't all that polite — he was quite rough actually." And Don Bradman? He was "very quiet ... did little but sit in his corner and keep to himself".

No sign of full-scale Bodyline yet, but plenty to write about and think about. And as the train transported the three young batsmen all the way back to Sydney, with the English team on board as far as Adelaide, Bradman confided to Fingleton and McCabe that he might not be playing in the big matches that season. More than that he refused to divulge. But during a round of golf in Perth he told Fingleton that he was very keen to get early runs to answer the questions about his ability to tackle what on paper seemed an English fast-bowling overkill.

Vic Richardson, during a chat with 23-year-old Bill Voce, possibly at the York races, was told that England were "not a bad side, and if we don't beat you, we'll knock your bloody heads off".[8] Alan Kippax was to hear from a friend that Voce was convinced that "if you can frighten them, you've got them more than half out".

WACA GROUND, PERTH, OCTOBER 27, 28, 29, 1932

MCC 583 for 7 dec (H. Sutcliffe 169, Nawab of Pataudi 129, W.R. Hammond 77, D.R. Jardine 98, E.Paynter 32 not out); **COMBINED AUSTRALIAN XI** 159 (S.J.McCabe 43, H.Verity 7 for 37) and 139 for 4 (J.H.W. Fingleton 53 not out, W. Hill-Smith 32). **DRAWN**

Don Bradman, Jardine's "little bastard", was feeling a great deal happier with life 10 days later, having scored 238 and 52 not out at Sydney for New South Wales against Victoria (for whom Bill Ponsford made 200). Bradman's was the fastest-ever double-century (172 minutes) in Sheffield Shield cricket, and was made against some testing bowling. Harry "Bull"Alexander, who finished with 7 for 95, was an unusually hostile fast bowler, while the combination of young Fleetwood-Smith, the left-arm spinner who could bowl the proverbial unplayable ball, and the two canny 50-year-old spinners, Bert Ironmonger and Don Blackie, demanded constant vigilance.

Right after this match Bradman was too ill to play against Queensland at Brisbane, but was to count himself well enough to face the Englishmen in the Australian XI match at Melbourne.

Before then, MCC had a match against South Australia at Adelaide. They were starting to look like a well-drilled team, Jardine's edict that all balls fielded should be thrown back to the wicketkeeper pre-empting by over half a century what is usually thought of as a modern intimidatory ploy. He also instructed Fergie, the factotum baggagemaster, to refuse an offer by a whisky agent who wanted to supply his tempting product free to the English team. An overture from the makers of Eno's Fruit Salt, however, was more successful. The team accepted, and Jardine's letter of thanks was used by way of endorsement in Eno's advertisements. (Was he ever aware — or did he indeed receive payment for it — that his photograph had been used as an endorsement for Gripu Sports Trousers in the *NSWCA Yearbook* of 1931–32?)

Social activities were an important part of the tour (the touring team had been made welcome by the exclusive Weld Club in Perth), and any suggestion of a night-time curfew was quashed by manager Warner, who knew full well — and told an enquiring reporter — that it would be detrimental for a cricketer to go to bed too early, only to wake up in the early hours and start worrying about the pressure of forthcoming events. In the fullness of time Warner himself was to lose more sleep than most over the dramatic twists of the 1932–33 tour.

A WELCOME LEG-STRETCH — AND FRATERNISATION — DURING A STOP ALONG THE NULLARBOR:
HEDLEY VERITY, STAN McCABE, DON BRADMAN AND VIC RICHARDSON.

At a stop along the Nullarbor Plain (only two trains a week ran to
Adelaide) the Englishmen bought boomerangs from the Aborigines and
tried — to little avail — to throw them properly, to the bemusement of the
black Australians. Some were so intrigued by the barrenness of the desert
outside, with just the occasional isolated shacks and mines, that their
feelings came close to horror. But boredom was the main problem on this
epic traversal. Picking all-time XIs helped pass the time. Final selection of
the Greatest Englishmen (as ever, without too pedantic a consideration of
birthplace) was: Nelson (captain), Wellington, Lister, Rhodes, Kelvin,
Simpson, Gladstone, Shaftesbury, Dickens, Shaw, Watt and Beaconsfield.
Three times they had to change trains, a welcome diversion, though not
the switch at six in the morning. Verity described the train as "primitive",
and the rails were so uneven that the jolting was apt to cause passengers
to "get jumped out of bed in the night".

It might have been on the journey to Adelaide that Tommy Mitchell got
into a panic when he found his wallet gone. Not only that but his false teeth
too. There were plenty of bottles of beer available for the players, and after

falling into a slumber Mitchell slowly came to and discovered his losses. For hours he wandered mournfully up and down the corridors, enquiring gap-toothed and anxiously about his wallet and teeth. As Hammond revealed, it was Mitchell's heartless team-mates who had hidden the missing vitals all along.[9]

Mischief was never far away when Mitchell was around. As he recounted in a 1986 interview with Guy Williams, at one stop on the marathon Nullarbor journey, Coolgardie, while standing talking with Stan McCabe and a couple of others he saw a goldminer passing them. He playfully pulled the peak of the stranger's cap down over his eyes. But the little miner had no sense of humour. He whipped out a pair of revolvers, and Mitchell found himself pleading with the man not to shoot: Mitchell had a wife and two children at home.

The South Australian Cricket Association had thoughtfully paid for special coaches to be added to the train from Port Augusta and for supplies of fresh fruit to raise the Englishmen's comfort level over the last four hours of their marathon.[10] They checked into the Richmond Hotel with the greatest relief and were guests at the SACA dinner that evening and at a tightly packed civic reception next morning at the Town Hall (which Verity considered as imposing as Leeds's) before net practice at the Oval, where many of the locals exercised their lungs. Jardine and Warner met Dr Robertson, the ACB chairman, together with Board member Bernard Scrymgour and secretary Bill Jeanes, at the SACA office in Pirie Street to go through the tour conditions. They came away with all their wishes met.

There was no shortage of social life and entertainment in Adelaide, the Australian city most deserving of the description "charming", to which was added a highly successful match from MCC's point of view. Clem Hill, still regarded in these parts as Australia's greatest left-hander, ran his keen eye over the tourists, and despite reservations about the Englishmen's fielding, he felt Australia would need to be at their best to win.[11] He particularly admired Verity's skill, and thought Freddie Brown's brisk legspinners and "wrong ones" could be nasty on a helpful pitch. Sutcliffe's century he thought spoilt by too many badly timed strokes.

Hill was unimpressed by Bowes: not fast enough. He might get plenty of wickets against "sedate professional batsmen" in county cricket, but it would be different in Australia: an earlier version of Rod Marsh's cutting observation in the late 1990s that English county bowlers are "pie-throwers".

Jardine won the toss again and sent Sutcliffe in with Leyland to open. Both made centuries against an attack headed by the 40-year-old spin schemer Clarrie Grimmett but lacking Tim Wall, who had a chill; Leyland had the great fortune to be missed before he had scored and again on 93. They put on 223 — Sutcliffe slow and steady until opening up after reaching his hundred, when he lobbed two sixes in among the seats — and this seemed the ideal pairing for the Tests, except that Jardine was a captain who believed in a flexible batting order. Poor Pataudi, lining up for a third hundred in three innings, was run out without scoring.

Vic Richardson had an extraordinary tale to tell about Hammond's dismissal, stumped off Grimmett for 27.[12] England's most dominant batsman had hammered Australian bowling mercilessly on his previous tour, and not once had he lost his wicket to Grimmett in the Tests. But Grimmett got him five times in the 1930 Tests, so now, at their first meeting on this tour, it was something of a private grand final between them. To his team-mates' astonishment, Clarrie whispered that he would get Hammond out with his fifth ball, five overs from now. For four overs he spun them down around Hammond's leg stump, with an appropriate field, luring the batsman into playing either to mid-on or aiming to penetrate the gap between the short legs. Came the designated ball: it drifted legwards as Hammond came down the pitch, and Charlie Walker completed the stumping. Hammond walked away cursing, and the young fieldsmen now knew that Grimmett was indeed a conjuror. Shane Warne would have been proud of such an episode.

Jardine, still preferring his Harlequin cap, made the third century of the innings, Larwood hammered 81 — mostly off Grimmett but with a long, straight six off Merv Waite — in 42 minutes (50 in 27 minutes) before Whitington held a stratospherically high catch, and Wyatt, going in at No. 8 after Verity had done the nightwatch, scored 61, an innings that he felt made his Test place safe, though he might have gone without scoring:[13] he trod against the leg stump as he hooked his first ball, from Grimmett, but the umpire didn't notice and gave him not-out. Wyatt and his skipper put on 135, and it is doubtful that this was Wyatt's last chance to impress, for Jardine must have made up his mind to have a break during one of the remaining preliminary matches, and Wyatt would take over the captaincy.

Three partnership records for MCC v SA were rewritten before Brown rushed the innings to the declaration at 634 by belting 27 in seven minutes.

South Australia's reply, which began promisingly, fell away for 290 and they followed on. Almost half those runs came for the first wicket. Vic Richardson batted for almost four hours for his delightful 134 and "Slinger" Nitschke (who was to become a wealthy racehorse breeder and pastoralist) took one painful blow on the shoulder from Larwood as he hit 69 in just under an hour and a half before perishing in an attempt to hit Verity for six for a third time. Larwood bowled only five expensive overs before a blister on the big toe forced him out of the match, but it was Bowes who was the centre of attention. The shorter he bowled the harder he was hit. "Can I have another man on the leg side, Skipper?" he asked. Jardine replied, "No, but you can have five." Feeling unfairly treated, Bowes bounced another, and Richardson took another four high to long leg. Same question from bowler; same answer from captain. More long-hops, more runs. Eventually Jardine took him off.

That evening Jardine said to Bowes, "I want to have a word with you." And the big, confused, bespectacled bowler said back, "Yes, and I want to have a word with *you!*" It was decided that they would walk back to the hotel together to sort this one out. They were at the other end of the scenic Torrens Park before the silence was broken. Bowes then told his captain that he'd never had a suggestion about field placings rebuffed like that, and if it happened again he would continue to bowl as he had until he got what he wanted or was taken off.

"Anybody who plays under me," snapped Jardine, "does as I say, or he goes home."

"Right," said Bowes, "I go home."

Jardine stopped and turned his piercing blue eyes onto him and asked if he really was prepared to go back to England on the next boat. Bowes confirmed his stance.

"Well, that's marvellous, Bill. Shake hands, forget it, and I'll do some talking." He then explained that in Australia it had to be either off theory or leg theory. You cannot spread the field.[14] Although Bowes was to play in only one of the Test matches and to take one wicket only — but what a wicket — he was converted on the spot into a fervent admirer of Jardine for his firmly decisive and extremely thoughtful captaincy.

Feelings between Bowes and vice-captain Wyatt were less pally. There was needle between them. Bowes taunted Wyatt by saying that he was scared of fast bowling (which Bowes himself must have recognised as an absurd accusation), to which the batsman retorted, "How the hell do you know? You're not a fast bowler!"[15]

Making his first-class debut for South Australia in this match was 20-year-old R.S. Whitington, who was to play for the Australian Services at Lord's after the war and write cricket books renowned for their entertaining prose and disregard for fine accuracy. He scored only 5 and 0, but his colourful Adelaide University cap caught Jardine's eye. The England captain sidled up to him as they left the field at one of the intervals and chatted to him for fully 10 minutes at the top of the Giffen Stand, among other things "asking me whether my ancestors came from his own birth-place, Guildford, Surrey". DRJ, of course, was born in Bombay, India. In 1956 Dick Whitington found himself responding to the toast to Australian Cricket, proposed by Jardine, at the Queen's Hotel in Leeds, and found him "an extremely delightful companion". The enigma intensifies.

Whitington also recalled that during this Adelaide match Jardine sought permission from the headmistress of St Peter's Girls' School for himself and Pataudi to take five of her pupils to Luna Park, the funfair at Glenelg.[16] Nearly 40 years later Whitington claimed that those girls, now "oldish married women", swore that the very sun shone out of DRJ.

On the fourth day MCC duly wrapped up an innings victory, with spinners Verity and Brown sharing 14 wickets and Wally Catchlove's four-hour 65 easily the top score for the State in the second innings. The Englishmen had earned their trip to the beach at Glenelg next day before catching the night train to Melbourne. The Adelaide match had been watched by over 50,000 during the four days, but there had been discord at times, and P.F. Warner felt disposed to criticise the barracking.

Off the field, unhappiness was starting to build up. Claude Corbett, the journalist to whom Jardine was so cutting in Perth, had let his readers know what he thought of the captain and had been critical of his late arrival for play one day in the Perth match. They had tried to become friends over a beer in Jardine's room in Perth but the attempt had patently failed. Now Jardine, having received some nasty letters, showed that his public image was, after all, of some importance to him. He decided that there should be a kind of peace conference in Adelaide, and summoned Corbett; Warner was also to be present. Jardine said he intended to ignore letters from Australians, but intended to reply to an English friend living in Australia. Was there anything Corbett would like to say for inclusion in that letter? "Yes, Mr Jardine," he said. "There *is* something you can add. You can tell him from me that my comment is this: You can go and *** ****!"[17]

Hugh Buggy first saw Jardine around this time, at the Hotel Richmond, and thought he resembled the Florentine monk Savonarola: "His eyes had the same intensity, he meant business and quickly revealed it." Earlier pleasant Press relations with England captains such as Arthur Gilligan and A.P.F. "Always Plays Fair" Chapman made this chap's presence all the harder to bear. When Buggy asked Jardine about the unprecedented fast-bowling battery he received curt answers.

Meanwhile, in convivial social settings Plum Warner was not short of a word. He spoke to the Adelaide branch of the Oxford and Cambridge Association, 90 men who had belonged to the two old English universities and who were playing host to the Varsity Blues from the English cricket party. Warner recited a limerick about a "young fellow of New [College, Oxford]" (Jardine) and told some jokes, all of which were unwrapped again at a similar dinner in Sydney.[18] While in Adelaide he and the team also enjoyed the hospitality of Government House, meeting the Governor, Sir Alexander Hore-Ruthven, who was soon to become a central figure in the most massive controversy cricket had ever known.

ADELAIDE OVAL, NOVEMBER 4, 5, 7, 8, 1932

MCC 634 for 9 dec (H. Sutcliffe 154, M. Leyland 127, D.R. Jardine 108 not out, R.E.S. Wyatt 61, H. Larwood 81, C.V. Grimmett 4 for 176); **SOUTH AUSTRALIA** 290 (V.Y. Richardson 134, H.C. Nitschke 69, F.R. Brown 4 for 81, H. Verity 3 for 45) and 216 (W.E. Catchlove 65, H. Verity 5 for 42). **MCC WON BY AN INNINGS AND 128 RUNS**

Soon after the team's arrival in Melbourne, Plum Warner was fluting another speech, this time at a reception in the Town Hall. Still saddened by the barracking to which Jardine had been subjected during his slow century at Adelaide, Warner asked: "Do you think it is quite dignified that the greatest cricket match in the world between the two greatest cricketing powers should be interrupted by a certain amount of noise?" At another reception later that day R.G. Menzies, the rabidly Anglophile, cricket-loving Attorney-General of Victoria, gave him Australia's answer: "Whether Englishmen hit out or sit on the splice, we will have the satisfaction of barracking them. It is our prerogative!" There was much laughter, even from the English cricketers.[19]

The Englishmen are again finding the great Australian barracker a source of annoyance—why not pay the bloke on the hill back with some of his own medicine!

WHILE AUSTRALIA WERE UNWILLING TO RETALIATE AGAINST BODYLINE BOWLING, TOM GLOVER CAME UP WITH THE INGENIOUS NOTION THAT THE ENGLISHMEN MIGHT CARE TO STOP THE BARRACKING BY PERFORMING SOME OF THEIR OWN — A SUGGESTION THEY WISELY NEVER PURSUED.

The visitors were impressed by the city's layout and atmosphere, and on the eve of the match they were guests at a performance of *The Gondoliers* at the Opera House. Strong opposition awaited them at the MCG, even with Ponsford absent with an ankle injury. Leo O'Brien and Len Darling, two of Victoria's five left-handers, had just rejoiced in a partnership of 301 against Queensland at the Gabba, and the solid Bill Woodfull, Australia's captain, headed the batting order.

But the chief concern was the left-arm wrist spinner Leslie "Chuck" Fleetwood-Smith, 24, who had taken 47 wickets with an array of largely indecipherable deliveries in only seven first-class matches to date, even though Bradman had punished him mercilessly a week earlier in a Shield match in Sydney. Wally Hammond was instructed by Jardine to hit Fleetwood-Smith out of the running for the Test series, a duty he performed like the best of the SAS. Fleetwood-Smith did have Paynter caught behind, and dismissed Duckworth too, but he went for five runs an over and Hammond finished with a magnificent 203, having been 169 not out over the rest day. A picture of athleticism and power, he played strokes to all parts, excelling in his trademark off-drive and reaching his century with a sweep to the boundary off poor Fleetwood-Smith. The weather was cold enough for some topcoats to be worn on the Saturday, but Hammond kept himself warm by pounding Fleetwood-Smith and the rest, though the craggy-faced oldtimer Ironmonger wheeled away very economically: in the day's second session 100 balls from him produced a mere *three* scoring shots. He was rewarded with Hammond's wicket when the Gloucestershire bat fell "with a stroke as rustic as a haystack" in Hobbs's view. Jardine, splendidly capped in the Harlequin colours, made a statuesque contribution of 19 in 68 minutes and attracted some mild barracking, to which he would have made not the faintest signal of recognition.

Paynter had to retire for a time with swollen lips and some loosened teeth after edging a lifter from Vernon Nagel onto his mouth. The Bendigo-born Nagel towered at 6 ft 6 in (198 cm); his brother Lisle was forced to miss this match after injuring his arm while trying to crank his car. The Englishmen would be seeing Lisle — more than they wanted to — in the contest which followed.

Victoria, batting first, owed almost everything to O'Brien and Darling, the stars of the recent Shield match at the Gabba (both would feature in some of the forthcoming Tests), and to Hec Oakley, who was left stranded on 83 after two hours' batting when the bowler deflected Ironmonger's drive into the stumps at the non-striker's end. Voce played his first tour match here, picking up four wickets without approaching top pace. In the State XI's second innings, after some rain (which had little effect on the pitch), only Woodfull and Oakley reached 20 as Allen, Verity, Hammond and Mitchell bowled them out for 94 to win another match by an innings and earn themselves a day off.

It was during this match that Pataudi uttered one of the greatest replies ever made to a barracker. "Hey, Gandhi! Where's ya goat?" The usual tittering came from the ranks on the public side of the railings. Turning with a bright smile and pretending to fix on one particular spectator's face, Pataudi said: "Ah, so there you are. Would anybody lend me a piece of rope?"[20]

The *Sun* reported that Jardine, at Bill Woodfull's invitation, visited

Melbourne High School, a pleasant interlude which surely would not have been conceivable in the atmosphere which prevailed by the time the team next came to Melbourne.

MELBOURNE CRICKET GROUND, NOVEMBER 11, 12, 14, 1932

VICTORIA 231 (L.P.J. O'Brien 45, L.S. Darling 45, H.H. Oakley 83 not out, G.O.B. Allen 4 for 45, W.Voce 4 for 55) and 94 (G.O.B. Allen 3 for 21); MCC 408 (R.E.S. Wyatt 74, W.R. Hammond 203, E. Paynter 37, H. Ironmonger 3 for 62). MCC WON BY AN INNINGS AND 83 RUNS

Hedley Verity documented the fact that some of the chaps had suffered mosquito bites just before the next game. But this inconvenience was quickly forgotten as events unfolded in the Australian XI v MCC match, a highly significant few days which *The Australian Cricketer* headlined without reservations as A SENSATIONAL MATCH. It was here and now that Australians first beheld full-blown Bodyline. And Douglas Jardine was nowhere to be seen.

Bob Wyatt was in charge, and his words are witness: "In that match we did for part of the time operate the leg theory, although not in so concentrated a form as it was used later. We noticed that Bradman was decidedly uncomfortable when he played this type of bowling from Larwood ... Afterwards I told Jardine what had happened."[21]

Against such typically cool English understatement is matched the anxiety of those who were shocked by what they had seen. In *The Australian Cricketer* the field set by Wyatt was described as "a fan shaped back wicket field", and the report made it clear that the batsmen were soon defending their heads. "The leg stump, or higher, was the target." After MCC had made an unspectacular 282 — even the pigeons, Mailey noted, wandered onto the square without being at risk — an audience of just on 54,000 on the Saturday saw the tall, high-scoring but somewhat slow-footed opener Woodfull take a thumping blow around the heart from a Larwood thunderbolt which necessitated a 10-minute hold-up while he recovered. But it was Bradman's behaviour that raised eyebrows furthest. He could have been playing for his State in Brisbane, and when the invitation to be part of this Australian XI arrived, he wisely let the NSWCA make the decision for him. They were happy for him to play in the Melbourne match. It is questionable that the right decision was made.

Against what was near to being England's full-scale fast attack of Larwood, Voce and Bowes (Allen's leg strain prevented him from bowling in the first innings), Bradman decided to be even more foot-nimble than usual, darting around the crease, hopping into position, swaying, ducking, going for his shots where possible. Ray Robinson later compared it to "jitterbugging". Other onlookers actually laughed, believing that Our Don was teasing the bowlers, clowning in order to get them to bowl like this in the Test matches. The truth was less appealing. With the intensive leg field, the bouncers at his person were pointed, and he had to devise something foreign to his nature if he were to survive and prosper. Anticipating a bumper, Bradman fell to a sitting position, bat over left shoulder, and the ball struck it and went out towards mid-on. Enterprisingly, he ran a single.

Hobbs was not supportive of the new tactics being unwrapped by England but observed that there was no legislation to prevent short bumpers, and that "they certainly chopped up Bradman's game".[22] Voce too was now getting into his stride, and bowled some ugly deliveries. There was no more apt description of the big Notts left-armer than that he resembled "an angry grizzly bear as he pounded up to the wicket".[23]

Perky little Leo O'Brien, who opened with Woodfull and top-scored with a defiant 46 (158 minutes), seeing the cluster of fieldsmen on the leg side as his partner walked to the crease to take guard at the start of the innings and thinking they were intended to be the slips cordon, had said to nobody in particular, in an effort to be helpful: "It's the right-hander down that end. I'm the left-hander." The Englishmen smiled but did not reply.[24] When he faced the bowling they left the field as it was, with five slips. No "leg theory" against the left-handers. It was the big fish they were after on this tour: Bradman, Woodfull, Ponsford, Kippax.

Bradman made some thrilling shots, including a square-cut and a hook to the railings off Larwood and a lovely late-cut, once taking 13 off an over from Bowes. But at 36 he was adjudged lbw as he moved across to that bowler. O'Brien said of him: "He was like a cat on hot bricks. One went for his head and he tried to get out of the way. As he did so he hit it like an overhead smash at tennis. It went between mid-on and square. There was no one there and we ran five. He could run like a rabbit. I can recollect hearing footsteps behind me and he had almost lapped me! The crowd laughed. They enjoyed it."[25] At one stage Larwood's experimental field was two long legs, two legs close in, and two slips standing very deep for any top-edged hook. O'Brien, Larwood's 1000th first-class wicket when he bowled him, thought that the Englishmen were actually starting to look rattled while Bradman was making runs at such a frenzied rate. But that dubious lbw verdict finished it, and another failure went into the scorebook.

In the second innings matters worsened. After Woodfull was caught behind off Larwood for a duck, Bradman was bowled by Larwood for 13. This time, having just been missed off the glove by Duckworth off Allen, the rebound eluding Sutcliffe, he flicked a smart four to third man off a sharp lifter. Manoeuvring in the same unorthodox fashion as in the first innings, as a misty rain swept over the ground, Bradman stepped back to cut a ball pitched well up and, to the bemusement of the silent crowd, his off stump was hit. This was enough for Bruce Harris, writing in the *Standard*: "Provided that Larwood retains his present demon speed, the Bradman problem has been solved. Bradman dislikes supercharged fast bowling."

The rainstorm which broke after little more than half an hour's play on the final day was acutely frustrating because the Australian XI needed only 125 to win, having shot MCC out for 60. Laurie Nash, the truculent Tasmanian fast bowler, more famous as an Aussie Rules footballer, failed to add to his three first-innings wickets, but Queensland offspinner Ron Oxenham took two lower-order wickets to add to his five first-innings victims. The outstanding show came from the lofty, fair-haired Lisle Nagel, who bowled with his injured elbow strapped. Using the crosswind and with wicketkeeper Ben Barnett sometimes standing up, he floated, bent and spun his medium-pacers so cleverly that he finished with 8 for 32 off 10 overs. (While six-ball overs were bowled in the Tests this season, all other first-class matches were played under the prevailing Australian *eight*-ball over stipulation.)

Nagel had no undue assistance from the pitch as over by over he earned himself Test selection. (Paynter later mischievously suggested that they were playing Nagel into the Test side.) He simply utilised the breeze and humidity while the Englishmen — without Hammond — showed a reluctance to move their feet. Paynter, having held a fine running catch to dismiss Keith "Perker" Lee, top-scored with 12. Sutcliffe and Brown each made 10. And all before a Monday crowd less than a third of Saturday's in size. Some would have noted that Herbert Sutcliffe's Bradman-like run of big scores at the MCG was thus terminated. This was his third tour of Australia and he had never before been dismissed for under 58 in his seven innings in this grand stadium. His four MCG centuries were all compiled in Test matches.

"Rubbishy" covers where bowlers landed their feet and damaged the pitch cost many overs of play, and what should have been a thrilling ending (Larwood was certain MCC would have won) was denied. Yet it remains a highly distinctive match: MCC humiliated, though it scarcely mattered, and their dastardly tactics unveiled. Alan Kippax, Stan McCabe and Bert Oldfield had withdrawn from the original selection, a decision which must have saved them a few bruises. And Jardine? He was having a fishing break with three friends 200 miles (320 km) away in the Bogong Valley. Their only problem had been three burst tyres. When the captain returned on the third day of the match, stand-in Wyatt told him of the extremely fast MCG pitch and how Larwood had made the ball fly off a length — Duckworth, standing 18 yards (metres) back, was often at full stretch skywards taking the ball — and how the fielders were placed on the leg side because there was little of what moderns refer to as "lateral" movement. And his description of Bradman's performance must have given Jardine the greatest satisfaction.

Years later, Bill O'Reilly, with typically uncompromising bluntness, suggested that Jardine had deliberately absented himself in case the Bodyline plan backfired.[26] If Bradman had sailed to a century, Wyatt would have been left carrying the can. Wyatt, of course, to his dying day protested that he had no foreknowledge of Jardine's plans. As for Bradman himself, when questioned about the prospects after these reversals, he replied, with the characteristic grin: "Don't worry about that. I'll be right as pie." More provocatively, as far as the touring side were concerned, it became known that he was determined not to get hit by Larwood.

Larwood knew he had rattled The Don but still believed that the batsman might prosper in the Tests because of his unique skills. Some of those crisp square-cuts in the Melbourne match sent familiar shivers through bowlers whom he had mistreated in the past. Nonetheless the "leg theory" had worked better than expected, even though the English camp was unprepared for the Press outcry.

"Stork" Hendry, having told Jardine to "go to buggery" four years previously, now wrote in Melbourne's *Truth* newspaper: "Douglas Jardine, captain of all the bally old English cricketahs, went trout fishing while Larwood was trying to decapitate Don Bradman and Bill Woodfull … Now, just why did Mr Jardine go off hunting for trout? Ah ha! Ah ha!" He went on to suggest that DRJ wanted to avoid the inevitable outcry when his fast men let loose this barrage. Hendry aired defiant views about Australia's Test chances — and then hedged his bet as he thought again about Harold Larwood.

A lot of people were now thinking about Larwood. In the *Argus*, R.W.E. Wilmot wrote scathingly about his hostility. That same morning Larwood ascended the steps to the Press box and asked to see Wilmot, who came forward, probably in some trepidation. The Notts cricketer then told him: "I would have you know, sir, that yesterday I was bowling to instructions." And with that he walked quietly away.[27]

And then there was the tour manager, P.F. Warner, who was worried by what he'd just seen. For him the nightmare had begun. Almost two years later he wrote revealingly and feelingly to Trevor Wignall outlining his difficulties on the 1932–33 tour (Wignall was a racy journalist on the staff of the *Daily Express* whose ignorance about cricket was a standard source of amusement in the Press box): "As for DRJ. He was 'my man', so to speak, and, therefore, all the trouble that his captaincy in employing BL [Bodyline] led to was, I assure you, a sore disappointment to me. Entre nous, DRJ in his Number One mood is a very nice fellow, and I am very fond of him. But he is not by any means an easy person, and he has not two moods, but about four. As a tactician he is very good indeed …

"The moment BL was used in the fifth match of the tour … I spoke on the matter, saying it would get us into grave trouble. I was in an awkward position as I was only a manager, and it was made more awkward by my having been twice captain in Australia (thrice if you count my captaincy of Lord Hawke's team in 1903). I did not wish in any way to appear as if, because of my experience, I was trying to boss the show. Besides, I was in the pavilion, and could not alter the tactics on the field if DRJ did not see eye to eye with me. I did all I could, and I think the team will tell you that I had not a little to do with keeping the side together, and avoiding a fearful internal row … I am devoted to cricket. It is a religion, almost, to me.

"You wield an attractive pen — shall I ever forget your description of your supper-party with Al Capone — and I want you to use that pen to bring cricket back to what it was, a modern order of chivalry."[28]

There will be those who believe that chivalry in cricket, as in so many other areas of life, has long been at death's door.

MELBOURNE CRICKET GROUND, NOVEMBER 18, 19, 21, 22, 1932

MCC 282 (H. Sutcliffe 87, M. Leyland 38, G.O.B. Allen 48, L.J. Nash 3 for 39, R.K. Oxenham 5 for 53) and 60 (L.E. Nagel 8 for 32); **AUSTRALIAN XI** 218 (L.P.J. O'Brien 46, D.G. Bradman 36, H. Larwood 4 for 54, W.E. Bowes 3 for 63) and 19 for 2. **DRAWN**

Which one of Jardine's four moods prevailed as the English team took the night train to Sydney is a matter for conjecture, though he must have felt satisfaction at the progress so far. His batsmen had all made runs and his heavy artillery was on target and close to full capacity. Newspaper criticism he would not be taking to heart. Besides, the huge gathering of cricket fans to welcome the Englishmen at Central station was all the reassurance needed at that stage. They were even applauded by enthusiasts gathered by the steps and marble columns at the entrance of the Hotel Australia in Castlereagh Street as they entered that fine establishment, which was to be their home for the duration.

New South Wales Premier B.S.B. Stevens, the Mayor of Sydney, and the Postmaster-General were at the top table at the welcoming dinner laid on by the NSWCA, with Association president, the white-bearded A.W. Green, in the chair; the conversation, at this stage of the tour, was still cheerful and polite. Had the dinner been held after the forthcoming match against the State it might have been otherwise. But for the moment there was no inclination to suppose that the English fast bowlers were adopting unfair methods. "People brought up to believe in the superiority of British values," wrote Philip Derriman, "including the ethic of fair play, just could not bring themselves to believe that a man of Jardine's background would do anything unfair."[29]

Behind the scenes, however, things were being said. And they were being said firstly by Don Bradman. He told some Board delegates (almost certainly those from New South Wales, among them Frank Cush, who was a fellow St George man and Bradman's landlord in Rockdale when the teenage cricketer first came up from Bowral) that he was concerned about the English bowling tactics in Melbourne. But his anxious observations were met with indifference. Jack Fingleton discovered years later that one Board member had decided to reserve judgment until after the New South Wales v MCC match. And what did he think then? To the astonishment of Fingleton, whose flesh was badly battered in that match, the official said he did not believe the MCC bowlers had been bowling at the body.[30]

He was correct only as far as Allen, Tate and the spinners were concerned.

The English cricketers wandered around Sydney ("Americanised" in Verity's view), marvelling at the recently opened Sydney Harbour Bridge, and then loosening up at the nets at the SCG No. 2 ground (where the Football Stadium stands today). State coach George Garnsey mustered some grade cricketers to bowl at them, among them Alan McGilvray, who had yet to make his New South Wales debut and would one day become as good a radio commentator as the cricket world has known. Thrilled though he was to be bowling his medium-fast stuff to the famous English names, he was to remember the occasion gloomily because of one incident. In the pavilion long bar afterwards, Jardine was asked for his autograph. "He swept the autograph hunter away with such arrogant disdain I was consumed with an instant dislike for him."[31] Like so many others, McGilvray discovered another Jardine later in life: "affable, gentlemanly" — though the former England captain was always to defend Bodyline robustly.

Although Larwood and Bowes were rested for the New South Wales match it was still a fiery, bouncy game, thanks to Bill Voce's performance. Allen stole the figures with five wickets, mopping up the tail, but in the early stages of the New South Wales innings the spotlight was on Maurice Tate, who had joined the team in Melbourne and was now greeted by the SCG patrons as the popular English hero that he'd been on two previous tours.

MARKED MAN. DON BRADMAN TAKES MORE EVASIVE ACTION.

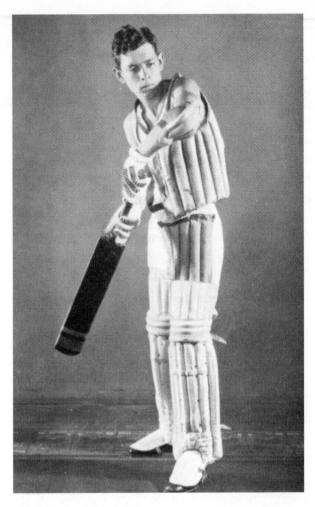

JACK FINGLETON, WONDERING WHETHER HE WOULD SURVIVE THIS TORRID SUMMER,
RESORTED TO SOME PNEUMATIC PROTECTION AFTER THE POUNDING HE TOOK DURING HIS
CENTURY FOR NEW SOUTH WALES AGAINST THE TOURING TEAM.

Not quite as nippy now, the big man, although (against custom) denied the new ball, still disconcerted the batsmen with movement through the air and off the seam, trapping Bill, Bradman (lbw), Kippax and McCabe and restoring not only his faded confidence but also his hopes of returning to the England XI. He was not to know that he was never a serious factor in Jardine's campaign plans. (Tate's successor as linchpin of England's bowling, Alec Bedser, on *his* third tour of Australia, in 1954–55, was similarly regarded by Len Hutton after one Test as surplus to requirements.) Some thought Tate had not been wanted in the first place, especially by Jardine: DRJ's biographer suggested that Jardine might have formed an antipathy towards Tate when Tate refused a run that cost Jardine his wicket — and what might also have been his first Test hundred — in the 1928 Old Trafford Test against West Indies.[32]

Apart from Wendell Bill (22), Stan McCabe was the only batsman to give opener Fingleton sustained support. Their fourth-wicket stand amounted to 118, and McCabe's 67 (83 minutes), which included 18 runs off one of Verity's overs, found him hooking and pulling Voce's short stuff with freedom and great confidence, often forcing the short-leg fieldsmen to consider their own safety. Fingleton, in contrast, drove handsomely but played a few false strokes at Tate's mixture and took a lot of the short leg-side deliveries from Voce about the body. There were several stoppages while he regained his breath after blows to the torso, but he gritted his teeth and battled on and was still there at the end, having carried his bat through the innings for 119 not out in 4½ hours. Film shot privately by a member down by the pavilion fence to this day causes sensitive viewers to flinch instinctively. Fingleton, never one to be intimidated on or off the field, was wirily built, with no excess flesh about his ribs, and Voce was playing on those ribs as if they were a xylophone. Wilmot noted that many of his deliveries pitched some way short of halfway.

It was a brave triumph for the batsman, but he carried a dozen or more bruises, and had to be attended to by the masseur for an hour that evening before leaving the ground — and his cricketing outlook was altered irrevocably. A century against MCC should have been the fulfilment of his youthful dreams, but instead Fingleton "was conscious of a hurt, and it was not because of the physical pummelling I had taken from Voce. It was the consciousness of a crashed ideal."[33] After a time the English fielders (Tate, Pataudi, Jardine, Hammond and Sutcliffe were in the leg-side ring) gave up commiserating with him when he was hit, for it would have seemed hypocritical. Dr H.V. Evatt, the cricket-loving High Court judge who would one day lead the Australian Labor Party and become President of the United Nations General Assembly, stated that he was so revolted by what he had witnessed that he lost, there and then, all desire to see any Test cricket that summer, a sentiment shared by Fingleton's mother, who must have felt the pain even more acutely each time her son was hit. What Governor-General Sir Isaac Isaacs — to whom the teams had been presented at lunchtime — thought about it all is not recorded.

Sir Philip Game greets N.S.W. and Eng. at Sydney Cricket Ground, Nov. '32.

AWAY FROM HIS POLITICAL BATTLES FOR A FEW HOURS, THE NSW GOVERNOR, SIR PHILIP GAME, MEETS THE TWO TEAMS DURING THE NSW v MCC MATCH.

Jardine won some plaudits for readily allowing Hammy Love, who was not even in the New South Wales twelve, to come in as wicketkeeper when Bert Oldfield went down with influenza, but the biggest concern was Bradman's health. He had contracted flu while playing golf on the Sunday of the Australian XI match, and was now confined to bed on the third day.

On the second day MCC laid the foundations of another big score, Sutcliffe unflappably 157 at the close of play, opening partner Wyatt having made 72 (lbw for the fourth time on the tour), Pataudi back to some sort of form with 61, and Hammond a turgid 20 after having his image as the world's best slip fieldsman dented by two misses on the first day. His long, drab innings was ended by a catch to Bradman who in taking it "seemed to play a bit to the gallery", according to Hobbs, the fielder turning a somersault in pocketing a dolly. Bradman also cost O'Reilly four runs with a wild overthrow. The tall, balding, long-striding O'Reilly, in his first appearance against English opposition, had a spell of 18 eight-ball overs of brisk, bouncing legspinners, topspinners and wrong'uns for a mere 26 runs. For the next six years he was to be England's foremost adversary with the ball, his ire tickled (never difficult) on this occasion when Jardine protested at the way he followed through down the pitch.

Bradman was having a bad match. He whistled a return just over a ducking Sutcliffe, drawing a scowl from the senior player, and when the MCC innings closed for 530 on the Monday he was in for yet another batting failure. (George Hele noted that on the previous English tour of Australia, in his second Test match, when Bradman was accused by Sutcliffe of throwing the ball at him the youngster coolly replied: "If I was aiming at you I would have hit you.")

On the Sunday the tourists were taken on a harbour cruise, exploring the inlets, gaping half-believingly at the Bridge, and enjoying a dip at Palm Beach, a few kilometres up the coast. "The beaches are full of people in swimming costumes," wrote Verity in his diary, long before the bikini was daringly baptised. "No-one thinks of being dressed." Paynter was to remember fondly the Palmer family yacht placed at their disposal, with Wally Hammond at the helm, and finding secluded beaches where they could enjoy their "bottles" of afternoon tea. Another Sydneysider, keen to make the visit enjoyable, had organised cars and a trip to the Blue Mountains, and later, crayfish suppers.

Les Ames got going at last with a three-hour 90, putting on 100 with Voce in even time and running MCC towards their imposing total. O'Reilly was the most impressive bowler, but the young legspinner Syd Hird, who had grown up with Archie Jackson in Balmain, toiled away with what *The Australian Cricketer* called "donkey drops" to finish with six wickets, half of them consummated by substitute keeper Love.

BRADMAN OUT OF POSITION FOR ONCE: HIS MANOEUVRE TOWARDS THE OFF SIDE FAILS HIM AS VOCE ELUDES THE BAT AND CLIPS THE STUMPS IN THE NEW SOUTH WALES MATCH.

The premier cricket State completed its slide towards an innings defeat. Almost 37,000 had witnessed Saturday's play, most discarding their coats and shoes — even their socks — as the sun blazed down, but there were only a third as many in attendance now as New South Wales lost three for 68 by the close, McCabe caught by Brown in hooking Voce, with Bradman yet to bat. Leaving his sickbed, he went in at No. 6 on the final day, and played a few reassuring shots to reach 23. Then Voce returned to the attack. The first ball was short but failed to rise as expected, and blue-capped Bradman, already over towards his off stump, defences wide open, was mortified to hear the ball crash into his leg stump. He had now scored 103 runs in six innings against the Englishmen, and his countless fans were beginning to fret.

Kippax was another to be caught when hooking, and Hird was snapped up in the leg trap. Frank Cummins, a cousin of Macartney, clubbed 71 at almost a run a minute, but the innings closed for 213, giving the English team their third innings victory on the trot against the southern States. What better lead-in could there have been to the first Test match? Australia were no longer quite such clear-cut favourites.

Hereabouts Jardine wrote revealingly to his friend Percy Fender back in England that, further to their pre-tour discussions, he was finding that more and more fielders were needed on the leg side for the fast bowlers and he may end up needing as many as seven.[34] Fender's collection of letters was lost in the Blitz, but years later he could still clearly recall DRJ's sentiments.

SYDNEY CRICKET GROUND, NOVEMBER 25, 26, 28, 29, 1932

NEW SOUTH WALES 273 (J.H.W. Fingleton 119 not out, S.J. McCabe 67, G.O.B. Allen 5 for 69, M.W. Tate 4 for 53) and 213 (F.S. Cummins 71, W. Voce 5 for 85); MCC 530 (R.E.S. Wyatt 72, H. Sutcliffe 182, Nawab of Pataudi 61, L.E.G. Ames 90, W. Voce 46, W.J. O'Reilly 4 for 86, S.F. Hird 6 for 135). **MCC WON BY AN INNINGS AND 44 RUNS**

A slight variation came with the version Fender gave his biographer, Richard Streeton, in 1981: "if this goes on I shall have to move the whole bloody lot to the leg side".[35] Fender, Jardine's live-wire predecessor as Surrey captain and a caricaturist's dream, was one of cricket's eternal thinkers. On his 92nd birthday, in 1984, he had a letter published in a newspaper in which he suggested a runs penalty for intimidatory bowling.

Aside from the famous evening with Jardine, Carr and Larwood and Voce at the Piccadilly Hotel grill-room in the late summer of 1932, Fender had taken some letters to show Jardine at the family home in Walton-upon-Thames. These letters were from Australian journalists who had been watching closely and listening, and had drawn the conclusion that England were going to send a team with an unprecedented squad of fast bowlers and that Australia's batsmen would have to make fundamental adjustments to their strokeplay.

RELAXATION UP THE RIVER AT PORT HACKING: JARDINE (IN SUNHAT) AND SUTCLIFFE
PREPARE FOR AN EXCURSION IN JOHN BAVIN'S BOAT AT ARTHUR ALLEN'S HOUSE, MOOMBARRA.
GUBBY ALLEN STANDS BY THE BOATHOUSE. (*COURTESY ROGER MANN*)

Alarms were ringing and the rumbles of criticism were growing ever louder. A horrified Tom Garrett, 74-year-old white-bearded survivor of the first Test match (Melbourne 1877), wrote to the *Sydney Morning Herald* to say that this was the first time he had ever seen bowlers deliberately bowling at the batsman — and he had been close to Tom Richardson and Ernie Jones. Garrett considered English cricket "tarnished", and urged that Australia should never retaliate. Dr E.P. Barbour, former New South Wales cricketer (he and Trumper still hold the Shield eighth-wicket record with 270 against Victoria in 1912–13), a *Sydney Mail* and *Referee* writer to whom ethics mattered deeply, and a New South Wales selector as well, also condemned what had been on show. After the Australian XI match in Melbourne he accused Jardine of placing himself morally on a par with the football captain who tells his team to "put the boot in" to a star opponent. In common with others, he was already regretting having written in terms of ridicule when he heard of Hobbs's objection to Bowes's methods at The Oval a few months previously.

Panic was not quite universal, however. The *Herald* asked its readers if Ernie Jones, Tibby Cotter, Ted McDonald and Jack Gregory, all hostile Australian fast bowlers, were so soon to be forgotten, and former players such as wicketkeeper Sammy Carter and left-hand opener Warren Bardsley defended the English bowling. But not all opinions were to remain fixed.

Within the English camp a split was beginning to widen, at first in the form of confidential grievances, as when Plum Warner wrote to his wife on November 29 a letter which would take about six weeks to reach her by seamail. Quoted in Gerald Howat's biography, Warner told Agnes that Jardine was "a very difficult fellow — such a queer nature — rather 'cruel' in some ways ... Hates Australians and his special hate is now Bradman! ... He is not the right fellow to be captain [Warner was on the panel which chose him] ... He says cruel things of people and his language is poor at times. Not often but he uses awful words on occasions in talking, e.g. of Bradman. He is very conceited, only he knows, and arrogant." Warner must have been grateful for the company of his brother-in-law Ormond, Agnes's brother, during a portion of the tour.

Mrs Warner had also had a letter from Gubby Allen, written near the end of the voyage, in which he confessed he was "terrified of Douglas", whom he described as for all his education "easily the stupidest I know and conceited" — though he was not saying he didn't like him.[36]

Warner was understandably shocked at a remark Jardine allegedly cracked as they stared, supposedly in wonderment, at the Sydney Harbour Bridge. Some RAAF aircraft flew over, and the England captain snarled: "I wish they were Japs and I wish they'd bomb that bridge into their harbour." (The Japanese had recently bombed and invaded Manchuria.)[37]

The cricketers' pleasure trip continued on its way, with enjoyable social engagements, such as the luncheon at Government House on the eve of the Sydney Test match. The menu featured Plums Warner and Fruits de Jardine, and the table was decorated with Australian wildflowers. Little dolls dressed as cricketers, half in Australian caps, half in English, were admired, as were the ices in the shapes of bats and balls on a cricket pitch. Governor and Lady Game had also invited 37 of "the prettiest girls in Sydney", and no one had more fun than the Governor's wife herself, for she sat next to Douglas Jardine, and "liked him so much" — the "so" underlined.[38] It seems that no RAAF aircraft flew over Government House during the festivities.

AUSTRALIA PLAYERS IN 1932-33 TEST MATCHES

Name and state	Nickname	Born	Died
William Maldon WOODFULL (Victoria)	Bill, Woody	Maldon, VIC, Aug 22, 1897	Tweed Heads, NSW, Aug 11, 1965
Harry Houston ALEXANDER (Victoria)	Bull	Ascot Vale, VIC, June 9, 1905	East Melbourne, VIC, April 15, 1993
Donald George BRADMAN (NSW)	Don, George, Braddles	Cootamundra, NSW, Aug 27, 1908	Adelaide, SA, February 25, 2001
Ernest Harvey BROMLEY (Victoria)	Slogger	Fremantle, WA, Sept 2, 1912	Clayton, VIC, Feb 1, 1967
Leonard Stuart DARLING (Victoria)	Len	South Yarra, Melbourne, VIC, Aug 14, 1909	Daw Park, SA, June 24, 1992
John Henry Webb FINGLETON (NSW)	Jack, Fingo	Waverley, Sydney, NSW, April 28, 1908	St Leonards, Sydney, NSW, Nov 22, 1981
Clarence Victor GRIMMETT (South Australia)	Clarrie, Grum, Gnome	Dunedin, New Zealand, Dec 25, 1891	Kensington Park, Adelaide, SA, May 2, 1980
Herbert IRONMONGER (Victoria)	Bert, Dainty	Ipswich, QLD, April 7, 1882	St Kilda, Melbourne, VIC, May 31, 1971
Alan Falconer KIPPAX (NSW)	Kippy	Paddington, Sydney, NSW, May 25, 1897	Bellevue Hill, Sydney, NSW, Sept 5, 1972
Philip Keith LEE (South Australia)	Keith, Perker	Gladstone, SA, Sept 15, 1904	Woodville South, SA, Aug 9, 1980
Hampden Stanley Bray LOVE (NSW)	Hammy	Lilyfield, Sydney, NSW, Aug 10, 1895	Mosman, Sydney, NSW, July 22, 1969
Stanley Joseph McCABE (NSW)	Stan, Napper	Grenfell, NSW, July 16, 1910	Beauty Point, Sydney, NSW, Aug 25, 1968
Lisle Ernest NAGEL (Victoria)		Bendigo, VIC, March 6, 1905	Mornington, VIC, Nov 23, 1971
Leo Patrick Joseph O'BRIEN (Victoria)	Mo	West Melbourne, VIC, July 2, 1907	Mentone, VIC, March 13, 1997
William Albert Stanley OLDFIELD (NSW)	Bertie, Cracker	Alexandria, Sydney, NSW, Sept 9, 1894	Killara, Sydney, NSW, Aug 10, 1976
William Joseph O'REILLY (NSW)	Bill, Tiger	White Cliffs, NSW, Dec 20, 1905	Sutherland, NSW, Oct 6, 1992
William Harold PONSFORD (Victoria)	Bill, Ponny	North Fitzroy, Melbourne, VIC, Oct 19, 1900	Kyneton, VIC, April 6, 1991
Victor York RICHARDSON (South Australia)	Vic	Parkside, Adelaide, SA, Sept 7, 1894	Fullarton, SA, Oct 29, 1969
Thomas Welbourn WALL (South Australia)	Tim	Semaphore, Adelaide, SA, May 13, 1904	Adelaide, SA, March 26, 1981

CHAPTER SIX

THE MAGIC OF McCABE

It is reasonable to suppose that the greatest fear of Australian cricket authorities — to say nothing of the millions who idolised him from afar — was that their prize asset, Don Bradman, would be seriously injured by Bodyline. Jigging about the crease, avoiding bodily contact with the lethal ball, he had made pitifully few runs against the touring Englishmen so far, but still the public "knew" he would come good. Look at his record. And his nimbleness—sometimes described as "antics"—had saved him from injury.

But it was no injury that caused him to miss the opening Test match. Instead he was brought down by illness, symptoms of which had curtailed his involvement in the New South Wales v MCC match. There have been all sorts of vague descriptions of this illness. Bradman himself informed the world in due course that he had been "completely run down" after all the strain of cricket, travel and argument. Jardine thought he must have been afflicted by a nervous breakdown, and stated so in his book on the 1934 Tests. Certainly Doctors Aspinal and Holmes à Court, who were brought in by the Board, while declaring him unfit to play, thought him "organically sound".

It was the most stunning news of the summer so far, and the trusted Ray Robinson, as a result of his friendship with Ponsford, was the first outsider to learn of it. The Victorian batsman sent a coded telegram to the journalist at the *Herald* office in Melbourne: "Three declared unfit." It was signed "Two". Robinson's editor was not convinced, so Bradman's withdrawal was tucked cautiously into the Stop Press, to become only a mini-scoop.[1] When Jack Hobbs spotted Bradman at the SCG he went over for a chat. He thought Bradman looked "drawn", but heard him say wistfully, "I would like to be out there, Jack, and not sitting here watching." He was echoing the nation's thoughts.

Another player was to step into The Don's shoes, if only for two never-to-be-forgotten days of this Sydney Test match. Stan McCabe's parents, and brothers Bill, Les and Bert had travelled in from Grenfell, a bush town about 200 miles (300 km) west of Sydney, and young Stan made sure their trip was worth the outlay.

The Australian selectors, Dr Charles Dolling, E.A. "Chappie" Dwyer, and W.J. Johnson (father of future Test player and captain Ian), had not been unduly stretched to construct a team around the huge crater created by Bradman's absence. Eight of the team had toured England in 1930; Fingleton's selection — and Nagel's too — were natural after recent performances; and O'Reilly seemed the finest bowling discovery of the age. Some felt uneasy that Bert Ironmonger was omitted from the original squad of 13 (Jardine for one was relieved), for he was seldom collared on a good pitch and could be unplayable on a damp one. But with the scheming Grimmett in support of O'Reilly the job could surely be done?

Syd Hird, made 12th man (and given a baggy green cap and blazer), was never to play in a Test match, for he was very soon to pursue a living with Ramsbottom in the Lancashire Leagues and in South Africa. Bradman had been saved for Australia when similarly tempted by an offer from Accrington after his contract with Mick Simmons, the sportsgoods shop, ran out. A £30-a-week employment package from F.J. Palmer's department store, radio station 2UE and the Sydney *Sun* newspaper had secured his future for three years — though therein lay another great problem that would soon need to be resolved if the world's greatest batsman was not to be lost indefinitely to Australian cricket.

For the first time, radio played a key role in public understanding of the Test series. For most Australians it was a luxury. A Tasma Tiger brand mantel wireless cost 16 guineas at Grice's in Queen Street, Brisbane, and a Baby Astor was offered for £11.15.0d, a sum that was three times the average weekly wage. As this exciting medium of communication planted itself throughout cities and suburbs and farflung bush regions, often even into the homes of the unemployed, it soon demonstrated a greater power of immediacy and dramatic impact than newspapers. Wireless was a means of "being there" for masses of people who could not have been accommodated at the Test cricket grounds, large as they were, even if they had been near enough and had the time and money to seek admission.

Not that it was so popular with those whose employees were distracted. Australia's favourite idiomatic writer, C.J. Dennis, scribbled a four-verse tongue-in-cheeker called *Dad on the Test*. "Who got Wyatt? Is Sutcliffe out? What do they care if I rave an' shout?" As the farm gets neglected and even the wife and daughters slacken off around the home Dad reaches a searing conclusion: "An' I reckon (said Dad) that a man's worst pests / Is this here wireless an' these here Tests."

Even business in the pubs expanded as drinkers lingered in convivial groups to listen to the commentary. They had little opportunity to glean progress scores from shop windows because police were soon issuing bans against blackboards and other displays: the public gatherings had caused too much congestion.

A concert at the New South Wales Conservatorium on July 1, 1932 had celebrated the formation of the Australian Broadcasting Commission, and it was estimated that there were already 370,000 licence-holders that year, served by the ABC's eight city and four regional stations. These were 2FC and 2BL Sydney, 2NC Newcastle, 3LO and 3AR Melbourne, 2CO Corowa, 4QG Brisbane, 4RK Rockhampton, 5CL Adelaide, 5CK Crystal Brook, 6WF Perth and 7ZL Hobart.

The commentators, as listed in an ABC pamphlet published the following season, were Charles Moses, E.L. "Gar" Waddy and Lionel Watt (all Sydney), Rod McGregor and Mel Morris (Melbourne), J.H. Holdsworth (Brisbane), and Len Ford and Steve McKee (Adelaide), with "special commentator" M.A. Noble. Live coverage was sometimes interrupted when land-lines were tied up, but studio staff would then grasp the initiative by carrying on a synthetic commentary based on messages sent from the Test ground by telegraph.

There had been cricket broadcasts in Australia as early as 1925 and in England since 1927, but the ball-by-ball commentaries of the five Test matches of 1932–33 were the first "live" and day-long international sporting broadcasts aired by the ABC, and set the pattern for many years to come. Commercial stations busily signed up Test cricketers for evening bulletins. Don Bradman, already on 2UE's payroll, sat in the stand during the first Test and broadcast each evening, giving a résumé of the play, score details for country listeners, and often concluding with a humorous story about a barracker or a team-mate. R.T. Corrie, author of *The Barracker at Bay*, a protest pamphlet distributed at the end of the series, wrote of his expectations concerning the radio offerings by Bradman and Woodfull after days of particular hardship for Australia's batsmen against Larwood and Voce: "Always I was disappointed. Never once did they disparage their opponents." Other Australian cricketers who aired their views in the evenings on local commercial stations — while being forbidden by the Board to write — included Stan McCabe, Vic Richardson, Keith Rigg, Alan Kippax, Wendell Bill, and sometimes even old Ernie Jones. Frustratingly, no recordings seem to have been made.

Even radio listeners in England had a realistic taste of the series through Radio Paris, which broadcast two 15-minute summaries daily and, most realistically, through Poste Parisien, who employed former Australian allrounder Alan Fairfax to cobble together a delayed "commentary" from piles of cabled information. Perched in a booth in the Eiffel Tower, Fairfax began talking at 6 am, giving two hours of concentrated synthetic description of the Bodyline Tests from start to finish, all financed through the sponsorship of a car firm and bearing the stamp of authenticity because of the cricketer's knowledge and confident style.[2] What English listeners, in their innocence, failed to realise was that the story was often doctored before being transmitted, so that the full extent of the physical punishment inflicted on the Australian batsmen by Larwood and Voce was disguised by euphemisms and omissions.

This has only recently been discovered. An archive preserved by the family of an executive of Gillette, one of the sponsors of the broadcasts, was purchased by the State Library of New South Wales in 1996 and opened up for public examination. *Sydney Morning Herald* journalist Philip Derriman, one of the first to look at the cables and the transcripts of the actual broadcasts, compared some of them and tabled the comparisons, one of which was: Cable — "fingleton clean bowled 234 dogged defence courage took innumerable blows". Broadcast — "Fingleton was clean bowled after he had been batting for 234 minutes. His was an excellent effort for Australia. He showed a dogged and courageous defence." Listeners could be forgiven for thinking that Fingleton had not once been touched by the ball.

The BBC, feeling a responsibility to match these commercial transmissions, deployed its Empire short-wave service to accommodate 10-minute round-ups direct from the Australian cricket grounds by the urbane Alan Kippax, who lost his place in the side after the first Test. Such a pronounced opponent of Bodyline tactics must surely have felt no urge to whitewash his summaries to audiences in England.

Percy Taylor, "Onlooker" of the *Argus* for many years, was one of many journalists who were staggered at the growth of the Press corps after Bodyline had first put cricket on newspaper front pages. "After the Bodyline tour, what a difference!! There were cricket writers from everywhere. I counted 60 in our Press box one day."[3]

The Australian Cricketer's editor, H. Drysdale Bett, described the gathering of writers even at the first Test match as "probably ... the greatest gathering of Press representatives in the history of cricket", and devoted space to listing them. Apart from the aforementioned Mant, Ingham, Hobbs, Armstrong, Harris, Wilmot, Worrall, Buggy, Mailey, Claude Corbett, Fingleton, J.C. Davis and M.A. Noble, there were:

Captain E.W. Ballantine, a South African (Exchange Telegraph, London); H.E. Stock (Reuters); F.S. Puddicombe (New Zealand Press Association); Charles Macartney (*Daily Mirror*, London, and Sydney *Truth*); P.F. Warner (*The Cricketer* and *Morning Post*); Frank Maugher (*Age*); E.H.M. Baillie and J.H. Corless (*Sporting Globe*); A.H. Thomas (*Telegraph*, Brisbane); C.H. Gardner (*Sun Pictorial*); Edwyn E. Oakes (*Sports Referee*); W. O'Connor (*Courier*, Brisbane); Frank Burke (*Daily Standard*, Brisbane); J. Corbett (*Herald*, Melbourne); A.G. Moyes (*Sun*, Sydney); Tom Goodman and H.W. Sherring (*Sydney Morning Herald*); G.L. Thatcher (*Labor Daily*); W.P. Tiernnan (Australian United Press and *Newcastle Herald*); F. Tierney (AUP); W.M. Rutledge, Alan Hulls, J. Russell and T. Glover (*Referee*, Sydney); E.W. Kann and S. Perkins (*Daily Telegraph*, Sydney); C.G. Simons (*Sunday Sun*, Sydney); A.R.B. Palmer (*Truth and Sportsman*, Sydney); P.B. Odgers (Country Press); Wendell Bill (Parisien Wireless); and B. Porter (Sydney Newspapers Ltd).

As the frantic summer wore on, others, of course, penned their opinions and drew their cartoons and wrote their funny verses — particularly in *The Bulletin*. Former Test captain Clem Hill gave his straight opinions to Adelaide papers, and Harry Kneebone ("Long On") contributed regular comment to the *Advertiser* in Adelaide. Former Test batsman Peter McAlister wrote for the *Leader*, B.J. Davie, another first-class cricketer, represented *The Referee* in Melbourne, and later Kenneth Slessor supplied satirical articles to *Smith's Weekly*.

As the first Test dawned, Warwick Armstrong sniffed pending trouble and said so in his cabled bulletin — the one containing the potentially electrifying word "unsportsmanlike" — to the *Evening News* in London. He was not alone in his apprehension, for many had been startled by the alarming events of the two preceding tour matches. Now, with Bradman a late withdrawal, Australia could not realistically start favourites.

Hours of play for the Test matches were 1½ hours from the noon start until lunch (45 minutes); 1¾ hours between lunch and tea (15 minutes); and the same between tea and the close at 6 o'clock, making five hours' play in all. No minimum-overs regulations — and resultant "overtime" — were then in existence or were even remotely thought necessary, for the bowlers turned smartly after following through and strode back to their marks, few had long run-ups, there were swift changeovers between overs and few delays for field changes or shillyshallying by batsmen.

The umpires were George Hele and George Borwick, who were to stand in all five Test matches. They had officiated in all five the previous summer, when South Africa toured Australia, and Hele had earned the respect of both sides in all five Ashes Tests in 1928–29. Jardine liked him (a feeling that was mutual), telling W.L. Kelly of the VCA (Victorian Cricket Association) that Hele and Frank Chester, the Englishman, were bracketed in England as the world's best. In the same letter to Kelly he said he would like to have a look at Borwick in the forthcoming New South Wales match. "Woodfull, I think, approves of him." Borwick passed muster in the final match before the Test and secured appointment.[4]

Adelaide-born Hele, now 41, had been named after the great allrounder George Giffen, and was once West Torrens's wicketkeeper. He made his first-class umpiring debut in South Australia's match against the 1920–21 MCC touring team, when Rhodes and Russell scored double-centuries, and he might have made his Test debut as early as 1924–25 except that he declined when he discovered that his appointment would have put an end to the career of the greatly respected Bob Crockett. Hele eventually stepped onto the Test field at Brisbane's Exhibition Ground in 1928, so he could look back upon a debut shared with Don Bradman. When Bradman scored his maiden Test hundred ("I've never seen a man more pleased") at Melbourne a month later, Hele watched as the Englishmen sat on the ground. They seemed to dislike the young Australian batsman, mistaking his *joie de vivre* for conceit. Larwood even wrote, in his book on the '32–33 tour,

THE ENGLISH (MCC) TEAM WHICH TOURED AUSTRALASIA IN 1932–33.
BACK ROW — G. DUCKWORTH, T.B. MITCHELL, NAWAB OF PATAUDI, M. LEYLAND, H. LARWOOD,
E. PAYNTER, W.H. FERGUSON (SCORER/BAGGAGEMASTER); MIDDLE ROW — P.F. WARNER (MANAGER),
L.E.G. AMES, H. VERITY, W. VOCE, W.E. BOWES, F.R. BROWN, M.W. TATE, R.C.N. PALAIRET
(CO-MANAGER/TREASURER); FRONT — H. SUTCLIFFE, R.E.S. WYATT, D.R. JARDINE, G.O.B. ALLEN,
W.R. HAMMOND.

that Bradman had been taunting the bowler by reminding the public of
what he had done to Larwood's bowling in 1930, going on to suggest that
Bradman's motto seemed to be "Australia? It is I!" Hele's opinion was that
"he was never conceited — merely a realist who loved batting and never
tried to conceal it".[5] Hele's blue–grey eyes would be trained with special
interest on The Don — when he eventually returned to Test cricket.

His umpiring partner throughout the series, George Borwick, was now
36. Born in Pyrmont, Sydney, son of a Finnish father whose surname was
Bjornvik, he was a small, genial man who had been a reader of gas-meters
before becoming a cashier.[6] This gave Yabba, the famous barracker on the
Sydney Hill, the perfect material for one of his shouts when Pataudi
descended into a trough of inaction during this Test: "Put a penny in 'im,
George! He's stopped registerin'!"

Australia may well have been without Bradman, but the English camp was suffering a frisson of panic of its own as Gubby Allen — already worried by criticism from Armstrong and Noble concerning his habit of running down the pitch after delivery — now crossed swords with his skipper. On the first morning Jardine said to him: "We all think you should bowl more bouncers, and with more fielders on the leg side." Allen replied: "Douglas, I have never done that, and it's not the way I want to play cricket." He told his captain that if he didn't like it, he should leave him out of the team. With that he walked away. Jardine, collecting himself, accepted it. "He never mentioned it to me again," said Allen. (He seems to have forgotten a letter he wrote after a similar confrontation with his captain just before the start of the next Test. The Sydney-born Middlesex amateur's refusal to bowl Bodyline made him a hero in the eyes of the multitude; but he nevertheless had no qualms about fielding at short leg, where he held five catches off Larwood during the series and acted as a visual deterrent who cut off numerous strokes played in the only direction possible against this bowling.)

Concluding on Jardine, Allen reflected: "I was probably his best friend on the trip."[7] Now this does not sit comfortably with remarks Gubby Allen made in letters to his parents during the tour. They came to light in 1992, after his death, and were sold at auction in Berkshire by Dreweatt Neate for £11,000 to the State Library of New South Wales. In one letter, following the Adelaide Test, Allen wrote: "Douglas Jardine is loathed and, between you and me, rightly, more than any German who fought in any war. I am fed up with anything to do with cricket ... He seems too damn stupid and he whines away if he doesn't have everything he wants ... Some days I feel I should like to kill him and today is one of those days."

Best friend? He seems not to have written about his enemies.

And how might Don Bradman have felt had he known of Allen's view on his batting during the Bodyline series? The two were to become staunch friends for life, and smoothly steered the Ashes series in Australia four years later when diplomacy and goodwill were urgently required by both nations. But in 1933 Gubby Allen wrote of Bradman (to "Darling Dads" from Government House, Canberra, after the series had ended) that he was "a terrible little coward of fast bowling!" This letter was understandably held back from public gaze until after Sir Donald Bradman's death in February 2001.

It was no great surprise when Jardine annoyed the Press again by with-holding his selected team until it was almost time to begin the match. Indeed, the final eleven was a secret even among his own team until just before the start. They had all had to get changed. It enhanced team spirit, Jardine believed. He lost the toss and duly led his men quietly out of the handsome old turreted SCG pavilion across a patchy outfield on a sunny day, with a cool breeze blowing. The most famous Test series of all time was under way.

AWAY AT LAST: THE CAPTAINS TOSS.

Larwood steamed in from the Randwick (Hill) end to bowl to Woodfull. At first there was a strong slips cordon with only a short square on the leg side. The sixth ball rose off the green-tinged pitch and just missed Woodfull's head, and then Voce took up the attack to a concentrated Bodyline field with no slip at all. Australian brows furrowed.

Larwood put all he had into his early salvoes against his old adversary Bill Ponsford, but the Australians survived, with much ducking and swaying, as it became clear that this pitch was not so very fast, though Ponsford took a sharp bang on the hip and walked about for some time hoping to relieve the pain. Allen replaced Larwood, Australia having survived the first round unscathed. But it was not to last. Woodfull played an incomplete hook at a Voce bouncer and was caught behind by Ames above his head.

Les Ames, who was preferred to Duckworth on account of his greater runmaking ability, had taken the Lancashire keeper's advice and put slices of steak into his gloves to soften the impact of this chain of fast deliveries. He had also had to sort out where to stand. If he stood too much to leg, where the ball was mostly flying through, he would be struggling to take anything outside off stump. He was to concede 73 byes during the series, and hold only eight catches, all off the fast men, while disappointing with the bat. Yet such was his calm demeanour and so valuable was his advice to the bowlers and his captain that no serious thought was given to restoring Duckworth.

Runs came very slowly, but nobody complained. The heavily padded Fingleton, bowled by a no-ball from Voce and lucky to survive a run-out attempt, coped with Larwood, whose bowling he had never tasted before, taking a stinging blow on the hip and surviving a trap set when Leyland moved deeper as Voce ran in. Fingleton hooked, but it was another no-ball. The square-leg umpire sometimes had to cross over when Voce's leg-side field thickened.

It was about this time that the celebrated exchange between Jardine and Pataudi took place. The Indian refused to field in the leg trap, whereupon the captain snorted, "I see His Highness is a conscientious objector! Very well, you go, Hedley." (Pataudi's insubordination may have been temporary, for he is identified in a diagram in Hobbs's book as a member of the cordon of short-leg fieldsmen in the next Test.) Pataudi got one back at Jardine when he detected that his captain had flinched ever so slightly while fielding in the close leg-side cordon: "Skipper," he said quietly, "you seem to have forgotten your own instructions!"

At the lunch break, with Verity bowling after Jardine had seemed to respond to a barracker's cry of "Give Variety a go!", Australia were satisfied with a scoreline of 63 for one wicket. But after only two runs had been added after the interval, Ponsford (32), having already been hit on the backside, moved to the off and lost his leg stump to a swinging Larwood delivery. Jardine — who later expressed disappointment at Allen's bowling — kept mixing his bowling, allowing Voce the benefit of the breeze. Having had a short breather before getting Ponsford out, and still without a full Bodyline field, Larwood had a straight-batted Fingleton (26) caught simply at short leg.

The temperature edged higher still when Kippax was hit glancingly on the head by Voce, and took one on the knuckles. He was soon lbw, giving Larwood a third wicket for seven runs: 87 for 4, and barely a sound from the vast gathering. The writer Denzil Batchelor, then aged 26 and living in Sydney, was to write that Larwood must have had a lunch of boiled dynamite with radium sauce.[8] (The bowler actually preferred a pint of beer and a fag. In this spell he had taken wickets in his first, third and fifth overs.)

"He's too bloody fast for me," Kippax is supposed to have lamented as he unstrapped his pads in the dressing-room. This prolific stylist's approach had been altered after two terrible injuries the previous season: a ball jumped from an iron peg securing the matting in a minor match at Grenfell and broke his nose, and soon afterwards he was hospitalised by a blow to the temple from "Pud" Thurlow's bowling in the Shield match at Brisbane in which Bradman was unseated by Eddie Gilbert, the Aborigine.

BILL PONSFORD TAKES A FAST ONE ON THE RUMP, HIS PREFERRED WAY OF DEALING WITH THE PERSISTENT SHORT BOWLING.

The Hill was now full, the ground attendance well over 40,000, and the noise was not always pleasant, especially when an Australian batsman was struck. Bob Wyatt, who spent a lot of time fielding in front of the Sheridan Stand, was pelted with orange peel and apple cores. It may have been on this very day that, as Jardine chased after the ball, Yabba bellowed from the Hill, in the best upper-class accent he could muster: "Mind your stays [corsets], old man!" And when he caught sight of Pataudi, another stentorian shout — not as compassionate as the usual Yabba utterances — rang across the SCG: "Go back to Africa, Pat O'Dea!" Some of the Hillites, perhaps embarrassed by raucous shouts at "the Nawab of Potato", had the courtesy to ask England's Indian batsman what he preferred to be called. "Just plain 'Pat' to you boys," he said with a smile.

It was odd, half a century later, to be told by an insistent Gubby Allen that Bodyline didn't start until the second Test. When queried again, he placed a hand on the author's arm and said huskily: "My dear chap, I was *there!*" So were many others, and short-leg fieldsmen were in predatory positions and the fur was flying. Some people believed that there was a sub-plot. If Bodyline was aimed at Bradman, he wasn't out there to cop it. But he was watching, and must have ridden every bouncer and every body blow.

STAN McCABE STRIKES OUT AT VERITY.

IF EVER THERE WAS A SERIES IN WHICH "NO PAIN, NO GAIN" COULD HAVE BEEN THE WATCHWORD,
THIS WAS THE FIRST. McCABE TRIES TO RUB THE DISCOMFORT AWAY AFTER A BLOW TO THE CHEST
AS ENGLAND PLAYERS PATAUDI, ALLEN AND SUTCLIFFE APPROACH TO COMMISERATE.

Vic Richardson, buoyed by his recent Shield innings of 203 against a
strong Victorian attack, now joined Stan McCabe, and the first truly stirring
hours of the series unfolded. Bravely the two took all that Larwood and
Voce could fire at them, dropping to their haunches or dodging where
necessary, ready for the full-length ball, hooking and pulling the short ones
when calculations permitted, always alert for quick singles. McCabe, who
had been in good shape for the State and had two grade centuries up for
Mosman already, remarked to his father just before going in: "If I get hit
out there, make sure you stop Mum from jumping the fence." And he was
not really joking. His mother stood for no nonsense, and on his father's side
too they were as quietly tough as they come. Stan's grandfather left the
Victorian Police back in the 1860s and rode hundreds of miles to join the
New South Wales gold rush, and his wife had followed with three
youngsters in the canvas-topped buggy and a rifle for protection, surviving
a brush with bushrangers near Albury.[9]

McCabe's 187 not out was to feature in every future self-respecting
anthology of the greatest innings ever played (and there were two more
masterpieces to come from him: at Johannesburg and Trent Bridge). It was
brave, exceptionally skilful, and, by his own admission, touched often with
good fortune as some balls found the bat's edge and some hooked balls just

eluded deep fielders. Asked many years later and high up in the SCG
Press box to indicate the scope of McCabe's shots, Bill O'Reilly thrust a
gnarled forefinger towards the gaudy advertisement boards that now
concealed the white pickets square either side of the pitch, and with
slightly misted eyes as he remembered his adored mate, he gasped: "There!
And there! And there! And *there!*" Film shows McCabe to have had a
beautifully balanced elegance of strokeplay that would have set him
comfortably into any era of batsmanship, though cricket is unfortunate in
that only a few frames of this Sydney classic survive: a pull shot and a hurried
defensive response to a short ball which lobs safely behind him as Gubby
Allen lurches from short leg.

He was 127 not out at the close, having lost Richardson after a fifth-
wicket stand of 129 in only two hours. Though Voce was still strong enough
to send four balls in a row flying over McCabe's cap, Larwood had tired.
England's back-up bowling — Allen's swift non-Bodyline attack,
Hammond's fine seamers and Verity's probing left-arm spin — was
continually testing, but Australia, even without Bradman, seemed to have
stumbled on a combination to frustrate the bowling which had struck fear
into the hearts of so many batsmen and onlookers. The way they dealt with
Voce reminded Mailey of what had happened at Trent Bridge two years
earlier. McCabe's crackling hooks brought roars from the depths of the
spectators' lungs, while his fine glancing, slashing cuts and sporadic drives,
some over mid-on, sent ripples of ecstasy around the ground. He even took
a quick step or two down the pitch to the fast men, his hands holding a
challengingly high grip on the bat-handle. Never reckless, he was
nevertheless on alert to punish anything he could, as if he knew that life out
there was probably programmed to be short.

He was only 22 years of age, and Richardson was 38; it was the older
man who, having continued on from his hundred in the South Australia
v MCC match with a determined display during which he took blows to
knee and thigh, and had his right thumb split by Larwood when he was 10,
finally lost his wicket for 49 when Hammond took a smart falling catch at
square leg off Voce shortly after the new ball had been taken. In retrospect,
the batsman was convinced that had the partnership been extended by
another hour or so, Bodyline might well have been smothered soon after
birth. Indeed, at the height of the resistance, when Richardson flicked
Larwood twice for four over the short legs' heads and McCabe took more

runs off England's ace, the Notts man seemed unhappy with the field setting and was taken off soon after, to calls from the crowd for him to be kept on. Earlier, when he was at his fieriest, one of his shortest balls prompted one of the more genial shouts from the outer: "Hey, Harold! That would have been a yorker if you'd bowled it from the other end!"

McCABE CUTS PAST A DESPERATE VOCE.

Oldfield lasted only four balls before snicking Larwood to Ames, but the 40-year-old Grimmett hung on till the close, wincing with McCabe as the young man took a clanging blow to the box from Voce and then hit the next ball for four. McCabe's century came after 161 minutes at the crease, and it came in style, with a handsome drive off Allen for four. The members and the mob cheered with pride and relief and sublime exhilaration. Denzil Batchelor, some years later, described McCabe's performance as colourfully as any who were there: it was, he said, "a sparkling thing of pure beauty, and yet a functional masterpiece as well, for it coped with, and, for the space of a few hours, dispelled the bogey just as fighter planes swept the sky of the peril of the [German] doodlebug".[10] The imagery which sprang from the nimble mind of Ray Robinson is equally compelling: McCabe's knock was "like a blood transfusion for a sinking innings".[11]

Next day, moving slightly stiffly as a result of bruising (his left hand was also sore), McCabe retained the initiative against refreshed bowling as Australia's tail shrivelled. First Grimmett, who often backed away and had just been dropped by Verity at short leg, was caught behind off Voce, then Nagel, at the other end and on Test debut, saw his off stump sent cartwheeling by Larwood. O'Reilly, relieved that his captain had urged him not to get hurt, was now further fortified by McCabe's assurance that not only would Larwood not waste a "sconer" on a No. 10, but he wasn't really all that fast. The big bowler took guard, watched wide-eyed as Larwood purred in, and almost had his head taken off. In shock, he stared down the pitch just shaking his head at his partner, "a rosy-faced, twinkle-eyed, sparse-thatched boy", and McCabe looked back at him innocently, with the suggestion of a grin about his cherubic chin.[12] O'Reilly slashed a no-ball from Voce for four but was soon bowled by him.

That left Tim Wall, the last man, a tall, quiet schoolmaster from Adelaide. The score was 305 for 9, better than many had expected, but probably still not enough to embarrass England, with their deep batting line-up. However, against all expectation, Wall held his end up while 55 more runs came in 33 minutes, with only one unintentional four from him as he survived 18 balls before falling to a catch at short leg by Hammond (who later wrote that McCabe's innings was a "joy to watch" even to an opponent).

For the first time, Jardine had been seen to lose his grip on the game, scattering the field this way and that; and overthrows were conceded. Of the last-wicket 55, McCabe stroked 51 (26 came off two overs from Voce) to finish 187 not out (four hours, 25 fours), and he finally walked off to thunderous applause from 58,000 people, many of whom had torn the boundary pickets away in front of the melting asphalt concourses by the Sheridan and Brewongle stands in order to get a better view. Now they stood and clapped and called until McCabe disappeared into the dressing-room.

There had been only three oblique chances: at 159 through Larwood at gully off Voce, and at 170 through Voce himself at slip, both times the ball streaking like a meteor, and when Jardine conceded that a better fielder than himself might have caught him at square leg off Larwood. McCabe had also been only a whisker from lbw just before tea on the first day. He had made his runs off all five bowlers, against leg theory and off theory alike: 40 off Larwood, 65 off Voce, 39 off Allen, 20 off Hammond, and 23 off Verity, though such was the general direction of the bowling that only 18 of his 187 runs came in front of the wicket on the off side. Nineteen times (13 hook strokes) "Napper" (he vaguely resembled Napoleon) hit the ball to the leg-side fence, mainly to square leg and midwicket. That his match fee for all this was a paltry £30 was completely laughable. But immortality was his.

Ray Lindwall, then an 11-year-old, was in among that packed house, thrilled by McCabe's dashing display but also much taken by Larwood's rhythmic approach and smooth, powerful delivery. With big brother Jack, Ray had taken an early train from Hurstville, walked from Central and joined the queue outside the SCG at half-past-six that morning. They sat on the Hill in front of the great concrete scorebox and were mesmerised.[13] Ray was to adopt elements of Larwood's action and become, on the other side of the looming world war, as fine a fast bowler as Australia has ever possessed. And by one of the charming little quirks of fate which life constantly spouts, Lindwall found himself sitting beside his English hero in 1948 at a farewell dinner to Don Bradman in London.

THE HILL WAS THE PLACE TO BE AS ENGLAND STARTED THEIR REPLY TO AUSTRALIA'S 360. FEELINGS WERE STRONG BUT HUMOUR WAS USUALLY IN EVIDENCE, AND THE DRESS CODE WOULD HAVE STUNNED SPECTATORS OF LATER YEARS.

As for Stan McCabe, a man with one size 5 foot and one size 6, he confessed he had taken chances: it was "Sydney or the bush", and when Chappie Dwyer later jokingly asked him if he'd got a swollen head after reading the newspapers, the young batsman replied, "But I haven't read any of them. I took a book to read on the ferry. I thought there might be a lot of exaggerated praise in them that it wouldn't do me any good to read."[14] Echoes of Trumper.

In an interview a third of a century later McCabe said: "I merely did what my impulse told me to do — that was to attack the bowling. The only shot to play against bodyline was the hook. It was my favourite shot ... It was just that, with the crowd yelling and clapping and my blood up, my reaction was to hit Larwood and Voce with everything I had."[15] The noise was such that Verity considered it greater than anything he had heard outside an FA Cup final. Wembley Stadium's capacity, of course, was almost double that of the SCG.

All the hullabaloo wasn't to everyone's taste. Lady Game, the Governor's wife, confessed in a letter that she knew little about cricket, but she was affected by the noise that constantly erupted on that Saturday at the SCG: "... they really are like children over it — screaming with excitement, yelling, clapping, cheering and almost going off their heads about their own men. It makes one feel that games are a mistake when one sees them behaving like that ... Mr Bridge goes so far as to say that Larwood's bowling 'isn't fair', I believe, and he and General Anderson, who is English to the core, could hardly be safely put together. Isn't it silly!"[16]

Most Australians in the crowd (there must also have been quite a few British immigrants of varying vintage in attendance too, but very few tourists) were drawn together by the unfolding drama, and some of them made new friends. One newspaper reporter spotted a girl dodging a misdirected tomato hurled down the Hill. She moved her head at the critical moment and the soft projectile splashed all over a young man's jacket. She went and offered him her handkerchief, and there the narrative trailed off.[17]

Facing Australia's 360, and with the prospect of batting last, England went about consolidating their innings, and so well did they progress that by stumps they had 252 on the board for the loss only of Wyatt. Sutcliffe and Wyatt had batted soundly and calmly, the former unruffled not only when Wall beat him four times in an early over but also when he played a ball from an inconsolable O'Reilly off his pad hard onto the stumps without disturbing the bails. As umpire Hele came in and verified that there was no dismissal the batsman merely leaned on his bat, other hand on hip, watching the seagulls winging over Moore Park. Sutcliffe was to advance from 43 to 194, his eighth, last and biggest century against Australia. Hair glistening with brilliantine, never ruffled, knees pumping rather stiffly as he ran, this cool and charming professional who thought of himself as a gentleman amateur was patience personified.

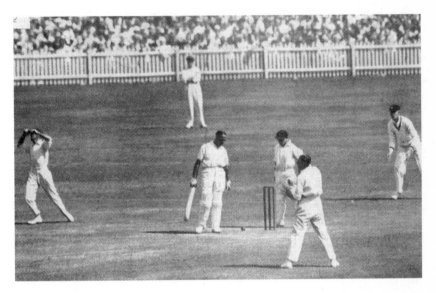

ONE OF THE SERIES' GREAT "NEARLY" MOMENTS: SUTCLIFFE PLAYS ON AT 43 BUT SURVIVES.

The near-record crowd was impatient. Roused by the last stages of McCabe's innings, they now wanted wickets. "Never get 'em out!" came Yabba's weary roar, while Drysdale Bett, in *The Australian Cricketer*, noted that the dense crowd "was restless and wriggled and squealed in the heat like a kennel full of pups". O'Reilly plugged on, and throughout the innings — during which he and Grimmett wheeled down over 60 overs apiece — the watchful Englishmen, unfamiliar with the long-striding O'Reilly, struggled to absorb the reality of such vigorous spin at such an irregular velocity. But the even taller Nagel was never the threat he had been in Melbourne.

Bob Wyatt, glad now to be some distance from the rubbish-throwers, coped with Grimmett's crafty legspin repertoire with less discomfort than in the past, and the mature pair posted 112 for England's first wicket in only

96 minutes — the first 50 in only 40 minutes — before Wyatt (38) fell to Grimmett as his bat caught in his pad-flap. It was the seventh time in eight innings that he had been leg-before, and although he considered some of the decisions against him marginal, he was satisfied with this one. Back in the dressing-room he told his skipper that the pitch was "dead easy" and that the ball wasn't turning. There was nothing to worry about. "You must be bloody well mad," was Jardine's rejoinder.[18]

"YABBA", STEPHEN HAROLD GASCOIGNE, THE "RABBITOH" FROM BALMAIN, WAS WOUNDED IN THE BOER WAR, BUT THERE WAS NOTHING WRONG WITH HIS LUNGS.

Hammond's feelings were as ardent towards the Sydney ground as towards any of his lady friends. Last tour he had scored 225 in the State match and 251 in the Test match.

Now he began with that glorious cover-drive and stroked his way to 87 by the close of play, when Sutcliffe was 116, their unfinished stand worth 140. How Woodfull wished that Ironmonger was in the Australian ranks. England's captain, for his part, was still so tense that he could scarcely bring himself to watch, half-hiding behind a pillar and peeking furtively at the play from time to time. (Jardine's daughter recently affirmed how highly strung her father was, recalling that his fingernails were constantly bitten down to the quick.) Now he began to relax, with England only 108 behind, nine wickets in hand, and the day of rest upon them.

Umpire Hele was staying at colleague Borwick's house in Glebe, and already they had both come to the grim conclusion that there was a risk that someone would be killed if England continued to bowl so many bouncers.

On the tram that evening they overheard many grumbles from home-going spectators.[19] The two umpires felt powerless to address Jardine. Nothing in the Laws seemed to entitle them to do so. Recently retired Test umpire Alf Jones, however, made it known as the series progressed that had he been standing in the Tests he would have intervened on the grounds that, under Law 43, "the umpires are the sole judges of fair or unfair play".

Douglas Jardine tried to relax on the Sunday rest day with a visit to Gubby Allen's uncle's country house, "where, on being teasingly threatened with rain from an alleged cloud no bigger than a man's hand, he had passed the day watching and praying on a corner of the verandah while lesser men sunbathed".[20] The Test pitch, of course, was open to the elements.

The atmosphere was heavier on the Monday after some overnight rain, and England continued to build, but slowly, on their promising start. Hammond was in prime form, his powerful shoulders firing a bat which was clearly intent on stroking almost everything through the off side, where control was easier and placement more precise. His partnership with Sutcliffe had stretched to 188 — beating Shrewsbury and Gunn's second-wicket record against Australia — in even time when Hammond's rubber grip twisted as he drove at Nagel on the up, and the imperfect shot lobbed the ball into cover's hands. England 300 for 2, and a nervous Nawab of Pataudi coming to the crease.

WALLY HAMMOND IN FULL FLOW ON HIS FAVOURITE GROUND.

Play became slower still, and the crowd of nearly 28,000 showed their frustration. Wall was bowling too wide of off stump, and the spinners couldn't penetrate. Yet another century stand — the third of the innings — was taking shape. The suave Sutcliffe, under orders to grind it out, added only 28 to his score in the 90 minutes before lunch, batting for the cause, as he had so often in the past. During the afternoon, while Mailey looked down from the Press box and wished one of the spinners would depart from the flat trajectory and float a full-toss, just as he so often did, Sutcliffe began to loft the ball into the outfield. His double-century was imminent.

But he was to be denied. Wall broke through with the new ball and Sutcliffe was lbw for an immensely dutiful 194 in 7¼ hours, leaving England 423 for 3. When Leyland, who might have lifted the run rate, was given out lbw next ball, though it probably just brushed his thigh, Jardine walked stiffly to the middle to avoid the hat-trick, and kept out Wall's inswinger. He steadied the ship until McCabe had him caught by Oldfield, and Verity was quickly dismissed. Four wickets had fallen for 56.

Pataudi was still there, having batted with elegance touched by a nervousness that had overtaken his game after his duck (run-out) in the South Australia match. He seemed overawed by the occasion. At one point Vic Richardson chipped him about his slowness. When Pataudi explained that he was gauging the pace of the wicket the Australian laughingly said, "Well, it's changed three times since you came in!"[21]

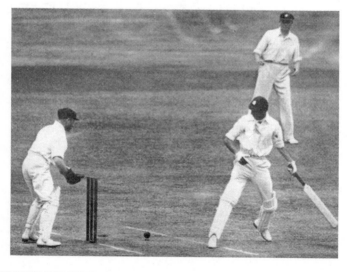

PATAUDI'S DETERMINED RESISTANCE ENDS, BUT HE HAD ADDED HIS NAME TO AN ILLUSTRIOUS LIST.

Pataudi, 80 not out overnight, returned to the crease on the fourth morning wearing the same clothes as yesterday out of superstition, and inched towards his hundred. After 5¼ hours of intense dedication, he nudged Nagel past gully to reach the treasured milestone, a moment captured by the newsreel camera. He thus joined Ranji and Duleep in having made a century on Test debut. Unlike them, having hit a mere half-dozen fours in his long innings, he got out immediately, last wicket to fall, bowled by Nagel. What had been left of the England innings had come crashing down, with O'Reilly getting belated reward for his toil with three lower-order wickets. England were all out at last for 524, with a lead of 164. And as the players left the field, Pataudi asked umpire Hele if he might have one of the bails as a souvenir. Hele (who claimed he lost a stone [6.35 kg] in weight during this match) invited him to go one better by taking the ball from his pocket. Some weeks later, to Hele's embarrassment, Pataudi gave him a gold wristwatch out of gratitude. "I thanked my lucky stars Pataudi did not play in another Test," said the virtuous umpire.[22]

It was to be a black time for Australia. Wickets clattered throughout this fourth day, which ended with their hopes in shreds: 164 for 9, the scores absolutely level. Whether Harold Larwood started his devastating spell of bowling after one of his enlivening sniffs of snuff is unknown,[23] but with grace, power and a certain beauty he earned figures of 5 for 28 that day, while Hammond's medium-fast accounted for the heaviest runmakers in the first innings, McCabe and Richardson. The bulky Ponsford, the only man to score two first-class quadruple-centuries, now looked inept.

He tore his glove off after being struck by a vicious Voce delivery. Then he tried to rock — as he thought — out of harm's way, only for a half-volley propelled by Voce to cannon into his leg stump. Woodfull, still scoreless after 20 minutes, had his stumps flattened by Larwood, whose speed was simply too great, even though he now had his side strapped after feeling a slight strain (he told Hobbs it felt as if a knife were in his side). The outgoing captain met incoming batsman Kippax and told him to go back, letting McCabe in next to join Fingleton. There followed the highest stand of this anaemic innings, 51, McCabe taking up where he left off in his memorable first innings, and hitting Voce for six, with Fingleton watchful, sometimes teasing the field, as was his habit, by threatening to run after tapping the ball, and once ducking a ball which failed to rise and escaping an lbw appeal. They saw off the opening assault.

FINGLETON WORKED HARD IN HIS FIRST ASHES TEST.
HERE HE HOOKS AND ELUDES THE DAUNTING LEG TRAP.

Hammond, told by Jardine that it was "now or never", skilfully moved the ball about and eventually trapped McCabe (32) leg-before with a slower delivery and had Richardson caught at slip via Ames's pad with the next ball. For all his great batting record, Hammond would have given much for a Test hat-trick, but Kippax averted it. At tea Australia were a sickly 61 for 4. Kippax resisted for a time, adding 39 with Fingleton. But then he played across the line to Larwood, who, with the leg field in place, continued to dismember the innings. Oldfield briefly batted well before holing out to Leyland in the deep leg side, and Fingleton's plucky 2½-hour vigil ended with a catch off another scorching Larwood delivery. Grimmett looked just as frightened as in the first innings until becoming "Killer" Larwood's fifth victim, caught at slip, and after some brave resistance from Nagel and Wall, the last pair held out as the clock ticked round towards end of play. England would have sealed an innings victory had Ames completed a stumping off Verity with Nagel well down the pitch. But they all had to trek back to the ground next morning, when Allen bowled a maiden and Voce castled O'Reilly with his third ball.

Sutcliffe calmly took the single needed off McCabe's opening delivery, and England's 10-wicket victory was sealed, before fewer than 100 people, with the Hill empty bar one man, who yelled "Never get 'em out!" a few times to cement his new-found celebrity.

Perhaps as yet unaware that Victorian Cricket Association president Canon E.S. Hughes (who had conducted the Bradmans' marriage ceremony) felt himself insulted by Jardine and intended to let it be known, the England captain was soon set up in front of the newsreel camera to give his polite and satisfied reaction to his team's success. The Englishmen then repaired to the nets rather than indulging in instant celebrations.

So England were one-up, Bodyline had been seen intermittently by thunderstruck Sydneysiders, and an innings that would never be forgotten, by virtue of its poise and its sparkling audacity, had been played. The Australian team dispersed, O'Reilly back to his schoolteaching responsibilities in Kogarah, where he let the boys go on experimenting with a rough form of Bodyline at each other, feeling that they must learn the hard way.

NO STOPPING THE AUDACIOUS McCABE: A HIT FOR SIX OFF VOCE.

ONLY THE VERY KEENEST TURNED UP TO SEE THE FEW BALLS BOWLED ON THE FINAL DAY.

McCabe had taken four body blows and Fingleton, who took eight, would write, when years had distanced him from the drama, that this season of Bodyline brought "incidents galore, oaths aplenty and unorthodox movements of strange design".[24] One booming piece of advice from the Hill to Bill Voce was along the lines that this was meant to be a game of cricket: "You're not playing baseball!"

And in the backwash of this opening Test at Sydney there was already movement behind the scenes: while Australian Board members might still have been unperturbed, NSWCA secretary Harold Heydon wrote a letter to his counterpart in South Australia, Bill Jeanes, who was, more significantly, also the Australian Board of Control's secretary.[25] Having watched England's fast-bowling hostility at the SCG, Heydon warned Jeanes that anything similar on Adelaide Oval during the forthcoming third Test could well lead to public disorder.

Already Bill Woodfull was being urged to consider retaliation to the short-pitched fast bowling. Future New South Wales Premier and Governor-General Billy McKell said it was the only way to counter rough stuff in Rugby League, a sport at which he once excelled.[26] Woodfull would have none of it. The editor of *The Australian Cricketer* later described him as a Puritan for not endorsing retaliation, and now valiantly claimed that Australia could still win the rubber, even allowing that "how to hit a head-

S.J. McCABE, WHO PLAYED THE INNINGS OF THE SERIES, ALMOST KILLING BODYLINE AT BIRTH.

high leg ball clear of seven leg fieldsmen was a conundrum that was not satisfactorily solved by the end of the first Test". The magazine's columnist, former Australia captain M.A. Noble, gave full credit to England, calling any suggestion of unfair play by their bowlers "humbug". He felt that Voce would soon be collared and that the Australian batsmen had been over-awed by the field setting. Many balls coming at the hip should have been punished. They should make him bowl straight; then he would tire and "his poisonous fangs would thus be extracted". One of the problems, Noble felt, was that Australia's batsmen had become too dependent upon Bradman. Well, Bradman would soon be back, all being well.

There was only one unhappy Englishman around. Denzil Batchelor knew him and described him as a ne'er-do-well. He had staked his steamer ticket home that England would win one Test by an innings. Ames's missed stumping on the fourth evening cost him the bet.

And on that fourth evening, with the match in the bag, MCC's manager Plum Warner booked a telephone call from the ground to his son at Eton College. Connections were made through Colombo and Paris, and father told son that the players were coming off the field as he spoke, with the scores level and Australia with one wicket left. Then they both became tongue-tied. Warner senior said it was hot in Sydney, and young John said it was cold in the college. End of phone call.[27]

Cyril Ritchard, the comical-looking popular actor and vocalist, was positively not lost for words. Performing in *Our Miss Gibbs* at Her Majesty's Theatre in Sydney, he added a topical verse to the show:[28]

Now this new kind of cricket,
Takes courage to stick it,
There's bruises and fractures galore.
After kissing their wives
And insuring their lives
Batsmen fearfully walk out to score.
With a prayer and a curse
They prepare for the hearse,
Undertakers look on with broad grins.
Oh, they'd be a lot calmer
In Ned Kelly's armour,
When Larwood, the wrecker, begins.

And when Ritchard asked another character in the play if he'd tasted the new Larwood cocktail, and the name of it was queried, he explained *sotto voce*: "Because it always goes to your head." Larwood, in his ghosted book on the tour, took exception to this "drivel" and to the money so easily earned by the performer.

FIRST TEST MATCH

SYDNEY CRICKET GROUND, DECEMBER 2, 3, 5, 6, 7, 1932

Toss won by Australia
12th men: S.F. Hird (A), E. Paynter (E)

Umpires: E.G. Borwick & G.A. Hele
Debuts: L.E. Nagel (A), Nawab of Pataudi (E)

AUSTRALIA

		mins	balls	4s			mins	balls	4s
*W.M. Woodfull	c Ames b Voce	7	38	34	-	b Larwood	0	22	19	-
W.H. Ponsford	b Larwood	32	93	79	-	b Voce	2	10	9	-
J.H.W. Fingleton	c Allen b Larwood	26	72	77	3	c Voce b Larwood	40	144	120	5
A.F. Kippax	lbw b Larwood	8	28	27	1	[6] b Larwood	19	37	35	1
S.J. McCabe	not out	187	242	233	25	[4] lbw b Hammond	32	65	68	4+
V.Y. Richardson	c Hammond b Voce	49	120	108	5	[5] c Voce b Hammond	0	1	1	-
#W.A.S. Oldfield	c Ames b Larwood	4	8	4	-	c Leyland b Larwood	1	14	21	-
C.V. Grimmett	c Ames b Voce	19	53	37	2	c Allen b Larwood	5	17	15	1
L.E. Nagel	b Larwood	0	2	1	-	not out	21	55	59	4
W.J. O'Reilly	b Voce	4	6	8	1	[11] b Voce	7	9	9	1
T.W. Wall	c Allen b Hammond	4	33	18	1	[10] c Ames b Allen	20	34	29	3
Extras	b 12, lb 4, nb 4	20				b 12, lb 2, w 1, nb 2	17			
Total	(102.2 overs, 356 mins) **360**					(63.3 overs, 214 mins) **164**				

+ plus 1 six

Fall   1/22 2/65 3/82 4/87 5/216 6/231 7/299 8/300 9/305 10/360   1/2 2/10 3/61 4/61 5/100 6/104 7/105 8/113 9/151 10/164

BOWLING	O	M	R	W	w/nb		O	M	R	W	w/nb
Larwood	31	5	96	5	-/1	Larwood	18	4	28	5	-/-
Voce	29	4	110	4	-/3	Voce	17.3	5	54	2	-/1
Allen	15	1	65	0	-/-	Allen	9	5	13	1	1/1
Hammond	14.2	0	34	1	-/-	Hammond	15	6	37	2	-/-
Verity	13	4	35	0	-/-	Verity	4	1	15	0	-/-

ENGLAND

		mins	balls	4s			mins	balls	4s
H.Sutcliffe	lbw b Wall	194	436	496	13	not out	1	1	1	-
R.E.S.Wyatt	lbw b Grimmett	38	96	91	3	not out	0	1	0	-
W.R.Hammond	c Grimmett b Nagel	112	192	242	16					
Nawab of Pataudi	b Nagel	102	317	380	6					
M.Leyland	c Oldfield b Wall	0	2	1	-					
*D.R.Jardine	c Oldfield b McCabe	27	68	82	2					
H.Verity	lbw b Wall	2	14	15	-					
G.O.B.Allen	c & b O'Reilly	19	63	66	2					
#L.E.G.Ames	c McCabe b O'Reilly	0	5	8	-					
H.Larwood	lbw b O'Reilly	0	6	7	-					
W.Voce	not out	0	3	1	-					
Extras	b 7, lb 17, nb 6	30					0			
Total	(229.4 overs, 609 mins) **524**					(0.1 overs, 1 min) 0 wkt	**1**			

Fall   1/112 2/300 3/423 4/423 5/470 6/479 7/519 8/522 9/522 10/524

BOWLING	O	M	R	W	w/nb		O	M	R	W	w/nb
Wall	38	4	104	3	-/3	McCabe	0.1	0	1	0	-/-
Nagel	43.4	9	110	2	-/-						
O'Reilly	67	32	117	3	-/3						
Grimmett	64	22	118	1	-/-						
McCabe	15	2	42	1	-/-						
Kippax	2	1	3	0	-/-						

ENGLAND WON BY 10 WICKETS

Attendances: 1st day 46,709, 2nd day 58,058, 3rd day 27,938, 4th day 25,488, 5th day c100: Total 158,293
Gate receipts: £14,883.16.8d
Close-of-play scores: 1st day Aus 6/290 (McCabe 127, Grimmett 17), 2nd day Eng 1/252 (Sutcliffe 116, Hammond 87), 3rd day Eng 6/479
(Pataudi 80), 4th day Aus (2) 9/164 (Nagel 21, O'Reilly 7)

CHAPTER SEVEN

DON'S ODD DOUBLE

The great concern now was whether Don Bradman would be fit to play in the second Test, which was due to start at Melbourne on December 30. There was nobody outside their own families that the majority of the Australian public cared more about. Even *The Australian Cricketer* remarked with some seriousness that there was some concern about Bradman's liking for stewed black tea, which might have explained his olive-brown complexion. It is a species of drug, the magazine warned, particularly if the tannin was allowed to rise. "But as he has a wife to look after him," came the comforting conclusion, "there should be little cause to worry."

Not that his physical and mental well-being were the only concern. He was also having to cope with the wrangle with the Australian Board of Control over his journalistic commitments.

The break away from everyday pressures which he and Jessie were glad to take, at physiotherapist Tom Langridge's secluded beachside shack, revived his appetite, strength and spirits, in spite of, or perhaps even partly because of, the distractions wrought by a threatening bushfire, a terrifying thunderstorm and straying snakes. Back in Sydney, Bradman called in to see A.G. "Johnny" Moyes, the fatherly and trusted journalist and former State batsman, to test in theory his proposed technique for handling Bodyline bowling. Fundamental to his proposed strategy would be the use of his speedy footwork to escape the danger. But that alone would not suffice. He had to score runs. The only way he felt able to do this was by moving to leg and hitting into the empty spaces on the off side. That would surely confuse Larwood and Voce. Moyes asked about the ball that failed to get up, or the yorker. Bradman felt he would be able to deal with them. If the ball were of full length he wouldn't move to leg. As for his famed hook, with Larwood bringing the ball from the off he believed that the stroke could not be relied upon.[1] So these were to be his tactics, and — with only spasmodic departures as circumstances dictated — he adhered to them throughout the series.

Some have since speculated that Bradman so despised Bodyline that he refused to bat in conventional style against it, for that would have been somehow to legitimise it and dignify it. Ray Robinson went so far as to state that the calm and self-possessed Bradman knew well enough that Bodyline could not be mastered and "could see no sense in getting himself knocked about in fruitless martyrdom for a hopeless cause".[2]

Meanwhile, the other dilemma hung heavily over him: whether to honour his newspaper contract and thus have to withdraw from the Melbourne Test or else try to sidestep his journalistic obligations in order to please the traditionally uncompromising ACB. Already somewhat peeved at the Board's willingness to allow Jack Fingleton to continue with his *full-time* journalistic work (the discreet Fingleton sat on some hot stories that summer), Bradman remained determined to take the former course of action if it came to the crunch. Of course, being held indirectly responsible for Bradman's absence from the Australian team would not have enhanced the newspaper's image, and the batsman must have recognised that as his trump card.

The position was resolved when Associated Newspapers' editorial chief R.C. Packer (grandfather of Kerry), backed by managing director Sir Hugh Denison, persuaded Bradman to accept a release from his contract. Only hours before the Test match it was announced, to the relief of all Australia, that Bradman would play. The abiding absurdity was that he and other players were permitted to make their broadcasts at the close of play each day, and the papers often reported their comments next morning. Not that Bradman was prepared just to leave it at that. He took his chance to chastise the ACB, composing a Press release which included words of gratitude to his employer, then: "I most emphatically protest against the Board's being allowed to interfere with the permanent occupation of any player. To my mind the Board was never meant to have powers directing the business activities of players."[3] The ACB might have squinted at the word "permanent", but the victory was actually theirs. And they would soon have even bigger things on their minds.

"Our Don" had returned to New South Wales colours a week before the Melbourne Test started, motoring to Melbourne and scoring 157 on Boxing Day against Nagel, Ironmonger, Fleetwood-Smith and the blustering pace of "Bull" Alexander. During that innings against Victoria he reached 10,000 first-class runs in fewer innings (126) than the previous holder (Ponsford, 161) and at a younger age — 24 years 121 days — than anyone previously (a record since eclipsed by Javed Miandad and Graeme Hick, though in both cases in many more innings). And 69 years later, Bill Brown, who suffered a cut eye in this match courtesy of Alexander, recalled something Bradman said to him about the Bodyline attack which had been unleashed on him in the Australian XI match a month previously: "You cannot believe how big the problem is unless you've been out there. You fellas have no idea what sort of summer this is going to be!"[4]

From their Test victory in Sydney the English cricket team moved out to Wagga Wagga for a match starting three days later against Southern Districts of New South Wales, and thence to Tasmania. Jack Hobbs, about to celebrate his 50th birthday, and his beloved wife Ida took the chance for a break in Warrnambool, much to the master batsman's relief when he learned of the rough crossing endured by the cricketers on their way back from Tasmania after their two matches on the Apple Isle.

Wagga: this, said Maurice Tate laconically, was what he'd been sent on tour for — though even here he was to bowl only 10 overs in the two innings. Tate, a great bowler, was ignored by Jardine much of the time. Compensation came with an unbeaten half-century stretched over nearly three hours, though the visit was rather spoiled for him when he left his suede shoes outside his door at the hotel only to find them next morning thickly smeared with brown boot polish. The misery was to intensify. When a dance was thrown in honour of Tate's baby son Michael (still unseen back in England) Jardine forbade any of the players to attend, including Tate. The infant benefited to the tune of £100.

Wagga, birthplace years later of Geoff Lawson and Michael Slater, was in the throes of the Riverina's busy harvesting season. The town had last seen an English cricket team 45 years ago, when G.F. Vernon's 1887–88 combination had beaten the locals by an innings in two days after drawing lots as to the batting order (one of the English stars, A.E. Stoddart, went in at No. 11). This time MCC were led by Bob Wyatt, in Jardine's absence, and Gubby Allen was rested, against his will it seems. In one of his letters to his parents he has another dig at his captain (and "best friend"): "Douglas changes his mind every five minutes and the idea now is that I am to miss the Wagga match." This was the letter in which he branded Jardine as "too damn stupid", whining away if he doesn't have everything as he wants ... "sometimes I feel I should like to kill him."

Les Ames found some form in Wagga with a hard-hit 91 in the stifling heat — around 100°F (38°C) — while Paynter and Brown also entertained. The outstanding performance, however, came from legspinner Tommy Mitchell, who gave the ball plenty of air and spun it lavishly for a reward of 12 wickets, four of them to stumpings by Duckworth. For the Districts XI, an 18-year-old named Sly seized the moment, Sadlier batted for two hours and also impressed the Englishmen with his wicketkeeping, and Bennett's half-century earned the Junee player a spot as 12th man for New South Wales in the match in late January against the tourists (though he was never to play in a first-class match). The match was drawn, and the touring cricketers had the opportunity to go duck-shooting.

WAGGA WAGGA, DECEMBER 10, 12, 1932

SOUTHERN DISTRICTS OF NSW 226 (S. Sadlier 31, L. Bennett 53, S. Sly 67 not out, T.B. Mitchell 7 for 77) and 68 for 7 (T.B. Mitchell 5 for 26); MCC 313 (E. Paynter 46, L.E.G. Ames 91, F.R. Brown 51, M.W. Tate 52 not out, J. James 3 for 80, M. Rumble 5 for 73). DRAWN

Now the MCC team sailed down to Tasmania for two matches before the second Test, Jardine taking the first off in order to get some more relaxation fly-fishing — though not before breaking his silence on the thorny issue of England's bowling tactics. He felt the criticism should be answered, and told Reuters that the leg theory his men were bowling was "exactly the same type of attack on the leg stump that has been tried times without number from village green to Tests. The only difference is that we place the field differently to that usually adopted." He said there was nothing dangerous in it and he hoped to go on being successful with it.

Jardine had been greeted on the quay by an old friend, to whom he honoured a promise to perform the prize-giving at a school in Launceston, where he was touched at receiving a presentation. Then off he went, with three others, to catch some brown trout, and perhaps some rarer rainbow trout too, in a lagoon at Penstock, over 3000 feet (915 metres) above sea level, halfway between Launceston and Hobart. Doubtless he stood patiently in his waders as if waiting in the gully position for a catch.

Back with the team, Plum Warner was having to endure further pressure. This time, W.M. Rutledge, in *The Referee*, had front-paged an accusation of inconsistency against the MCC manager: Warner had condemned Bowes's tactics at The Oval in August, yet now, when he surely had the power to censure England's tour captain over similar tactics and halt them, he was holding back. "He is, by his official indifference, helping to breed a feeling of bitterness, not only between the opposing teams, but between the peoples of the two countries of the Empire."[5] This would have wounded Warner deeply.

Two letters were now penned to MCC secretary Billy Findlay at Lord's. Warner wrote of the hostile feeling England's fast bowling had created and expressed his fear that there could be a "terrible accident". The captain, too, sent a missive to headquarters telling Findlay that England's bowling had been an "unpleasant surprise to the old hands in Australia" and, disdainfully, that the newspapers "have put up a squeal rising to a whine about bowling at the man". It was, he continued to contend, nothing of the sort.

The skipper, pensive with his fishing-rod, missed seeing his batsmen gorge themselves in the first Tasmanian match at Launceston. Four made centuries before throwing their wickets away, Sutcliffe, Pataudi (missed twice), Ames and Paynter all batting at a fair rate, Ames the longest (169 minutes), the last seven wickets then falling for only 75 as Gerald James, a fast–medium bowler, gathered his reward for steadfast work. The Tasmania innings suffered rain interruption. After a good start by Owen Burrows and the prodigious 18-year-old Clayvel Lindsay "Jack" Badcock, who had a short peak-and-troughs Test career ahead of him (one century and failure to reach double figures in his other 11 innings), they lost the services of their captain Alf Rushforth after he twisted an ankle while fielding, and were bowled out for 229. Syd Putman, who was only 20, used his feet well in making a brisk half-century but Tasmania had to follow on. Tommy Mitchell had another enjoyable time, spinning six out in the first innings (three stumped by Ames) and five in the second, amazing the locals by sometimes getting through an over in 46 seconds. This time the pint-sized Badcock, already known as "the Tasmanian Bradman", had the distinction of carrying his bat through the innings, hitting but one four in his unbeaten 43, and being applauded warmly by his opponents as he walked off.

NTCA GROUND, LAUNCESTON, DECEMBER 16, 17, 19, 1932

MCC 502 (H. Sutcliffe 101, R.E.S. Wyatt 33, Nawab of Pataudi 109, L.E.G. Ames 107, E. Paynter 102, G.T.H. James 6 for 96, S.W.L. Putman 4 for 156); TASMANIA 229 (C.L. Badcock 57, A.O. Burrows 41, S.W.L. Putman 56 not out, T.B. Mitchell 6 for 70) and 147 (C.L. Badcock 43 not out, F.R. Brown 3 for 28, T.B. Mitchell 5 for 74). MCC WON BY AN INNINGS AND 126 RUNS

Four days later, down in Hobart, the Englishmen began their second match on the island, with Jardine back. He brought the rain with him — and further controversy. Only 48 minutes' play was possible on the opening day, during which Tasmania scored 13 for the loss of both openers. So wet was the field on the second day that Jardine firmly declined to play, not wanting to risk injury to his bowlers or fielders; the umpires prevailed, however, and out they went, Jardine to display his understandable displeasure by using non-regular bowlers such as Paynter and Ames — and himself. He usually bowled slow legbreaks, from a "pensive, halting run-up",[6] and once took 6 for 6 for Oxford University against a bemused Essex. Now, as the batsmen, surrounded by slush and mud, played him watchfully, suspiciously, on the sodden pitch, he bowled 10 overs for 21 runs, employing a towel to dry the ball after each delivery. Many in a crowd numbering 3665 booed and shouted. Paynter gleefully nipped in with some wickets as fieldsmen sought islands of firm ground upon which to stand, and when Ames had a bowl he rolled his trouser-legs up to the knees.

It was an uncanny echo from 38 years previously, when Drewy Stoddart, England's tour captain in the outstandingly thrilling 1894–95 Ashes series, caught a chill through batting in the rain in Hobart after strong persuasion from officials who were anxious not to disappoint the crowd. So marked was Stoddart by his costly sacrifice that he declined to take his team to Tasmania on the next tour, in 1897–98, which concluded with another parallel to Jardine's mission: Stoddart objected (in an interview in *The Referee*) to Australian barracking — and lost points for doing so, even though he was in fact upset at the way players from *both sides* were jeered.[7]

The farcical conditions on Christmas Eve 1932 eventually prompted

Tasmania's skipper "Snowy" Atkinson to declare the innings closed at 4.50 pm, and by stumps MCC were 56 without loss, Wyatt and Leyland batting. After the merriment of a coolish Christmas Day, spent at the old convict centre of Port Arthur, with many a thought devoted to loved-ones at home so many miles away, most of the English batsmen continued to enjoy themselves on the final day of the match (Ames 52 in 38 minutes) until a further declaration put Tasmania to the test. Bowes bowled a particularly hostile spell, taking four wickets at one point for only seven runs before the match ended in a draw. That night the players were invited to a Boxing Day dance.

TCA GROUND, HOBART, DECEMBER 23, 24, 26, 1932

TASMANIA 103 for 5 dec (A.O. Burrows 38, E. Paynter 3 for 40) and 89 for 4 (A.O. Burrows 33 not out, W.E. Bowes 4 for 18); MCC 330 for 7 dec (R.E.S. Wyatt 51, M. Leyland 65, F.R. Brown 35, L.E.G. Ames 52, H. Verity 54 not out, S.W.L. Putman 3 for 72). **DRAWN**

It had not quite matched the notable visit Larwood and Jardine had enjoyed four years previously. Then, Jardine had scored 214 and Larwood had propelled a bail the incredible distance of 66 yards (60.32 metres). Now, in 1932, there was an acrimonious editorial in the Hobart *Mercury* branding Jardine as a "sulky schoolboy", a condemnation from Joe Darling, long settled in Tasmania, who said he had played on far worse pitches in England, and another from a man who mocked Jardine's old school's motto — Manners Makyth the Man — concluding with the remark that Mr Jardine would be remembered as "the undertaker and gravedigger of the traditions of English cricket".[8] There were also letters of complaint on their way to the ACB — possibly conveyed on the very same ship, SS *Mariana*, in which the team were tossed by terrible gales all through the night on their way back to the mainland; most of the passengers clung to bunks between vomits during a voyage that must have felt as if it would never end.

Those letters contained protests at Jardine's negative behaviour during the saturated Hobart match and were written by the Tasmanian Cricket Association chairman, the secretary, and the team vice-captain, as well as by the monolithic Charles Eady, solicitor, Member of the Legislative Assembly and former Test batsman (who had scored 566 in a club match 30 years before).[9] All Board secretary Bill Jeanes felt he could do with the letters was pass copies to MCC in London.

At the end of this season Burrows and Walsh, who had bowled with little success for Tasmania in the matches against MCC, unleashed some Bodyline when Victoria needed a mere 24 to win in their second innings at Punt Road Oval, Melbourne.[10] They took two wickets each, all caught — the brilliant young Lindsay Hassett was a victim — before the match was lost. As far as can be seen, no protests ensued from this episode.

The touring cricketers went about their pleasures while in Tasmania, in their various ways, as the festive period approached and passed. Sutcliffe, Pataudi, Ames and Duckworth were photographed with Mrs Jack Gregory (Miss Australia 1927), seated lawnside at the tennis championships. Tommy Mitchell, feeling bored in Launceston, had got even with a local obsessive who kept prattling about the fish he'd caught by buying a load of fresh fish down at the harbour and having it dumped at the chap's door.[11] "We had a good party and got up to some larks behind closed doors," recalled the diminutive old legger years later. For others there were more cerebral and reflective ways of passing the time. Hedley Verity, who took a wicket with his first ball in Tasmania, travelled in the tram out of Hobart town with his bosom friend Bill Bowes towards Mount Wellington, and had a highly rewarding time every inch of the way up that great maternal mountain, culminating in some glorious views from the summit.

For the second Test match, set to start at Melbourne on Friday, December 30, Australia fielded a much-changed team from the one which had lost so heavily in the opening Test, at Sydney: Bradman back (at the last minute); Ponsford relegated to 12th man, Fingleton moving up to opener; the shaky Kippax dropped, left-hander Leo O'Brien in for a Test debut; Nagel out in favour of the ancient left-arm spinner Bert Ironmonger; and Queenslander Ron Oxenham, who had impressed the Englishmen in the Australian XI match as well as on the previous MCC tour, omitted from the squad of 13. Mailey made the potent point that the omission of Kippax was the first sign that leg theory "interferes seriously with the brilliant batting artist, and has a tendency to produce batting plodders".

As for England, on the first morning of the Melbourne Test, just as there had been stiff words between Douglas Jardine and Gubby Allen at the start of the Sydney Test, there was now another sharp exchange, the nature of which has been preserved in another of Allen's letters to his father. There are few — if any — comparable examples of a cricketer revealing so much of himself in one letter: "DRJ came to me and said the following, 'I had a talk with the boys, Larwood and Voce, last night and they said it is quite absurd you [Allen] not bowling bouncers: they say it is only because you are keen on your popularity.' Well! I burst and said a good deal about swollen-headed, gutless, uneducated miners, and that if it had been a question only of popularity I could have bowled bouncers years ago. I concluded by saying if he didn't like the way I bowled he still had time to leave me out not only of this match but until he came to his senses ... He said, 'Well! I am afraid you will have to or Larwood won't try.' I told him I had no intention of doing it but he had walked away by then and the matter was left. I bowled my ordinary way." (Dick Whitington reckoned that Allen taunted his captain with the words, "I'd better get my golf bag from the Windsor [Hotel] then Douglas, hadn't I?"[12])

So Allen remained involved, on his terms, and with Paynter still 12th man, the only change in the England XI from the Sydney Test was Verity's replacement by Bowes, leaving them with an all-pace attack of four plus Hammond. It was a long way from being the wisest piece of team selection. In fact it caused disbelief in some quarters, and was to look even more crazy when Bert Luttrell's pitch turned out to be much slower than expected. Most of the English party suspected a conspiracy. The counter-argument was simply that days of rain had hampered preparation and the pitch had been under a tarpaulin. When Jardine examined the sacred patch of ground he had simply drawn the wrong conclusion.

On the opening morning the players beheld with amazement the long queues curling around the MCG and across the surrounding parkland. People had turned up before first light, and when the final count was made, the attendance on this first day was a world record: 63,993 passed through the turnstiles, many of them destined to have less than a complete view of the proceedings, such was the crush. And this figure was to be bettered on the third day, Monday, the New Year's Day holiday, when 68,238 crammed into the stadium ("one huge bowl of staring faces", wrote Hobbs, who could remember no other Test match starting in such a tense and dramatic atmosphere).

SECOND TEST MATCH.
Scenes of the memorable match on the Melbourne Cricket-ground.

A section of the world's record attendance of 63,993 on the first day.

MORE PEOPLE THAN EVER BEFORE CRAMMED INTO THE MCG ON THE OPENING DAY,
THOUGH THE ATTENDANCE FIGURE OF 63,993 WAS BETTERED ON THE THIRD DAY.

So desperate was the desire to be there that a nightwatchman actually fired a warning shot from his revolver when he spotted two intruders trying to get over the wall behind one of the outer stands at 3 o'clock in the morning. Trembling, the men explained that they had simply wanted to see Bradman bat, and felt there might not be room later on.[13] They were marched out, still carrying their lunch packages. And Bill O'Reilly was telephoned in his room one morning about half-past-seven by a friend frantically seeking a ticket. The bowler later declared this to be the most interesting Test match in which he ever played.[14] *The Australian Cricketer* waxed lyrical too: "The tension was almost unbearable. How the players stood it, only they themselves know."

The Australians were disconcerted when the reappointment of Bill Woodfull as captain (or even as player) was deferred until it was almost time to start the match. Jardine tut-tutted in sympathy when told that the toss would have to wait because of this. Some criticism and concern hung about Woodfull, and there was even speculation that his refusal to consider retaliatory Bodyline was held against him by officialdom. But the upright, square-jawed Victorian now served his country well by winning the toss and taking first use of the slow wicket, which, according to Larwood, was cracked from the start. Newsreel footage shows Woodfull walking out with

Fingleton to open, heads erect, black armbands high on their shirt-sleeves, respecting the memory of Jack Blackham, Australia's great spade-bearded wicketkeeper from 1877 to 1894, who had died in Melbourne two days previously, aged 78.

Fingleton took strike to Larwood, who had the breeze and the slight slope in his favour; Voce operated from the other end. Tension soon gave way to farce. The Wisden ball (Jardine would not countenance Australian balls) split after a couple of overs and a replacement, at Woodfull's insistence, had to have the equivalent of two overs' wear applied to it. So Jardine tossed the ball gently to Woodfull, who patted it back. This hilarious procedure lasted several minutes, though the humour was lost on England's captain, even when Fingleton decided to join in.

WITHOUT A TRACE OF EMBARRASSMENT THE CAPTAINS PLAY PAT-BALL,
WITH FINGLETON WAITING IN RESERVE.

The Bodyline field was set straight away: as Arthur Mailey put it, "Just with a nod of the head Jardine signalled his men, and they came across on the leg side like a swarm of hungry sharks."[15] The ball then began to fly, and fast. Fingleton strolled down the pitch and patted a divot — possibly imagined — almost at the far end. Larwood glared and bounced him some more. The batsman smirked. His little scheme was paying off. Fearing Larwood's screaming late outswinger on a full length, he actually felt safer seeing the ball dug in short. He swayed out of harm's way for the most part, though painful hits, courtesy of Larwood and Bowes, were noted to his knee, hand, hip, thigh (causing a lengthy hold-up) and thumb.

148

LARWOOD'S BOOT PROBLEM CAME AT AN INCONVENIENT TIME. HIS CAPTAIN LOOKS
AT THE SPLIT IN THE LEATHER, BUT WAS SOON FUMING WITH FRUSTRATION.

Jardine was soon irritated further when Larwood's left boot split from
the toe to the heel and he had to leave the ground (to jeering). Back he came
wearing a pair of Duckworth's size 7s, but the replacement boot went on
Larwood's second ball. Altogether he went off four times, totalling almost a
full hour, while a cobbler worked at a hectic rate, and Larwood's toes were
gradually skinned. In desperation he put on his spare, unused pair. They
were tight and soon he was in agony, but he was reluctant to go off again
because the crowd, despite his attempts to clarify the problem, was in
uproar, some laughing at him, others suspecting that he was leaving the
field for a rest. (Some still remembered S.F. Barnes going off at Sydney
during the 1911–12 tour for a rub-down and a cigar.) When Larwood did
return to the dressing-room his socks were soaked in blood. Jardine, in his
account of the tour, much of which reads like a legal document, wrote icily:
"Test matches have been won and lost by lack of attention to such details.
No cricketer, and particularly a fast bowler, can be too careful in this
respect."[16] For some time his disgust prevented him from even speaking to
his star bowler.

Allen bowled with real pace, seaming the ball from the off, and he struck
Woodfull in the chest. (There were times during the day's play when Allen
had five men on the leg side.) Then the Australian skipper moved across his
wicket and was unexpectedly bowled after the ball cannoned into his pads.
First loss at 29, and Leo O'Brien in for his first Test innings. In the dressing-
room Bradman had given a quizzical, disbelieving look when he saw

O'Brien padding up after Woodfull had pinned up the batting order. "You don't seem to have much confidence in me, Leo!" he said. The newcomer replied that *he* was down as the No. 3. Bradman unbuckled his pads and walked away without a further word.

O'Brien diligently scored 10 off 47 balls, and a snippet of surviving film shows him employing his sharp boxer's footwork to jerk out of the path of a vicious delivery from Larwood. The English attack seemed on the verge of wilting in the heat when he was run out after the lunch interval. Fingleton embarked on a chancy run, ignoring his partner's warning shout, and O'Brien generously sacrificed himself, Pataudi's wide throw being scooped up on the half-volley by Ames, who broke the wicket. A section of the crowd booed the surviving batsman for causing the local favourite's dismissal, but the noise was soon drowned by a thunderous reception for Don Bradman as he emerged from the shadows and into the sunlight and slowly made his way to the wicket. As he crossed with the outgoing O'Brien, the Victorian, trying to be helpful, said, "He's slowed down a good bit." Then, as Bradman passed Sutcliffe, he managed to hear the Yorkshireman cordially say, "A wonderful ovation, Don," to which the batsman replied, "Yes, but will it be so good when I come back?"[17]

This was the moment. England's most prized quarry had suffered all manner of discomfort in the lead-up games, but now there was a mild pitch awaiting him, a bowling attack that was apparently losing its sharpness, and he was wearing his baggy green Australian cap. A million or more ears were alert, close to radio speakers all around the nation as he took guard: two legs. Bowes, at the Richmond end (where no monolithic stand yet stood), prepared to bowl, but the acclaim for Bradman continued tumultuously. To fill in time the bowler motioned to one of the leg-side fieldsmen to move a metre this way or that. He tried again, but the cheering persisted, so he fiddled with his field again.

Eventually a hush descended over the ground. The lumbering, blond, bespectacled Bowes shuffled in. A radio commentator set the scene: "Bradman is preparing to receive the first ball ..." Bowes heaved a short one down, a long hop rather than a demanding bumper (deliberately so, he was later to claim), and Bradman stepped to the off and swung into a hook shot. The ball flicked the under-edge of the bat and crashed into the stumps. *"HE'S OUT!"* screamed the commentator, though there were some listeners who thought he might have been kidding. But The Don was truly

OVER SO SOON: AFTER ALL THE BUILD-UP BRADMAN LOSES HIS WICKET TO HIS FIRST BALL OF THE
SERIES, A PROSPECT WHICH EVEN JARDINE COULD HARDLY HAVE DARED CHERISH.

out first ball, for cricket's most famous duck until 1948, when he fell second
ball at The Oval in his final Test innings. Hammond was to write that the
"O-OOH!" from the mass of spectators would remain with him till his
dying day.

The stunned silence that blanketed the thousands of onlookers at the
MCG, seated in the shade or standing on hot asphalt, was a statement in
itself. This was an Australian disaster of the worst magnitude. A tram could
be heard jangling over the rails some way from the ground, and of course
there had been a shout or two from the centre as the Englishmen took in
what had happened. But, of all things, the captain, at short leg, was spotted
for once free of his characteristic composure. As Bowes gleefully recalled:
"Jardine, the sphinx, had forgotten himself for the one and only time in his
cricketing life. In his sheer delight at this unexpected stroke of luck he had
clasped both his hands above his head and was jigging around like an
Indian doing a war dance."[18] Professor Manning Clark, the historian, was
there, a keen teenager then, and he recalled a remark made to him many
years later by Jack Fingleton, the non-striker: "He told me that in the great

hush that descended upon the ground when Bradman was bowled, Bowes just put his hands on his hips and turned round to Jack and the umpire, and said to them in broad Yorkshire: 'Well I'll be foocked!'"[19]

Another youngster with a big future, Keith Miller, then aged 13, was present that day, disappointed as much by the exclusion of his hero Ponsford as by Bradman's failure. (Miller's form-master at Melbourne High School was none other than W.M. Woodfull, who seemed to show no great interest in the school 1st XI, which was captained by Bluey Truscott, later killed while serving as a fighter pilot.)

And far away in Pudsey, Yorkshire, 16-year-old Len Hutton, mesmerised by Bradman's 334 at Headingley in 1930, now thrilled at the news that a fellow Tyke had got him first ball. Bowes, of course, was to bowl Bradman again, 19 months later in the Headingley Test … for 304. And when the organisers of the 1977 Centenary Test match in Melbourne persuaded Larwood and Voce to walk to the middle during an interval, and the ageing "heroes" were cheered to the echo as they jokingly removed their coats as if preparing to bowl, I happened to be standing beside the towering figure of Bill Bowes. "They should have invited you out there too, Bill, after the Bradman duck," I murmured in sympathy. "Oo, noa," came the bass whisper, with a dismissive chuckle. But it left me wondering.

And what if Jardine had still been living in 1977? Would he have accepted the invitation to attend the great Melbourne event? Would he have deigned to go out to the middle? Would he even have been invited to do so? And would the teeming thousands of Australians, amidst the all-pervasive atmosphere of celebration and goodwill, have forgiven him and applauded him, or simply given him the raspberry? (Jack Fingleton wrote that as the audience of almost 200 former Test cricketers stood to applaud Sir Donald Bradman's speech at the ACB's gala dinner during the Centenary celebrations, Messrs Larwood and Voce remained seated, as did a few others, including Ian Chappell.[20] What might Jardine's reception have been on such a grand occasion?)

Bradman's sensational Melbourne dismissal (Bowes's only wicket in the series) was filmed not only by a newsreel camera from a high position behind the wicket but also by another on a tripod at third man. The cameras may not have captured what Hammond later claimed was a beaten batsman's face, "dark red with mortification" as the ear-splitting yells of disappointment rose to the skies, but there was no risk of this thing being forgotten. What is little known — and it really deserved banner headlines — is that this Bradman duck probably saved the lives of three children. A man named Hancock was listening to the Test broadcast in a hotel in Launceston, and was so disgusted and frustrated at what Bowes had done that he got up and went for a walk. As he neared the river he spotted three youngsters — the youngest only 2½ — struggling in the water. He dived in, fully clothed, and saved them from almost certain drowning.[21]

So many vivid personal memories were cast that afternoon. During the war an RAAF flight sergeant based at the Melbourne Cricket Ground spoke of his nostalgia for the place. His father had brought him to watch cricket there. After that black moment a dozen years before, when the dreaded scoreline Bradman b Bowes 0 was etched, "Dad got the sulks and didn't speak for half an hour."[22]

There was no question of Bradman sulking. He left the field with his head high. Just emerging from the shower when Bradman re-entered the dressing-room he had so recently vacated, Leo O'Brien was startled to see him back so soon. "He said he'd been bowled — didn't mention that he'd played on to Bowes. Very modest bloke."[23]

Meanwhile, a little charade had been going on down by the boundary railings. Bob Wyatt had been forced to listen to the repeated taunt, "Wait till our Don comes in!" Wyatt kept his powder dry for a time, but after another wicket or two had fallen he turned to the men who had been so voluble and asked straightfaced, "When's your Don coming in?"[24] There were a few sick chuckles.

The Australian innings never quite recovered. Voce deserved more wickets than went his way, and Bodyline was put on hold for periods while the other bowlers kept things tight to a cleverly placed field. After tea (120 for 3), soon after Hammond had missed him, McCabe's fine cameo ended with a catch to Jardine at gully and Richardson, as if in a Fairbanks role, went on the attack against a fresh round of Bodyline, employing his prolific hook stroke to such effect that the close fielders prudently inched back. With little more than an hour remaining, Fingleton, having seemingly cemented his place at the top of the Australian order but now showing signs of weariness, was bowled by Allen for 83; most of his runs had accrued behind the wicket. The muscle between his right thumb and forefinger ached for a week after the pounding it had taken from the bat-handle as he fended off Larwood and Voce during a resistance lasting almost four hours.

RICHARDSON, SECOND-TOP SCORER, IS CAUGHT BY HAMMOND.

The dapper Oldfield looked in good shape and batted as well as anybody, but Richardson's bright hand ended with a catch to Hammond at backward square, and no sooner had Sutcliffe taken that fieldsman's place, rubbing his hands in anticipation, than the tentative Grimmett fed him a catch, the bat being knocked from his grasp. Australia were 194 for 7 at the close (5.55 pm after a light appeal), having reached the boundary only nine times (five by Richardson).

In the January 7 edition of *The Australasian*, John Worrall wrote of "this bodyline attack" as being "all brute strength and no guile…just a succession of battering rams". The old Test player reckoned that "if our batsmen survive his [Larwood's] battery this season they should be able to earn a living as acrobats", but after witnessing McCabe's downfall he believed "our men were getting themselves out, there being nothing in the bowling to be afraid of" — which suggests slight confusion in the eye of the observer.

Saturday's crowd was much down on the first day, as much as anything because Our Don would not be batting; also, news had spread that a hundred or so spectators, overcome by the intense heat on Friday, had been taken out on stretchers. But the second day was less oppressive. Larwood took the new ball as soon as the 200 was up and bowled to an orthodox field with four in the slips. (Wyatt kept the old ball as a souvenir, as he had done in the Australian XI match at the MCG. In the earlier match the wear and tear from 200 runs had left the ball in tatters. This Test match ball, however, still looked fairly new, which demonstrated how little abrasion occurred on this much softer pitch. Wyatt presented both balls to Lord's.)

The second run-out occurred when Oldfield played the ball down and took off, and his partner, Wall, failed to beat the stumps-destruction carried out by short-leg fielder Allen (another of the few incidents to be captured on film). O'Reilly swished powerfully through the covers, always mindful of his personal safety. Ironmonger, one of those No.11 batsmen whose entry unfailingly prompted the horse automatically to position itself between the shafts of the heavy roller — the horse seemed to sense that Ironmonger would not bat for long, and so was ready to pull the roller out to level the pitch before the other side began their innings! — hit what Vic Richardson considered the most memorable stroke of the entire series, a clanking cover-drive to the railings off Larwood. (Begging forgiveness for tabling yet again a very well-cooked chestnut, it was Ironmonger whose wife is supposed to have telephoned the ground as he went to bat. Upon being told he had just gone in, she said she'd happily hold on, knowing he was certain to be back very soon.) For this glorious hit off Larwood, the batsman modestly claimed to have closed his eyes as he swung his old bat.

Australia's slow 228, which owed so very much to Fingleton's gritty 83, disappointed not only Hobbs, who — while reckoning that fewer balls lifted here than in Sydney (the slowness of the pitch would explain that) — could not recall the initiative ever having been surrendered to this extent. Voce was generally considered the best of England's bowlers in this innings.

A cricket match seldom adopts meaningful shape until the sides have had an innings apiece, and as Australia took the field O'Reilly confided to one of the umpires, after enquiring as to the state of his eyesight and hearing, that he'd "need them both, for I'm after 'em today, and I want plenty of wickets".[25]

The big man got them, first five in this innings, off almost 35 overs from which under two runs an over were scored: brisk, bouncing topspinners mixed with nasty wrong'uns, some legspinners too fast for any but the most ambitious batsman's footwork, and the occasional well-concealed slower ball. The demands facing England were ominous, with Wall bowling penetratively — after a fast but perverse beginning when he bowled leg theory with an off-side field — and O'Reilly's spin accomplices Grimmett and Ironmonger (with their combined age of 91 years) bowling cannily.

Wyatt had a particularly torrid time before O'Reilly got him in what seemed the only fashion known to this batsman, lbw — even the scrupulously fair Oldfield joined in the appeal — shortly after he'd hit the brisk spinner for six to leg off a no-ball. England's vice-captain shouldered his bat at a straightish ball and was plumb. The most important wicket, that of Hammond (who had cut his foot swimming while in Sydney), soon followed, when the heavily padded batsman tried to force Wall off the back foot and was bowled by one which came back sharply and kept a little low. The crowd in the outer cared little what the ball had done: he was out and they were dancing with joy.

The fielders crowded around the batsmen, and it could have been immediately even better for Australia, but Pataudi was lucky to find Bradman's lightning throw going to the wrong end, and Sutcliffe, a perennially lucky batsman, saw a few chances missed, the most glaring being a stumping at 30 when he was well down the pitch, which Oldfield mishandled, to Grimmett's deep frustration. McCabe had just missed him off a fairly simple chance at slip.

The crowd were fooled when Sutcliffe was "caught" off a no-ball and pretended to walk off. The jocular gesture was a risky challenge to the fates.

Just before tea the textbook style of the cautious Pataudi let him down: he dragged a ball from O'Reilly into his stumps, and when after the break Sutcliffe went, soon to be followed by Jardine, England were in a miserable state at 104 for 5. Richardson had been a very fluid backward short leg, moving position frequently, causing Sutcliffe to glance round every ball. Now, pulling Wall, he gave that sure-handed fieldsman a catch and was on his way for 52, top scorer for the third innings running and passing 1000 first-class runs (average 111) for the tour before the year ended, the first Englishman to achieve this. It was, all the same, "absolutely the worst half-century I have ever seen in a Test", in John Worrall's view.

Jardine was well caught by the dapper Oldfield, making ground to a glance off Wall. Wall then bowled Ames, whose unfortunate stroke reminded everyone of Bradman's the day before as the stumps exploded. A fastish googly from O'Reilly then sent the obstinate Leyland's stumps flying as he aimed a forceful shot and the ball skidded through. (In retirement, O'Reilly would react tigerishly to any suggestion that this left-hander usually held the upper hand against him: "You just check how many times I got him out!" The answer is nine times in 16 Tests, but with decreasing frequency. In their Test encounters Leyland made 1412 runs at an average of 56.)

Wall and O'Reilly in particular were grateful when Ponsford brought out the drinks.

NO DOUBT ABOUT AMES'S DISMISSAL, CASTLED BY WALL.

The crowd reacted when O'Reilly, operating with three short legs and a silly point, struck Larwood painfully on the glove but expressed frustration when Bradman missed him off a skyer. They became ecstatic again when O'Reilly hit Larwood's middle stump. There was just time for Allen to produce a few defiant hits before Grimmett got the compensatory wicket of Voce, and with England in a mess at 161 for 9, the Australians left the arena to prolonged cheering. Wall (who had been fighting to control indigestion) and O'Reilly led them off.

Jardine is said to have posted a spy in the England dressing-room to watch out for any tampering with the pitch during the Sunday of rest — New Year's Day. He was trusting nobody. As for the day's play, he was to write in all honesty that "there can be no excuse for our very feeble batting performances".

That night there was a dinner thrown by the Victorian Cricket Association, adjudged by *The Australian Cricketer* to be the best such event in the country that season. It was somewhat incongruously linked to the first-ever English cricket tour 71 years ago. The Australian Cricket Board had originally intended that the Australian players should not be invited, but the VCA were not so unenlightened. Canon Hughes — he who imagined himself subjected to insult by the England captain in Sydney — presided, and the "most brilliant speech ever heard at a cricket dinner in Australia" was delivered by the Minister for Railways, a certain R.G. Menzies. One point cleverly made by the future Prime Minister and statesman concerned

Vic Richardson. One writer had called for the 38-year-old to retire. Menzies said that reluctantly he had to agree: "After all, we who have been watching Vic at silly mid-off have not failed to notice that he stands six feet [183 cm] nearer to the bat than he did once. True, he never misses; but clearly his eyesight is not what it used to be!" There were loud cheers from the players and a baleful glare from the journalist.[26]

D.R. Jardine, in his speech, rued the batting failure not only of himself but of his opposite number, Woodfull. The music was provided by the Sundowners' Quartette, and the magazine regretted that cricket-mad Melbourne wasn't able to tune in to a broadcast of the evening's delights. "The situation seemed to affect Mr Warner a little, but maybe he was more affected by the thought that he was watching his last Test in Melbourne."[27]

Or perhaps he had something else on his mind: not just the growing burden of objections from many quarters against his captain's tactics, but perhaps — as revealed in Gerald Howat's 1987 biography of Warner — the distraction of having met (at a dance) a certain "Miss EH", a dancer. She was to follow him back to England in due course, became his mistress, and would be quietly supported by him for years to come, with the tacit awareness of Warner's wife. In EH, the bothered manager was to find some desperately needed solace as the tour entered its roughest waters.

The biggest crowd of the match watched the third day, over 20,000 forming a queue three hours before the start. Some of the fittest among those who could not afford the admission climbed the sturdy trees for a view of the cricket, "roosting aloft like big birds".

Only eight runs were added before the England innings closed. Allen fell to another good catch by Richardson — chin-high, and just in from the railings at midwicket — giving O'Reilly his five-for and leaving Australia cock-a-hoop with a first-innings advantage of 59. Woodfull and Fingleton now sought to build on this; in the England dressing-room, Jardine had delivered a stirring pep talk. Mailey noted that Larwood looked around at the packed stands and waving flags as the team took the field, "sniffing the air and scenting battle". Once described by his team-mate and friend Bill Voce as "a little ball of muscle", he now began the attack — downwind, with off theory.

O'BRIEN, ANOTHER TO SUFFER COMPREHENSIVE DISMISSAL, BOWLED BY LARWOOD.

There were two early wickets, separated by a four-wides by Allen: Fingleton was caught behind off the speedy Allen's fourth ball from the southern end, and O'Brien, again having looked in control, was suddenly yorked by Larwood, the stump going into orbit. This brought England back into the picture. It also brought Bradman in, facing a pair. "As he walked in you could see 'Not this time!' written in letters of fire across the sky!" Hammond was later to write.[28] Australia's darling, a smile about his lips, took block, glanced at Larwood's intensive leg field (there was nobody forward of point on the off side) and calmly played his first ball, to a universal sigh of relief from the nervous crowd. Two sizzling leg-side bouncers flew by. Larwood had changed ends to benefit from the wind. Soon Bradman was facing Bowes, the first-innings axeman, who tried another bouncer on him. He hooked it crisply for four — a shot similar to the one which had brought him down on the first day — and there were whoops of joy and relief. Then he top-edged him for a single.

Bradman and his captain eased the score along steadily through till lunch, when Australia held the ascendancy again: 65 for 2, 124 ahead, Woodfull 21, Bradman a brisk 25. Afterwards, the total grew to 78 as Hammond bowled a high-class variety at medium pace; Larwood bowled five balls in one over which grazed Bradman's hip pocket, and one short ball was repelled by the batsman with a tennis smash. The Hammond–Bradman duel was finely balanced, and the two were exchanging looks ball after ball as neither got on top of the other.

Then the breakthrough: Woodfull propped tamely at a straightforward fast delivery from Larwood and gave Allen a catch. When McCabe fell without scoring, edging a widish ball from Allen into the stumps, England could see an opening. But now came the crucial partnership, as Richardson joined Bradman. It was worth 54 and took Australia close to an overall lead of 200, which was reassuring on the wearing pitch — the Glenroy soil was so dissimilar to the bone-hard Merri Creek black-soil MCG surfaces of past years, and there were three spin bowlers waiting to do their duty. Richardson played some false strokes at the start, and had to leave the field for attention when Larwood hit him on the back of the thigh. He was then hit on the elbow by Allen, but went on looking for runs.

Denzil Batchelor wrote vividly of Bradman's performance that afternoon: "He played that fantasy of a stroke, half square-cut, half drive, that went faster to the boundary than any other shot in anybody else's locker. He used his feet audaciously. He was prepared to move away from the line of the ball on the leg stump, and cut it sumptuously through the desert once inhabited by the slips."[29]

Not that he adhered to his specific strategy throughout. There was much orthodoxy in his innings — permitted by the lack of fire in the pitch — and it seemed that the caricature he had presented in those preliminary matches might indeed have been conceived to fool the opposition as much as anything. Again, bowlers tired as the Bradman–Richardson partnership steadied the innings. Bowes had caused Bradman anxiety with only one ball, but Hammond now impressed his captain by continuing to operate man-fully into the strong breeze, aiming to spin the ball. In turn Jardine impressed his majestic allrounder by his courage as he remained the only close-in fielder on the leg side, intercepting many of Bradman's stinging pull shots and finishing with hands that "were black and blue afterwards, for he never flinched from one of them," wrote Hammond; "I wondered who would be killed first — Jardine from one of those cracking hook shots, or Bradman from a rising ball."[30] Three of Bradman's fierce pulls to midwicket are preserved on newsreel, Bowes and Allen doing the chasing. A kind of delirium reigned in the crowd, and during a rare moment of silence amidst the hubbub a lone voice rang across the ground: "Good on you,

Don! Everyone in Australia's behind you except me, and I'm a Pommie!"[31]

Hammond broke the stand when Richardson, having played a memorable straight-drive and a pull off Voce, was leg-before for a precious 32, and Australia were half out for 135. The last five batsmen were now able to contribute only a feeble nine runs between them as Voce and Hammond each struck twice. Oldfield lost his off stump to a swinger, and the game entered a cat-and-mouse period as bowlers and fielders tried to keep Bradman away from the strike. Grimmett was exposed and done for by Voce with a slower ball which shot through low.

Bradman was 77 at tea, having scored 52 runs in the 105-minute session, and the nation wrung its hands in mass entreaty that he should reach his hundred. He now took nine off a Larwood over, but runs were declined as he manoeuvred the strike. Then a resounding drive by Bradman was brilliantly cut off by Jardine. By the time the supportive Wall was lbw he had moved to 96. But when Hammond took another wicket, O'Reilly's, Bradman was still two short, and Ironmonger, allegedly the world's worst batsman, was coming in. The hopes of a Bradman hundred seemed dead. Only a year before, he was left 299 not out against South Africa at Adelaide when the last batsman, Thurlow, was run out.

"Don't worry, son, I won't let you down," said the big, old, tanned Queenslander. Everybody — even policemen and ground attendants — peered anxiously towards the centre. Hammond ran in and Ironmonger kept his bat firmly in the blockhole as the ball whizzed by. Same again, and as the slips fielders threw their hands aloft and Hammond muttered a curse the anticipatory cheers bore an element of hysteria. Bradman was now on strike against Voce.

The first ball of the over defied run-scoring, as did the next and the three after that, which left one ball before England could get at Ironmonger again. Voce sensibly dug it in. But Bradman swung at it and tonked it over the leg field into the lush grass towards midwicket, and they ran hard for three to take him to 101. A greater roar than ever went up, and the Englishmen applauded as round after round of cheers rose to the heavens. M.A. Noble thought the reception given to "our marvellous genius, Bradman" was even greater than G.L. Jessop received after his 75-minute Test-winning century in 1902 — and Noble was on the field that day.[32] (The attendance at The Oval 30 years earlier, it ought perhaps to be remembered, was only a fraction of that at the MCG.)

On and on went the ecstasy of public delight as the scoreboard signalled what to this day is often reckoned to have been the innings of Don Bradman's life. Worrall described it as "beautiful and perfect ... the most perfect hundred I have ever seen" (and he was a team-mate of Trumper's). Like the first-innings first-baller, this hundred, viewed against the background of the unprecedented campaign plan to bring Bradman down, was almost too far-fetched to be a real-life event.

THE HUNDRED ALL AUSTRALIA HAD PRAYED FOR: DON BRADMAN CRASHES VOCE TO MIDWICKET TO SCAMPER THE THREE RUNS THAT BROUGHT HIM PERHAPS THE FINEST OF ALL HIS TEST CENTURIES.

It was Bradman's fifth century in the last five Tests in which he had batted — if further proof were needed that he was cricket's ultimate batting phenomenon — and no lower Australian total (191) has contained a century. It was a three-hour, chanceless hundred, built with near-perfect judgment, with no more than seven fours, and despite his determination to withdraw where possible and hit to the unoccupied off-side space when Bodyline was being bowled, only a quarter of his runs came on the off side. He had become the first Australian to score seven centuries against England (another 12 were to follow), and his unbeaten 103 came out of 164 runs scored while he batted. A lasting memento was to be a grand piano, purchased from a testimonial fund set up by Melbourne Cricket Club and presented to his wife.

And still the cheers rang out. Eventually, after two more runs, he tried a quick single to keep the strike and Ironmonger failed to make his ground. Australia all out, and England in need of 251 to go two up in the series.

Bareheaded, Bradman ran from the ground, clapped by the Englishmen, patted on the back by the luckier ones in the wide swarm of spectators — several women threw their arms around him and planted quick kisses on his face — and cheered by a crowd on the verge of hoarseness.

England had three-quarters of an hour to bat that evening, and Jardine sent in the county colleagues Sutcliffe and left-hander Leyland in the hope that a positive start could be made. To that point it was a successful move, for 43 runs were made before the end without loss (though Leyland's first run came from an edge over the slips), leaving England slight favourites in the eyes of many.

On the fourth morning O'Reilly broke through Sutcliffe's defence with an exquisite legspinner of some pace before he had added to his overnight score (umpire Hele said it was the best ball he had ever seen), and Leyland, having added nine, was bowled by a Wall inswinger that rebounded off his pads and rolled into the stumps. So England were soon in some disarray.

Hammond and Pataudi prospered for a time, the former nearly playing a ball on from Wall before he had scored, and Pataudi seeming to umpire Hele to be "on the brink of panic". Then came the collapse. Ironmonger, with that stub of a forefinger on his left hand, legacy of a sawmill accident, spun sharply off a perfect length, and Pataudi played him tamely to slip; then, third ball, Jardine also edged to slip: 70 for 4. The skipper had worn a new-looking Harlequin cap — "gay, and not at all out of place", stated *The Australian Cricketer* — and later told Hele that he had never faced three such wonderful deliveries in a row. Hammond found himself limited by O'Reilly's leg-stump direction and stretched by his slower, flighted balls. This was a real fight.

WITH A PEARL OF A BALL O'REILLY BREAKS THROUGH SUTCLIFFE'S BROAD DEFENCE.

Ames disappointed again, lifting one from O'Reilly to be caught at square leg. Three wickets had crashed for a mere seven runs. Hammond, as if on the scales with Bradman in opposition, held the key to the result. Wyatt went to the crease, a fine defensive batsman, the last of the specialists. Soon, to Hammond's horror, he was out: in his endeavour to take the initiative he had belted O'Reilly for a lofted four, but then miscued a shot, and was caught at deep cover by O'Brien, a sure fieldsman. At lunch the score was 102 for 6 and Australia were close to victory.

But there were more nerve-jangling minutes to come in this extraordinary Test match. Wyatt and Allen played sensibly against spin bowling which was not only well directed but was also aided by rough patches at both ends. This resistance saw another 50 runs added to England's score and an edginess developing among the Australians. O'Reilly was given a rest after bowling 12 overs on this hot day, taking 3 for 23. Woodfull continued to make fine adjustments to the field, and now put all his money on O'Reilly and Ironmonger, to the partial exclusion of Grimmett. There were periods of near silence when it was hard to realise that over 30,000 people were present.

Then Wyatt's pads were rapped yet again and up went the umpire's finger. (No dismissal was more ironic than this, for Wyatt had provided

George Hele with a ticket for his wife Matilda's sister so they could sit together in the guests' enclosure: his reward was to be given out lbw twice by Hele.[33]) Next over Allen had a swing at Ironmonger and the dapper Oldfield whisked off the bails in a flash. Larwood and Voce thrashed desperately but to no avail, both falling to outfield catches, and by mid-afternoon Australia were victorious. The scramble for the stumps as souvenirs was still in progress as hundreds of spectators raced across the field. Umpire Hele had an armful but was quickly dispossessed by Fingleton, Ironmonger and Woodfull — the captain no doubt feeling more satisfaction at the triumph in this match than in any other of his career. Soon he was being raised aloft by admirers and chaired from the ground as singing broke out and a few hats were tossed high into the very warm air.

"We want Woodfull!" The cry went up. So did another, calling for boos for the Board, but there was no support for this. The crowd were feeling uplifted and generous, and gave even Jardine a throaty cheer when he addressed them briefly and almost inaudibly on the balcony. (In *Cricket Caravan*, a book co-written by Keith Miller and R.S. Whitington in 1950, there is a claim that Jardine needed some persuasion to go out onto the committee balcony. Once there, he "muttered approximately the following sentence to the happy throng: 'Well, you have won. Why not go home?'") Woodfull, now in his dark suit, came out onto the Grey Smith Stand and said the things the members and others expected to hear.

Many remained for hours, reluctant to leave this coliseum, talking about the match, souveniring chunks of the turf, watching the players leave, seeking their autographs. Some might have agreed with Jack Hobbs that the result of the match went with the toss. The majority probably accepted the general view that England's cardinal error was going into the match with no specialist spinner. If there had been a Man of the Match award in those days it would have taxed the adjudicators' skills and emotions quite considerably. Should the medallion and cheque have gone to the doughty Fingleton for his patient innings of 83 or to the destructive, persevering O'Reilly for his 10 wickets or to the man now firmly restored as National Hero No. 1, D.G. Bradman? Whatever the case, Bradman's reputation had been restored, Australia's cricket prestige had been revived, and Bodyline had shrunk just a little, from its initial form as a distasteful threat to something that could be worn down and repelled … on a pitch slower than is customary. Milliseconds matter.

SECOND TEST MATCH

MELBOURNE CRICKET GROUND, DECEMBER 30, 31, 1932, JANUARY 2, 3, 1933

Toss won by Australia
12th men: W.H. Ponsford (A), E. Paynter (E)

Umpires: E.G. Borwick & G.A. Hele
Debut: L.P.J. O'Brien (A)

AUSTRALIA

		mins	balls	4s			mins	balls	4s
J.H.W. Fingleton	b Allen	83	234	227	3	c Ames b Allen	1	6	9	-
*W.M. Woodfull	b Allen	10	53	33	-	c Allen b Larwood	26	85	71	-
L.P.J. O'Brien	run out (Pataudi/Ames)	10	65	47	-	b Larwood	11	21	13	-
D.G. Bradman	b Bowes	0	1	1	-	not out	103	185	146	7
S.J. McCabe	c Jardine b Voce	32	76	58	1	b Allen	0	5	5	-
V.Y. Richardson	c Hammond b Voce	34	74	66	5	lbw b Hammond	32	44	48	3
#W.A.S. Oldfield	not out	27	84	66	1	b Voce	6	15	15	1
C.V. Grimmett	c Sutcliffe b Voce	2	7	6	-	b Voce	0	6	5	-
T.W. Wall	run out (Allen)	1	10	3	-	lbw b Hammond	3	34	22	-
W.J. O'Reilly	b Larwood	15	15	13	1	c Ames b Hammond	0	7	8	-
H. Ironmonger	b Larwood	4	5	4	1	run out (Larwood/Ames)	0	6	2	-
Extras	b 5, lb 1, w 2, nb 2	10				b 3, lb 1, w 4, nb 1	9			
Total	(86.3 overs, 326 mins)	**228**				(56.5 overs, 216 mins)	**191**			

Fall 1/29 2/67 3/67 4/131 5/156 6/188 7/194 8/200 9/222 10/228   1/1 2/27 3/78 4/81 5/135 6/150 7/156 8/184 9/186 10/191

BOWLING		O	M	R	W	w/nb		O	M	R	W	w/nb
Larwood		20.3	2	52	2	-/2	Larwood	15	2	50	2	-/-
Voce		20	3	54	3	-/-	Allen	12	1	44	2	4/-
Allen		17	3	41	2	2/-	Bowes	4	0	20	0	-/-
Hammond		10	3	21	0	-/-	Voce	15	2	47	2	-/1
Bowes		19	2	50	1	-/-	Hammond	10.5	2	21	3	-/-

ENGLAND

		mins	balls	4s			mins	balls	4s
H. Sutcliffe	c Richardson b Wall	52	156	182	5	b O'Reilly	33	53	63	4
R.E.S. Wyatt	lbw b O'Reilly	13	56	51	- +	[7] lbw b O'Reilly	25	54	50	3
W.R. Hammond	b Wall	8	9	7	1	[4] c O'Brien b O'Reilly	23	51	43	2
Nawab of Pataudi	b O'Reilly	15	60	78	-	[3] c Fingleton b Ironmonger	5	34	36	-
M. Leyland	b O'Reilly	22	68	62	2	[2] b Wall	19	58	51	2
*D.R.Jardine	c Oldfield b Wall	1	11	7	-	[5] c McCabe b Ironmonger	0	2	3	-
#L.E.G. Ames	b Wall	4	9	10	1	[6] c Fingleton b O'Reilly	2	8	10	-
G.O.B. Allen	c Richardson b O'Reilly	30	69	74	3	st Oldfield b Ironmonger	23	51	63	1
H. Larwood	b O'Reilly	9	11	11	1	c Wall b Ironmonger	4	11	7	-
W.Voce	c McCabe b Grimmett	6	29	30	-	c O'Brien b O'Reilly	0	3	5	-
W.E. Bowes	not out	4	6	9	-	not out	0	2	2	-
Extras	b 1, lb 2, nb 2	5				lb 4, nb 1	5			
Total	(85.3 overs, 251 mins)	**169**				(55.1 overs, 173 mins)	**139**			

+ plus 1 six

Fall 1/30 2/43 3/83 4/98 5/104 6/110 7/122 8/138 9/161 10/169   1/53 2/53 3/70 4/70 5/77 6/85 7/135 8/137 9/138 10/139

BOWLING		O	M	R	W	w/nb		O	M	R	W	w/nb
Wall		21	4	52	4	-/2	Wall	8	2	23	1	-/1
O'Reilly		34.3	17	63	5	-/-	O'Reilly	24	5	66	5	-/-
Grimmett		16	4	21	1	-/-	Ironmonger	19.1	8	26	4	-/-
Ironmonger		14	4	28	0	-/-	Grimmett	4	0	19	0	-/-

AUSTRALIA WON BY 111 RUNS

Attendances: 1st day 63,993, 2nd day 36,944, 3rd day 68,238, 4th day 31,460: Total 200,635
Gate receipts: £16,172.4.2d
Close-of-play scores: 1st day Aus 7/194 (Oldfield 13), 2nd day Eng 9/161 (Allen 26), 3rd day Eng (2) 0/43 (Sutcliffe 33, Leyland 10)

The Englishmen returned to their quarters at the city end of the parklands, the elegant Hotel Windsor, where many years later Harold Larwood's tour contract and sweater would be put on show in a glass case in the Cricketers' Bar. (A pair of his boots went to the Melbourne Cricket Club museum.) Soon Jardine would be receiving more letters, some friendly, some less so, including several which accused him of throwing the Melbourne Test. It was alleged that some of the English cricketers were laying heavy bets, absurd charges that he dismissed in his book with characteristic disdain.[34]

Don Bradman wrapped up his Melbourne radio duties on 3DB, his nightly viewpoint having contained some criticism of team-mates and of Hammond, too, for what he perceived as recklessness on the final day, which bent back some ears. But, as one R.T. Corrie was to point out, neither Bradman nor Woodfull ever complained on the air about Bodyline, and The Don nearly always closed with a humorous little anecdote about a barracker or a team-mate.[35]

Meanwhile, contrary to the widespread latter-day view that cricket-lovers in pre-television England were left in complete ignorance of what was going on in the Australian Tests of 1932–33, a glimmer of concern was shown as early as January 4, 1933, the day after the Melbourne Test ended, when a Mr Horace Hill wrote to *The Times*, mildly pointing out that "the stumps are not bowled at, endeavour is made to make the batsman hit the ball either in order to defend himself (not his wicket) or to make a run. He can be caught off a good stroke. The application of the leg-trap theory, therefore, is an artifice, and such a thing, in some opinions, is foreign to 'cricket'."

CHAPTER EIGHT

ADELAIDE EARTHQUAKE

In one sense there were two English teams touring Australia: the professionals and the privileged amateurs, who sometimes vanished on social jaunts at which it was felt — not without cause — that the working-class cricketers would not be comfortable. Plum Warner had sallied off for Christmas at Sir Alan and Lady Currie's property, Ercildoun, where from distant England King George V's broadcast came over the wireless loud and clear, the first Royal broadcast ever. The visitor was understandably transfixed by an exhibit in the smoking-room: the skull of a bushranger who had been shot some time in the 1870s. "You could see the bullet holes in the skull," he later wrote.[1]

Not inappropriately, Warner took centre stage in the house-party charades, performing the Clive Brook part in *Shanghai Express* opposite "Marlene Dietrich": "What have you been doing all these years?" "Usual routine of a soldier. Couple of years in the Sudan, three in India, six months in Egypt." "And did you ever think of me?" "Every second of every minute of every hour." Paraphrased, it might serve as an exchange between any international cricketer and his lady.

Warner returned to Ercildoun after the Melbourne Test, taking Palairet, Jardine, and the polished Sutcliffe with him, causing the local trout population to suffer severe depletion. But there was an unhappy consequence of Jardine's temporary departure. He left the team-sheet for the Bendigo match in the letter-rack at the Shamrock Hotel, where the team were staying. When Larwood, having a quiet drink in the hotel bar, saw the names he was furious. He had just bowled 35 overs flat out in the Test match. His feet were hurting too after the bursting-boots episode. In need of a rest, he had planned an outing in the bush next day. But there he was on the sheet — as *12th man*! He saw red. Grabbing a pencil, he scratched through his name.

A local happened to be passing, and remarked: "I hope you never get another wicket in Australia!" Larwood rounded on him and the man apologised, saying he hadn't meant to serve an insult; he had actually tried to pay Larwood a compliment. They had a friendly drink on it.[2]

When Jardine and the managers returned that evening they went to see Larwood in his room, and the bowling ace showed them "suppressed anger". Word was about to circulate that he felt himself too great a player to serve the drinks, which was a gross misrepresentation of a conscientious, honest, hard-working cricketer. Jardine devised a clever escape plan. The Victorian Country XIII would all bat and so would the MCC XII, which would spare Larwood from being seen as merely 12th man. Both sides would have only 11 in the field. Gilbert Mant, Jack Ingham and Bruce Harris made a pact not to report this fiasco for fear it would land Larwood in trouble at Lord's.

Looking back over 30-odd years as he put his autobiography together, Larwood accidentally merged Bendigo with Ballarat (where the team was to play — but without him — a fortnight later) by saying that Alexander played in the Bendigo match.

It had to happen: Victorian Country's second-wicket pair, Ron Porter (captain) and Ray Ratten, got settled against the bowling of Tate, Verity, Mitchell and Brown, and were closing in on a century partnership; so Larwood took the field in place of Tate and Jardine tossed him the ball. Porter hit him for four to raise his half-century. Larwood lengthened his run. Porter hooked him for another four. In went the Bodyline field.[3] Another short one, but this time the pace was too much for the Country batsman, and Duckworth held the catch. The stand amounted to 99 in 2½ hours, and the two local men, although they hit only three fours each, had become local heroes.

Jardine opened with Sutcliffe and played on for 11, but on the Monday the runs flowed, Sutcliffe hitting powerfully and striking two sixes before overdoing it when in sight of a century, Hammond also driving a very long six, and Pataudi, as ever, preferring to concentrate on style. MCC led by 71, and then the reluctant Larwood tore the head off Victorian Country's second innings, and Tate and the spinners all picked up wickets as the local thirteen crumbled for 75 just as time was called, so close to a win and loss. Stubborn batting by Best (32) and Stan Hammill (9) squeezed the Victorians to safety. The scoreboard might have been embarrassing, but the authorities were delighted at a record take for the ground of £715.

UPPER RESERVE, BENDIGO, JANUARY 7, 9, 1933

VICTORIAN COUNTRY XIII 215 (R. Porter 55, R. Ratten 48, H. Verity 3 for 43, T.B. Mitchell 3 for 58, H. Larwood 4 for 29) and 75 (W.L. Best 32, H. Larwood 3 for 15); MCC XII 286 (H. Sutcliffe 91, W.R. Hammond 67, Nawab of Pataudi 37, F.R. Brown 32, F. Moore 4 for 23). DRAWN

A little indigestion had been caused at tea by the delivery of a telegram from W.H. Jeanes, the ACB secretary, questioning on whose authority this two-day match was played by such odd team numbers. The calm reply was to the effect that Bendigo and MCC had come to a mutual agreement. And so to Adelaide for the third Test match and the boiling climax to the tour.

The match began on Friday the 13th. Nor was that the only dark omen, for when the Englishman had net practice at Adelaide Oval, watched by several thousand fans, the abuse hurled at Jardine — most pointedly when Bowes hit Jardine's stumps — was so upsetting that the England captain, who believed anyway that a few pence admission should have been charged to raise something for charity, cut short the practice and told the authorities he wanted nobody to be let in when the next day's net took place. The "display of hooliganism", he said, made the practice a "farce". The demand was met and next day there were police guarding the gates. Reporters were none too happy, but the dilution of Test previews in the papers did nothing to deter people from coming to see the match.

The largest shadow over the touring team was Jardine's own uncertainty about whether he should play, for his batting had been extremely disappointing. He left the room while his fellow selectors discussed the issue, "only to be met on my return with a flat *non possumus*".[4] In other words, they wanted their skipper to remain at the helm.

Press rumblings included an attack, in Melbourne's *Truth* newspaper, on "the hypocritical humbug of Captain Jardine" and "the seemingly guileless evasions of manager 'Plum' Warner". It so happened that this newspaper was refused a Press pass for the match, as was the *South Australian Worker*.[5]

More disturbing still were scandalous stories concerning Maurice Tate. One weekly ran a claim that he had thrown beer over his captain, another that they had come to blows. "Everyone in the team congratulated me on my throw," Tate later wrote, "because Jardine and I were 60 miles [97 km] apart at the time the incident was supposed to have occurred."[6]

As for the blow which is supposed to have left the big Sussex man with swollen knuckles (another absurd newspaper yarn claimed that McCabe had got stuck into Paynter), Tate pointed out that if that were true he would have been sent home on the next available ship. Tate suspected a chambermaid of concocting this story for money. One morning he was going down to breakfast when he met his skipper returning from his bath. Jardine asked if Tate would step into his room for a moment. "Yes, certainly, sir," replied Tate. (Both men happened to be freemasons.) Jardine then told him how sorry he was that he could not be included in England's Test XI and complimented him on the way he had taken it. "You can always rely on me," said the yeoman cricketer. "If you want me, I'll be there." Tate then concentrated on enjoying Glenelg beach, whose sand he wished were a feature of Brighton's great stretch of pebbles.

The MCC party were staying at the Pier Hotel, out at Glenelg, and soon became aware of the drawing power of this Test match as thousands poured into Adelaide by road, rail and sea. Scarcely a room was left for rental in city or suburbs as packed express trains from Melbourne came in four times a day, depositing 1800 passengers during the week. A second-class return ticket cost £2.10.0d, the best part of a working man's weekly wage. All cabins booked, the coastal steamers *Westralia*, *Manunda* and *Katoomba* converged on Port Adelaide. And a one-day record was set when 100 motor-cars from interstate crossed the River Murray on the Wellington punt.[7]

South Australian Cricket Association secretary Bill Jeanes was later accused of complacency for not making reservation of seats a priority, but he was not alone in failing to anticipate something of a stampede when the gates were opened at 10 am on the opening morning: long queues stretched from King William Street, and over 37,000 filled Adelaide Oval almost to the limit. Even worse discomfort followed on the Saturday, when over 50,000 squeezed in. Some women had even infiltrated the men's reserve, sparking a few more letters of complaint. This was no longer peaceful Adelaide, stately queen among Australian cities.

Jeanes did at least make sure that players and officials were well cared for in the guests' areas: the wives and daughters of SACA officials attended to their needs. Extra gatemen, police constables (400 at the ground on foot) and St John's Ambulance people were also engaged. And the secretary had shrewdly applied to the City Corporation for permission to raise admission prices, knowing full well that interest was sky-high. Three newsreel companies — Fox, Herschells, and Movietone — had applied for permission to film the Test match, and each was glad to pay £20 for the rights.[8] The cans of film would take three weeks to reach British cinemas.

Of all the newsreel shot at Adelaide and elsewhere during the series — and with due lamentation for all the footage tossed away into the rejection bins in the cutting-rooms — the surviving clips of Bill Woodfull and Bert Oldfield being struck by balls from Harold Larwood, and Bradman's Melbourne duck, of course, remain important, and in a sense iconic, moving-image records of the most dramatic moments of all. They will speak forever. And of what does the footage of the two injuries actually speak? Not of Bodyline, but of straightforward balls such as the ones which have felled many dozens of batsmen in Test cricket. Yet these incidents lit the short fuse to cricket's most ear-splitting and resounding explosion.

The contest began with honest expectation. S.P. "Sonny" Foenander, a cricket identity from Ceylon, noted particularly the enthusiasm of the females: "As for shrill shrieks the Australian girls are second to none in the world. They queue up very early in the morning of a big match outside the Adelaide Oval, every one of them carrying her luncheon basket, stuffed with sufficient food for at least two persons for a day, a cushion perhaps and a copy of a souvenir, that is usually on sale, giving all particulars about the two teams. At least for two hours before play begins these spectators sit patiently in the stands, chatting, watching others come and go, eagerly awaiting the arrival of the players on the ground ... 'There's Don' would be shouted out as Bradman's dapper little figure appeared."[9]

Nobody expected fireworks on the genial Alby Wright's pitch, for Adelaide had long been a batsman's hunting-ground, even if scores had been modest in the last two first-class matches there. Bert Tobin had delivered a notably fiery spell against Queensland on the opening day of the Shield match just before Christmas.

Capless and smiling, Jardine was well received by the crowd as he shook Woodfull's hand and at last won a toss, sticking to his call of "tails" and with the moral support of a miniature figure of a black cat lent him by Leyland. Having hopped over the rope to examine the pitch, he chose to bat, only to find within the hour that this pitch, in Bradman's words, had some sort of imp in it, a venomous spirit on that first morning after a little rain the day before.[10]

England were fortified by the return of Verity at the expense of Bowes, while Pataudi, whose rich seam of runs had come too slowly, gave way to Eddie Paynter, whose left-handedness it was hoped would counter Australia's three spinners, who all broke mostly from leg. When Clem Hill remarked, as the captains came off, that it should be a close game, the England captain, confident in his long batting line-up and bowling strength, retorted that the old Australia captain obviously hadn't heard who had won the toss.

But by lunch England were in serious difficulty. Jardine, after discussion with his senior players (who were aware of his exceptional nervousness as he waited to bat down the order), opened the innings himself with Sutcliffe, facing Wall and O'Reilly. The fourth ball kicked sharply and hit Sutcliffe on the shoulder, something the crowd seemed to relish. After 20 minutes, with only four runs posted, Jardine (wearing his navy-blue MCC touring cap) was bowled off his pads as he shuffled this way then that and tried to glance a swinging delivery from Wall. The newsreel cameraman made sure he got that one. Hammond soon followed, having shown discomfort at some "headers" (the topical expression) from Wall. One delivery forced him to duck, and the ball freakishly hit his bat as he withdrew it behind his legs. Wall at his fastest soon had him. As he slashed wildly the nimble Oldfield caught him almost in front of first slip. Disturbed by the frequency of the short balls, Hammond was heard by O'Reilly to growl as he walked off, "If that's what the bloody game's coming to, I've had enough of it!"[11] Umpire Hele even thought he might have thrown his innings away.

Sutcliffe then fell to O'Reilly, hitting tamely to short square leg, where

Wall dived forward to take a top-class one-handed catch, Borwick confirming the dubious dismissal. After paddling around for some time to no real effect, edging more than once and being bowled by an O'Reilly no-ball, Les Ames, whose poor form was inhibiting him, was bowled by a faster ball from first-change bowler Ironmonger. That made it four down for 30 just before lunch (Allen and Verity were seen rushing to the dressing-room to get into their flannels), and a mere 37 at the break, made in an hour and a half. The crowd was in a high humour.

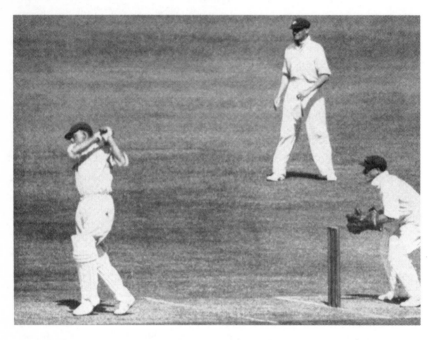

THE USUALLY CAUTIOUS WYATT AMAZED MANY WITH HIS SIX-HITTING AT ADELAIDE. HERE GOES ONE OFF GRIMMETT.

With England perched unsteadily, Leyland and Wyatt, both fighting cricketers, knuckled down for a salvation partnership of 156 which lasted into the third session, the pitch calming into a lovely batting strip. It was the best innings among many solid scores by Wyatt during the series, rendered untypical by three hits for six (winning the huge sum of £65 for the team kitty from a sponsor: the professionals were the beneficiaries, but they bought Wyatt the latest model in miniature cameras in return). After the first two sixes, smashed off Grimmett's legspin, the batsman caught sight of his skipper leaving his seat at the front of the pavilion and retiring to the dressing-room. It was then that Wyatt — who was dropped at 54 by McCabe at slip — remembered what Jardine had told his batsmen at lunch: go cautiously. The third six was a hook off Wall which just cleared Bradman's upstretched hands at long leg; Wyatt must by now have been hoping that a certain barracker was watching all this. In another match, this man had screamed out: "For God's sake get out, Wyatt! We've seen all your strokes but one, and that's sunstroke! The sooner you get that, the better!"[12] Early in the morning in England, Wyatt's mother switched on the wireless just in time to hear a description of that third six hit by her son.[13] R.S. Whitington speculated that Wyatt was perhaps inspired by his new happy friendship with local golf champion Kathie Rymill.

During this crucial stand there was a *contretemps* when Leyland, the carpenter from Yorkshire, lodged an objection against Ironmonger, the former timber worker from Queensland, on the grounds that he believed the bowler was smearing resin on his bowling hand (the significant stub of a left index finger too) to help his grip of the ball, in shades of the J.W.H.T. Douglas incident on this very ground in 1911–12. Old Bert, known as "Dainty" and sometimes as "Darkie", whose bowling seemed to lose something following this challenge, turned out his pocket and shook his handkerchief in the breeze to establish his innocence and Leyland apologised.[14] A newspaper recorded that "the old chap looked rueful and resentful"; R.T. Corrie, of course, was among those whose fury was inextinguishable. In *The Barracker at Bay* he thundered that this embarrassing spectacle was insulting to Ironmonger. He had been portrayed as "a thief caught in the act". But umpire Hele was to recollect that Ironmonger "emptied the wrong pocket and Leyland never thought to insist he empty the other one".[15] Complicating matters further, it was known that Ironmonger, among others, kept eucalyptus oil about his person. It was useful for keeping the flies away. It also rendered leather rather sticky.

"He's got a yo-yo in his pocket, Maurice," came a cry from the outer, causing people to laugh even if they weren't quite sure why.

Nor were the spectators pleased when later in the day Jardine sent a message out to the umpires to stop Richardson moving his position behind the batsman (it was a similar manoeuvre that sparked the ugly Mike Gatting/Shakoor Rana flare-up at Faisalabad in 1987). Richardson's response to the "petty" accusation was "forcible and free", according to R.W.E. Wilmot.

O'REILLY TOILS ON. HE SENT DOWN 100 OVERS IN THIS TEST MATCH.

Leyland, who started with a hooked four off Wall, moved down the pitch and clipped Grimmett twice to the long straight boundary, and gradually the innings was transformed. Wall, off that long run and with that idiosyncratic thrust of the stiff left leg just prior to release, tried some leg theory to Wyatt, without a crowded leg-side field, but the batsman whacked the ball over square leg's head. At tea England were 154 for 4, the century stand having come in only 90 minutes. Soon O'Reilly adopted a "leg theory" field: five men on the leg side and four on the off. And then the innings was distorted again. Having survived a stumping off Grimmett when Oldfield fumbled and then a catchable stroke over the ducking Fingleton, Leyland, facing O'Reilly from the river end, was bowled via bat and pad by a faster ball into the blockhole. Wyatt for once then advanced to Grimmett but lifted the ball to Richardson at mid-off: 196 for 6. After this fine rescuing partnership of 156 both were gone and the innings was still in the balance, leaving Wilfred Rhodes over in England wishing — not unreasonably — that Leyland would be England's regular opener with Sutcliffe.·

It was now Paynter's turn to serve with distinction. Already 31 years old, he had played only twice for England, having made a debut on his home ground at Old Trafford against New Zealand in 1931, and a year later scored a fifty at Lord's in the sole Test against India. Unafraid to loft the ball, he now brought his renowned tap-dancer feet into use from the start, creaming Grimmett through the covers — only to lose Allen to that bowler soon after he had cut McCabe long-hops twice to the fence. Allen's long net practice during lunch was of little use. Verity saw the day out with Paynter, Australia having taken the first drinks of the day and the new ball at 200. Woodfull and his men could be pleased with their work as they headed for the showers.

Probably this was the evening when a local lad named Dennis Monkhouse, waiting with others for a sight of the cricketers after play ended, spotted Jardine and Allen emerging from the dressing-room and politely asked the evidently suspicious England captain if he might carry his bag for him to the car. "He looked at me ... he looked *through* me," Monkhouse recalled 50 years later. Gubby Allen resolved the situation by suggesting to the youngster that he might care to carry *his* bag across the ground.[16]

Bradman and Woodfull hurried off to carry out their broadcasting duties at 6.55 pm for 5AD (sponsored by Vacuum Oil), Bradman, with characteristic directness, expressing concern at O'Reilly's several no-balls, the skipper praising his bowlers for their efforts.

The Saturday brought in a staggering attendance of 50,962, the largest ever at Adelaide Oval, for cricket or football. In the outer they stood literally shoulder to shoulder, the men and boys nearly all wearing jackets and hats. None there that particular day — and one paper assessed that there were many Englishfolk among them — could ever quite forget what happened.

Paynter and Verity resumed their partnership, Paynter needing to banish from his mind a nasty incident an hour earlier. As he and four other players were walking along the pavement approaching Adelaide Oval he was charged from behind and sent toppling full-length (all 5 ft 6 in [168 cm] of him) to the ground. His team-mates, almost as shocked as he was, could only give vain thought to chasing the assailant and his four mates, for they ran off and quickly vanished.[17]

As with any eighth-wicket defiance worth as many as 96, the Paynter–Verity stand was a source of deep frustration to Australia. Paynter, who had clobbered his partner's bowling in last season's Roses match, was a revelation, driving crisply, smothering O'Reilly's spin with a long stretch forward, having no problem with Grimmett's googly, and punching through the covers off the back foot, while Verity reflected his very inner nature by backing Paynter doggedly and sensibly, allowing himself a bold drive through point off Ironmonger, both batsmen also alert for the quick single. Once, Paynter slipped, and if Fingleton's throw from side-on had hit he would have been well out. And Verity had some luck when an edge off Ironmonger was too swift for O'Reilly, who was probably standing too close at slip. "You'll never get 'em out!" came the corny cry from the grassy mound, while up in the branches of the trees the youngsters were having their say. In the Press enclosure Hobbs was wondering why Woodfull didn't try Bradman in an endeavour to break up the partnership; his introduction had to wait until the second innings, and then it would be notable.

"I must tell you this," wrote Hobbs. "During the big stand by Paynter and Verity I went into the dressing-room to talk to Herbert Sutcliffe, but was quickly ordered back to my position in the Press box. It is a cricket superstition that something happens if anyone in the dressing-room changes position during a big stand."

Lunch came, with 79 having been added and no further loss, but Paynter was out soon afterwards, caught behind square leg for 77 as he tried to pull a ball from the refreshed Wall from in front of his face. He was given a loud and genuine reception as he climbed the steps. The same bowler then bowled Voce as he moved across and exposed his leg stump. Verity, having survived a run-out chance just before lunch and catches to McCabe low at slip and Richardson running at extra cover, soon followed, after an invaluable 2½-hour 45, as England finished with 341, a figure beyond reasonable expectation when they were four down for 30 just over a day previously. Wall walked wearily off with the best figures, 5 for 72, the unfulfilled O'Reilly just as tired after his 50 overs.

In mid-afternoon Woodfull and Fingleton strode out to open Australia's innings, tea having been taken between innings, leaving England to field for 2¾ hours. A few minutes later Fingleton, one of the heroes of Melbourne, was on his way back, caught behind in Allen's second over. To affectionate and expectant applause Bradman marched in.

THE BLOW THAT INFURIATED A NATION: BILL WOODFULL STAGGERS FROM THE FORCE
OF A BALL FROM LARWOOD WHICH BRUISED HIS CHEST NEAR THE HEART.

Then came the first rumbles of the most awful human thunder. Larwood galloped in from the Torrens end for his second over and whooshed the fifth ball inches from Woodfull's head. In he came again, and this time the Australian captain ("essentially firm-footed and almost immobile", as Larwood classified him in his tour book) was caught over the crease by a shortish ball directed more or less over middle stump. It thumped him over the heart and he staggered away, dropping his bat, clutching his chest, doubled up with shock and pain, facial features screwed up. The suggestion that a ball from Larwood had greater force than a shrapnel bullet was clearly an exaggeration, but not by so very much. Nearer the mark was the likening of it to a pebble on a lake: the ball skidded through, and if that wasn't enough for a batsman to contend with, the bounce might vary.

Woodfull managed to stay on his feet, and as English players gathered around to enquire and sympathise Gubby Allen ran to get a glass of water. So much happened in such a short space of time. Hooting and angry jeering spread from section to section, from spectators not only on the grassy mounds but in the members' seats. Wally Hammond, sensing Larwood's alarm at the cacophony from all around the ring, called across to him: "Don't take any notice of them!" But they couldn't hear each other above the din.

And when the blow had struck, Jardine, as much for non-striker Bradman's benefit as anything, cried out to his bowler, "Well bowled, Harold!"

Larwood was later to dictate to his ghost-writer that "Bradman and Woodfull were the only ones who used to 'show' a little when they got out of the way of a rising ball. Their mannerisms made the crowd think I was trying to kill them."[18] But Woodfull was not playing to the gallery. He was hurt, and had the pericardium been full of blood at the peak of a heartbeat, he might have been killed, a fate suffered by more than a few batsmen — one in a first-class match in Pakistan in 1959; another Martin Bedkober, Jeff Thomson's flatmate, who took a fatal blow to the chest in a Queensland grade match.

Gwen Woodfull, who was at home in suburban Melbourne with the two young boys but in regular touch by phone with Bill, lived in fear through-out this torrid summer, and later expressed the opinion that the chest blows her husband took during the 1932–33 season hastened his death (at 67, in 1965).[19]

The hold-up lasted a few minutes before Woodfull, after unbuttoning his shirt for a quick look at his bruised chest, indicated that he was able to continue. Bradman took runs off Allen, and then the ball was back in Larwood's hand again. Now we have divergent recollections of what led to the immediate setting of the Bodyline field as Woodfull prepared to face up. Jardine, having reasonably pointed out that Woodfull was welcome to retire hurt if he felt the need, was to claim that Larwood made a sign to him that he wanted a leg-side field. Larwood, in *his* book, insisted that his captain stopped him in mid-stride by clapping his hands and then motioned the fieldsmen over into the leg trap, with only Voce standing on the off side, deep at backward point. Over they went to join Allen at short square: Verity, Jardine and Sutcliffe strengthening the cordon, Hammond out at long leg.

Groans from the crowd, highlighted by escalating cries of abuse, rang in the ears of the English cricketers, and possibly echoed still in Jardine's many years later when he quietly confessed (to Bob Menzies, among others) that he wished he could have that five minutes back again. There can be no adamant belief that the England captain and his key fast bowler desired to put the boot in at that particular moment — it was about time for the scheduled switch in the field setting anyway, and Bradman would soon be on strike — but few of the irate spectators, whether in the outer, the members' enclosure, the committee-room, the Press box or the Australian dressing-room, could see this as anything other than a case of kicking a man when he was down.

Australian selector Bill Johnson was to declare it "the most unsportsmanlike act ever witnessed on an Australian cricket field", while Canon Hughes, the VCA president, was approaching a point of such outrage that he was to say, "Cancel the remaining two Tests. Let England take the Ashes for what they're worth."[20] Jack Fingleton was told by R.G. Menzies that he was sitting next to a stranger who showed himself to be quietly spoken, cultured and most interesting as they conversed before play began. After Woodfull was struck, however, Menzies's new friend was a changed person. "He was on his feet and his face was choleric. He shouted, he raved, and he flung imprecations at Larwood and Jardine because of what his eyes had seen."[21] There were many like him.

Dick Whitington, in the midst of his 1970 O'Reilly biography, reflected on his own experience at the match as a 20-year-old: "I saw some of Adelaide's octogenarians in the members' enclosure rise to their feet, flush scarlet of face and, with their Adam's apples throbbing, count Jardine and his team out. Respectable Adelaide men they were, professional and business men, scions of Adelaide's Establishment. I knew some of their daughters. They had not seen Bodyline bowling before … they did not want to sit without protesting while it was being aimed at the heart and head of a badly stricken man, a man who in their opinion stood for all the finest qualities that had come to be associated with cricket. Australia had taken it until then."

Here and there, with very good reason, it was written that if either Bill Woodfull or Don Bradman had been seriously injured now by a bouncer there must have been a riot. Other venues may be recognised as more volatile, but Adelaide Oval had been stirred into an unprecedented fury, and if one hothead had leapt the pickets the mob would have needed no further incitement to storm on: it has since happened time and again on the cricket grounds of the world, often for no substantial reason. And all those Adelaide mounted policemen could have done little about it. It was not merely a matter of what was happening before their very eyes: spectators were seeing the violence "in the general context of events" as Ray Robinson put it, knowing full well that the English fast bowlers (except Allen, of course) had been doing this for two months now and seemed intent on continuing to do it.

IMMEDIATELY AFTER RECOVERY, THE SHAKY WOODFULL, NOW FACING A BODYLINE FIELD SETTING, HAS HIS BAT KNOCKED FROM HIS GRASP BY ANOTHER ROCKET FROM LARWOOD.

Woodfull, having next had his bat knocked from his grasp by a Larwood thunderbolt, popped a ball just wide of a short-leg fielder, and Bradman spooned the next straight into Allen's hands at short square: 18 for 2, and more historic newsreel as The Don loses his bearings on the way back to the dressing-room and is seen walking beside the pickets to the exit gate. Not long afterwards, facing Larwood, McCabe (8), now lacking the fortune which escorted him through his legendary 187 at Sydney, gave Jardine a catch in the leg-side ring off the splice of the bat. Bodyline at its most deadly was on show. And the crowd howled.

Back in the side at the expense of O'Brien, Ponsford prepared to go to the middle, his outline swollen by extra padding. (Some of the Australians, including Bradman but not as yet Woodfull, were now wearing rubber chest-guards, suspended inside the shirt by straps around the neck.) A friend called across to the laconic Ponsford: "Where are you staying?" — that's to say, which hotel? The reply was calm and collected: "Out in the middle for as long as I can."[22] And brandishing his Big Bertha bat and taking one resounding blow after another to the thighs, back and rump, which was his chosen method of dealing with Bodyline, Ponsford was to stay for 3½ hours while compiling a brave 85. Fortune favoured him only in that no ball kicked quite high enough to strike the back of his head, and as the Englishmen who were close enough to do so looked on — some of them with silent concern and admiration — wicketkeeper Les Ames in particular constantly enquired if he was all right.

There are varying assessments of the number of serious bruises Ponsford acquired in that remarkable innings, but it must have been about a dozen, and at one stage Woodfull gave an overpriced assessment: "A fiver per bruise, Ponny!" He said he'd gladly take more if he could get to 100. There were dark imprints of the ball surrounded by purple, with yellow haloes, and when one of the newcomers to the side in the next Test match caught sight of them he was left wondering if Bill Ponsford was suffering from a strange disease.[23]

He had the required luck, being missed early wide at slip by Hammond off Allen, and the pounding came from the start, though in *Cricket Casualties* R.H. Campbell bothered to list only two blows, a hit on the shoulder from Voce when Ponsford was 3 and a crack on the back from Larwood when he was 15.

The famous and highly prolific pairing of Woodfull and Ponsford, usually seen at the top of the order, remained intact for only a short time now, for Woodfull, having sustained a few more hits about the body, had his middle stump sent flying by Allen when the ball kept low and he got a touch with the bat. The captain had fought on for an hour and a half for his 22. That made it 51 for 4, statistically the lowest point of the day for Australia.

But Ponsford and the mature local hero Richardson saw it through to stumps, having the odd narrow escape from dismissal and injury, and Ponsford once inflicting a stinging blow on Allen at short leg. The fieldsman, maintaining his diplomatic responsibilities, doffed his hat and graciously bowed. There were times when Ponsford, from his crouching stance, ducked balls which zoomed only just above the bails, but he was a different character entirely when facing the slower bowling, once banging Verity back high through his desperate hands and also using his feet well to clip the ball to the distant long-on boundary. The bringing out of further drinks made the onlookers even more irritable.

Voce had left the field (Brown substituted) with a damaged ankle after tea, which led to a brief loudspeaker call for a doctor. This persuaded many of the hoarse and unhappy spectators to spring to the conclusion that it must be Woodfull who was in serious need of medical attention. Angry rumbles of contempt rose afresh from the terraces. Larwood was barracked and counted out: "One! Two! Three! [through to] Nine! OUT! You Pommie bastard!" Jardine bravely, perhaps masochistically, took them on, if only for one over before Brown switched with him. England's stern-faced captain went out to a fielding position in the deep and faced the consequences. The shortest of Anglo-Saxon expletives were fired at him, together with the spluttering protests of normally placid, decent people: "D'you call this sport?" "Why don't you play cricket, Jardine?" A newsreel cameraman seized the chance to set up his equipment and persuade a bunch of well-dressed male spectators to shout some epithets for the benefit of posterity. Self-consciously they barked, "Hey, Larwood, bowl them at the wicket, not his head!" Then there was laughter. It was a mild and far from representative sequence.

ADELAIDE OVAL HAD NEVER BEEN SO CROWDED AS ON THE SATURDAY, WHEN OVER 50,000 CRAMMED IN. THEY BEHELD SENSATIONAL INCIDENT AND AIRED THEIR OPINIONS FORCEFULLY.

And so this wretched day's cricket came to an end. Australia, licking their wounds, stood 232 in arrears with six wickets in hand. Ponsford, now with a replacement bat after Allen had taken a chunk out of his first one, and Richardson were given a sympathetic reception as they left the field, but for the Englishmen there was hardly a handclap.

George Hele remembered teetotaller Woodfull's reaction when McCabe told him they were out of beer and that the steward had replied that Mr Jeanes would not send more in: they had had their quota. Woodfull told Jeanes: "No beer, no play on Monday, and I mean that." The Australians soon had their refreshing beer.

The crisis was about to escalate dramatically, firstly through what has become known as the Adelaide Leak. Although he did not wish it, the strength of feeling of Australia's discreet and greatly respected captain William Maldon Woodfull at last became known to the nation. He had seen it thus far as his duty to battle on without complaining in public. But in the privacy of the dressing-room he could contain himself no longer when Plum Warner, in his favoured panama hat, and Dick Palairet called later that Saturday afternoon to enquire after him in view of the knocks he had taken, especially the severe chest blow.

Condemnation of the English managers for their gesture would be misguided. It was the decent and courteous thing to do, and they were experienced enough to time the visit appropriately. There have been many versions of the exchange, the most colourful coming in later years by 12th man Leo O'Brien. Woodfull, having showered, stood with a towel around his waist. (There are impressions — including Jack Fingleton's — that depict him lying on the massage-table having attention to the bruising, but this might owe something to the narrators' desire to boost the dramatic content of the scene.)

Having expressed their sympathy and concern, the English gentlemen were then taken sharply aback by the normally reticent Woodfull's response (Warner's version — and as Gubby Allen enjoyed saying of himself, Plum was *there*): "I don't want to see you, Mr Warner. There are two teams out there. One is trying to play cricket and the other is not." The English manager then recalled saying, "Apart from all that, we most sincerely hope you are not too badly hurt." The captain of Australia replied, "The bruise is coming out."[24]

Fingleton, who was one of those within earshot, added to Woodfull's dialogue: "This game is too good to be spoilt. It is time some people got out of it."[25] Shocked and close to tears, Warner departed, with Palairet at his heels. In *The Referee*, W.M. Rutledge recorded yet further words. Woodfull, he wrote, went on to say, "The matter is in your hands, Mr Warner, and I have nothing further to say to you. Good afternoon." And an interesting variant was scorer Ferguson's, who had Woodfull saying, "If these tactics are persevered with, it may be better if I do not play the game."[26]

The genteel Plum Warner cannot have been so humiliated — outside the recent brushes with Jardine — since his schooldays at Rugby.

In 1983 "Mo" O'Brien told me[27] that he was alone in the dressing-room with Woodfull, apart from the masseur, who was deaf, Alan Kippax, Jack Ryder and Ernie Jones (whose unique opinion of Larwood was: "Him fast? Why, s'welp me, he wouldn't knock a dint in a pound of butter on a hot day"[28]). O'Brien was adamant that neither Bradman nor Fingleton was in the dressing-room. However, some confusion could have arisen from the fact that most of the Australian players were not far away, watching the play from the gallery which backed on to the dressing-room, and they probably overheard the Woodfull–Warner exchange.

O'Brien was seized upon by others after the 1983 interview, and inconsistencies in his story began to emerge. Additionally, Ryder's son protested that his father was a man of integrity and would not have made the outburst a matter for public consumption. Bill Ponsford — the droll character remembered by Fingleton as having devised a hushed warning to players not to speak when reporters were in the vicinity ("Nit, the Press is about!") — then described as "just plain rubbish" any suggestion that Woodfull was lying injured on the massage-table.

W.M. WOODFULL (LEFT) AND D.R. JARDINE AS SELDOM SEEN ON THE 1932–33 TOUR AFTER THE INITIAL SOCIAL CONTACT.

Later correspondence with O'Brien put more flesh on the subject: firstly, what of other writers' complaints of discrepancies in versions of Leo's recollections? "I have soon adjusted their ideas to some order." And what, therefore, is the full list of suspects? "There were about 20 persons outside in the players' enclosure," he wrote in June 1983, "when I went outside and told the details of Plum and Palairet's visit. Included in the group were players, selectors, and several members of the Board of Control, and any one of those could have spilt the news." Then, disarmingly: "The only two you'd eliminate were myself and no doubt WM [Woodfull]." Ten years later O'Brien teased with another possibility: "In the UK party was a journalist who could have entered the field."

At this point, lest there be any incomprehension as to why the passing to the Press of the substance of this dramatic private exchange between the captain of Australia and the eminent MCC gents should have fired such horrified reaction, it needs to be appreciated just how acute sensitivity in such matters could be in those times. Leakages, breaches of trust, unauthorised scoops, "whistle-blowing" are fairly commonplace nowadays. In 1933, when courtesy, discretion and respect were more cherished commodities than they are today, this sort of thing was regarded as a moral offence of the first order. In pre-war society respectability, manners and etiquette were upheld as fundamental qualities.

But not by everybody. There were many — Australian cricketers among them, and perhaps some English too — who, with a sense of frustration, felt that as long as Woodfull made no public pronouncement then cricket-lovers might continue to nurse the ingenuous belief that he had no strong objection to Bodyline. Now they knew. He deplored this kind of bowling as intensely as did the rest of them. So it was time for something to be done about it. Across Australia the floodgates of revulsion could now be flung open, for Billy Woodfull hates Bodyline too. His strong words, even though they were never intended to reach the outside world, had a decisive impact.

Of course, none of the cricketers wished to be associated with the leak. However, Warner, when he saw the story in Monday's papers, immediately assumed that the only full-time journalist in the Australian team must be the culprit, and he instantly offered Larwood a reward (£1) if he got Fingleton out in the second innings.

It was nearly 10 years before Fingleton got to hear of Warner's assumption. He was in military uniform, and had just acquired Warner's book *Cricket Between Two Wars*. He was so upset that he wrote to Warner, who confirmed that, yes, it had been his conviction that Fingleton was the source, but if he cared to present the facts, a correction would be published. Fingleton let it lie, though for the rest of his days he believed that people who mattered, not least the Australian Board, held him responsible, and that this cost him a place on the 1934 tour of England. There were possibly allied causes: criticism of his fielding cropped up in a newspaper column written by Bradman; and (an O'Reilly theory, this) Fingleton's abrupt reaction to

Woodfull when the Victoria captain invited him to return to the crease after he had wrongly been adjudged run out (when he was 86, during an opening stand of 340 with his rival for the 1934 tour, Bill Brown). Missing that 1934 tour cost Fingleton a lot of sleep in the years ahead.

Subsequent years have brought further enlightenment — and some puzzlement too. While Fingleton was to write[29] that Woodfull told him some time later that it was a pity that the attachment of blame did indeed cost him a trip to England in 1934, a letter written by Woodfull to him in June 1943 stated, "I can assure you that I did not connect your name with the passing on of that conversation. Indeed, I seem to recall that you told me on the day that it was published that you had nothing to do with it. I still do not know who was responsible for the leakage as I have always expected cricketers to do the right thing by their team-mates."[30]

As for Warner, Bill O'Reilly claimed that following the Englishman's "unpardonable mistake" in accusing his mate Fingleton, the two Australians confronted him one morning during the 1948 tour as they all converged on the hotel breakfast-room. There, Warner answered Fingleton's pointed question — did Sir Pelham still believe Fingleton was the culprit in Adelaide? — with an emphatic negative. He had been hasty, he was sorry, and he apologised.[31]

In the Press box at The Oval during the 1968 Ashes Test, Jack Fingleton, who was always stimulating company, suddenly broke away from our rambling conversation during a dull period of play to tell me that the leak was provided by Don Bradman. "But don't you breathe a word of this while I'm alive!" he said, with a glare that persuaded me it would be best to keep this to myself. Then, in 1978, to my astonishment, and in the unlikely context of a biography of Victor Trumper (which was some way from being his finest work), Fingleton threw off any inhibitions and pointed the finger at Bradman: "The story as told me by Claude Corbett, then writing for the *Sun* and a colleague of mine, was this: 'I got a ring on the phone that night at our hotel. It was from Don Bradman, who told me he wanted to tell me something. Don was also working in a third sense for the *Sun*... We arranged a rendezvous on North Terrace and, while we sat in his car, he told me all about the Warner–Woodfull incident. It was too hot a story to run on my own, and I gave it to all the Press.'"[32] (Fingleton often declared that as a journalist he had ignored numerous opportunities of scoops during the 1932–33 series. He did offer a close-up profile of Jardine but his editor wasn't interested. The cricketer/journalist, somewhat surprisingly, gave it as his opinion that not even his hallowed Trumper could have coped successfully with Bodyline: he didn't fancy Foster so how could he have been comfortable against Voce and Larwood?)

CLAUDE CORBETT, THE FIRST NEWSPAPERMAN TO HAVE ACCESS
TO THE STORY OF THE LEAK. (*COURTESY HELEN CORBETT*)

Bradman hotly denied Fingleton's story of the rendezvous with Corbett and tossed the accusation back two years after Fingleton's death in 1981. In a book written by Michael Page, with the close co-operation of Bradman, it is stated: "It seems certain that Jack Fingleton, the professional journalist, was the man who snapped up this tit-bit ... Fingleton soon realised he had stirred up a whirlwind and he always denied responsibility for this breach of confidence ... he attempted to shift the blame onto Bradman, against whom he carried a grudge for an incident that had nothing to do with bodyline. Shortly before he died, he circulated an absurd fabrication about Bradman having a clandestine night-time meeting with the sportswriter Claude Corbett, and leaking Woodfull's words to him. However, he did not make this allegation until Corbett was dead and unable to deny it."[33]

Fingleton's executor, Malcolm Gemmell, swiftly responded to these words in an article in *The Australian*, citing Fingleton's earlier accounts of the matter and quoting at length from his writings. He then gathered some circumstantial factors to support Fingleton's claim that it was Bradman who was responsible for steering the leak for public consumption: he worked for Corbett's paper, the *Sun*; he was the prime target of Bodyline and had already urged the Board to object to it; he was in dispute with the Board. And Gemmell reminded readers that it was not necessary for anybody wishing to pass the story on to have heard the exchange *first-hand*.

Some years later, in 1997, Fingleton's brother, the Reverend Wally Fingleton, entered the fray with a letter to the *Sydney Morning Herald* in which he gave Jack strong posthumous support, concluding with: "Foremost ethical sports writer of the period, Claude Corbett, revealed the source, or one of the sources [now there's a thought!], of that Adelaide leak, and it was not Jack Fingleton. Bradman says that it was not he. Corbett says it was." (As late as 1995, in *87 Not Out*, the television feature conducted by Ray Martin, Sir Donald Bradman snapped "It wasn't me!" almost before the interviewer had finished uttering the inevitable question concerning the origins of the Adelaide leak.)

GILBERT MANT, LAST OF THE BODYLINE REPORTERS.

Now for a late development. Reuters' man on the tour, Gilbert Mant, lived out his retirement years on the New South Wales north coast, and I was fortunate enough to spend time with him in Brisbane and to correspond with him regularly. After his death in 1997 at the age of 94, his widow sent me a package. It contained a letter to me in which Mant pledged me not to publish any part of the typescript enclosed during his lifetime (which he knew was fast drawing to an end) or that of Sir Donald Bradman. The last survivor of the Press corps from that tour, Gilbert Mant had written a résumé of The Leak, observing firstly in the article (unpublished) that both Bradman and Fingleton would have been aware of the importance of getting the widest publicity for Woodfull's outburst for the sake of cricket. "The leakage was not exactly a heinous crime and few of us at the time thought so." He was surprised that the person responsible didn't own up immediately and maintain that the breach of the code of silence was justified.

Mant clear-headedly pointed out that once Leo O'Brien had spread the news to his team-mates — those who might not themselves already have overhead Woodfull — it spread like wildfire, and *any* of the players — with the possible exception of Ponsford and Richardson, who were batting at the time — might have alerted any of the large assembly of Pressmen in the vicinity. There seems no question about Corbett's having fired off the news to his paper and then sharing it with others (in order perhaps to smokescreen the source) that Sunday at the hotel after a happy day up at Seppelts winery in the Adelaide Hills.

Mant then touches on the long vendetta between Fingleton and Bradman, and on how the fireworks continued even after Fingleton's death, when the archive of his letters entered the public domain: "in many ways he [Bradman] was a little, churlish man" (1980); "playing under him was different to chaps like Woodfull or Richardson. One sensed [they were] playing for Australia; with Bradman it seemed like for his own personal glory" (1981).

The alleged cloak-and-dagger rendezvous in North Terrace? Why would Bradman have resorted to that? "Things were rough at times during the tour but I don't think our telephones were bugged," wrote Gilbert Mant.

Mant then refers to Jim Swanton's story of Bradman's final-Test duck in 1948, when Fingleton and O'Reilly, in the Oval Press box, were so overjoyed that it seemed they were risking a stroke, so heartily were they laughing after his dismissal. "My admiration and respect for O'Reilly diminished somewhat," wrote Mant, "when I read about this disgusting behaviour."

Mant then goes on to say that in correspondence with Bradman in 1992 he learned that The Don continued to claim that Fingleton was the "culprit" and would never forgive him for the "dastardly lie he concocted about me". Bradman further told the aged journalist that as the only person left, now that Moyes was dead, Mant could counter Fingleton's accusation with authority. "My personal rebuttals are seen as biased whereas a neutral view by someone like you would have helped to put the record straight." (Mant was working on his book *A Cuckoo in the Bodyline Nest* at the time.)

Bradman then confirmed the causes of Fingleton's animosity towards him, citing the problems of the opposing religions (suggesting that Fingleton wanted a Roman Catholic rather than Bradman in charge from 1936 onwards) and his [Bradman's] preference for Bill Brown as batsman. Warming to his task of getting a clear conclusion to his investigation once and for all, Mant then wrote to Leo O'Brien: "A few months later he telephoned me in Port Macquarie. It was an unsatisfactory conversation and he was very evasive in answering my direct questions ... I was told later that he had been ill at the time with lapses of memory."

Delving further, Mant rang Claude Corbett's son "Mac" and was told that Claude never mentioned the dressing-room incident to his family. "But," writes Mant, "I was in for a shock when I questioned his sister Helen. She told me that after Claude's death [in 1944] her mother confided to her that Claude had told her that Bradman had been the culprit, confirming the secret of the after-dark meeting as alleged by Fingleton."

Poor Mant. He'd been told what he didn't want to hear: "Now where does that leave us? I believe implicitly in Bradman's denial and have no reason to doubt [Helen's] story. Claude Corbett was a down-to-earth, hard-drinking and convivial character, fond of a practical joke. Perhaps he had perpetrated a gigantic leg-pull on Fingleton but it was scarcely conceivable that he would do the same thing to his wife."

At Gilbert Mant's suggestion I telephoned Claude Corbett's daughter, and she confirmed what she had told him, adding that her father remained friends with Don Bradman, and had once written that "to know Bradman is to know as clean a type of young manhood imaginable".

Whoever was responsible for feeding the story to Corbett — and we have a choice as to which version we accept — the leak should today be seen as having served cricket well.

By way of plaintive endnote, Sir Donald Bradman remarked in a letter to me in May 1992: "So Gilbert Mant is telling his story. He was a pal of mine and was always very much on the ball."

In due course P.F. Warner issued a statement to the Press in which he claimed that Woodfull had expressed regret for Saturday's incident, that the matter was now closed, and that "we are now the best of friends". This was swiftly followed by a statement from W.H. Jeanes on behalf of

Bill Woodfull in which he strongly repudiated any suggestion that he had *apologised* to Mr Warner for any statement he had made. He had merely said that there was no personal animosity between them.

As for Jardine's reaction when the shaken Warner returned and told him, it was a characteristic "I couldn't care less." Gubby Allen recalled that the captain then locked the door and relayed to the gathered team what had transpired in the Australian dressing-room, then warned them not to speak to any of the newspapermen — or anyone else for that matter.[34] With that, Jardine and Allen went off to spend the rest day with friends at Victor Harbour.

There, as he turned in for the night, Jardine said to his host, Ian McLachlan (father of the future Cambridge and South Australia batsman and Federal Minister), "Well, it was an interesting day, laddie." McLachlan replied, not without geniality, that although they had agreed not to talk cricket, "I do want to say this. If this goes on it's going to muck up cricket because you're going to have cricketers playing in things like baseball masks." He was told not to be silly: "It'll be stopped. I've got an instrument in my hand whereby I can win a series against the little man [Bradman]. It's good for England to win a series against the little man. But don't worry. It'll be stopped."[35] D.R. Jardine, it seems, knew the matter would be taken out of his hands. It was just a matter of when.

Warner later wrote to his wife that "thank heaven, the most unpleasant tour ever" was nearing its end. Looking back to Adelaide, he told her that Woodfull had made "a complete fool of himself" and had been "fanning the flames".[36] Warner's biographer, Gerald Howat, suggests that by now, in face of the flow of letters from Plum — which had been his safety valve throughout the long tour — Agnes must have been alternating between worry and boredom. Nor was it likely that "Miss EH" could provide Plum with much comfort politically.

The pressure on poor Warner and Palairet was escalating, for during the Adelaide Test members of the Australian Board had asked them to engineer a cessation of Bodyline. They could only plead that they had no control over the England captain in respect of playing matters. The ACB men then decided that a message had to be sent to MCC in London without further delay. And so the drafting of The Cable began.

On many a Monday morning it seems that the world has changed for the worst, and irrevocably. On Monday, January 16, 1933, the newspapers carried material depressing to cricket-lovers. It was all about the injury to Woodfull and the squirm-inducing follow-up concerning Woodfull and Warner. In England the slant of the headlines was unsympathetic: "Woodfull Sulks in His Tent", sniped the *Sketch*; "Woodfull Snubs Warner", snapped the *Daily Mail*; "Not Cricket!" bugled the *Daily Telegraph* on its front page; "Woodfull Rebukes English Manager", blared another paper; and Neville Cardus's concern was headed "Hooligans" (though he made it clear in his piece that he was still in England).

Among those who had been at the ground on Saturday and were still reeling from the unprecedented ugly noise was the Roman Catholic Bishop of Toowoomba, Dr James Byrne, who had popped in to Adelaide Oval (presumably by special invitation in view of the massive crowds that queued) on his way home from Rome. "I was watching every ball," he told a reporter, "and the one that hit poor Woodfull was more like a cannonball than a cricket ball. It was enough to kill an average man. To see batsmen dodging for their very lives reminded me of coconut shies at country fairs — not of the sport that is the backbone of England."

The attendance on this third day was still a big one, over 32,000 at its peak, the onlookers including Ike Fisher, who had umpired in Adelaide's first Test match, in 1884, and E.G. Phillips, who had fielded as a substitute in that match. And sobering details began to circulate in light of Saturday's ravages by pickpockets in the crowd. A lot of cash was stolen from the packed assembly and from people queueing, and one accountant who had not very shrewdly brought £219 in seven envelopes with him to the match was horrified to find them all gone.[37]

The Ponsford–Richardson stand, the biggest of the innings, was broken when 80 had been added. Allen got a ball through as Richardson, after a patient 28 (with 17 singles), played on. Oldfield was then seen at his best as he supported Ponsford, whose reputation was being restored with every over and upon whom so much now depended. The wicketkeeper imperiously straight-drove Verity and delicately late-cut him for boundaries. Voce, returned but still unable to trust his ankle fully and bowling over the wicket at lesser pace, almost had Ponsford caught by Verity off a hook, but that batsman continued to handle Verity's bowling with ease. He also coped with Larwood (with a 5–4 off-side field) and with Allen, even when he dropped short. If no reaction with the bat seemed prudent, Ponsford simply turned his back and suffered the consequences as the ball thumped against flesh or padding.

Hammond needed careful watching, and when the ball was hit away there was Paynter haring around the boundary to cut off many runs. The sixth-wicket partnership showed promise. Larwood, who was to take exception in his tour book not only to Woodfull's words of protest but to newspaper accusations of hypocrisy by English players who had gathered anxiously round him when he was hit, now returned to the attack, and his second ball rocketed past Oldfield's ear. The leg trap was adopted anew and the crowd roared disapproval yet again. When Jardine chased a ball to the fence a torrent of catcalls and booing greeted him. The welcome lunch interval came with Australia 185 for 5, Ponsford 20 away from what would be a valiant century.

With a new ball soon available, Jardine opened the afternoon session with Hammond and Voce. It was noted that Woodfull and Bradman had gone down to meet Sir George Murray, the Acting Governor of South Australia, though there is no record of whether they engaged in smalltalk or greater matters were discussed. Half an hour after lunch, Oldfield having narrowly escaped a leg-side catching chance to Ames off Hammond, Ponsford's resistance was ended, partly by his own misjudgment, just after he had escaped a run-out against Larwood's wild throw from cover. Not for the first time, he moved across to glance, exposing the leg stump, which Voce hit. The bruised Victorian had made 85 in 3½ hours, and the door was ajar for England to crash through.

Grimmett, fanning at off-side balls, perhaps imagining he was still giving slips-catching practice to pupils at St Peter's College, again scarcely looked up to the task; even less so when Larwood and the impressive Allen took the new ball. Grimmett's theory that if you left all the bouncers alone the bowlers would soon tire was simply not working. To his chagrin this was to be his last Test match for a while. At 212 he became the seventh wicket to fall, well taken at slip by a diving Voce, another dismissal captured on film. England's latest concern was Paynter, who damaged an ankle as he collided with a concrete step while chasing the ball. He was helped from the field by Jardine and Hammond, and Brown came on until he was able to return.

Wall joined Oldfield, who was dodging bumpers but still managing to take runs off Larwood's scorchers, film showing a four through the leg

THE MOST DRAMATIC BLOW OF ALL: BERT OLDFIELD IS CRACKED ON THE SKULL.

field and a quick, friendly exchange between batsman and bowler. When he tucked a four through the covers, Larwood said, "Good shot, Bert." It took the little wicketkeeper's score to 41, and Larwood was still bowling to a conventional field.

The next ball was a fraction short of a length and not quite as fast. Oldfield lost it against the low sightscreen, changed his mind, switching his intended cut to a pull, and deflected the speeding hard lump of leather onto his temple. The impact was clearly heard over the radio and Warner, seated next to R.G. Menzies, was chillingly reminded of the sound of the impact on the skull when Larwood knocked South Africa's Jock Cameron out at Lord's in 1929.[38] Oldfield reeled out towards point, clutching his head and tumbling to his knees. In a reflex action he started to remove his cap but then pulled it on again. Allen was the first to reach the prone figure. Umpire Hele ran from the bowler's end, as did Larwood, and the injured batsman was soon surrounded by England players. Allen ran off to get a jug of water and a towel, and Woodfull, dressed in a business suit and having been a guest in the Governor's box, brushed his way through the throng and crossed the outfield towards his stricken player. His stride was deliberate, and bespoke anger as well as anxiety.

The bowler instantly apologised and was relieved to hear Oldfield murmur, "It wasn't your fault, Harold." (Oldfield was later quoted in

Smith's Weekly as denying that he had called it "a fair ball". He then spoke out in unmistakable terms about the "unsavoury incidents" at Adelaide.) Yet even if the masses had been able to overhear any words of forgiveness, it would have made no difference. The hooting and shouting, the expression of indignation and outrage, rose to a new intensity. Obscenities rang out and men were jumping up and down, waving their fists. "Go home, you Pommie bastards!" was one of the more moderate cries as the ground-fire persisted.

Once more it seemed that a riot must break out, and Larwood was not the only one to eye the stumps as potential defensive weapons should the hordes run on. The policemen in their dark uniforms and white helmets tensed all around the ground and moved into some sort of strategic position, the horses of the mounted section now restive. The SACA office put in a call to Angas Street police headquarters asking for reinforcements to be sent. Some came on motor-cycles. An Adelaide barrister standing by the pickets at the front of the Giffen Stand was actually invited by a mature police inspector to jump the fence if he wished: "I won't stop you."[39] It was a shameful but almost understandable reaction.

Maurice Tate, sitting with the non-playing English cricketers, said he was getting out of there: somebody was going to get hurt. He wrote subsequently of the Adelaide Test that it was a war: "I call it a 'war' advisedly after having gone all through France [with the Royal Artillery], and why it did not end in heavy casualties I don't know."[40]

No onlooker then, and surely few who have seen the newsreel sequence since, would necessarily endorse the commentator's remark after Oldfield went down: "... Larwood again being the unlucky bo-lah!" (Oddly enough, in *Body-Line?* Larwood himself referred to Alf Gover, after he had flattened George Gunn with an accidental beamer in a 1932 county match, as "the unlucky bowler".)

Bert Oldfield, the somewhat unlucky batsman at Adelaide Oval, had blood trickling from a linear fracture of the right frontal bone. An inch either way and he would have been killed. This was a man — seventh child of an upholsterer from Manchester — who had served in the 15th Field Ambulance and been critically wounded by a German shell during the fierce fighting in Polygon Wood in 1917. It exploded under his stretcher party, killing the other four men and leaving him buried for hours in the mud. Corporal Bert Oldfield's head and back injuries and his resultant shellshocked condition confined him for months in hospital in Rouen and then Gloucester.[41] A steel reinforcement plate was inserted into his skull.

It was a dreadful realisation of the worst fears held by so many: as Bodyline crashed its awesome path through the summer, sooner or later somebody surely must get hit on the head and suffer serious consequences.

By one of the most poetic ironies known to cricket, Harold Larwood and Bertie Oldfield were to become staunch friends in later years, and the former was to act as pallbearer at the latter's funeral in 1976. In October 2000, Oldfield's cap, which may just have saved his life in 1933, sold for $28,000 at Christie's saleroom in Melbourne (where Woodfull's 1932–33 cap sold a year previously for $23,000).

Woodfull, having been handed Oldfield's discarded bat by the umpire, eventually helped the dazed batsman from the arena: "Come along, Bertie," he said gently. The captain later regretted not closing the innings there and then as a mark of disgust, as Bishan Bedi was to do 43 years later at Sabina Park, Jamaica as a protest against intimidatory bowling, with India 306 for 6. He did the same in the second innings when India were 97 for 5, with two batsmen nursing head injuries, one a broken finger and two tailenders with hands damaged while fielding. He later amended his statement: the innings had finished with these five unable to bat. The match was lost by 10 wickets 13 days after India had scored 406 for 4 to beat West Indies — who had three spinners — in Trinidad.

At Adelaide Oval, in a rather different context (there was no booing this day), when Bob Willis hit Rick Darling in the chest in 1979 he fell to the ground unconscious, and his life was almost certainly saved by swift attention from John Emburey and umpire Max O'Connell. The young South Australian was carried away on a stretcher, and the tension around the ground was intense — never to be forgotten by anybody who was there. News of his condition was awaited for some time afterwards. At last a loudspeaker announcement to the effect that Darling had recovered brought sighs of relief, and he was able to bat later, resuming his opening partnership with Graeme Wood in the second innings, enabling them to continue pursuing their practice of running one another out.

As Oldfield walked shakily from the field on that Monday afternoon in 1933, it was noticed that Larwood was lying full stretch on the ground at the end of his run-up, tossing the ball from hand to hand. The tall, gangling O'Reilly had taken an inordinately long time to reach the middle, partly through a natural reluctance and also because highly agitated spectators had spilt across the pathways. He had pushed his way through. His feelings about the dangers have been firmly chronicled: "We bade sentimental farewells to each batsman as he made his way out to bat. We had a genuine feeling they were making a journey from which they might be borne back on a stretcher."[42] As the Australians watched their team-mates batting, silence usually prevailed in the dressing-room, apart from when runs were scored or when there was a near thing. "Oh 'struth, look at that one!" was O'Reilly's customary reaction.[43]

With the crowd still in a state of uproar — and now, surely, if there had been a stampede towards the jittery England cricketers it would have spelt the end of Australia v England Test cricket for who knew how long? — O'Reilly provided a comical sequence, fanning at six of Larwood's flying deliveries from a safe distance before becoming a simple, scoreless victim.

WOODFULL (IN SUIT) GOES TO THE STRICKEN OLDFIELD AS GUBBY ALLEN WALKS AWAY CARRYING TOWEL AND WATER. UMPIRE BORWICK, SUTCLIFFE AND LARWOOD ARE TO THE LEFT OF THE GROUP, UMPIRE HELE AND JARDINE TO THE RIGHT.

Few realised that Oldfield had deflected a *non-Bodyline* ball onto his head, and fewer still would have cared to make the subtle distinction. So the fury bubbled on. Wilmot, while branding Bodyline a "perversion", described the abuse still being directed at Larwood as "senseless and wicked". Unemotional as ever, Jardine was to write in his account of the tour that Oldfield's assurance to the Englishmen that it was his own fault for losing sight of the ball "increased our regret for the accident to this splendid cricketer". Soon after the white-hot moment, a newspaper editor was spotted waving his panama hat in the direction of Hugh Buggy in the Press box and yelling, "This is disgraceful! Put the boot into them!"[44]

Brave to the point of near-madness, Jardine had moved himself from leg gully down to field by the fence, in front of the scoreboard mound, where the invective was quickly directed at him specifically. The more polite shouts included, "You're not game!" and "Why don't you have some pluck?" Pluck, as it happened, was one commodity in which the England captain was certainly not lacking. An added ingredient in the invective was the still-fresh memory that this man had banned them from watching the pre-match practice. He did not stay long in the deep. The barrage of orange peel was too persistent.

Hammond bowled Wall and Australia's innings closed at 222, putting them 119 in arrears on first innings. The Englishmen walked from the field in an eerie silence, with a smattering of applause mixing with a crossfire of insults as they mounted the steps to the dressing-room.

Walter Hawker, a Federal Minister, wrote in the Adelaide *Advertiser* that on this third day he had positioned himself in the public area behind the bowler's arm and had noted 34 balls from Larwood that were Bodyline balls against 38 in the same spell which were at the stumps or outside off. He observed that the five balls which preceded the blow to Oldfield were all Bodyline balls, and that the near-fatal delivery was in line with middle and leg. Voce bowled Bodyline but Allen's bowling was "unobjectionable". As for Australia's lone fast bowler, at the start of England's second innings Tim Wall released 54 balls of which only two, by Hawker's assessment, were Bodyline.

At the end of the Australian innings Bert Oldfield was still stretched out on the treatment table in the dressing-room. Having been examined firstly by Dr Dolling, one of the Test selectors, he was found to have concussion and to be suffering from shock. He was then taken by ambulance to

Glenelg, where he was seen by Dr Kenneth Steele, a former South Australia fast bowler, who arranged an X-ray and patched the wound. Oldfield considerately issued a statement exonerating Larwood from all blame and promising that he would be back tomorrow ready to resume play, a promise which proved over-optimistic.

Soon the most dramatic film sequence cricket had produced to date was showing on cinema screens throughout Australia and Britain: distressing clips of both the Woodfull injury and Oldfield's. Years later visual recordings of similar incidents were to become commonplace — and in full colour on television. But in 1933 the shot of Oldfield being hit and reeling away, falling to his knees, was unprecedented, and had a shock effect on a wide-eyed public. Even the still photograph had more impact than anything seen before on a newspaper or magazine page. There had been images of Ernest Tyldesley, hands to face, after Jack Gregory had bounced one at him in the 1921 Trent Bridge Test; of Warwick Armstrong's great bulk, horizontal at Lord's after Durston had laid him out; of Cameron being borne away on a stretcher after the knockout ball from Larwood in poor light; and of Arthur Gilligan, motionless on the turf after a blow to the heart. Oldfield, though, was the first cricketer to be projected onto the giant silver screen as a writhing, involuntary victim of violence.

Meanwhile, Jardine revealed another side to his complex nature by sending a telegram to Oldfield's wife Ruth expressing the hope that her husband would soon recover. He then arranged for a friend of his in Sydney to deliver a pair of Shirley Temple dolls to the Oldfields' little daughters.

Now, though, he had work to do. With his ears still smouldering from the raucous shouting, Jardine might have chosen to take some quiet refuge in a corner of the dressing-room while Leyland or Wyatt opened the second England innings with Sutcliffe. Instead, he strapped on his pads, placed his colourful cap on his head, pulled on his gloves, and strode forth, a few cheers being detected among the hoots. "Hit 'im on the bloody 'ead, Tim!" barked one fan. With Bradman often staring at him from silly point, Jardine displayed his bloodymindedness to the full for just over two hours until the close of play. He chipped 24 runs, stirred up further widespread vocal protest and inspired some barracking that has entered cricket's thesaurus.

"Take that back to Jardine!" advised one chap when he spotted the groundsman picking up some horse manure near the heavy roller. When Jardine was scoreless for an hour one exasperated onlooker shrieked to

GLAD TO BE ALIVE: BERTIE OLDFIELD BACK HOME WITH WIFE RUTH AND THEIR
TWO DAUGHTERS, HIS INJURY ON THE MEND.

Woodfull, "Get a tin-opener and extract the Sardine!" His bat broke, and
when a replacement was brought out this gave one wag the opportunity to
holler: "You won't need it, you bastard!" Gubby Allen particularly enjoyed
recalling how one spectator, spotting a pigeon take off from the outfield
when Jardine was fielding, shouted at it: "Come back here! He's at mid-
off!"[45] And when drinks were taken and Woodfull handed his opposite
number a glass of cordial, somebody thundered: "Don't give *him* a drink!
Let the bastard die of thirst!" Allen regretted that the catcalls were not
always as amusing as that.

As for the very admissibility of barracking, Jardine would have welcomed
legislation against it, while Larwood scoffed at the Australian barracker's
apparent belief in himself as both an important and funny figure and
identified this lot as the grandsons of the men who invaded the ground at
Sydney in the late 1870s, when they were met by Lord Harris, "Monkey"
Hornby and George Ulyett armed with stumps. Yet, despite all, the right to
shout had few more persuasive advocates than R.G. Menzies, who insisted

in the course of a speech that the patrons "must say something or die" and that barracking "is their prerogative". Bert Oldfield later wrote that Australian spectators usually had a greater knowledge of the game than did English spectators, and recalled the particularly hostile reception the Australians had had at Old Trafford in 1921.

Perhaps the favourite piece of barracking, uttered as Jardine waved a persistent fly from his face, was: "Hey, leave our flies alone, Jardine! They're the only flamin' friends you've got here!" He seemed faintly amused himself as the "commentary" continued. But there was never the slightest chance that he would lift his game. He was making his adversaries on both sides of the pickets suffer. And he took a few knocks and developed a few colourful bruises of his own, never once flinching or complaining. When the scoreboard had scarcely flickered for several overs he turned to O'Brien at short leg and remarked that he had indeed been a bit slow. There had not been much conversation between the England captain and the opposition.

O'Brien was fielding as substitute (Merv Waite took over the 12th man duties), and Richardson, probably South Australia's greatest-ever allround sportsman, was keeping wicket in Oldfield's absence, a task that was to extend through almost 200 overs in more than nine hours, with three of the world's greatest spinners in action. It was tiring, demanding work, but Richardson's shiny black hair was barely ruffled, even if, as Wilmot noted, he just failed to hold a few chances that a first-class keeper might have pouched. The deputy was two days older than the injured first choice — though Oldfield, who never complained about the false birth year, possibly having engineered it in the first place, was believed for many years to be three years younger than he actually was. He was born in 1894, not 1897, so they were both 38.

England's only loss on that third evening was Sutcliffe (7), whose steepling hook was held by the leaping O'Brien in the deep to complete a rare double failure for the master batsman. As he passed the catcher he said whimsically, "Only a bloody Irishman would have tried for it!" Throwing his mind back 60 years to that afternoon, O'Brien recalled that a deliberate Australian throw had just missed Sutcliffe's chin, causing him to wheel round in alarm; and that when O'Brien in turn had a golden chance to hit Jardine's back with a throw he abstained, to the disappointment of one or two team-mates, who believed this to be the only form of retaliation open to them.[46]

Wyatt, missed at slip by O'Reilly when 9, ended the day on a steady 47, having restrained himself from hitting any sixes, and England's overall lead in this timeless Test match was now 204, with nine wickets in hand. Ironmonger's 13 overs had produced a mere 12 runs.

Some irate spectators hung around afterwards to boo the England players as they emerged from the dressing-room, but a policeman walked close to Larwood (who was glad to have his heavyweight mate Voce by his side as well) and there was nothing physical. As the English players strolled along the beach and around the amusement park at Glenelg that evening, sensation-seeking journalists lurked in hope.

Having showered and changed, Jardine and Allen went off to the Haywards' for dinner — the former having telephoned to say he would like now to take up the earlier invitation. But even in social gatherings Jardine was not safe from condemnation. Dudley Hayward was almost in a blind fury over what had happened at Adelaide Oval that day and on Saturday. The family agreed that cricket talk must be avoided. But that was like expecting flies to bypass a cow-pat. Hayward responded grumpily when Jardine asked him if he had been to the cricket, and alternative matters were discussed — until, some time later, somebody innocently spoke of the recent death of Blackham, the great wicketkeeper. There was naturally a chain reaction as one keeper's name was reminiscently followed by another, right down to Oldfield, at which point Hayward thundered, "And *now* we have Vic Richardson!"[47]

That evening one of the newspaper placards bore the words: PREMEDITATED BRUTALITY — M.A. Noble. Allen picked it up and teasingly handed it to his captain: "Here Douglas, you'd better have this for your archives!"[48]

It was not surprising that the shrewd old cricketer Wilfred Rhodes, writing for the *Yorkshire Evening Post* so far away, while conceding the negative aspect of England's current method, took a different stance: "The leg theory which is being employed by our fast bowlers has got the Australians rattled as badly as the terrific bumpers of Gregory and the pace of McDonald got our batsmen rattled ... neither Voce nor Larwood will look anything like so formidable to the batsmen as Gregory did when he was over here and at his best in 1921. He hit a few men." To rub his point home, Rhodes recalled Armstrong's objectionable slow leg theory too.

WYATT WELL CAUGHT BY WALL: OR WAS IT REALLY A BUMP BALL?

The rest of the match may quickly be described. The Tuesday was over-shadowed as much as anything by news of the increasingly forlorn search for one of Australia's favourite record-breaking aviators, Queenslander Bert Hinkler, whose Puss Moth aeroplane had come down somewhere in the Apennine mountain range, near Florence, in Italy.

England batted in curmudgeonly fashion through this fourth day, losing five wickets and adding 211 runs to tighten their grip. It was hotter, the attendance was down, and so was the barracking, to everyone's relief. Wyatt fell to a marvellous catch close-in by Wall (the batsman thought it might have been a bump ball but the umpires consulted and Borwick's finger was raised), and Allen's elevation in the order didn't pay. A mere 45 runs came in the pre-lunch session, and Jardine was seen literally to watch the ball onto the face of his dead bat, patting back half-volleys. Eventually he pushed Grimmett wide of mid-on for his fifty, which contained one solitary boundary. It came as an enormous relief when Ironmonger had him lbw for an ever-more-tedious 56 in 4¼ hours. Hammond and Leyland, duly applauded, now played a few strokes, none more delightful than Hammond's trademark drive off the back foot off the medium-pacer McCabe. No longer faced with brisk lifters on a fresh first-day wicket, Hammond had only one real moment of discomfort, and that was when a ball from Ironmonger hit him in the face, though not severely.

Watched by Oldfield, who sat in the stand, plaster covering his injury, the bowlers toiled away in the heat. Wall's walk back to his mark seemed to be in slow motion. Mailey timed Wall's overs at a disappointing three minutes. (Fortunate he was to be spared the crawl of the fast men of the late

20th century.) Leyland's 42 was terminated by an excellent catch by Wall, who this time held a skyer in spite of the close proximity of a hesitant Fingleton. The runs slowed again as Hammond and Ames played for tomorrow, Ames spending an hour and a half over his 18, but just before stumps were due to be drawn Bradman was called up for a bowl, and with what Hobbs called "the most hopeless full-toss you ever saw" he bowled Hammond for 85 as he swung mightily at it and got but a touch.

There are many other accounts of this dismissal, including Hammond's own, and they are all in accordance with regard to the nature of the ball. But Don Bradman, a few decades later, vigorously denied that it was a full-toss, taking the author to task in spite of my attempt to smoothe the matter over by referring to the fact that Mailey often took wickets with full-tosses, even the batsman usually finding it amusing, and everybody living happily ever after. This vehement denial merely showed how memory can play false, for in the 1938 edition of *Don Bradman's Book* Bruce Harris repeated his quote from Bradman's very own broadcast during the match, which had first appeared in Harris's book on the tour: "Three minutes before time Billy Woodfull said to me: 'Are you fit to bowl an over?' He had just seen me chase a ball to the boundary, so thought I must be. I tried to bowl a good ball, but instead sent along the rankest of full pitches. Hammond, presumably thinking that these balls come only once in a lifetime, tried to hit it into the river. He seemed to hit at it too hard, the ball flicked his bat and went on to his wicket — and I realized I had bowled him." (These broadcasts by players were another thing to which Larwood objected. In *Body-Line?* he accused them of selling their souls to the microphone, making money and damaging the game.)

This unexpected breakthrough allowed the Australians to leave the field with a communal grin, but Hammond was most certainly not amused. Gilbert Mant popped his head around the door to check with him: "A moody man at any time, Wally exploded into a torrent of bad language. I was left in no doubt that it was a so-and-so full-toss and would I so-and-so get out of his so-and-so sight as soon as so-and-so possible. I withdrew hastily and reported back to my colleagues, 'Wally says it was a full-toss'."[49]

It is possible that this was the evening, described in Wilmot's book, when the successful bowler (Bradman) played billiards with Pataudi at the home of Harry Hodgetts, a stockbroker who was to set up an attractive deal to bring The Don to Adelaide a year or so hence. It is also possible that this was the evening when, at the Richmond Hotel, where the Englishmen were staying, Mant was sitting in the lounge having a peaceful drink of ice-cold beer with Jack Ingham, Tom Goodman (of the *Sydney Morning Herald*) and Hedley Verity when a waiter told Verity that three gentlemen were waiting to see him. Who were they? "They're from the Adelaide branch of the Rechabite Society."

There was a hasty scramble as the other three took all the beer to a dark corner of the room while Verity quickly obtained a lemon squash as the members of the strict abstainers sect entered the lounge. "We watched," wrote Mant, "three cadaverous-looking men with long beards approach him and sank his beer between us. I mention this only to illustrate that bodyline was such a deadly thing it could even drive a Rechabite to drink."[50]

Ames escaped a stumping off Grimmett when 10 on the fifth morning, but Verity batted soundly again, though nearly bowled by Wall, the ball going for four byes past poor Richardson's borrowed gloves. Ames, displaying confidence at last, reached his only half-century of the series with a beautiful cover-drive, having punished the erratic spin of Bradman — who had the honour of opening Australia's "attack". Soon after lunch, when the Ames–Verity stand was two short of the century, O'Reilly ripped a wrong'un through Ames's defence just after the batsman had thrown himself out of the way of a ferocious return by Fingleton — and he copped some derision from the crowd when he slipped while running.

Larwood was greeted by cheers from the members' area and boos from the outer. Bradman caught him at deep mid-off and almost brought off a nifty double, but his outstretched hand could not quite hold a chance from Voce. With the lead already over 500, the limping Paynter, with Leyland as his runner, was rather needlessly sent to the crease at No.10. His blackened, swollen ankle was strapped, and a doctor had advised him to rest for a week. But this was D.R. Jardine's grind-'em-into-the-dirt policy at its most blatant. Like General William Tecumseh Sherman, and the odd previous captain in Ashes Test series, he would answer that war is war and not popularity-seeking.

As the Australians trooped off at last the weariest heroes among them were O'Reilly, who had laboured through 50.3 overs, and Ironmonger, 23 years his senior, who had bowled even more (and still, in the eyes of some of the Englishmen, with a dubious arm action). Middle-aged Grimmett had contributed 35 overs too, and never had any of the bowlers given anything less than their concentrated best. With this 9½-hour innings England had amassed an overall lead of 531, which would have been greater still had not several straight drives smacked into the far stumps.

There was just time that evening for Fingleton to record his second duck of the match, bowled by the ball he dreaded from Larwood (who thus secured the £1 promised him by Warner). It pitched middle-and-leg and hit the off stump and was, of course, extremely fast. Like McCabe and, as was soon to be realised, Ponsford too, Fingleton struggled in this series after having prospered on one grand occasion. To his mild surprise he received commiserations on his pair from Jardine, who said, "Don't worry. Some very good men have had the same experience."

THE BRADMAN PLAN: STEPPING BACK, HE CUTS A LEG-SIDE DELIVERY INTO THE WIDE OPEN SPACE ON THE OFF SIDE.

Ponsford went back up the order to first drop, but was soon snapped up by Jardine in the gully, and Larwood had 2 for 1. Bradman came in to partner Woodfull (who now wore pneumatic padding under his shirt) and lifted spirits with a hook to the fence off Larwood and then a back cut. The bowler left the field briefly (Pataudi substituted for him, decked out in a Harlequin cap) before returning and marshalling his leg field into position in response to the runs accruing from leg glances. (Larwood had actually been cheered for maintaining an off field to this point.) This prompted Bradman to swing his bat with almost manic intent, and turning his attention to Verity's slow left-arm he played shots that had the oldtimers thinking about Trumper. As he reached his fifty in only 64 minutes, his spectacular assault was dividing opinion to the extent that there were some who did not think of Trumper at all: they were quite put out by the desperate, cavalier assault.

M.A. Noble, in *The Australian Cricketer*, granted that Bradman had at first been "brilliantly audacious" but condemned his subsequent "insatiable desire to score off everything, regardless of the safe-keeping of his wicket". The shrewd old Test captain felt that England's bowlers were smiling inwardly at the indiscretions, sensing that he would play into their hands. "No doubt," he wrote, "most of the crowd were thrilled by his versatility and power, but the older hands watched his display with feelings of doubt and misgiving, and were not surprised when he became a victim to his own daring. Brilliant as was his hurricane exhibition, it was not Test cricket." He believed that Woodfull should have curbed his young partner's aggressive intent.

Bradman's penultimate ball was whacked into the members' reserve and damaged a woman's arm, ambulancemen rushing to her aid. It was The Don's first Test six. Never before had he hit one in a first-class match in his homeland. But in aiming to blast the next ball in the direction of the Moreton Bay fig trees at the northern end, he hit Verity back hard and the bowler held the catch, ending a 73-minute innings of 66 which came off 71 balls, in a stand of 88 with Woodfull. As Bradman left the field he was seen to slam the gate behind him.

When questioned in the dressing-room about his hectic approach, Bradman replied frankly: "Oh, I wanted to hit one bowler [Verity] before the other [Larwood] hit me." Ray Robinson, who kept in fairly close touch with the Australian players during the series, went as far as to say that Bradman's "instability" caused consternation from the moment some time earlier when they heard about his request to bat a little lower in the order. The writer referred to him in this context as the Reluctant Dragon.[51]

Hedley Verity, bowling in his second Test against Australia, had at last claimed his first wicket. Before the war brought the curtain down, he was to claim Bradman's prize scalp a further seven times.

Australia sustained one further loss this evening as McCabe, having stroked Allen beautifully through the covers for four, hooked and was caught by Leyland out near the fence. One newspaper reported that somebody had placed a "dummy cavalier in his bedroom clad in armour and with steel helmet, and marked: 'You'll need it tomorrow'." Whether the intent was jocular or sinister, and whether or not it played on McCabe's mind, we shall never know.

At the close, half an hour early after Richardson's appeal when heavy cloud came across, Australia needed a further 412 for victory with six wickets in hand, with Oldfield unlikely to be fit to bat. Had it been 1930, with Bradman still in, not everyone would have dismissed Australia's chances. But this was a much-changed world.

Richardson, stiff from his long wicketkeeping stint, accompanied Woodfull to the middle on the sixth morning, and they held their ground for some time. The captain swayed out of danger or played the ball down from in front of his throat and sometimes picked up a run or two. On a pitch that seemed to have lost all life, Larwood and Allen ran in and strove for the breakthrough that would put this most sensational of Test matches finally to rest. Allen, brisk as ever, raced across the ground, making a final loop with his arms as he held the ball with both hands, then moving into an elastic delivery, an explosion of power, but with his sights firmly set on the off stump, his followthrough taking him into a mild convulsion, hair flopping over his forehead.

The crowd, now admitted for half-price on this day of Australian obsequies, still numbered just over 7000, and there were more rainclouds about. Still there were noises of disapproval from the terraces when England had drinks brought out. Woodfull was picking up runs through Larwood's thickly populated leg field — which was duly intensified — and the fifty partnership came. Then Richardson, who had been tied down (Verity smoothly bowled four consecutive maiden overs), hooked a four safely through Larwood's leg-side concentration only to misjudge an attempted repetition and thumb the ball painfully into a gentle loop which the agile Allen intercepted to his left just before it touched the ground. Wyatt later recalled that Jardine went across to Larwood and congratulated him for getting that ball to "rise nicely onto his thumb". "It was a form of English upper-class humour!" said Wyatt.[52] It was typical Aussie humour that led to one spectator screaming out as Jardine chased the ball with his stiff-legged run, "Come on, Phar Lap!" (The long-legged Englishman made it clear in his tour book that the taunts, apart from the genuinely good-humoured ones, were so repetitive and "threadbare" as to become "a weariness of the flesh".) At least Jardine went across to congratulate Woodfull on his half-century.

Grimmett proved easy meat again, a vast slips cordon having been set for him before Allen bowled him as lunch beckoned. He did the same to Wall after the interval. The crowd had laughed loudly not only at the five-man slips setting but at Grimmett's snick through it for four. Larwood uprooted O'Reilly's unguarded off stump, and the inept Ironmonger became the fifth bowled victim of the innings, leaving Bill Woodfull 73 not out (with only two fours) and smiling self-effacingly amidst the ruins of the match.

It was the second time he had carried his bat through Australia's innings against England. At Brisbane Exhibition Ground in 1928 he had hung on or 30 out of 66, with two men unable to bat. He had also batted through on two other occasions against English opposition: at Blackpool in 1926 and for Victoria in 1928–29. Truly did this strong, patient, valiant man of integrity deserve his nickname of The Unbowlable (and also The Wormkiller, a tribute to his bat, which was straight and usually scraped the ground as he played resolutely forward). Plum Warner said that bowling at Woodfull was like throwing stones at the Rock of Gibraltar. Some spectators ignored Woodfull's resistance and carried him shoulder-high to the pavilion, but rumours of his possible withdrawal from the series continued to worry the majority of Australians.

The margin of 338 was England's largest victory over Australia (in terms of runs) apart from the Brisbane debacle of 1928 (675 runs; Bradman's maiden Test). As the last man dismissed, Bert Ironmonger was in a position of advantage to grab the stumps as souvenirs, and as he trotted from the field with an armful, Maurice Leyland came across and pretended to rugby-tackle him, asking if he might have a stump. As a final measure of how low England's standing had slumped over the past few days of cricket combat, a female spectator, down by the fence and wearing the *de rigueur* cloche hat, cried out, "Don't give it to him, Bert! Hit him over the bloody head with it!"[53]

Five minutes later it was raining.

THIRD TEST MATCH

ADELAIDE OVAL, JANUARY 13, 14, 16, 17, 18, 19, 1933
Toss won by England
12th men: L.P.J. O'Brien (A), F.R.Brown (E)

Umpires: E.G. Borwick & G.A. Hele
Debuts: none

ENGLAND

		mins	balls	4s				mins	balls	4s
H. Sutcliffe	c Wall b O'Reilly	9	46	43	-	[2] c sub (O'Brien) b Wall	7	13	11	1
*D.R. Jardine	b Wall	3	20	18	-	[1] lbw b Ironmonger	56	254	266	2
W.R. Hammond	c Oldfield b Wall	2	15	15	-	[5] b Bradman	85	221	247	8
#L.E.G. Ames	b Ironmonger	3	39	38	-	[7] b O'Reilly	69	169	173	7
M. Leyland	b O'Reilly	83	181	190	13	[6] c Wall b Ironmonger	42	108	93	5
R.E.S. Wyatt	c Richardson b Grimmett	78	164	176	3+	[3] c Wall b O'Reilly	49	133	138	4
E. Paynter	c Fingleton b Wall	77	185	216	9	[10] not out	1	17	15	-
G.O.B. Allen	lbw b Grimmett	15	37	30	2	[4] lbw b Grimmett	15	52	59	2
H. Verity	c Richardson b Wall	45	154	147	2	[8] lbw b O'Reilly	40	115	131	2
W. Voce	b Wall	8	14	13	1	[11] b O'Reilly	8	7	10	-
H. Larwood	not out	3	3	4	-	[9] c Bradman b Ironmonger	8	14	12	1
Extras	b 1, lb 7, nb 7	15				b 17, lb 11, nb 4	32			
Total	(146.1 overs, 437 mins)	**341**				(191.3 overs, 560 mins)	**412**			

+ plus 3 sixes

Fall 1/4 2/16 3/16 4/30 5/186 6/196 7/228 8/324 9/336 10/341   1/7 2/91 3/123 4/154 5/245 6/296 7/394 8/395 9/403 10/412

BOWLING	O	M	R	W	w/nb		O	M	R	W	w/nb
Wall	34.1	10	72	5	-/3	Wall	29	6	75	1	-/2
O'Reilly	50	19	82	2	-/4	O'Reilly	50.3	21	79	4	-/1
Ironmonger	20	6	50	1	-/-	Ironmonger	57	21	87	3	-/-
Grimmett	28	6	94	2	-/-	Grimmett	35	9	74	1	-/-
McCabe	14	3	28	0	-/-	McCabe	16	0	42	0	-/1
						Bradman	4	0	23	1	-/-

AUSTRALIA

		mins	balls	4s				mins	balls	4s
J.H. W.Fingleton	c Ames b Allen	0	6	8	-	b Larwood	0	8	14	-
*W.M. Woodfull	b Allen	22	89	65	-	not out	73	235	208	2
D.G. Bradman	c Allen b Larwood	8	18	17	1	[4] c & b Verity	66	73	71	10+
S.J. McCabe	c Jardine b Larwood	8	21	25	1	[5] c Leyland b Allen	7	21	19	1
W.H. Ponsford	b Voce	85	216	213	8	[3] c Jardine b Larwood	3	13	11	-
V.Y. Richardson	b Allen	28	95	81	1	c Allen b Larwood	21	83	76	3
#W.A.S. Oldfield	retired hurt	41	123	114	4	absent hurt	-	-	-	-
C.V. Grimmett	c Voce b Allen	10	29	24	1	[7] b Allen	6	10	8	1
T.W. Wall	b Hammond	6	22	19	-	[8] b Allen	0	1	4	-
W.J. O'Reilly	b Larwood	0	8	9	-	[9] b Larwood	5	11	10	1
H. Ironmonger	not out	0	3	-	-	[10] b Allen	0	1	1	-
Extras	b 2, lb 11, nb 1	14				b 4, lb 2, w 1, nb 5	12			
Total	(95.4 overs, 332 mins)	**222**				(69.2 overs, 235 mins)	**193**			

+ plus 1 six

Fall 1/1 2/18 3/34 4/51 5/131 6/194 7/212 8/222 9/222   1/3 2/12 3/100 4/116 5/171 6/183 7/183 8/192 9/193

BOWLING	O	M	R	W	w/nb		O	M	R	W	w/nb
Larwood	25	6	55	3	-/-	Larwood	19	3	71	4	-/2
Allen	23	4	71	4	-/-	Allen	17.2	5	50	4	1/2
Hammond	17.4	4	30	1	-/-	Voce	4	1	7	0	-/-
Voce	14	5	21	1	-/1	Hammond	9	3	27	0	-/-
Verity	16	7	31	0	-/-	Verity	20	12	26	1	-/1

ENGLAND WON BY 338 RUNS

Attendances: 1st day 37,201, 2nd day 50,962, 3rd day 32,527, 4th day 19,821, 5th day 24,529, 6th day 7321: Total 172,361.
Gate receipts: £16,241.5.7d.
Close-of-play scores: 1st day Eng 7/236 (Paynter 25, Verity 5), 2nd day Aus 4/109 (Ponsford 45, Richardson 21), 3rd day Eng (2) 1/85 (Jardine 24, Wyatt 47), 4th day Eng (2) 6/296 (Ames 18), 5th day Aus (2) 4/120 (Woodfull 36, Richardson 0).

Although he had not seen the match, Wisden's new editor, Sydney Southerton, had sufficient eye-witness material on his desk to be able to proclaim this as "probably the most unpleasant" match ever played. "Pandemonium reigned", he recorded. The whole atmosphere was "a disgrace to cricket". With sympathies clearly favouring England, he felt that Jardine's captaincy was touched by genius: and Jardine showed great pluck in fielding near the boundary, where he became an easy target for "offensive and sometimes filthy remarks". An Australian paper warned, however, that cricket was at risk of degenerating into a "dog fight".

Australia's only cricket magazine editor, Drysdale Bett, kept his calm. Beyond all the acrimony and public uprising he had seen enough impressive batting, bowling and fielding to declare: "Still, it was quite a good match." And in many ways it had been, even if Larwood's assessment was slightly simplistic: "It was won because Australia's batsmen cannot play fast bowling that pitches on the wicket and off it on the leg side, instead of, futilely, wide on the off side."[54] Sutcliffe was the only top-order England bat to fail twice, and all their bowlers performed well. If Jardine put down a catch or two, Arthur Mailey pointed out that he had been seen at the hotel putting cold water on a badly bruised hand. The determination and resilience shown by Woodfull and Ponsford, "Mutt and Jeff", were not easily to be forgotten, Oldfield had looked good until tragedy struck, and there was that hour of sheer rainbow brilliance from Bradman. Australia's bowlers had all stuck to their task manfully. So, yes, it was an above-average cricket match, with Australia scoring much faster than England (44 runs per 100 balls against 34). But it was stained forever with odium, and some time before it ended it had become the lever which would cause the great granite boulder which is Test cricket to rock and sway threateningly.

Both skippers managed unemotional addresses after the match, though D.R. Jardine's words could surely have come only from such a man: "What I have to say is not worth listening to. Those of you who had seats got your money's worth — and then some. Thank you." W.M. Woodfull, too, revealed his disciplined character: "This great Empire game of ours teaches us to hope in defeat and congratulate the winners if they manage to pull off the victory. I want you to remember that it is not the individual but the team that wins the match."[55] Words worthy of the son of a church minister.

Some time before the Test ended Jardine had decided that he could not go on with Bodyline if there were any serious reservations within the team.

He believed that it would not be fair to his players to persist with it if they were not behind him or if they felt they were about to be overwhelmed by the upsetting reaction of the crowds and some sections of the Press. Harold Larwood, for instance, said that a little girl had pointed at him when he went to the theatre in Adelaide and remarked to her mother, "Why Mummy, he doesn't look like a murderer!"[56] Elsewhere he was spat at and abused, and at times the need was felt for a police presence at the team hotel. By the end of the tour, according to A.W. Carr, half the England team had vowed never to return to Australia (although Larwood personally benefited in one respect: any pressure he felt from Australian spectators and Press merely served to make him bowl even faster — to the discomfort not only of batsmen but of wicketkeeper and slips fielders too[57]).

The England captain, perhaps forced to reconsider his position after having the door shut in his face and being made to wait when he went to see Woodfull, now felt compelled to ask his players to decide. His wavering confidence, despite the victory, may have been affected also by a recent conversation with Tom Goodman, a gentle and conservative sports-writer, who had asked him to confirm a cable which stated that Jardine's fiancée had broken off their engagement. Jardine read the message then snapped at Goodman that "the Australian Press has had its last jibe at Jardine", and walked off. He must soon have discovered that the communication was not fraudulent. (Wyatt, looking back, said his skipper had a few girlfriends in Australia, but "he wasn't any kind of playboy or lady-killer".[58] Larwood wondered if, while in Tasmania, his skipper might not have impressed at least one attractive woman with his charm, culture and strength of character.)

Jardine and the managers did not attend the crisis meeting, which was chaired by the senior pro, Herbert Sutcliffe. From it emerged a statement which did not please some of the Australian newspapers, for it assured the outside world that all was harmony in the England camp:[59]

> The members of the MCC England team have no desire to enter into public controversy, for they deplore the introduction of any personal feeling into the records of a great game. In view, however, of certain published statements to the effect that there is, or has been, dissension or disloyalty in their team, they desire to deny this definitely and absolutely, while assuring the public of England and Australia that they are, and always have been, utterly loyal to their captain, under whose leadership they hope to achieve an honourable victory.

Rather as a battalion would follow the captain into the conflict even while certain junior officers and men bore reservations about the strategy, they remained bound to honour not only the uniform but also the oath of allegiance (and possibly, in the case of the cricketers, their tour contracts). One day, perhaps, they would be free to air their grievances. Les Ames, later in life, confirmed that he and Hammond (to name but two) disapproved of Bodyline, but added: "Had we spoken out no-one would have said or done anything."[60] Meanwhile, Maurice Leyland spoke for his captain's supportive majority when he quipped, "What, give up leg theory just because it's got 'em licked?"[61] This stout-hearted Yorkshireman, so Bill Bowes's story went, was not even affected by having a cushion, a flour-bomb, an empty beer bottle and then a full one tossed past him as he fielded near the boundary. He picked up the full bottle and asked if anyone had an opener.[62] That won them over.

The newspaper stories about dissension in the camp had been started, Larwood thought, by the Nawab of Pataudi, who seethed for some time at having been dropped so soon after making his Test century. "Before I left England several people told me that there were many qualities I'd like in Douglas. Well, I've been with him now for nearly three months and I haven't found one yet that I care for."[63]

Further complicating Jardine's feelings in victory and in the vote of support from his men was the recall of his visit to the Australian dressing-room in quest of an apology for an alleged reference to Larwood as a "bastard". Vic Richardson answered the door. Upon being told of the nature of Jardine's call he turned to the players inside and said, "Hey, which of you bastards called Larwood a bastard instead of Jardine?"[64] A variant came in a cartoon drawn years later in which Richardson is asking, "Which one of you bastards called this bastard a bastard?"

What a generous-spirited cricket series it was.

CHAPTER NINE

CABLES AND LABELS

It was time for an official Australian protest — or at least that was the feeling of the majority. By no means unanimously approved of throughout Australia, the complaint was sent by the Board to MCC at Lord's on Wednesday, January 18, 1933, the fifth day of the Test match, but it was not backed by all members of the Australian Board.

Only four of the 13 delegates were present at the Adelaide match: B.V. Scrymgour, H.W. Hodgetts and R.F. Middleton, all of South Australia, and W.L. Kelly, representing Victoria. These were the men who drafted the protest cable and telegraphed a copy to the chairman, Dr A.W.D. Robertson, in Melbourne for approval. Telegrams were then fired off seeking the backing of the remaining eight Board members. Five (R.A. Oxlade, W.C. Bull and F.M. Cush, all of New South Wales, and M.J. [Roger] Hartigan and J.S.Hutcheon, of Queensland) voted against sending the cable, being dissatisfied with the wording — and probably having at the forefronts of their minds the revenue expected from the upcoming Test matches in Brisbane and Sydney. The three votes of support, which came from Dr Ramsay Mailer (Victoria), Harold Rowe (the first batsman — 25 years earlier — to score a century for Western Australia against an English touring team) and Harold Bushby (Tasmania), produced an 8–5 majority in favour, and so the cable was sent off to London.

There had been an attempt to persuade Woodfull and Bradman to associate their names with the cable but they declined. The wording was seen by some as clumsy, and opinion was divided as to whether it was too late or too early to have sent such a communication. R.G. Menzies

MOST OF THE PRINCIPAL AUSTRALIAN CRICKET BOARD DELEGATES OF 1932–33 ARE SEEN IN THIS 1936 GROUP. STANDING — S.H.D. ROWE (WA), CLEM HILL (SA), H.W. HODGETTS (SA), R.F. MIDDLETON (SA), K.O.E. JOHNSON (NSW), J.S. HUTCHEON (Q), R.L. MORTON (VIC), C.H. BUSHBY (TAS), A.W.D. ROBERTSON (VIC), H. BUSHELL (VIC), M.J. HARTIGAN (Q); SEATED — F.M. CUSH (NSW), R.A. OXLADE (NSW), W.H.JEANES (SA).

did not have a hand in its composition (it entirely lacked elegance, if further proof of the fact were needed), but he did see it and then gave as his personal — and possibly his gratis legal — opinion that Woodfull and Jardine should best be brought together for private discussions. In *Afternoon Light*, his memoirs (published in 1967), Australia's most renowned statesman describes Jardine as a cricketing Coriolanus. He also explains how the Woodfull incident at Adelaide altered his feelings. Until then he had been on Jardine's side. Why should the fast-rising ball outside leg be any less legitimate than the fast-rising ball outside off? Now he knew.

Bill Jeanes (an estate agent in Glenelg who happened to have been born in West Bridgford, close to Larwood–Voce territory in Nottinghamshire) summoned most of the Pressmen to his SACA office at Adelaide Oval on that fifth day of play. He had written out the text of the cable in a quiet corner of the Australian dressing-room ("We all agreed with 'unsportsmanlike'," claimed the unstoppable O'Reilly), and now, having sent it on its way to Lord's, Jeanes read the communication out to the assembled newspapermen:

217

AUSTRALIAN BOARD OF CONTROL TO MCC, January 18, 1933:

> Bodyline bowling assumed such proportions as to menace best interests of game, making protection of body by batsmen the main consideration. Causing intensely bitter feeling between players as well as injury. In our opinion is unsportsmanlike. Unless stopped at once likely to upset friendly relations existing between Australia and England.

There were some stunned expressions in that room. Gilbert Mant's duty now as Reuters' correspondent was to make contact with London himself as rapidly as possible, no matter what time it was. He cabled a summary of the sensational Board move, and sent it urgent rate. The Board, without thinking the matter through, had its cable dispatched at normal rate. Mant's reached London almost instantaneously, in the early hours of the English morning. The Board's did not land until it was almost lunchtime. The agency story hot in their hands, frantic newspapermen in London tracked down the MCC president, Viscount Lewisham, and awoke the gentleman from a sound sleep at about half-past-two in the morning. It was, wrote Mant, Reuters' first major scoop since the assassination of Abraham Lincoln.[1]

When allied to the perhaps excusably aggressive tone of the cable from Australia, this unhappy piece of mistiming had the same effect that a rock thrown through the Lord's committee-room window might have had. Admittedly, after the Woodfull–Warner incident an MCC official *had* told an Australian newspaperman (dateline Monday, January 16) that should there be any official protest then "the whole position of the leg theory" might be discussed later in the week. But Lord's hardly expected that its lofty figurehead would be shaken from his slumbers in this way in the middle of a winter night. And to level any accusation of unsporting behaviour at a nation which prided itself on sportsmanship above almost any other quality was to slap the Imperial face with a very heavy glove.

Australian newspaper reaction was on the whole unsympathetic to the Board's action. In Melbourne the *Herald* drew the image of Australian cricket holding a pistol at the heads of the English cricket authorities, and the *Age* simply concluded that nothing could justify the terms of the cable.

In time it became clear which cricketers and other major figures approved or disapproved of the sending of the cable. Among the top players, Wally Hammond felt the protest justified but thought it would have been better to have held it back till the series was over.[2] Vic Richardson said he

"NEVER MIND, OLD 'ROO — THAT FELLOW DIDN'T PLAY CRICKET" — TO WHICH THE WOUNDED KANGAROO REPLIES: "SH-SH! NOT A WORD MORE ABOUT THAT JUST NOW. THE TIME TO SQUEAL IS WHEN WE'RE WINNING." AS TED FARFIELD SAW IT IN *THE BULLETIN*.

was the only senior Australian player to oppose it, and gave some sound reasons:[3] Englishmen could have no conception of what was going on; MCC would be inclined to support its team; the word "unsporting" would be a red rag to a bull; and sending it when Australia had just gone 1–2 down in the series made it seem like squealing. Richardson favoured sending a secret (and therefore immune from Press hysteria) report to Lord's at the end of the series.

Australia's sinking situation in the Test series was certainly seized upon by some sectors of the Press as cause to depict them in a poor light: the *Daily Herald* in England coined the memorable description "undignified snivelling", an insult partially offset by a cartoon by the paper's Australian cartoonist, Will Dyson, who drew a bruised, bandaged and supplicant Australian batsman pleading to the League of Nations: "Tell 'em I'm here, cobber. It's urgent."

But the man who summed up the probable effect most accurately was Gubby Allen, who displayed an exquisite relish many years later in recalling what he said to Douglas Jardine after they had been shown the gist of the Australian Board's cable: "I'll always remember Douglas saying to me,

'Have you seen the cable?' And I said, 'Yes, I have, and I think it's dreadful.' He said, 'I know they'll let me down at Lord's.' I said, 'No, Douglas, you're wrong. No-one can call an Englishman unsporting and get away with it. They've lost the battle with the first shot they've fired.' I can still see the smile that came over his face."[4]

The MCC secretary, Billy Findlay, a former Lancashire amateur batsman, Oxford Blue and an old Etonian, was quickly at work on a draft reply, though it had to pass through many hands. He also had cabled messages from Jardine and Warner on his desk. (These documents were not to survive the years.[5]) While Australia waited, chairman Allen "Robbie" Robertson, Collins Street specialist born in 1867 of humble origins, unmarried, intolerant of rude language, and currently also serving as president of Melbourne University Cricket Club, expressed his somewhat drastic views to Jeanes in a letter: "I would go so far as to cancel the next Test games and all the Test games for the next 10 or 12 years, but of course I am only one of the number."[6]

His bitterness might have been concentrated by a letter which Woodfull wrote to the Board. It went beyond concern for his players. He revealed his worry about international relations: "Since entering Test cricket [1926] I have not been sure that it is for the good of the Empire that in times when England and Australia need to be pulling together large sections of both countries are embittered."[7] This was very much something for the politicians and economists of both nations to chew on, no matter how much Bill O'Reilly, half a century later, scoffed at suggestions that Bodyline and the cables had threatened Empire unity.

MCC took a while to reply, and that kept Australia on edge. The Test had been over for some days before the Australian Board took delivery of the reaction. Findlay had first composed the following for consideration by the MCC committee:

> Much regret contents of your cable. Marylebone assured that no English bowler bowls at the man but at leg stump which is said to be the weakness of certain batsmen. Cricketers of today have not had great experience of fast bowling and the open stance of batsman necessarily increases risk. Of all considerations friendly relations and the game itself paramount. If remaining Tests cannot be played in this spirit and appreciated by players and spectators alike would it not be well to consider substitution of state games?

It might have been better if this first draft by Findlay had been sent. MCC's secretary semi-privately regarded the Australian Board members as "rather tiresome gentlemen", and in another private letter they were "very difficult people".[8] The cable eventually sent by MCC would turn them into rather angry people. Viscount Lewisham chose to have Findlay's first effort reworded. This time there was reference to the possibility that Larwood was simply too fast for the Australians on their current pitches. That would have seemed a slur on the very manhood of Woodfull and Ponsford and Richardson and McCabe ... and Bradman.

WILLIAM FINDLAY, MCC SECRETARY IN THE HOT SEAT.

All these words were scrapped, and after five days of tight breathing the ACB took delivery of the following communiqué, finalised at Lord's after a two-hour meeting, the authors having been Viscount Lewisham (the president) and Sir Kynaston Studd, Baronet (one of a distinguished brotherhood, an Etonian, MCC committee member since 1878, a Lord Mayor of London, and — not least — one of the Cambridge XI which beat the 1882 Australians):

MCC TO AUSTRALIAN BOARD OF CONTROL, January 23, 1933:

We, Marylebone Cricket Club, deplore your cable. We deprecate your opinion that there has been unsportsmanlike play. We have fullest confidence in captain, team and managers, and are convinced that they would do nothing to infringe either the Laws of Cricket or the spirit of the game. We have no evidence that our confidence has been misplaced. Much as we regret accidents to Woodfull and Oldfield, we understand that in neither case was the bowler to blame. If the Australian Board of Control wish to propose a new law or rule it shall receive our careful consideration in due course. We hope the situation is not now as serious as your cable would seem to indicate, but if it is such as to jeopardise the good relations between English and Australian cricketers, and you consider it desirable to cancel remainder of programme, we would consent with great reluctance.

One newspaper's comments might serve adequately to summarise the nature of these cables for impartial readers: Australia's protest, suggested the *Daily Herald*, had been "a little rude" while "our reply was unnecessarily stiff". Clearly, much unthawing remained to be carried out.

One of MCC's most senior figures (not that any of the committee seemed young in any sense) was the 6th Earl of Dartmouth, now 81, a man of charm, once Conservative Whip in the House of Commons, MCC president in 1893, and now a trustee of the club, with strong cricket connections with Kent, I Zingari and Staffordshire. He also happened to be father of the current MCC president Viscount Lewisham. The Legge family's barony had been created by King Charles II, 250 years previously. The elderly earl, being an incurable versifier, now felt his best contribution to the storm of debate swelling out of Australia's protest was to offer some verse:

We have fought,
We have won,
And we have lost,
But we have never squealed before.

His son William, now Viscount Lewisham, Lord Great Chamberlain, and aged 52, faced greater immediate responsibilities as MCC president than his aged father had ever countenanced, with the rumbles of the most ferocious row the club had ever known growing ever deeper. Still, he was a man of great fortitude, having commanded the Staffordshire Yeomanry during Allenby's Palestine campaign in the First World War. Being awoken at 2.30 am would have been nothing new to him.

VISCOUNT LEWISHAM, MCC PRESIDENT IN 1933. *(COURTESY MCC)*

The worrying tailpiece to MCC's response (floating the option of cancellation of the remainder of the tour) was inserted after "Lord F's" suggestion to secretary Findlay. Who was Lord F? Might it have been the former H.W. Forster, Eton, Oxford, Hampshire, MCC president in 1919, an imposing figure who had been a popular Governor-General of Australia from that year until 1925?

The gathering of the committee at Lord's on January 23 to discuss and approve this response to the ACB's cable comprised so many members of the aristocracy, men of government and public service, with high scholastic and sporting achievement, and even close proximity to the Throne, that it might have been a sitting, in miniature, of the House of Lords. And all to debate the future of Test cricket between its earliest protagonists.

The matter was placed in the hands of an inner group of MCC committee members. These were the president (Viscount Lewisham) and the treasurer (Lord Hawke, the towering figure in Yorkshire cricket as captain and president for several decades), along with Viscount Bridgeman (former Home Secretary, First Lord of the Admiralty, and MCC president in 1931) and Sir Stanley Jackson (triumphant captain of England in the 1905 Ashes series, Boer War officer, Conservative Party chairman, and Governor of Bengal from 1927 to 1932, when he survived an assassination attempt; he also had the boy Winston Churchill as his fag while at Harrow School). There was also Sir Francis "Ben" Lacey, Findlay's highly respected predecessor as MCC secretary. He had held this position for 28 years, during which his diplomacy and management skills were brought to bear in further elevating the club's role and image. A barrister and now aged 73, Lacey was a trustee of the club, his cricket credentials secured by his record innings of 323 not out for Hampshire against Norfolk in 1887. Sir Kynaston Studd made up the group of six "executive" committee members. Billy Findlay was also on hand, notebook at the ready. (In *From a Window at Lord's*, published in 1937, E.H.D. Sewell, claiming that the names had never before been published, listed all these apart from Lacey, but with the additional names of Lord Hailsham and prominent Oxford and Surrey figure H.D.G. Leveson Gower.)

They held the fate of Anglo-Australian cricket in their hands, and they were all variously inter-connected either through their public schools or Oxford or Cambridge, or their club and family and social allegiances. It was truly a formidable legion of cricket governors that the Australian Board delegates had taken on. By comparison, several among the Australian XIII seemed a little unworldly and short of stature beyond the modest cricket clubhouse.

With scarcely any of the MCC special committee *really* comprehending what had gone on of late at the Sydney Cricket Ground, Melbourne Cricket Ground, and Adelaide Oval, these gentlemen, whose input into the matter was greatest, were backed up by other committee members at Lord's, members who were quite as much allied to the ruling classes of Great Britain or at very least to the Conservative Party, and all born in the Victorian age. They were: Brigadier-General the Earl of Lucan, Field-Marshal Lord Plumer (who led a force to relieve Mafeking and whose life was now very near its end), Viscount Ullswater, Lord Aberdare, Brigadier-General Viscount Hampden, Stanley Christopherson (a prominent figure in the City, who had played against Australia in the Lord's Test of 1884), and Lieutenant-Colonel Christopher Heseltine (a Hampshire amateur who once dismissed Bobby Abel three consecutive times for ducks), together with former MP and gentleman cricketer for Norfolk Michael Falcon, recent England captain A.P.F. Chapman, R.H. Mallett (a Durham identity who gave long service to Minor Counties cricket and to arranging international tours into and out of the UK), and the two MCC managers currently in Australia, P.F. Warner and R.C.N. Palairet. Added to which, one of the trustees of the club was the Duke of Buccleuch.

Among the complexities facing these august gentlemen as they deliberated over the crisis was the belief that the senior tour manager, Warner, had not as yet informed the captain, Jardine, of his disapproval of this particular brand of "leg theory"— or so it appeared from remarks made in a letter by Findlay to Lacey dated January 18. Throughout the tour there had been a steady flow of letters between secretary Findlay and both the captain and manager in Australia; these must have left Findlay the best informed — and also probably the most confused — of all the men involved at Lord's. In *Cricket and Empire*, the Sissons/Stoddart book published in 1984, examples of Findlay's contradictory state of mind are given: to Viscount Ullswater (January 20), "I hope and believe they will support Jardine", and to Lord Bridgeman (same day), "I hate these five men on the leg side".

At least the Marylebone club could congratulate itself that the cabled response met with the approval of Stanley Baldwin, friend of many of the committeemen, and himself leader of the Conservative majority in Ramsay MacDonald's national government at Westminster.[9]

Meanwhile, a suggestion (cabled January 26) from South Australia's Acting Governor, Sir George Murray, to the Governor, Sir Alexander Hore-Ruthven, who was in England, failed to produce results. The suggestion — which was nothing if not super-optimistic — was that MCC should persuade Jardine to state publicly that fast bowling to a leg-side field would be instantly abandoned.

The Australian Board now felt it necessary to convene an emergency meeting rather than rely on telephone hook-ups, though it would take time, rail journeys being so lengthy and tedious. The delegates gathered in the NSWCA's rooms in Sydney on January 30 with the purpose of constructing a response to MCC's awkward cable of January 23. Sydney Smith junior, an influential figure (though he was not one of the Board's three New South Wales delegates), had served as Board secretary himself from 1911 until 1926 and managed Australian teams in England in 1921 and 1926 (his span of cricket administration extended across *76 years*, stretching from a school commitment when he was 10 until his 30 years as NSWCA president ended in 1966). He had been in a central position during the 1911–12 Board versus rebel players stand-off — literally so when selectors Clem Hill and Peter McAlister came to blows in Bulls Chambers, in Martin Place, Sydney. A career with the Department of Agriculture was shaped to allow of maximum involvement in cricket matters, and Smith was swiftly behind the microphone at 2UW to denounce the sending of the Board's January 18 cable, though parts of his reasoning were faulty: Bodyline had *not* been bowled since the start of the tour, and the umpires did *not* have powers to stop it. However, the NSWCA did have the foresight to alert the SCG that the sort of crowd violence threatened at Adelaide could become a reality during the fifth Test. The New South Wales Commissioner of Police gave assurances.[10]

As for Messrs Oxlade, Bull and Cush, the New South Wales Board members, they made their disapproval clear at the January 30 meeting, the spectre of possible lost revenue high in their considerations. (An anomaly followed three weeks later when the NSWCA voted by the slimmest margin of 16–15 against E.L. Waddy's motion to dissociate itself from the cable of January 18. Ted Adams, once Bradman's club captain at St George, who became Sydney's town clerk, and Syd Webb, a Queen's Counsel who was to manage the 1961 Australian team in England, both supported the cable.[11] It was beginning to seem like a country divided.)

The long ACB meeting in Sydney on January 30 struggled for anything resembling unanimity, and it surprised nobody when a subcommittee was set up, comprised of Allen Robertson (the Board chairman), Roy Middleton and Bernard Scrymgour from South Australia, Aubrey Oxlade from New South Wales, and Jack Hutcheon from Queensland. The surprise was that Hutcheon, rather than Robertson, was elected chairman.[12]

The subcommittee's main mission, to frame a reply to MCC's reply, was completed with some difficulty. It was clearly a miserable meeting, and even the minutes were erratic and incomplete. At last a cable was written and agreed and dispatched with hope, the wording reiterating the concerns expressed in the original cable while showing keenness to keep the show on the road. Where it erred was in its refusal to redress the offence caused by the word "unsportsmanlike". They'd called the Poms cheats, and left it at that. On the very day that Adolf Hitler, with his plans that might destroy the civilised world, was installed by Marshal Hindenburg as Chancellor of Germany, the Australian Board sent off its second cable:

AUSTRALIAN BOARD OF CONTROL TO MCC, January 30, 1933:

We, Australian Board of Control, appreciate your difficulty in dealing with matter raised in our cable without having seen the actual play. We unanimously regard bodyline bowling as adopted in some of the games in the present tour as being opposed to the spirit of cricket and unnecessarily dangerous to players. We are deeply concerned that the ideals of the game shall be protected, and have therefore appointed a committee to report on the action necessary to eliminate such bowling from all cricket in Australia as from beginning 1933–34 season. Will forward copy of committee's recommendation for your consideration, and, it is hoped, co-operation, as to its application in all cricket. We do not consider it necessary to cancel remainder of programme.

By now, having played their match at Ballarat and the return game against New South Wales, the Englishmen were entering the Queensland leg of the tour; the fourth Test was due to begin at Brisbane on February 10. As matters stood, this Test match was highly unlikely to start. That charge of questionable sportsmanship still irked MCC and, equally significantly, it greatly irked their captain in the field, D.R. Jardine. Thus the ball came back over the net without much delay this time:

MCC TO AUSTRALIAN BOARD OF CONTROL, February 2, 1933:

We, the Committee of the Marylebone Cricket Club note with pleasure that you do not consider it necessary to cancel the remainder of programme, and that you are postponing the whole issue involved until after the present tour is completed. May we accept this as a clear indication that the good sportsmanship of our team is not in question? We are sure you will appreciate how impossible it would be to play any Test match in the spirit we all desire unless both sides were satisfied there was no reflection upon their sportsmanship. When your recommendation reaches us it shall receive our most careful consideration and will be submitted to the Imperial Cricket Conference.

Warner gloated some years later that the MCC committee have had their detractors "but they are pretty good at drafting telegrams".

The Australian Board agonised over the dilemma: should they climb down even further? With financial considerations of paramount importance, the continuation of the tour must not be threatened. But there was an understandable reluctance to allow such pressure as they had seemingly mustered against the very "proprietors" of English Bodyline bowling now to evaporate. Even the slowest-thinking ACB delegate would have known that MCC simply could not amend the Laws of Cricket without months of preamble, worldwide consultation and preparation, so the best that could be hoped for was a decision to instruct Jardine to aband-on it immediately. Thought had to be given to withdrawing the one comment that seemed to have shaken that mighty fortress in St John's Wood, London NW: that their cricketers were playing in an "unsportsmanlike" fashion.

Findlay had sent off another cable, this one direct to P.F. Warner, expressing hope that MCC's cable to the Board would facilitate *his* negotiations. He was referring to Warner's personal plan to have a sort of peace agreement signed by Jardine, Palairet and himself on behalf of MCC and Dr Robertson and Woodfull for the Australians. Perhaps not unexpectedly, Warner's draft consisted of high-flighted rhetoric which failed to tackle the specific problems. The 11th chapter of Jardine's book on the tour is a masterly document. In it he analyses the problem in all its magnitude and demonstrates how clear-minded and determined he was: Warner's "formula", while admirable, was pious, rumoured, he thought, to be the work of politicians, and probably thought up as a tentative feeler. Jardine was currently interested in one thing only, and that was the withdrawal of the word "unsportsmanlike". No withdrawal, no Test match — for the skipper at least.

Everyone seemed keen to air an opinion, even if it was little more than a way of briefly distracting the mind from the everyday hardships. Was cricket a man's game? Were "Sardine" and his team worth two bob? Was Test cricket (at a time when it was largely only England v Australia that mattered) really worth preserving? Many would have been surprised at Jardine's remark in his forthcoming book on the tour. Test cricket was at the crossroads, he thought, and there was a common tendency to attach an importance to Test matches "which is out of proportion to their true worth". What might he have thought of Test cricket today, with 10 countries taking part and sometimes three Tests going on at the same time in various parts of the globe?

Before piecing together the diplomatic manoeuvres going on in high places and quiet corners during the first weeks of 1933, the kaleidoscope of opinions that bounced around the cricket world needs to be viewed, if only to demonstrate the wide range of disparate attitudes. Everyone, it seemed — player, ex-player, spectator, and the man on the Sydney tram or pub barstool — had to express himself at this emotional time, for the Adelaide Test had been like no other, contested in an atmosphere classified by Alan Kippax as one of "hostility and sinister gloom".

Plum Warner must have lost quite a bit of sleep after receiving a letter from a man in Tasmania who accused him — after the Adelaide Test — of being "a liar of the lowest order" for shielding himself behind thousands of miles of communications.[13] His discomfort grew worse by the hour, the remark of his old Test adversary Clem Hill adding to it substantially when he countered Warner's anguished "What can I do?" with a straightforward "You can come down off the fence for a start, Plum."[14]

Editor Bett, of *The Australian Cricketer*, who actually thought the Adelaide Test was "quite a good match", nonetheless fired off a condemnatory front-page editorial in his February issue spotlighting the accusations from afar that Australia's batsmen were cowards and damning those accusations with words that would have made Lord's — and even Whitehall — blanch, should they have flown that far: "None of them would say it to our cricketers' faces. And everyone knows to whom England would look if she was threatened in war again. Even the Germans have never pointed the finger of scorn at the Australians."

There was a certain justice in Bett's objection. He reasonably pointed out that Australia had taken their 1–4 defeat by England in the 1928–29 series without comment. With a picture of Harold Larwood — "The Terror of the Tests" — on the magazine's front cover and under the heading LEG THEORY HEADERS MUST GO, Drysdale Bett aired the general worry that viciousness might enter "an absolutely clean game", rendering the crowds "bloodthirsty".

He was still broadminded enough, three months later, to give his "coaching editor" a page and a half to expound on how to play Bodyline; and in the March issue he had praised Jardine's captaincy for its uncanny touch in bowling changes and alterations to the batting order.

Quoted in one of E.W. Swanton's autobiographies is one of the more provocative insults from the Old Country, cloaked in satire, with a trace of Newbolt at the tailend:[15]

Indignant daughter of the South,
We always have admired your pluck;
But now you're rather out of luck
Why not preserve a firmer mouth?

Where is that tough Australian grin?
When, Digger, did you learn to faint?
Can you not take without complaint
A dose of your own medicine?

Finish this futile brawl today!
We won't believe the paradox,
A whining Digger funking knocks;
Come on! One up, and two to play!

Swanton, who did not identify the source of this ditty (it came from the pen of J.C. Squire, and appeared in the *Evening Standard* and *London Mercury*), went on to write that after publication of his earlier autobiography he had received one of the most hate-filled letters he'd ever had, written by somebody from Bourke, New South Wales "whose antipathy to the Crown and all things British" apparently stemmed from the events of the Bodyline series played 40 years before.

Squire's mocking verse inspired a response from cricket-loving New South Wales district judge John Sheridan:

And when we say the grand old British game
Is butchered by the present British team,
And voice our protest to the mother land,
And send it by Marconi's wondrous beam,
Yet Mr Squire says what we do is whine,
(So thieves asperse the victims of their theft),
For me I'd sooner slake my thirst with brine,
Than show myself of decency bereft.

Neville Cardus, already at the apogee of his career as a cricket essayist, was among the first Englishmen to accept Australia's word that Bodyline was bad. In the *Manchester Guardian* he challenged its morality, displayed his revulsion at violence and intimidation, and probably had a guiding hand in the paper's leader which suggested it might be best to cancel the last two

Tests and abandon international cricket for 10 years (a sentiment he might have endorsed afresh 60 years and more later, in view of the ill-feeling so recurrently generated by some countries unto others).

As ever, *The Times* reflected the opinions, liberally sprayed with Latin phrases, of many a gentleman at his breakfast table. The early optimism of reader Charles Gilmore ("The great art of batting must be given a chance to see how it can meet this new Giant Despair") was followed by N. Shore's satire (the latest street game in Somerset comprised bowlers trying to hit batsmen who, when touched by the ball, have to lie down and be carried off). Next day, January 21, 1933, tough old Viscount Buckmaster was regretting how the perfection of pitches had meant the loss of the low scores and the physical dangers of old.

Before the month was out, Leonard Crawley, a fine amateur batsman (and golfer) who came close to selection for the tour, lodged his objections to England's tactics, saying that if Bradman could not survive then no great batsman of the past could have. He suggested that cricket, like rugby, should have the power to punish offenders, citing bowling aimed at a batsman's body as being on a par with a footballer's hacking and tripping of an opponent.

On the last day of the month a correspondent calling himself "Austranglian" pointed the finger at the barrackers, who were mainly "larrikins, habitual loafers, and grass-chewers [deadbeats]" whose favourite amusements were throwing paper bags full of banana-skins at those who stood in front of them. He remembered cascades of bottles being thrown on the field at Sydney when there was a delay through rain, Plum Warner being the English captain. One Australian player told him he would willingly have turned a machine-gun onto the crowd at times. (This might have been Alan Fairfax, who quit the game in disgust in 1931.)

On February 6 a letter was published from B.J.T. Bosanquet (Oxford, Middlesex and England), first major purveyor of the googly 30 years earlier and a considerable batsman too. What about the fast inswingers of Bart King the great American, and Tom Richardson's fearsome breakbacks, he asked. The ball passing to leg should simply be left alone. He and his contemporaries had had to cope with Australian stump-smasher Tibby Cotter bowling head-high stuff at Melbourne with eight men on the leg side. "Bosie" invited Australians to come to England later in the year to see whether his own countrymen squealed against the "really fast" Constantine.

A certain Mr Akenhead (a clever *nom de plume* perhaps?) from Western Australia wrote to *The Times* to say that England's 1932–33 tour had done big cricket in his State "a tremendous lot of good". They had been getting swelled-headed, and there had been far too much "Bradmanitis" in the air.

"The Thunderer" seemed unwilling to venture into the ethical aspects of "the so-called bodyline bowling" because it considered the matter *sub judice* in view of MCC's position *vis-à-vis* the Australian Board, but it gave space to letters, and the one which has seemed to attract most attention came from a famous literary figure, A.A. Milne, creator of Winnie-the-Pooh. The bitter feeling aroused by the colour of Mr Jardine's cap had been intensified, he noted, by the direction of Mr Larwood's bowling. He thought it "the laugh of the year" that after so much discontent over high scoring the bowlers were now on top, and that batsmen, having protected their wickets with their persons, were put out now that bowlers were bowling at their persons. His assessment was flawed in one respect: when he averred that the centuries by McCabe and Bradman were scored at rates four times faster than Jardine's. He seemed unaware that McCabe had declared — not out of modesty alone — that it had just been his lucky day, Bradman was operating in a state of near-panic, and Jardine was deliberately grinding Australia towards a position of hopelessness at Adelaide. Milne closes strongly, how-ever: "let us admit frankly that the game is made for the batsmen only".[16]

As to the danger inherent in Bodyline bowling, the voice of the Law was raised with an opinion from John Sheridan, the Australian judge, who believed that any injury suffered against such bowling would be covered by criminal law. It was a view shared by a group of law students, who let it be known that they thought any fatality should mean that the fast bowler responsible would face trial for manslaughter. Reminding Judge Sheridan of Dr Johnson's advice that big words should be kept for big occasions, the *News Chronicle* over in England laughed at the judge's pronouncement, saying that cricket might be more thrilling if police equipped with handcuffs lurked on the lookout for any bowler who bowled down the leg side.

What was the simple cricket-lover to believe? He might have read — unexpectedly too — in *The Bulletin* that the Australian Board's cable was a "hysterical protest" which cast Australians as small-minded people who "can't win without skiting or lose without squealing", an angle taken up in gentler language by the *Sydney Morning Herald*. But even before the

Adelaide Test had finished, J.C. Davis, in *The Referee*, had sounded the first warning that Australia's next tour of England, in 1934, could be in jeopardy. Furthermore, Davis quoted remarks by a "leading citizen of the Commonwealth" in a letter to him: the English players were "revealing very little spontaneous sporting pleasure" and that "the cricketing air to the players is becoming like the atmosphere of war". He warmed to his subject with some of the most passionate words coined during this hot-tempered period: "the feeling is that the English tactics in this direction are what Britishers often described the German tactics in the war. [Surely Davis did not suspect Larwood of using mustard gas?] Those tactics, in the end, helped to defeat those who used them. It will be the same in this cricket business, but the effects will last for generations, and the men responsible will not be held up as paragons in pushing their game forward as a great Empire-builder."

Davis then asked what England would have said if these "inglorious and indefensible tactics" had been devised by Australia, South Africa, New Zealand or West Indies. It was now a time, he urged, for some real action by "real fighting men to preserve the game's pleasant, personal and international relationships from utter discord". The crunch question came at the end:"Is the sportsmanship for which the Marylebone Cricket Club has stood for a century still sound to the bone?"

But England didn't cable a protest to Australia after Ernest Tyldesley's horrible facial injury at the hands of Jack Gregory's bowling in 1921, A.G. Gardiner pointed out in the *Star*. Like Clive Lloyd so many years later whenever his West Indian fast men came under critical attack, Gardiner was among those who felt it significant that the umpires had not seen fit to intervene when Larwood bowled.

"An Englishman" who had lived in Australia for 12 years wrote an impassioned letter to an Australian newspaper, picking up on the word "unsportsmanlike" and insisting that if it were anywhere applicable it was when Great Britain, fighting back after conceding points in the Rugby League Test in Sydney the previous year, were vociferously intimidated by the Australian spectators, especially when a place kick was being taken. It was applicable too, he wrote, when the Adelaide crowd cheered after Wall hit Jardine's body and made Paynter duck and dodge further bouncers, when Hammond was hit in the mouth by Ironmonger "also with musical honours", and when Larwood was counted out as he ran in to bowl.

The writer favoured discontinuing Tests between England and Australia —
cricket and football — until the crowds could be properly controlled and
learned how to behave.

A Dr Yates, who described himself as a former Sydney googly bowler,
wanted the ACB to withdraw its cable: "The Board showed its resentment in
a crude and undignified way, making the Australians look like Latins and
not Anglo-Saxons."

And yet L.V. Manning, sports editor of the *Daily Sketch* in London, was
moved to write that the situation was one that "will make all true cricket-
lovers want to bow their heads in shame and wish the English cricketers
had never left home".

Among the few who thought it all merely funny were foreigners such
as a writer for a Chicago newspaper. England hoped to regain the Ashes,
he wrote, by using the "bean" ball, with cricket likely to become a brother
to baseball.

So much for the *vox populi*. The opinions that counted, one might have
thought, were those of players and former players. But if unanimity were
to be expected in that quarter, it was notably absent.

J.T. Hearne was one of the oldest of Test veterans to make his opinion
public when questioned in an *Evening News* interview after the series had
ended. To Jack Hearne's credit attaches the greatest of all Test hat-tricks,
at Headingley in 1899, when he got Clem Hill, Syd Gregory and Monty
Noble with consecutive balls. He was a much-respected professional of
impeccable demeanour, who had toured Australia with Stoddart's side in
1897–98, and he thought the Bodyline controversy would best be put right
by the cricketers themselves. "If a man does anything against the spirit of
the game let him suffer for it." But in common with most cricketers, he
rarely forgot what mattered: "But I cannot forget that Gregory and
McDonald were very terrifying to our players in 1921, especially Gregory,
who delivered right on the return crease." The implication was clear:
that meant that Gregory was angling the ball towards the batsman. This
was also a specialty of Larwood's.

An even older hand, J.W. Trumble, elder brother of Hugh (Australia's
most successful bowler against England before Dennis Lillee) and a Test
allrounder himself in the 1880s, brought his legal mind to bear on the thorny
issue of Bodyline in an article in the *Argus* after the Adelaide Test. Larwood
thought it so supportive that he ran it in full in his book on the tour. Trumble

thought the term "Bodyline" ungenerous but admitted that calm consideration was difficult while feelings were running so high. He thought this type of bowling was legitimate and justifiable in Test matches, and referred to past similarities. There was Ted McDonald's bowling for Lancashire against Yorkshire in 1927, when he bowled with no slips and four "leg traps". Trumble himself had been hit 20 times while facing Turner and Ferris at Lord's on "a pig of a wicket". He concluded a longish feature by expressing the wish that more ex-players were serving on the Australian Board, a lament that has been repeated many times over the years.

One of the very earliest complaints, printed in *The Field*, Madras, when the tour had barely got under way, came from the old Surrey and England fast bowler Bill Hitch, but his disapproval was on practical grounds and stemmed from leg theory's negative nature: not so many slips catches, he lamented, and reduction in off-side strokes. Leg theory, he knew, took "all the brightness and beauty out of our national game". Jack Fingleton had taken precisely the same line: "Bodyline prostituted the art of batting. It knew not the delicacy of the back-cut; it denied the grace of a cover drive, cricket's most graceful stroke. The glorious straight drive, majestic off drive or lofty shots over the off field might never have been born for all birthright bodyline conceded them." This season the Australians were forced to employ cow and dog strokes instead and a form of aeronautical loop-the-loop shot as if on the village green.[17]

A slight divergence of attitudes which caused wry amusement came from Frank Mitchell, who wrote as "Second Slip" in *The Cricketer*. Even as the magazine's proprietor, Mr P.F. Warner himself, was on his way home from the tour, Mitchell, a Cambridge and Yorkshire cricketer who captained South Africa, summarised the tour at length, relying on what he had read during the winter and producing a balanced review, full of praise for the victors, with only the faintest expression of apprehension about the possible acceptance and further spread of leg theory. He did, however, put his finger on the greatest need: an amendment, in favour of the bowler, to the lbw law.

In the *Daily Sketch*, "What kind of effeminacy has entered Australian cricket?" asked E.H.D. Sewell, the old cricketer/sportsman who loved shooting tigers — and much else that moved — in India. Not at all, thought the great Frank Woolley: Larwood was so fast and good that he didn't need to resort to Bodyline. Once it was seen how relations between the two countries were endangered, the veteran Kent and England left-hander believed, "it should have been abandoned forthwith ... even at the cost of the rubber".[18]

Lionel Tennyson, a supporter of Jardine's strategy, declared after Adelaide that "Test cricket has been reduced to a state of war" (and he knew something about the real thing), but wrote in the *Evening News*: "Play the game, Australia. If cricket is impossible without squabbles and screaming let us be content with our domesticity and the Village Green." It sounds more entertaining if read while adopting His Lordship's difficulty with the letter r.

Fred Root, key figure in the development of a leg theory that was hardly physically dangerous, was naturally keen to have his say too, and having proclaimed that England's Jardine, Sutcliffe and Allen could play leg theory with a walking-stick (though Hobbs disliked it), he told readers of his column that Australia must either learn to play leg theory or switch to playing with tennis balls. Duleepsinhji's outlook was similar: they may as well use a soft ball and convert cricket into a game solely played by girls: "Half the thrill in playing cricket is the element of personal danger involved."

Several county captains were polled. Brian Sellers, the no-nonsense Yorkshire skipper, surprised nobody by declaring the Australian Board's cable as "perfectly ridiculous". H.M. "Whiz" Morris (Essex), George Rudd (Leicestershire) and Maurice Turnbull (Glamorgan), who had thrashed the Notts attack only a few months previously, were all of like opinion.

The diminutive Indian, Ranjitsinhji, has been one of the few batsmen to warrant the label "genius", and yet he, as a Cambridge undergraduate in the early 1890s, had forced himself to overcome fear by employing Tom Richardson and Bill Lockwood, the world's best fast bowlers, to bowl at him in the nets while he tied his right foot to a peg to prevent any backing away. Now, seemingly as confused as most other people, and on his way back to India to die, he continued to cable his views to the newspapers, airing the conviction that he would rather lose than win over the bruised bodies of his opponents, but also urging Jardine to continue with his strategy, the governors of cricket to seek the fullest evidence, and his readers to believe him when he said that he did not think things were as dangerous as was being made out. This was just about Ranji's final known utterance on cricket.[19]

Nigel Haig, who had had a brief but bitter taste of Gregory and McDonald in his one Test during the 1921 series, was opposed to Bodyline; it remains an unanswerable but nonetheless tempting question to ask what influence his uncle, Lord Harris, the great power at Lord's for so many years, might have had on matters had he lived beyond March 1932.

The unequivocal views of Arthur Gilligan, perhaps the most popular England captain ever to tour Australia (1924–25), came to light unexpectedly many years later when a letter of his went on the market.[20] "This bodyline bowling is disgusting," he wrote, "and it is a miracle that Jardine has completely got away with it ... I admire Woodfull for the way he behaved in such a horrid situation. I regret to say it, but Jardine is a pig dog of the worst description and he should never have been sent as a skipper. His tour of office has put the game back 50 years, and I know that Australians will never forget his criminal proceedings ... Percy Chapman and I ... agreed that Jardine was a rotter." The verdicts of two England captains for the price of one. (During the Adelaide Test, Chapman had put his glass down for a moment to air his own view on matters: few people would be sorry to see the end of this Test match, he thought: "It has contained much that is nasty and regrettable and foreign to the spirit of the game.")

Gilligan wanted an Anglo-Australian committee set up to investigate the problem (Arthur Mailey also saw this as the most likely solution). Had one been established, Dr Reg Bettington was the sort of man who might have served on it. Parramatta-born, he was a spin-bowling allrounder for Middlesex and New South Wales, Australian amateur golf champion in 1932, and Jardine's captain at Oxford in 1923. He detested Bodyline too.

The Reverend Jack Parsons, soldier, clergyman and punishing batsman for Warwickshire, also let his voice be heard. All the glorious shots were eliminated by this kind of bowling, which "encouraged brute force and ignorance". Of Bill Bowes's short-pitched bowling prior to the tour, he said it was "a disgusting show and I have told him so". England captain in the Edwardian years, the regal (and usually penniless) Archie MacLaren, was another to condemn without quite understanding the intermittent nature of Bodyline attacks: "There is nothing to recommend this pounding of the body throughout an innings."

The *Daily Telegraph* in London scoured around for some reactions during the Adelaide Test, and found three unsympathetic to Australia's complaint and two in support. George Gunn, one of Nottinghamshire's greatest batsmen until his recent retirement at the age of 53 after being struck on the skull (by Gover) once too often, gave the time-honoured reply: "They have a bat in their hands and should take care of themselves." Only three years previously Gunn had caused ripples of laughter around the Caribbean by advancing to the West Indian bouncers, playing them in front of his face with a straight bat, and blowing a raspberry at the bowler.

Arthur Carr — owner of racehorses called Notts For Ever and Bodyline — predictably supported Gunn: "If a fast bowler is to be told how to bowl the sooner we give up the game the better." Harold Gilligan, too, felt the complaints were unwarranted: "One thing this leg-theory business shows, and that is that those people who have been hit are very slow on their feet." Any conversation he might have had with brother Arthur at that time might have been worth overhearing.

The kindly Andrew Sandham, Gunn's 39-year-old opening partner on the 1929–30 tour of the West Indies, warned that "if this leg-theory business has come to stay, it will spoil the game as a spectacle". His Surrey team-mate, the tiny wicketkeeper Herbert Strudwick, agreed. "Struddy" loved Australia, having toured with Warner in 1903–04 and 1911–12, and twice more in the 1920s. He believed that Larwood would never try to hit a batsman, any more than would Jack Gregory, who once hit Strudwick (usually last man in) over the heart with three successive balls. But if the leg theory was now killing cricket from the spectator's point of view it would be best to stop it "for the sake of clanship".

The newspaper's columnist, Howard Marshall, who was also a mellifluous radio commentator, thought that the recent incidents in Australia might have been magnified. He knew that leg theory was nothing new, though he wondered at its effectiveness with Larwood bowling "breast high" with four short legs. Gregory and McDonald, he recalled, had four *slips*. (McDonald also had things to say at this time — that he and Gregory never bowled Bodyline, and that the only way for Australia to stop it was to retaliate. But his old fast-bowling partner had made it a policy never to speak to the Press.)

Contrary to popular acceptance, then, cricket followers huddling through their English winter of 1932–33 were not left in complete ignorance of what was happening on Australia's Test pitches. News of a sort was coming through. Strong opinions were circulating, even if much was being left to the imagination. The majority of the population has always been accustomed to buying its opinions. Now, once again, it was simply a matter of where one should shop. As for the gentlemen of MCC, there must have been plenty of telescopes and blind eyes in the committee-room even as the true picture was slowly forming.

As for the former Australian Test players, they did not all automatically line up against Bodyline. Charlie Macartney, square-shouldered, short of stature, the greatest batsman between Trumper and Bradman, was full of praise for Larwood at every opportunity. As a 40-year-old he had faced the raw young miner during the 1926 tour of England, and his respect had sprung from there. Macartney was one of the few to take the trouble to compliment England's leg-trap fieldsmen for their work. The concentration needed by them, with a touch of bravery too (none wore helmets or shinguards), has usually been overlooked.

The remarkable and likeable Arthur Mailey, too, remained reluctant to condemn. In his book on the tour, which revealed occasional inattention to detail but was threaded throughout with his lovely sense of whimsy, he is generous to all who took part in the series. Modern readers would be stunned to see his reference to "we Britishers" on page 2 and intrigued by his profiles of the Englishmen, with whom he became so friendly, as was his wont. The severest thing the old googly bowler could say about Jardine was that he "adopted a relentless Napoleonic attitude" and ought not to have declared war on the Australian Pressmen. A typical Maileyism concerned the cure for barracking: simply keep Jardine away from Australian cricket grounds. Leg theory, he wrote, was "vivid, risky and adventurous", unlike off theory, which was as outdated as crinoline. He did concede that if Bodyline continued, batsmen would be compelled to wear baseball masks. And look at the huge crowds! Everyone sat up and stared when Larwood had the ball.

Which leaves the serious minds of M.A. Noble, Australia's studious captain in the Edwardian years, and Jack Ryder, easy-going and respected skipper last time England were in Australia. Noble persuasively classified Bodyline as "preventable cruelty" while remaining unforgiving as far as Bradman's performances went. He berated him for his "sensational desire to score off everything", and was unhappy that Woodfull had not checked him in this style of play. (He was not to know that the captain disapproved to the point where he was tempted to vote for Bradman to be dropped.) Noble believed that England "revelled in his indiscretion and laughed up their sleeves because they knew he was doing just what they wanted".

While exonerating Larwood over the injury to Oldfield, Noble said in a broadcast that Woodfull's protest was understandable — "outraged feelings reaching breaking point" — and he could not understand how the MCC managers could stand by and not insist that an end be put to this type of bowling.[21]

According to Kippax,[22] Hugh Massie, Jim Kelly, Jack Gregory, Herby Collins, Roger Hartigan and C.T.B. Turner were other Australian Test veterans opposed to Bodyline. Ryder was one of the many whose minds were changed by the events of Adelaide. Previously he had reckoned leg theory to be yet another challenge to batsmen. Now he saw the pitfalls and believed that Australia should give it back, should retaliate. Many of England's batsmen, he believed, would not stand up to such a battering. If he had still been in charge of the Australian side, or if Vic Richardson had been brought in to replace an overwrought Woodfull, what carnage there might have been.

And what about the opinion of the man who stood literally at the bullseye of the whole affair, D.G. Bradman? On January 30 he wrote a confidential two-page typed letter to the MCC secretary.[23] It was a plea for "the betterment of our glorious game of cricket" and he "dared to write" it only after considerable thought. Its tone was humble, its wording slightly stilted. He hoped it would be placed before the committee. If they were prepared to listen to his suggestion he would feel "very honoured".

His constructive thought was that, having helped bowlers by increasing the size of the wicket, the lawmakers might now consider extending the lbw law to allow for dismissal by inswingers and offcutters pitching outside the line but heading for the stumps. This would make for more willing strokeplay, more slips catches, more lbws, and better prospects for legspinners when they encountered left-hand batsmen. "Unquestionably teams would make less [sic] runs. To my mind it would be in the best interests of the game if this was so." (How generous can you get?)

Bradman ended with apologetic — self-defeatingly so? — words about his inexperience when compared to the members of MCC and apologised for troubling them. The letter deserved a thoughtful reply. It received none at all.

CHAPTER TEN

SILENT
MANOEUVRES

We look now at the intrigue going on behind the scenes, beyond the whispering and the strained conversation in the ACB's chambers and various State cricket association offices, beyond the nodding and guffawing in St John's Wood, beyond the newspaper outbursts, beyond the speculations and concerns afflicting the agitated and bemused man in the street.

Certain files and records at Lord's and in the Australian Board's archives were lost long ago. How lost? We can but guess. Even a file opened by the Australian Prime Minister's Department (748/1/291: English Cricket Team 1932), Phil Derriman discovered in 1984, is no longer visible.[1] Nor, as Sissons and Stoddart found in writing *Cricket and Empire*, also in 1984, is there any trace among the official records of the Australian or British cabinets of any formal discussion about Bodyline. Laurence Le Quesne, during research for his 1983 book, established that a file in the Dominions Office — which he assumed would have been "very bulky" following formal meetings known to have taken place between principals — had been destroyed. Sissons and Stoddart found that the Public Record Office, London file F20436/2 concerning the Dominions Office involvement in discussions over Bodyline (it lists 43 entries up to June 1934) has not been preserved; even the index to it is closed to the public. Of the Dominions Office's extensive interest in the matter and activity at the time there can be no doubt (it is known, for instance, that it even allowed MCC to use its diplomatic cipher codes when cabling Jardine and Warner), and the

Secretary of State for the Dominions, the fascinating J.H."Jimmy" Thomas, played a colourful role, probably applying a little political "guidance" to the gentlemen of Lord's.

As for MCC, the club's archivist explained to Le Quesne that some papers had probably been disposed of during the war, when the RAF commandeered Lord's (and, let it be added without trace of suspicion, at a time when P.F. Warner — now Sir Pelham — was acting as MCC's "deputy secretary"). There was also a nationwide waste-paper drive for the war effort, though this fails to explain why many older files still remain intact. If reputations were being protected, the weakness of such strategy — if sensitive minutes, letters and reports (not least those written by Warner and Jardine) were indeed spirited away — lies in the fact that responsibility for any "poor fielding" at Lord's during the Bodyline crisis will rest forever with *all* those eminent men on the committee collectively. It is not as if they remain anonymous. Their names have already appeared here (as have those of the Australian Board members) and are laid out elsewhere, most accessibly in *Wisden* for 1933.

A certain amount of additional material has surfaced, and it seems unlikely that anything further of real significance will come to light to alter our understanding of how the matter unfolded. The amount of back-room diplomacy which transpired from the moment that ball pounded into Woodfull's chest is quite extraordinary. The disapproval of the ACB's first cable, expressed in a telegram from Victorian parliamentarian Wilfred Kent Hughes to the Board, signalled but the start of concern at political level.

The cardinal figure, in that he was the most influential of go-betweens, is the Governor of South Australia, Sir Alexander Hore-Ruthven. Had he still been in Adelaide instead of enjoying a break in England when the third Test was played, Bodyline might well have been extinguished there and then, and Anglo-Australian relations, instead of being stretched to breaking point, could perhaps have been swiftly repaired as the Governor gently banged certain heads together. Of all people, he might have been able to persuade Jardine that it was time for a rethink. As it was, the England captain, according to one of Gubby Allen's letters in January 1933, was already a changed man: "The whole thing has given Douglas a great fright and seems to have done him good. He is less bumptious and seems to look on the leg theory in a more gentlemanly light." (Allen thought the Australian cable a "common outburst" but MCC's reply "magnificent, so dignified".)

Hore-Ruthven was a genial, physically impressive and approachable man, second son of Lord Ruthven, of distinguished Scottish lineage, born in Windsor in 1872, christened Alexander Gore Arkwright, known to close friends as "Sandy", and educated at Eton.

SIR ALEXANDER HORE-RUTHVEN, GOVERNOR OF SOUTH AUSTRALIA, DISTINGUISHED SOLDIER AND CRICKET-LOVER. HIS CONCERN FOR ANGLO-AUSTRALIAN TRADE AND FRIENDSHIP CAUSED HIM TO PRESS HARD FOR A SOLUTION TO THE BODYLINE IMBROGLIO.

The shining feature of his curriculum vitae was his Victoria Cross, won in 1898 for saving a wounded officer from advancing Dervishes in one of his many actions in the Sudan. Numerous other military decorations followed, and as he moved into the realms of the vice-regal his duties as Military Secretary to Lord Dudley, the Governor-General, took him to Australia, following earlier visits with Dudley and with Lord Kitchener. In Elliott Monfries's little book *Not Test Cricket*, Hore-Ruthven is pictured alongside such luminaries as George Giffen, Hugh Trumble, Frank Laver, Vernon Ransford and Gerry Hazlitt in Lord Dudley's team in 1910. The outbreak of the First World War saw Hore-Ruthven returning to action as an officer in the Welsh Guards and being severely wounded at Gallipoli, where he was awarded the DSO.

His term as Governor of South Australia began in 1928, and the popularity of this soldier–statesman was widespread from the start. No sooner had his departure from Government House, Adelaide in 1934 been lamented than he was back in Australia, this time as Governor of New South Wales. He was soon to succeed Sir Isaac Isaacs as Governor-General of Australia, and became Lord Gowrie of Canberra and of Dirleton in 1935. An MCC member from an early age, he became the club's president in 1948.

In 1930 some strictures which he (as Governor) had passed against, as *The Times* put it, "a small, active and noisy element of hotheads" had annoyed the Australian Trades & Labor Council, who lodged an official protest. This did not prevent the Labor government from extending Hore-Ruthven's term, and his constructive intervention probably underlined his eminent qualification for sorting out the mess made of Anglo-Australian relations by Bodyline bowling. The trouble was, he happened to be 12,000 miles away when it mattered most.

But he had a private secretary, the "Comptroller", a man named Cyril Legh Winser, English-born but long resident in South Australia, a State he represented as wicketkeeper in five matches either side of the First World War. Winser had once kept to the bowling of S.F. Barnes and played against W.G. Grace, but his cricket gave way to golf, and in time he was to win the 1921 Australian Amateur Open at Royal Melbourne. Winser served under six successive governors of South Australia from 1915, but it was his term with Hore-Ruthven in which cricket featured with unique significance, for it was Winser who arranged for a cable to be sent to his Governor in England to say that senior citizens in Adelaide were extremely alarmed at what was happening. He urged his boss to speak with the Dominions Office in London without delay.

Legh Winser died in 1983 in his 100th year, but in the early 1970s the file of correspondence — to and from Sir Alexander Hore-Ruthven — which Winser had stored for nigh-on 40 years was sent to Lord's for safe keeping at the instigation of a neighbour, Geoffrey Adams, a director of a newspaper group in Victoria. Adams happened to be a former Hampshire amateur batsman who had scored 31 against Notts in 1930, finishing up "black and blue all up the left side" (Larwood wasn't playing but Voce was). Cricket owes something to Adams for his alertness; the papers could so easily have been dumped or destroyed. However, in keeping with Bodyline's theme of confrontational difficulties, researchers were refused access, and in time the

Hore-Ruthven (Gowrie) family laid claim to the papers, the rest of the Hore-Ruthven archives having already been deposited in the National Library of Australia. Adams had told would-be interviewers during the 1980s that "there was stuff in there that I thought the Press boys in Australia shouldn't get hold of". (He was also convinced that the intimidatory fast bowling now widespread in Test cricket was far more dangerous than 1930s Bodyline.) Some — probably all — of those papers have been perused in the MCC Library in the course of the writing of this book.

Legh Winser's own diary (now kept at the South Australian State Archives) is crucial in plotting the chain of off-field events. On January 11, two days before the Test match, there was an official dinner at the elitist Adelaide Club. It was hosted, in the Governor's absence, by his deputy, Lieutenant-Governor G.R.J. Murray, KC, who came from one of Adelaide's most distinguished pastoralist dynasties. With Warner, Palairet and Jardine present, the other guests in what may safely be assumed to have been an Anglophile gathering included Sir Walter Duncan, another leading pastoralist and a Member of the Legislative Council.

Five nights later, in the thick of the Test match, another important dinner was held, this time with Sir Walter Young, head of the great Australian rural trading company Elder Smith, at the head of the table. In view of the injuries to Woodfull and Oldfield, there must have been little else but anxious cricket talk. The following day, Winser recorded, MCC manager P.F. Warner called upon the Lieutenant-Governor, Sir George Murray. His mission must surely have been to seek support in high places for his so-far-futile efforts to put an end to Bodyline bowling while getting the ACB to recant on its use of "unsportsmanlike", for ugly cracks in the Old Relationship were starting to appear.

In Adelaide there were many who cared. In addition to Murray, Duncan and Young, mentioned above, there was Sir Wallace Bruce, chairman of the federal committee set up to look into the acute economic problems facing Australia. There was also Sir John Duncan-Hughes, a war hero, senator and very prominent civic figure with considerable industrial interests.

Out of all the anxious discussion emerged a trio — Sir Walter Young, and the manager of the Adelaide *Advertiser* newspaper, and his editor, Lloyd Dumas — who strongly urged Winser to persuade the Acting Governor to cable the Governor in England, as previously mentioned.[2] Hore-Ruthven accepted the message with due gravity and went to see J.H. Thomas, the Dominions Secretary, in Downing Street, London on February 1. The continuation of the Test series was still in the balance. Yet another heavy-weight figure was in attendance: Sir Thomas Inskip, the United Kingdom Attorney-General. So too were four members of the MCC committee: Viscount Lewisham (president), Viscount Bridgeman, Sir Kynaston Studd and Sir Stanley Jackson. By now there was an added threat that not only Jardine but many — possibly all, perforce — of his team would quit the tour if Australia did not withdraw the word "unsportsmanlike". All parties at this conference declined to comment afterwards, though Thomas uttered an aside to the effect that "any idea that I am intervening in the dispute is more of a leg-pull than leg-bowling".

Nonetheless it seems that progress was being made. Hore-Ruthven sent a telegram next day to his deputy in Adelaide, Sir George Murray, and followed it with a letter. The cable informed Murray that MCC realised the results of the Tests were unimportant when set beside Empire relations, but they strongly resented "unsportsmanlike" in the Board's cable. "MCC will make every effort to arrive at amicable solution on the basis withdrawal this charge." So there was hope.

The lengthier communication, the letter, was responded to by Murray six weeks later, and survives as part of the Winser cache of correspondence held at Lord's. Murray was keen to reach the Governor before he sailed back to Australia. He told Hore-Ruthven that he had shown that letter, in confidence, to Walter Young, Duncan Hughes, Fred Downer and Legh Winser, and they all felt obliged to him for making the approach to MCC, and to the committee for their "sympathetic interest". He moved on to air an opinion that Jardine was "a curious person". During the final tour match Warner and Palairet had invited Murray, among others, to dinner. "Jardine refused to come because Hodgetts, a member of the Board of Control, was a guest, but he had dinner in mufti at another table beside us." It was almost as if Jardine were prescient, for Hodgetts's career as a stockbroker was to end in disgrace and jail 12 years later. In September 1945 he was found to be bankrupt and guilty of fraudulent conversions and false pretences. Don Bradman, his trainee and office manager, who had stayed — with Jessie — at Hodgetts's luxury home while their own house in Kensington Park was being built in 1935, then benefited from the overnight adoption of Hodgetts's entire client list.

Sir George Murray penned an opinion on the Australian Board's opening cable to MCC, the one which had been dispatched during the Adelaide Test. He was certain, he said, that it was not sent because Australia were losing: "It was inspired, I believe, by putting an immediate stop to the danger batsmen were exposed to by the new mode of attack. If it had been sent after the second Test in Melbourne or after the whole series had been completed, it would have had little or no effect. A protest should be prompt." These remarks were reinforced by the imposing letterhead: Judges' Chambers, Supreme Court, Adelaide.

From a letter Hore-Ruthven wrote to Dominions Minister Thomas after his return to Australia and with the tour now over, the conclusion has to be drawn that, like the majority of people so far away from the scene, even *he* was *still* not completely aware of the ocean of feeling that had been stirred up in Australia by Bodyline.

It was typewritten and dated June 21, 1933. Hore-Ruthven remained concerned at the damaged feelings still evident between the two nations. He had observed a "deep sense of injustice" in Australia which sprang from the knowledge that matters had been unfairly represented in England and that MCC continued to display no sign of regret over Bodyline. (How could they, some were asking, without betraying the team they had selected?) But when he returned to Australia the Governor had had his eyes fully opened to the realities. He had spoken to "sound, reasonable men" and found himself "forced to the conclusion that the Australian case had far more justification than one would have been led to suppose at the other side of the world".

He conceded that leg theory and barracking were separate issues ("how can you control fifty thousand indignant people?") and that MCC had erred in making Jardine captain while being aware of his "temperament and reputed antipathy towards Australia which had not escaped notice in the previous tour". Then Hore-Ruthven tabled the growing fear that the 1934 tour might not go ahead. This would widen the breach, and "our prestige as sportsmen will suffer all over the world".

Hore-Ruthven next unwrapped his plan (to further lubricate Anglo-Australian relations and allow the 1934 tour to proceed) for J. H. Thomas's consideration: if MCC are not prepared to bend (on the matter of future bowling tactics and any amendment to the laws, which would be seen as a climbdown), then it would be beneficial if the newspapers in England, free of all shackles, would project a fair presentation from *both* sides:

"it would have a very good effect here [Australia] and pave the way to a reception of the Australians if they go to England next year". He emphasised how restrained the Australian newspapers had been, and their players too. But he deplored the "ill-timed effusions of Jardine and Larwood" after they returned to England and cited a recent headline which stated that Australia had received a "well-deserved snub" from MCC.

Australians, he said, were susceptible to criticism, but they were also susceptible to sympathy and consideration, and all that was probably needed to break the impasse was an indication, "however slight", that there was some justification for their attitude (which was one of deep resentment, though the Governor was too tactful to say so).

Then he played his ace: "That feeling rankles even to the extent of reluctance to buy English goods, which business men inform me is going on to a certain extent in this city [Adelaide] today." The UK newspapers could be the "best instrument" to bring about a relaxation of the tension. Then "these unfortunate misunderstandings would disappear and we could resume our cricket contests in the happy and friendly spirit which has always existed in the past". (And Britain's export trade to Australia would be restored to maximum potential, he scarcely needed to add.) Of all Hore-Ruthven's many letters written that year, this one seems to embody sufficient comment to give us a full appreciation not only of the political complexities but of his personal understanding and anxiety.

After the explosions of the third Test match, the newspaper editors of Adelaide did exchange correspondence with some of their opposite numbers in England, but in the case of *The Times* and its editor, Geoffrey Dawson, the communications were considered in retrospect to have been "not over-warm". Lloyd Dumas in particular was keen to reduce the level of ridicule aimed at Australia, many of the inflammatory remarks having been picked up by the Australian papers.

In the Legh Winser file held at Lord's, a five-page letter by Dumas, written on June 17, 1933, on the letterhead of the *Advertiser*, is by way of a draft for Hore-Ruthven's approval before it was circularised to the editors of all Britain's major newspapers. Its main objective was to give them "something which will make them realise that there is an Australian viewpoint, and that it cannot be ignored without possibilities of serious harm".

Dumas referred to the injury to Woodfull. An "audible wave of sympathy swept through the crowd. But there was no outburst against Larwood, for the field at that moment was an orthodox one, and cricket-lovers know that, with a fast bowler of Larwood's calibre, such an accident may happen at any time." He was scathing in his recall of how the field was switched to leg for bumpers to be bowled at a "disabled man". Then came the unprecedented demonstration, a spontaneous expression of anger from every part of the ground. "Nothing has caused more resentment in Australia than the calm assumption by English critics that nothing unusual occurred out here." He believed that 95 per cent of those who saw it felt with passionate sincerity that it was unsportsmanlike, "and these included men like Darling, Hill, Noble, Woodfull and others". He then cited Walter Hawker's statistics on dangerous deliveries.

"We know sales in England of Australian wines and other commodities fell off considerably," Dumas concluded. "The manifestation of feeling at this end, fortunately, has not taken that form. But it may do so. The possibility is one to cause grave concern; for history is full of instances where serious consequences have followed upon the most trivial causes." He then remarked that his and other Australian newspapers had refused for months to open their columns to discussion on the subject.

Reverting to early February 1933, there can be no reasonable doubt that J.H. Thomas conveyed Hore-Ruthven's sentiments to his Cabinet colleague Viscount Hailsham (Leader of the House of Lords, Secretary of State for War). Being president-elect of MCC, Hailsham would in turn have conferred with his friends on the club's committee. Yet another man of great distinction, not least on the battlefield (he had also narrowly escaped death by bullet in the Boer War), Hailsham had attended the Ottawa Imperial Conference in 1932, and was among those who would not want the country's — or the Empire's — economies damaged by some blasted cricket match. Thomas must also have passed on such general but pertinent comments as Hore-Ruthven conveyed to him in a separate confidential report about the people of South Australia — that they tended towards insularity and had much to learn from the outside world: "The slightest hint from an outsider that all is not perfection causes offence at once. The narrow and confined outlook of the people is in inverse proportion to the breadth and expanse of the country, and accounts a good deal for the lack of progress."[3]

RT HON. J.H.THOMAS, SECRETARY OF STATE FOR THE DOMINIONS, ONE OF WHOSE MAIN DUTIES WAS TO GUARD AGAINST ANYTHING HARMFUL TO IMPERIAL RELATIONS. *(COURTESY LABOUR PARTY)*

Jimmy Thomas, this central figure, was a Welshman, born into poverty in 1874. He left council school at 12 and rose through the ranks of the railwaymen, starting as an engine-cleaner and becoming a moderate general secretary of the National Union of Railwaymen in 1918. In Ramsay MacDonald's Labour government, overcoming the disappointment of having lost his seat on the Labour Party executive to Oswald Mosley, he had impressed with his eloquence, joviality and tact while serving as Secretary of State for the Colonies, and now he was being brought into an international dispute, his lowly origins and trade union commitment rendering him an unlikely agent for persuasion against the powers at Lord's.

Thomas, whom the King befriended, was renowned for "a defiant avoidance of the aspirate". He liked a beer and a joke, and this quality would have eased his negotiations with all at governmental and sporting levels, even if he was approaching a sorrowful end as a politician. He "developed a proneness for intemperance"[4] and his political career ended in 1936 when a judicial tribunal found he had leaked Budget secrets to friends. ("I don't think Jim deliberately gave anything away," said Stanley Baldwin, who was by then Prime Minister. "What he most likely did was to let his tongue wag when he was in his cups.")

We can only guess what the vanished Dominions Office files contained, but it is a fair assumption that those records would have revealed concern at the highest level about matters over which Bodyline cast a shadow: the serious threat to trade to and from Australia in those frightening times of falling production and mounting debts, and to relations within the Empire, perhaps even to future military co-operation. The files must surely also have included minutes — however sparely written — of meetings the purpose of which was to encourage MCC to do whatever was necessary to patch up the quarrel, notwithstanding the fact that the majority of Britons, whether in government positions or not, preferred to see Australia continuing to be reliant upon Britain. The force of the economic factors which formed the background to Bodyline should never be underestimated: Australia's high protectionist tariffs on goods from Britain caused continuing offence, as to Australians did the magnitude of loan interest imposed by Britain on her former colony. Australia's parlous economic position, relying as heavily as the young nation did on British favour, affected all thinking, not least in the cricket committee-rooms.

A versifier named MacFlecknoe (to judge from the clever message and irregular beat he might have been a relative of Spike Milligan's) summed it up succinctly in five smart verses in the *New Statesman*, the last three of which read:[5]

> *Dimly one can see the process — say that British exports fall:*
> *"If you'll give us further preference, Larwood shall not bowl at all."*
> *While if meat should be in question then experience suggests*
> *An increased Australian quota, in return for four-day Tests.*
>
> *But while thus employing cricket to cement the Commonwealth,*
> *We shall make it clear that Britons don't play cricket for their health;*
> *If a Test match should be cancelled we shall tax at higher rate*
> *All Australia has to send us, to recoup the vanished "gate".*
>
> *So the weapons that have banished unemployment from our land*
> *And impressed the Irish voter with the weight of Britain's hand*
> *Shall be sharpened and perfected — that is how it seems to me —*
> *By the aid of Jimmy Thomas, Larwood and the MCC.*

If British sympathy towards Australia has diluted in some quarters in recent times, in 1933 it was only six years since the British government had chosen to spare Australia an enormous embarrassment. In his in-depth report on the 1915 Gallipoli military campaign, the compiler of the official

British history of Gallipoli, Brigadier-General Cecil Aspinall, found himself (in 1927) challenging the hallowed myth of Anzac performance as chronicled in 1921 by the Australian war historian C.E.W. Bean. Aspinall apparently had no intention of hurting feelings, and must have been relieved when the War Office and many of the principal military figures gave their approval to his work. But the Australian government lodged a strong objection to certain passages, and these were expunged before the account was published. There was a leak, followed by predictable outrage in some quarters, but with certain areas of Aspinall's evidence duly suppressed the official British account of Gallipoli now harmonised with the Australian history and imperial relations escaped fairly bruise-free.[6]

The author of the 1933 anti-Bodyline tirade The "Sporting" English? chose to close his 88-page book with lengthy extracts from the Melbourne newspapers of September and October 1927, which had suggested there were no justifiable grounds for Aspinall's conclusions. General Sir John Monash, the Australian commander who knew as much as anybody about what went on at Gallipoli, branded the findings as "just another of those depreciations of the Australian soldier which appear every two or three months in England". He refuted the claim that his men were "an ill-trained, ill-led, disorganised rabble" and stated that the Dominion generals had a very poor opinion of the efficiency, discipline and leadership of some of the British troops, with the exception of the 29th Division at Cape Helles. Mention is made of how the Australians filled the breach opened by the helpless collapse of the British 5th Army at Mondicourt, France in 1918, leaving the reader to wonder if the term "Allies" had much meaning after all.

Would Bodyline, which nobody seemed able to suppress, now prove just as damaging to relations between the two countries? And might the Gallipoli wrangle of 1927 even have caught Jardine's eye and strengthened his desire to demonstrate how much tougher than his Aussie counterpart the British soldier (cricketer) inherently was? During the Brisbane Test, in acknowledging Paynter's triumph over physical hardship, he was certainly quick to summon visions of the resilience of the British troops in the 19th century Afghan War .

It so happened that the aforementioned Australian military historian Dr Bean was among those who fired off letters to the Sydney Morning Herald at the height of the Bodyline furore. He reminded readers that schoolboys had always been taught that bowling at the body was a mean trick for which the school colours could be withdrawn, while in decent club cricket it was normally ruled out of order. He feared that batteries of fast bowlers would be developed to win matches by bowling at the man, and that a leading batsman might soon be killed. The game, he said, would soon have an element of the prize fight. He stopped short of recalling how even the Turks and Aussies were capable of sportsmanship in rare moments amidst the blood-letting at Gallipoli.

A few frank words from the engaging Jimmy Thomas at a farewell function at Claridge's for Sir Julien Cahn's private cricket team before it left for Canada in August 1933 provided proof, should it still have been sought, that the behind-the-scenes activities in Downing Street and at Lord's earlier in the year had caused Thomas, for one, a headache or two: "No politics ever introduced in the British Empire caused me so much trouble as this damn bodyline bowling!" So much for "a spokesman's" denial that there had been any official interference. Whether he had his tongue in his cheek or not we shall never know, but Thomas urged Cahn not to take Larwood to Canada with him. (Cahn, a wealthy furniture merchant in the Midlands, had already made clear his support for Harold Larwood. At a dinner he had said, with all the pomposity he could muster, "I am not going to have anything said against Larwood, because he is a member of my club." Here in the making was one of cricket's great *volte-faces*.)

Then in the following year, at a function at the Criterion welcoming the 1934 Australians, a few more words from Thomas were preserved on newsreel: "Bodyline bowling?" he chirruped. "As Dominions Secretary I'm strictly impartial! The Prime Minister [looking across mischievously at Ramsay MacDonald] tries to talk about it. About the only game he knows about is marbles!" A clever little piece of obfuscation at which Bill Woodfull and his players laughed with relief.

If MCC remained unshiftable early in 1933 and resisted whatever pressure the British government might have put on it (it is equally possible that Thomas and others were telling Lord's to hold fast), the Australian Board, in its currently weaker position, was vulnerable to political pressure. In the gap between the third and fourth Test matches the tour had somehow to be saved, though any pressure to persuade England to abandon Bodyline seemed to be based on wishful thinking. The financial and moral requirement to keep the series going depended on one thing now: soothing England's indignation by rescinding the allegation of unsportsmanlike play levelled at them in the opening cable.

It was supposed by some that had Warner telephoned Lord's he would have been given plenipotentiary power to control Jardine's strategy. Assuming Jardine would not simply then have told Warner to go away and not bother him, the captain, alternatively, might have felt obliged to listen to Warner and abandon Bodyline. But he was much more likely to have walked out. He was, after all, not a subservient paid professional. Warner, with time still on his side, was convinced that the ACB would soon withdraw the offending word, allowing the tour to continue. In a letter to Agnes dated January 27 he expressed this view and vented his feelings about the clumsy remarks coming from both sides of the world: the Board's cable had been "silly, tactless and rude", while Lord Hawke's outburst about Australian hostility during the 1921 Tests caused his old friend to write that he wished Lord Hawke would not make speeches: "he always says something stupid". Not all was grimness, however: Warner also told his understanding wife that he and Jardine had made up a four for a supper party and dance, and that his partner at said party and dance had told him that she wished some of the young men danced as well as he did. Another dinner party and piano recital and some weekend tennis alleviated the hardships.[7]

The crucial step that saved the tour was taken by Warner on February 1. That was the day he sent a telegram to E.T. Crutchley, who, without having the full status of High Commissioner, was nevertheless head of the British Mission in Canberra. There, as Sissons and Stoddart outlined in their book, Crutchley had forged an important friendship with Keith Officer, of Australia's External Affairs department. Officer and Crutchley were both Gallipoli survivors and both cherished the Anglo-Australian bond. Officer had met the touring English cricketers in Melbourne, and introduced Crutchley to people who mattered when Crutchley was a somewhat unconnected newcomer to Canberra. In addition Crutchley was friendly with R.G. Casey, a rising Australian diplomat, winner of a DSO at Gallipoli, member of Lyons's cabinet, and a future Governor-General. Casey was currently in London, and had opened further doors for Crutchley. There was no shortage of men anxious to resolve this ugly cricket conundrum.

Ernest Crutchley was somebody whom J.H. Thomas himself ought perhaps to have contacted by now, but apparently he had not. Crutchley had been a passenger on *Orontes* as she bore the English cricketers to Australia, and he came to know them well. In his diary he had actually predicted trouble, penning this thought after a shipboard dinner: "The usual stuff about the Test team being ambassadors of Empire. I wonder! If the crowd are as hostile to Jardine as they have been in the past I can see anything but good coming of the visit."[8]

ERNEST CRUTCHLEY, ANOTHER OF THE AGENTS IN THE WIDE-RANGING DIPLOMATIC NETWORK.

In this desperate hour Warner clearly realised that a direct approach from himself to the Australian Prime Minister would be improper. Having already filled Crutchley in on details of the unpleasant Adelaide episode, he turned to him once more, in the hope that Crutchley could persuade the PM, J.A. Lyons, to bring pressure to bear on the Australian Board.

Even here embarrassment flushed cheeks. This time it sprang from mischief on the part of a clerk in the telegraph office. He leaked Warner's uncoded communication to the Press. When questioned in Toowoomba, Palairet confirmed that the contact had indeed been made and said he hoped good would come of it. Crutchley, although aghast at the leak, acted swiftly, telephoning Prime Minister Lyons in Melbourne. The weight of the Depression had broken numerous governments, and Lyons's coalition was one of several similar unlikely groupings charged with the virtual salvation of states. The general stance of the Federal government, and of most of the States' too, was not hostile towards Britain.

AUSTRALIA'S HIGHLY REGARDED AND LONG-SERVING PRIME MINISTER, J.A. LYONS.

Fortunately, Lyons was also sympathetic to cricket's cause. His first reaction to Crutchley's appeal was that it looked as though they were leading two opposing armies, but the PM immediately sought contact with ACB chairman Robertson, to whom he stressed the perils to Australia's economic stability posed by the unrelenting interest burden of the British conversion loans. Robertson now sent a telegram to Board secretary Jeanes which included an inadvertently false indicator. This, introduced earlier in Lyons's questioning of Crutchley, was to the effect that England might consider significantly modifying their bowling if the Board withdrew the "unsportsmanlike" charge. Warner had to make it clear now that no condition could be attached to the withdrawal of "the obnoxious word".

This was not the first high-level exchange on the cricket crisis for Lyons. He had been asked by his resident minister in London, S.M. Bruce, even while the Adelaide Test was in progress, if he might somehow reconcile the control bodies of the two countries. Stanley Melbourne Bruce, who somewhat reluctantly became Australia's Prime Minister (1923–1929), a constructive leader at that, might almost have stepped out of the Lord's committee-room himself to judge from his voice and appearance. A Cambridge man who rowed for the university in the 1904 victory over Oxford, he was admitted to the English bar and also saw action in 1915 at Gallipoli, where he was wounded and won the Military Cross and Croix de Guerre. This eminent Australian statesman, who lacked the common touch and was detested by most of the working class, wore spats and moved in the top circles of both government and society — usefully too, during these fevered weeks for cricket.

FORMER PRIME MINISTER S.M. BRUCE, A SPATS-WEARING ANGLOPHILE WHO,
DECEPTIVELY, WAS AUSTRALIAN THROUGH AND THROUGH.

It was S.M. Bruce who was Australia's chief representative and tough negotiator at the 1932 Ottawa economic conference, a gathering which went some way towards preserving the Empire. When Britain's Chancellor of the Exchequer, Neville Chamberlain, was proving obstinate about meat quotas, Bruce employed typical Australian frankness to move the matter on: "I saved the bloody Empire on Monday," he cracked. "It's your turn to save it now." The stability in trade established at that conference was to last many years.

Now, like so many others in 1933, S.M. Bruce, even though he occupied yet another heady post as Australia's representative at the League of Nations, knew that any attempt to apply pressure on Lord's would be a waste of time.

It would be he who would one day propose the toast to MCC at its 150th anniversary dinner. But that was four years off. Soon he was to speak at the welcome-home dinner given for Jardine and his team in London, and he took that opportunity to compare the controversy of Jardine's Harlequin cap with his own spats. Bruce recalled how his fellow Australians had objected when he brought some spats back from London. When he spotted some lampoonery in a newspaper he ordered six more pairs "and had to wear the wretched things for four years". He reflected that Australian crowds have true sporting instincts, and ill-feeling only comes when they are roused and believe they are right: "Whenever it is necessary to straighten out troubles, do it, for God's sake, by personal contact and not by exchanging notes."[9] Sometimes easier said than done.

Speculation was everywhere, for there had been yet another leak during the English team's long train journey up to Queensland. Warner's faintly desperate, unfettered remark that Bodyline would ruin cricket, his first uttered public criticism, was gleefully radiated by the journalists who were privy to it. Now, as the Australian Prime Minister and the Board members tried to rescue the tour, Warner engaged in further urgent, hopeful chat with the Queensland delegates, Hutcheon and Hartigan (the same Hartigan who had scored a century against England on his Test debut in 1908 at Adelaide).

Meanwhile, Crutchley came up with a suggestion: why shouldn't the Australian Board make Bill Jeanes, its secretary, the scapegoat and sack him so that the cabling could start all over again?[10] Mercifully, such a shabby injustice was not transacted.

As he awaited the arrival of the MCC team, the Governor of Queensland, Sir Leslie Wilson, was fully in the picture, having corresponded after the Adelaide Test with Legh Winser, Hore-Ruthven's secretary. He knew that "these Tests are doing a lot of harm as regards the good understanding within the Empire!" He had close friendships with both Warner and Jardine, and hoped to "pour oil on the troubled waters". He believed that trouble had been developing for 10 years — or even longer, when he thought of the upset at Sydney in 1903–04, when Warner was captain. "And this is supposed to be cricket!!" Hutcheon and Hartigan had already appraised Wilson of the unhappy feeling between the teams, leaving him doubting the wisdom of arranging any joint entertainment while the Englishmen were in Queensland.[11]

The excruciating suspense which for three weeks had gripped the nation, and in particular the cricket fraternity, was about to ease. The players had known little more than the general public as they relied on the thin and largely speculative coverage in the newspapers. But now, at last, Jack Hutcheon's subcommittee having done its job, the Australian Board, cognisant of the wider implications as laid out by Prime Minister Lyons, composed a carefully worded cable that brought smiles to the faces of the gentlemen at Lord's and relief to the embattled MCC cricketers, who had been waiting either to pad up for the Brisbane Test or pack up their bags for home.

AUSTRALIAN BOARD OF CONTROL TO MCC, February 8, 1933

We do not regard the sportsmanship of your team as being in question. Our position was fully considered at the recent meeting in Sydney and is as indicated in our cable of January 30. It is the particular class of bowling referred to therein which we consider is not in the best interests of cricket, and in this view we understand we are supported by many eminent English cricketers. We join heartily with you in hoping that the remaining Tests will be played with the traditional good feeling.

It was no abject climbdown. It actually marked a slight change in the tide. The remainder of the tour was no longer in jeopardy, the financial worries had been alleviated, and yet the flavour of Australia's objection to Bodyline had been neatly sustained. The onus of responsibility now swung to England, if not in the shorter term then most positively in the longer, for only a year hence Australia were scheduled to tour England. They wanted certain assurances beforehand and knew that MCC would be fully conscious of the need to uphold the Ashes tradition and protect the game's finances.

Lighten grief with hopes of a brighter tomorrow, wrote Horace, adding cautiously: Temper joy, in fear of a change of fortune.

CHAPTER ELEVEN

FROM A
HOSPITAL BED

On the day when stability of a sort was secured by the Board's cable, Plum Warner, in a letter to his wife, below a Queensland Club letterhead, vented further deep misgivings about Jardine: "Nothing can compensate me for the moral and intellectual damage which I have suffered on this tour," he wrote. "DRJ is very trying and is now a bundle of nerves ... DRJ is half-mad but the men are splendid and stick to me when I tell them that only the end matters. Bear with him until we win (or lose) and then say what you like to him ... DRJ must not captain again. He is most ungracious, rude and suspects all. He really is a very curious character and varies like a barometer. He is very efficient but inconsistent in his character and no leader. I ought to get a prize for patience or tact and good temper if not a knighthood!! 75% of the trouble is due to DRJ's personality. We all think that. DRJ has almost made me hate cricket. He makes it war. I do hope the Test will go happily. I rather dread it."[1]

After the Adelaide victory the Englishmen had moved on to Ballarat for a two-day match against a Victorian Country XIII. Some thought that the inclusion in the local side of Harry "Bull" Alexander (Essendon and Victoria) meant that the MCC batsmen were about to absorb some retaliatory Bodyline, but the ACB sent a caution to Ballarat that this was not to be allowed. Besides, the pitch was too soft and slow. Even so, a Ballarat fast–medium bowler named Stalker bowled leg theory without a concentrated leg field and took four wickets, starting with Jardine's (bowled), a reward that would have been even better but for dropped catches. The large crowd relished the discomfort displayed by the Englishmen as they fended off deliveries from Stalker and the nippy Alexander, leaving *The Australian Cricketer* to surmise that they would have done no better than the Australians if faced with full-blown Bodyline in the Tests. Neither Sutcliffe nor Allen was comfortable, while Leyland and Pataudi "performed various contortions in trying to get away from the leg balls". The rolypoly Yorkshireman tried dancing down the pitch when Alexander was bowling but it availed him little.

Here in the old gold-mining town the atmosphere was not as relaxed as is usually the case with touring teams' visits to country centres. Councillor Harrison, the acting mayor, set the pattern. Instead of the customary welcoming speech, he launched into a diatribe on Bodyline: "Woodfull has not adopted leg theory bowling by fast bowlers and I am gratified that Australia has not done so. That is your method … We in Australia are admirers of skill … We should not like to see brute force brought in to suppress skill." Jardine would not be drawn at length in his reply, but simply threw in the red herring about the high number of batsmen Larwood had bowled out.[2] The England captain was still smarting at a suggestion from one of the Pressmen that it was impossible to libel a cricketer. Plum Warner was at his historically allusive best, saying that while von Moltke (Chief of the German General Staff in the First World War) could be silent in seven languages, he (Warner) could be silent in one.

Percy Beames, Ballarat-born and aged 21, a future Victoria batsman and in time a well-respected sportswriter, recalled half a century later that "they never spoke to us and Jardine acted in a very supercilious way on the field".[3] The Victorian Country skipper, Bert Rogerson, found Jardine little interested in getting the game under way after rain on the Monday; he seemed more concerned about what was on at the cinema. When play was called off, only an hour's action having been possible, the English cricketers left the ground to collect their possessions from the hotel and then headed straight for the train to Melbourne. While waiting on the platform, Jardine caught sight of a locomotive warming up and began to study it with that stern gaze of his. Just to be friendly, the engine-driver scooped some hot cinders into his shovel and shouted across: "Hey, Mr Jardine, here are the ashes! Would you like to take them back to England with you?" DRJ tossed back his head and ignored him.[4]

The professionals in the side had formed The 77 Club. It gathered in the bar each Saturday night, sometimes with special friends, even Australians. The club tie was coloured blue, and had a rooster embroidered on it. (The "ground staff" — players such as Freddie Brown, who played little during the tour — had a brown tie bearing a little red rabbit.) A fine of five shillings was extracted from anybody found not to be wearing the 77 tie to breakfast on a Monday morning, the money going into a drinks kitty, with Larwood the collector of the penalties. On their Saturday night in Ballarat the English pros were having a merry and noisy time of it when their captain rang, asking for baggagemaster Fergie. As soon as the players realised it was Jardine on the line they raised the level of noise, shouting, whistling, clinking bottles, until it was almost impossible to continue with the phone call. "Who is making all that noise?" barked Jardine down the line. Fergie said he couldn't quite hear him. On the Monday, upon his return to the hotel Jardine made some enquiries, but got nowhere.[5]

CITY OVAL, BALLARAT, JANUARY 21, 23, 1933

MCC 255 (Nawab of Pataudi 84, M. Leyland 62, W. Stalker 4 for 62); VICTORIAN COUNTRY XIII 84 for 8 (M.W. Tate 3 for 22, T.B. Mitchell 4 for 31). DRAWN

Then came the return match with New South Wales, who had Fingleton hoping to get his Test place back and Bradman keen to show that he was not the disappointment that several of the oldtimers had portrayed him as (outside his Melbourne century). Immediately after the Adelaide Test match he had been able to get back to the most enjoyable kind of cricket, playing for Australian & English Press against a team from the Australian Navy. Over 4000 fortunates saw Bradman and Hobbs batting at the charming Rushcutters Bay Oval, just east of Sydney's city centre, with oldtimers M.A. Noble and Arthur Mailey among other great names treading the smooth turf, and with Admiral Dalglish in attendance.

While the Australian Board continued to cogitate over MCC's stiff cable of January 23, Jardine — Larwood too — took the New South Wales fixture off; the ankle injuries to Paynter and Voce kept them out of the match. The State team was lacking the injured Oldfield, and McCabe, O'Reilly and Hird had decided not to play. Still, the Australia Day crowd of over 23,000 had The Don to look forward to, and so were well pleased when Alan Kippax won the toss and took first use of the pitch.

Unhappily for the Sydneysiders, after Bowes and Tate failed to make an immediate breakthrough, legspinner Tommy Mitchell made a triple strike, first bowling Fingleton round his legs and then breaching Bradman's defence with a topspinner when, with only a single run to his name, he was caught in two minds. Mitchell then held Kippax as he tried to save his face from a Bowes bumper and bowled Cummins for 0, meaning that by just after lunch, all dreams of a day of merry runmaking by the star players were dead. But Bill Brown, the stylish Queenslander, aged 20 and in only his fourth match for his adopted State, gave a pointer to the future with a handsome 69 in 2¾ hours, drawing from Hobbs the ultimate in compliments when he wrote that Brown reminded him of Archie Jackson. Ray Rowe, a 19-year-old left-hander from the Cumberland club, was on first-class debut and was just as impressive, striking 70 in an hour and a half, though his drives, played from a crouching stance, tended to go in the air. The Brown/Rowe partnership for the fifth wicket amounted to 101, but there was little else. Brown had the misfortune to edge one of Bowes's lifters wide into the slips, in light so poor that the players were then forced from the field, having left it because of rain not so long previously. It was a bowlers' day, and would have been even more so if all catches had been held — Tate and Bowes suffered most.

The last five New South Wales wickets went down for four runs next morning, three to Hammond's offspin (with three short legs), two to Verity. But MCC fared little better on a wet pitch that was a joy to bowl on, even if their attitude seemed to be more relaxed than if it had been a Test match. Whereas Wyatt batted with the perfect combination of concentration and power, Hammond was caught in the deep and hardly seemed to care. Leyland and Brown (29 apiece) both hit sixes, the left-hander hampered by a stiff thigh muscle before falling to a catch by Rowe close to the pickets, and it was Verity's 33 that became second-top score in an innings that was only slightly bigger than their opponents'. Hughie Chilvers, the English-born legspinner, took the bowling honours for New South Wales. *Evening Standard* reporter Bruce Harris was touched by the discriminating behaviour of a Hill barracker who protested when Tate was hit by a short ball: "Hey, *that's Tate!*" he cried. The Sussex man was probably Sydney's favourite English cricketer.

The State lost Fingleton that evening, lbw to a Tate inswinger, before the small deficit was wiped off, and the third day started with Brown 18, Bradman 10. The Friday crowd of 15,000 sat in the cold, hardly knowing what to expect. Hedley Verity went to the middle before play began and pressed his thumb into the sodden turf. Turning to Wyatt, the MCC captain, he murmured, "Poor Don." It was thought that Bradman was watching from the pavilion and, if not actually lip-reading, could well imagine what the canny Yorkshire bowler had said. Hammond saw Bradman, when he reached the wicket, give Verity a very hard look. In all, Bradman batted for a little over two hours in this innings, to finish with a watchful and at times quite brilliant 71 that has sometimes been invoked as prime evidence that he could make runs on a dodgy pitch after rain when he put his mind to it. Anyway, Wyatt, with his peculiar sense of humour, never let Verity forget this.

Hammond picked up six wickets in the innings, nearly all caught very close to the bat in the leg trap. They included Bradman, who was snapped up off a kicking delivery by Ames, who was not keeping wicket. Brown again batted patiently, this time for 25. The pitch was not especially spiteful before lunch, but Hammond's eventual rich pickings left the impression that Verity, an accredited killer on such pitches, simply had an off day. As for poor Tate, who might have cleaned up, he was barely used.

MCC's target was 110, and at one stage they had lost six wickets for 70. But Brown and Tate saw them home. Bill Howell, son of the offspinner who had played for Australia at the turn of the century, opened the bowling with Bradman, Chilvers and Fingleton fielding in the leg trap, Brown, Kippax and Rowe also on the leg side, and no slips. Howell hit Wyatt three times in one over, and it was suggested that Larwood, sitting in the pavilion, might have been considering an action for breach of copyright. Then Chilvers, the flighty wrist spinner, had the unusual experience of getting two stumpings from different wicketkeepers. First, Love whipped off the bails as Hammond (24) walked into the shot but missed a legbreak, and after that keeper had been hit over the eye by Chilvers, Fingleton took over behind the stumps and brought off a slick stumping to send Ames on his way. After tea it was Leyland's straightforward belting of the ball (he had first Pataudi then Duckworth to run for him) followed by Tate's hearty strokeplay that brought the visitors victory. It was a match that had been high in entertainment value and more like a good old-fashioned game of cricket than Adelaide could ever have been. As for Bradman's attractive contribution, in reality, with Larwood and Voce not playing, it had been made against England's 2nd XI.

SYDNEY CRICKET GROUND, JANUARY 26, 27, 28, 1933

NEW SOUTH WALES 180 (W.A. Brown 69, R.C. Rowe 70, T.B. Mitchell 3 for 32, W.R. Hammond 3 for 22) and 128 (D.G. Bradman 71, W.R. Hammond 6 for 43); MCC 199 (R.E.S. Wyatt 63, H. Verity 33, C.J. Hill 3 for 39, H.C. Chilvers 5 for 73) and 110 for 6 (M. Leyland 33, H.C. Chilvers 3 for 29). MCC WON BY 4 WICKETS

The train that took the MCC team away from Sydney at 7.30 pm did not disgorge them in Brisbane until just over 21 hours later. They admired much of the scenery through the windows — from the Hawkesbury right up to the northern rivers, where Jack Hobbs was enchanted by the railway bridge over the Clarence that replaced the old punt, which had always cost passengers so much time. He was relieved that there was no hold-up at the border, in the wooded hills around Wallangarra, where there used to be a compulsory time-consuming change of trains because of the different gauges. Some of the cricketers had even left the train at breakfast time for a quick splash in the sea at Coff's Harbour.

For the first time in weeks the Englishmen were about to be "bathed in the spirit of good fellowship" as R.T. Corrie put it, for they were entering Queensland, whose average citizen was "fuller of nature's kindliness than the man from more closely settled States".[6] It would surely, though, be too much to expect that further jarring notes were not about to be sounded.

This time it was government entertainment tax that was the trivial cause of unpleasantness. MCC's treasurer, Dick Palairet, objected to the deduction of a very small amount (a penny on each five-shilling stand ticket) from the gate takings at the forthcoming matches in Queensland and strong words flew back and forth. Toowoomba cricket president Cecil Roberts calculated that the dispute was over £4.

The continuation of the tour was still in the balance at this stage, the ACB having as yet to satisfy MCC that they did not after all regard the English cricketers as lacking in sportsmanship. The flames would continue to flicker and leap as long as the public debate lasted. One of the strongest statements around this time was by Victorian judge W.H. Moule, who had taken three wickets for Australia in the Test match at The Oval in 1880. Responding to an article in the English journal the *Saturday Review*, Moule wrote:

Permit me, as an old cricketer, and as one who has founded my whole idea of cricket on what I deemed to be the standard fixed by England, to protest against your articles appearing in your issue of January 28. I feel it is my duty to protest against the vituperative expressions you have used ... I was present at the Test match played in Melbourne and at the match against the Australian XI, and thus had an opportunity of watching the fast bowling of England. I have no hesitation in saying that Larwood bowled AT the man ... If a fast bowler bowls often enough at a batsman he may well intimidate him, and so in the end hit the wicket ... Bowling at the man was the one complaint Australia made. It is not cricket and was never meant to be cricket ...

From Brisbane, the team immediately headed west for Toowoomba, which nestles in the picturesque Darling Downs. There, at the Showground, Hammond and Ames made hard-hitting centuries, Ames landing three sixes into the crowd, and the mighty Voce indulged in some big hits as MCC piled up 376 runs in only 261 minutes. The Queensland Country XII would have been stronger had Frank Sides (Townsville), Eddie Gilbert (Barambah), and Otto Nothling (Maryborough; he had played in a Test against England in 1928–29) been available, but there was a gifted 16-year-old in the side, Don Tallon, who earned praise from one and all for his wicketkeeping. Only a few years earlier he had helped push Bert Hinkler's aeroplane down the dusty main street of Bundaberg upon the aviator's triumphant homecoming. Now he stumped the great Herbert Sutcliffe off Hunter Poon (the first Sheffield Shield cricketer of Chinese descent: he finished with the extravagant analysis of 2 for 123 off only 15 overs). In time, Don Tallon was to play in 21 Tests for Australia; late in his life Bradman rated Tallon the best wicketkeeper he ever saw.

The Country team, led by Mo Biggs, were soon in big trouble at 29 for 5; Larwood was showing no mercy. Then Lew Litster and Brittle rallied the innings before Litster was bullied out by Freddie Brown. The first shout for leg-before found the umpire looking blank; the hectoring Surrey spinner appealed with even greater force, and up went the finger. Ralph Raymond stayed with Brittle while 108 runs were added in only 80 minutes, the highest-ever stand against an English touring side at Toowoomba (teams had been visiting since 1894–95). Larwood returned to blow away the last four wickets (including Tallon for 2) and finish with 8 for 28, though he was never quite at full stretch.

On the second day, a Thursday, MCC gave an exhibition of batting, the prime exhibit being the captain himself. Jardine's runmaking on this tour had fallen well short of the lofty level of 1928–29 and he remained worried as to whether he should keep himself in the Test XI, so the lovely drives that helped him to his unbeaten 77 gave him — as well as the true cricket-lovers of Toowoomba — much satisfaction. The unhappiest Englishman, as they departed, was Bill Voce, whose latest setback was an attack of influenza.

TOOWOOMBA SHOWGROUND, FEBRUARY 1, 2, 1933

MCC 376 (W.R. Hammond 101, L.E.G. Ames 121 not out, W. Voce 32, H. Larwood 36) and 187 for 3 (E. Paynter 45, D.R. Jardine 77 not out); **QUEENSLAND COUNTRY XII** 210 (L. Brittle 65 not out, R.C. Raymond 53, H. Larwood 8 for 28). **DRAWN**

The Englishmen rumbled off to Brisbane, via Ipswich, in an old charabanc which, according to Tate, rocked like a ship. He compared the 100-mile-or-so (about 160 km) journey with that rough sea voyage from Tasmania. The jovial warrior unpacked in the same room at the Belle Vue Hotel as he had occupied on the two previous MCC tours, although this time there was not quite the same sense of anticipation: "As leader of the MCC team there was another Pharaoh who knew not Joseph, and though I was still Maurice Tate to the locals and in my own heart, I was no longer regarded as the chief bowler in the side. It was a galling thought."[7] A consolation was a trip 50 miles (80 km) down the coast to see Governor Sir Leslie Wilson and his wife at their summer residence at Southport, on what is today called the Gold Coast.

As they had entered friendly Queensland, it was Governor Wilson who was undertaking to clear the way for the MCC cricketers through the oppressive background of the rumpus over "that word". But tension could not be banished so simply. While the Queensland Club was prepared to offer honorary membership to the English amateurs, it was not willing to allow its premises to be used for a dinner for the team.[8] Anyone caught acting dishonourably now — in Queensland at least — was said to be "coming a Larwood".

One incident fell just short of homicide. While Larwood, Voce, Ames, Duckworth and Mitchell were having a quiet drink at the Belle Vue one evening with the publican Mick Maguire, reporter Gilbert Mant and Tom Lawton (a Wallaby — rugby union player), in walked a big, bearded man who soon began to needle little bespectacled Tommy Mitchell (who, it must be said, seemed to be particularly talented at winding people up). With a beer or two already inside him, Mitchell removed his glasses and shaped up to the giant — who suddenly produced a revolver and began waving it around. Larwood and most of the others ducked for cover, but Maguire, a former boxer, flattened the menace, probably with the burly figure of Lawton as his second.[9]

In his 1992 memoir of the tour Mant reflected that Maguire had three beautiful teenage daughters, who often ran along the hotel verandahs in the morning "rather scantily clad", and that Douglas Jardine "took a shine to one of them". One of the girls became a film star, another married an English peer, and Jardine was never destined to take any of them home with him. As for the old Belle Vue Hotel, across the road from Brisbane's Parliament building, it was later bought by the State, and was eventually torn down in 1979.

Brisbane seems to have been one of the wildest towns in the Empire — for the English cricketers had yet another close encounter with a gun in the hotel bar! This time it was Bill Bowes, who recalled that he was with Leyland, Larwood and Voce when a "bushwhacker" came over and wanted to talk about Bodyline. Larwood was not keen to talk cricket but invited the man to have a drink. The man persisted though, and slammed his revolver on the bar, saying, "This'll probably make you." Larwood called for his much larger friend, Bill Voce, to come over, and Voce suggested that the fellow put his gun away. He argued, so Voce hit him. "What happened then I don't know," said Bowes, "because the bar emptied like a flash."[10]

Then there was Eddie Paynter's quite different version.[11] He was remembering either a third terrifying incident or an amalgam of the two previous tales. He placed it at the end of the Brisbane Test, when the players were enjoying themselves at the bar and some drunken locals kept calling them "Pommie bastards". This time it was Larwood who wanted to take them on, only for Bill Voce to restrain him and Micky Maguire to move him away when he saw one of the troublemakers reach into his pocket. Maguire telephoned for the police, and they all escaped with their lives.

The match against Queensland at the Gabba was over in three days, and still clearance for the tour to continue (or otherwise) had not been received. Warner's speech on arrival in Brisbane was laced with emotional phrases, touched in parts with a sense of desperation. "I pray for peace as much as any statesman ever prayed for peace … I hope and pray that the sky is clearing … If you stretch out your hand to us we shall grasp it eagerly. England and Australia are two great cricketing powers. We are the masters of cricket. We stand for everything in cricket. Anything that ruffles the calm surface of English and Australian cricket affects cricket all over the world. I say from the bottom of my heart that England and Australia in cricket must never drift away from each other." The man seemed close to breakdown, as he came close to confessing in his letters home.

Jardine, on the other hand, no matter what Warner wrote about his mental condition at this time, was in no mood for a long speech. He settled for a brief statement: "In the present trials and tribulations in the cricket world I hold very strongly that the least said the soonest mended. Believe me, it is not always very easy to remain silent."

When the Australian Board's cable of February 8 was published, relieving the pressure and allowing the tour to continue, Jardine was still not satisfied until he had spoken personally to Lord's by telephone, a longish and expensive call at £2 a minute. His only remaining reservation now was, once again, whether he should drop himself from the side for lack of batting form.

Queensland's captain, Frank Gough, made it clear there would be no "body bowling" if he had anything to do with it. It would cause the married men to withdraw, he said. The traditional Queensland hospitality was spoiled only by the mosquitoes, and the pre-match talk centred on whether Eddie Gilbert, the little Aborigine — he was only 5 ft 7 in tall (170 cm) — whose pace had sometimes been up with Larwood's, would give the Englishmen a taste of their own medicine. All kinds of lurid predictions were being made, for although Gilbert was not quite as fast as a year or two previously, and was now worried by an inflamed shoulder socket, the taunt had reached Larwood — from some of Gilbert's fans — that Gilbert had knocked Bradman's bat from his grasp, and that was something the Englishman had never managed to do. Bob Wyatt said that "one or two of our lot took him [Gilbert] to one side and said that if he did this [tried to intimidate the MCC batsmen] Larwood would knock his block off — so prudently he gave up". But not before hurting Jardine.

EDDIE GILBERT, A SOURCE OF FASCINATION — AND OFTEN FEAR — AMONG BATSMEN.

Eddie Gilbert had been no-balled a year earlier by umpire Andy Barlow at Melbourne, when he adjudged Gilbert to have thrown eight balls one evening and five next morning before Gough mercifully took him off. But he was back, and he would be bowling for a few years yet, even falling foul of umpire Borwick at Sydney in 1936 for intimidatory bowling. Many wished he was in the Test side, though Vic Richardson was not among them. In common with a few other contemporaries, he was convinced that Gilbert's action was illegal.

R.G. Menzies told of a warning to Pataudi that Gilbert would knock him out in the Queensland v MCC match, to which the Indian is supposed to have replied: "Not at all. When Eddie sees me standing at the wicket he will say 'No, I cannot kill a brother!' and will bowl slow."[12] Jack Fingleton said that Jardine told him that the morsel of barracking he most enjoyed during the tour was bellowed as he walked out to bat: "Get stuck into this ******* Pommie, Gilbert! It was his ******* mob that took all that land from your ******* mob!" The Jardine family had indeed owned land in Queensland's early days.[13]

At a still-primitive Gabba ground, where poinciana trees provided much-needed shade but barbed-wire partitions kept sections apart, Queensland batted first on a day of pleasant warmth against England's Test attack — apart from the unwell Voce. And they acquitted themselves capably until the tail collapsed. Tiny left-hander Roy Levy was caught by Allen out of the blinding sun when he miscued Larwood's second ball of the match, but Geoff Cook shaped an admirable three-hour half-century which included a six off Verity, the talented former New South Wales batsman Charlie Andrews stayed for 100 minutes until pulling Larwood straight at a doubled-up Allen, and Lew Litster, with no Freddie Brown to yell into the umpire's face this time, batted for almost 2½ hours before being yorked by Bowes. The innings was overshadowed, however, by The Oxenham Incident.

Ron Oxenham, the 41-year-old former Test allrounder, played a ball from Larwood to Allen for what appeared to be a straightforward catch. The Englishmen idly tossed the ball to each other before noticing that the batsman hadn't budged. After an appeal, the umpire, claiming he was unsighted, consulted his colleague, who was none the wiser. Oxenham was given not out, so Larwood snorted, stomped back to his mark, and ran in full pelt, letting loose bouncer after bouncer, Oxenham dodging as best he could, the crowd hooting loudly. Larwood was simply seeing red. He resented the barracking, for in his view the Queenslander was the player who had behaved unsportingly. It was a relief all round when Oxenham was bowled in Allen's next over.

Jardine — opening in the hope of recovering his lost touch — and Verity played out the final 10 minutes, finding that tales of Gilbert's speed off a run-up of only four yards (3.7 m) were not exaggerated. His body fell away in delivery and his arm was low, but it was also unusually long for a man no taller than Larwood, and the ball hurried through at a disconcerting height and pace. One ball struck Jardine on the hipbone, to the glee of the crowd, some of whom had made it their business to abuse the MCC captain. In pain, his face white with shock, he waved fielders away and saw it through to the close. In the dressing-room he told someone to shut the door then fell almost in a faint onto the masseur's table. When his trousers were removed an ugly, raw, sticky weal on the point of the bone showed clearly. He had the Sunday to get over it, and that was the end of the matter.

On the Monday, MCC's innings crawled along, fairly obviously being used as batting practice for the Test (if indeed there was to be a Test), though liberties could not be taken with Gilbert or with Oxenham's offbreaks. The

18-year-old Jack Govan's legspin brought him three wickets, but his six eight-ball overs went for 59 runs, Hammond and Wyatt plundering 22 off one over. Les Ames brought some vivacity to the innings with 80 in 76 minutes, with a six driven off Gilbert just missing the sightscreen, but catches were missed and wicketkeeper Len Waterman had one of his worst days, three times missing Wyatt, twice off possible stumpings. Leyland (beaten at 2 by Gilbert's extra-quick ball) and Paynter (19, batting at No. 8) were the only two of the first nine batsmen to fail to reach 20.

So MCC forged a lead of 142, which was to prove more than enough for an innings victory. Larwood crashed through the second innings, taking 4 for 15 before lunch and six wickets altogether, two courtesy of Jardine's low catches in the gully, and Verity took four in the lower middle order. Once again Larwood had cause to stare disbelievingly: not at a batsman who refused to walk, but at Herb Gamble, the former Victoria fast bowler, batting at No. 8 — here was a left-hander who closed his eyes (said Larwood) and whacked him for six over extra cover. Gamble's 14 was second-top score to Oxenham's 17; Cook was the only other batsman to reach double figures. Queensland all out 81 in a mere 100 minutes, no Bodyline bowling on display, all four Sheffield Shield sides now crushed by innings margins, and all eyes now sharply concentrated yet again on the Australian Board — whose secretary, Bill Jeanes, was able to report to his chairman that he had taken his wife out last night, the first time for weeks he had dared leave the telephone.

The ACB's conciliatory February 8 cable to Lord's enabled Queens-landers to settle back in anticipation of only their fourth Test match, only the second at the Woolloongabba ground. Last time Bradman had made a double-century and Bert Ironmonger had taken nine wickets. What now?

Relaxation came in the form of a match at Nundah between the Wanderers and the Press, watched by 3000 people. Being supernumeraries to whom injury would not have mattered, Pataudi, Brown and Duckworth played; the Indian hit three lovely sixes off an over by Mailey, and Brown landed a six on the Premier's limousine. Surprisingly, however, Jack Hutcheon, the feared boss of Queensland cricket and delegate to the Australian Board, laughingly called for everybody to field on the leg side when the Press XI's innings began. Over they went, including Sir Leslie Wilson, and Pataudi proceeded to bowl well wide of the off stump. Was he sending a plaintive message to his captain?

WOOLLOONGABBA GROUND, BRISBANE, FEBRUARY 4, 6, 7, 1933

QUEENSLAND 201 (G.G. Cook 53, W.C. Andrews 45, J.L. Litster 67, W.E. Bowes 3 for 43) and 81 (H. Larwood 6 for 38, H. Verity 4 for 20); MCC 343 (D.R. Jardine 34, H. Sutcliffe 35, R.E.S. Wyatt 40, G.O.B. Allen 66, L.E.G. Ames 80, R.K. Oxenham 4 for 70, J.M. Govan 3 for 58). **MCC WON BY AN INNINGS AND 61 RUNS**

It would have advanced matters if, by some supernatural process, the Australian Board could have shown members of the MCC committee at first hand what was happening in minor cricket all around Australia. At Moore Park, alongside the Sydney Cricket Ground, an offended batsman threatened to hit a would-be Bodyline bowler over the head with his bat. A match on the Domain — where the first-ever English team had played in 1862 — ended in a free-for-all after a quarter of an hour because of intimidatory bowling. A junior match in Adelaide broke up in similar disarray in even less time than that. According to ambulance officers, head injuries in matches played in Centennial Park's expanses quadrupled. The NSWCA deemed it necessary to send out a circular to all affiliated clubs urging them to discourage intimidatory bowling. In an Adelaide district match University laid on full-blown Bodyline against Glenelg, prompting the SACA to impose a ban on it.

GOVERNOR WILSON AND JACK HUTCHEON, WHO ENDEAVOURED TO MAKE THE VISIT OF THE ENGLISH CRICKETERS TO QUEENSLAND A HAPPY ONE AFTER THE RUCTIONS OF ADELAIDE.

As far as England's tour was concerned, the recent cable had gone some way towards clearing the air, even if little had been achieved in practical terms. Bodyline could still be employed if England chose, although with Voce missing the Brisbane Test because of influenza it would be left to Larwood. Legspinner Mitchell, who had bowled Bradman for 1 in the New South Wales match, came in for Voce as the only change, earning a place ahead of the frustrated Brown, who was 12th man again, while Captain Jardine's self-doubt had been swept aside once again by his senior players. He was persuaded not to drop himself. In keeping with his customary thorough approach, the skipper had taken Mitchell to the middle after the Queensland match finished and had him bowling on the worn pitch in a kind of visualisation exercise. He believed his little Derbyshire slow bowler might have the beating of Bradman again, and Woodfull too.

There were several peculiarities about Australia's selections. To replace the convalescent Oldfield they brought in Hammy Love, even though he was by no means universally regarded as the second-best wicketkeeper. Ben Barnett of Victoria, Charlie Walker of South Australia, and even tiny (he was little more than 5 foot [152 cm] tall) Cyril Parry of Tasmania were thought by many to be better keepers. It was to be Love's final first-class match. Fingleton was harshly dropped after his Adelaide pair and Grimmett was also withdrawn from the front line. Their misery would have been lessened had they known that neither of their Test careers was over. Richardson moved up to open the batting, and in came two Victoria left-handers: Len Darling, 23, and Ernie Bromley, 20, the latter the first West Australian to play Test cricket. "Slogger" Bromley had batted only once this season in first-class cricket, scoring 84 in a Shield match against New South Wales, and had been stumped off Mitchell without scoring in the recent tour match in Ballarat.

But the strangest selection by far in the original XII was Bert Tobin, a tall 22-year-old fast bowler from South Australia. He could hardly believe it when he was told, though having taken no wicket for 92 runs in the recent Shield match, his feet were soon back on the ground when he was made 12th man (never to play Test cricket). Tobin later told friends that the Australians had dubbed him the best drinks waiter they had ever had — and if ever drinks have been needed it has been during Tests at the sultry, tropical Gabba. Tobin later sailed off to Lancashire League cricket and married a rich woman.

Tobin's omission left Australia with seven specialist batsmen and only three front-line bowlers, a high-risk strategy even though Tim Wall's stocks (and Bradman's for that matter) had risen sharply since the Adelaide Test. On the Friday before the Brisbane Test, in South Australia's match at Sydney, Wall, the fast bowler with the magnificent pair of ears, had taken all 10 wickets in the first innings for 36 runs, the first instance of an all-10 in Sheffield Shield history — and further proof, said the cynics, that the current crop of Australian batsmen simply could not handle fast bowling. Watched by just over 7000 gaping spectators, Wall had 1 for 31 at lunch, then cleaned up afterwards with a highly dramatic spell of 9 for 5, including four wickets in one over, using a strong crosswind. Of New South Wales's 113, Fingleton scored 43 and Bradman 56. But in the second innings Bradman added a 97 (bowled by Perker Lee) in New South Wales's 356, and the South Australians went home empty-handed after all.

DON BRADMAN (IN PANAMA HAT) WITH WELLWISHERS BEFORE THE BRISBANE TEST MATCH.
HE SEEMS TO HAVE BEEN DETERMINED TO RETURN HOME TO SYDNEY IN ONE PIECE.
(IMAGES OF BRADMAN)

So Bradman was in good touch — though Fingleton was later to claim that The Don confided to a friend before the fourth Test that he "would sooner return from Brisbane with a pair of ducks than a pair of broken ribs".[14]

All sorts of parts of the body had been broken and bruised at the Gabba only a few months previously. In the Rugby League Test between Australia and Great Britain in June 1932 players of both sides nursed wounds so severe that, despite their protests, several were dragged from the field for treatment — three times in the case of Ernie Norman, Australia's concussed five-eighth. It was a brutal encounter, repeatedly interrupted by brawls, with Australian forward Dan Dempsey defiantly staying on the field after his forearm was broken and halfback Hec Gee losing part of his lower lip as he was knocked out (fullback Frank McMillan had also been knocked senseless, earlier). One Australian and two Britishers needed stitches to facial injuries — all this in an era before the game became soft by allowing substitutes. The Battle of Brisbane, fought before more than 26,000 awestruck spectators, ended on a thrilling note. Leading 10–6 and with little time remaining, Australia resisted strong British pressure before Eric Weissel, ignoring a badly sprained ankle, broke away and ran 75 yards (about 70 m) to set up Gee for a famous try. The series was level, but Great Britain went on to win the decider at Sydney 18–13, winger Stanley Smith completing a hat-trick of tries in the dying moments.

Brisbane's sporting fraternity therefore felt a greater sense of anticipation than usual as Jardine and his less-than-popular crew took on Woodfull's battered boys. There was an atmosphere rather like that at a bullfight as over 22,000 filed through the Gabba turnstiles on the opening day, a Friday, filling the little wooden stands or grouping in close bunches under the Moreton Bay fig tree at the Stanley Street end. Most of them, but not all, wore hats, some were even in collars and ties, and many sheltered from the sun's rays beneath black umbrellas. A Gabba crowd of the 1930s was less knowledgeable than its southern cousins, according to Bill Brown, and "much rougher, cruder and more partisan".[15] They were also subjected to the most acute discomfort as they squeezed along gangways and struggled against the odds to get comfortable in the overcrowded stands at this ramshackle venue. The congestion and poor facilities prompted a man to write to the *Courier* complaining vehemently about the "disgraceful over-crowding" and the fact that hundreds had been "imprisoned in the stand from 8 am until stumps at 6 pm", many without food and drink.[16] Lucky were the children who watched from the cool verandahs of the school across the road.

The Englishmen, in their wise choice of panama hats and white neckerchiefs, were less stressed in the field under the broiling sun than some of the onlookers. Not that this lasted, for the early Australian resistance was much stronger than in any of the previous Tests. Woodfull won the toss and proceeded to construct, with Richardson, a first-wicket stand way beyond anything Australia had managed so far. The skipper had given his partner a reminder he hardly needed: that Larwood must be denied an early wicket at all costs. Without the support of the steady Voce, his regular Bodyline partner, Larwood faced a heavy burden, and the Australians knew it. "I'll show the bugger he can't bowl!" growled Richardson, who was soon astounding everyone by jumping out at Larwood and lofting him over mid-on.[17]

The pitch had been covered by protective matting during the Queensland match. Jardine, wanting a fast surface for the Test, objected to this, but curator Jack Farquhar stuck to his guns. That pitch had to be protected. Now, it seemed, with the wicket bland and Larwood bowling with only conventional back-up, Australia had a golden chance to put a giant first innings on the board and level the series if Wall, O'Reilly and Ironmonger then hit the spot.

When Jardine saw that one end was livelier than the other he swung Larwood round, much to Allen's chagrin. With only sparing use of a Bodyline field (six in the leg cordon) and in the troublesome heat and humidity, Larwood seemed far less effective. The Australians were showing a new determination. In the first hour Woodfull nudged seven runs; Richardson, sometimes edging close to Jardine in the gully, collected 18. Both let many deliveries fly past either side of the wicket, swaying or ducking. Mitchell's arrival helped — Woodfull cut two fours in his first over — and by lunch the total was an encouraging 56.

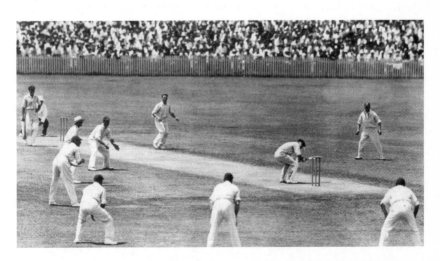

THE BEST-KNOWN — ALMOST ICONIC — BODYLINE PHOTOGRAPH: WOODFULL DUCKS A LARWOOD BOUNCER IN THE BRISBANE TEST WITH THE FULL LEG-SIDE SQUAD IN ATTENDANCE: FROM FORWARD SHORT LEG TO FINE LEG SLIP — LEYLAND, ALLEN, JARDINE, SUTCLIFFE, HAMMOND, AND VERITY, WITH MITCHELL AT SHORT COVER.

While the film shot here by Pataudi's tripod-mounted movie camera may or may not still exist, there is clear and fairly familiar newsreel footage of Larwood bowling a few bouncers in this Test, with Australian batsmen tumbling to the off side or sometimes placing the ball for singles. One clip shows Ames reaching up and failing to hold a high ball cleanly. The camera angle — from long-off — seems to reveal a kink in Larwood's right elbow just before delivery, and when I watched the film with Les Ames in 1977 he gasped and said, "Well, I never!" He too was left wondering whether the action was impure, though he and other contemporaries were always adamant that there had never been a serious challenge concerning the legitimacy of Larwood's action during his playing days.

After lunch Larwood increased the bouncer ration. One, failing to rise, hit Woodfull on the hip, close to lbw. Richardson, unlike his captain, was forever seeking runs, and his forceful shots had close fielders Leyland and Allen backing away. At one point he said to Allen: "Gubby, I'm going to stand two inches outside the leg stump and if I have to duck you've got to admit they've bowled *at* me." To which Allen replied, not without a certain pomposity: "Vic, you can stand anywhere you bloody well like, but I do not discuss that with you or anyone else."

By mid-afternoon, with Jardine frequently changing the bowling and the field placements, there were signs of scrappiness in the field. A huge roar greeted the century partnership. Richardson, having punished Allen in spite

VIC RICHARDSON, PLAYING HIS BEST INNINGS OF THE SERIES, FEARLESSLY PULLS LARWOOD OVER THE LEG CORDON IN THE BRISBANE TEST.

CAPTAIN TO CAPTAIN: WOODFULL NEGOTIATES ANOTHER LEG-SIDE BALL SAFELY DOWN
TOWARDS JARDINE IN THE LEG TRAP IN THE GABBA TEST. IT WAS "A GREAT CAPTAIN'S INNINGS"
SAID THE ENGLAND SKIPPER.

of his "modified leg-theory field", and once having hooked inches short
of Sutcliffe in the deep, now looked more confident than ever. The crowd
loved every minute of it, even if the conditions were stifling. There may even
have been a reprise of Jardine's nickname in these parts —"Rainbow"— first
shouted four years earlier at the Exhibition Ground, when people were
mesmerised by his Harlequin cap as he contributed 100 thought-ful runs in
the match towards England's 1928 victory by 675 runs. On the current tour
Bruce Harris overheard a message from a paying spectator who was not
completely familiar with the Scriptures. "There's only one man entitled to
wear a cap of many colours," he boomed. "He's Joseph, and he's dead!"
Harris also enjoyed a remark that greeted a Sutcliffe single after a long
period of inactivity: "That's right, Herbie; now go and have a rub-down!"

DISMISSAL BY DESIGN, IF MUCH LATER THAN INTENDED: RICHARDSON STUMPED BY AMES.

Having battled against heat and persistent England bowling for just over 2½ hours, Richardson was stumped down the leg side by Ames off Hammond, a successful dismissal this time — an earlier attempt to bring it off (when Richardson was only 11) had failed. Having registered his highest score against England since his century in the Melbourne Test eight years before, the batsman looked tired but well content with his 83 as he passed the newsreel camera on his return to the iron-roofed dressing-shed. It was still uncomfortably hot: Tate recorded apologetically that those not playing sat watching with their coats off, almost as if they felt "regimentally undressed".

TIME TO REST THE LEGS AND TALK TACTICS: JARDINE HOLDS AN IMPROMPTU TEAM CONFERENCE ON THE GRASS DURING A BREAK IN THE SWEAT-SOAKED ACTION.

So Australia had the sturdy start required — 133 for the first wicket. Now in came Don Bradman. He had difficulty in middling the ball at first, and his captain outscored him and displayed more certainty of touch, hitting Verity to the pickets once or twice, and Larwood too, in his own sweet time. Bradman miscued a hook and sent the ball lobbing over Larwood close in at mid-on, and was guilty of the odd inside edge. A thick touch screamed past Hammond. Still, the 200 was reached for the loss of only Richardson. A major distraction occurred when a hectic chase through the crowd ended with the arrest of two notorious pickpockets.

SOME BLOWS HURT MORE THAN OTHERS. THIS, TO McCABE'S UPPER ARM, CAUSED A HOLD-UP.
BRADMAN WENT TO COMFORT HIM, AND FURTHER COMPASSION IS ABOUT TO EMERGE FROM AN
UNEXPECTED QUARTER. *(IMAGES OF BRADMAN)*

Then Australia's painstaking captain, Bill Woodfull, who had looked dead tired at the tea break, was out soon after the interval, untypically dancing out to Mitchell and hitting around a ball of full length. His 67 runs had been etched from four hours of studied devotion: "a great captain's innings", Jardine later wrote. Since he had taken strike in the second innings at Adelaide, Woodfull had defied England's best continuously for eight hours, facing 440 balls before losing his wicket.

McCabe was hurt when Larwood hit his left arm. He dropped his bat and was bemused to find that the fieldsman who was rubbing the flesh and sympathising was none other than Jardine, soon assisted by Larwood himself. Was solicitude for the enemy part of the new unwritten accord? England had one further success that afternoon when McCabe, after a somewhat reckless innings of 20 and with slight numbness still restricting arm movement, was held by Jardine at gully: the captain simply thrust out his left hand and found the ball in it.

ONE OF THE MORE STARTLING CATCHES OF THE SERIES:
JARDINE — PART LUCK, PART REFLEX — HOLDS McCABE IN THE GULLY.

Ponsford opened his account with an all-run four to leg, and by now Bradman had found his touch. Bulky in thigh-pads and chest-protector, he seemed to be taking advantage of every scoring opportunity, often driving punishingly. At 48 he reached 1000 runs for the season. Sutcliffe was the only other to touch the milestone that summer. Although the "heroic" (Jardine's carefully chosen description) Verity's every second over was a maiden ("doing my quietening stuff again", as he put it), Australia remained on top, even when Larwood braced himself to give his all with the new ball in the hot evening. It was noticed that throughout this extremely hot day he did not bowl Bodyline to new batsmen until they had been in for an over or two. The exhausted spectators, faith restored, wended their way out with visions of a big, big stand by Bradman and Ponsford next day.

The tourists' efforts had taken a lot out of them this day, and Hobbs noted that Gubby Allen looked "positively ill, with sunken eyes, though he said he felt well". One euphoric headline (*Sydney Morning Herald*) went so far as to announce: LEG THEORY MASTERED. So concerned was Jardine now that he took it upon himself to upbraid some cricket writers in the hotel bar for plying the thirsty Larwood with what he suspected, rightly or wrongly, was too much drink. The fast bowler, for his part, had bet Hugh Buggy and a couple of the others that he would get the "Boy Wonder" (Bradman) within three overs the next day. He was currently nursing unfamiliar figures of 0 for 65 off 20 overs.

In Jardine's view, Bradman was "inclined to be over-sensitive to adverse criticism"; this perhaps explained his hesitant start on the opening day, for after his Adelaide batting he had been the target of derogatory comment from Australian oldtimers. Now he was determined to redeem himself, and at 71 not out overnight, being optimistic by nature, Bradman, like the Brisbaneites, must now have felt another century coming on — or even one of those double-centuries he so relished.

It was now reported that S.M. Bruce, speaking at a London sports club dinner, had proclaimed that the leg-theory controversy was all due to a misunderstanding. It would resolve itself, he said, if only the two countries did not take the things they said about each other too seriously. The trouble (at Adelaide) had begun in a small section of the crowd, the Press had taken it up "and the people became hysterical". Australia's Minister in London also considered the Olympic Games to be a cause of misunderstanding and rancour, and said he had no wish to see that sort of thing carried into the British Empire.

The players awoke — those who had managed to sleep at all, that is — with sheets and pyjamas soggy with perspiration. It was like a Turkish bath inside the Gabba again on the Saturday, with an even larger crowd — almost 29,000 — crushed into the enclosures. Most coats, ties and waistcoats were removed early. Freddie Brown took Paynter's place in the field when Paynter conceded that he was far from well. It was thought the left-hander would not take any further part in the match — the first act in a famous drama.

Larwood was briefly reinvigorated after yesterday's exertions, and not long into the day's play — after Ponsford had delighted the fans by playing Larwood's first ball to the square-leg boundary — he swung the match by dismissing Bradman and Ponsford in quick succession. Bradman had first ducked a ball that just cleared the stumps. When he moved back and tried to cut the next ball, his leg stump was dislocated. It was another dark moment for Australia captured on film, the error destined never to be allowed to fade after such comments as Jack Hobbs's: "If a schoolboy tried to cut a ball on the leg stick you would smack his head, yet here was Bradman doing it."

A couple of minutes later Bill Ponsford, having clipped a ball straight at Allen at short leg, was also bowled by Larwood, yet again moving across and exposing his leg stump.

PONSFORD CAN SCARCELY BELIEVE IT AS HIS LEG STUMP IS RAPPED YET AGAIN.

Apart from brief resistance from the two new batsmen, Darling and Bromley, this was, astonishingly, just about the end of the innings, all being watched glumly by non-paying spectators sitting on the galvanised-iron roofs of neighbouring houses. As Wilfred Rhodes observed from half a world away, the Kangaroo seems to have a long tail.

Darling, whose first ball in Test cricket came straight at his nose, loved to hook, and did so with dubious results and then with heartening success, while Bromley had one close scrape after another, first getting a steepling hook just over Wyatt's head at long leg then top-edging a pull, the ball landing between cover fieldsmen. The colt would never forget his first encounter with Larwood. Umpire Hele shuddered as the first ball flicked Bromley's cap-peak, bringing a wry look to the bowler's face, and the second sat him on the seat of his pants faster than any batsman in Hele's memory. But he took a dozen runs off one Larwood over, and the crowd loved him for it. Jardine seemed just a little flustered, perhaps distracted by a cry from the mob that he must keep Larwood on.

Allen got a richly deserved second wicket when Ames held Darling, who had shown a tendency to be insecure outside off stump. Mitchell had Love lbw, and the cameras were rolling again as the inexperienced Bromley, having gone after the bowling with "a few flashy shots" (Verity) now that all the recognised batsmen were gone, became an archetypical Bodyline victim after the lunch interval, caught at short leg by a quick-to-react Verity off a lifter played off the chest. O'Reilly gave his usual clownish performance before becoming yet again one of Larwood's rabbits, and old Ironmonger clubbed a defiant four and gave Larwood an unwanted century just before the end of an innings that had seen the last seven wickets fall for 76.

Wyatt believed this the hottest day of cricket he ever experienced, and complimented Larwood and Allen on the "terrific guts" they had shown. In air that was so humid you could feel the sogginess, the vice-captain believed that these two put on the best fast-bowling display the game could ever have seen.

Only later did Jardine reveal that the hidden factor behind England's revival was champagne. But not too much. His own very sober explanation was: "We were indebted to our manager, Mr R.C.N. Palairet, for a very good suggestion. He did not often say much, but what he said was always as helpful as it was sound. On this occasion, in view of the terrific heat, he suggested that our bowlers should be given half a dozen sips of champagne. All of us, I think, are agreed that the less use made of stimulants in all sport the better, but on this exceptional occasion the champagne proved an unqualified success. That we were not extravagant in its use will be appreciated when I say that three-quarters of a bottle sufficed for four individuals to have three drinks each. Further, it made it possible for some of them to eat a little lunch."[18] Four individuals? Five men bowled, leaving one to wonder who was unlucky.

MOSTLY COATS OFF BUT FEW BARE HEADS: THE BRISBANE CROWD GAVE ENGLAND
A MORE CORDIAL RECEPTION THAN THEY HAD BEEN GIVEN AT ADELAIDE. PAYNTER THOUGHT,
TOO, THAT THEY PROBABLY REMEMBERED MORE OF HIS INNINGS OF 83 THAN HE DID.

Jardine went on to say that this was the greatest day known by English cricket for 20 years. His reasoning stemmed from the bowling/fielding fightback after the worrying situation on the first evening and the steady reply he and Sutcliffe mustered on the second. In reply to Australia's 340, England were 99 without loss in the final serene 2¼ hours, as a haze built up and the temperature dropped. Sutcliffe, notwithstanding a few edges and an unaccepted chance to Love, dealt with O'Reilly's leg attack with his usual calm and resisted Wall's plan to have him taken in the outfield off a hook, making most of his runs with the distinctive cut-push. Bromley, slow–medium left-arm, had his first bowl in Test cricket and troubled both batsmen, but an appeal against the light was upheld at 5.52 pm, soon after Wall had shot one or two balls past their heads. Many spectators had already taken their leave. In keeping with the series trend, England were scoring their runs at a much slower rate than Australia.

Film of the opening pair striding to the wicket provides a surprising vision of Jardine. He preferred an MCC cap this time (as did Sutcliffe) and is chewing gum, something which adds an air of nonchalance uncharacteristic of the man. But what catches the eye most is the shirt. Its sleeves are cut so high that they finish only a few inches down from the tip of Jardine's square-set shoulders. What about the sunburn warnings? What about sartorial propriety? Had the tropical sun got to him?

Bill Woodfull, as he often did as they filed out of the dressing-room, might just have stirred his devoted men with the football rallying cry: "Come on, youse! Straight up the centre — no short passes — boots and all!"[19] If it failed to have the desired effect that Saturday evening, it worked on the Monday, Brisbane's hottest day of the year. One paper concluded that it was nothing short of cruelty to expect cricketers to play in Brisbane at this time of year — cruel to spectators too, since the ground authorities had now cut off the four hose-taps in the outfield from which boys on Saturday had filled their drink bottles in order to survive.

Against an Australian team mostly wearing sunhats — though Richardson stubbornly went bareheaded — England lost wickets at a steady trickle. Jardine's 3¼-hour vigil ended at 46, when he misjudged a sweep off O'Reilly and helped the ball into Love's gauntlets. The batsman departed reluctantly and later testily asked scorer Ferguson, "How have you got me out in your book — umpired out or cheated out?"[20] The opening stand had just outstripped the 112 by Sutcliffe and Wyatt in the first Test.

There had been a further clash of wills before play started. Jardine wanted the 10-minute rolling of the pitch to be split into two five-minute operations so that any moisture drawn up would evaporate between the two rollings. It went wrong, for as the second rolling began the Australians were entering the field. Umpire George Hele ordered the roller to be removed from the ground, whereupon Jardine told him to mind his own business. Hele's order to the groundsman was repeated, and off creaked the roller, leaving an irate England captain to snarl at Hele that he had umpired his last Test match. Woodfull consoled the umpire: "Don't worry, George, I had my watch on him too." Jardine apologised to Hele at lunchtime, saying he had checked the rulebook and the umpires were right. "You knew that all the time," said Hele, at which Jardine walked away, saying, "Forget it."[21]

England ground out only 52 runs in the 90-minute pre-lunch session as the two Australian spinners slowed their pace and gained more turn. The only excitement for the well-behaved crowd, apart from Jardine's dismissal, was a six smashed by Hammond off an O'Reilly full-toss and two near-run-outs when Sutcliffe called for tight singles. The England score had grown to 151 for 1 at lunch, but both these master batsmen went quickly after the interval, O'Reilly getting his reward at last when Sutcliffe was given out lbw and Hammond being bowled for 20 by a yorker from McCabe after an hour and a half of studious batsmanship. O'Reilly was Australia's rock once again, his figures to date being 2 for 69 off 38 intense overs.

After a short spell of Bromley's slow left-arm, Ironmonger, who had been wheeling that kind of stuff down before Bromley was even born, found the edge as Wyatt played back. Leyland swung at O'Reilly and was caught on the run at wide midwicket by Bradman, almost unrecognisable in his large white sunhat. Allen smacked O'Reilly straight for six before touching Wall to the keeper after the tea break, and soon after Paynter had gone to the wicket, Ames, having spent nearly an hour and a half making 17, had a dart at Ironmonger and was caught at mid-off. The bowler clapped Darling with great enthusiasm, a gesture which attracted notice in an age when even hugging was a spectacle unseen on cricket fields. Larwood belted Ironmonger for a six and a four before McCabe yorked him, making England 264 for 8, still 76 behind and with the prospect of batting last on a pitch that was taking spin.

And the wonder of it is that almost all the action described in the previous paragraph has been preserved on film.

The big story of this third day, of course, was the unexpected appearance of Eddie Paynter. It was a tale that has long been part of cricket's folklore, and not just in Oswaldtwistle, his hometown. Jardine was displeased when he first heard that Paynter was unwell. He assumed Paynter must have known before the match started and should therefore have declared himself out of it. Paynter claimed he had first felt his throat sore during the second day's play, when his temperature was found to be a raging 102. He was taken to Brisbane General Hospital, and diagnosed with tonsillitis. He remained in hospital throughout the Sunday and for much of the third day's play on the Monday. But he knew his country needed him, groggy though he still was.

What happened next is best told in his own handwritten recollection:[22]

If I can think correct & I am sure that it was Bill Voce that came to the hospital and we had the wireless on, one or two wickets went down so I asked Bill to get a taxi for us to go to the ground. I got my dressing gown on & was just going down the ward when sister appeared. She wanted to know where we were going. I said to the Cricket Ground, she played hell & said if we must we were doing it at our own risk & she nor the doctor would be responsible for our action, so we left for the ground. I had just got changed when G.O. Allen got out so I went into bat, and as you know I was 24 not out at the close of play, and then back to hospital for a good night's rest.

The following day I went in with H. Verity & made 83. I do think the sweating did me a lot of good. For after match was over I was smashing and all the rest of whole tour.

In his ghosted autobiography Paynter gave a little more detail: on the rest day he was comfortable in the hospital bed, tonsils painted and plenty of tablets down him. The day was a "sickly maze" of sleep and visits from team-mates, with regular gargling, and tasty gruel brought by Mick Maguire from the Belle Vue Hotel. Jardine visited Paynter too, and put the thought into his batsman's head that even if he had to "bat on crutches" he would do so. Any coercion was apparently no stronger than that, though Wyatt felt, in retrospect, that Jardine did put considerable pressure on Paynter.

Monday brought a slight improvement in his condition, but he was told firmly by the doctor that he would not be taking any further part in the Test match. Then came England's slide, and a new urgency swept through the little Lancastrian. Voce helped him to a taxi while the ward sister went off to find somebody to stop him.

A FAMOUS INNINGS PLAYED IN ADVERSITY: EDDIE PAYNTER, STRICKEN WITH TONSILLITIS, OVERCOMES MUZZY VISION AND ACHING MUSCLES TO DRIVE FOR PRECIOUS RUNS.

The taxi was soon at the Gabba and the two slipped from Vulture Street into the dressing-room, Paynter's appearance causing Jardine to do a double take. No sooner had the invalid buckled on his pads soon after tea than Allen was out. To thunderous applause the little man under the wide-brimmed panama transported himself slowly to the wicket, pale and trembling. Ames, equally astonished, greeted him. Woodfull patted Paynter on the back and sportingly offered him a runner but he declined. Fortified by egg and brandy, a warm shower, and sips of champagne (some of this or all of this: the memoirs of those who were there are not short of suggestions), he was just in time for the new ball. He held on for the remaining 75 minutes, making 24 precious runs, Larwood's passive partner in a vital stand of 55 after Ames was out. Larwood's six off Ironmonger helped offset a memorable period of play during which only 10 runs came in 50 minutes. Paynter was too weak to hit with any power, but held on to the close, with Verity as his watchful partner. He then tugged his pyjamas back on, donned his dressing-gown and returned to hospital in a bit of a daze. He had saved England. They had steadied to 271 for 8, a mere 172 runs having been chiselled out of the five hours' play; even McCabe conceded well under two runs an over in his 19 overs.

The ward sister greeted Eddie Paynter with a "Well done!" followed by a "Get into bed!", and he had a good night's sleep. He felt appreciably better next day and, pockets bulging with tablets and gargle mixture, he returned to the Gabba.

With the steady — and often fortunate — Verity he continued the England resistance, playing strokes to all parts, taking England into the lead, stopping twice to gargle and take his medicine, and receiving great cheers when he reached fifty. On a pitch rendered tranquil after Jardine ordered the heavy roller at the start, the pair were still together at lunch, Paynter having picked up most of his runs on the leg side. Again the heat was scorching, and a newspaper described the Australians as "looking hopelessly stewed". When Paynter finally fell at 83, lifting a drive off Ironmonger to Richardson, who had finally accepted the wisdom of wearing a cap, a navy-blue one, there was the rare sight of Australian cricketers clapping an England batsman as the small figure withdrew to the dressing-shed.

As at Adelaide, Paynter and Verity had put together an extremely important partnership of 90-plus, and Paynter's courageous innings was already bringing him rewards. Admirers in Melbourne collected £40 for him, while a warm telegram of congratulations from his old workmates in the brickyard was among the first to come in.

England's innings of 356 lasted 10 hours — seemingly an eternity for the bowlers, fielders and spectators. Weary Wall's efforts were seen by Mailey as tedious: the long, slow walk back and the high proportion of deliveries flying harmlessly outside off stump had spectators yawning. O'Reilly's noble labours through not far short of 70 overs of windmill action and great accuracy brought him a fourth wicket when he trapped Mitchell, the last man, lbw, while Ironmonger, the heavily built quinquagenarian who, in O'Reilly's opinion, deserved the Victoria Cross this day, had wheeled down 43 overs, each seemingly slower than the last, from which only 69 runs were taken. The performance of Australia in the field was criticised, catches going begging and Bradman throwing unnecessarily hard to Love at close quarters.

The loss of body fluid in that steamy heat was incalculable, and O'Reilly, who had been off the beer most of the summer — and paid for it with nocturnal cramps and weight loss — was now told firmly by a doctor friend to return to it. Meanwhile, as "Tiger" and Ironmonger flopped in the Gabba dressing-room, McCabe suggested to the teetotal Woodfull that champagne might help his weary bowlers. But the dressing-room attendant, the old Queensland player Sid Redgrave, came back empty-handed and clearly embarrassed. Jack Hutcheon, the czar of Queensland cricket, had refused the request. So Woodfull put on his blazer and purposefully strode off to see QCA president Hutcheon. He returned with the prescribed magnum.

England, thanks in the end mainly to the Paynter–Verity alliance, were 16 ahead rather than heaps of runs in deficit. Verity's 23 not out — he was sometimes referred to as "Sutcliffe gone stale" — had taken 2¾ hours, and he had survived a leg-side stumping chance, a catch to Wall at short leg, a catch off a no-ball nobody heard at first, and a catch off a huffing O'Reilly which fell between the hesitant Ponsford and Bromley. He managed only one four in all that time.

MRS PAYNTER IS GRANTED USE OF THE LATEST MIRACLE IN COMMUNICATION, THE INTERCONTINENTAL TELEPHONE, TO SPEAK TO HUSBAND EDDIE, WHO HAS JUST BECOME A HERO.

Having batted himself to the brink of collapse, Paynter now took the field when Australia batted again, enjoying the calls from the crowd: "Very good, Eddie" and "Well done, Paynter" — a different tune to the one at Adelaide. But he was too weak to stay out there for more than a couple of hours. Freddie Brown took his place and he returned to hospital for a third night — to be woken up at midnight by a most unexpected modern miracle, a telephone call from his wife May in Manchester. The enterprise of the organisers of the Telephones and Telegraphs Exhibition had made this brief and restricted call possible, and it was just the tonic the English cricket hero needed. His name was suddenly on everybody's lips and was even mentioned in the House of Commons, prompting cheers. A testimonial was set up by warm-hearted Australian cricket-lovers, though Eddie was too shy to go along on his own to receive the cheque. He took Duckworth and Leyland with him for moral support.

Worse followed upon his return to England, for he had to overcome his bashfulness and deliver a response at the dinner his Lancashire captain threw in his honour in Oxford. None was better qualified to reiterate Paynter's words than Neville Cardus: "'Mr Eckersley an' la-ads', he said. 'Ah can't mak' any speech. Ah can only say thanks. Ah did me best at Brisbane for England an' for Lancashire ... but as for talk about mi leavin' a sickbed at risk of mi dyin' — well, beggin' your pardon, Mr Eckersley, that were all rot. It were nowt more than a sore throit.'"

D.R. Jardine put it another way. He could never really countenance one of his batsmen lying semi-conscious in a hospital bed while there was urgent rescue work to be done at the crease. He thus drew upon a stirring vision of heroism and hardship in Britain's war in Afghanistan, just over half a century past: "What about those fellows who marched to Kandahar with fever on them?"[23] Lord Roberts, VC, and his 10,000 British heroes on their 320-mile (515-km) bleak and dangerous mountain trek were not forgotten yet.

THE WATER TAPS AT THE GABBA WERE CRUCIAL TO THE AVOIDANCE OF DEHYDRATION.

This was merely a cricket match, but one which contained much fighting cricket all the same. There had been less Bodyline in it than in any previously in the series, and the tension built on the fourth day as Woodfull and Richardson again made a steady start. Such was the heat that Jardine gave Larwood and Allen alternate overs after the formal opening spell. A series of Larwood bouncers was cracked so viciously by Richardson that Allen backed away from his sentry post close on the leg side, and another pull almost grazed Leyland's head. The crowd reaction to the spectacle of Bodyline, this being Queensland, was "languid" hooting. Towels were brought out with the drinks. Then Richardson, who had started so confidently, though lucky to survive a high chance to Leyland at deep square leg, got carried away, slamming Verity high to mid-off, where Jardine leapt and held the catch.

Bradman (who had not been the only batsman to confide to scorer Ferguson that he had no intention of getting severely hurt in the cause of cricket and would rather give up the game[24]) began cautiously again, and there was amusement when Verity signalled Jardine at silly point to go in closer to the batsman. When Larwood returned as usual to direct his special attention to Bradman, the batsman eschewed the early protection Woodfull had clearly arranged for him (keeping him away from the strike) and clipped two flashing square cuts off the stumps in one over, the umpire (as so often having to stand on the off side) throwing himself out of the firing line. More bouncers followed, and four leg-byes as an lbw appeal went up. Then there was a slight adjustment to the field on the wide open off side, and once more, to the desperate disappointment of millions, Bradman got out cheaply. With 24 beside his name, Woodfull having just had a word with him, and having just felt a bouncer pass his chin, he clipped Larwood straight into the hands of the lone cover fieldsman Mitchell, who had wandered a few yards from his original position. "Well caught, Tommy," said Jardine, "but *I'll* move you when it's necessary."

Worse followed for Australia. Ponsford flicked Allen to square leg, where Larwood dived and thrust out his left hand to hold a blinding catch inches from the grass. It was to be the only duck recorded by Ponsford in his 48 innings through 10 years of Test cricket, and to Larwood's words of commiseration the batsman simply retorted, "Go to blazes."[25] Ponny's long-term partner Woodfull dropped his bat in shock. As if reciting some Sherlock Holmes script, Jardine wrote in his tour account: "I felt bound to admit to the delighted bowler that, the very next ball, I had intended to suggest that Larwood should be moved three or four yards squarer — another example of good luck."And little comfort to the scowling Ponsford.

And the match lurched further away from Australia when, near the close of play, Woodfull, after a patient 19 in a total of 91, edged a Mitchell leg-break to slip. Hobbs could not recall one shot Woodfull had played during his 109-ball tenure, and an Australian paper described the fatal final stroke as that of a tired man, "perhaps depressed". McCabe swept Mitchell for four but almost fell to a badly timed pull against Allen. He survived, with Darling, to face the fifth day, having driven one ball hard at Jardine's shin, which brought some cruel laughter from the outer as the Englishman lay on the ground, face contorted by pain.

Not all hope was gone, though, for even if Australia's tail was long, these two were capable of big innings. It was surely time for McCabe to repeat something resembling his grand Sydney performance in the first Test. And there was always the possibility that rain and then the usual hot sun might come to transform the wicket. Bert Ironmonger had taken 11 for 24 against South Africa on such a surface at Melbourne a year ago.

Alas for vain hopes: Australia's last six wickets were swept away for only 67 on the fifth day. It began promisingly when Larwood, having compelled McCabe to duck fierce deliveries four (or was it six?) times in one over, temporarily left the field. The exertions in the relentless sticky heat were taking a toll, and the tiring express bowler did not exactly benefit from a spectacular collision with the stumps as he delivered one ball. Made of Queensland ash, the stump snapped off at the base like a carrot and the off-balance bowler was sent sprawling heavily. Two balls from Hammond hardly bounced, a worrying sign for England. But the breakthrough came at 136 when McCabe, trying to force Verity to leg, played the ball onto his leg stump as it, like many others, kept low.

Bromley, after some heart-stopping escapades in running with Darling (a surf lifesaving club team-mate of his), was smartly caught by Hammond at slip off Allen.

The lead was 153, the match finely balanced, when in the over before lunch Len Darling was run out for a game 39, the innings' top score. It was a needless catastrophe, as are most run-outs, and poor Hammy Love seemed to be the culprit. He played to mid-on, started to run, but went back when he saw bowler Larwood darting across to gather the ball and throw it to Mitchell at the stumps. Darling could never have got to safety in time, but Love should have sacrificed himself. He didn't, and that was effectively the end of the innings, for straight after the interval the last three wickets fell for six runs. Well might a fan have shouted out "Come on, dears!" during the Darling–Love partnership.

Love went lbw to Larwood first ball upon resumption; Jardine caught Wall — one-handed and knee-high — at third slip off Allen, who was operating in spite of pain from a side strain; and finally O'Reilly's Russian roulette brought him a four down the ground off Larwood before his wicket was demolished. Australia all out for a disappointing 175, England 160 runs from regaining the Ashes.

ERNIE BROMLEY, THE PROMISING YOUNGSTER, FALLS TO A CATCH BY THE CONSUMMATE
SLIPS FIELDER HAMMOND.

Laughter was in short supply during this Test series but Pataudi generated some while acting as 12th man. Taking the empty glasses back to the dressing-shed, he stumbled on the steps, creating an alarming jangling and tinkling. There was applause from all within earshot, to which the neglected young batsman reacted with swift wit, saying, "I still have my public."[26]

The pitch was swept, and Jardine this time ordered the light roller. There was an encouraging early breakthrough for Australia when Sutcliffe, having jabbed down on a shooter from Wall and then been missed at slip by McCabe off O'Reilly, ran out of luck: Wall bowled yet again outside off and he steered a catch to backward point. Leyland, the left-hander shrewdly elevated to No. 3, now joined Jardine in a tense fight against desperate bowling. Ironmonger sent down six overs for a solitary run, and by tea England had crawled to 45 after 100 minutes' vigilant batting.

With Leyland opening up a little, a further 62 came in the third session for the loss of Jardine, whose grim innings of 24 lasted over two hours before he was leg-before to Ironmonger, who conceded only two runs from his first nine overs. One spectator remembered, years later, how he had gone into the Stanley Street bar to calm his thirst with a couple of beers, and when he returned some time later to watch the game he saw that Jardine was *still* on the same score.[27] He went *82 balls* without scoring at one stage, fixed for 63 palsied minutes, seven minutes short of the Test mark set on this ground a year before by Bruce Mitchell of South Africa (equalling Billy Murdoch's 70 minutes at Sydney in 1882–83), and four minutes short of Will Scotton's unwelcome England record, set at The Oval in 1886. Many batsmen have out-waxworked Jardine since then, some with just as much at stake, some without. The Brisbane audience displayed their own special humour by applauding his forward defensive strokes.

That evening Bill O'Reilly had his first real conversational exchange with the England captain he so despised. Jardine came onto the verandah of the dressing-room draped only in a bath-towel and watched the groundsman laying tarpaulins on the pitch as the sun went down. O'Reilly ventured a compliment: "Well batted, Douglas." Jardine looked him straight in the eye and said: "Really, Bill, really. Don't you think I was like an old maid defending her virginity?" The tired 27-year-old, who was to marry his Molly in three months' time, replied: "Sorry, Douglas, I am too short in experience to answer that question."[28]

For a cricketer who could claim, as did O'Reilly, that he wouldn't care if he never played against England ever again — were there any Englishmen worth playing against? — he was suddenly having rather a lot to do with his despised opponents, for on the Saturday of the Brisbane Test he had bumped into Jardine in the foyer of the Belle Vue. The captain invited him to the Englishmen's Saturday night meal, and he went — out of curiosity. There at the head of the table sat Jardine, with one of Mick Maguire's teenage daughters beside him; O'Reilly years later confessed that he enjoyed the occasion.[29]

After Jardine's dismissal Leyland and Hammond saw to it that England suffered no further loss before they came off for bad light at 5.50 pm, Hammond hammering the ball into the covers, a specialty of his, and

Bromley once diving like a goalkeeper to deny him. Like all Australian crowds, this one was enthusiastic about good fielding. They also felt their chances drifting further away when Wall left the field, limping from a sore heel hit earlier by Leyland. Tobin, who would never play in a Test match, now tantalisingly came onto the Test field as substitute.

The sixth and final day began with a complexity of emotions. With England needing a further 53, with eight wickets in hand, the sound of heavy rain (parts of Queensland were in flood) conjured up exciting visions of another rout by Ironmonger of helpless batsmen on a "sticky". But desperately sad news was also circulating. Just after midnight, Archie Jackson, 23 years of age, once thought to be another Victor Trumper, had finally succumbed to tuberculosis.

ARCHIE JACKSON, ADMIRED AND CHERISHED. HIS EARLY DEATH WAS LAMENTED BY THE WORLD OF CRICKET AND CAST A SHADOW OVER THE BRISBANE TEST MATCH.

Four years before, the Glasgow-born batsman had scored a memorable century in his first Test innings — driving Larwood to the fence to reach it — when he was not yet 20 years old. He toured England with the Australians in 1930 and contributed 73 to a fourth-wicket stand of 243 with his "big brother" Don Bradman in the final Test, at The Oval, where Bodyline was said by so many to have been conceived. Not long before his final breath was drawn, the elegant and modest youngster sent a telegram to Larwood from the Brisbane private hospital: "Congratulations magnificent bowling. Good luck all matches. Archie Jackson." It was a souvenir the English cricketer would treasure all his days.

Several of the players from both sides had visited him at Ingarfield Hospital before the Test. His family was up from Sydney, and shortly before he died he became engaged to Phyllis, his petite dancer girlfriend from Brisbane. Jackson had played grade cricket for Norths until very recently, gasping for breath and often aided by a runner, but desperate to go on doing what he loved best, playing strokes and making runs. He scored 77 in his final innings. Optimistic despite his desperate health, he wrote to a friend in England that he expected to be over there with the 1934 Australians. Nor did he think complaints about Bodyline were justified. He believed the Australians, Bradman and McCabe aside, lacked quick footwork. And he believed his friend Larwood would not intentionally hurt a fly. In handwriting almost as elegant as his batting, Jackson wrote: "the Australian batsmen are beginning to squeal — certainly a rotten thing to say — but it's a fact and is creating a good deal of unnecessary trouble".[30]

The flags at the Gabba were at half-mast and the Australians wore black armbands as they entered the field for the final session of an intriguing match. A few umbrellas were raised among the smattering of spectators, who had had to pay only half-price to get in for this day of decision. The start was delayed only five minutes and the heavy rain held off, though enough had touched the pitch for the ball to be clearly doing more now for O'Reilly and Ironmonger. The big wicket of Hammond soon came — yet another dismissal of a batsman trying to drive Ironmonger. It was Hammond's first attempt at real aggression after more than an hour at the crease. Bromley held the catch. Ames came in, but just when it seemed that Leyland was carrying England home on his broad shoulders a nasty ball from O'Reilly had him caught at slip for a laudable 86, constructed over 3¾ hours. Twenty-two needed, and who should enter but the slight figure of Eddie Paynter, his "throit" now much better.

AWAY SHE GOES: PAYNTER HITS THE SIX THAT WON THE ASHES.

Almost bowled first ball, he hooked a four off O'Reilly, who then conceded a six to Ames over long-off, the batsman wiggling his bat towards the dressing-room as he earned another £5 for the team kitty.

But the drizzle that had begun earlier now began to intensify. Lunch was approaching. So these professional batsmen went after the runs, and when McCabe bowled a full-toss with the greasy ball, Paynter unleashed his favourite hook shot and sent it out of the ground to win the match — and recover the Ashes won by Australia in 1930 by Bradman, Grimmett and company. Paynter was later glad to give the retriever of the ball a bat in exchange for it, and 57 years later — some time after Paynter's death in 1979 — that historic ball fetched £4400 at auction in London. (A commemorative ashtray given by Jardine to Paynter at the end of the tour made £1100.)

The players grabbed the stumps and bails as souvenirs while the crowd, such as it was, surged across the Gabba ground. The policemen in their white topees had no problems to sort out, which is not to say that there was no pandemonium around the cramped dressing-room area. Plum Warner had returned, having gone off to find a radio commentary, unable to bear the tension of the last few overs, and Bill Woodfull and his players (O'Reilly doubtless still moaning that with Grimmett they could have won) went into the England room to offer congratulations as champagne flowed. Jardine was whisked off by Bruce Harris to speak by telephone to the *Evening Standard* in London, and there were formalities now in the presence of Governor Wilson.

There were speeches by Jack Hutcheon, and Jardine and Woodfull, who found the right words, the England captain surprisingly nominating the Melbourne Test, which he had lost, as the "greatest Test in history" and quoting Kipling on triumph and disaster, those "two impostors". He also expressed his team's condolences to Archie Jackson's family. Warner, having permitted himself an exuberant little outburst ("If we are happy like Sunshine Susie at our victory it is only natural"), spoke of O'Reilly's great bowling and then inevitably drew upon history, quoting Lord Roberts: "The men have been splendid." The great British soldier had attended Warner's wedding in 1904.

The men had done the job just in time too, for it rained for the next 12 hours. As the Queensland Governor told Legh Winser in a letter, he saw every ball bowled in the match and observed that there had been some barracking, though it was good-tempered. "In fact, so far as I could gather, the crowd would have been disappointed if Larwood had not bowled the leg theory with an on field. The play of the Australians was the best answer to all the controversy — Richardson, Darling and others hit Larwood about by standing up to him while Bradman, O'Reilly and others got out because they did not! Jardine was splendid in his management of the team and in his complete disregard of criticism which has won him the admiration of the crowd."

It would seem from this that the resident dignitaries of the governors' houses in Brisbane and Adelaide could have had themselves a fairly heated debate on the subject.

Meanwhile congratulations flowed in: from the King himself as patron of MCC ("... I have followed with closest interest the ups and downs of the match"); from the British Prime Minister, Ramsay MacDonald; from MCC and from its president Viscount Lewisham; and from Dominions Secretary Jimmy Thomas ("Bravo. The Ashes are won. But they are secondary to the great fighting spirit and good sportsmanship shown by both sides"). There was also a warm telegram from Prime Minister Lyons of Australia.

The Englishmen had a celebration dinner-dance that night, and there were schoolboy shenanigans back at the Belle Vue, with bedclothing, shoes and whatnot strewn all over the hotel. But they were heading south to Newcastle by train next day, hoping for a drop in temperature. The Australians were aboard too, as was a casket containing Archie Jackson's body, to be conveyed to Sydney, where thousands would line the route to the Field of Mars cemetery. The pallbearers were Woodfull, Richardson, Bradman, Oldfield, McCabe and Ponsford, with Kippax taking McCabe's place when he became ill. Plum Warner later spoke at a memorial service at Balmain Central Methodist Mission, and a number of Jackson's contemporaries broadcast tributes, among them Bradman, who described his one-time junior partner as a "batting genius".

Several weeks later a cricket match played at the SCG in aid of the Archie Jackson Memorial Fund was distinguished by the scoreline "Bradman c Macartney b Mailey 98". Earlier, Bradman had set a Bodyline field against State coach George Garnsey. Unlike the full-toss that got Hammond at Adelaide, this delivery bounced four times.[31]

A REFRESHING 450-MILE (725-KM) VOYAGE DOWN THE COAST FOR THE LUCKY ONES, INCLUDING AMES, VERITY AND PAYNTER, IN THE COMPANY OF JIM PIKE, THE JOCKEY (SECOND FROM RIGHT). (COURTESY ROGER MANN)

Sparing themselves the long and tedious train journey, Jardine, Allen, Larwood, Paynter, Verity, Ames and Hammond voyaged aboard *Orungal* down to Sydney — with the late Phar Lap's jockey Jim Pike a fellow passenger. The absence of so many stars from the Newcastle match meant that Jack Hobbs and Plum Warner had to be enlisted for the three-day game.

Their slipping into flannels, while delighting the nostalgia buffs, seemed to disappoint the majority, who wanted to see the entire Ashes-winning team. Jardine's shrewdness was again in evidence. This boat journey was aimed at refreshing his tired warriors. The skipper was scornful of Newcastle for "putting itself on the map as one of the few places in the world which have no desire to see Messrs Hobbs and Warner play cricket!"

His iron resolve and self-discipline enabled him to contain any excessive glee at winning the Ashes — at least in public, though it is easy to imagine him doing his Indian war dance in the privacy of his room; his plan had been laid out rigidly and he had endured heavy criticism. Had he lost, his insistence on utilising Bodyline would have brought the greatest humiliation down upon him. He had won because of his alert captaincy and his better batting line-up (England's last four completely outbatted Australia's), and because of superior bowling resources and fielding. *The Australian Cricketer* was not alone in bewailing Woodfull's shortfall in imagination and originality. By general consensus he was not only captain of a disjointed crew but had been continuously outgeneralled. M.A. Noble felt the Australians were now completely overawed by Harold Larwood and were too willing to duck, while Bradman's method was surely undermining the other batsmen.

The newspapers, almost without exception, gave credit where it was due. Claude Corbett's view was that Jardine was a "born leader" who had allowed no obstacle to prevent him from reaching his goal. Had Australia levelled at 2–2, he believed England would have unleashed their shock attack with more severity than ever before in the final Test. In Manchester a doubting Neville Cardus had read enough (and had probably been to the newsreel cinema too). He turned to Dr Johnson's words: "knock the man down first and be compassionate afterwards". And yet even Cardus was not immune to the schismatic thinking that Bodyline has induced: he wrote that "the sturdy little man from Nottingham has got rid of stalemate" (after the "fatty degeneracy" of batsmen making copious centuries on featherbed pitches). He advocated that a statue of Harold Larwood be erected in London, for his performance was of the kind that Tom Richardson, the outstanding fast bowler of the 1890s, would have recognised and loved.[32]

On the broader front opinion was split — as it always will be — as to whether England could have won the 1932–33 series without using Bodyline.

FOURTH TEST MATCH

BRISBANE (WOOLLOONGABBA) CRICKET GROUND, FEBRUARY 10, 11, 13, 14, 15, 16, 1933

Toss won by Australia
12th men: B.J. Tobin (A), F.R. Brown (E)

Umpires: E.G. Borwick & G.A. Hele
Debuts: E.H. Bromley, L.S. Darling, H.S.B. Love (A), T.B. Mitchell (E)

AUSTRALIA		mins	balls	4s		mins	balls	4s
V.Y. Richardson	st Ames b Hammond	83	159	146	6	c Jardine b Verity	32	64	64	2
*W.M. Woodfull	b Mitchell	67	244	232	7	c Hammond b Mitchell	19	104	105	1
D.G. Bradman	b Larwood	76	156	138	11	c Mitchell b Larwood	24	32	31	3
S.J. McCabe	c Jardine b Allen	20	28	28	4	[5] b Verity	22	82	75	1
W.H. Ponsford	b Larwood	19	48	40	2	[4] c Larwood b Allen	0	4	4	-
L.S. Darling	c Ames b Allen	17	29	21	2	run out (*Larwood/Mitchell*)	39	109	80	3
E.H. Bromley	c Verity b Larwood	26	65	52	2	c Hammond b Allen	7	34	30	-
#H.S.B. Love	lbw b Mitchell	5	31	24	-	lbw b Larwood	3	12	14	-
T.W. Wall	not out	6	32	25	-	c Jardine b Allen	2	5	4	-
W.J. O'Reilly	c Hammond b Larwood	6	7	11	1	b Larwood	4	8	4	1
H. Ironmonger	st Ames b Hammond	8	11	13	1	not out	0	3	2	-
Extras	b 5, lb 1, nb 1	7				b 13, lb 9, nb 1	23		
Total	*(121 overs, 411 mins)*	**340**				*(68.3 overs, 244 mins)*	**175**		

Fall 1/133 2/200 3/233 4/264 5/267 6/292 7/315 8/317 9/329 10/340 1/46 2/79 3/81 4/91 5/136 6/163 7/169 8/169 9/171 10/175

BOWLING	O	M	R	W	w/nb		O	M	R	W	w/nb
Larwood	31	7	101	4	-/1	Larwood	17.3	3	49	3	-/1
Allen	24	4	83	2	-/-	Allen	17	3	44	3	-/-
Hammond	23	5	61	2	-/-	Hammond	10	4	18	0	-/-
Mitchell	16	5	49	2	-/-	Verity	19	6	30	2	-/-
Verity	27	12	39	0	-/-	Mitchell	5	0	11	1	-/-

ENGLAND		mins	balls	4s		mins	balls	4s
*D.R. Jardine	c Love b O'Reilly	46	190	191	3	lbw b Ironmonger	24	132	112	2
H. Sutcliffe	lbw b O'Reilly	86	266	244	10	c Darling b Wall	2	9	11	-
W.R. Hammond	b McCabe	20	90	93	- +	[4] c Bromley b Ironmonger	14	71	75	-
R.E.S. Wyatt	c Love b Ironmonger	12	47	44	2				
M. Leyland	c Bradman b O'Reilly	12	45	48	1	[3] c McCabe b O'Reilly	86	222	235	9#
#L.E.G. Ames	c Darling b Ironmonger	17	82	65	1	[5] not out	14	40	36	- +
G.O.B. Allen	c Love b Wall	13	26	31	1+				
E. Paynter	c Richardson b Ironmonger	83	238	218	10	[6] not out	14	12	11	2+
H. Larwood	b McCabe	23	33	27	2+				
H. Verity	not out	23	162	157	1				
T.B. Mitchell	lbw b O'Reilly	0	1	4	-				
Extras	b 6, lb 12, nb 3	21				b 2, lb 4, nb 2	8		
Total	*(185.4 overs, 599 mins)*	**356**				*(79.4 overs, 247 mins) 4 wkts*	**162**		

+ *plus 1 six*   # *plus 1 five* + *plus 1 six*

Fall 1/114 2/157 3/165 4/188 5/198 6/216 7/225 8/264 9/356 10/356 1/5 2/78 3/118 4/138

BOWLING	O	M	R	W	w/nb		O	M	R	W	w/nb
Wall	33	6	66	1	-/2	Wall	7	1	17	1	-/-
O'Reilly	67.4	27	120	4	-/1	O'Reilly	30	11	65	1	-/-
Ironmonger	43	19	69	3	-/-	Ironmonger	35	13	47	2	-/-
McCabe	23	7	40	2	-/-	McCabe	7.4	2	25	0	-/2
Bromley	10	4	19	0	-/-					
Bradman	7	1	17	0	-/-					
Darling	2	0	4	0	-/-					

ENGLAND WON BY 6 WICKETS

Attendances: 1st day 22,516, 2nd day 28,794, 3rd day 14,177, 4th day 16,992, 5th day 8793, 6th day 1591: Total 92,863
Gate receipts: £10,909.8.0d
Close-of-play scores: 1st day Aus 3/251 (Bradman 71, Ponsford 8), 2nd day Eng 0/99 (Jardine 41, Sutcliffe 51), 3rd day Eng 8/271 (Paynter 24, Verity 1), 4th day Aus (2) 4/108 (McCabe 14, Darling 8), 5th day Eng (2) 2/107 (Leyland 66, Hammond 8)

CHAPTER TWELVE

THE FINAL
SHOOT-OUT

There was one match — the three-day game (without first-class status) against Northern Districts of New South Wales — in the week which separated the fourth and fifth Tests, and the Englishmen were seen, perhaps understandably, as being below par. They were certainly well under strength, and local resentment was such that the Newcastle Cricket Association sent a deputation to the MCC party — in vain — and appealed to the Australian Board for compensation for the shortfall in gate money resulting from the absence of star players such as Larwood, Hammond, Sutcliffe, Allen, Verity and the now-legendary Paynter — perhaps even Jardine too?

Jack Hobbs, now 50, was quite hurt at the negative reaction to the appearance in the match of Warner and himself, and having registered his disappointment, he refrained from describing the play in his book, though he mentioned in the closing chapter that he sustained a knee injury. The 59-year-old Plum Warner would have been equally annoyed by the shouts of "Go it, Grandpa!" as he went about his fielding duties.

Bob Wyatt led MCC and there was no Bodyline bowling in this match. There were, though, two enforced retirements when Northern Districts batted. Jim Donnelly, who had played three times for New South Wales (outscoring Bradman in both innings of the only match they played together), went off, still without a run to his name, after a freak encounter with the ball: he accidentally trod on it and damaged his ankle. Then the

No. 6 batsman, Rayford Robinson, an 18-year-old who was to play in a Test match four years later, was hurt so badly by a ball from Voce which crashed into his groin (he then fell into the stumps but was given not out) that he was not able to bat in the second innings.[1]

There were several interesting pointers to the future in this match. Robinson, with a plaintive gaze about him not dissimilar to Justin Langer's, was a stylish local batsman from Stockton who made his debut for New South Wales two years later, and in his sole Test, at Brisbane in 1936, Bradman's first as captain, he scored 2 and 3 (on a rain-damaged pitch), caught by Hammond off Voce both times. In Warwick Franks's delicately chosen words, Robinson was "a player of enormous potential whose gifts were compromised by his propensity to personal indiscipline".[2]

Ray Little, from Armidale and still only 18, also went on to play for the State, beginning an eight-match career in 1935 with two ducks at the hands of Eddie Gilbert. Hal Hooker's career at Shield level had just ended, but not before he had placed his name beside two notable entries in the record books during his enjoyable 1928–29 season. Together with Alan Kippax (260 not out), at Melbourne, mostly throughout Christmas Day, he established a world record of 307 for the tenth wicket. Then a month later, at Sydney, again with Victoria the opposition, Hooker took four wickets in four balls, including a hat-trick that wrapped up the first innings. He now captained the Northern XI.

But of all the home talent on show at Newcastle, Arthur Chipperfield was to have the most distinguished cricket career, playing in 14 Tests (scoring 99 at Trent Bridge in the first of them, and later a century against South Africa at Durban) and touring England twice. It was here, against the 1932–33 MCC side, that Sydney-born "Chippie", already 27 and player–coach at the Wickham club, a fine batsman, legspinner and slips fielder, was to make his name.

Reg Beatty, another destined to wear the light-blue cap of New South Wales, was the first to get going, making a half-century before Little and Chipperfield engaged in a stand of 103. Chipperfield's stroke-filled 152 took him only 208 minutes, his greatest chunk of luck coming when Duckworth missed a stumping off a Mitchell teaser when he was 95. He reached three figures in only 105 minutes and raised the Districts' total to 322, a challenge slightly beyond the weakened MCC side, who finished 68 short after the first innings. There would have been acute embarrassment without the contribution of an unbeaten 94 by Pataudi, who was nursing a chipped finger-bone. As for Hobbs, the old master, who opened the innings with Wyatt, he soon found his touch, though it was now five months since he had made the last of his 1460 runs for Surrey in the previous season (averaging 54.07, well ahead of the next man, a certain D.R. Jardine). His 44 (with 26 singles) was the neatest of ripostes to the local Philistines. Vic Wright, a left-arm spinner from Maitland, used the crosswind skilfully and came away with the best figures, the undoubted prize among his half-dozen scalps being John Berry Hobbs. Plum Warner, going in just before tea at the fall of the seventh wicket, managed only a single before being bowled as he tried to hook. This caused particular amusement, since he frequently cautioned others against the use of this shot on Australian pitches.[3]

The weather was so dull towards the end of the second day's play that car headlights were trained on the scoreboard for the benefit of spectators.[4] On the final day, Ray Little (a most impressive 117 in under three hours) and fellow colt Baker, from Wyong, had a stand of 102 in the second innings, when Voce went for 36 runs off his four overs. But Bowes and Mitchell got among the wickets. So a target of just over 300, had there been a fourth day, would have been a nice challenge for the makeshift touring team. But there was a Test match to be played, a supremacy to be underlined if possible in Sydney. The 100-mile (160-km) journey was embarked upon without further ado.

NEWCASTLE SPORTS GROUND, FEBRUARY 18, 20, 21, 1933

NORTHERN DISTRICTS OF NEW SOUTH WALES 322 (R.G. Beatty 53, R.C.J. Little 40, A.G. Chipperfield 152, W.E. Bowes 3 for 64) and 236 (R.C.J. Little 117, A. Baker 50, W.E. Bowes 3 for 58, T.B. Mitchell 4 for 62); MCC 254 (J.B. Hobbs 44, M. Leyland 31, Nawab of Pataudi 94 not out, T.B. Mitchell 32, V. Wright 6 for 79). **DRAWN**

Although the daily attendances at the second of Sydney's Test matches compare unfavourably with those at the first, in the innocent days of early December, the final daily average for the series was to show an increase of over 4000 a day (30,436 to 26,030) against the previous MCC tour, in 1928–29. The State associations all pocketed weighty profits and MCC took home nearly £10,000 (perhaps half-a-million in modern money). Well might English billiards champion Melbourne Inman have complained that he wasn't drawing the crowds. "What do you expect if you come over here in Larwood time?" he was told; to which he is supposed to have replied,

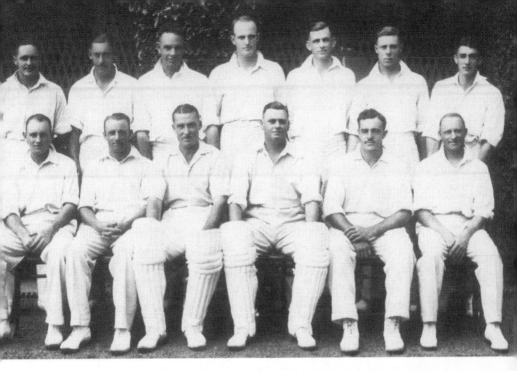

THE AUSTRALIA SQUAD FOR THE FINAL TEST. IT WAS NOT THAT THEY DECIDED TO FIELD
13 MEN IN THE HOPE OF OVERCOMING ENGLAND. INJURY PREVENTED WALL FROM PLAYING AND
BROMLEY WAS MADE 12TH MAN. STANDING — L.S. DARLING, P.K. LEE, H. IRONMONGER,
W.J. O'REILLY, T.W. WALL, E.H. BROMLEY, L.P.J. O'BRIEN; SEATED — S.J. McCABE, D.G. BRADMAN,
V.Y. RICHARDSON, W.M. WOODFULL, H.H. ALEXANDER, W.A.S. OLDFIELD. THE DIFFICULTIES OF THE
SUMMER CAN BE MEASURED IN PART BY COMPARING THIS TEAM WITH AUSTRALIA'S XI IN THE
FIRST TEST: NO PONSFORD, FINGLETON, KIPPAX, GRIMMETT OR NAGEL.

"**** me! You don't expect me to come over here in *lilac* time, do you?"[5]

The opening day of the fifth and final Test, a Thursday, was a working day — for those fortunate enough to be employed — and drew just over 26,000 spectators to the SCG, so the extra security arrangements inspired by ACB secretary Jeanes's message after the near-riot at Adelaide Oval five weeks previously was unlikely to be stretched, though had the Ashes still been at stake, the attendance might well have doubled.

Australia made four changes from Brisbane. Bromley was made 12th man as O'Brien returned, maintaining the quota of left-handers. Ponsford was dropped and in came Perker Lee, the South Australia allrounder. Bert Oldfield seemed fully recovered from the head injury, so Love was out. And two days before the start Wall had to withdraw, the heel injury sustained at Brisbane still troubling him. With Lisle Nagel unable to get leave from his employers, Victoria fast bowler Harry Alexander came in. It was to be his only Test match, but he left a vivid mark on it — or rather on Jardine.

There was only one change in England's line-up. Voce was fit again, so Mitchell had to make do with that one Test on this tour. He could go back to slipping into Australia's dressing-room, supposedly in quest of autographs — but in reality to carry out a secret mission: his captain wanted him to find out what the Australians were talking about. This Derbyshire character had firm views about captains: he thought Jardine was a great skipper, but Fender was better. As for Wyatt, his captain in later Tests, Mitchell claimed "he couldn't captain a box of lead soldiers".

Nor was Jardine much good at winning tosses. He now lost his fourth of the series and was soon leading his team out on a scorchingly hot day. Bushfires were crackling on the outskirts of Sydney. He had impressed upon his men the need to win this final Test, yet if there was an outstanding feature to England's performance in the field this day it was the huge number of dropped catches. To date only one difficult chance had been spilt by the tourists during the series, a telling factor in their success. But now came a veritable cascade of misses. During the lunch break Jardine gathered his players together to discuss the problem, and the air was blue. When he dropped a catch himself soon afterwards some of his players struggled to conceal their giggles. It might have been at that moment that the stubbly, waistcoated Yabba roared another of his celebrated statements from his post on the Hill: "What about a clap for Captain Bligh!"

It had all begun so well for England. Beneath an overcast sky Richardson took guard to Larwood and fed Jardine a straightforward catch in the gully off the fifth ball. This brought Bradman to the crease. He had a bad cold. Surprisingly, it was his first Test on his home ground, although he had played already in a dozen against England. And this was the final Bodyline challenge — for some time to come at least. All summer, through all the gunshot and smoke, the central duel had been Bradman v Larwood. And, it being Sydney, it was as if Larwood felt extra pressure now. He was to write: "On his own dunghill so to speak, right in the bosom of his enormous family, since the whole of Australia's inhabitants are as his brothers and sisters, he came to put things right once and for all. His last chance in Australia until 1936–37."[6]

Don Bradman approached the wicket slightly more slowly than usual, and in the Press box Arthur Mailey considered the welcome to be subdued compared with the usual tumultuous acclaim. Bradman "played in a lifeless sort of way", in Hobbs's opinion. Soon he was cutting Larwood for four and flicking him over slips for another. Then came a back-foot stroke through the covers for three. For his fourth over Larwood swung the leg field into position. It was here that Sutcliffe's influence was clearly observed. When Allen was about to take the ball to measure out his run, the senior pro, as if captain himself, gestured towards Voce and tossed the ball to him.

Jardine kept adjusting the field and switching his bowlers throughout the session, concerned at the below-par performance of Allen and Voce, neither of whom was fully fit. Woodfull was ducking even to balls that barely rose, and Sutcliffe, for one, never ceased to believe that the Australian captain's tactics were misguided: "He went down on his hands and knees to allow the ball to go over the top. He was hit on the backside a number of times and we appealed for lbw!"[7] This time Larwood, in his second spell, bowled him after a laborious 14 runs in just over an hour. Woodfull played on as he tried to avoid a shortish ball outside leg which rose less than he expected. The preceding ball had been, in close fieldsman Jardine's considered opinion, the fastest he had ever seen.

Larwood was galloping in as if it were the first match of the season. His beautifully balanced approach climaxed with a perfect side-on action, left arm high, right foot landing parallel to the crease and scraping audibly during release. Among those watching closely was Eric Barbour, cricketer, selector and writer. Having studied the newsreels, he believed that the England fast man was getting away with a few no-balls. The umpires bent low and continued to do their best.

Bradman had been busy, carving Allen (two overs for 21) to all parts when he replaced Voce, sometimes with little movement of the feet. So the left-armer returned and banged the ball in with a six–three leg field, looking perplexed when Bradman stepped back and cut. So he bounced even more ferociously, causing the batsman to unleash one of his overhead "tennis" shots. Then, when Bradman saved his collarbone with a prop towards short leg, Allen was unable to reach the catch, having been forced back.

Only a few minutes after Woodfull's dismissal, a fine cut to the pickets off Larwood suggested that Bradman was outwitting Bodyline. But for how long might he be expected to do so against the leg attack from both ends? The next ball from Larwood was well up and Bradman moved across to glance, exposing the leg stump, and the ball crashed into it. Once again the newsreel cameraman was fully alert. Bradman's 48 had come from only 56 balls, seven of which were dispatched to the boundary. But it was inadequate — not only for his team and his personal requirements, but also in the face of public demand and expectation.

BRADMAN B. LARWOOD 48 — OUTMANOEUVRED AGAIN. IT WAS THE FOURTH TIME IN SIX WEEKS
THAT THE NOTTINGHAM MAN HAD DISMISSED HIM IN TESTS. IT WAS TO BE THE LAST TIME.
(IMAGES OF BRADMAN)

Larwood now had three wickets for 14. And to think that just before
the match he had asked Jardine if he might be excused from this final
contest: "I've bowled my inside out and we've won the Ashes," he pleaded.
The captain would have none of it: "We've got the bastards down there,"
he purred, twisting his thumb against the table-top, "and we'll keep them
there."[8] It is a colourful interlude to visualise, but its credibility is under-
mined when the next anecdote in Larwood's book concerns an exchange
he is supposed to have had with an opposing batsman in the Newcastle
match: Larwood did not play in Newcastle.

Australia were 67 for 3 at lunch, O'Brien and McCabe a single apiece,
play having been held up briefly when McCabe was hit yet again on the
shoulder by a Larwood flyer. Their partnership gradually rectified matters.
They put on 99 in even time after O'Brien, the left-hander, had played and
missed three times in Larwood's first over following the 45-minute interval.
In intermittent sunshine, with a south-easterly breeze flowing, strokes

were freely played when length allowed, the most striking being McCabe's stand-up pull, which took minds back to his unbeaten 187 in the opening Test. Was he about to do it again? Though he was not enjoying the best of health this summer, he was nevertheless due some runs, having managed only 121 in his seven Test innings since that glorious first of the series.

O'Brien brought up the hundred with a drive to the fence off Hammond. Paynter was running his little socks off at cover, but while England's ground fielding was fine, their catching was not. Larwood bowled exaggerated off theory to O'Brien with only one leg-side fieldsman and five slips, and when the Victorian snicked to Voce the big man floored the hot catch. In the next over O'Brien snicked again between second and third slips, and Voce was deemed to have given him another let-off. Then wicketkeeper Ames missed a wide chance, again off Larwood.

Superstition, whether springing from religious foundations or otherwise, can have a strong bearing on cricketers' thinking, and that day Leo O'Brien must have felt his luck was in. The Catholics in the side all had St Christopher medals, but O'Brien's talisman somehow became separated from his person, perhaps as he adjusted the protective sock in the pocket of his flannels. McCabe, a fellow "Tyke", found it on the grass and returned it to him. Earlier in the season Fingleton had had the rosary beads in his pocket crushed by a ball from Larwood as it thudded into his thigh. He, of course, owing to selection quirks following his pair at Adelaide, failed to see the series through.[9]

Like a massive swarm of bees spread thickly across the mounds at both ends of the Sydney ground and in the stands, the crowd were poised to applaud the century partnership when O'Brien, having dominated the stand with his brisk — if lucky — 61, tried to pull Voce, only for Larwood to shoot his hands up and hold the catch: 163 for 4, and the crowd subdued. Larwood later recalled in his tour book that the Hill was fairly quiet all day, as was normal when Australia did well. Any outbursts, he told his ghost-writer, were caused by "their own ingrained inability to take a licking".

To the warm satisfaction of all Australians, more resistance followed. Len Darling joined McCabe — Darling, the confident left-hander so fondly remembered in later years by O'Reilly as being dismissive of Bodyline: he reckoned his sister could have played it. In five innings against this English attack while Larwood was part of it, Darling never once lost his wicket to him, and it could be that the Australian selectors missed a trick by delaying his selection until the Brisbane Test. This square-jawed batsman, an All-Australian baseballer, had made his first-class debut at 17, and as his pal O'Reilly was keen to record, "his famous hook shot took lots of paint off boundary fences in Australia, England and South Africa".[10] Nonetheless, Ray Robinson had evidence that in the end "even such bold spirits as McCabe and Darling confessed that they were intimidated by Larwood's tactics".[11]

How much better remembered today would McCabe and so many of these Australian batsmen have been had there never been a Bradman?

LEN DARLING FEARLESSLY PULLS ALLEN DURING THE SYDNEY TEST.

The McCabe–Darling stand for the fifth wicket, begun just before tea, was worth 81. Darling was missed by Sutcliffe high to his left at slip off Hammond, and when he was 12, Allen — off balance — put down a return catch. The new ball was taken when the 200 came up, just before 5 o'clock, but Larwood, understandably, showed not quite the fire of the pre-lunch session. It still made tactical sense for McCabe to suggest that his left-handed partner should take most of the new ball, which swung away from him. Wyatt had a try, and went for 12 runs, mainly to Darling, in two overs of medium-pace.

Then at 244 Verity had McCabe caught at slip for a stirring and smoothly made 73. This brought in a tense-looking Oldfield, to sympathetic applause. He held an end while Darling sought more runs, his footwork eye-catching. They put on 52 before the close, strengthening Australia's position just when a late breakthrough would have diluted all the earlier hard work. Larwood even resorted to flat-out Bodyline to Oldfield for the final over of the day, fortunately causing no harm. Had he hit the diminutive Australian on the head again, surely a lynch mob would have charged onto the field.

The 296 runs (21 extras) in the five hours' play constituted not only a fine recovery but the highest return for the first day of any of the 1932–33 Tests.

Even more (298) came on the second day, under a cloudless blue sky. But more catches went down, too, prompting *The Australian Cricketer* to brand much of the cricket as disgraceful for even had it been a third-grade match. (An eerie explanation was also suggested, to which we shall come.) Oldfield might have been caught off the very first ball, when he played Allen close to Larwood at short leg. Darling twice drove Allen for four, bringing up the fast bowler's century on the magnificent SCG scoreboard, though he had no wicket to date. Impatiently he took off the strapping which was intended to ease his strained side muscles. At drinks Sutcliffe didn't bother coming up from his position at deep third man, risking a few gulps from a friendly spectator's bottle at the base of the Hill instead.

Paynter continued to field like a terrier, and just when a memorable century was in the offing for Darling, Verity, who had been underused on the first day, yorked him with his faster delivery, after a 2½-hour 85. His stand with Oldfield had yielded an important 84, and had spanned the crucial first few overs of the day, when a breakthrough by fresh bowlers was most feared.

Now came the fourth successive resistance of over 50, as Keith Lee joined the solicitous Oldfield. The strongly built Perker Lee was an extrovert. Only a few months previously he had been reprimanded by the SACA for jumping the fence to confront a heckler during a district match in Adelaide.[12] Now he watched with amusement as Oldfield was first dropped by Verity at leg slip off Larwood, and then missed off his bowling by Allen, who flung up a desperate hand at forward short leg.

Runs came. Lee hit hard, mainly through the air, and Australia's highest total of the series, 360 on this ground in the first innings of this torrid summer, was surpassed. Lee hit Verity for four, and four again, and nearly a third time, Paynter fielding well by the fence, before the canny bowler held one back and had him caught — for a useful quick-time 42 — by Jardine off a steepling hit at extra cover. O'Reilly swung lustily ("Here they are, Harold! You can have 'em!" he called, pointing at the stumps), just clearing Sutcliffe at long-on. And Oldfield rode his luck further with an edge just wide of Hammond before surviving another chance, this time low to Ames off Larwood, the umpire having to bring his upraised finger hurriedly down again. O'Reilly thick-edged Allen over Voce, and the comedy continued with Verity's spillage of Oldfield just after he had reached his fifty with a scintillating hook for four. The second new ball seemed just as semi-visible to the fieldsmen as the previous one, despite the brightness of the day.

George Duckworth, the forgotten man on this tour, tried to cheer up his team-mates during lunch by recalling a morning when Lancashire's catching was so abysmal that — allegedly — 14 catches went down off Ted McDonald's bowling *before lunch*. It seemed that England were now out to match that record, for straight after lunch (taken with Australia 411 for 7) Jardine could do no more than get a hand to a fast gully catch from O'Reilly's flailing bat off Allen (which may well have prompted another liverish letter home to Mummy and Daddy).

As so often happens in this kind of ongoing adversity, the fielding side got a wicket with a run-out. O'Reilly tried to run away from Larwood's bowling and Oldfield paid the price as Paynter broke the stumps from mid-off. Oldfield's 2¼-hour innings constituted a heartwarming rehabilitation for the figure last seen crumpled beside the Adelaide pitch and wobbling off with a damaged head. It needs little imagination to appreciate how he must have felt as he renewed his contest with Larwood's speed and bounce.

Alexander swung his bat merrily until it fractured, and stirred Larwood's wrath by cutting him to the fence. And when O'Reilly lost his off bail to Allen, that bowler must have felt that there was a God after all. Larwood finally added to the three wickets earned about 24 hours earlier with the easy clean-bowling of Ironmonger. Australia had amassed 435 at better than a run a minute and were ready now to get stuck into England, Ashes or no Ashes. The big total, reflected Larwood, proved that "the howling against Leg-Theory was just so much nonsense".[13] He hoped Australian Board members had been watching and had realised how foolish their first cable had been. So too, he believed, was their setting-up of a special committee.

"Bull" Alexander began the attack from the Paddington end to Jardine, switching to the Randwick end to benefit from the breeze after only one over. It did not take long for this fearless fellow to upset the experienced Englishmen. First Sutcliffe, the non-striker, objected to the way Alexander ran down the pitch, just as he had done four years ago in MCC's match against Victoria. Alexander's bootmarks were setting up ideal rough patches for Ironmonger later on, and the umpire referred it to Woodfull. The bowler made adjustments, although switching to around the wicket hardly helped matters.

Such was Alexander's aggressive demeanour that the Hillites dubbed him the Wild Man of Borneo. As film attests, he was short but strongly built, and had a bustling run-up which culminated in a virile, long-armed delivery off a high leap, his thighs clashing violently against each other in the followthrough. He was nowhere near as fluent as Larwood, nor as fast or accurate. Egged on by Richardson, Alexander put all he had into it. "What about a square leg, Bill?" he panted to his captain. "No, Harry," came Woodfull's unhesitating reply, "too much like Bodyline."

Jardine benefited from two missed catches — what was it about this match? — Alexander's luck was truly out as keeper Oldfield and McCabe at slip between them let a chance go and Lee at third slip failed to secure another sharp low chance. Then Jardine complained about Alexander's straight followthrough, which set the barrackers off again — "in marked contrast to the silence in which Woodfull objected to Allen doing the same thing in the first Test", as one paper noted. England's stubborn captain, however, lasted little longer, for O'Reilly had him glancing fine to avoid the short legs and Oldfield swallowed the catch.

SUTCLIFFE, WHO LOVED TO HOOK, SHOWS ALEXANDER THE SHOT THAT HAD BEEN BRINGING THE YORKSHIREMAN RUNS AGAINST AUSTRALIA AND NUMEROUS OTHER TEAMS FOR SEASONS GALORE.

A seemingly carefree Hammond came in and was soon landing O'Reilly onto the white pickets and hitting Lee along the ground and then through the air for fours. This was Hammond the giant of old. Like Bradman's, his average was now roughly half of what it had been at his glorious best. Some put this down to Australia's concentration on his leg stump, others to the amount of bowling he was now doing. Yet others felt that the distraction of Bodyline bowling, which simply did not appeal to him, gnawed at his concentration.

Sutcliffe too seemed restored. He had often looked to be awkward and inordinately lucky in previous innings. Now there were glimpses of the artist who had made runs seemingly at will on his previous two visits. He dealt more comfortably with O'Reilly and had the freedom to punch short balls from Alexander into the wide spaces on the leg side, for Woodfull went on firmly resisting pleas to strengthen the field there, having no wish to be seen to be adopting leg theory in even the remotest sense.

Sutcliffe's stand with Hammond climbed to 122 ("classic batsmanship", thought Hobbs). Further spillages occurred when Hammond edged Ironmonger to McCabe and Alexander to Richardson. And further objections were lodged with umpire Borwick by the batsmen as Alexander trampled on the pitch (with a predictable reaction from the crowd). There was little time remaining on this second day when Richardson suddenly snapped up Sutcliffe at short leg off the first ball of a new spell from O'Reilly. It was a wrong'un: 153 for 2.

LARWOOD'S TALENT AS A BATSMAN WAS CONCEALED BY THE NEED TO BAT HIM LOW DOWN BECAUSE OF HIS FAST-BOWLING EXERTIONS. HERE AT SYDNEY HE BEGINS TO TAKE BATTING SERIOUSLY. PERKER LEE IS THE GULLY FIELDSMAN.

HAMMOND MADE PILES OF RUNS AT SYDNEY, AND HERE IN THE FIFTH TEST HE UNLEASHES
HIS GLORIOUS COVER DRIVE YET AGAIN.

Verity had been nominated as nightwatchman should a late wicket fall, but Wyatt, for reasons best known to himself, later claimed that he persuaded Jardine to send in Larwood instead. The weary fast bowler had got through 32 wholehearted overs and had just showered when the news was imparted to him. He was fuming. If only his captain had explained that he wanted Larwood to have his innings early so he would be fresh to bowl in the second innings, and that any runs he made would be scored at a faster rate than Verity's.

When Sutcliffe was out Larwood snatched up his bat and said to Ames, "Get your bat ready, Les, because I'm going to get myself out."[14] He stomped out to the middle, whacked the first ball from O'Reilly to Bradman at cover and raced off for a suicidal single. Hammond shouted a warning but found himself responding. It was the most irresponsible thing Larwood did all tour. It could have cost Hammond his wicket. But Bradman threw hard at the bowler's end, missed, and conceded four overthrows to Larwood.

So England finished the day 159 for 2, still 276 behind.

Urged on by screams of advice from the Hillites next day, Alexander bounced Larwood, but there was no serious contact between flesh and ball. Had he not been the fastest bowler in the world, Larwood would have made many runs higher in the order, though he confessed to preferring fast bowling. Still unhappy about having to bat, he went after Alexander with cuts and slashes and a hook or two, exchanging friendly banter with

Oldfield as balls just missed his nose. Nor did Ironmonger cause him much trouble. He thumped him to leg for a four and then just eluded Bradman at square leg for another.

Hammond, sedately getting the feel of the pitch, was lucky to escape when O'Brien backpedalled and overbalanced after a looping mis-hit into the sun off O'Reilly. The majestic Hammond swung O'Reilly for four next over, and entered the nineties. Handsome drives off McCabe brought him only singles, but another glorious stroke off Lee took Hammond to 99, and a single to third man off Ironmonger brought up his seventh hundred against Australia, his third in successive Test innings at Sydney. He was very annoyed to get out next over, sweeping offspinner Lee.

Leyland entered, and Larwood, although uncomfortable against O'Reilly, continued to pick up runs, having reached his fifty with a pleasant on-drive off Ironmonger. Then he just cleared Alexander at mid-on off that bowler. At lunch he was 62, and upon resumption he hooked Alexander's short stuff almost as if making a statement that this was how to do it: except that Alexander was no Larwood and had no heavily populated on-side field.

A straight six off Lee followed by an edged two over the slips and a pick-up through square leg for four took Larwood to 98. Lee bowled again and Larwood this time — not fully accustomed to chalking up centuries — spooned weakly towards mid-on. His hopes, for a split second, were high. The fieldsman was the plodding Ironmonger, and so few catches had been held in this match. But the old boy moved to his right and got his hands into position just below the knee to secure the catch.

LARWOOD HOLES OUT FOR 98, AND THE SYDNEY CROWD GIVE HIM A SPORTING AND SYMPATHETIC SEND-OFF THAT BRINGS UNANTICIPATED LUMPS TO MANY THROATS.

So Harold Larwood missed his Test century. But his dismissal brought out the very best in the Sydney crowd, for the appreciative cheering was as great as if it were Don Bradman who was leaving the field. The members stood and, feeling that handclapping was inadequate, gave their feelings vocal release. Larwood was yet again affected by the mass reaction, so different this time from what he had been accustomed to hearing, and he broke into a trot as he neared the pavilion gate. His captain awaited him: "You little bastard — I knew you could play," were Jardine's words, as recalled by Larwood in his life story.

He had made 98 of the 157 runs registered since he had entered so sullenly the evening before, and it was now left to Leyland and Wyatt to advance on Australia's tall total. There was a mirthful interlude when Wyatt's bat broke as he got off the mark against Alexander. The replacement was not to his taste when he played a false stroke off Alexander close to Richardson's grasp, so Freddie Brown ran out during the drinks break and suddenly Wyatt was seen to be trying out a child's bat. This simple, small joke at the tailend of the bitterest Test series ever contested was very welcome, and was enjoyed to the full by the 33,000 spectators there, who had not lost their sense of humour.

The same could not be said for Maurice Leyland when he was run out after a mix-up with Wyatt. The left-hander played towards square leg — always the trickiest zone for judging a run — and Wyatt would have none of it. Leyland was stranded, and gave his vice-captain a piece of his mind as he departed. It was the first run-out suffered by England in the series.

LESLIE AMES IS GIVEN RUN-OUT. TODAY HE WOULD ALMOST CERTAINLY HAVE BEEN REPRIEVED, PROTECTED BY TELEVISION'S ALL-SEEING EYE.

Ames, surprisingly preferred to Paynter at No. 7, pottered around for a time before becoming another run-out casualty, though a photograph in the papers next day supported the view that he must have been safely home before Oldfield gathered Bradman's brisk but slightly wide throw and broke the wicket.

So they trooped off for tea, England 349 for 6, still 86 behind, and Ames, to a team-mate's enquiry as to whether he could get him anything, replying with a rueful, "Yes, a pistol to shoot myself with."[15]

It was during this interval that pandemonium and despair ran through the English camp at the discovery that the tattered MCC flag was missing. Plum Warner had carried it to Australia on his two earlier tours as captain and it was a powerful sentimental token of recurring success. One minute it was draped over the balcony railings in front of the England dressing-room, then it was gone. Warner was greatly distressed by the apparent theft.

There was an innocent explanation. It had slipped to the ground, and one of the pavilion attendants forgivably saw it as old rag. (Or did he really know?) For a time it was used as just such — one account stated that it was being used to mop up the beer on the pavilion bar counter — but when a full-scale search was launched on the rest day it was found in the storeroom and handed back to a profoundly relieved Warner.[16] Perhaps now the luck would revert once and for all to England.

PLUM WARNER'S SEEMINGLY PERSONAL ENSIGN HANGS FORLORNLY, DESPITE HAVING REPRESENTED THREE TRIUMPHANT MCC VENTURES TO AUSTRALIA OVER 30 YEARS.

The final session on the Saturday was slow. Paynter had his off stump pushed back by a spinner from Lee, leaving Allen to work with Wyatt to close the gap, the latter broody after the two run-outs. They put on 44, Allen lucky when O'Brien let a catch sail over his head, Wyatt bringing up the 400 with a glanced four off Ironmonger and then logging his second half-century of the series with a leg-side four off O'Reilly. To his horror he then drove a full-toss into Ironmonger's hands at mid-on in the final over of the day.

At a banquet staged by the New South Wales government, attended, it seems, by everybody who was anybody, the State Premier, B.S.B. Stevens, made an anodyne speech which included such platitudes as "our visitors have played cricket in the best traditions of the British people". He said that this function was "primarily to show our appreciation of the sportsmanlike manner in which [England] have played the game".[17] It was almost too much for the sentimental and grateful Warner, who spoke in his emotional reply of his hopes that "the little ruffles on the surface will be forgotten and everything unpleasant relegated to the dustheap of oblivion" (like — nearly — his treasured old flag).

As throughout the tour, Warner's public face disguised the anguish he felt and continued to release in his letters to his wife. "D.R. Jardine is a trial," he now wrote. "I never wish to see him again. His outlook and mentality are all wrong. Wyatt and Gubby say 'he is the man who made the game impossible'."[18]

Monday brought England a small advantage on first innings — thanks almost entirely to Allen — and a few pleasures and shocks for what grew to be the biggest attendance of the match, just over 43,000. Alexander soon snapped up Verity, caught by Oldfield off a dangling bat, giving the newcomer his first wicket, at a cost of 115. Voce then helped Allen add 20 before the amateur fell to a brilliant catch by Bradman as he sought his half-century. The ball swirled high while the fieldsman turned and flew after it, holding the catch with outstretched hands. Hobbs was impressed, though, as on a previous occasion he had felt that Bradman "rather spoiled things by ending with a theatrical flourish". So Lee took the bowling honours, following his worthy innings of 42, in his only Test against England. And O'Reilly could put his throbbing feet up at long last.

Australia, batting again and 19 in arrears, suffered the worst possible start, for Richardson tried to pull his second ball, which thudded onto his thumb and shot up over Allen in his usual close-in position. The fielder thrust up his left hand and caught the ball on the rebound with his right. The brave and pugnacious Vic Richardson thus ended the series with a pair. He had seen Allen at short leg out of the corner of his eye throughout the series and had been privy to some of his departures from standard English. "How's the language today, Gubby?" he used to ask. "Oh, fluent!" came the convivial reply. Knowledge of this persuaded Bruce Harris to write that cricket needed one reform: the hanging of a microphone over the pitch with loudspeakers connected all round the ground. "Why shouldn't we hear our cricket as well as see it; share in those little asides that so frequently leave us guessing?"

The crowd remove pickets from the fence.

DESPERATE MEASURES, BUT IMPERATIVE: OUT COME A FEW PALINGS FOR A BETTER VIEW.

And so, for the last time (*ever*, as it turned out), Bradman faced Larwood. The huge assembly watched transfixed, the youngsters down at the very front peering through the gaps where pickets had been knocked free, and radio listeners all over the nation hushing their families. A collective whoosh of relief came as Bradman drove his short-pitched second ball tennis-fashion for four. There was no doubting his intentions.

Woodfull was almost caught when he edged Larwood in front of Hammond at slip, and when Larwood switched to Bodyline he took a blow between the shoulder-blades which caused a short hold-up. A couple of runs later he was hit painfully on the thigh by the same bowler, and at 24 Voce struck him on the shoulder. But he battled on, cutting the following ball for four.

LIKE A HIDE-AND-SEEK GAME THAT HAD LASTED ALL SUMMER, THE CHALLENGE BRADMAN
HAD SET HIMSELF (NOT TO BE TOUCHED ABOVE WAIST LEVEL BY ANY BALL FROM LARWOOD)
REACHES A CONCLUSION OF SORTS AS THE BOWLER STRIKES HIM ON THE UPPER ARM.

The score at lunch had been 32, all but 10 of them to Bradman, who now continued to dance about the crease, exploiting whenever possible the off-side spaces — and splitting his bat in driving Larwood. The Monday crowd had increased noticeably during the interval, a phenomenon known as The Bradman Factor.

And then came the moment Australia's pride and joy had vowed would never come. Larwood hit him. He hit him with a short ball which smacked into his left upper arm, causing him to drop his bat. Bradman thus became the last of Australia's major batsmen to be "branded" (though he had taken a few blows on his padded thigh during the series). The crowd howled its displeasure — and again, next over, when a bumper from Voce hit Woodfull.

Fingleton thought this Bradman innings to be "the riskiest and most thrilling batting imaginable", and concluded that Larwood was not interested in hitting the exposed stumps. It seemed to be that "Larwood was anxious to claim a hit on Bradman".[19] Might there have been a pint of beer on it — or more — with Bill Voce? We shall never know.

It was some time before the muscle stiffened, so Bradman was able to go on blazing away at everything he could reach, with Voce now straining every sinew and the pitch playing at uneven heights. Bradman's fifty, reached with a crisp square-cut four off Verity, came in only 76 minutes. The second half of the century partnership came in a mere 33 minutes, and when Larwood's new spell ended abruptly Australian hopes rose.

The stark reality for England was that Larwood now carried a very serious foot injury, and his dream of taking six of the remaining nine wickets and thus pass Maurice Tate's record of 38 in an Ashes series, let alone claiming Bradman's wicket for the fifth time in their past six Test encounters, was shattered. There was a sharp exchange between bowler and captain, for Jardine found his champion's breakdown not only unbelievable, but unacceptable. To please him, Larwood had to finish the over.

It was a pathetic picture. All Larwood could do, with Jardine utterly determined to keep him on the field as long as Bradman was there, was stand at the crease and wheel his arm over. The bluff was based upon a mirage: that the injury was no more than cramp. Just as poignant was the sight of Woodfull patting back the slow deliveries; someone of a less gentlemanly disposition — O'Reilly, perhaps — might have helped himself to 20 runs.

"I can't run. I'm useless. I'll have to go off," Larwood pleaded.

"Field at cover point," snapped Jardine. "There's a man covering you there. You can't go off while this little bastard's in."[20]

Freed for the time being at least from the greatest menace, Bradman became if anything even keener to add to this wondrous necklace of runs. Having survived (at 37) a "catch" by Jardine in the gully off Allen which was called as a no-ball, he had even escaped poisoning, if a barracker's wry shout was to be believed. As Jardine offered a glass to Bradman during drinks the cry came across the ground: "Make him taste it first, Don!"

Verity takes up the story. On a river bank on the rest day he had sat in his familiar state of deep meditation, thinking over what Jardine had said about the footmarks left by Alexander. He visualised those roughened patches and deduced that they were not much use to him as they were almost completely outside the line of a right-hander's leg stump. But he made a fine calculation that if, bowling over the wicket, he could pitch the ball on a small strip about a foot long and three inches wide (30 cm by 7.5 cm), the ball would bite. Moreover, with the right field placing, batsmen (one in particular) might be tempted to exploit gaps deliberately left.

"The first two balls I bowled to Woodfull hit the spot and turned sharply," wrote Verity, "and just as sharply a midwicket conference was held between the batsmen. Don was down at my end next over, and bang! — four runs came to him through the vacant cover field. Yet another followed: but then, suddenly he was out — bowled in attempting to repeat the stroke off a delivery that pitched outside the leg stump."[21]

The crowd groaned, for a Don double-century had been the wish — and had seemed a distinct possibility. Now he left the field, to loud appreciation and with Jardine clapping his hands to draw Larwood's attention — "Right, Harold, you can go now!" The Englishman limped from the Sydney arena alongside Bradman, neither of the two arch gladiators saying a word. It was one of the most dramatic exits in Test history, but no cameraman, it seems, considered it worth filming.

The Woodfull–Bradman partnership amounted to 115, but the innings now folded for only 67 more runs, the next-highest stand being 20 between Woodfull and O'Brien. By the close of the fourth day England had made 11 without loss, seeking 164 for victory. And there had been further spitefulness.

After Bradman's dismissal Woodfull gave Ames a stumping chance, but three byes resulted. Then O'Brien was caught off Voce at point, which had always seemed a likely fate. An out-of-sorts McCabe quickly went, taken by Jardine at gully off a weak stroke, also off Voce, bowling now over the wicket, and at tea Australia were 139 for 4. (McCabe was admitted for a tonsils operation soon after the match ended.) Mitchell substituted for Larwood in the field, having fielded previously while Wyatt had a bruised wrist strapped up. Meanwhile, a doctor had gone to the England dressing-room to examine Larwood's swollen left foot.

While Woodfull plodded on in the final session, Verity, bowling into the wind, persuaded catches from Darling, obsessively pulling, and Oldfield, driving, both held by Wyatt. Then, when it seemed certain that the captain would carry his bat through yet another innings, Woodfull played on to Allen at 5.10 pm, after three hours of unwavering concentration and self-assurance.

Verity now bowled a flailing O'Reilly and trapped Alexander lbw first ball, a rich little spell which would have ended with a hat-trick had the ball he got past Ironmonger not missed the stumps by the thickness of a cigar. It would have been a succulent way for the calm Yorkshire left-armer to end the series. Instead, Gubby Allen finished it off, uprooting the leg stump of Lee, who was one of only three batsmen to reach double figures. It was considered one of Australia's poorest efforts of the summer.

Jardine took Wyatt rather than Sutcliffe in with him, holding the experienced Yorkshireman back in case of a collapse. Did ever a captain specialise in chopping and changing his batting order like this one? There was not quite half an hour left for play as Alexander measured out his long run and hurtled in, bent on atoning for his dismal first-innings figures, rendered so bad by the inordinate number of dropped catches. But in his second over he was in trouble again for running down the pitch.

When Jardine appealed to the umpire, the bowler swore at England's captain and said to Borwick, "Round the bloody wicket!" This only brought another objection from the batsman, who wondered if Alexander might consider changing into sandshoes. The racket from the Hill was deafening, and the bowler had steam coming out of his ears by now. ("I did my nana," he confessed years later.) He took nonsense from nobody, and when Jardine began patting marks on the pitch Alexander bent down, picked up a blade of grass, and proffered it to him with the words, "You missed this, Douglas." He was, of course, ignored.[22]

Bowling, in his own opinion, as fast as Larwood, Alexander roared in and just missed Wyatt's ear with a bouncer, then cracked Jardine on the gloves as he fended off another nasty rearing ball. Then in his second over he again struck Jardine, this time hard on the hip. Jardine was obviously hurt, and there were hoots and whistles from the crowd, with some counting him out with the slow, doomful "One! Two! Three! ...", a callous reaction that had many Australians squirming as they thought back to the second-most explosive word of the summer, "unsportsmanlike". The England captain straightened up as soon as he became aware of the sound of the blood-lust, and resumed guard. The bowler later said that Don Bradman, fielding down by the Hill, was seen to have a broad grin on his face at this stage; Leo O'Brien reckoned that Alexander jumped for joy when he hit Jardine and yelled "I've killed him! I've killed him!"[23]

How might the series have been conducted if this rugged "Bull", with his William Powell moustache, had been let loose in all the Tests?

In the England dressing-room Jardine said nothing, though his hip-bone, hit by Gilbert in the Queensland match three weeks before, was bleeding. But his duty was done for the day, and he resumed next morning, as unsmiling and uncommunicative as ever. Looking back 60 years on, Harry Alexander said: "He didn't flinch. He had some guts. I didn't like him as a man, but I admired him for the guts he had. He was a peculiar man. He gave the impression he loved antagonising people."[24]

That evening a Londoner named Crudgington asked to see D.R. Jardine. He was an old soldier of the Royal Garrison Artillery and represented the

Mons Veterans' Association, eight of whose members had watched the day's play. (Mons, in Belgium, was the scene in August 1914 of the first major British engagement in the Great War. Aside from the mystical vision of the Angel of Mons, it became a bloodbath as the German cavalry overran the British lines.) This cricket-loving survivor, who had probably emigrated to Australia, presented a silver ashtray to Jardine to mark the winning of the Ashes. The cricketer told him that he regretted being too young to have fought, but the memento, he said, would be treasured as one of the nicest gestures made to him in Australia.

On the fifth-day wicket, could Ironmonger now prosper like Verity? With the attendance amounting to no more than a fifth of the previous day's, atmosphere was lacking, and as Jardine and Wyatt cautiously eased the total up, a sense of inevitability cloaked the scene. Ironmonger's very first delivery leapt from the rough (referred to as "Alexander's ragtime patch") and went for two byes, but although he was to bowl for the rest of the innings and concede scarcely more than one run per over, he was not to run amok, and neither was the grimacing O'Reilly.

A DISAPPOINTING SERIES WITH THE BAT ENDS FOR D.R. JARDINE AS RICHARDSON
SNAPS HIM UP AT SLIP ON THE FINAL DAY.

Ernie Bromley fielded as substitute for Bradman, whose left bicep had stiffened after the blow from Larwood; this led to the unusual sight of the world's best batsman bringing out the drinks. The only real excitement came when Ironmonger drew Jardine forward and had him caught at slip and 12 minutes later bowled Leyland for a duck as the batsman raised his bat high only for the ball to jag back off his knee-roll. This rotund left-hander ended his otherwise profitable series as he began it: scoreless. Ironmonger had 2 for 8 off 11 overs. People craned forward. Could this be the breakthrough?

Hammond and Wyatt made sure it wasn't. They batted with care, punishing anything loose, and it was now that Arthur Mailey, who knew spin bowling inside out, declared that it was Australia's batsmen who had let the side down. His reasoning was simple: he considered Ironmonger a better bowler than Verity, and the Australian now had a pitch even more worn upon which to operate: ergo, England's batsmen had a greater task ahead of them than had the Australians; but they did not fail.

Hammond attacked the spinners, once landing O'Reilly for a massive six over wide long-on and using his feet to get at Ironmonger without taking undue risk. The six landed high in the stand and the ball bounced down a stairwell that led to the luncheon-room. They continued to look for quick singles, and Hammond touched Lee through the vacant slips area, there being nobody behind the wicket apart from Oldfield. He scored off McCabe to reach his fifty, and then the century stand arrived. For a time Wyatt kept pace with his partner, punishing Lee and completing almost as important a batting double as Hammond. When the weary O'Reilly bowled Wyatt it was swiftly seen to have been a no-ball. The bowler addressed a few muffled words to nobody in particular.

England's third-wicket pair made sure of victory, which came at 3.40 pm with a huge six off Lee from Hammond's cultured bat. This great shot, symbolic of the closure of such a long and unhappy chapter, and very properly captured on film, landed the ball in the lower reaches of the Sheridan Stand. There was a scuffle for the ball by spectators, as there also was in the middle by players seeking souvenir stumps and bails, much to the annoyance of long-serving curator Bill Stuart.

England thus won the Bodyline series of 1932–33 four Tests to one, and the overall balance between the two countries now stood at 51 victories each. The principal protagonists came away with fine figures, Bradman with a batting average of 56.57, Larwood with 33 wickets at 19.52. And yet both would have liked better. Bradman's figure, viewed against his overall career performance, was harshly perceived as failure.

When it was over there was relief — of varying hues — all around. The mass of spectators gathered by the pavilion had their calls for the captains unrewarded. Bill Woodfull walked through the Long Room to the England dressing-room to congratulate Jardine, having himself been given three rousing cheers by his own players at the behest of Vic Richardson. And Jack Hobbs went down to congratulate his county captain, who told him it was a great performance to have won four Tests after having lost four tosses.

Not the least relieved of the participants were umpires Borwick and Hele, whose concern for batsmen's safety had been on red alert from the first day of the series. In terms of nervous tension alone they had earned their £15 per Test (£10 if in their hometown). If they made mistakes, few among the three-quarters of a million people who watched the Tests would have known.

Compared with the bevy of important people and the feelings of international goodwill at the NSWCA's welcoming dinner early in the tour, the farewell function at the Hotel Australia was a subdued affair. For one thing, there was not a current Australian cricketer in sight. Still, the Association met its diplomatic obligations by presenting a cigarette box each to Jardine and the two managers. The boxes were made from Australian cabinet timbers and were each surmounted with a kangaroo and boomerang. The craftsman, had he been a cricket-lover, must have been tempted instead to stick a set of gallows on each box.

The Australians returned to their headquarters at the Coogee Bay Hotel after the match, eager to pack up and go home. But before catching the train back to Melbourne, Woodfull met umpire Hele and *Age* writer Frank Maugher by Coogee beach, where they talked for three hours about possible solutions to the Bodyline problem. They agreed that imposing limits on the leg-side field was not the answer, for medium-pace leg theory, while not attractive, did not pose serious physical threat. They concluded that it would be best if the umpire were left to decide whether or not a bowler intended to intimidate.[25]

This eventually was very close to the amendment which was adopted. But as Harold Larwood then and many since have known, it became a law reliant on mind-reading, and was therefore unsound.

FIFTH TEST MATCH

SYDNEY CRICKET GROUND, FEBRUARY 23, 24, 25, 27, 28, 1933
Toss won by Australia
12th men: E.H. Bromley (A), T.B. Mitchell (E)

Umpires: E.G. Borwick & G.A. Hele
Debut: H.H. Alexander (A)

AUSTRALIA		mins	balls	4s			mins	balls	4s
V.Y.Richardson	c Jardine b Larwood	0	4	5	-	c Allen b Larwood	0	1	2	-
*W.M.Woodfull	b Larwood	14	69	59	-	b Allen	67	185	168	5
D.G.Bradman	b Larwood	48	71	56	7	b Verity	71	97	69	9
L.P.J.O'Brien	c Larwood b Voce	61	107	88	6	c Verity b Voce	5	22	20	-
S.J.McCabe	c Hammond b Verity	73	172	129	11	c Jardine b Voce	4	6	6	1
L.S.Darling	b Verity	85	148	129	8	c Wyatt b Verity	7	10	13	1
#W.A.S.Oldfield	run out (Paynter)	52	138	96	4	c Wyatt b Verity	5	22	25	-
P.K.Lee	c Jardine b Verity	42	35	44	7	b Allen	15	30	21	2
W.J.O'Reilly	b Allen	19	37	27	1	b Verity	1	2	3	-
H.H.Alexander	not out	17	17	17	2	lbw b Verity	0	1	1	-
H.Ironmonger	b Larwood	1	4	4	-	not out	0	2	3	-
Extras	b 13, lb 9, w 1	23				b 4, nb 3	7			
Total	(108.2 overs, 410 mins)	**435**				(54.4 overs, 198 mins)	**182**			

Fall 1/0 2/59 3/64 4/163 5/244 6/328 7/385 8/414 9/430 10/435 1/0 2/115 3/135 4/139 5/148 6/161 7/177 8/178 9/178 10/182

BOWLING	O	M	R	W	w/nb		O	M	R	W	w/nb
Larwood	32.2	10	98	4	-/-	Larwood	11	0	44	1	-/-
Voce	24	4	80	1	1/-	Allen	11.4	2	54	2	-/3
Allen	25	1	128	1	-/-	Hammond	3	0	10	0	-/-
Hammond	8	0	32	0	-/-	Voce	10	0	34	2	-/-
Verity	17	3	62	3	-/-	Verity	19	9	33	5	-/-
Wyatt	2	0	12	0	-/-						

ENGLAND		mins	balls	4s			mins	balls	4s
*D.R. Jardine	c Oldfield b O'Reilly	18	33	50	1	c Richardson b Ironmonger	24	58	57	2
H. Sutcliffe	c Richardson b O'Reilly	56	155	137	4					
W.R. Hammond	lbw b Lee	101	207	205	12	[4] not out	75	123	140	6+
H. Larwood	c Ironmonger b Lee	98	138	148	9+					
M. Leyland	run out (Darling/Oldfield)	42	77	87	6	[3] b Ironmonger	0	12	16	-
R.E.S. Wyatt	c Ironmonger b O'Reilly	51	161	196	5	[2] not out	61	195	215	4
#L.E.G. Ames	run out (Bradman/Oldfield)	4	32	27	-					
E. Paynter	b Lee	9	39	29	1					
G.O.B. Allen	c Bradman b Lee	48	102	104	6					
H. Verity	c Oldfield b Alexander	4	14	14	-					
W. Voce	not out	7	29	35	-					
Extras	b 7, lb 7, nb 2	16				b 6, lb 1, nb 1	8			
Total	(171.2 overs, 500 mins)	**454**				(71.2 overs, 195 mins) 2 wkts	**168**			
			+ plus 1 six & 1 five					+ plus 2 sixes		

Fall 1/31 2/153 3/245 4/310 5/330 6/349 7/374 8/418 9/434 10/454 1/43 2/43

BOWLING	O	M	R	W	w/nb		O	M	R	W	w/nb
Alexander	35	1	129	1	-/-	Alexander	11	2	25	0	-/-
McCabe	12	1	27	0	-/-	O'Reilly	15	5	32	0	-/1
O'Reilly	45	7	100	3	-/2	Ironmonger	26	12	34	2	-/-
Ironmonger	31	13	64	0	-/-	Lee	12.2	3	52	0	-/-
Lee	40.2	11	111	4	-/-	McCabe	5	2	10	0	-/-
Darling	7	5	3	0	-/-	Darling	2	0	7	0	-/-
Bradman	1	0	4	0	-/-						

ENGLAND WON BY 8 WICKETS
Attendances: 1st day 26,143, 2nd day 25,687, 3rd day 33,032, 4th day 43,380, 5th day 8604: Total 136,846
Gate receipts: £11,782.14.5d
Close-of-play scores: 1st day Aus 5/296 (Darling 66, Oldfield 13), 2nd day Eng 2/159 (Hammond 72, Larwood 5), 3rd day Eng 8/418 (Allen 25), 4th day Eng (2) 0/11 (Jardine 6, Wyatt 5)

TEST AVERAGES 1932-33

AUSTRALIA

BATTING	M	Inns	NO	HS	Runs	Av	50s	100s	Catches	Stumpings
D.G. Bradman	4	8	1	103*	396	56.57	3	1	3	-
S.J. McCabe	5	10	1	187*	385	42.78	1	1	4	-
L.S. Darling	2	4	0	85	148	37.00	1	0	2	-
W.M. Woodfull	5	10	1	73*	305	33.89	3	0	0	-
P.K. Lee	1	2	0	42	57	28.50	0	0	0	-
V.Y. Richardson	5	10	0	83	279	27.90	1	0	7	-
W.A.S. Oldfield	4	7	2	52	136	27.20	1	0	6	1
J.H.W. Fingleton	3	6	0	83	150	25.00	1	0	3	-
W.H. Ponsford	3	6	0	85	141	23.50	1	0	0	-
L.P.J. O'Brien	2	4	0	61	87	21.75	1	0	3+	-
L.E. Nagel	1	2	1	21*	21	21.00	0	0	0	-
H.H. Alexander	1	2	1	17*	17	17.00	0	0	0	-
E.H. Bromley	1	2	0	26	33	16.50	0	0	1	-
A.F. Kippax	1	2	0	19	27	13.50	0	0	0	-
C.V. Grimmett	3	6	0	19	42	7.00	0	0	1	-
W.J. O'Reilly	5	10	0	19	61	6.10	0	0	1	-
T.W. Wall	4	8	1	20	42	6.00	0	0	4	-
H.S.B. Love	1	2	0	5	8	4.00	0	0	3	-
H. Ironmonger	4	8	3	8	13	2.60	0	0	2	-

+ includes 1 as substitute

BOWLING	O	M	R	W	Av	5w/i	Wides	No-balls
T.W. Wall	170.1	33	409	16	25.56	1	0	13
W.J. O'Reilly	383.4	144	724	27	26.81	2	0	12
H. Ironmonger	245.1	96	405	15	27.00	0	0	0
P.K. Lee	52.4	14	163	4	40.75	0	0	0
D.G. Bradman	12	1	44	1	44.00	0	0	0
L.E. Nagel	43.4	9	110	2	55.00	0	0	0
C.V. Grimmett	147	41	326	5	65.20	0	0	0
S.J. McCabe	92.5	17	215	3	71.67	0	0	3
H.H. Alexander	46	3	154	1	154.00	0	0	0
A.F. Kippax	2	1	3	0	-	0	0	0
L.S. Darling	11	5	14	0	-	0	0	0
E.H. Bromley	10	4	19	0	-	0	0	0

ENGLAND

BATTING	M	Inns	NO	HS	Runs	Av	50s	100s	Catches	Stumpings
E. Paynter	3	5	2	83	184	61.33	2	0	0	-
W.R. Hammond	5	9	1	112	440	55.00	2	2	6	-
H. Sutcliffe	5	9	1	194	440	55.00	3	1	1	-
R.E.S. Wyatt	5	9	2	78	327	46.71	3	0	2	-
Nawab of Pataudi	2	3	0	102	122	40.67	0	1	0	-
M. Leyland	5	9	0	86	306	34.00	2	0	2	-
H. Verity	4	5	1	45	114	28.50	0	0	3	-
H. Larwood	5	7	1	98	145	24.17	1	0	2	-
G.O.B. Allen	5	7	0	48	163	23.29	0	0	7	-
D.R. Jardine	5	9	0	56	199	22.11	1	0	9	-
L.E.G. Ames	5	8	1	69	113	16.14	1	0	8	2
W. Voce	4	6	2	8	29	7.25	0	0	3	-
T.B. Mitchell	1	1	0	0	0	0.00	0	0	1	-
W.E. Bowes	1	2	2	4*	4	-	0	0	0	-

BOWLING	O	M	R	W	Av	5w/i	Wides	No-balls
H. Larwood	220.2	42	644	33	19.52	2	0	7
T.B. Mitchell	21	5	60	3	20.00	0	0	0
H. Verity	135	54	271	11	24.65	1	0	1
W. Voce	133.3	24	407	15	27.13	0	1	6
G.O.B. Allen	171	29	593	21	28.24	0	8	6
W.R. Hammond	120.5	27	291	9	32.33	0	0	0
W.E. Bowes	23	2	70	1	70.00	0	0	0
R.E.S. Wyatt	2	0	12	0	-	0	0	0

CHAPTER THIRTEEN

SACKCLOTH
AND ASHES

Douglas Jardine and the bulk of his team were not yet free to go home. While the injured Larwood was repatriated to England and Pataudi headed back to India to attend to some business, the Englishmen had to meet their obligations with State matches in Melbourne and Adelaide before the brief New Zealand visit. It was anticlimactic, but there was some animated cricket still to come.

Larwood and Pataudi travelled westwards together, company for each other across the vast Nullarbor. At Quorn late one night a mob of noisy youngsters came aboard the train and began booing and hissing at the two cricketers, Larwood in particular. They spat pomegranate pips at them, and Larwood feared there would be serious trouble. They reached Perth safely, however, and a reporter got wind of the matter, misquoting Larwood — apparently — by writing that he never wanted to see Australia again.[1]

English heads may just have cleared by the time they batted against Victoria, three days after their Sydney Test victory. It was no surprise when Woodfull withdrew from the Victoria team, Keith Rigg leading in his stead. Nor was Ponsford anywhere to be seen.

Australia's captain was a tired man after batting for over 19 hours during this most turbulent of Test series, averaging 16 runs an hour as time and again he tried to hold the fort, taking more of the Bodyline onslaught than any of his team-mates. His fortitude, coupled with his refusal to retaliate, led curiously to the convictions that (a) it was fortunate for *Australia* that such a strong leader was there, and (b) that it was fortunate for *England* that such a forbearing man presided over the opposition. Had a Richardson been in charge it might have developed into an all-out fast-bowling brawl. Wyatt, who was captaining MCC in this match, had sympathy for Woodfull and thought that he must now have forgotten what a friendly game of cricket, like this one against Victoria, was like.

Sutcliffe would have been interested to see Alexander measuring out his run again to start proceedings at the MCG, where 10,000 spectators scattered themselves around the vast bowl. But the tearaway bowler was no more successful now than in the Test: less so, in fact, for he failed to take a wicket. Perhaps the absence of his old friend Jardine somehow diminished his ardour. Sutcliffe made a two-hour 75 and Hammond was well worth watching for his swift 59 (eight fours, two sixes, with 33 runs off two overs from Fleetwood-Smith, who eventually had him caught, after so much torture in the two matches in which they confronted each other). But the cake was taken by the half-forgotten Tate, who thumped 15 fours in his 94 not out. Neither Ironmonger nor Fleetwood-Smith worried any of the batsmen, and the last-wicket stand of 53 that Tate had with Bowes (run out for 20) was a riotous affair. Amusement was never far away when Tate was about. So embarrassed was he by the warmth of the reception as he stepped into the arena that he went to raise his cap only to find that he wasn't wearing one.

Len Darling, one of six left-handers in the Victoria side, further heightened his reputation with a century — it was only the *fifth* century scored against the tourists in their 17 first-class matches — and Hec Oakley, who made 83 not out in the November match, now stroked 50. Hans Ebeling, who along with four other members of this Victoria side was to tour England in 1934, made an unbeaten 68 batting at No. 8 and had an unlikely 10th-wicket stand of 40 with Ironmonger (6) that gave Victoria a token lead.

Victoria's two left-arm spinners got good results in the second innings as MCC set about giving Victoria a decent target, the second day's play having been reduced by rain to only 45 minutes. Hammond was more cautious this time, and Allen, nursing a recurrence of his side strain, fell just short of a half-century, lbw to the confusing spin of Fleetwood-Smith.

The challenge was set at 178 runs in 109 minutes (overs not coming into it, of course, as regulations then stood). There was excitement immediately, as O'Brien was caught low by Allen at mid-on first ball. The batsman hesitated, the umpire gave him out, but Allen signalled that the ball had touched the grass and O'Brien stayed. But not for long. After two wickets had gone Rigg and Bromley laid into the bowling, but 78 runs were still needed, with only 38 minutes remaining. At half a minute to six, with five runs needed, the umpires ordered one more over. Bowes bowled seven tidy balls. And with one run needed off the final delivery, and a thick off-side field in place, Rigg tried to hook but merely lobbed a catch to Mitchell at mid-on. Although Victoria still had seven wickets in hand, under prevailing rules the match was declared a tie, the first ever in Australian first-class cricket.

The Australian Cricketer published an epic verse to mark the exciting finish. The creator "WJN" wisely retained his anonymity, but, for the record, the final stanza went:

Thus Captain Rigg (at first twelfth man)
Missed immortality
In the closest match the game had seen
In Nineteen-thirty-three!

MELBOURNE CRICKET GROUND, MARCH 3, 4, 6, 7, 1933

MCC 321 (H. Sutcliffe 75, W.R. Hammond 59, E. Paynter 30, M.W. Tate 94 not out, H. Ironmonger 3 for 82) and 183 for 9 dec (W.R. Hammond 64, G.O.B. Allen 48, H. Ironmonger 5 for 31, L.O'B. Fleetwood-Smith 3 for 66); **VICTORIA** 327 (L.S. Darling 103, H.H. Oakley 50, H.I. Ebeling 68 not out, W.E. Bowes 3 for 93, F.R. Brown 3 for 63) and 177 for 3 (K.E. Rigg 88, E.H. Bromley 56 not out). **TIED**

At the luncheon put on by the Victorian government, Dick Palairet made what Arthur Mailey, a keen judge in such matters, considered the most appropriate speech of the entire tour. It was an indication that MCC did not exploit its oratorical resources sufficiently, for Warner always seemed to think he was in church and Jardine that he was in a Winchester College classroom. Palairet, with his sad moustache, had a winning way about him, though it had been slow to reveal itself outside the travelling team. The problem was that he was usually well down the pecking order when it came to speech-making. Given the opportunity at last, he proved highly entertaining. Amidst his happy remarks he thanked the Melbourne tramways department for painting "Safety Zone — MCC" all over the city's streets (knowing full well that it stood for Melbourne City Council).

When he told baggagemaster Ferguson that the managers and a couple of the amateurs would not after all be accepting an invitation to Canberra to meet Governor-General Isaacs because the captain had no wish to do so, Fergie pointed out that the managers should be making these decisions. "Oh, well," said Palairet with a shrug, "we don't want to have any bother."[2] So they did meet the Governor-General, who took the opportunity to urge Warner to do what he could to mend Anglo-Australian relations when he got back to England, a plea Ernest Crutchley would have been keen to endorse.[3]

And so to the final tour match, back in Adelaide, where the volcano had rumbled and erupted two months previously. Here Vic Richardson showed what might have been as he let his two fast bowlers — Wall was not playing — indulge in some Bodyline, while Jardine, with a depleted team (Sutcliffe was already on his way to New Zealand), showed what he thought of Adelaide by ordering a go-slow with the bat and then taking the mickey in the matter of headwear. It was no rare sight to see all the Englishmen in their navy-blue MCC caps while their skipper wore his Harlequin cap, but when towards the end of this match the procedure was reversed and they all donned borrowed multi-coloured caps while Jardine wore his MCC cap it caused a chuckle or two around the thinly populated terraces. His heart must have been full of joy at the prospect of never being the target of abuse on a cricket field ever again. "Ay, Jardine! Where's the butler to carry ya bat for ya?" may have been worth an imperceptible smile, but he had had to endure far worse than that.

Nobody could be bothered laying on any official functions this time for the English team, so the caps nonsense helped brighten a low-key atmosphere, break down the sense of boredom and combat the fatigue. As for the admissibility of a Harlequin cap in an international cricket match, Jack Fingleton was rightly adamant that no cap should take precedence over your country's. (He would turn in his grave if he could have beheld some of the sponsors' headwear forced onto cricketers for television interviews today.) As for that Harlequin cap, Australian historian Professor Manning Clark, himself a former Melbourne first-grade wicketkeeper who had played for Oxford University in 1939, said in an interview with writer Jack Egan in 1989: "But if you knew anything about Oxford, there was nothing very odd about what he was doing, really. It was just a cap for people who played good cricket. I even got a Harlequin cap at Oxford, so there was nothing very unusual about it."[4]

MCC crawled to 240 for 4 on the first day against South Australia, Paynter and Wyatt scoring at a reasonable rate but Leyland and Jardine, who followed them, batting tiresomely before Ames came to enliven matters. It was *The Australian Cricketer*'s view that the visitors must have been using bats that were too heavy and perhaps suffered from paralysis of the arms. The dreariness of some of the English batting during the summer was objected to: "we want some more of that West Indian style of cricket".

Grimmett, deposed from the Test team after the first three Tests (and author of two recently published books on spin bowling), took three wickets in the match but paid over 200 runs for them. Still he finished with 55 wickets for the season, second only to O'Reilly's 62, though at much greater cost, and the two were destined to pair up profitably again, on the next tour of England and beyond.

Verity had opened the innings with Paynter, and fiddled around for 42 minutes for his 12 runs, while the oddest dismissal was Jardine's: he got a fine touch to a ball from Tobin which then grazed a stump on its way to keeper Walker's gloves without budging the bails. That evening Vic Richardson was critical on radio about MCC's sluggish scoring, but he paid the price next day when Bowes had him caught off a bouncer by Verity at slip second ball of the innings, giving him three ducks in his last nine balls from this English attack.

South Australia batted at only slightly greater speed, though Jack Palmer, in his only first-class match, sniffed around for 81 minutes for his 15. "Bulla" Ryan, top scorer, got on with it, his 61 coming in an hour and a half, while Maurice Tate was another happy man for having shared the new ball with Bowes. Duckworth opened with Paynter in MCC's second innings, and the Englishmen could scarcely believe their eyes when they saw Tobin and Williams bowling bouncers to a Bodyline field setting.

MCC batted through the Monday, Leyland and Jardine having a fourth-wicket stand of 142 in even time after Wyatt had taken three blows from the tall Williams's bowling. But the South Australia pair were simply not fast enough to make it count, and according to Hobbs, not only did the crowd not seem to have any opinion on the matter but the Englishmen (Wyatt apart, perhaps) considered this attempt at retaliation as a bit of a joke. Who could have foretold that young Graham Williams would be cheered at Lord's 12 years later when he went out to bat for the Australian Services in a "Victory Test", having recently been released from a German prisoner-of-war camp? After taking the wickets of Hutton and Hammond, Williams was now given what Keith Miller described as "a great ovation that compares with anything ever given Bradman, Lillee or Richards". But this was different: "Everyone stood up. They all knew about Graham's captivity. He was a big fella, but he was gaunt from his experience, and he just walked round for a while as if in a trance."[5]

During his undefeated 152 (264 minutes) Maurice Leyland was hit on the head, but not full-on, the glancing blow bringing four *leg*-byes. Voce applied the finishing touches before the declaration on the fourth day with 33 not out in 15 minutes, and the State XI were set a fanciful 479 to win. Richardson got off the mark this time and made 20, and Nitschke pounded 87 before Mitchell had him lbw. But Voce, as if to show how leg theory should be bowled, made a few batsmen hop about before Tobin took a lifter full in the face when 32 and was knocked out, recreating fearful visions from the Test match. He had to retire for a time but gamely returned to see the innings through with Grimmett and force the draw. Bowes was rendered thoughtful and miserable by seeing four catches go down (three in succession) off his bowling in seven deliveries.

Jardine, having given himself a ceremonial over from which 13 runs were taken, had entered the match, Mailey imagined, with a sulky, mischievous imp sitting on his shoulder saying: "This is where the old fossils sent the unsportsmanlike cable from, Duggie ... Bat as slowly as you can. Don't even try to win ... Stop for drinks every half hour, and lie down when you get them."

Po-faced R.W.E. Wilmot was distraught when he saw the fancy caps on the heads of the English cricketers: "No-one could suggest that either Ames or Mitchell were 'Harlequins' or that Leyland was an 'Incogniti', Paynter a member of St John's College, Cambridge, or that Voce was a 'Crusader'." Precisely. But Hobbs, the eternally respectful professional, saw it as a "joyful spectacle" that England's players wore all manner of club caps "as a sign of rejoicing that they were going home".

ADELAIDE OVAL, MARCH 10, 11, 13, 14, 1933

MCC 298 (E. Paynter 62, R.E.S. Wyatt 43, M. Leyland 36, D.R. Jardine 48, L.E.G. Ames 63, B.J. Tobin 3 for 65, C.V. Grimmett 3 for 124) and 371 for 8 dec (E. Paynter 47, M. Leyland 152 not out, D.R. Jardine 65, W. Voce 33 not out, R.G. Williams 3 for 107, P.K. Lee 3 for 65); **SOUTH AUSTRALIA** 191 (H.C. Nitschke 38, A.J. Ryan 61, W.E. Bowes 3 for 60, M.W. Tate 3 for 36) and 313 for 8 (H.C. Nitschke 87, A.R. Lonergan 36, B.J. Tobin 52 not out, W.E. Bowes 4 for 95). **DRAWN**

No homeward journey just yet though. They dashed back to Melbourne and played a soccer match next day against Hakoah, a Jewish team which had won the Victorian premiership. MCC lost 1–3 in front of an appreciative crowd of 3000 while playing robustly, Paynter's skills catching the eye and Hammond, the captain, reminding everybody of his professional days with Bristol Rovers. Hammond's face "wreathed in smiles", they took the train up to Sydney and from there the most despised — and equally the most successful — English team ever to visit Australia sailed away across the Tasman Sea for a refreshing and record-breaking fortnight in New Zealand. That graphic journalist Frank Browne wrote of their departure from Australia as if they were jackbooted Germans who had stamped across the Lowlands: "Australians watched them go with the sullen hatred of a conquered nation. Not an Australian cricketer farewelled them. It looked as though what had all started in Melbourne 66 [actually 56] years before might have finished."[6]

AS ARTHUR MAILEY SAW IT. THE PALLBEARERS ARE SMILING, BUT THE SOBERING HEADING
SERVED AS A WARNING THAT THERE COULD YET BE MORE OF THE SAME.

The future was indeed still uncertain. The Australian Board's climbdown before Brisbane had allowed the tour to continue, but the matter of Bodyline's future — and whether Australia would agree to tour England in 1934 — continued to hang heavily in the air. Cricket administrators, diplomats and people with vested interests in Anglo-Australian relations continued to work feverishly behind the scenes.

Warner's biographer, Gerald Howat, made three most telling remarks in his book. First, "It says a great deal for the ethics and conventions of the day that a party containing two managers at mild variance, an autocratic captain, and players who had private differing views on policy could represent such an image of collective loyalty to the outside world over eight months. In our own times, and over a much shorter period of time, dissent would certainly 'out'. It also says something for Warner."

Second, in explaining Warner's apparent weakness in his failure to curb Jardine: "To have done that would have needed the rhetoric of Cicero and the courage of Scipio. Nor could he have been assured, in December 1932, that the senators from Lord's would have backed him up."

And third, in looking at the broader picture, and in words upon which Warner himself could hardly have improved: the Bodyline episode in some ways "heralded the dawn of a new world in which politics and sport would become inextricably associated, in which the imperial bonds unifying cricket would become weaker, in which — after Warner's time — the role of MCC would be diminished. Lord's, no more than Westminster, could not forever arbitrate upon an Empire which had ended."

Political intervention in international cricket has been in evidence time and again since Bodyline, principally over the South African issue and almost certainly following the ball-tampering allegations surrounding Pakistan (newly returned to the Commonwealth) in the early 1990s. Cricket, once a meadow game, was now a major tool in the jungle of world affairs.

There was to be no Bodyline bowling in New Zealand. For one thing, the injured Larwood was on his way home aboard *Otranto*, to be met at Port Said by his county captain Arthur Carr, who escorted him for the remainder of the voyage, as a sort of minder, while penning his own thoughts for the *Daily Sketch*. Carr's mission was condemned by Nottinghamshire CCC (and by MCC, who had warned Larwood not to speak or write publicly about the tour, advice backed up by Lord Belper, another of MCC's bigwigs and Larwood's neighbourhood aristocrat). Larwood was being swamped with tempting big-money offers to sign newspaper articles about his recent experiences. He resisted … for the time being. Lord's would later deny Jardine too when he requested permission to write.

Thousands waited to greet Larwood. He travelled overland from Toulon, and as the train from Dover reached Victoria station he was reunited with Lois. There were many more Notts folk cheering him at Nottingham station when the train pulled in just before midnight. If he had any reservations about where he stood, this must have erased them. Having given his little daughter June a big hug and a koala doll (Billie Bluegum), he had to stay indoors, for his house was besieged by newspapermen. When the rest of the team arrived home on May 6 the tour was officially over. The next day Harold Larwood's thoughts appeared in the *Sunday Express*. The edition sold well.

Larwood would have enjoyed New Zealand. Everyone else did. For a start, there was no barracking. The tourists marvelled at the scenic splendours, were treated like heroes and showered with hospitality, and they met the King and Queen of the Maoris. The Australian Board had opposed this appendix to the tour of Australia, a demand that Jardine for one considered quite unreasonable and felt was connected to the larger country's disdain for the cricket prowess of the smaller. He made a few cracks about Australia in his speeches and in conversation, and while staying with relatives of Percy Chapman (who had married the sister of one of New Zealand's finest cricketers, Tom Lowry), Jardine allegedly not only kept on complaining retrospectively about Australia's flies but "evinced symptoms of acute paranoia", fearing that he might be assassinated and keeping the back door open for a quick getaway.[7]

The English team were greeted by New Zealand Prime Minister George Forbes at a reception at Wellington Town Hall, and two Test matches were scheduled during the brief stopover after a two-day opener against Wellington. There, after a first-day washout, 16,000 people crammed into the Basin Reserve to see Paynter and Hammond make half-centuries, the latter with a runner because of a septic knee, as MCC scored 223 for 8 declared, to which Wellington only had time to reply with 141 for 2, Stewart Dempster hitting 47.

The night ferry took them to Christchurch, on the east coast of the South Island, for the first Test, where Wally Hammond lit up Lancaster Park with a powerfully made 227 in England's total of 560 for 8 declared. With Ames, who made 103, Hammond, though still hampered by his bad knee, put on 242 for the fifth wicket, the double-century stand coming in a mere 110 minutes. Brown hammered 74, Voce 66, this pair adding 108 in 45 minutes, all this after England's first two wickets had gone for four runs. Sutcliffe was caught behind off the first ball of the match, from Ted Badcock, and Paynter was bowled by a swinging delivery (his first in Test cricket) from Otago 20-year-old Dennis Smith. Tate took the new ball again for England and, with Voce, Allen, Brown and Verity, bowled New Zealand out for 223. On the third afternoon, however, with the New Zealand follow-on innings hardly started, high winds and a dramatic dust-storm interrupted play. Rain followed, and the match was left unfinished.

Back in the North Island, off the Englishmen went to the hot springs of Rotorua and a variety of entertainment at the chateau at Mount Ngauruhoe. Eddie Paynter took particular notice of the Maori rendition of *Now is the Hour*, which became one of the favourites of the Lancashire Lass herself, Gracie Fields.

Four days later, in the second Test, at Auckland, without the services of Tate (who was upset at being tossed aside again, it being intimated to him that he was "getting too old"), England bowled out New Zealand for 158. Bill Bowes, back in England colours for the first time since he dismissed Bradman for a duck at Melbourne, bowled Mills and Weir with his first two balls and finished with six wickets, all bowled, for 34. Stewie Dempster, having arrived late, dashed to the crease to prevent Bowes from taking a hat-trick, and made a superb 83 not out. It turned out to be the last of Dempster's 15 Test innings, leaving him with an average of 65.73. The departure of *Tainui* was held up for him to board, eventually setting off and taking him to his new life on Sir Julien Cahn's staff in England.[8]

Now came Hammond again at his thunderous, carefree best. In 318 minutes he scored 336 not out, a new Test record, overtaking Bradman's Headingley 334 with an exultant cry of "Yes!" as the quick single was run. Hammond hit 10 sixes — a Test record for many years to follow — three off consecutive balls from left-arm medium-pacer Jack Newman, and 34 fours, and reached century marks in ever-faster times: 100 in 134 minutes (signalled with a booming six), 200 in 241 minutes, 300 in 288 minutes.

Borrowing Tommy Mitchell's (little-used) bat when his own broke late in the innings, he gave only one hot chance, at 134. It was all the official scorers could do to keep up with the batting rampage, and the resultant run chart resembled a penny-farthing bicycle wheel as seen by a man with double vision. His partners had been little more than close-quarters spectators; Paynter, for instance, made only 36 in their third-wicket stand of 149. One small spectator on the grassy embankment which then almost completely encircled Eden Park was nine-year-old Bert Sutcliffe, who would one day become New Zealand's finest left-hander and end Hammond's Test career 14 years later with a catch in the 1947 Christchurch Test, which was Sutcliffe's first.

Wyatt was leading England (Jardine was nursing his rheumatism at Rotorua), and on April 1 he mercifully declared England's innings closed at 548 for 7 as soon as it had been double-checked that Hammond had the record. But after the rest day, weather again intervened, when New Zealand were 16 without loss on the third day. Hammond thus took away with him an average of 563 for this two-Test series. He had also racked up 1003 runs in the seven Tests of the Australasian tour (739 at 369.50 in his last three Tests), leaving everyone to wonder whether he might have regained his crown from Bradman as the world's greatest batsman. (He certainly reigned supreme as an *allround* cricketer, though less so as a deep-sea fisherman after his venture in quest of swordfish.) Tommy Mitchell was one bowler who would rather bowl to Bradman than Hammond.[9]

Jardine's farewell utterances included words of comfort and encouragement to New Zealand cricket, while Warner, back after 30 years, felt the batting had improved though the bowling had not. Then they sailed from Auckland on *Aorangi* on April 4 — the newly married journalist Gilbert Mant still with them — to complete their global journey, stopping at Suva, Fiji for a few hours, and Honolulu before the Pacific crossing terminated at Vancouver. They were completing what was a round-the-world trip known as the Red Route, since every stop (bar Hawaii) was in territory coloured red/pink on the map as part of the farflung British Empire.

In Suva, where a proposed cricket match was washed out, Jardine was honoured by the local chieftain's presentation to him of a whale's tooth (some believed a shark's tooth might have been more appropriate). The chieftain was given a bat in return, signed by the team, who ceremonially drank kava from coconut shells — a drink Paynter compared to antiseptic.

In Honolulu on Good Friday they were rendered wide-eyed again by the scenery — especially Maurice Tate when he thought a shark had got him by the ankles as he stood in the surf at Waikiki. But it was only the ship's hairdresser having a lark. The British Consul entertained the team, and somehow while in Hawaii Tate got to dance with Ginger Rogers.[10] Fred Astaire's legendary partner must have felt it a challenge to keep clear of the biggest feet in international cricket.

As *Aorangi* sailed away, the huge cross on the hill was illuminated by searchlights from other ships and a great shadow was cast onto the cloud beyond, leaving the cricketers emotionally touched and thinking of home now more than ever. But there was much sea still to be crossed, and while Mailey might spend time writing and sketching (he drew a neat caricature of Wyatt playing deck quoits and saying, "They can't give me out leg-before at this game"), Wyatt made continuing good use of his gramophone. Just about every morning of the tour the strains of *Today I Feel So Happy* boomed down the hotel corridors — until somebody mysteriously broke the record.[11] Mailey went one better (in terms of teasing Wyatt) in his booklet commemorating the series (*Cricket Sketches and Short Stories 1932–1933*). He drew Wyatt with bats instead of pads strapped to his legs to avoid lbws.

Crossing the International Date Line, which meant that the same day started all over again, had Hammond reflecting that it would be extremely useful to have this facility during some cricket matches.

Jardine's boredom was such that he buried his nose in books, even during a concert, when he carried on reading as if alone while the distinguished English actress Violet Vanburgh performed a beautiful reading for the audience, who all — bar England's cricket captain — showed their appreciation. This rudeness was noted by Gilbert Mant for the book he was writing.

In a cabin near his, Bruce Harris was busily scribbling away at his tour book, in which he took the party line. Jardine, presumably already having completed his own book on the tour (such was his self-discipline), contributed a foreword to this one in which he pronounced the term "body-line bowling" as "meaningless" and warned that the newsreel film of the Adelaide Test should be watched only when "armed with two wads of cotton-wool". Harris had so earned Jardine's trust that when he needed to check on a detail during the Brisbane Test he ventured to knock on Jardine's hotel door late at night. "Come in!" came the response. Harris switched on the light and, addressing the captain through his mosquito netting, found him quite welcoming.

Harris's book was soon published, of course, but Mant's was not. His efforts to obtain clearance from the head of Reuters, Sir Roderick Jones, was thwarted when Mant told Jones that he disapproved of much of what he had witnessed. Jones did not want the news agency to become embroiled in controversy. Gilbert Mant's book did eventually get written — all of 59 years later.[12]

NEVER BEFORE — AND, FOR THAT MATTER, NEVER SINCE — HAS A TEST SERIES PROMPTED SO MANY BOOKS. THE FIRST CAME OUT SOON AFTER THE FINAL BALL HAD BEEN BOWLED.

The team disembarked at Vancouver, where they stayed two days, feted by local cricket enthusiasts, before boarding the well-appointed Canadian Pacific train for four days of seat-bound sightseeing that compared very favourably with the Nullarbor trip. Through the Rockies they steamed, the air freezing with embarrassment when one of the players pretended to drop Bill Bowes's diary of the tour out of the window as the train curved its way around a deep ravine. The carriage suddenly lurched and Bowes's precious journal floated to oblivion.

At one stop Tate had 20 minutes to dash by taxi into the town to buy some whisky, since the train was "dry". His breathless entry into the saloon bar had customers ducking for cover, thinking it was a hold-up. He made it back just in time. There was a quick taxi ride around Winnipeg, and they clacked on across the Prairies — the screeches of the Australian barracking becoming ever more distant — before taking an excursion to Niagara Falls during their two-day stop in Toronto, where they attended more official engagements. Montreal, with six-foot (1.8-metre) snowdrifts all around, finally came into view, and they then boarded *Duchess of Atholl* for the trans-Atlantic crossing. It was among the first vessels to sail down the St Lawrence River that spring. The river is closed in winter.

This was as rough as any of the sea journeys they had undertaken since leaving England over seven months before. The ship's furniture was chained down as they manoeuvred south to avoid the numerous icebergs.[13] Australian cricket fans would have rubbed their hands with glee at the sight of it all. Eventually, having been diverted north from Liverpool because of the amended course, they slipped into Greenock on May 6, too late to see the Cup final, as Tate lamented: Everton 3, Manchester City 0. A pipe-and-drum band greeted them, and among the sizeable welcoming party was the mayor, who of course insisted on making a speech.

The 77 Club was formally disbanded as the Scottish coast neared, the proceeds of the collections having been spent on a silver cigar box engraved with all the players' signatures, which the team presented to D.R. Jardine. Inside the lid was the St George and Dragon badge, and a heartfelt inscription: "In appreciation and admiration of his leadership and wonderful courage". R.C.N. Palairet was given a toast-warmer. P.F. Warner had been given a similar cigar box during the trans-Pacific leg of the journey, because he had secured permission from MCC to leave the tour at Toronto and give himself a break in New York, a city he was anxious to see while the chance was there. He explained to Agnes in a letter that he intended to find a cheap hotel somewhere but did not bother stating the obvious: that he would thus dodge the media attention that would undoubtedly await the team and its principals on their arrival back in Britain. He would leave Jardine and Palairet to do the talking. After all, they got on so well together, while he felt the cool/cold shoulder from both of them. (Palairet was to write the foreword to Jardine's book, with Warner scarcely mentioned in it, and also to attend Jardine's wedding in 1934, to which Warner was not invited. Warner regarded Palairet as "not a pleasant travelling companion", and noted that he was sometimes very rude to the servants.) "Plum" was quite fed up, and desperately needed to get away from it all. He told scorer Ferguson that he would not tour again even for £10,000. He did not land back in England until May 13, by which time things were a lot quieter.[14]

Bachelor Gubby Allen had also left the team before the Atlantic crossing — at Vancouver, to sail down to Los Angeles at the invitation of friends. He was keen to see Hollywood and had a high old time of it, meeting stars such as Leslie Howard, Robert Montgomery, Katharine Hepburn, C. Aubrey Smith, Nigel Bruce and Douglas Fairbanks Jr, and becoming friendly with Marlene Dietrich. He then travelled east, saw the sights of Chicago and New York, and fell in love with a girl who was to die two years later.[15]

The Bodyline rumpus might well have been left 12,000 miles (19,300 km) behind them in geographical terms, but it continued to be a global topic of enormous dimensions. Even during the voyage home Jardine was asked what he thought of the latest proclamation to come from Australian officialdom. R. A. Oxlade, whose influence had grown within the chambers of the Australian Board (he was a past and future chairman), had expressed as the view of the NSWCA that Bodyline bowling was against the best interests of the game and must be discouraged by all affiliated clubs. It was a "canker" on the game, and unless it was removed there would be no Australian tour of England in 1934. What did the England captain think of that? Jardine compared it with the utterance of the deputy mayor of Ballarat in January, who had gained for himself an "hour's notoriety" by commenting on this matter after it had become *sub judice*. He was surprised at Aubrey Oxlade's remarks because, being a member of the ACB, Oxlade ought to have borne in mind that the Board's "hasty action" (the first cable) had rendered the matter *sub judice*.[16] One lawyer to another.

The English cricketers dispersed, Paynter and Duckworth off to Preston together, the hero of Brisbane embracing his wife before being bundled into a taxi and whisked off to a reception at Enfield Cricket Club. Duckworth would soon be preparing his lantern slides for public showing. Tate lugged all his baggage down to Brighton, thankful that he had sent his stuffed North Queensland crocodile on ahead. At long last he was about to see his baby boy, born so soon after his departure. Ten days later he was playing against Larwood and Voce in a county match at Hove.

One newspaperman cleverly headed straight for scorer/baggageman Bill Ferguson, knowing he must have been privy to so much that went on in hotel and dressing-room. He held out a tempting handful of £1 notes, saying there was plenty more where that came from. Fergie kept his counsel for 20-odd years, and even then was discretion personified. In his book he reserved his strongest opinions for Larwood and Jardine. The fast bowler, "as inoffensive a chap as I have ever met, had to endure some of the most disgusting treatment ever meted out by a nation which prides itself on its fair dealing and sportsmanship". He was not alone in finding Jardine "an odd mixture of a man" — at times the most delightful companion, a friend to everyone, but sometimes guilty of issuing snubs. Fergie thought him "a nervy type, highly-strung, invariably tensed-up". These intimate opinions would have sold lots of newspapers in 1933.

Hedley Verity was met in Glasgow by his father and a friend, and they drove through the dark night — and a thunderstorm — to Rawdon. The journey was slow because Hedley had messages to deliver to people in Yorkshire from Northcountryfolk domiciled all over Australia. The quiet hero was soon given a civic reception hosted by the local cricket club and the Council chairman, who happened to be Mr Verity senior. Over 2000 admirers stood in heavy rain for another homage to Verity at Micklefield Park. Jardine wrote a warm letter to Verity senior. He said, talking about England slow left-armers, that Rhodes had been ineffective in Australia in 1911–12, Jack White had been successful in 1928–29 and Hedley, the latest, had "come through his first tour triumphantly". On and off the field he had been a friend and "grand help" to his skipper.[17] Verity was to name his second son Douglas.

DRESSED FOR THE OCCASION: DOUGLAS JARDINE ARRIVES AT LORD'S
TO PRESENT HIS REPORT ON HIS VICTORIOUS CAMPAIGN.

As for D.R. Jardine's reception, contrary perhaps to his expectations, he and several of his team were welcomed warmly in London. Lord Hawke, Viscount Lewisham (outgoing MCC president), Sir Kynaston Studd and Billy Findlay joined Jardine's parents and innumerable back-slappers to greet them at Euston station. He escaped the tumult and acknowledged the continuing rapt attention from the window of his hotel. Three days later, dressed in top hat and swallowtail coat, the captain presented himself at Lord's to hand in his official report on the tour, as did Palairet. Warner's was submitted later, upon his return home. All of these reports have long been items on the list of Bodyline's Vanished Documents, though we must surely have a fairly accurate notion of their individual flavours.

In June, Warner, Jardine and Palairet (whose brother Lionel, epitome of the Golden Age batsman, had died on March 27) were called to Lord's for interview, as were Larwood and Voce and Ames. No minutes of these meetings — if they were ever written — survive. Wyatt was not called and nor was Allen, though the latter had made his feelings known to doubting secretary Findlay in no uncertain terms: "The sooner you try to find out what's been going on, the better for cricket!"[18] For two years thereafter Allen and Findlay did not speak to each other.

During Warner's interview, in the presence of MCC president Lord Hailsham and fellow peers Belper, Bridgeman, Hawke and Ullswater, together with Sir Stanley Jackson and Sir Kynaston Studd, the tour manager was observed by prying newsmen through the committee-room window. As the barons of English cricket watched gravely, Warner mimed a batsman ducking and weaving. So transfixed was the old Middlesex captain A.J. Webbe that his pipe went out three times. Warner's gently uttered discourse and little pantomime persuaded MCC to set up a special subcommittee.[19] In a letter to Hore-Ruthven written later that year, Warner confirmed that in giving his evidence before the committee he had condemned Bodyline "in every way". The barracking had been bad, certainly, but three-quarters of it was caused by this type of bowling. What was needed urgently now (August) was a conference: "Can you use your great influence to bring this about? Cables are not much use." The public were dead against Bodyline, he wrote, after seeing it at Manchester (where West Indies gave it a try: a description follows).

In the edition of May 20, 1933, Warner had written one of the most demanding editorials he would ever have to prepare for his magazine *The Cricketer*. He praised Jardine, while expressing regret at his lost batting form, and complimented Wyatt on his improved fielding and his collection of Maori and Hawaiian gramophone records. Pataudi had become too "pawky" (hesitant). Brown had lost his rhythm but could still bowl his legbreak from a standing position. Sutcliffe won praise, and Hammond even more, not least for his bowling, which Warner considered in the S.F. Barnes class in the first Test at Sydney. Man by man they were congratulated in print: Larwood for his magnificent fast bowling, Verity for his studious skill, Duckworth for his uncomplaining role as non-player for most of the tour. Allen was tipped as a future captain, and Bowes alone was criticised for the shortness of his bowling length. Interestingly, Warner wrote of Paynter that he is "particularly well endowed in the lower part of his anatomy".

POLITICS ASIDE FOR THE MOMENT, LORD HAILSHAM (RIGHT) REJOICES IN ENGLAND'S
SUCCESS IN COMPANY WITH THE MAN OF THE MOMENT, D.R. JARDINE, AT THE DORCHESTER.

Beyond all the seriousness, there was a major celebration on July 19, with
an Ashes victory dinner at the Dorchester Hotel, a black-tie affair, no
military medals, no band, Stanley Baldwin in attendance, the Prince of
Wales unable to be present, 30 shillings a ticket for the unprivileged.
A roving tape-recorder would have resulted in some extremely interesting
conversations. New MCC president Lord Hailsham brought a blush to
Jardine's cheeks by referring to him as "probably the best captain in the
world" and describing his team as a "gallant band of sportsmen" who had
"worthily upheld England's reputation". Clearly His Lordship had not been
sitting on the Hill at Sydney. S.M. Bruce, Australia's High Commissioner
in London, reflected Australia's attitude in the suavest manner possible.

From an item in *Punch* drifted a welcome whiff of humour: "Among
the latest exhibits at Madame Tussaud's is a model of Jardine, but we are
unable to confirm the overseas rumour that the absence of Larwood from
the Chamber of Horrors is due to 'boot' trouble."

The hornets' nest had been most seriously disturbed by Larwood's
newspaper outpourings the moment the tour was deemed to be over.
Provocative extracts from his forthcoming book appeared in the *Sunday
Express* on May 7, 1933. (E.H.D. Sewell had lined up serialisation in the

Sunday Dispatch, but William Pollock belatedly secured the scoop for the *Express*, leaving Sewell out of pocket and Larwood carrying blame for failing to honour the earlier agreement.[20] Larwood had tried to stop the *Express* article and even returned the modest cheque, but since he had already signed the proofs, sports editor Charles Eade went ahead with publication.)

Larwood let rip: he was playing for his side; the angry barrackers knew nothing about the finer points of cricket and were there only to see Bradman score runs and Australia win; leg theory requires more accuracy than any other kind of bowling; Woodfull was too slow and Bradman too frightened; Richardson and McCabe played him all right; the crowds wanted to see Larwood fail but while they succeeded in upsetting him on his first tour (1928–29) "this time I was inspired"; he gritted his teeth and bowled harder, saying a few things under his breath; false stories of squabbles in the England camp were spread by the Australian Press. As for the Australian Board of Control, "it cannot even control its own crowds, and half of its members could not tell you the weight of a cricket ball. When the Australians come here they are treated as gentlemen. When we go to Australia we have to suffer cheap wit and abuse from an unsportsmanlike gang."[21]

The reaction from Australia was swift and strong. Walrus-moustached former ACB chairman E.E. Bean considered Larwood's remarks "offensive" and "so surcharged with personal spleen" that it seemed like an act of insubordination, leaving MCC in a difficult position. Future England tours were, in his view, now in doubt. Arthur Mailey wrote a balanced reaction but made a point of questioning the charges levelled at Woodfull and Bradman, a defence supported by Alan Kippax. Australian selector W. J. Johnson branded the accusation of cowardice as "hysterical", while Bradman himself retorted that Larwood's statements were apparently a financial success but he had better watch out for the opinions of the Australian crowds when he returned in 1936. Fingleton acknowledged Larwood's "genius as a fast bowler" but regretted that he now seemed to have "thrown his mental balance to the winds". Vic Richardson lamented the fact that the gentlemen of MCC had not seen it all, and believed that Australian crowds had been libelled.[22]

In Sydney, *Smith's Weekly* tried to frighten the Australian newspapers which had reprinted Larwood's "lying slander" by suggesting that they might have brought themselves within the scope of the Defamation Act should Bradman decide to "vindicate his manhood".

For the defence, Northants captain V.W.C. Jupp said that newsreel film supported the view that Bradman had been scared, while George Duckworth claimed that "some of the Australian wizards were frightened to death of Larwood". Even Larwood's mother had her say: "It was good cricket but they can't take it and that is all there is to it." And just to emphasise yet again the inconsistency in opinion, *Sydney Truth* described Australia's players and legislators as "petulant schoolboys": the legislators should resign *en bloc* for they had "put a stigma on Australians generally; branded them as a pack of squealers". England had not cabled Australia in 1921 asking them to call off Gregory and McDonald. Batsmen had had their day. Now it was the bowlers' turn. As for barracking, take no notice of it.[23] R.C. Robertson-Glasgow, fast making a name for himself as a cricket essayist, simply believed that Larwood had every right to express himself, particularly after the abuse he had endured.

Jack Hobbs's book came out in June, much of its contents straight and uncontroversial, though he was critical of the "very rough time" given the English team by the barrackers. Towards the end, like the man muttering at the rear of the hall while listening to an irritating speech, the old batting master declared at last that leg theory was not in the best interests of the game. This added much weight to the argument against it. He had not wished to embarrass Jardine or his men during the tour by giving the Australians another peg on which to hang their fierce attacks. England's bowling contained "marked elements of danger" and was "a most venomous thing" which robbed cricket of its attractiveness, a fact which would be reflected in falling attendances. (He was not to know that in the far-off late 1970s this very fact — an over-abundance of hostile bowling and the possibility of serious physical injury — was unashamedly used as promotional meat for television coverage in Australia.) Not least significantly, Hobbs feared for the safety of young boys starting to play the game. How opponents of Bodyline wished he had spoken out months earlier.

Hobbs, who played in 10 Championship matches for Surrey in 1933, averaging 47.88 in his penultimate season, also had to deal with criticism aimed at himself. Lord Hawke felt that he had been hard on his former opening partner Sutcliffe in his recent Test reports from Australia, leaving the gentle Hobbs to ask why Lord Hawke attacked him so often. "Almost every year he has a go." He thought the demand made by Hawke for him to apologise to Yorkshire was silly.

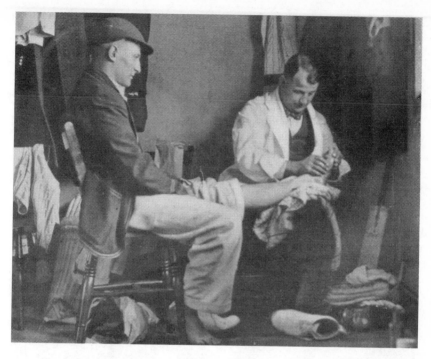

THE MOST FAMOUS FOOT IN CRICKET HISTORY? HAROLD LARWOOD HAS A FURTHER
ASSESSMENT OF THE DAMAGED BONE AS HE STRUGGLES THROUGH THE 1933 SEASON.

At Gamages, the London department store, Larwood gave exhibitions
of Bodyline — and a darn sight more convincingly than Jack Durston in a
starchy newsreel feature. And he played in a dozen Championship matches
for Nottinghamshire in the 1933 season — as a batsman. He averaged
24.50, with a highest score of 62 not out at Worcester, but the fractured
sesamoid bone in his left foot permitted him to bowl only 10 overs in May
before it became clear that he needed more time to recover; he made the
Glamorgan match in early July his last for the moment. There had never
been any serious question of his playing Test cricket again just yet. With his
tour fee and the £388 raised by the shilling fund, headed by the Lord Mayor
through the local newspaper for Voce and himself, he extended the chicken
farm into a market garden, so that his miner father could live above ground
in more congenial conditions.

At close of play during Surrey's June bank holiday match at Trent Bridge,
Jardine made the shilling-fund presentation to the popular Notts and
England fast bowlers, who also, in the presence of their wives, took
possession of silver salvers. A crowd of little short of 20,000 applauded and

called out affectionate remarks, and speeches were made on the pavilion balcony, Jardine stiff and formal as ever as he tried to beam an amiable disposition, Larwood struggling with aspirates and nerves as he thanked his Test captain, whom he described, reading from a sheet of paper, as "a great sportsman and a true friend".

England's line-up for the three Tests against West Indies that summer was much altered from that which had played in Australia, for all kinds of reasons. Voce seemed to have lost his zing, Allen was keen to pursue his new career in stocks and shares, and Lord Hawke, who had taken over from Warner as chairman of selectors, had preferences of his own. The most telling decision was the reappointment of Jardine as captain.

TANGIBLE REWARD FOR ALL THE HARD WORK: VOCE AND LARWOOD, IN THE COMPANY OF THE MAYOR OF NOTTINGHAM AND A LARGE BODY OF SPECTATORS, RECEIVE THEIR TESTIMONIAL CHEQUES FROM THEIR GRATEFUL TOUR CAPTAIN, JARDINE.

Gubby Allen was persuaded to play at Lord's in the first Test against West Indies, where he dismissed another candidate for the title of world's best batsman, George Headley, in both innings. On the opening day, a Saturday, Allen found himself in conversation with his monarch. King George V had talked privately with Jardine during a rain interruption and now he enquired of Allen as to what had really been going on in Australia. "I didn't know you took an interest in cricket, sir," said the allrounder who had tried so hard to play ambassador on tour. "I take great interest in my subjects," His Majesty replied. "My secretaries mark items in the papers for my attention — sometimes I also look elsewhere."[24] Might Gubby have enlivened the old King's day by confiding to him how he could so easily have killed the captain during the tour and that Don Bradman was "a terrible little coward"?

Again the conundrum: if the King were seriously concerned about relations between Britain and Australia, and if the Dominions Office and other bodies were worried too, why had they not leaned on MCC to act in the common interest, commanding Jardine to stop Bodyline or stand down?

When Jardine went in to bat in this Lord's Test match, which England won by an innings (top scorer Les Ames, 83 not out), he was given a standing ovation. He had been cheered pointedly as he took the field as MCC's captain against the West Indians in May, and would be cheered just as lustily by the Bramall Lane cloth caps in July as he scored a century against champions Yorkshire — including Bowes and Verity and all — shyly doffing his Harlequin cap to all corners of the ground and, according to Bowes, needing to pull out his handkerchief, ostensibly to blow his nose but also furtively to wipe away a couple of tears. And the reception was also heartfelt at Old Trafford, when he played one of Test cricket's most emblematic and moving innings against West Indies.

Headley and Ivan Barrow had made centuries for West Indies on a slow pitch, and England were a precarious 118 for 3 in reply to the visitors' 375 when Jardine went to the crease on the second day. Hammond, shocked at having Bodyline bowled at him, was hit on the shoulder-blade when he ducked and then had his chin split by a bouncer from Learie Constantine. Retiring for repairs, once more he was heard to mutter that if this is what the game had come to he might as well bloody-well quit. He returned with two stitches to the wound and some covering plaster, and approached Constantine. "Let's stick to cricket," he said, as no Australian had ever said to Larwood. "It was nicer when we first met, wasn't it?"[25] — presumably meaning in the Caribbean in 1926: in which case his memory was faulty, for a feature of their encounter then had been a spray of bouncers. In time Hammond was able to reflect philosophically on the matter by saying, "We started it, and we had it coming to us."[26]

But Jardine weathered the West Indian Bodyline, once nearly suffering Hammond's fate but time and again playing the ball down off the splice of a perfectly straight bat held firmly in front of his face as he stood to his full height. Sometimes he swayed out of danger and sometimes he scored runs through the leg trap, though forswearing the hook. Sometimes he was hit about the body. Those who knew him were not in the least surprised that he never stopped to rub the spot, and never showed pain. First with Ames and later with Walter Robins, Jardine eased the threat of a West Indies breakthrough, and after making 127, his only Test century, in just under five hours (with only five fours) he was caught by one of the Bodyline purveyors, Constantine, off the other, Manny Martindale.

The West Indians had no more affection for Jardine than the Australians did; his 83 against them on this Manchester ground in the Test five years earlier was the innings during which he persuaded the umpire not to give him out hit-wicket. Now, with the brilliant allrounder Constantine released by his league club Nelson for his one appearance in the 1933 series, and already one down in the series, the West Indians decided that the employment of some Bodyline was the best way to go about levelling the series. To date, beginning in 1928, they had played four Test matches in England and lost them all by innings margins.

So the leather was flying, and Ames, for one, was none too happy. Noting this, Jardine called out, "You get yourself down this end, Les. I'll take care of this bloody nonsense."[27] Constantine tore in, his trousers held up by a black belt, and whirled into his delivery. Martindale's action was slightly more disciplined, but he was also unmistakeably quick. Even Vincent Valentine's pace was above the ordinary. Ames (47) succumbed to the new ball, which he fended into a short leg's hands, and after Jim Langridge's brief innings Robins joined his captain, who was 68 at the close of play, England 263 for 6.

And next day Jardine reached his hundred. It was the perfect response, though he might have had greater difficulty making it on the faster surfaces of Lord's or The Oval. Newsreel film survives to show him, stiff-legged at the crease, Harlequin cap centrally positioned, calmly playing a couple of balls downwards to leg. Also shown is Hammond striding off, hand cupped to bleeding chin, face like thunder.

Jardine was eventually held by Constantine in the gully, the catch being taken so close to the turf that the batsman waited for confirmation. Robertson-Glasgow, who had recently replaced Plum Warner as the *Morning Post*'s cricket correspondent at a salary of nine guineas a week, wrote that he had never heard such cheering as greeted Jardine upon his return to the pavilion.[28] Umpiring was E.J. "Tiger" Smith, standing in his first Test after keeping wicket for Warwickshire for years, and to the bowling of Barnes and Foster in Australia in 1911–12. He had no great liking for Jardine, but had to admit that his innings here was the bravest he had ever seen. (He had not seen the Australians recently against Larwood, of course.) Smith, in old age, could still picture Martindale and Constantine, operating at times around the wicket, banging in four balls an over around Jardine's chest and head. Although the batsman (who wore no chest padding) dropped his bat several times, he never complained and he never touched the spot where the ball had just thumped him.[29] As a footnote, Smith recalled that so delighted was Headley that West Indies had held England to a draw that he had quite a few celebratory drinks.

What would not have pleased Jardine was the wider reaction to the style of cricket on display at Old Trafford. Established sources were quick to acknowledge his courage and skill, but this was the first demonstration of Bodyline in England at the highest level, and eyebrows were raised. Few liked what they saw, or, at breakfast tables across the land, approved of this kind of bowling as visualised from the reports they were reading, for Ted "Nobby" Clark, the Northants fast left-armer, also bowled it in West Indies' second innings, though with little effect. Jim Langridge, the Sussex slow left-arm bowler, now actually outbowled Verity, taking 7 for 56 on Test debut, with Hammond back to his silkiest form as a slip catcher. (The other fast bowler, George Macaulay, was sidelined by a foot injury during this match. He was not especially fast, but he knew how to bowl to a leg trap.)

D.R. Jardine was destined not to play in the last Test. Nor was there much cricket in store for him for the rest of the summer after Surrey's match against Kent at The Oval a week later, when he took a wicked blow on the shin while fielding in his proprietorial gully position. It was another irony that he should be hurt in the field after dodging and deflecting so much heavy artillery while batting in the recent Test match.

A sidelight to the drawn Old Trafford Test was the dismissal of Robins for 55 after his seventh-wicket stand of 140 with skipper Jardine. He was stumped (a common form of dismissal for this batsman) off a wrong'un from "Puss" Achong, and his exasperated utterance — "Fancy being stumped off a bloody Chinaman!" — gave life to that term for a left-arm spinner's googly.

Was the West Indian decision to bowl Bodyline at England born of impulse, or of desperation at having lost by an innings at Lord's, or of some other prompting? Jack Grant, West Indies' white captain, recalled only that they simply decided to try it out at Old Trafford, without any previous practice. It rattled Cyril Walters and Sutcliffe — and, of course, Hammond, who decided to "have a go" after his chin was cut. Wyatt and Ames succumbed to it, but Grant, like everyone else there that day, attested that Jardine stood tall, never flinched, and never lost his nerve. Later to become a missionary, Grant also made it clear that he disapproved of Bodyline, for he and brother Rolph (who was struck on the head and retired hurt) weathered a ferocious dose of it when England toured the West Indies in 1934–35 under Bob Wyatt. Both sides had bouts of bounceritis during this tour.[30]

Learie Constantine had a clearer memory of events in 1933. He and Martindale had been criticised for bowling bouncers against MCC at Lord's in May, though he protested that he had only three men on the leg side. *Wisden's* editor, C. Stewart Caine, had written in the recent edition of the *Almanack* that it was "inconceivable" that England's fast bowlers would bowl at the man. Now Sydney Southerton, who was to succeed Caine upon his death a year later, was writing that the West Indian bowling was "unpleasant, not to say dangerous". This annoyed Constantine, the future barrister, rights campaigner and peer.

He had rejoined the touring team at Harrogate for the Yorkshire match, only to find that a pudding of a pitch had been prepared. He took nine wickets, but Verity took seven wickets in each innings and the county won by 200 runs. In Yorkshire's second innings, Jack Grant, a little peeved, ordered Constantine and Herman Griffith to bowl Bodyline. ("The private soldier does not argue with his General," wrote Constantine, taking a leaf out of Larwood's book.[31]) Sutcliffe scored 86, Arthur Mitchell 67 not out, and it did not prove very effective. The last match before the Old Trafford Test was at Stoke-on-Trent, and on the train to Manchester, Grant discussed Bodyline again with Constantine, who by now was quite eager to experiment with it against England. He was tired of reading about it, thought it a good idea to give England a taste of what they had been giving Australia, and although he would have enjoyed batting against it rather than delivering it, he proceeded to let rip in the Test and only regretted that the pitch was so slow.[32]

The fascinating backdrop to all this is that in Sydney, Don Bradman had suggested in his newspaper column that MCC had a fine opportunity to arrange for the West Indians to provide them with a special viewing of Bodyline on a fiery wicket at Lord's. Did the travelling West Indians know they had the backing of The Don?

Jardine's dramatic Old Trafford century prompted P.F. Warner to write a long letter to the *Telegraph* expressing gladness that England had now seen Bodyline first hand, though he was quick to point out that Constantine was two yards slower (*less fast*, perhaps?) than Larwood and not as accurate. In one sense he was sorry that "my countrymen" (he had been born in Trinidad, youngest of Attorney-General Charles Warner's 18 children) had resorted to Bodyline (which he continued to asterisk as an Australian term), but it served the useful purpose of showing England what it was like. In his unwaveringly gentle manner he pointed out that there had been many fine fast bowlers down the ages, but only now was there the problem of direct attack and intimidation.

Warner's neatest point was probably this: "To suggest that the Australians are 'squealers' is unfair to men with their record on the battlefield and on the cricket field. Rightly or wrongly [pity about the equivocation] they believe that such bowling is contrary to the spirit of the game."

Retaliation remained an option — and not only in the eyes of Australians. James Agate, the theatre critic and prolific writer, a Manchester friend of Cardus's, wrote that he hoped the Australians were "raking the bush for some Hercules who can bowl faster than Kortright, in order that, without regard to length and aiming solely at the batsman's head and heart, he shall, next season, try on the English goose the sauce that has been deemed proper for the Australian gander".

Warner in his letter would have none of this: "I should be sorry indeed to see a Red Terror from the Never-Never, some Saltbush Bill of Richardsonian proportions, exploiting this bowling against England in a Test match at Lord's, or anywhere else." The courtesy of combat would vanish, and anger, hatred and malice would be bred. He was opposed to altering the Laws — reposing rather too much faith in human qualities, perhaps? — but if they had to be amended he favoured a line across the halfway point on the pitch. This silly suggestion has been adopted by several otherwise intelligent cricket people over the years, people who seemed to think that only balls pitched shorter than halfway can be dangerous.

But Warner deserves sympathy. His heart, whatever its size, was in the right place. During the Australian tour he had belaboured a reporter with an off-the-cuff thesis on Tradition. "They've got it all wrong in Australia, you know. It means nothing more than loyalty to the scene of your happy schooldays ... being proud of getting your colours in the Australian XI ... This modern scoffing at tradition is a product of super-democracy ... It's [Tradition's] what takes a regiment through hell. Good God, you fellows out in Australia have a great tradition. What fighters you are! What is it, do you think, that makes your soldiers fight to the last man and your cricketers to the last ball? It's tradition, of course."[33]

It was traditional, too, to appoint the captain for the forthcoming winter tour as soon as possible, and on July 10, between the Lord's and Old Trafford Tests, MCC announced the name of the skipper for the 1933–34 expedition. It did not please P.F. Warner, or several others. The captain was, of course, D.R. Jardine, who was not only keen to display no willingness to back down from his victorious strategy last winter in Australia but nursed a strong desire to play in the land of his birth. His acceptance had not been without a pause. Percy Fender was among those he consulted before deciding to tour. He would take with him only one member of his 1932–33 side, Verity. And MCC minuted the fact that Lords Hailsham (president) and Hawke (treasurer) were to have a private word with him before departure, doubtless along the lines that he must not upset the Indians as he had upset the Australians. (Hailsham personally wrote to Jardine's employer requesting permission for him to be given leave. The letter, to Alfred Wagg, a keen cricket statistician who also happened to be Jardine's godfather, contained two significant opinions, which were also slightly at odds with each other: DRJ was the "best cricket captain in England" and he felt "a little ashamed of the doings of our team last winter".[34])

Whenever possible Jardine relaxed, a proud man after his Manchester century, a sore man with his damaged shin, and an amused man at the Foyle's literary lunch at Grosvenor House, London on August 16, when the speakers included H.D.G. Leveson Gower and Alec Waugh. Sir John Squire welcomed the England captain as the Monster from the Antipodes, Douglas the Killer, the cave man. He took all this smilingly and made some perceptive remarks in his speech: that people would probably have much more leisure time in future, that the test of a culture was the ability to make good use of one's leisure, that cricket needed writers who could bring out the romance in cricket — and "some genius who could draw an accurate picture of Australian barrackers in full cry". He then drew on that favourite definition of his, that cricket was a "beautiful, beautiful game that is battle and service and sport and art".[35] While this is almost the perfect definition of cricket, the knowing will have attributed nine-tenths of Jardine's appetite to the "battle" bit.

There was a lot of serious physical damage on the first-class cricket fields of England during the 1933 season. Most of it was inflicted by varying degrees of Bodyline bowling.

In the MCC v West Indians match at Lord's in May, Joe Hulme, who played cricket for Middlesex and football for Arsenal, was hit about the thighs and ribs by four balls in a row from Constantine at his fastest, as he opened MCC's reply towards the end of the first day. He rubbed the spots furiously and helplessly, and was clearly distressed with what was happening. He lashed out desperately at the next ball and set off for an easy run, only to find that his partner, W.B. Franklin, had his hand firmly raised and was calling out: "Go back! I know where I'm well off!"[36] The *News Chronicle* sympathetically commented that "Hulme's football colours are red [Arsenal]: his cricket colours are likely to be black and blue."

HENDREN BATS IN HIS ODD-LOOKING PROTECTIVE CAP.

This was the match in which Patsy Hendren, now aged 44, emerged from the pavilion wearing a peculiar piece of headgear, a cap onto which his wife had sewn an extra padded peak either side so as to protect his ears. One of those ears had been lacerated two years earlier when a bouncer from Larwood knocked his friend cold. Some very anxious hours followed as Hendren was rushed to hospital, still unconscious. This time, reassured by his padded cap, he topped the innings with 61.

His anxiety had been worsened by George Headley's second-innings injury. Having made a beautiful century in the first, Headley took a fierce blow to the chest from Bowes and was out to it for a chilling five minutes. The West Indians went on to secure a joyous victory, but Headley did not feel well enough to play for another 10 days.

In late May, Bowes caused further damage at Cardiff when he bounced Glamorgan to defeat, angering the crowd as he dropped short time and again, hitting Turnbull and tailender Clay on his way to figures of 6 for 82 and moving Yorkshire towards victory. In June the big, bespectacled, scholarly Bowes seriously injured two other leading English batsmen. Lancashire's Frank Watson took a juddering blow to the head that rendered him senseless in the Roses match and sent the Old Trafford crowd into an indignant frenzy. "Killer!" they screamed. But Bowes went on bouncing — though not in this match, for Sellers wanted his spinners to get to work on a dusty track. Towards the end of June, at Trent Bridge, the recognised hotbed of Bodyline, after Larwood and Voce had made half-centuries in Notts' first innings, Bowes flattened Walter Keeton, striking him on the cheekbone, one of the more delicate zones of the head.

Nor was it just the professionals who took a liking to "fast leg theory". In the Varsity match — always a special fixture, not least socially — Ken Farnes did just as he had done in 1932: he put the fear of God into Oxford with rapid, short-pitched balls that came at their skulls, with a ring of close leg-side catchers perched in the soggy sawdust, many deliveries whooshing well wide of leg. Unlike Larwood, Farnes dished it out to tailenders too. Jahangir Khan and Rolph Grant bowled medium-pace offspin with a leg trap, and Oxford could scarcely believe what was happening to them. P.C. Oldfield, the No. 11 (and a wicketkeeper, like his Australian namesake), was hit on the jaw and bowled, and in the second innings opener David Townsend was out hit-wicket when struck on the neck. Alan Melville, the South African, took a paralysing blow to the ribs and Vivian Jenkins and

Gerry Chalk endured considerable punishment as they denied Cambridge victory in this drizzle-interrupted match. It was as if the poetry-dabbling Farnes, bounding in from the pavilion end, had lost all reason.

Now that Bodyline had been shown at Lord's, letters of protest were fired off to the papers, a group of eminent people sending one to *The Times*. Farnes, in his book, while confessing to bowling with a conscious aim to intimidate, expressed resentment at the criticism, believing that the wonderful catching in the leg trap had been overlooked.[37] He had been encouraged by his university captain, Denys Wilcox, and had even spoken to Bill Bowes about field settings for leg theory. (Farnes was to perish in the forthcoming war, as were three of his opponents and one of his team-mates in this notorious match.)

At the end of July, following Jardine's heroics in the Manchester Test, Notts entertained Leicestershire for a Championship match, and in another contest of exceptional significance one of the arch designers of Bodyline, Notts captain Arthur Carr, now became the biter bit. Fed up with Voce's rib-pounding aggression, Leicestershire's Haydon Smith retaliated by bouncing the Notts batsmen. They were unused to this treatment. Having Larwood and Voce in their line-up was usually a deterrent. But Smith let rip, and Carr was hurt and scared. Twice he came close to oblivion as the ball streaked past his face. There and then he decided on a moratorium: "E.W. Dawson, the Leicestershire captain, and I felt that this sort of thing was not good enough and we mutually agreed that we would not stand for it."[38]

This was a very big breakthrough for the pacifists. Knowing full well that he would be accused of hypocrisy, Carr made a Press statement: "Somebody is going to be killed if this sort of bowling continues, and Mr Dawson and myself considered that the game would be much more pleasant if it is stopped. Sooner or later something will have to be done so why not do it now?"

Two matches later Voce was bouncing at the throat again in a high-scoring match at The Oval, where patrons booed the left-armer every time he hit their old favourite, Jack Hobbs (who nevertheless survived to score his 196th first-class century, having made 221 for MCC against the West Indies in May).

An even greater slab of double-dealing by A.W. Carr was to follow on November 23, when he was one of only three county captains who voted against banning Bodyline bowling, Jardine (predictably, and by proxy) and

Vallance Jupp (Northants) being the others. Fourteen captains, therefore, had seen and heard enough. This gentlemen's agreement was a major factor in saving the game — for the time being. Only a few months earlier, while the Test series was raging in Australia, Reggie Ingle, of Somerset, had seemed almost alone among the county captains in stating that it was not really cricket.

Cricket's finest essayist, Neville Cardus, had long ceased to sit on this particular fence. He now wrote: "Everybody is getting to hate the sight of the leg trap and the short bumper. Bodyline would vanish tomorrow if cricketers here governed the game." Did he mean that players and captains were not free to control the kind of cricket they wished to play? If they weren't, who was? County club committees have always been seen as comprised mainly of ambitious enthusiasts and businessmen who little understand the game's real anatomy, and have frequently been among the last to see reality in all its fullness.

Even within the 1933 England v West Indies series there was intrigue. The tourists were so much stronger with Learie Constantine in their ranks, so they tried to have him released by league club Nelson again for the final Test. The deal was set up, with Stan Nichols of Essex substituting for him that Saturday at Nelson. When Jardine heard of this he persuaded his fellow selectors to pick Nichols for England, so the Constantine deal came to nothing.

Bodyline, like so many of Britain's creations, was exported further afield. In Trinidad no inhibitions prevailed when Barbados fast bowlers Manny Martindale and C.D."Pampie"Spooner let fly in February 1934. One bouncer flew from Rolph Grant's skull almost for six leg-byes. The batsman was carried from Queen's Park Oval, but resumed next day and bravely pushed his score to 152.

While the bruising English season of 1933 was playing itself out, feverish efforts were being made not only to resolve the Bodyline problem but to save the 1934 Australian tour of England.

A major new figure had entered the picture, though his presence was hardly visible to the world at large. Dr Robbie Macdonald was born in Melbourne, played for Queensland, and was QCA secretary in 1894–95, having qualified in 1891 (in Pennsylvania) as a dentist. He became honorary secretary of Leicestershire CCC in the 1920s, having batted with notable patience for the county between 1899 and 1902. In 1901 he made a 6½-hour 127 against Sussex at Hove and two other lengthy hundreds, one of them against WG's London County. It was noted that he preferred to spend English winters in Queensland.

Protective of and optimistic about Queensland cricket, Macdonald had batted with Australia's 1888 captain Percy McDonnell and the irrepressible Arthur Coningham for Queensland and played against both of Stoddart's English touring sides in the 1890s. And he endured for 4½ hours to score 59 against Warner's 1903–04 MCC team. His dogged batting led C.B. Fry to remark that "his methods are ultra-Australian; that is to say, he pays extreme attention to not getting out, and has no regard for the time he takes to make his runs ... Bumpy fast bowling on an imperfect wicket might bother him a bit, as he is not tall, yet I don't know that he would be got out by it."[39]

DR ROBBIE MACDONALD, AUSTRALIA'S ASTUTE SPOKESMAN, PICTURED YEARS EARLIER,
WHEN HE WAS JUST AS DETERMINED AS A BATSMAN.

In other words, patient, determined, and fiercely opposed to bullying bowling, Robbie Macdonald, now aged 63, was the ideal individual to act as Australia's key agent in cracking Bodyline. Now based in Leicester, he was one of the scattered band of Anglo-Australians who felt perhaps a great deal more than ordinary concern over the bowling crisis which had driven an ugly wedge between his two countries.

Macdonald had represented the Australian Board several times at

Imperial Cricket Conference gatherings at Lord's. Now, suddenly, he was a key player in the drama, consulting with MCC, advising the ACB, never hesitating to apply pressure. He had handled the advance tour arrangements for the 1932–33 enterprise, and now, in retrospect, he was endeavouring to clear up a mess which had been none of his making.

As early as March 13, 1933 he cabled home to the Australian Board notifying them that there was evidence that English feeling was beginning to mount against "body bowling". "Respectfully submit we should maintain inflexible attitude making tour next year conditional on ban," was his readily accepted suggestion.[40]

The ACB's new subcommittee, set up after the Board's January 30 meeting, comprised M.A. Noble, M.J. (Roger) Hartigan, Bill Woodfull and Vic Richardson, and they were to look into the matter of intimidatory bowling, with the aim of devising a cure. Their conclusion was to recommend that a no-ball should be called for any delivery which was bowled "with intent to intimidate or injure" the batsman. Harold Larwood was to devote many paragraphs in his tour book to deriding this proposed "thought reader's" charter. "In cricket," he wrote scornfully, "*English* cricket, the real cricket, we do not condemn people on suspicion."[41] For once he had written something with which his masters at Lord's might readily agree.

Nonetheless, the Australian Board were happy to act upon the recommendation of their widely experienced subcommittee, and on April 28 the new Law 48B (No ball) was adopted for Australian cricket as from the forthcoming 1933–34 season:

> Any ball delivered which, in the opinion of the umpire at the bowler's end, is bowled at the batsman with intent to intimidate or injure him shall be considered unfair, and "no ball" shall be called and the bowler notified of the reason. If the offence be repeated by the same bowler in the same innings he shall be immediately instructed by the umpire to cease bowling and the over shall be regarded as completed. Such bowler shall not again be permitted to bowl during the course of the innings then in progress. Law 48A shall not apply to this law. [*The last remark refers to the existing clause covering the need for the umpire to call no-ball "instantly upon delivery".*]

The Australian Board tried MCC out on April 28 by cabling their additional clause for examination and, it was fervently hoped, MCC's approval. Many anxious nights passed before Lord's cabled a reply. It was a long one, and not to Australia's liking:

MCC TO AUSTRALIAN BOARD OF CONTROL, June 12, 1933

The MCC Committee have received and carefully considered the cable of the Australian Board of Control of April twenty-eighth last. They have also received and considered the reports of the captain and managers of the cricket team which visited Australia 1932–33.

With regard to the cable of the Australian Board of Control of April twenty-eighth last, the Committee presume that the class of bowling to which the proposed new law would apply is that referred to as "body-line" bowling in the Australian Board of Control's cable of January eighteenth. The Committee consider that the term "body-line" bowling is misleading and improper. It has led to much inaccuracy of thought by confusing the short bumping ball, whether directed on the off, middle or leg stump, with what is known as "leg-theory".

The term "body-line" would appear to imply a direct attack by the bowler on the batsman. The Committee consider that such an implication applied to any English bowling in Australia is improper and incorrect. Such act on the part of any bowler would be an offence against the spirit of the game, and would be immediately condemned. The practice of bowling on the leg stump with a field placed on the leg side necessary for such bowling is legitimate and has been in force for many years. It has generally been referred to as "leg-theory". The present habit of batsmen who move in front of their wicket with the object of gliding straight balls to leg tends to give the impression that the bowler is bowling at the batsman, especially in the case of a fast bowler when the batsman mistimes the ball and is hit.

The new law recommended by the Australian Board of Control does not appear to the Committee to be practicable. Firstly, it would place an impossible task on the umpire, and, secondly, it would place in the hands of the umpire a power over the game which would be more dangerous and which any umpire might well fear to exercise.

The Committee have had no reason to give special attention to "leg-theory" as practised by fast bowlers. They will, however, watch carefully during the present season for anything which might be regarded as unfair or prejudicial to the best interests of the game. They propose to invite opinions and suggestions from county clubs and captains at the end of the season with a view to enabling them to express an opinion on this matter at a special meeting of the Imperial Cricket Conference.

With regard to the reports of the captain and managers, the Committee, while deeply appreciative of the private and public hospitality shewn to the English team, are much concerned with regard to barracking, which is referred to in all the reports and against which there is unanimous deprecation. Barracking has unfortunately always been indulged in by spectators in Australia to a degree quite unknown in this country. During the late tour, however, it would appear to have exceeded all previous experience, and on occasions to have become thoroughly objectionable. There appears to have been little or no effort on the part of those responsible for the administration of the game in Australia to interfere or to control this exhibition. This was naturally regarded by members of the team as a serious lack of consideration for them. The Committee are of opinion that cricket played under such conditions is robbed of much of its value as a game, and that unless barracking is stopped or is greatly moderated in Australia it is difficult to see how the continuance of representative matches can serve the best interests of the game.

The Committee regret that these matters have to be dealt with by correspondence and not by personal conference. If at any time duly accredited representatives of Australian cricket could meet the Committee in conference, such conference would be welcomed by MCC.

Don Bradman's reaction, although politely restrained, spoke for almost every Australian:"astounding". In his *Sun* column he pointed out that when 50,000 people protested at a cricket ground there had to be a reason, and that reason was that they did not like the bowling methods. He wanted an "ambassador" to be sent to Lord's, and suggested Bill Woodfull.[42] At a time when one could not simply climb aboard a fast-flying Jumbo jet, it was not a practical suggestion, even had Woodfull waited until school broke up.

The Australian Board were merely left speechless. What indeed could they now say?

It was to be three months before their next communiqué to Lord's. In the meantime they allowed the pressure to build up in the matter of the 1934 tour. England and Australia were at heart equally keen that the tour should go ahead, and were both quite heavily dependent on the revenue from it. So it now became a game of bluff.

In August, Bradman wrote an article in which he urged the Board to obtain an assurance from MCC that there would be no Bodyline: "After all, it is the players who have to face the music."

But how could MCC give such an assurance without considerable and embarrassing loss of face? It was their team, their captain, their bowlers, their victory. How could they now say, yes, we agree it was a slightly stained victory and we're sorry and it won't happen again? Those high-ranking politicians and soldiers gathered in the committee-room at Lord's had won a war against the Kaiser not so very long ago, which emphasised the might of the British Empire. It was no time to bow the knee to a dominion.

THE HONOURABLE F.S. JACKSON EMPLOYS HIS UMBRELLA TO SHOW HOW THE THROAT BALL SHOULD BE PLAYED. HE IS WATCHED BY ANOTHER TEST VETERAN, GEORGE HIRST, WHO KNEW A THING OR TWO ABOUT CONVENTIONAL LEG THEORY.

One of those rulers of cricket, Sir Stanley Jackson, once captain of England and an excellent allrounder, had evaded not only Australian bouncers but also an assassin's bullets in Bombay. Writer John Marshall went to see him at his Pont Street home and was enthralled at "Jacker's" private demonstration of how Bodyline should have been played: "With a Malacca cane he hooked them right off his neat cavalry moustache ... I can see, in the mind's eye, the ball soaring heavenwards somewhere between square leg and midwicket to land high up in the Mound Stand — or, it seemed to me in view of our location, in the centre of Cadogan Gardens."[43]

Despite his innate bullishness, Jackson gave Robbie Macdonald cause for optimism soon after the unhelpful MCC cable had gone off on June 12. When they met at Lord's the influential Sir Stanley indicated to the Australian that he was now opposed to the kind of bowling England had used in Australia and that he was sure it would not recur. As revealed in a letter dated April 25, 1933 to "My dear Ruthven",[44] Jackson stated that he doubted if "the Body Line will be exploited here — I think there is a lot of feeling against it ... I don't think MCC quite realise that the team which played it out there was <u>their</u> team, tho' they ought to realise that their team had a very disagreeable tour and they must ask the reason why ... I think we must all try to forget the last trip and begin over again but this can only be done if 'Body Line' bowling is declared to be against the spirit of the game — and that means exit Jardine!!!" (Note that in referring to MCC he uses "they" and "their" rather than "we" and "our".)

Macdonald could hardly contain his joy as he conveyed news of the clearly impending breakthrough to ACB secretary Jeanes.

Macdonald's finest moment came during discussions with the autocratic Lord Hawke. Hawke, together with MCC president Viscount Hailsham and Jackson and Findlay, had emerged from an MCC meeting which had followed the ICC gathering earlier that day, July 31, 1933. Macdonald and R.H. Mallett, an all-purpose English cricket identity, had represented Australia at the ICC meeting (P.F. Warner was wearing yet another hat, as one of South Africa's two delegates), and Macdonald managed to persuade Jackson to manoeuvre Australia's proposed amendment (Law 48B) into the deferred basket rather than having it kicked out.

LORD HAWKE IN HIS PLAYING DAYS. NOW HE WAS ONE OF THE WEIGHTIER CHARACTERS IN THE COMMITTEE-ROOM AT LORD'S, NEVER LOST FOR AN OPINION.

Now, in an episode that for years remained undisclosed, referred to simply as Macdonald's "secret letter" (written to his Board: even the State associations were not permitted to view it), the bold little Australian politely informed the four esteemed gentlemen of Lord's that the Australian Board needed an unequivocal assurance that their team would not face Bodyline in 1934, otherwise there would be no tour. And when he sensed that they were simply going to pad the suggestion away by saying they would gladly talk to the Australian captain and manager *after* the team had landed in England next year, he unblinkingly slipped in the thought that an alternative might be for Australia to come over armed with four fast bowlers, double the customary number in that era (England's four in 1932–33 had been seen as overkill). The menacing notion was conveyed with a figurative sweet smile.

Lord Hawke reacted like one of the bewhiskered old colonels in a Roy Ullyett "Colonel Blimp" cartoon. "Reprisals, by Gad!" he exploded. To which Macdonald calmly replied: "No, I would call it reciprocity, merely mutual action and reaction."[45] There was, Macdonald reported, a friendly reception to his remarks, with even a little laughter.

Since this frank exchange and evident English enlightenment came only a fortnight after the British government had finally eased the terms of the loans to Australia — a concession that would have created a wealth of goodwill had it only been made some months sooner — Australia's sun was just beginning to shine again, and by September 22 the Australian Board felt ready to send another cable to MCC:

AUSTRALIAN BOARD OF CONTROL TO MCC, September 22, 1933

We note that you consider that a form of bowling which amounted to a direct attack by the bowler on the batsman would be against the spirit of the game. We agree with you that leg-theory bowling as it has been generally practised for many years is not open to objection. On these matters there does not appear to be any real difference between our respective views. We feel that while the type of bowling to which exception was taken in Australia strictly was not in conflict with the Laws of Cricket, yet its continued practice would not be in the best interests of the game. May we assume that you concur in this point of view and that the teams may thus take the field in 1934 with that knowledge? We are giving consideration to the question of barracking and you may rely upon our using our best endeavours to have it controlled in future tours. We are most anxious that the cordial relations which have so long existed between English and Australian cricket shall continue.

The carefully worded phrase "type of bowling to which exception was taken" was inserted upon Macdonald's urging. Any use of the pejorative "Bodyline" would have set the negotiations back weeks, if not years.

The power base of Australian cricket administration had now shifted. Dr Robertson's term as chairman ended in September, and Aubrey Oxlade, the lawyer from Manly, was in the chair. But the Australian Board of Control for International Cricket was no more unified in outlook than before. Five of its 13 members — Robertson, Kelly, Mailer, Hartigan and Hutcheon (the first three in Victoria [Kelly had managed Australia's 1930 tour], the others in Queensland) — retained a hard line on the '34 tour, insisting that assurances of no Bodyline should be *demanded*. The two Queensland members, particularly, distanced themselves from the remainder of the Board's eager acceptance of MCC's airy assurances and made their resentment clear: "The responsibility of letting Australia down is off our shoulders."[46] When Dr Macdonald was appraised of this lack of unanimity, fearing that his diplomatic efforts in London were being jeopardised when all had seemed settled, he shot off a cable to ACB secretary Jeanes in Adelaide on October 21:[47]

> Respectfully hope matter be regarded as gentlemen's agreement. Marylebone position difficult … Risk of repetition bodyline infinitesimal. Overwhelming majority English captains and cricketers and all Imperial Conference delegates condemn it. Any attempt to reopen negotiations will be grave tactical mistake. Marylebone's cable promised warm welcome and every effort to make visit enjoyable. This assurance reveals the certain abandonment of bodyline.[47]

The MCC cable to which he referred had been dispatched from London 12 days previously and had appeared to seal peace. It had helped matters, of course, that Australia's cable of September 22 had omitted any reference to the dreaded word "Bodyline", which had been regarded at Lord's as almost as inflammatory as "unsportsmanlike". In cricket's lexicon the English for "Bodyline" was "direct attack".

MCC TO AUSTRALIAN BOARD OF CONTROL, October 9, 1933

The MCC Committee appreciate the friendly tone of your cable and they heartily reciprocate your desire for the continuance of cordial relations. In their view the difference between us seems to be rather on the question of fact than on any point of interpretation of the Laws of Cricket or of the spirit of the game. They agree and have always agreed that a form of bowling which is obviously a direct attack by the bowler upon the batsman would be an offence against the spirit of the game. Your team can certainly take the field with the knowledge and with the full assurance that cricket will be played here in the same spirit as in the past and with the single desire to promote the best interests of the game in both countries. The Committee much appreciate your promise to take the question of barracking into consideration with a view to ensuring that it shall be kept within reasonable bounds. Your team can rely on a warm welcome from MCC and every effort will be made to make your visit enjoyable.

Presumably because of the scattered thinking in the ACB ranks — together with the ill-timed claim in Larwood's latest newspaper outpourings that he intended to bowl leg theory if picked for the 1934 Tests (Macdonald, now in America, told the Board that this was best disregarded) — it was 38 days before the Board responded to MCC's cordial dispatch:

AUSTRALIAN BOARD OF CONTROL TO MCC, November 16, 1933

We appreciate the terms of your cablegram of October 9 and assume that this cable is intended to give the assurance asked for in our cablegram of September 22. It is on this understanding that we are sending our team next year.

Governor Hore-Ruthven called this a "stupid and tactless" cable and in a letter to Warner he gave the wording which he knew to have been originally intended for dispatch:

We accept your cable as creating a gentleman's understanding that matches shall be played during the 1934 tour in same spirit as in former tours and with the single desire to promote the best interests of the game both in England and Australia.

The reason this was not sent, the Governor explained, was that although it was passed by an 8:5 majority "the minority then bluffed the majority to send a substitute. Hutchings [Hutcheon] opposed — he'd hoped to be sent to England as a delegate to discuss the matter with MCC". Others to oppose the approved draft were Hartigan, Dr Robertson (just superseded as chairman), Dr Mailer, and Kelly (also disgruntled — in his case because "quite rightly" he was not chosen as tour manager). These five, said Hore-Ruthven as he strove to conceal his disgust, "allowed personal feelings to override the interests of cricket". He referred to a very nice talk he had had with Woodfull while he was in Adelaide: "He has got absolutely the right outlook and is only anxious that the whole spirit of the game should be put back onto its old footing and will do everything he can to ensure that end." The Governor had long since become the focal figure at the Australian end of the dispute. Among surviving letters is one scrawled to Hore-Ruthven by one of South Australia's ACB members, Harry Hodgetts. It said little, but it is added testimony to the fact that letters concerning Bodyline and its likely solution were flying back and forth in so many directions and in such profusion as to make an enormous cat's cradle.

When the contents of the Australian cable of October 9 became known, P.F. Warner naturally felt impelled to write to Sir Alexander Hore-Ruthven, kicking off with a jubilant if somewhat premature "Peace reigns again." He explained that some of the MCC committee had been slow to grasp the difference between plain leg theory and the direct attack, just as they had been loath to accept that Jardine hated 95 per cent of Australians and "conceived this bowling in hate". He begged the Governor to take no notice of Larwood's "outbursts": "He is paid to make them by the Daily Express! He will be muzzled presently." Jardine's book is "a rotten one" and Warner thought him "a bit 'mad'" — "Toone [prominent Yorkshire administrator and MCC tour manager in Australia in the 1920s] always thought so, Hawke tells me."

Before responding to the November 16 cable, MCC waited to see what might happen at the heavyweight meeting at Lord's on November 23. Convened were members of the Advisory County Cricket Committee, the Board of Control of Test Matches at Home, and 14 of the county captains, together with representatives from the other three county clubs. Under consideration was the circular sent out by MCC concerning fast leg-theory bowling. The conclusion was that no change would be made to the Laws but that it was the captains' responsibility to see that the spirit of the game was not violated by any direct attack. This went only part of the way towards resolving the problem, but the principle was affirmed by the ICC at its meeting on July 25, 1934.

The best MCC could do now, even though it smacked of further brinkmanship, was commit to the wires the following:

MCC TO AUSTRALIAN BOARD OF CONTROL, December 12, 1933

Reference your cable of November 16, you must please accept our cable of October 9, which speaks for itself, as final. We cannot go beyond the assurance therein given. We shall welcome Australian cricketers who come to play cricket with us next year. If, however, your Board of Control decide that such games should be deferred, we shall regret their decision. Please let us know your Board's final decision as soon as possible and in any event before the end of the year.

There was no hesitation on the part of the Australian Board:

AUSTRALIAN BOARD OF CONTROL TO MCC, December 14, 1933

With further reference to your cable of October 9 and your confirmatory cable of December 12 in reply to ours of November 16, we, too, now regard the position finalised. Our team will leave Australia on March 9.

By return came the message that so many had dreamed about receiving for so long:

MCC TO AUSTRALIAN BOARD OF CONTROL, December 14, 1933

Thank you for your cable. We are very glad to know we may look forward to welcoming the Australians next summer. We shall do all in our power to make their visit enjoyable.

The telegraph wires could cool at last. The stream of shilling-a-word missives through the drawn-out crisis was at an end. Anglo-Australian cricket had been saved. The tour was on. Disadvantaged though its delegates were by being scattered across a continent, the diplomatic skills of Australian cricket's governing body — crucially guided by Macdonald — had belatedly won the day, though MCC's special subcommittee felt it had done its job too. Chairman Viscount Hailsham is actually known to have preened himself upon having achieved a settlement.[48] Not that it should be questioned that a major element in settling this thorniest of disputes had been the persuasive powers and insight of this MCC president, Secretary of State for War, and Leader of the House of Lords (who was to be carried from the bombed ruins of the Carlton Club in 1940 on the shoulders of his son, himself one day to become Lord Chancellor).

Australian embarrassment at the first, gauche protest cable during the Adelaide Test now seemed to have evaporated. "The Board must be awarded some points," *The Australian Cricketer* was soon reflecting, "for the blind courage it showed in launching its bull-like charge on the citadel of world cricket ... The temerity of the attack ... apparently turned Marylebone blind with fury ... Obviously another dragon had to be slain, a dragon that had been masquerading in sheep's clothing, or was it a kangaroo's?"

To chairman Aubrey Oxlade went the closing honours on the Australian side. This whisky-drinking diabetic 47-year-old smoker was devoted to cricket, and had served the game in the New South Wales and national committee-rooms for almost a quarter of a century already. From his early soft line on Bodyline had emerged stern disapproval, and his strong-willed attitude and powers of persuasion were directed to effecting not just a solution to the problem but one by which Australia would not be compromised. There were suggestions within the Board that he had exceeded his powers by sending the cable of December 14 which clinched the tour: "we, too, now regard the position finalised". But Oxlade had the required majority, and his predecessor, Allen Robertson, could but gnash his teeth.

The British establishment certainly thought Oxlade had batted well. He was appointed CBE in the 1934 New Year Honours, *Punch* giggling that he had been in line for the Order of the Garter but there had simply been no garter big enough for leg theory. Plum Warner's prolific correspondence included a letter scrawled to Hore-Ruthven (it was now "Sandy" and "Plum") on January 3, on Conservative Club notepaper: "Much comment over here Oxlade's CBE in the New Year Honours. Personally I think it will do good. It is a gesture, but fancy they don't much like it at Lord's — think it a little premature. Some construe it as saying Board were right in their view, though everyone here is certain that their original cable was a terrible blunder. Anyway Australia will no doubt take this CBE as a friendly gesture."

Warner himself had to wait another three years before he got his knighthood.

He went on to tell the South Australia Governor that a circular (*"entre nous"*) was going to the county clubs urging them to prevent barracking. The danger was greatest in Nottinghamshire (Larwood "if he is able to bowl fast again, which I doubt") and Yorkshire (Bowes).

But one major problem remained: what was to be done about Douglas Jardine? "The real trouble is Jardine," Warner continued. "Is he to be capt[ain]? At present I say 'No' unless he makes a most generous public gesture of friendliness and then I am not sure that I would trust him. He is a queer fellow. When he sees a cricket ground with an Australian on it he goes mad! He rose to his present position on my shoulders, and of his attitude to me I do not care to speak. It is hoped he may retire at the end of the Indian tour, but in many quarters here — where they do not know the truth — he is a bit of a hero. If he is captain in first Test and is not friendly he will not capt in the 2nd — but I would not have him at all, as I do not believe in honouring a man who has done untold harm to cricket and its spirit and traditions. His book is full of contemptuous and disparaging remarks of Australia and Australians, and in his chapter on the IVth Test, at Brisbane, he actually has the impertinence to justify his questioning of the umpires' decisions; and he the captain of England!! But, please, keep <u>my own</u> opinion on DRJ to yourself."[49]

CHAPTER FOURTEEN

CONSEQUENCES

The *Australian Cricketer* magazine's summary was eloquent:

> Cricket diplomacy has quickly reached a high standard. Australia softly cooed that she was going over, and England was asked to be good. England gently whispered that she had not done anything, but it would not happen again. Most of the sympathy is now with Marylebone. The old club was entitled to a gentlemanly way out of an awkward position, and Australia was wise enough to offer the chance. So far there is nothing to be taken exception to, except the opinion in Australia that if Marylebone is unable to control Larwood's newspaper barracking, the Australian Board cannot be expected to have much control over a hundred thousand ordinary spectators ... Bodyline is officially dead. Public — and cricket — opinion has killed it ... A few dying kicks may be expected, but the wide arms of cricket can absorb many of these.

The predicted dying kicks, when they came, were enough to spread fears that Bodyline was not dead and perhaps, like some creature in a horror film, never could be completely vanquished.

First, there was D.R. Jardine's continuation of the tactics in India in defiance of any warnings given to him by Lords Hailsham and Hawke. Indeed, MCC had had a nasty scare before the team even sailed. The Indian Board of Control cabled to say that the under-strength side England had selected was a disgusting insult to India. Unless half-a-dozen star names were added the tour would be cancelled. The corridors of Lord's filled with fresh tension, and heads gathered. Then the cable was revealed to be a hoax, the mischievous prank of a lowly, disillusioned clerk. The Indian Board were even more horrified than MCC.[1]

Second, the printed words that appeared in ever-increasing abundance kept the embers aglow. It seemed that Australia's damaged psyche might never recover. Alan Kippax's book *Anti Body-Line* (written in collaboration with Eric Barbour, who died a year later at the age of 43) was a calmly expressed, reasonable and sad little book which spelt out the dangers of allowing Bodyline to continue to be legitimate. It was aimed at an English readership and utilised letters of outrage written to Australian papers during the series, including those from C.E.W. Bean and Tom Garrett previously referred to. Of Larwood's post-tour "literature", Kippax wrote that "abuse is not argument, and self-praise is no recommendation". He believed that the "body-liner" was on an exact par with the footballer who puts in the boot. While not approving of Bradman's strategy, Kippax acknowledged that Bradman played shots no other living batsman could have managed; and, of course, he still topped the averages. A family man could afford to play against Bodyline only if he was very well paid and heavily insured, Kippax claimed; he also hated it because it would breed fast bowlers armed only with brute force, against whom runs could only be made from occasional pushes for singles and twos through the packed leg-side field. This ugly bowling must be outlawed or else it would spring up again and again. (As it has done repeatedly in the years following Kippax's death in 1972.)

But there were much more robust attacks on Bodyline — and the species responsible for generating it — in *The "Sporting" English?* and *The Barracker at Bay*. The former was a small board-bound publication compiled by "A Man in the Street" (thought to be W.R. Staton) and published by the Macquarie Head Press, and the latter was a 32-page pamphlet written by a young man from Melbourne named R.T. Corrie. A copy of *Barracker* was sent by Raymond Corrie to every player who had taken part in the series. Larwood sent an acknowledgment, saying it was always interesting to hear the views of others "providing they are not biased"; Jardine, as he awaited the arrival of his copy, thanked the author by means of a typical riposte: "I can at least congratulate you on your courage in claiming to speak for 95 per cent of so large and varied a country."

Corrie's case for lifting blame from the barrackers rested on two things: their right to express their opinions (they had paid for that right) and the fact that only the tiniest proportion of their offerings was objection-able. England had used the anti-barracking argument as a red herring. He further claimed that the average Australian spectator was more knowledgeable than his English counterpart, though in citing the generous Australian cheering of English players he compares the barrackers with unsophisticated boys at heart. "While liking them as individuals, we [the barrackers] were forced to regard them unfavourably as a team." He quoted Vernon Ransford, the former Test left-hander, who philosophised: "What does it matter if we lose the Ashes? … I think the real Australian will say good luck to the Englishmen … MCC is quite true in saying the English-men have not infringed any of the laws of cricket, but there are laws that are not in print."

P.F. Warner surely shuddered when he read Corrie's verdict on his role: the MCC manager's "apparent hypocrisy has disgusted many of his former admirers in Australia". The word "former" must have hurt like a hornet's sting.

And yet there were passages that would have touched the heartstrings of the cricket governors of England, a nation that "makes a fetish of sportsmanship". Corrie acknowledged with relief that there were those over the other side who had expressed their distaste for Jardine's scheme. "The great tree of sportsmanship and chivalry was implanted and grew through the centuries in England. Today, that tree is finer and grander than ever. It is far, far too strong a tree to be permanently affected by the plague at present despoiling its foliage. All that it needs is a courageous gardener to wield the pruning knife, to cut out the unclean thing in its midst and to allow its beauty to show forth unblemished."

Corrie closed his case with a persuasive claim: "If the hooting acted as the slightest restraint on the use of bodyline, then the barrackers did a great service for cricket."

The "Sporting" English? went in much harder. "England entertains a pleasant fiction," the author teased, "that the Duke of Wellington declared that the Battle of Waterloo was won on the playing fields of Eton. That complacent epigram has inspired countless smug boys-of-the-bulldog-breed for a century, and they still talk of one Englishman being better than five Frenchmen — and what is worse, they believe it! 'An Englishman knows not when he is beaten — ', of course he doesn't, that's the devil of it; and he won't even accept the umpire's decision about it!"

Ben Travers's comedy *A Bit of a Test* is referred to: when it closed after three nights in Melbourne in May 1933 the playwright blamed the unwillingness of Australians to see themselves caricatured. Well, not by an Englishman, one would suppose.

"Man in the Street" reproduced a number of newspaper articles, throwing all he could find at England and English cricket mores: didn't an American once say that "the ordinary Englishman is a man of few words, and these are generally disagreeable"? Sport in England was subject to cant and hypocrisy. "Poor, petulant, slow-witted Larwood" is lampooned: the hero/villain wrote a stinging, ridiculous article, refused the payment cheque, regretted the article, regretted sending back the cheque, then went ahead with the article and pocketed the resultant cheque. Larwood and Jardine "had a mutual and unhidden dislike of each other".

There was so much more: the separation between amateurs and professionals in English cricket was a contradiction of the true spirit of sport. (Wilfred Rhodes once described it — without a trace of resentment — as "English apartheid".[2]) The field change after Woodfull's Adelaide injury was unsportsmanlike and cowardly. An unnamed Australian batsman is supposed to have said that if there is nothing in the rules to stop Bodyline bowling, well then there's nothing in the rules to stop him walking up the pitch and clouting the bowler with his bat either. And C.J. Dennis was called in once more to lighten the mood. The last verse of his *We Mean to Say* was probably deliberately intended to sound like Lord Hawke:

> *There's the code, you know — our code, we would remind you.*
> *We made it for ourselves, and mean to stick to it.*
> *And to try to knock us flat*
> *With a boomerang like that –*
> *By gad! It isn't done! It isn't cricket!*

"Man in the Street" drew repeatedly on recent history: how *The Times* had condemned the barracking of Jack Gregory at The Oval in 1921, especially after he had struck Andy Ducat twice — without any Bodyline field, needless to say. From that period he appended Norman Campbell's satirical view of English spectators, published in *The Bulletin* (last stanza only):

At 'Ome, of course, we Play the Game,
The crowd behave decorously,
They never criticise or blame,
But say "Bravo!" sonorously;
"Played, sir!" they chirp, or cry "Well run!"
But barrack — haw! — it isn't done.

This side-swipe was backed up by Warwick Armstrong's claim that the barracking in Yorkshire was worse than anything heard in Australia. Then *The "Sporting" English?* summarised all the unpleasantness of the 1932–33 tour: the incidents in Perth, Adelaide, Hobart, Bendigo, Toowoomba and Brisbane. Some indefensible criticisms of Australia by all kinds of Englishmen in the past were laid before the reader before the author wound up with his rekindling of the miserable wrangle over the British and Australian official histories of the First World War.

Why, he asked, had Australia, alone in all the Empire, been singled out for the Bodyline attack? He would not have uttered that question had he known what Jardine was about to get up to in India.

Meanwhile, there was more than enough damage to be cleared up following the Tests of '32–33. The ripples had spread even into Asia. Australian journalist J.S. Hughes reported that the *North China Daily News* was editorially pro-Bodyline. "It was remarkable how the bodyline business had militated against Australia in certain quarters of the Far East," he wrote. "It was impossible not to be struck by the heat it had engendered and by its bad effect on our commercial interests in China. This may seem rather far-fetched, but it is nevertheless a fact that Australians engaged in business in Hong Kong and Shanghai have been embarrassed by it. I know of several deals lost to Australians because of it."[3] This, alongside observations (such as Sir Alexander Hore-Ruthven's in his letter of June 21, 1933 to Dominions Secretary Thomas) that Australians were showing a reluctance to buy British goods, presents a picture of vast common sacrifice at the feet of Messrs Jardine, Larwood and Voce.

The task of the peacemakers was rendered difficult by the apparently never-ending flow of provocative remarks — a year, two years, and longer still after the series, until the Second World War caused suspension of all such disturbing sentiments. A.W. Carr's disputatious book, *Cricket With the Lid Off*, which came out in 1935, featured letters he said he had received during the Bodyline series, sent to him in recognition of his role in formulating this method of attack. Some were supportive, some slightly abusive. Voce should have bowled underhand; MCC should have asked Mr Woodfull to pick the England team; thank God there are men like you and Jardine in cricket today who don't care a damn for MCC; and one which began: "I have lived in Australia and served with the Australian Light Horse in the war, and my experience is that, with the exception of Americans, Australians are the world's worst losers."

Memories were not going to fade in a hurry. A couple of years after the Bodyline Tests a South African football team played in Sydney. One of their forwards was named Bastard, and when the denizens of the Hill spotted him they gave him disproportionate attention, being divided only as to whether to screech "Larwood!" or "Jardine!" at him.[4]

Such was the lingering odour that many Australians altered their attitude towards English immigrants, whether or not the immigrants had supported England's cricket strategy. The potential for friction between the settled Australian populace and newcomers from Britain has been rampant since shortly after Captain Phillip disembarked his fleet of unenthusiastic emigrants in 1788. Mutual resentment — often with good cause — between people from the old country and the new must simply be regarded as inevitable and unavoidable. Bodyline intensified it. A young university student, English-born Graham McInnes, enjoyed many a passionate conversation on cricket while in Tasmania, but after the Adelaide Test he found himself shunned and cut off, even though he had no more liking for Bodyline than had his Australian friends. In his autobiography, *Humping My Bluey*, McInnes wrote of the crowd roars coming from the wireless speaker.[5] Every corner of Australia was being touched by commentary on the electrifying cricket. The revulsion felt was certainly not restricted to the "live" spectators alone.

Even an enquiring German political activist named Egon Erwin Kisch took an interest in the Bodyline phenomenon. Suspected — not without cause — of being a Communist, he was at first refused entry into Australia in 1934. Kisch went to great lengths to gain both entry and the time to wander around the country, and in his book *Australian Landfall* he devoted a whole chapter to Bodyline, first tracing the development of cricket in Australia and making much of the amateur/professional divide in English cricket, then writing of "the poetic movement of the former coal-heaver

Harold Larwood" and the fact that Don Bradman's wax image was to be seen at Madame Tussaud's. Given the option, claimed Kisch, of choosing a black man (Eddie Gilbert) to represent Australia or sending a protest to Lord's, the Australian cricket administrators followed the latter course. Referring slightly anachronistically to Viscount Hailsham (identified not only as Secretary of State for War but as a Vickers Armstrong shareholder), he noted that England's bland response turned Australian into a "veritable volcano". Let England henceforth get her wool from and play cricket against South Africa, he said! Kisch saw the statue of Queen Victoria's husband, Prince Albert, in Sydney defaced: the word BODYLINE! was painted on it and an ear had been knocked off. That only an ear went missing, suggested the writer, was because the rock-throwing vandal's aim was not as good as Larwood's. His final assessment was that "Bodyline, after all, has not changed the map of the world."

Meanwhile, poor Major the Honourable Gerald French, DSO (Wellington and Devon), having failed to find a publisher for his complete record of the 1932–33 tour, consigned the typescript to the MCC Collection at Lord's, where it rests to this day, a 664-page tome which steers meticulously clear of controversy. Based on agency and newspaper reports of the matches, its chief attractions are the 97 illustrations clipped from contemporary newspapers. Among the few personal opinions expressed in the compilation is French's remark that when he first saw Woodfull batting — in the nets at Lord's at the start of the 1926 tour — he assumed he must be a bowler or wicketkeeper, so unsophisticated was his style.

Rueful protest came in the shape of *Bodywhine: a Treatise on the Jardinian Theory*, a 40-page booklet which Rigby published in Adelaide in 1933. R.W. Blundell's cartoons were supported by V.M. Branson's words. In addition to a satirical film compilation soon after the Adelaide Test, Pathe Newsreel did their bit by releasing a short diagrammatic cartoon called *The Bodyline Argument*; it was the creation of Joe Noble, and concluded with a batsman's head being knocked clean off: "And that's how bodyline bowling was born!" It was as unconvincing as the melodramatic demonstration in front of the camera by the gap-toothed Middlesex and England fast bowler Jack Durston had been.

Lennie Lower produced an amusing little essay, *Bradman and the Burglar*, in which the power of the radio cricket commentary was emphasised. An intruder becomes as distracted by the broadcast as the family he has come to burgle and the police constable who comes to investigate. They all sit down to listen to the exploits of Bradman, McCabe and Larwood, all else forgotten.

Of the numerous topical cartoons sketched in both countries, one of the more dramatic was David Low's imaginative effort in the *Evening Standard* after the Adelaide Test. A ball from Larwood strikes Bradman on the jaw, prompting the batsman to hurl his bat at the bowler; the England fieldsmen then pick Bradman up and chuck him into the stumps and Jardine sinks his teeth into Woodfull's leg. Australia then declares war.

Long after the dust had settled, in 1949, Scottish author A.G. Macdonell — better known, and rightly so, for his classic *England, Their England* — published a slab of nonsense entitled *How Like an Angel*, which tells of a chap named Hugo Seeley who is plucked out of obscurity to bowl his "levin-bolts" (flashes of lightning) at the Borealians' leg stump. When 10,000 Borealians riot and storm the field the England players shelter in the Mound Stand, and the Dominions Secretary is soon promising that "We'll 'oof that blighter out." Poor Seeley is banished to America.

Bodyline, it seems, simply cannot be banished from public consciousness. As recently as 1985 there was a hilarious spoof, "Bodyline Revisited", by Christopher Booker and Ian Hislop, in *Private Eye* magazine. Little Don Bradman's mother believes that one day he'll "smash those snotty-nosed poms". When he hits 25 consecutive sixes soon afterwards England are worried at the prospect of losing the Empire. Comes the man to fix the problem. It is Jardine, and his weapon is a machine-gun. Is he going to kill Bradman? "No. [Smiles evilly.] I'm going to do what the British ruling class has always done. Get some member of the working classes to do their dirty work for them." Larwood kills Bradman but the Empire collapses all the same, to *Rule Britannia*, played on a ukelele.

This skit was inspired by the recent showing of the Kennedy Miller television drama–documentary *Bodyline*, which was made for Network Ten in Australia at a stated cost of $5 million. It received some scathing reviews, particularly in England. The *Daily Mirror* dubbed it "*Bodylies*".

In addition to the laughable characterisations, there were numerous careless errors of fact. The ship supposed to be *Orontes* leaves England with two funnels and reaches Australia with three. The English professionals are shown wearing suits instead of dinner jackets on board. (This of course did not entitle them to address Jardine as "Douglas". He was still "Mr" or

"Skipper": the writers got that right.) But even cricketing ignoramuses must have recognised the falsity of the cries of "Howzat!" that go up after a batsman is caught in the outfield, the umpire then raising his finger. Ames sometimes crouches up over the stumps to Larwood's express bowling. (The real-life Ames thought the cricket scenes were "phoney".) Non-striker Bradman picks the ball up after it is driven back and hands it to the bowler, and elsewhere he drinks beer, though he was regarded as a teetotaller in real life. O'Reilly and McCabe have thick hair hanging over their foreheads, and Warner is bald — glaring oversights. Some of the sweaters belong only on village greens. Ironmonger is dropped by Jardine (played by Hugo Weaving) when Bradman (Gary Sweet) is 98 not out (this simply didn't happen). The crowd — with women in the members' stand — bursts into *Our Don Bradman* when he reaches his hundred. Jardine as a boy is shown bowling left-arm and scoring a century against Eton (he did neither). Sir Stanley Jackson is elevated to "Lord". Lord Harris is far too fat. Gubby Allen is much too tall, Bill Voce much too short. The years given for Warner's knighthood and Larwood's emigration are incorrect. Percy Fender is depicted as an outrageous Bertie Wooster type. Bowes somehow finds himself in the Piccadilly grill-room scene. Oldfield was not forced out for the season by his head injury. The quantity of booze sunk in hotels and committee-rooms is simply beyond rational belief. The British flag is shown being burned at the top of the SCG pavilion, an incident unrecorded in any contemporary source and clearly provocative. And even when the Test matches shown are being enacted at Melbourne or Adelaide, that beautiful and instantly recognisable Sydney pavilion is forever in the background.

All the same, and allowing for much further distortion that might be considered legitimate in the interests of dramatic licence, the production has a few humorous moments and some that are quite touching, such as the final confrontation between Jardine and Warner. The captain — with a curl of the lip — accuses the manager of being weak. Warner, eyes moist, responds with the comment that while that may be true, at least he was sane.

Among the media critics, Richard Coleman found the greatest excitement in the scene where Jardine's fictitious girlfriend removes her stockings. Julian Barnes's main objection was the slow-motion filming of the cricket action, which concentrated the viewer's eye on the slowly flopping jowl and filled the ear with "wicked-dragon amplified breathing".

Veteran writer and former Oxford and Surrey cricketer E.M. Wellings, in a letter to me, described the cricket shots as "too ludicrous for words" and pointed out that Bradman, far from being the Australian dressing-room favourite, wasn't particularly close to his team-mates by 1932. The character assassination of Jardine, Larwood and Lord Harris was "repulsive to one who knew the players of that time".

Bob Wyatt, who was depicted sympathetically, declared the seven-hour series to be "trash from beginning to end". Gubby Allen found it "repulsive". The young Don and Jessie Bradman were fetchingly portrayed, though the real Bradmans scoffed at the mild hysteria displayed by Jessie in the post office upon the arrival of Don's Test selection telegram. As for Bill O'Reilly, he almost choked in his armchair as he watched the series, and when he had recovered he rubbished it in his *Sydney Morning Herald* column. A major objection concerned the portrayal of himself: "I must congratulate my counterpart, Ross Hall [the actor who played him in the series], for his initiative in escaping all the hard work which came my way that season. Surely it will surprise him (he got away with one ball delivered from half my usual run) that I had to bowl more than 380 overs. That is more even than Larwood and Voce's contributions put together."

After the Larwoods had received some abusive and obscene phone calls during the transmission of *Bodyline*, Lois said, "The series showed Harold with hate in his eyes. My husband never had hate in his eyes." As for the scene of his Nottingham upbringing, Larwood (played by Liverpool migrant Jim Holt) said, "I've never seen slums like that anywhere."

Tony Pawson hit the bullseye in his review in *The Observer* of this "mendacious" film: "Larwood posed the Australians the question: 'Would you have behaved in similarly outrageous fashion to me had I been Tim Wall bowling for Australia?' Time has supplied the answer with the Australian spectators baying for blood as Lillee and Thomson bowled a more lethal form of bodyline to chants of 'Ashes to ashes, dust to dust — if Thomson don't get ya, Lillee must!'"

The programme probably set Anglo-Australian relations back 20 years. It will probably be shown again. Viewers are advised to expect a few evenings of sporadically compelling entertainment — and to keep a sizeable pot of salt close at hand.

Around the same time the English film-maker David Puttnam was planning a full-length feature on Bodyline, but for one reason or another it was not pursued, although Kerry Packer was said to be prepared to put up most of the money. A script by Paul Wheeler was converted into a novel with the intention of providing "pure entertainment", but once again several of the Test cricketers of 1932–33 were appalled when the book came out in 1983. Freddie Brown threw it into the dustbin, Gubby Allen described it as a "ridiculous distortion" and Bob Wyatt was critical too. Jardine was not a cheat, he said. "He was a man of great principle and we must not let him down."

If Puttnam had gone ahead with a movie he planned to eliminate any reference to lbw because the Americans would not have comprehended that particular law. The more one thinks about fictional dramatisation, the more sacred and precious becomes the truth.

In 1983 came the finest television documentary on Bodyline to date. Produced by Alan Patient, the BBC *Forty Minutes* programme incorporated interviews — not always in friendly harmony — with Larwood, Wyatt, Bowes, Allen, Ames, O'Brien, Alexander and O'Reilly, together with much newsreel from the series. This is one production that must never be allowed to be wiped or go adrift, as has so much else from the vast BBC vaults.

Warm wafts of conciliatory words between administrators and others prevented a complete breakdown in relations in the gushing wake of Bodyline, and kept hope alive. When the next English team toured Australia — the 1934–35 *women's* team — they were greeted in friendly fashion wherever they went, and at the end of the tour George Garnsey, the New South Wales (men's) coach, wrote to the captain, Betty Archdale, concluding his letter with an encouraging remark: "We all know of the brotherhood, and I should add sisterhood of cricket, and it will take more than a piffling dispute on bodyline to upset that fellowship."[6]

Walter Hammond, whose aversion to Bodyline soon became public knowledge and who believed that Jardine and Larwood might not have foreseen quite how dangerous Bodyline would be, wrote — a few years later, when passions had calmed — that some Australians had refrained from protesting because they feared being labelled cowards. He went so far as to attribute much of the force of the barracking to the frustration felt by men who had placed heavy bets on the outcome of the Tests. Nobody had been really seriously injured, and he believed the damage done to Empire relationships and personal friendships was not beyond repair. "It was an unhappy affair; and that cricket has survived with so few scars to show means that Australians and Englishmen have tried hard since to understand each other better."[7] This, it should be noted, was written before the 1946–47 Ashes series, when he and opposing captain Don Bradman hardly exchanged a word after an umpiring incident in the first Test.

Soon, however, there were signs of an easing of tension in Australia following MCC's pacifying words.

When the 1934 tour had been confirmed, *The Australian Cricketer* saw fit to publish an inconsequential parody of Macaulay entitled *The Larwood–Bradman Duel*, which began: "Larwoodus spied Bradmanus, and dashed across the main — Ho Bradmanus, I have sought thee in many a hard-fought game. One of us two, O Bradmanus, henceforth will reign alone — So! Lay on for Australia, and I'll lay on for Home."

Even the advertising copy-writers picked up on Bodyline. As promotion for the show *Rebecca of Sunnybrook Farm*, newspaper readers were tempted by a three-verser called *Leg Theory at Sunnybrook Farm*. The first four lines will suffice:[8]

There's an Animal Test match at Sunnybrook Farm;
And the Board of Control can't keep itself calm
For as soon as the centipede went in to bat,
A cow bowled leg theory and knocked ten legs flat.

When the New South Wales team went to Adelaide for the Sheffield Shield match just before Christmas 1933, some of the players took part in Kerwin Maegraith's stage production of a skit called *It Ain't Cricket* at the Theatre Royal on the Sunday. Arthur Mailey provided topical sketches, Jack Scott, the nuggety umpire and former fast bowler, took the part of Larwood, and Don Bradman was, not surprisingly, the batsman. He hit tennis balls at a delighted audience, and at one point Vic Richardson tried to throw a ball to the Governor and Lady Hore-Ruthven, up in the dress circle. It was remarked that the cricketers' "repartee was so well done that most of the audience thought that it was impromptu". Proceeds from the event went to the testimonial fund for Ernie Jones, the old fast bowler who was South Australia's coach. He had fallen on hard times and his wife was ill.[9]

For the moment, the word that best soothes the Great Argument can come from Robert Gordon Menzies, then a barrister, and witness to the sensations at Adelaide Oval in 1933, who wrote 30 years later: "Great Britain and Australia are of the same blood and allegiance and history and instinctive mental processes. We know each other so well that, thank Heaven, we don't have to be too tactful with each other."[10] Forty years on the claim may have lost a little of its validity, but still should not be dismissed as worthless.

And so to India with Jardine.

"I never understood the fellow," said the stylish batsman C.F. Walters, his tour vice-captain, who finished second to Jardine's 52.19 in the first-class averages. "During the tour he seemed always to have a large book tucked under his arm. When the Indian officials and others lined up as he walked into a reception, one of those in the group was an uncle. You could tell too, for he had the same huge nose as Douglas. Douglas just walked straight past him."

What was it like batting with him? "He disliked batting on the matting. Amar Singh was very fast and made the ball curve and then cut several inches on the mat. I played back to him most of the time, and Douglas lunged forward and got out, saying afterwards that he was sick of watching me play back all the time."[11]

The MCC side sailed from Tilbury aboard *Mooltan* on September 22, 1933 and reached Bombay on October 12, to begin a gruelling 19-week tour that was not without its outdoor and indoor recreation and relaxation. Of 34 matches in India and Ceylon they lost only one, to the Vizianagram XI at Benares; two of the three Tests were won. But a trail of damage was left behind.

Tours planned for 1930–31 and 1931–32 had been called off because of civil disorder across the land — generated by the Indian nationalist movement — and because of the threat of boycott or violence. This 1933–34 tour was therefore undertaken in circumstances even more sensitive than those prevailing during the recent campaign in Australia. For a variety of reasons, Wyatt, Hammond, Sutcliffe, Allen, Paynter and Ames declined to tour this time, and of course there were no Larwood and Voce. Instead, the pace bowling was in the hands of Nobby Clark of Northants and Stan Nichols of Essex. Hoping for a peaceful tour, MCC appointed as manager Major E.W.C. Ricketts, a solid-looking man with a moustache who probably knew all he needed to know about Jardine, and to whom Plum Warner must surely have sent his special blessings.

It is not necessary to recount the events of the tour in detail, other than to analyse the part played in it by the two fast bowlers. The captain, now engaged to Miss Irene Margaret Peat, was noticeably more "at home" in old-fashioned India, a fact registering in his more relaxed speeches. Jardine was as determined as ever to achieve victory, and the scorecards would suggest that his spin bowlers did most towards realising this. Countless Indians were spellbound by the guiles of slow left-armers Verity (23 wickets in the three Tests) and Langridge (10) and elsewhere of "Father" Marriott's legspin and Les Townsend's polished medium-pace offspin to a leg-side field, an intellectual study for the keen onlookers. The batting of the Englishmen, stylish or aggressive or studious, was admired too, and these first Test matches on Indian soil were later to be seen as the beginning of developments that would lift India (and Pakistan too — after its birth in 1947 — although along a separate path) to the game's heights. Fifty years hence, India, in spite of the ceaseless bitter tribal infighting which hampered its administration, would be one-day World Cup champions. Jack Hobbs's comment on their 1933–34 approach has long since been buried by time: "I am afraid that the Indians do not take Tests seriously, for there was a happy-go-lucky kind of picnic air about them."

Sometimes Jardine's fast bowlers wilted in the punishing heat, causing him on one occasion to say heartlessly, "Thank God we have one bowler in the side" — a reference to the cricketer he probably admired above all others, Hedley Verity. But when the fast pair Clark (left arm around the wicket) and Nichols were in action, with the Bodyline field in position, there were casualties ... considerably more, in fact, than were seen in the series in Australia.

At Calcutta, in the second Test, big, bald wicketkeeper Dilawar Hussain was hit on the back of the head by a ball from Nichols and had to be carried from the field. He came back, the wound bulging under the bandage, to score a fifty in each innings (with a further retirement when Clark cracked his thumb). Dilawar was not alone in experiencing pain as bowlers on both sides got the ball to kick. Mahomed Nissar, operating at times with a Bodyline field, was as big and aggressive as a right-armed Voce, and Arthur Mitchell, Jardine and Townsend all sustained bruising blows. In another match Nissar crushed the brim of Bakewell's solar topee with a bouncer.

TED "NOBBY" CLARK, THE NORTHANTS REDHEAD WHO RIPPED INTO INDIA —
AND, THOUGH WITH LITTLE SUCCESS, AUSTRALIA AS WELL IN 1934.

At Madras, in the third Test, opener Naoomal Jeoomal received a horrible crack above the left eye while attempting to hook Clark early in India's first innings. He was taken from the field by stretcher with blood oozing from the wound and was out of the match. Sections of the crowd became frenzied, and were screaming "Bahdee Line! Bahdee Line!" When Clark was fielding at square leg a large pebble was thrown at him. At the end of the over the red-headed bowler, renowned for his volatile temperament, walked slowly towards the onlookers behind their wire-netting enclosure. They fell into deathly silence. Watched by his anxious captain, Clark reached the boundary line, where he gently placed the stone onto the ground before returning to the middle. Peace had been restored.[12]

There were other worrying moments. Soon after Naoomal had been felled, the young giant, Yuvrajah of Patiala, came close to taking some rearing balls full on the turban. His proud admiring onlookers were incensed, and made so much noise that Jardine felt it prudent to take Clark off. And another revered young cricketer, Vijay Merchant, whose name was to rise very high in the annals of the game, had his chin cut, courtesy of Nichols. He went off for stitches and returned to bat determinedly, leaving Jardine with the impression that here was the soundest batsman in India. The England captain showed his respect for Merchant by bringing his fast bowlers back on as soon as he reappeared. Merchant believed in swaying from the path of bouncers and letting them sail by wherever possible.

The Dilawar incident at Calcutta had deep repercussions, for the umpire was Frank Tarrant, the highly gifted Victorian cricketer who played for Middlesex for many seasons before making a lucrative living in India dealing in racehorses, with Indian princes among his clientele. Tarrant warned Jardine that unless Clark calmed down he would stop him bowling. In return, Jardine, who might not have expected to have the riot act read to him by an Australian in India, curtly replied: "I will stop you from umpiring." And he did. (Jardine was already suspicious of the number of lbws granted against the Englishmen by Tarrant and had cabled Lord's for guidance and support. The Australian was in the employ of some of the princely rulers of India.)

Years later Tarrant wrote to Jack Fingleton with details of the goings-on (the letter fetched just on £600 at auction in 2002).[13] When the England captain threatened to have him removed from his umpiring role Tarrant replied that it was immaterial to him: "I wrote to MCC at Lord's and explained everything, how I had heard Clark say There will be some bobbing today, and he will take this one ... well at any rate, Jardine never played again ... Clark at Colombo dug the wicket up ... while he was batting, he deliberately walked down the wicket and rubbed his spikes where a good length ball pitches, it was so bad that the batsman [Bryan Valentine] at the other end apologised to the captain."

Tarrant genuinely feared that Clark might kill someone with his wild short-pitchers. He was quoted in a Melbourne paper, the *Star*, in early 1934. He believed that Clark was bowling to hit the batsmen, and named C.P. Johnstone as one of the targets. Annoyed when the batsman backed away, Clark nominated what would happen next: "He will take this one."

A bouncer followed, which the batsman managed to duck. Tarrant felt sure that the crowds had come close to rushing the field, especially when the young Yuvraj was under threat from the short balls. In Larwood's absence it seemed England had another *enfant terrible* on their hands.

The Quetta earthquake was felt by the cricketers, and there were tremors of a different kind when a match to raise funds for earthquake relief was threatened with a boycott by Hindus and Muslims because too many Europeans had been chosen in the local team. Being of common purpose for once, the Hindus and Muslims who had been invited to the banquet in Jardine's honour also stated that they would not attend. The Calcutta Test was spoilt by a partial boycott by the fans because no Bengali was included in the side.

Jardine unquestionably enjoyed the tour of his native land, not least when he scored a century in Bombay, city of his birth. And in the minds of many he left with, curiously enough, a reputation for sportsmanship, springing from the first Test, when Lala Amarnath reached an exquisite century and a sizeable proportion of the Bombay Gymkhana crowd ran onto the field to place garlands around the batsman's slender shoulders. This greatly annoyed Jardine, but when he spotted India's captain, C.K. Nayudu, striding down the pitch to congratulate young Amarnath, with the ball not yet dead and on its way to wicketkeeper Harry Elliott from the outfield, England's captain was seen to shake his head, forbidding the keeper from completing the run-out.[14]

Jardine's sterner side was nevertheless still unfurled whenever he felt it necessary. He invited the Maharajah of Patiala to play for MCC in one of their tour matches, only for the Viceroy to declare it ill-advised. Jardine ignored the protest. Then when the Viceroy's XI batted at New Delhi, after a pitch-rolling of illegally long duration, he unleashed Nichols at his fieriest, and the Viceroy's men were blasted out for 63.

There had also been disturbances during the Ceylon leg of the tour. In a situation reminiscent of Adelaide, Jardine objected strongly to the extreme noise emanating from students in their enclosure in the first Colombo match and some were ejected from the ground. Then mechanical problems with the antiquated taxis caused late arrival by the Englishmen at the Galle ground, and further criticism — both ways.

The English players — most of them — reached home on March 28, 1934. But D.R. Jardine, having scored 65 and 35 not out in his final Test, stayed on for a holiday in Mysore, Torai and Nepal, where he would add yet further to his tally with the gun.

On March 31 he shifted his aim from Indian wildlife and fired a bolt from the blue at English cricket. His article in the *Evening Standard* revealed that he had "neither the intention nor the desire to play cricket against Australia this summer". The deep sighs of relief must have stirred the trees in St John's Wood and in Adelaide, Melbourne and Sydney.

Not only did Jardine have a wedding to look forward to; he also had a living to earn. So much of his time had been devoted to cricket in the past few years that the personal exchequer was in need of replenishment. Beyond that, his soul must have suffered such erosion from the constant cascade of criticism that even his outstandingly obstinate sense of purpose must have worn thin by now. That comment to Ian McLachlan during the Adelaide Test — "But don't worry. It'll be stopped." — probably foreshadowed this moment. The heavy jaws of inevitability were closing.

D.R. Jardine had captained England in 15 Test matches, winning nine and losing only when Bradman made his Melbourne century. In all, he had played in 22 Tests and been on the winning side 15 times, the losing side only twice. Small wonder that Englishmen — and a few others — believed that Bodyline, with its consequent deletions of Jardine and Larwood from England team-sheets, cost England the 1934 and 1936–37 Ashes series.

Nor would he ever play for Surrey again, though the club had to wait for him to make this clear. Several cables from the secretary remained unanswered before the matter was clarified: he certainly would not be playing regularly, if at all. Errol Holmes was appointed captain as his successor.

Lord Hawke had recently shown rare sensibility in a letter to the brother of E.R. Wilson (ERW had forecast that his former Winchester pupil Jardine might win the Ashes and lose a dominion). Hawke told the Reverend Clem Wilson that the problem was to stop Bodyline "without letting down Douglas Jardine too badly".[15] But others wanted to be rid of Jardine unconditionally. On January 2, 1934, continuing to pursue his scout/commando role on behalf of Australian cricket, Robbie Macdonald wrote to the Board saying he had told MCC that if Jardine continued as England captain the 1934 Tests would be played as "a veiled vendetta". He described Bodyline methods as "wholly Teutonic" and linked Jardine's victory-at-any-cost outlook to that of Attila: "If I do Attila an injustice by this simile I tender an apology to his belated memory."[16] As descriptions of Test cricketers go, Dr Macdonald's was an unparalleled piece of hyperbole.

Hore-Ruthven's prolific two-way correspondence with P.F. Warner reveals the strength of feeling that still prevailed at high level. In a typewritten letter dated February 5, possibly in direct reply to Warner's previously quoted letter of January 3, Governor Hore-Ruthven pleaded:

> The Jardine question is very important and from what I can see of the signs out here, the only thing that could disturb the harmony which players and public are all anxious to maintain, would be to put Jardine in charge again. The whole atmosphere will be altered at once if he is made captain. The players will go on the field with the feeling of irritation and suspicion, and it will play into the hands of the extreme element here who wanted to demand guarantees that Jardine would not be captain and that body-line bowling would not be allowed, and they will at once say that "Gentlemen's Agreements" are no good to them, and in future we must have the written guarantees. And, moreover, the sensational section of the Australian Press will make the most of it and start the controversy all over again.
>
> So if you want the game to be played in the proper spirit and the whole controversy buried once and for all, keep Jardine out of the picture on any plea you can find. Surely he has earned a rest after three strenuous seasons in succession?
>
> I know the difficulties of not appearing to let him down, but the question is so vital, not only from the point of view of cricket, but of the friendly feeling between the two countries, that some excuse must be found for leaving him out. As, once a sore is opened again it is going to be very difficult to heal, and all the soothing syrup we have administered of late will be wasted.
>
> We can't get away from the fact that the root of the trouble was the selection of a man of Jardine's temperament as captain, so why go on pouring sand into the machine until in the end you smash it up?
>
> You may think that I am exaggerating the facts that Jardine's captaincy would give rise to, but it has been my business to make a careful study of Australian mentality for the last six years and I have no doubt as to the repercussions this would cause on men's minds out here.

Warner had continued to stir the pot. A letter to MCC secretary Findlay, written on February 22, referred to their recent conversation, during which the secretary had indicated that MCC would want certain guarantees from Jardine before reappointing him as captain for the Tests against Australia.

"I believe you realise that I was his best friend and supporter," wrote Warner (what might another "best friend", Gubby Allen, have made of that?). "I have no axe to grind and my objections to his methods and manners was [*sic*] because I considered them contrary to the ideals and interests and the prestige of MCC."[17]

After Jardine's resignation — which was swiftly followed by the announcement that he would be writing on the forthcoming Tests for the *Evening Standard* — Warner seized on the chance to give the knife a twist by suggesting to Findlay that the words in Jardine's Press statement were "most discourteous and deliberately flout MCC's expressed wishes and desires". He sought the committee's agreement to look at the matter and consider whether any steps should be taken, given that Jardine was still on the cricket and selection committees. This letter plopped onto Findlay's desk on the day that Don Bradman was launching his second tour of England with a menacing message, an innings of 206 at Worcester.

CHAPTER FIFTEEN

THE CORPSE TWITCHES

W.A. Brown, the last surviving member of the 1934 Australian team in England, recalled (in his 90th year): "No, I didn't have any particular apprehension as we set off for that tour." So the word was that the assurances given by England to the Australian Board that there would be no Bodyline were thoroughly reliable? "That sounds about right." How about the Notts match and Bill Voce? "Well, Voce was absolutely ropable about not being picked in England's Test side. 'All over this bloody leg theory,' he said."

Bill Brown scored 27 in a first-wicket stand of 70 with Woodfull in that game. What was it like? "I spent all my time face down on the wicket! Next day we saw Voce hobbling but we were all doubtful about that."[1]

With Jardine gone and Larwood known to be hesitant about playing for England (Sir Stanley Jackson had summoned him for a heart-to-heart chat in April), Voce was the most dangerous survivor from the Bodyline series still in operation — though Bowes also bounced merrily on. But England declined to select Voce even though he was picking up bundles of wickets for Notts. Clark's season was interrupted by injury and inconsistent form, though he was chosen for two of the Ashes Tests, while Nichols's performances were not such as to appeal to the selectors for the moment. Instead, England capped Farnes and turned again to Bowes in their efforts to tame Bradman, Woodfull, Ponsford, McCabe and the rest — who had been welcomed at Waterloo Station by the top-hatted outgoing MCC president, Lord Hailsham.

During the winter Harold Larwood had undergone surgery at the London Clinic on his damaged foot. (From the clinic he had written to A.W. Shelton, who was a major benefactor of Trent Bridge, expressing his thanks for Shelton's help and complaining that "the Press have worried the life out of me".) Larwood returned to play for Notts early in May of 1934, when there was immense Press and public hope and expectation that he would return to the Test side to continue his high-profile duel with Bradman. He was, after all, still not yet 30, and had won the past few rounds. But something now occurred which filled him with disgust and dampened his desire to represent his country.

While playing in a warm-up match at Sir Julien Cahn's private ground at Stanford Hall he was approached by the wealthy Notts patron: "He talked for a few minutes and I knew he was buttering me up for something," Larwood was to write.[2] "Finally he said: 'Harold, I'm afraid you'll have to apologise to the MCC.' *Harold!* Usually I got called plain Larwood."

A statement had been prepared. If Larwood was willing to sign it the way would be clear for his return to the England XI. It was a letter of apology for his bowling during the 1932–33 tour of Australia. Dominions Secretary Jimmy Thomas was behind it, according to Arthur Carr. It seems certain that Thomas and Cahn discussed more than the Canadian weather at that farewell function at Claridge's in August 1933. And to think that not so long ago Cahn had said, "I am not going to have anything said against Larwood, because he is a member of my club."

"Apologise, sir? What for?" the incredulous Larwood now blurted.

"For your bowling, Harold."

"I have nothing to apologise for, sir."

"Oh, but you must, Harold. You must apologise to the MCC for your bowling and you must agree to bowl legitimately in future. If you do you will be picked in the Tests against Australia. But unless I have your word, I'm afraid you will not be considered at all."

All kinds of visions flashed through Larwood's mind: the extreme physical effort he had put in, exhorted by his captain, day after steaming day during the Australian tour; the pain from body, legs and feet which he had consistently forced himself to ignore; and not least, the cables of congratulation after the first, fourth and fifth Tests from ... MCC.

Although his mind seemed already made up, Harold, as a good son should, asked his mother for her opinion. Should he sign the apology?

Looking at him over her spectacles, she said, "If you do, you won't ever see me alive again."[3] His father was just as dismissive.

This was all to remain unrevealed for years. Larwood's absence from the first Test was explained away by reference to his bruised foot. Yet he was fit enough to take 5 for 66 against Sussex at Horsham, where the *Daily Express* reporter found him "too scared to comment after Australia had won the first Test". Public frustration mounted at the continuing absence of England's greatest fast bowler.

But just before the second Test, at Lord's, where Bill Brown made a century but which Verity won for England with 15 wickets, a bombshell dropped, and this time it had Larwood's name chalked on it. He would probably have been selected for the Lord's Test, though he would have been told he could not place his own field. That would be Wyatt's exclusive responsibility: he would be following the peace accord to the letter. Selector Peter Perrin had asked Larwood outright if he would play for England, while Lord Hawke, MCC treasurer and major influence, approached A.W. Shelton several times that summer. An earlier letter from Hawke expressed hope that Larwood would play, and one dated July 10 stated that it was Board policy that no cricketer can write for the Press as well as play for England. After registering regret at Arthur Carr's recent heart attack, Hawke clarified the selection situation, stating the obvious to Shelton: "until your committee see their way to lead Larwood to play the game for his country I am afraid no-one else can do so".[4]

Then the bombshell: in the *Sunday Dispatch* of June 17, Larwood told the world: "It is time the public knew the truth … I have definitely made up my mind not to play against the Australians in this or any of the Tests. I doubt if I shall play against them again … I am unrepentant about leg theory. There is a big hush-hush campaign to bury leg theory and brand me as a dangerous and unfair bowler." He asserted that if his methods had been right in Australia then they must be right now. Bill Voce also let fly in the *Sunday Express*.

J.H. Thomas vigorously denied having put pressure on MCC to squeeze Larwood out, and outgoing MCC president Hailsham protested that the suggestion was "the most extraordinary moonshine" he had ever heard. "Whose is this political influence and what is it supposed to do?"

Larwood's county captain, Carr, waded in, uncaring of his own position: "I believe Larwood is right in not playing for England when the rulers of the game have so completely deserted him ... I am not going to dictate to my bowlers." Cahn and others now began to dwell on the Notts skipper's own position.

Carr warned his bowlers just before Larwood's explosive article appeared that their approaching match against Lancashire (eventual champions in 1934) would lead to a protest. He had inside information, he said. Larwood at first refused to play, then said he would bowl at half-pace.

"Bill Voce and I played and it was an easy wicket. Several players ducked and drew away on purpose ... I bowled nowhere near my customary speed. I don't think I hit anybody but Bill bowled some leg theory and hit one or two batsmen a few times." Larwood took six wickets for one run in a spell of 29 balls. How empty the England XI seemed without him.

The newspapers immediately ran stories that Lancashire would not play against Notts unless leg theory was stopped. Published pictures of George Duckworth's bruises prompted Larwood to seek him out and ask, "What the hell have you been up to?"

"Nothing," said the little wicketkeeper, "I just protested about your bowling."

Later he told Larwood that Lancashire chairman Tom Higson wished to see him.

"Look, George," Larwood said, "if he wants to see me let him come and ask me and not send a little **** like you to tell me."[5] Higson, of course, was a Test selector and had helped pick Larwood for the Australian tour. He was also a bumptious little man who seemed to think the world revolved around himself.

Plum Warner told of arriving at Old Trafford for the third Test and being confronted by the sight of Duckworth with an arm in a sling, bandaged elsewhere and limping. Duckworth told his former tour manager that Bodyline had been bowled at him at Trent Bridge.

"What, your old friends, Larwood and Voce?" Warner asked.

"Aye, they nearly knocked out Mr Lister and our skipper [P.T. Eckersley], and I got a few. The worst was here ..." And he pointed to his neck.

Warner then reminded Duckworth that he (Duckworth) used to lecture after his return from Australia, defending Bodyline. "Maybe," said Duckworth, "but it's tough — too tough — and makes trouble. I am not for it now." Nor were Lancashire. They refused to play against Notts in 1935.[6]

"Tiger" Smith umpired in that match, and had this to say many years later: "There was a lot of hysteria at the time about bodyline. I remember Lancashire sending a photo to Lord's of George Duckworth's left thigh looking like a piece of liver after facing Larwood and Voce. I had to point out that they'd been bowling at the stumps, not at George, who was a small man and whose stance was a bent-kneed, low one … If I'd thought the batsman was being intimidated I'd have had a word with the skipper."[7]

Knowing that all over England leg theory was being bowled (legally and without protest) by medium-pacers — and by Bowes, Farnes and Clark — "Lol" Larwood, the great but excommunicated fast bowler, was now completely exasperated.

And so was his equally stigmatised mate Voce.

Nottinghamshire's match against the touring Australians was set down for August 11, 13 and 14, with the Test series standing at one apiece and the deciding fifth Test due to start at The Oval four days later. Bradman had broken out of an untypically moderate run in the first three Tests (highest score 36) with his second Test triple-century in the fourth Test at Headingley. What a showdown it would have been if Larwood had suddenly appeared in England's ranks for the Oval Test. But he was not even interested in playing for his *county* against the tourists. The committee accepted his decision, probably with some relief.

Voce, however, had other ideas.

Bill O'Reilly remembered the county match: "No bowler had bowled sconners at us on the tour so far, but we all viewed our Trent Bridge engagement with a certain amount of suspicion. We arrived at Victoria Station in Nottingham City about 9 pm to be greeted by a large, hostile crowd who hooted loudly and offered insults which, expressed in a broad vernacular, were difficult for us to translate. But they left us in no doubt whatever that they didn't like us … and that they thought we were all chicken-hearted no-hopers. To make sure that we got the message fully they lined the streets all the way down to the Black Boy Hotel where we were to be housed during the match. It turned out to be a shocker."[8]

O'Reilly seemed to have forgotten that Bowes was bowling short enough to threaten heads in the Lord's and Headingley Tests and to draw a hushed complaint from the Australian tour manager Harold Bushby, who spoke to the three England selectors about it at Lord's. Yet another of the lawyers who trod the Bodyline boards, Tasmanian Bushby pointed out that there was a risk that England were "departing from the agreement". He asked

Jackson, Higson and Perrin "to deal with the matter as if I had not taken it up with them". (Bushby was later to be seriously concerned at the methods employed by Nobby Clark.[9])

This was probably what caused England captain Bob Wyatt to go across to Bowes during the Lord's Test and tell him he had just been handed a message from the pavilion which read: "Ask Bowes not to bowl short."

"And what do you say as captain?" Bowes asked.

"Well," said Wyatt, "if they want it friendly, perhaps they'd better have it that way."[10]

During the Headingley Test, Bradman, as he cruised to 304, made only 10 false shots in seven hours at the crease, nine of them against Bowes, by Ray Robinson's calculations. After a series of short balls, Bradman walked slowly well beyond the halfway mark and patted down marks in the turf, while the Yorkshire crowd yelled their disapproval.[11]

Back at Trent Bridge for the Notts encounter, with the Bodyline field in position, Voce let the Australians have it. Bradman was being rested — probably a doubly wise precaution — but McCabe, according to A.W. Carr, was heard to say, "I don't care if Voce does play tomorrow or how he bowls. I'm going to have my innings."

Brown, McCabe, Kippax, Darling, Woodfull, Chipperfield, Barnett, Wall — they were all caught off the heavyweight left-armer, five of them in the leg trap as flesh was occasionally battered, runs were somehow garnered, and wickets toppled until the tourists' innings was over for 237, Voce finishing with 8 for 66. Although it was subsequently concluded that Voce's bowling on this first day did not quite infringe the new guidelines, it was clear that Bill Woodfull and others were far from happy, believing that the new guidelines had been ignored.

When the Australians went in for their second innings, late on the second day, Voce bowled two overs — in poor light — of which 11 balls flew through head-high or higher, the Trent Bridge crowd howling with joy. Manager Bushby and tour treasurer W.C. Bull now went to see the Notts honorary secretary, Dr G.O. Gauld. He had already had a visit from the two umpires, who informed him that they thought Voce had been guilty of direct attack.

"I told him," wrote Bushby, "that if Voce continued to bowl on the following day in the same way Woodfull would be advised to close the innings and we would recommend to the Board that the match against Notts should be eliminated from the fixture list next tour. Dr Gauld expressed regret at what Voce had done and agreed to see that it did not occur again the next day. Voce had complained on the first day of the match to Lilley (acting captain) about his leg, which had previously troubled him, and on arrival at Trent Bridge ground on the third and last day of the match, Dr Gauld called him into the office and enquired how his leg was. Voce still complained and Dr Gauld after examining him stated he was not fit to play. Voce took no further part in the game. Voce left the same day for Southampton with the Notts team but was not included in the side owing to the condition of his leg."

BILL VOCE BECOMES THE NEW PRINCIPAL NAUGHTY BOY AS HE BOUNCES THE 1934 AUSTRALIANS IN THE NOTTS MATCH WITH A BODYLINE FIELD IN POSITION (THOUGH NOT APPARENTLY EXPECTING MUCH TO COME THEIR WAY). WOODFULL (FACING) SCORED 81 OF THE TOURISTS' FIRST-INNINGS TOTAL OF 237.

Bushby reported the matter to MCC as a breach of "the agreement". They in turn invited the Australians to send a delegation to Lord's. Bushby, Bull and Robbie Macdonald duly went to a meeting with Lord Cromer (the new MCC president), Sir Stanley Jackson and Bob Wyatt on September 20, 1934. Lord Cromer said he regretted that no players had come along. Bushby soon put it to him that he thought MCC might by now have a proposal to put in lieu of the new law concerning intimidation which Australia had proposed — without success — at the ICC meeting on July 25. The president explained that MCC would make a pronouncement when they were in a position to do so.

Bull referred to bowling which the Australians had encountered during the tour and which he did not consider in the best interests of the game. The MCC group reacted by putting four questions to their visitors in an effort to establish what they might consider as constituting "direct attack". The Australians pondered the options before nominating fast bowling on or outside leg stump and short of a length, *with or without* a concentrated leg field.

Jackson, England's victorious captain in the 1905 series, asked if any untoward bowling had been witnessed in Tests or other matches this summer, to which Bull said the final Test at The Oval had seen some. Jackson rejected such a notion.

The Australian delegation confirmed that they had no authority to bind their Board to any arrangement but would report the proceedings to them.[12] Then they left Lord's and probably found somewhere quiet to order some stiff drinks.

Bodyline simply would not expire.

The Voce affair raised a rare furore at Trent Bridge. The belief persisted that "Tangy" had been forced to fake injury and make a diplomatic withdrawal from the match. His absence from the following game, against Hampshire at Southampton, lent a touch of authenticity to the injury claim, but he was back three days after that, taking nine wickets against Derbyshire at Ilkeston, and nearly 70 years later his close friend Eric Marsh confirmed to the author that Voce had often told him that he had indeed been forced to stand down midway through that match against the 1934 Australians.

Arthur Carr, who suffered a heart attack on July 7, was to be sacked by Notts just before Christmas. It was another messy process, for the Press informed the nation before Carr had received the committee's letter. His continued support for Larwood and Voce and their hostile methods had simply become too much of an embarrassment. All the rows and troubles which began in Australia when D.R. Jardine's team were there (Carr was to write) bit by bit narrowed down to Nottingham.

Lancashire had no intention of playing against Notts in 1935, and Middlesex took similar measures when Voce knocked out Len Muncer and hurt tailender Bob Beveridge at Lord's soon after the county's controversial

Australian match. Jardine was one of many advocating Voce's inclusion in the England side. That so much powerful English fast bowling continued to be sidelined for political reasons was proving extremely exasperating for English fans. Even Pud Thurlow, the Queenland fast bowler, was sympathetic. In the Australian paper *Truth* he denounced his country's batsmen for "refusing to face the music", and pointed to their inability to handle real fast bowling. Some had been bowled while ducking, he scoffed. They should "grin and bear it". The batsmen should cease wailing and screaming: "Their attitude is branding us as a nation of bad sportsmen ... We don't want to be called dingoes." Bill Voce would have enjoyed this particular outburst, having claimed in the *Sunday Express* that Australia now seemed to have the power of veto over English cricket.

The contrast in views continued to surprise. Thurlow was an Australian supporting Larwood and Voce. But another eminent Englishman, Lord Hankey, secretary to the British Cabinet, reported to the Dominions Office during his trip to Australia late in 1934 that deep down Australians admired the British, but because of that very admiration the "ridiculous" Bodyline controversy had caused bitterness. In simple terms, "They hated to feel that we had lowered our standard of sportsmanship."[13]

The repercussions of Voce's withdrawal with "sore shins" at Trent Bridge were near-riotous. When the Australians took the field they were booed loudly, only a diminutive parson sympathising with their situation. He demonstrated his support for the visitors by walking, hat under arm, alongside Woodfull's players almost to the wicket, clapping ostentatiously.[14] When Voce's wife Elsie arrived at the ground, keen to know if Bill was among the wickets again, she was amazed to be told that he was nursing sore shins and unable to bowl. "Where's Voce?" screamed the frustrated onlookers.

In the following winter, at a meeting of Notts CCC, solicitor Douglas McCraith read a detailed report of the goings-on to a large gathering of fellow committeemen and members. McCraith had said publicly in June that Larwood had been "sacrificed on the altar of imperialism". Now, however, he claimed that Voce had indeed been genuinely injured. In this he was supported by Dr Gauld, who, in his broad Scots accent, told of his intention on that final morning of the match against the Australians to advise the Notts players that the cricket must be friendly and free of unpleasant incident. But before he could do this he had been called to examine Voce's painful shins. The bowler had allegedly told him he was in pain even on the first day, when he took his eight wickets. On that last morning, Dr Gauld ordered Voce to rest for a few days, though he admitted that he would have liked a second opinion from the club's surgeon, who was not available.

Nottinghamshire sent an apology to Middlesex and to the Australian Board for the incidents that had so upset them in 1934. But thousands of the club's members were up in arms about Carr's sacking and about the unhappy circumstances surrounding their heroes, Larwood and Voce. So a special meeting was called. The Albert Hall in Nottingham was packed to the rafters and the deposed Carr was seated in the front row. There was excitement at a prepared statement from Voce that was read out at the start, claiming that he had been "fit and willing to play" that morning, and the animation mushroomed by the minute: cries of "Shame!" when Carr's blunt dismissal was referred to, "Hear, hear!" when Carr himself spoke in support of Voce: if he had still been captain, Voce would have carried on bowling, even if the Australians had walked off the field.

George Gauld, who had captained Notts in a few matches before the Great War, was grilled mercilessly by the leader of the protest group, a former Nottingham Lord Mayor named H. Seely Whitby, who described Bill Woodfull as "a duck in a thunderstorm" and referred to hundreds of letters of support for Voce. He moved that the apology sent to the Australians should be expunged from the records. Then came the biggest bouncer: a vote of no confidence in the Notts committee was tabled — and carried. The committee resigned *en bloc*.

And yet two months later, at the club's annual general meeting, the no-confidence result was rescinded. The former committee was reinstated, and five members, including Arthur Carr, were added. In a persuasive speech McCraith explained how Notts' very existence depended upon getting its house in order. The damage from the storm had been costly. Even the president, the Duke of Portland, wanted nothing more to do with the club. Apologies were tendered for any apparent reflection on Dr Gauld's honour and he was asked to resume his position with the club, and R.G. Hogarth, the surgeon, now appeared, saying that he had considered Voce unfit before, during and after the Australian match. And that he had also declared Larwood unfit to play beforehand. The rebels broke in with loud interjections, but the repair work was somehow carried out. A.C. Adams seconded the resolution, remarking: "Whoever invented the odious phrase 'body-line bowling' should be hung, drawn, and quartered." He may not have realised how very far-reaching was his other observation: that with the new intent-to-intimidate rule coming in he pitied the poor umpires.

Australia regained the Ashes in the final Test at The Oval, the match finishing on August 22, Woodfull's 37th birthday. He had had a similar anniversary reward four years earlier. This time the victory was set up on the first day, when Ponsford (266) and Bradman (244) put on 451 for the second wicket in 5¼ hours, and although Bowes (9 for 219 in the match) and Clark (7 for 208) banged down occasional bouncers and Clark often bowled to a leg field, Wyatt knew full well that he would have been hauled before a black-capped Lord Hawke had he arranged for a full-blown display of Bodyline. Anyway, the scoreboard made a mockery of whatever England tried: 472 before the second wicket fell, 626 before the fifth, an all-out total of 701, the second-highest to date in Ashes history. Bradman lost his wicket in both innings when hooking short balls from Bowes, but since he scored 321 runs in the match nobody was too bothered.

The England side which slid to defeat by the massive margin of 562 runs contained eight cricketers who had been part of the Bodyline tour. Matchwinners Larwood and Voce were not, of course, among them, and neither was Jardine, who sat in the Press box instead.

It would be 19 years before England next took possession of the little urn.

In place for the 1935 English cricket season were two momentous revisions: (i) an experimental note to the lbw law (fully adopted in 1937 after two seasons of trial, though Australia was not instantly receptive to it) whereby a batsman could now be given out to a ball which pitched outside off stump; and (ii) the captains' agreement having failed, new measures for curbing intimidatory bowling. On November 21, 1934, two years almost to the hour since Larwood had unleashed his "leg-theory" tornado against the Australian XI at Melbourne, the Advisory County Cricket Committee endorsed MCC's new ruling: "direct attack" was now a matter for umpires' consideration. Direct attack was now officially branded as unfair, and since Law 43 clearly stated that "the umpires are the sole judges of fair or unfair play ...", the men in white coats were told that the matter was henceforth in their hands.

Umpires, therefore, being universally fearless, infallible people, and skilled mindreaders as well, were going to save the game.

Posterity knows otherwise. The three lines of print which constituted Law 43 in the 1930s have swollen to *six pages* of fine print today (now Law 42 Fair and Unfair Play). Law 42 chronicles the procedure to be adopted by umpires against all manner of unfair play: ball-tampering, distracting or obstructing the batsman, time-wasting, damaging the pitch, stealing runs unfairly, and, with its antique aroma, intimidatory bowling. Captains are now also nominated as being responsible for the maintenance of "the spirit and traditions of the game", alongside the umpires' continuing sole responsibilities as judges of unfair play. We also, of course, have match referees to police international matches. What a commentary on the morality of the modern cricketer. And how broadly the ghost of Jardine must be smiling at the mounds of paperwork forced upon the game just because so many reprobate cricketers from so many nations since the Second World War have failed to behave like decent sportsmen.

THE OVAL TEST, 1934: PONSFORD IS CAUGHT IN THE LEG TRAP BY HAMMOND OFF CLARK FOR 22. DESPITE PALE SHADOWS OF BODYLINE, THERE WAS NO FAST BOWLER ON SHOW TO MATCH THE ABSENT LARWOOD. NOR HAD AUSTRALIA EVER GOT ANYWHERE NEAR 700 IN THE SERIES OF '32–33.

For the record, the members of the MCC subcommittee which recommended the 1935 amendment were the Earl of Cromer (MCC president), Lord Hawke, Viscount Lewisham (president when the Bodyline rumpus first erupted), Sir Stanley Jackson (now chairman of selectors), Sir Kynaston Studd, Lord Hampden, P.F. Warner, Michael Falcon, G.R. Jackson

(Derbyshire), R.H. Twining (Middlesex) and R.H. Mallett. The recommendation they handed to English cricket was wrapped in the hopes that no further action would be necessary and that the world would accept it.

Sydney Southerton, the idealistic editor of *Wisden* born in the Victorian era, was disappointed that such an amendment concerning direct-attack bowling had been found to be necessary. He wished, idealistically, that the game and its players had been capable of sweeping away the mess without recourse to legislation. He looked back upon the 1934 season as "unpleasant", coming as it did after "we" had won the Ashes series in 1932–33. But it was not the fact that England had now lost that upset him so much as the "insane desire constantly to stir up strife" displayed by certain sections of the Press. He deplored the "tittle-tattle of a mischievous character" and questioned whether Test matches were any longer worth staging. It was a view expressed elsewhere by D.R. Jardine.

After the lengths to which Southerton imagined that MCC had gone to accommodate the Australians, he found it "an ungenerous and misleading gesture when some of the visiting batsmen, as we all saw in several matches, ducked or turned their backs to balls which got up, not head high, but about a foot above the stumps. If that was meant as a sign of silent resentment, it carried no conviction whatever, even to those who abhor short bowling that bumps."

He deemed Wyatt's captaincy to be lacking in inspiration. The editor had no real need to mention Wyatt's predecessor's name by way of reminder of what England had lost in terms of strong, even ruthless, leadership. And Larwood was condemned for dashing into print and putting himself beyond the pale. The writer seemed unaware of the underhand and scandalous attempt to save everybody else's face by having the pilloried fast bowler sign a humiliating public apology.

Nor did Southerton live to see the new interpretation of the laws on the field, for he died in March of 1935, having just proposed a toast to Cricket at a club dinner at The Oval.

Bodyline, as Jack Fingleton wrote, was followed by an era of extreme righteousness in Test cricket.[15] "Everybody was so very, very careful to do the right thing that the red-blooded fast bowler who so far showed his distaste of modern marl wickets and modern batting methods as to bowl

an old-fashioned 'bumper' found, while hysterical onlookers were feverishly shouting 'Bodyline', that he was regarded in the best quarters as a
bit of a bounder — if not, perhaps, an utter cad."

Gilbert Mant, attached to the next (1936–37) MCC Test side to tour
Australia, went as far as to say: "There was a large contingent of Press representatives this time, hoping for more sensation and violence. Alas, all was
sweetness and light. The desire for reconciliation became so cloying that
sometimes I yearned for the bad old days of bodyline."[16]

Bouncers had flown during the 1934–35 West Indies v England series,
the tourists being outgunned for pace by Martindale, Constantine and
Hylton, and skipper Bob Wyatt finishing the last Test on a stretcher, carried
to hospital with a broken jaw, courtesy of Martindale. Unable to speak,
Wyatt grabbed a pencil just before he was driven away and wrote down a
revised batting order. Later he exonerated the bowler from blame, saying the
ball had leapt from a length.

Former Australian player Arthur Richardson, during a coaching stint
in the Caribbean, stood as umpire in the Trinidad and British Guiana (now
Guyana) Tests and did find it necessary to caution West Indies captain G.C.
Grant when his fast bowlers began to overdo the leg theory. "Fortunately
no trouble followed and the series of Tests were played in a good spirit."[17]

A non-Test-playing tour of Australasia by MCC in 1935–36 went some
way further in smoothing relations between Australia and England. Wyatt
having declined to captain the side, it went instead under E.R.T. Holmes,
the Surrey amateur. Not one of its members had toured in 1932–33. Eight
well-bred, fun-loving amateurs travelled alongside six carefully chosen
professionals, and the six matches played in Australia — before the major
segment, in New Zealand — went off without a hitch: a perfect public
relations exercise. Bradman had the decency to score no more than 50
against them for his new State, South Australia, and the Essex amateur
fast bowler "Hopper" Read kept his ferocity within bounds.

The Australia Test team, without Bradman, was touring South Africa at
the time under Vic Richardson's captaincy, taking the series 4–0. Fingleton
was rehabilitated, with a century in each of the last three Tests, and forged
a successful opening partnership with Bill Brown, and O'Reilly and
Grimmett restored spin bowling's good name with bucketfuls of wickets,
the 44-year-old Grimmett finishing with 44 in the five Tests at 14.59 in
what mysteriously proved to be his final series. And McCabe, at the Old

Wanderers ground in Johannesburg, played an innings of 189 not out that compared with his Sydney 187 against Bodyline. So lethal was his strokeplay in poor light that the South Africa captain, fearing his fieldsmen would be injured, successfully appealed to the umpires.

Global sensitivity was such that Ernie McCormick, Australia's extremely nippy and strongly built fast bowler, caused mild hysteria in one of the Johannesburg Tests when he came in off his extremely long run-up and dropped a few short. There were cries of "Bodyline!", just as there were to be in 1938 when he bowled for the Australians at Leicester. But those who protested had obviously never seen the real (and now outlawed) thing in action.

All eyes, of course, were on the 1936–37 Ashes series. Eight members of Jardine's team returned to Australia, including Bill Voce, who had given MCC the assurance they sought that he would never again bang the ball at the batsman's skull. Almost as if by way of God-given reward, England were granted a beast of a Brisbane pitch to bowl on after rain, and Australia, bowled out for 58 in their second innings, lost heavily. Fingleton had the personal compensation of a century in the first innings, but the reformed villain Voce took 10 for 57 in the match — by conventional means.

At Sydney, Australia went two down after another Hammond double-century and more rain to dog the home side's prospects. Voce, whom Fingleton rated a much better bowler on his second visit to Australia, took 7 for 76 in this match, and Bradman went for another duck. Already Bradman's captaincy was being called into question — as if he controlled the spin of the coin and the weather too. By contrast, his counterpart, the popular Gubby Allen, could do no wrong.

Then it all changed. Rain at Melbourne caught England out, and with Bradman (270) and Fingleton (136) going in late in the order and putting on 346 for the sixth wicket, a huge victory was engineered. Fleetwood-Smith, four years after Hammond had knocked him out of the reckoning, cleaned up the tail with 5 for 124 on his long-awaited Ashes debut. Then Australia levelled at 2–2 at Adelaide, after another double-century by skipper Bradman. Here Fleetwood-Smith realised all that potential spotted years earlier, taking 10 wickets in the match and swinging the game by bowling Hammond on the last day.

The decider, at Melbourne, was Australia's from lunchtime on the first day. Ken Farnes bowled fast, heroically and with no suggestion of the sort of direct attack he employed in the 1933 Varsity match. Bradman, McCabe and Badcock made centuries, the ill-fated Ross Gregory — he was killed in 1942, serving in the RAAF — celebrated his 21st birthday with 80 in his second and final Test, and Australia ran up a gargantuan 604; Farnes, scarcely daring to drop short, earned the fine figures of 6 for 96. Laurie Nash, McCormick, O'Reilly and Fleetwood-Smith kept on taking wickets as England folded up, not only losing by an innings but also creating history by losing a series they had just about won after 2½ Tests.

Not that the series was free of behind-the-scenes anxiety over fast bowlers' good conduct. The Australian selectors, Dwyer, Johnson and Bradman, had to fight the Board to secure acceptance of the selection of Laurie Nash for this final Test. Nash was a no-holds-barred, very physical and famous footballer, and a fast bowler who had taken five wickets for next to nothing against South Africa on a terrible Melbourne pitch five years earlier in his only previous Test. Australia now needed the most penetrative attack available for this deciding Test, and the selection panel had to threaten resignation to get it. A compromise attitude, which may well have been argued by the selectors, was that Nash was no more than what we today might refer to as a nuclear deterrent *vis-à-vis* Voce, should the Englishman be tempted to shift his line towards leg.

Nash, who came from an "industrial" background, always claimed that he could have ended Bodyline in '32–33 in two overs, and without the leg field. The England batsmen, he contended, couldn't hook. In his ignorance, he thought he might impress Woodfull in a South Melbourne v Carlton district match and thereby win himself a place on the 1934 tour of England. Still high from his performance in the VFL grand final before a massive MCG crowd the previous Saturday, when he was carried shoulder-high from the field, Nash now gave Woodfull a real going-over, one ball replicating the blow over the heart twice inflicted by Larwood during the torrid summer of 1932–33. He then caught-and-bowled Australia's captain, still perhaps not realising that there was no way in the world Woodfull would take this wild and slightly uncouth cricketer with him to England in the current political climate (or, perhaps, any other).[18]

Now, in 1937, Woodfull was in retirement and an Ashes series hung on a thread. Nash was in, and he played his part, taking five more Test wickets without decimating the Empire. But there had been some strained scenes before he stepped onto the field. In Victoria's match against the Englishmen

Nash had been selected out of the blue, after a three-year absence from first-class cricket. He dropped a few short and drew some old-fashioned looks from Charlie Barnett and Wally Hammond, although Hans Ebeling, his captain, was far too sensible to set a Bodyline field. Nash snatched four wickets at little cost in this low-scoring draw and won selection in the fifth Test ahead of Ginty Lush, who had just taken 13 wickets for New South Wales against the touring team.

Gubby Allen was rigid with anxiety when he saw Nash's name on Bradman's team sheet. "What!" he snorted. "Are you going to have a go at us?" Australia's captain, his old friend Don, is said to have replied that an opposing captain could not dictate who should or should not play for Australia. So Allen went to the umpires: George Borwick, who was a happier man now that Bodyline was apparently a thing of the past, and Jack Scott, who had once loved bowling it. In a paraphrase of Woodfull's sentiment at Trent Bridge in 1934, England's captain spelt out his feelings: "If there is one ball bowled straight at my men in the game, I'll bring them off the field. Nash deliberately bowled Bodyline in our game against Victoria."[19]

Scott was displeased, and asked Allen if he had any reservations about his ability as an umpire. There the matter settled. Dr Allen Robertson, in the second of his three terms as chairman of the Australian Board, had also made cautionary noises. But Bradman's position was about to be greatly strengthened — by this stand against the Board, by his insistence on including Nash (who, of course, was permitted to bowl fast but straight, and not too often short of a length), and, not least, by winning the match and the series. Cardus wrote of Nash and McCormick that "this was good-mannered fast bowling which observed the unwritten ruling of the Council of Trent Bridge. But nobody liked it."[20] Wrong: the batsmen did.

A neat touch was that Australia's Prime Minister, Joe Lyons, the Tasmanian who had played a part in resolving Bodyline, was there at the MCG to see two players from Tasmania (Nash and Badcock) helping Australia secure the Ashes. And when it was all over, Dr Robertson made an astounding speech from the MCG balcony during which he expressed regret that England had not won the series. How far could rapprochement be taken?

There were a few other hot spots during the 1936–37 season. Arthur Mailey viewed with alarm the great influx of general reporters who crowded into the Press boxes in the hope of finding — or even creating — headline news from something peripheral to the cricket. Mailey called these journalists "incident-spotters", and lamented the fact that regular cricket-writers now felt a need to respond to the new challenge by spicing up their material and widening their writing to encompass matters little connected to the actual play. "Some of us viewed the future of cricket journalism with a certain apprehension."[21]

The sensation-seekers would have relished an incident which is supposed to have taken place in the Melbourne dressing-room during a Shield match in November 1936. When Don Bradman was given a terrifying burst of bouncers by McCormick he was so ruffled that he protested to Victoria's captain, Hans Ebeling, that this was Bodyline. How could it be, Ebeling replied, with only two short-leg fieldsmen? The umpires had not intervened. Bradman pressed him again, only to be told, "You captain your side and I'll look after mine."[22]

Bradman managed to survive McCormick's fire-spray and settled down to make 192, the last 42 coming in only 16 minutes towards the end of play. South Australia were still in arrears when he holed out at long-off soon after being dropped at long-on. He had punished McCormick when the bowler returned for a later spell, his primary energy spent, but the fast man would be back with a new ball after the rest day, and it was felt by Grimmett, for one, that Bradman had thrown his wicket away rather than face a reinvigorated McCormick on Monday. "Ha!" Grimmett is said to have scoffed as Bradman took off his pads, "you were thinking about the new ball on Monday morning, weren't you? You didn't want to go through it again." When O'Reilly told this story in an interview which was published posthumously in 1995, Bradman vehemently denied that he had thrown his wicket away, describing O'Reilly's claim as a "complete fabrication".[23] For his part, O'Reilly attributed his pal Grimmett's subsequent exclusion from the Test team to this alleged altercation.

Looking back to the period between Bodyline and the war, O'Reilly stressed that the bouncer had become taboo: "A bowler was regarded as a social leper if he appeared to let one go with malice aforethought. Should he exasperatedly let one fly, he was always very quick to say, 'Sorry, it slipped.'"[24]

It was natural that Bradman was being scrutinised. He had been the prime target of English Bodyline, and now he was to all intents and purposes free of the terror. But had his approach and style altered? Many thought so, including Dick Whitington, who batted with him in the second South Australia v MCC match during the '36–37 summer. With his 270 in the third Test just behind him, The Don went in at No. 4, nursing a leg strain and having a runner for much of his innings of 38. The English attack was at its sharpest, with Voce, Allen and Farnes in operation, and Whitington was "amazed to see the great batsman playing back defensively to rib-high balls from Farnes with his feet six inches to a foot [15–30 cm] outside his leg stump, his bat 18 inches [45 cm] to the off side of his head and line of vision. Don was tapping these balls softly down onto the off side."[25]

Whitington suggested to Ames that it was perhaps Bradman's injured leg that was causing him to draw away. "Oh, no," replied the wicketkeeper, "he has been doing that ever since he got the habit in the Bodyline series." The player–author went on to remark that in the next Test Bradman scored 212 without retreating an inch. "He could certainly prove an enigma when he liked."

If the ghost of Bodyline haunted cricket grounds for years to come, in the 1935–36 season it materialised into fleshy form during the Shield match at Sydney between New South Wales and Queensland, when Eddie Gilbert was warned for intimidation and told that any repetition would result in his removal from the attack. The Aborigine, who had been no-balled for throwing a few seasons earlier, damaged the hands of two batsmen before attracting the attention of George Borwick, who had yearned in vain for such powers of intervention during the Bodyline Tests.

There was further wry amusement all round in the 1937–38 season when, before the Victor Richardson–Clarrie Grimmett testimonial match at Adelaide, umpire Jack Scott, himself a bouncer merchant from way back, called the fast bowlers together (McCormick and Lush were the fastest and bounciest) to warn them against excesses. Anybody who got bouncer-happy would be reported to the Board. The chief attraction, of course, was Bradman, and Grimmett was beside himself with glee when he bowled The Don for 17 on the first morning. "I thought he said I couldn't spin!" he chuckled to Richardson. His fellow beneficiary quietly pointed out that he had probably just spun them out of £1000 each from the afternoon gate money.[26]

So seriously were cricket's new guidelines taken that Governor Hore-Ruthven of South Australia went as far as telling Plum Warner that a certain "gentleman" ought not to be allowed to cover the 1936–37 Ashes tour as a journalist, even if it needed the persuasion of Australian High Commissioner S.M. Bruce in London. The person referred to may just have been Harold Larwood, but was very much more likely to have been Douglas Jardine, who regularly penned his thoughts for, and made part of his living from, the *Evening Standard*. Hore-Ruthven dreaded a resurgence of the friction and ill-feeling of four years before.[27] And of course he was far from being alone in that sentiment.

Even in the summer of 1937, Warner was still hopeful that Larwood might recant, so that he might return to the fold for MCC's 150th anniversary celebrations. He wrote to A.W. Shelton asking if Larwood could be persuaded to write "as Voce wrote", to which Shelton replied that Larwood continued to feel strongly about the matter, "and the Press goad him". A week later Shelton told Warner that he had met Larwood privately and established that the cricketer felt badly let down by MCC and was following his father's advice. Shelton had left a draft letter with him but did not feel optimistic. Later that year Larwood wrote to Shelton, on the letterhead of Larwood Bros Florists, Seedsmen, Etc. He thanked Shelton for the birthday greetings and said it was nice to know he had at least one friend on the committee. He had just turned 33 and his form had fallen away. He was considering his future — which probably made an agreeable change from thinking about the past.[28]

CHAPTER SIXTEEN

GATHERING
OF THE GHOSTS

Where did it all go wrong? The volcano erupted, as cricket's natural evolution dictated that it should, and the game's caring administrators managed to cap the lava flow and bury the casualties. In the years which immediately followed, umpires and the batsmen themselves policed the game and kept it cleansed by — as Bill O'Reilly graphically put it — turning any bouncer-bowler into a social leper.

Then the world became embroiled in real war. Certain limited sanctions against Bodyline bowling remained dormant on cricket's statute book during the anguished years from 1939 to 1945, but, like so many other moral restraints, many of the reservations and restrictions which prevailed in cricket and in broader society during the immediate pre-war summers were blown away.

The first signs of post-war excesses happened to be seen in matches in which Don Bradman played. It was noted that in the 1934 Tests he seemed to be batting in a manner that told the bowlers, "I'll take risks. You've got a chance."[1] Never would he have condoned anything resembling Bodyline. Hostility verging on intimidation? That was a different matter, particularly when he found himself in command of some heavy artillery in the late 1940s.

His flexibility of outlook on bouncers was demonstrated during the Gentlemen of England v Australians match at Lord's in 1948. His old friend Walter Robins, a Test selector who had been critical of the way English batsmen had handled the bouncers of Ray Lindwall and Keith Miller throughout that difficult summer, came to the crease. Some of the England players had suggested that the Australian fast men might like to try him out. Miller's first ball nearly parted Robins's hair. Bradman laughed heartily.

Six months later, in the Kippax–Oldfield testimonial match at Sydney, the impish Miller decided — "for the amusement of the crowd" — to try a bouncer or two at his 40-year-old Test skipper, who was playing his penultimate first-class match. Bradman hooked the first one immaculately. But the second nearly took his head with it, and the batsman looked daggers at the bowler. Miller, "for sheer devilment", decided that a third bumper was worth a try, and Bradman mistimed a pull and was caught at mid-on. In the millisecond before that ball reared off the turf, it is possible that Bradman not only pictured the Larwood of 16 years ago bent into his mighty delivery but suffered a flash of outrage as well. He certainly departed from the crease an unhappy man. Not so long afterwards the Australian team to tour South Africa was announced, and Miller, the world's greatest all-rounder, was omitted. He was never to know for certain whether it was those bumpers that were the root cause of his exclusion, or his incurably nonchalant attitude. All he knew was that "Bradman, like so many others, took the game far too seriously."[2]

During the Australians' highly successful tour of England in 1948, Miller had been roundly booed at Trent Bridge when he unleashed a stream of bouncers at Hutton and Compton in the gloom. Here was a visitor doing just what their Nottinghamshire heroes had done — and been punished for by the authorities — in the 1930s. The debonair Miller, wartime flyer and major pin-up of his era, flashed a broad grin and merely rolled his right sleeve back up to the elbow and strutted back to his mark. For years after the Larwood affair the spectators at Nottingham let their feelings be known to visiting Australian teams. In 1938 Jack Fingleton, touring England at last, felt obliged (and supported by skipper Bradman) to sit down until the barracking stopped during his backs-to-the-wall innings.

England opener Cyril Washbrook revealed in his book that during the Old Trafford Test of 1948, when Lindwall and Miller were bouncing frequently at Bill Edrich and himself, he was astonished to hear Bradman apologising. "I hope you don't think this is my wish, Cyril. It isn't," Washbrook recalled the Australian captain saying. "I don't mind an occasional bouncer but I don't agree with using them consistently." The

Lancastrian replied that it was all right, he wasn't worried, carry on.[3] But he was left wondering that the most powerful player in cricket apparently could not calm and control his fast bowlers.

And so the resurgence of hostile bowling was under way. The isolated excesses of Lindwall and Miller were followed by accusations of bullying against Fred Trueman after he bounced the Indians in 1952. As the years unfolded, new names became synonyms for terror: Neil Adcock, Curtly Ambrose, Ian Bishop, Sylvester Clarke, Colin Croft, Wayne Daniel, Winston Davis, Allan Donald, Joel Garner, Roy Gilchrist, Charlie Griffith, Richard Hadlee, Wes Hall, Peter Heine, Rodney Hogg (who so reminded Leo O'Brien of Larwood), Michael Holding, Merv Hughes, Imran Khan, Brett Lee, Garth Le Roux, Dennis Lillee, Malcolm Marshall, Craig McDermott, Glenn McGrath, Ezra Moseley, Len Pascoe, Pollock (father and son), Mike Procter, Andy Roberts, Gordon Rorke, Sarfraz Nawaz, John Snow, Jeff Thomson, Frank Tyson, Courtney Walsh, Wasim Akram, Chester Watson, Bob Willis. Unlike their pre-war counterparts, some of these stooped to verbal abuse to embellish their assault. Others settled for vulgar body contortions and gestures, B-grade movie glares and pulling nasty faces.

Viewed against the trail of destruction and havoc of the past half-century, Bodyline seems comparatively harmless. First the frantic waves towards the pavilion as blood streams from the gash, then the batsman helped from the field or carried off unconscious, sometimes to be rushed to intensive care: the list of severe injuries from Test matches of the past 30 years — and in spite of the helmets and other protective equipment — is far too extensive to catalogue here. Nobody present at the time easily forgets such incidents. Some actually enjoy them.

If one casualty may be cited as having a strange historical link, it was the near-fatal head injury suffered by India's left-hand opener Nari Contractor in Barbados in 1962. A bouncer from Griffith fractured his skull, causing bleeding from his nose and ears and partially paralysing him. His life was despaired of, and West Indies captain Frank Worrell was among those who gave blood while a brain surgeon was summoned from Trinidad. Manjrekar was hit in the face in the same innings, and Griffith was called for throwing. The interlude was described by *Wisden* as "sordid and unhappy".

Contractor, unconscious for six days, survived, but never played Test cricket again. His place as India's captain was filled by "Tiger" Pataudi (who bagged a pair in that Barbados match). At 21 years 77 days, he was the youngest man ever to lead in a Test match. The historical circuit was completed by the fact that he was the son of the Nawab of Pataudi, the gentle youngster and "conscientious objector" who could never quite hit it off with D.R. Jardine on the Bodyline tour.

Pataudi the Younger exacted some sort of revenge for his father's treatment by bettering Jardine's batting record at Winchester College with 1068 runs in 1959, though Jardine did not live to know it. The Pataudis became the first father and son to score centuries in the Varsity match.

CONTRACTOR IS HIT. AT FIRST THERE IS CURIOSITY. THEN, AS THE BATSMAN SHOWS CLEAR SIGNS OF SERIOUS INJURY, STOMACHS CHURN AND ALARM ESCALATES.

Bodyline left much disillusionment not only among cricket-lovers but in the ranks of players on both sides. As they reflected on it from the perspective of old age — those who were lucky enough to pile up the years — they exuded a subtle gratitude for having lived and played when they did. They were not blind to the greatly increased financial rewards enjoyed by modern cricketers. They were grateful for the more relaxed environment in which they played — the 1932–33 season usually excepted — and for the leisurely pace of tours and the camaraderie. But some of the more reserved among them, such as Woodfull and Ponsford, lost much of their affection for the game that had once meant so much to them, but which had gone into a severe spasm that brought havoc and discontent. They both toured England again, Ponsford finishing with 266 in his final Test, as if to say that he could really have gone on until … well, until the Hitler war.

Bill Woodfull too was disenchanted, though he had his career in education to pursue. This man, who was so truthful, according to Ray Robinson, that he was incapable of telling even an off-white lie, spoke little about the 1932–33 series, even to his family. As Fingleton pointed out, to hold his players together during this maelstrom as Woodfull did was no mean feat. In 1936, in airing a few philosophical thoughts in the *Sunday Sun* that revealed humour and insight, Woodfull made one point neatly: "In the development of confidence, the captain acts as the spark plug to the whole team, and it is well for him to remember that:

The battle of life doesn't always go
To the stronger or faster man,
But sooner or later the fellow who wins
Is the fellow who thinks he can."

Late in 1934 he declined a knighthood, saying he might have accepted the offer had it been for his educational work (in recognition of which he was made OBE in 1963). Woodfull the Unbowlable died in 1965, at the age of 67, while playing golf. In 1995 his great-niece became engaged to Bill Ponsford's great-grandson.

The equally reticent Ponsford reached the age of 90, having served on the office staff of Melbourne Cricket Club for many years. After his mammoth scores in the 1920s were overshadowed by young Bradman, he was able to smile from the corner of his mouth whenever anybody speculated as to whether any batsman had ever retired while still such a heavy runscorer, for he and Bradman had a partnership of 388 in Ponsford's second-last Test and 451 in his final Test. It was some compensation for the multicoloured bruises inflicted by Larwood and Voce.

Jack Fingleton, having got his tour of England at last in 1938, established an outstanding reputation as writer and broadcaster, oddly enough on cricket in England and India but mainly on politics in Australia. Though frequently testy, he was nonetheless a fascinating companion and raconteur, whose writings on Don Bradman are the most rounded that we have. He toured England frequently as a journalist before a stroke slowed him down, without quite preventing one further visit, during which a deerstalker hat became the last of his jokes on his fellow man.

Stan McCabe gave up cricket when aged only 31 because of foot trouble. His 232 in the Trent Bridge Test of 1938, following his 2000 runs on the 1934 tour, showed English audiences why he was held in such rapt esteem by Australians. He ran a sports shop in George Street, Sydney, where visitors might have been forgiven for surmising that the pleasant, bald-headed man at the counter had hardly played cricket in his life. He was only 58 when he fell to his death from the end of the garden of his harbourside home in 1968. The flags were lowered to half-mast at The Oval, where an Ashes Test was in progress and where he had made his highest score: 240 against Surrey in 1934.

Leo O'Brien, like Ponsford, was to become, in his turn, the oldest surviving former Australian Test cricketer. After a crowded lifetime in sport he took up residence in a nursing home for his final years, having put the cat among the pigeons with his account of the Adelaide Leak during the Bodyline series in which he batted so bravely. When he died in 1997, aged 90, only Bradman remained from the 33 playing participants in the Bodyline Test series.

Alan Kippax's prolific career seemed to have been shut off by Bodyline, so difficult had he found it following the head injuries of the previous season. But he toured England in 1934, and though hampered by illness, gave spectators at Hove something to remember with a graceful innings of 250. When he retired, at 38, he had the exceptional first-class batting average of 57.22. After he had been outrageously overlooked for the 1926 tour of England, when at his peak, he too set up a sports shop in Sydney, in Martin Place. To visit him in his Bellevue Hill home was to be transported into a calm 1930s world of silk smoking jacket, cigarette-holder and art deco trimmings. He died in 1972, aged 75, leaving an estate valued at $330,000.

Kippax's boon pal, Victor Richardson, "The Guardsman", was 41 when he led Australia — Bradman being unavailable — on a highly successful and convivial tour of South Africa, where he played his last Tests. Like Woodfull, he had a capacity for attracting the utmost loyalty and effort from his men, as did his grandson Ian Chappell, who inherited his dash and broadmindedness. Greg, another grandson, was more austere: would even Jardine have ordered Larwood to bowl a vital final ball along the ground? Richardson served in Burma and India during the war. He was created OBE in 1954, and gates bearing his name were erected at Adelaide Oval. Ambitions to enter Parliament were frustrated. A side-effect of this was that radio listeners had the benefit of pleasant and memorable between-overs chats through several post-war Test series when he and former England captain Arthur Gilligan were at the microphone. Richardson died in 1969, aged 75.

Bert Oldfield was yet another Sydney sports-store proprietor. He played his last Sheffield Shield match in 1938, when he was 43, and retired with 400 catches and 262 stumpings to his name, not one of his victims having cause to feel he had been cheated. In fact, like visitors to Oldfield's shop, batsmen were treated with the utmost courtesy. This charming little man, who had survived a German shell-burst in 1917 and a Larwood thunderbolt in 1933, was created MBE in 1970 and died six years later, aged 81, leaving $234,368.

Clarrie Grimmett came back from the decline of 1932–33 and not only successfully toured England again and South Africa (where he became the first bowler to 200 Test wickets), but should, in the opinion of many, have gone to England in 1938. Instead, he carried on weaving his magic — even experimenting with new types of delivery — into his 50th year. In his last full season, 1939–40, he took a staggering 73 wickets, and ended up with 513 Shield wickets, over double the aggregate of the next man (Fleetwood-Smith) at that time. Grimmett loved coaching and was especially good at it, and that was what occupied him for much of the rest of his long life. He died in 1980, at the age of 88.

Bill O'Reilly, until the end of his 86-year life, enjoyed pretending that he was still in shock from the Bodyline series. When war broke out he was considered the finest bowler in the world — and possibly of all time — even if his last Test before the hiatus was at The Oval in 1938, when his 85 overs on a featherbed left him with figures of 3 for 178 as England amassed 903 for 7. He wrote on cricket until he was 82, biased and outspoken and steeped in old wisdom to the end. He persuaded himself to accept an OBE from the British government in 1980, and in 1988 a towering stand at the SCG was named in honour of this towering bowler, who died four years later.

Tim Wall played his last match for South Australia in 1936, and seemed to miss the buzz of big cricket hardly at all. He went quietly about his teaching and lived until 1981, when he was 76.

Bert Ironmonger reached his 90th year, his true age something of a mystery until much later. He was 51 when he strapped himself up for his final first-class match, at Sydney in January 1934: he bowled to Fingleton while he made a century and to Brown as he scored 205. "Dainty", who was considered by Jardine, among others, to be a chucker, vacated the scene appropriately by being bowled for a duck.

Len Darling's promise secured him a trip to England and another to South Africa, but his 85 in the final Bodyline Test was to remain his highest score in 12 appearances for his country, a disappointing outcome. In his retirement in Glenelg North he remembered going to a boxing match at Rushcutters Bay, Sydney with some of his team-mates, and seeing Larwood and Voce there. "We became good friends. They were two villains in the series, but quite good friends off the field." Darling died in 1992, aged 82.

Ernie Bromley was another whose great promise was never fulfilled. He toured England in 1934 and played in only one Test, being dismissed twice by Verity in the debacle at Lord's, having just got off the mark. Nor did he go beyond 56 in any other match, poor health sometimes hindering him. His fielding always attracted praise. He actually played alongside Larwood for Europeans in the Indian domestic competition in 1936, but he was only 26 when he played his last first-class match, and he died when only 54.

Lisle Nagel, the extra tall man who wrote headlines with his 8 for 32 against the Englishmen prior to the first Bodyline Test, never added to his first Test cap, and played little further first-class cricket. He came back five years after his last Shield match to play in the Melbourne Cricket Club Centenary match, and on that convivial occasion he bowled Bradman and had McCabe caught. Nagel died in 1971, just over two years before his twin brother, at the age of 66.

Harry Alexander lived until 1993, having inherited the title of Australia's oldest surviving former Test player, willing to the end to give Jardine credit for his "guts". A year after Bodyline he was gone from first-class cricket. Having served with the Australian Army in Crete, the Middle East and the Pacific, "Bull" eventually settled out of Melbourne, as a wool classer in Euroa, where he became a councillor and leading figure in the community. He greeted several English touring teams and was among the oldtimers who were recognised all over again during the incomparable gathering of Test players at the Melbourne Centenary Test in 1977.

Hammy Love was another one-Test wonder, his appearance for Australia at Brisbane being also his final first-class match. He played grade cricket for Mosman for a time, and died in that Sydney harbourside suburb in 1969, aged 73.

Perker Lee missed selection for the 1934 tour of England after playing in the trial matches, and played for South Australia for the last time in 1934–35. He died at the age of 75 in 1980.

Don Bradman, having survived the 1932–33 series and the criticism that came his way from the hard-headed oldtimers, toured England three more times, and in the remaining 15 years of his career he played in only four losing Test matches against England. In that time Australia won 13 Tests and never lost an Ashes series. Aside from these 24 post-Bodyline Ashes Tests (in which he scored 2990 runs at 85.43), it is a peculiar fact that Bradman played in only five other Tests in that period. These were against India at home in 1947–48, a series won 4–0 by Australia, with the 39-year-old captain averaging 178.75. And during that season he became the first non-Englishman to score 100 first-class centuries.

Late in the 1934 tour of England Bradman fell so close to death that the obituaries were placed ready in the trays of newspaper editors. Added to the lassitude observed in preceding weeks was the problem of a badly torn thigh muscle, which had laid him up between his 304 in the Headingley Test and his 244 at The Oval. He found true relaxation in the woodlands while recuperating on the estate of Sir Douglas Shields, the Australian surgeon who had overseen his treatment, an experience which gave rise to The Don's remark that "nothing in this world has ever appealed to me more than England as nature made her".[4] But at the tour's end he fell seriously ill, was operated on for appendicitis, lost much blood, and suffered ominous complications. Jessie, deeply anxious, sent a famous cable to her husband: "It's all right, Don, I'm coming." As she reached Melbourne she "learned" that he had died. However, by the time her long journey by rail and sea was over, she found him on the mend. A long convalescence followed.

His post-war Test cricket might have been limited to one match had he failed at the Gabba in the opening Test. At 28 he edged a ball from Voce which finished in Ikin's hands in the slips. All the Englishmen thought it was out, but umpire Borwick gave it not out, and Bradman went on to score 187 and demonstrate to the owner of that 38-year-old body that it could still manage the demands of international cricket.

The glorious 1948 tour of England followed, the moment of highest drama coming when The Don played his last Test innings, an effort at The Oval which lasted twice as long as his first-innings performance at Melbourne in the 1932–33 series, with the same sad end product. A more enjoyable occasion followed: the presentation to him of a replica of the beautiful Warwick Vase, purchased from a shilling fund subscribed to by the readers of a British newspaper. The piquancy of the occasion was heightened when the formal presentation at the Savoy Hotel was made by none other than Lord Gowrie, VC, the former Alexander Hore-Ruthven, prime solution-seeker during Bodyline and now president of MCC — who also, at the instigation of Lord Nuffield, had a hand in the move to seek a knighthood for Don Bradman.

After his retirement as a player, Sir Donald Bradman attended to his business activities, wrote on cricket, continued as a selector, and became chairman of that same body, the Australian Cricket Board, which had hauled him over the coals in the early 1930s over such matters as published writings on tour, journalistic commitments while playing, and wives accompanying players on tour. As the years passed, with no lessening of his reclusiveness, so his public stature continued to grow, until the sense of reverence and unquestioning worship left many of his contemporaries scratching their heads in wondering admiration. With the establishment of the Bradman Museum and Trust in Bowral, a fresh and concentrated round of commercialism took off. So hallowed became the name that his image appeared on coins and postage stamps, and the compulsive desire to obtain his autograph drove many thousands of strangers each year to write to him. Seldom was a personal response not promptly received.

Just about every conceivable honour in cricket came his way, or was offered. No sportsman anywhere in the world has ever had to withstand such a colossal weight of expectation and demand upon time and energy, and Bradman was generous in response. Not only was his supremacy scarcely ever challenged, but all kinds of analysts deduced that he was not only the greatest batsman ever but, in terms of the great gulf between his performances and those of the rest, the most outstanding sportsman of all time from anywhere in the world.

And just as the oldtimers had launched forth on how inadequate his technique and approach to Bodyline had been, so the middle-aged Bradman subtly amended his view on certain matters. When Denis Compton was doing his best against the Lindwall–Miller assault in 1948, the Australian captain offered a suggestion: "I can't understand why you fellows don't step inside them and hit them to the leg fence."[5] And when Compton returned to the crease at Old Trafford with plaster over a stitched cut inflicted by a Lindwall no-ball which the bat of England's most popular player diverted close to his eyes — an injury not all that dissimilar to Oldfield's — there was no great outburst of protest when the bowler greeted him with further bumpers. The mild and affable Lindwall kidded the batsman that he was going to knock the plaster off. The humour behind the remark was lost on Compton.

When Len Hutton just managed to get his head out of the way of a vicious Miller bouncer at Sydney 18 months earlier, the batsman happened to catch sight of the Aussie skipper at cover smiling broadly. At Trent Bridge, after a similar barrage in 1948, when a Pressman questioned the Australian captain about it Bradman replied: "They have a bat in their hands, haven't they?"[6]

Intriguingly, Plum Warner revealed in his autobiography that after that outbreak of bouncers in 1948 "private correspondence between the authorities subsequently put matters on a calmer basis". There was no need for cables this time, but the letter-writers — conceivably MCC president Gowrie (the former Hore-Ruthven) and Warner himself among them — did the trick.

Bradman had been just as uncompromising in the Brisbane Test of 1946, the first Ashes contest after the war. On a mud-heap on which — according to Keith Miller — Blind Freddie could have got wickets, Miller's slowed-down deliveries were thumping into Hammond's body and leaping even more frequently and painfully off a length into little Bill Edrich's. Miller recalled that Bradman came over to him and urged him to bowl faster. Later the skipper told his new boy that when you play Test cricket you didn't give these Englishmen an inch. You play it tough, flat out the whole way. "Grind them into the dust," he said. Miller thought differently: "A war had just gone and a lot of Test cricketers and future Test cricketers had been killed and here we are just starting after the war, everyone is happy and now we have to grind them into the dust. So I thought, bugger me, if that's Test cricket then they can stick it ..."[7]

Bradman had joined up in June 1940 with hopes of becoming an observer in the RAAF but, perhaps tired of waiting, transferred to a commission in the Army (as a PT instructor) which, as it transpired, seemed to afford safer prospects, as his critics were quick to point out. According to E.W. Swanton (whose own status as a prisoner of the Japanese has lately been the subject of curiosity),[8] Bradman acted on the advice of Lord Gowrie, the Governor-General, and for once was guided by somebody else into a dubious course of action. The upshot was even unhappier: brought down by acute fibrositis and found to have surprisingly ordinary eyesight, he was discharged from the service a year later.

It is warming to recall that at least a certain measure of reconciliation between the Bodyline adversaries took place, though it took years. During the 1948 tour, then by chance in 1952 in Martin Place, Sydney, and again during the festivities surrounding the 1977 Centenary Test, when over 200 veterans of Ashes Tests mingled and talked at the MCG and at a series of functions, Don Bradman and Harold Larwood briefly conversed.

There were even "conversations" between Bradman and Jardine, when somebody with an odd sense of occasion positioned them side by side in the Press box at Headingley for the 1953 Test match. It has been generally understood that they gave each other no more than a cursory nod and a clipped "Good morning" — until Bradman recalled much later in a filmed interview that they had actually had an occasional "argument" over what was happening on the field, though not much else was said.[9] Even by 1948 there had been no thaw: they were observed arriving simultaneously at Australia House, London for a reception, neither acknowledging the other.[10]

The diminutive Australian who had been the cause of all the fireworks, rancour and contorted manipulations in 1932–33 became a widower in 1997, and with his grievous loss came a discernible and not unexpected wilting of spirit. While there was broad expectation that a man who so seldom had fallen in the nineties would go on to complete the greatest century of all, he fell short. The last surviving player from the Bodyline series, Sir Donald Bradman died in February 2001 at the age of 92. Media coverage and the quantity of retrospectives were nothing short of phenomenal. Anything less than that would have been a bigger surprise than a soft Larwood half-volley.

During the tense years of war, cricket — and Bodyline — was acknowledged in the midst of the carnage. Not only did Field-Marshal Montgomery promise to hit "Wommel" for six out of Africa, but when Mussolini was yorked comprehensively and strung up, a British Member of Parliament chortled in the House: "We have got Ponsford out cheaply but Bradman is still batting."

The Don would have cared less for that analogous reference to Hitler than to his name being used in a coded message to Allied forces in the Mediterranean before the assault on the Italian mainland in 1944. It read: "Bradman will be batting tomorrow."

Meanwhile, England was suffering a terrible and unexpected late German assault in the summer of 1944 by the V1 flying bombs, which were succeeded by something even worse, the faster-than-sound V2 rockets, over 2000 of which exploded on and around London, causing massive destruction and loss of life. Somehow the launch sites had to be found and destroyed. This was achieved by radar plotting. The flight paths of the missiles were traced backwards, and the bases were located and then bombed. This tracking operation was known as The Bodyline Watch, a nice tribute to cricket.

Sir Pelham Warner lived into his 90th year. When he died in Sussex in 1963, his wandering mind set on cricket until the end, it marked the closure of an era in more senses than one, for the English amateur–professional division was being abolished. Henceforth all cricketers would be players and paid as such, irrespective of education and social background. Eternally kind and courteous, Warner had continued to chair selection panels and write for the *Telegraph*. He also produced several significant books on cricket (writing more than once that if he had to pick a team to play for his life, Jardine would be captain: he proclaimed him a master of tactics, adept at preserving fast bowlers' energy and possessed of a great capacity for taking pains, which is a mark of genius). And to his unconfined joy, Warner was invited by his predecessor, the Duke of Edinburgh, to become MCC president for 1950. In 1958 he was present at the official opening of the Warner Stand at Lord's, and when he died his ashes were scattered on the ground in front of it, close to where his first boundary had been stroked as a Rugby schoolboy in 1889.

Dick Palairet, having left his position as Surrey secretary in 1932, associated himself in later years with his old county, Somerset, and was president of the club from 1937 to 1946. Having seen service as a staff captain in the Devonshire Regiment in the First World War, he was an air-raid warden in the Second. Palairet suffered from failing health for years, and died in Budleigh Salterton in 1955, aged 83, nine days after learning that England, under Hutton, had won the Ashes at — of all places — Adelaide.

Two years later, and in Bath, not far away, Bill Ferguson, Fergie the faithful scorer and baggagemaster, died, having had to withdraw from his duties with the 1957 West Indies team. He was 77.

Of the English players who toured Australia in '32–33, Eddie Paynter, who bestowed his name on the Brisbane Test, a rare achievement in any Ashes match, was grievously underused by his country. In 20 Tests during the 1930s he averaged a shade under 60 (84.43 against Australia), and his dancing footwork brought him double-centuries against Australia and South Africa and a triple-century in a county match at Hove. Later he became an umpire. He saw out his days quietly and without wealth, stacking wool in a Yorkshire mill. In a 1957 interview with Raymond Glendenning for BBC Television, Paynter's major recollection of his Brisbane heroics ended with the vivid memory that he "chairnged strairt int' me cricket material, went strairt in t'bat after Gooby Allen had got ote". He told the interviewer that he topped the bowling averages on the 1932–33 tour: "That's surprised you, hasn't it!" Paynter died at 77, in 1979.

Wally Hammond switched to amateur status and captained England from 1938, confirming his place as his country's greatest cricketer of the 20th century without, after all, outstripping Bradman. His commanding batting nonetheless persuaded most spectators that he was very close indeed to being the ultimate human creation in terms of style and power. For once figures give some idea of a man's accomplishment: 50,551 runs at 56.10, 167 centuries, 819 catches, 732 wickets (best figures 9 for 23). In a match against Surrey in 1928 he scored a century in each innings for Gloucestershire and held 10 catches. His final Test tally of 7249 (58.45) was a world record at the time. War service in the RAF took Hammond to an age — 43 — when it might have been wiser to have retired, or at least declared himself unavailable for the 1946–47 tour of Australasia. Glimpses of the majesty were still seen, but his struggle to make runs diminished his 1939 reputation. There was also a distressing divorce, followed by remarriage and migration to South Africa, where, in the wake of a bad road accident, his health declined. He died in Durban in 1965, shortly after his 62nd birthday, and his ashes were conveyed back to England and scattered at the Bristol ground.

Herbert Sutcliffe played his last Test in 1935 and ended with the imposing average of 60.73, having averaged 50 in his last Ashes series in 1934. At his retirement he had a first-class average of 52.02 from 50, 670 runs. His friend Jardine caused amusement by sending him an umbrella on the eve of his benefit match. Ever the unruffled gentleman, Sutcliffe ran a successful sports shop, served for a time as a Test selector, and charmed all who met him with his courtliness and rich reminiscences, not least when he sat comfortably, gin and tonic in hand, watching a Test match or acting as match award adjudicator at a one-day game. His son captained Yorkshire. In 1978, soon after Sutcliffe lost his wife (her nightdress caught fire), he himself died, also in a Yorkshire nursing-home, aged 83. Gates named in his honour had been erected at Headingley cricket ground.

Bob Wyatt was England's oldest surviving Test cricketer at the time of his death at 93, in 1995. He batted grittily on until 1951, having switched from Warwickshire to Worcestershire after the war, and was a Test selector from 1949 until 1954. His statistics too are impressive: 39,405 runs (40.05), 85 centuries, 901 wickets. In his later years he became a sought-after figure at Lord's as he watched younger generations at play. This man, to whom cricket seemed all, reminisced colourfully, with inevitable allusions to the lbw law, his passionate but unfulfilled wish being that the pre-1935 rule should be restored in order to discourage negative inswing and offspin bowling. Of Bodyline he would speak only if pressed, recalling how he had breakfast with Gubby Allen to discuss the situation each morning, and reaffirming his admiration for Jardine. It was not as if he couldn't take the rough stuff himself. Bowes bombarded him with Bodyline at Scarborough in September 1933, but he reached his century before lunch.[11] He enjoyed the 1932–33 tour as much as any of the many others he made. Years later, among his papers he found a 1935 note from Jardine observing that "Whiskers" (F.S. Jackson) was no longer a selector. Warner had returned to the panel. There would clearly be a leaning towards Gubby Allen as England captain now, so Jardine warned his old vice-captain: "Don't let them think they can do anything and you will take it smiling. It's Christian but it isn't respected and doesn't pay! — 'Ware Warner and Higson!" Even as Wyatt struggled in old age against the legacies of his broken bones and several strokes, he could always find one more reminiscence, such as this: "Kodak gave Pataudi a film camera which he used to leave lying about and I used to pop some embarrassing pictures on it such as Wally Hammond getting out of the bath, which surprised his girlfriends when he took them to Kodak to see his latest film!"[12]

The Nawab of Pataudi — later Iftikhar Ali Khan — played once more for England, in the first Test in 1934 (without success, though he topped the first-class averages that summer with 78.75), and he had several further seasons with Worcestershire. Then in the first post-war season he led India on their tour of England, his class again being obscured as he managed a top score of only 22. He was not to know of his son's great success for Oxford, Sussex and India, for he died in 1952, aged only 41, when he suffered a heart attack while playing polo in New Delhi.

Maurice Leyland continued to be one of England's mainstays against Australia, averaging 56.83 in Ashes Tests and contributing 187 to England's 903 for 7 at The Oval in 1938. There his fellow Yorkshireman Hutton laid out his 364 and the pair had a stand of 382, following which Bradman damaged an ankle and was unable to bat, just when the expectation was that he would surely score 500 himself this time. Leyland, who boyishly claimed, "I'm a lucky lad" when he found himself on board ship bound for Australia, was always popular there because of his joviality in the field. He coached Yorkshire after retirement, and died in his hometown of Harrogate in 1967, when 66.

Hedley Verity quietly and with dignity bestrode the 1930s as England's premier spin bowler, finishing with 1956 wickets at only 14.90 apiece. Twice he took all 10 wickets in a county innings and seven times he bagged nine. His 144 wickets in 40 Tests came at 24.37, and at the outbreak of war, like so many cricketers, he still seemed to have plenty of summers ahead of him. When in 1943 he was taken prisoner after being brought down by enemy fire in Sicily — he was serving as a captain in the Green Howards — among the first messages of sympathy received by his wife Kathleen was one from Jardine. Verity, severely wounded, was captured and taken to mainland Italy, but died on July 31, 1943. He was 38. On their way to Australia in 1954, Len Hutton's team found the military cemetery in Caserta where Verity was buried and visited his grave.

Gubby Allen lived until 1989, and at 87 he was still keen to impart his views, though by then he, like Wyatt, was reliant on walking sticks to get around (when his Bentley wasn't to hand). From the early all-ten against Lancashire at Lord's his promise was fulfilled, but only when business permitted him to play. Following his important contributions to the on-field success of the 1932–33 tour, he went on to captain England on and off, first against India in 1936, then on the topsyturvy 1936–37 peacemaking tour of Australia, and finally, and ill-advisedly, in West Indies in 1947–48. As he battled on past the age of 50 to play the game he loved, he was dubbed Regius Professor of Elastoplast by a fellow Free Forester. Power at Lord's was his for the taking, and over the years Allen served as chairman of selectors, Middlesex president, and treasurer and president of MCC, his long service to the game being capped by a knighthood which rendered him practically unrecognisable as Sir George Allen. In many an interview he stated that the sooner Bodyline was forgotten the better. After his death great sums of money were paid at auction for his scrapbooks and photograph albums of the tour. A lifelong bachelor, he left £928,987 nett.

Maurice Tate left £824 gross, nil nett. He finished his days as a publican at the Greyhound in Wadhurst, having played for Sussex until 1937, when he was brusquely dismissed. No more would his big boots and the broad grin be seen on an English first-class field. In all he took 2784 wickets at only 18.16 each, 155 of them for England. So often Tate with the new ball seemed unplayable. He never quite got over being marginalised by Jardine on his final tour of Australia. After that late call-up at Christchurch, in Larwood's absence, he played for England in one more Test: in 1935, when he was 40. Thereafter it was league cricket, wartime cricket (he was in khaki again, serving on the home front this time), newspaper work, coaching at Tonbridge (where Colin Cowdrey was still a student) and life behind the pub counter. He would have been far too polite to have a chip at Jardine when the two of them, plus Sutcliffe and others, lined up for an Old England XI in 1946 in a match to mark the centenary of Surrey CCC. Soon after Tate died in 1956, aged 60, memorial gates were opened at Hove.

Les Ames played on into the post-war era and even added his name to the scroll of those with 100 centuries. He finished with the estimable Test average of 40.56 and completed 97 wicketkeeping dismissals, a figure overshadowed by his 1121 in first-class matches. In the season following his return from the Bodyline tour he made his highest score, 295 against

Gloucestershire, and the longer he played the more obvious it became that he had underperformed on that tour. He was the first professional to become a Test selector, in 1950, and he was manager on several MCC tours, winning praise for his calm demeanour under pressure. Long a member of Kent's administrative staff, he was appointed CBE for services to cricket, and died in 1990, one of seven Bodyline tourists who lived beyond 80. Asked at Lord's how his lumbago was these days, even at 80 Ames was able to drop to the wicketkeeping crouch and spring back again to his full height.

Bill Voce was fed up with Bodyline and, being in a state of inanition on the subject, preferred in later years to talk about other things. Part of the reason for this was that, unlike his great friend Larwood, he had made his peace with cricket's puppetmasters and played on full-time until 1947, touring Australia again both sides of the war (and considered by many a better bowler in 1936–37, when he took 26 Test wickets at 21.53). None of his 16 Test appearances was in England. He was an uncomplicated soul. Carr said early on that this big lad, who had played for Notts to support his widowed mother and brothers and sisters, and "needs a lot of skippering", was rebuked by Jardine for clowning about at catching practice during the tour. Life was meant to be kept simple. Having been at school with Larwood at Kirkby Woodhouse during the First World War and worked down the mine too, Voce returned to work in the coal industry, though he did a great deal of coaching for Nottinghamshire CCC and at MCC's Easter classes. When he removed his coat to bowl to his pupils they needed to fend off the occasional delivery kicking up at their ribs. It was Mr Voce's natural delivery, it was explained, and he could not really help it. Against the county batsmen he still liked to dig it in, chuckling at the rib contact. Contentedly married for over 50 years and living in the same house in Hucknall all that time, Voce never wrote a book and scarcely ever gave interviews. Shortly before his death in 1984 at the age of 74, speaking to John Arlott during a rainy interval at Trent Bridge he paid tribute to his fast-bowling partner Larwood, recalling how fast he was in the first Sydney Test, when the catches "came through like bullets". In a radio interview in 1970 he said that Plum Warner's post-tour criticism came as a little bit of a shock. To Murray Hedgcock he said: "Bradman didn't like Bodyline, but he didn't show it the way some of them did. Kippax was scared stiff, and he let you see it. But Bradman had the right idea: he always knew the best defence was attack. He was very quick on his feet, and he could get out of trouble so fast. He wanted a lot of reckoning out."[13]

Freddie Brown returned to Australia 18 years after Bodyline, when he was 40. He had been the youngest member of Jardine's team, and frequently 12th man. Now he was in charge, a rosy-cheeked John Bull figure, white cravat and pipe at the toss with tiny Lindsay Hassett, displaying the last vestige of the old world of the robust amateur. Australia were four up with one to play in that 1950–51 series, but England won at last at Melbourne, their first success against Australia for 12½ years, with Brown's legspin (5 for 49) showing the way. He always made his feelings clear about Bodyline. He deplored it. In fact so strongly did he dislike bouncers that he told Lindwall and Miller not to bowl them at him in Sydney, and then scored 79. Moving from Surrey to Northants after the war (during which he was taken prisoner at Tobruk), he played on stoutly until 1953, when he returned to play in his 22nd and final Test, while chairman of selectors. Captain of England in 15 Tests, MCC president, tour manager, chairman of the Cricket Council, and appointed CBE, Brown made a huge contribution to English cricket, though he trod on some toes along the way. Confined to a wheelchair in his final months, he died in 1991, aged 80.

Bill Bowes was another who endured a long, punishing period as a prisoner-of-war, having had several peak cricketing seasons deleted by the conflict. He and Verity had helped Yorkshire to seven Championships during the 1930s, and it was while Bowes was helplessly confined in the PoW camp that he learned of his great friend's death. He was very menacing on English pitches, and claimed 1639 wickets at only 16.76, but he played in a mere 15 Tests altogether, 13 of them at home, contrasting with Voce's 16 all away. A thinking cricketer, Bowes proved a worthy addition to the Press box, and was always warmly welcoming at Headingley. His lost tour diary is one of so many documents that would have added even further to our know-ledge of the Bodyline adventure. The big man died in 1987, in his 80th year.

George Duckworth was a loyal also-ran on the Bodyline tour and was destined to be deputy to Ames in Australia again four years later, having made his raucous presence felt in a handful of Tests in between. He finished with almost as many first-class dismissals (1096) as Ames, and enjoyed being part of five Lancashire Championships. After the war he managed Commonwealth sides on tours of the subcontinent and was a clued-up baggageman–scorer on MCC tours. Duckworth died in 1966, at 64.

The last of the Bodyline tourists to die was Tommy Mitchell, the team clown, who found it hard to stop talking. Hopeless batsman that he was,

he still launched into a treatise on tour, prompting his capt
60:1 on a penny that he wouldn't score a fifty, even in an up-
"Tommy's hard-earned penny reposes in my waistcoat pocket as I wii,
recorded Jardine in his tour book. Mitchell was a better bowler than the
tour record suggests. He took all 10 wickets at Leicester in 1935, the year he
played the last of his five Tests, but he had barely any success during his two
Tests against Australia in 1934. His record for Derbyshire, however, places
him among the best of the spin bowlers: 1417 wickets at 20.20. Having
relished a spate of interviews generated by his longevity, Mitchell died in
1996, at the age of 93.

Which leaves the two key English figures, D.R. Jardine, Esquire, and
Larwood, H.

The story of Harold Larwood post-Bodyline is one of immense
frustration and ultimately heartwarming recognition. Although never as fast
ever again following the foot injury, he was still for some years England's
best — but of course unchosen — fast bowler. In 1934, while English
cricket-lovers moaned at his partially self-inflicted exclusion, he took 80
wickets for Notts at a meagre 15.03. Some of the edge had left his bowling
come 1935, but he still took 61 wickets at 21.16 and was able to look forward to a benefit next season. It was a good one, £2098, a Nottinghamshire
record, with some donations coming from Australia. At Lord's in the
Middlesex match, bowling at his very best, he claimed 11 wickets. Near the
end of the season he took 22 wickets in consecutive matches against Kent
and Surrey. If only he had been going to Australia with Gubby Allen's side.

There were offers to write for newspapers on tour. Instead he went to
India on a coaching contract, but soon returned to England, bored and
"flat broke". Another season with Notts brought Larwood moderate
success. The fires were dying. On July 22, however, he nearly became one
of cricket's saintly figures, cut down in the prime of life after the glory and
the banishment. A car accident in Northamptonshire left him with severe
head abrasions and a bruised neck.[14] It so happened that on that same day
Ted McDonald, the great Australian fast bowler and sometime purveyor of
Bodyline, was killed in a motor accident in Lancashire.

A knee injury led to fewer appearances and lesser performance, and
Notts released Larwood in 1938 with the briefest of acknowledgments for

his years of service. Never again in a first-class setting would that smooth, power-packed run-up be seen, the broad shoulders and deep chest, the economical approach, brown hair blown back, head steady, long arms moving into the perfectly co-ordinated bowling action, back foot scraping the ground — except on film, thank God.

With a plant nursery and some poultry as his main means of livelihood, Larwood boosted his earnings with a league contract with Blackpool (taking McDonald's place).

He was soon reaping bags of wickets. During the war he grew flowers and vegetables in Nottingham, and he settled in Blackpool in 1946, opening a small confectionery shop in a sidestreet. He refused to put his name on the premises, and worked 12 hours a day.

Into that shop in 1948 walked Jack Fingleton, one of his old Australian punching-bags, escorted by George Duckworth. Fingleton dropped the suggestion to Larwood that he and his family might be happier in Australia, a suggestion which strained Larwood's credulity as he reflected on the abuse he suffered as he had gone about his business in 1932–33. A rousing reception at a farewell lunch to the 1948 Australians helped him decide. When it was announced that he was considering emigration, offers of employment and accommodation came to him from Australia.

On April 28, 1950, Harold and Lois Larwood sailed in *Orontes* from Tilbury with their five daughters, Harold having had a final round of get-togethers: Jardine took him to his club for lunch, with Sutcliffe present, and Jack Hobbs opened champagne at his club. John Arlott and other Pressmen saw the Larwoods off, but nobody from Lord's went to Tilbury, though he was one of several eminent former professionals who had recently accepted honorary life membership of MCC. Symbolically, as the ship prepared to cast off, it snowed.

One of the unlikeliest of odysseys had begun. Larwood was taken by Bill Jeanes to the now-silent Adelaide Oval for old times' sake, and in Melbourne he was whisked off to see Bill Woodfull in his study at Melbourne High. Fingleton — and many others — were there to greet the family as *Orontes* docked in Sydney, and within weeks the Larwoods were in a home of their own in Kingsford, where the old England fast bowler was to spend the whole of the second half of his life, surrounded by photographs and souvenirs, none more cherished than the ashtray inscribed TO HAROLD FOR THE ASHES — 1932–33 — FROM A GRATEFUL "SKIPPER". Without their knowing it at the time, the rent during those first few weeks had been subsidised by Australia's Prime Minister, Ben Chifley. Fingleton later enjoyed describing the incomprehension written all over both their faces as Chifley, broad Australian, and Larwood, broad Nottingham, tried to make themselves understood to each other when they met in Canberra in 1951.

For some years after his arrival in Sydney, Larwood was employed on the production line at the Pepsi-Cola factory; he was later a nightwatchman, glad of the obscurity. He did occasional ghosted newspaper work on the Tests and was an easy-to-listen-to studio guest on radio. He never quite got over the warmth of the friendly reception that awaited him. Bert Oldfield took him to lunch, and Bill O'Reilly and Stan McCabe were soon shaking his hand. Succeeding English touring teams in Australia were less welcoming, Freddie Brown giving him what Larwood saw as a cold shoulder in 1950–51. West Indies skipper Frank Worrell was much more considerate a year later. It was not until Fred Trueman, Colin Cowdrey and a few others extended invitations that he began to feel more relaxed about relations with English cricket. In 1995, Darren Gough was thrilled to get a congratulatory phone call from Harold Larwood after his half-century and six wickets at the SCG.

FACING HAROLD LARWOOD'S ACCURATE EXPRESS BOWLING TRANSFORMED MANY A BATSMAN INTO A CHICKEN. NOW, HIS CRICKET CAREER ALMOST DONE, HE AND WIFE LOIS TEND THEIR OWN POULTRY AS HE COMES TO GRIPS WITH MAKING A LIVING BEYOND CRICKET.

As belated recognition goes, Larwood's MBE in 1993, when he was 88 and almost completely blind, takes some beating. It was bestowed at the instigation of Prime Minister John Major — the mix of cricket and politics yet again — and was followed by a congratulatory telegram from Sir Donald. Larwood was inclined to view the insignia as a belated apology and gave an aside to one newspaper about Major: "I wish I knew he was planning to throw 30,000 blokes out of the pits. I'd have given him a right ear-bashing."

The MBE drew an unusually profound comment from Britain's *Sun* newspaper: "If he did that today [bowled Bodyline] would we send him to Coventry? Would we hell. He'd be given the freedom of Britain ... It was easier, of course, to blame a working-class Nottinghamshire miner for this national disgrace than the well-spoken public school captain."

"At last," roared the headline in *Today*, "the ruling classes honour the man who carried the can for their savage arrogance."

Harold and Lois returned to England for visits, but their commitment to Australian life was total. As he sat in his little garden he could sometimes pick up the roar from the Hill on big match days. Other belated gestures were his honorary life membership of the Sydney Cricket Ground, where he had triumphed in three Test matches so long ago, and (in 1985) the opening of the Larwood and Voce Stand and Tavern back at Trent Bridge.

Larwood despised some of the modern antics, such as players hugging and kissing and dancing. When he got Bradman or anybody else out he saw it as merely doing his duty, and he would sit down and rest before the next ball. He also disliked one-day cricket, and felt there was too much money in the game, and that it had become more violent. "When I hear the commentators today saying: 'Oh, what a beautiful bouncer, it only just missed his head' I wonder what the game has come to. I might sometimes have bowled at a batsman's ribs, but never at his head," he told John Woodcock of *The Times* in 1990.

His idol remained Hobbs, but to Bradman he now unconditionally accorded the title of best batsman of all. And some time before the end he withdrew the claim that The Don had been scared of him. Just as England had long since taken Bradman to its heart, so Australia embraced Larwood. He never departed from his belief that Australia were hampered by Woodfull's caution to his batsmen to restrict the hook stroke. It played right into England's hands.

When Harold Larwood died he left a widow, five daughters, 13 grandchildren and six great-grandchildren. Lois followed him six years later; her ashes are interred beside his in a memorial wall at Holy Trinity, Kingsford.

When he was old and sightless, the gunslinger of 1932–33 would always smile and nod knowingly whenever he heard Sinatra on the radio crooning *My Way*. That song, recalled daughter Enid, was regarded by her Dad as his very own personal theme-tune.

Douglas Jardine will remain the most complex of figures. We've all known people like him: affable one minute, impossible the next. Attempts at analysis inevitably follow. Was it the separation from his parents as a child, the prep-school days at Horris Hill, the stoic regime at Winchester (though he had the great support and friendship of Andrew Lang, the wise old Scot), the upsetting barracking in Australia on two tours? Was it an innate and overwhelming shyness? His strength — unwavering determination — sometimes became a catastrophic weakness.

"Alas," wrote Robertson-Glasgow in a letter to Jack Fingleton, "with all his fine (and, when known, numerous) gifts Douglas Jardine has that streak of highbrow and iron unforgiveness and stern contempt for what is not worth either despising or disliking which have ever been the despair of his pals."[15] He considered it an appalling misjudgment that DRJ was sent as captain in view of his feelings after his maiden tour. But then again, if some higher force mapped out that campaign there probably would have been no other leader sufficiently strong-willed to see it through.

"Off the field he could be quite amiable," wrote Bert Oldfield, "but changed immediately he stepped into the cricket arena. [This is what certain Test cricketers of today call the 'white line syndrome' to justify their excesses on the field.] He would order his men about with the firmness of a general marshalling his troops."[16]

If politicians inside or outside the MCC committee did set Jardine up as the architect of Bodyline, he accepted the undertaking with scarcely any hesitation. And whether or not he was secretly forced to retire, he knew he had carried out his mission, and never showed the slightest remorse — except in respect of his decision to switch Larwood's field so soon after Woodfull was hit at Adelaide.

When it was all over, to be half-forgotten until revival of interest long after his death, he revealed time and again glimpses of the sense of humour ("delicious", Fingleton called it) that his few close friends had always known was part of him. Even early on the tour, at a lunch laid on for his team by the Millions Club, Jardine displayed some intelligent humour: "When it doesn't rain in this country we feel like handing round the hat for the pastoralists. But, on this occasion, the politician should be grateful to us for distracting attention. I think it is great, in these hard times, to forget our cares. As a parson remarked, the only wages that have not been reduced are the wages of sin."

He wrote a book (*Ashes — and Dust*) on the 1934 tour by Australia, remarking at the start that he was surprised that Bradman, with his peerless ability to hook and keep the ball down, had been a "comparative failure" against Larwood. As was expected of him, Jardine wrote a chapter on the latest manoeuvres concerning leg theory, branding the enforced withdrawal of Voce during the Notts match as "the only openly ugly scene of the tour" and congratulating Wyatt on placing a leg field for his bowlers in the last Test — ineffective though it proved to be. Why, he wondered, was it all right for Clark to bowl with this leg field when it was not all right for the not-so-fast Voce at Trent Bridge? And he opposed the pending broadening of the lbw law.

By no means did Jardine become reclusive. He was among the welcoming parties that greeted touring teams to England — the 1936 Indians (he wrote that if Duleep and Pataudi had been in the team they would have been favourites to win) through to the 1953 and 1956 Australians. He also accepted an invitation in 1953 to become the first president of the Association of Cricket Umpires — to be succeeded in due course by Gubby Allen — and was president of the Oxford University Cricket Club from 1955 to 1957.

Soon after the 1936 Indians arrived in England, Jardine's mother died. A surviving letter from that time, when he gave Sands End, Hayling Island as his address, expresses an unwillingness to play in a friendly match: "At the moment I do not feel inclined to take on any additional interest in cricket." Later that year, however, he wrote a bright letter (from 21 Bentinck Street) in his strong hand to Charlie Barnett, who was about to undertake his first tour of Australia: "Play Grimmett your natural way (like Wally) — only remember not to go forward <u>every</u> ball of the over ... Grimmett likes it to be all forward or all back — even I used to play forward sometimes just to upset him!"[17]

This was the year his coaching book was published, a 234-page work filled with wise and dogmatic advice, in which he poked gentle fun at his own severe facial expression in an illustration of the batting stance. A slim booklet came out the same year: *Cricket — How to Succeed.* "Cricket is like life," he told his readers. "In it, and through it, you are given training and opportunity to practise keeping your head, and with it your temper." His advice to a cricketer was that, upon rising, he should brush his teeth, wash his mouth out, blow his nose twice, strip, rub himself down with a rough towel, and go through a series of exercises. That the foreword was contributed by Lord Somers, who was MCC's latest president, suggests some sort of mutual and subtle forgiveness.

Jardine married in 1934, and his wife Margaret presented him in time with a son and three daughters. Dick Palairet, having written a loyal foreword to Jardine's book on the tour, was invited to the wedding. Warner was not. In 1937 Jardine returned briefly to first-class cricket and made 50 and 47 for Free Foresters against Cambridge University. For some who shared the cricket field with him in club cricket and special matches, whether he batted, fielded or umpired, he was an object of fascination in view of his special fame; some others, though perhaps a distinct minority, will have seen him only as a figure of infamy, with Bodyline the ever-lingering stigma.

His sardonic humour was never far away. He revealed that he bought his I Zingari tie at King's Cross station rather than from the Savile Row suppliers, thus saving half the price. He excelled at golf when the "whoof" system was played. Each player was allowed three whoofs during the round to distract his opponent. Jardine usually won without uttering a whoof but merely threatening to do so, that tight mouth pursed.[18]

By 1939 he was writing for the *Telegraph* — and well, too, having learned to relax. After war broke out he was commissioned into the Royal Berkshire Regiment, the "Iron Duke" in uniform at last at the age of 39. He went into Belgium to make contact with a platoon, only to find that it had been wiped out. Stranded, this man who by Bill Bowes's reckoning had so much courage he would have tackled lions bare-handed, now commandeered a troop-carrier and drove himself through the enemy lines back to Boulogne. With his feet badly cut, he volunteered to go in and help hold Calais, but his commanding officer refused him. Only single men were to remain. From the confusion on the beaches of Dunkirk he was among the last to escape back to England. For a time amidst that organised pandemonium he lost contact with his batman, but they were eventually reunited and scrambled aboard a vessel named HMS *Verity*. "We're bound to be all right now, sir," said the batman. "She's called after your favourite bowler."[19]

For a time he was a staff officer in St Albans, arranging transport. A fellow officer found him polite, shy and diffident, the humour peeping out again as he jested that the War Office might send him to serve as liaison officer with the Australian Army. Though it meant leaving Margaret and his young family, he was probably not altogether disappointed to be sent to India for the rest of the war, posted to Quetta and then Simla. His biographer has suggested a reason why Jardine, the great England cricket captain, was not used in Britain and Europe but rather sent to a marginal war sector: "He was unwilling to submit to the sort of authority for which he had no respect. [There is something very Australian about that.] In the army, his concern for the problems and welfare of those under his command lessened his effectiveness as a leader in the eyes of his superiors. Humanity, the very quality he has been said to have lacked, prevented him from being given more crucial work."[20]

Dennis Castle, an actor and writer, befriended him in India. He had been "barracked" by Jardine during a stage routine at the troops' Gaiety Theatre in Simla. "What guard do you want with that?" he called out when Castle came on stage with an enormous double bass. Castle gave him a reply with a Bodyline connotation, and later wrote: "I felt his wiles would have been better employed combating Rommel in the desert than handing out military provisions in that Kipling Raj backwater. When we had sundown drinks together, he would speak almost longingly of his boyhood there. We even played a couple of cricket matches there, but Indian umpires were far too eager for his scalp for him to enjoy them."[21]

With peacetime's return, Jardine and his family lived for a time in Drayton, Somerset before moving to Radlett, and he obtained employment as paper manufacturers Wiggins Teape's company secretary. By now he had a strong interest in Hinduism, and used Hindustani almost as a second language. The man once dubbed by R.W.E. Wilmot as The High Priest now frowned upon several aspects of Christianity, having been particularly disillusioned by the religious undercurrents of the Abdication (King Edward VIII's, not his own).

Wearing his Harlequin cap, he scored a polished 54 in the Surrey Centenary match at The Oval in the spring of 1946, but in the following winter his father, Malcolm, died, at the age of 77. In his obituary in *Wisden* it was cheekily observed that his son had led England successfully in 1932–33, the bowling, described as "body-line", "since copied by Australian teams without objection by England or adverse criticism".

DRJ himself was a loving but none too tolerant father. Watching two of his daughters playing cricket at their boarding school, he was so disappointed when they were out for next to nothing that he turned away in disgust, gasping "Jesus wept!"[22]

In the cricket Press box, where he was now something of a fixture, he had made the same early mistake so many newcomers commit to this day, transgressing against the unwritten rule which forbids applause. Jardine, as J.M. Kilburn remembered, "once stood up in the Lord's Pressbox to clap an outgoing batsman. Nobody spoke a word; nobody moved or so much as creaked a chair or shuffled a foot. Jardine's burst of clapping stuttered, slowed and ceased. In impressive silence he sat down."[23]

He performed some radio work, his delivery slow and his tone suggestive of an undertaker. It provided a modicum of extra income, challenging his view, expressed in a pre-war speech to the English Speaking Union in London, that international cricket had outlived its usefulness beyond raising money for the county clubs.

Bill O'Reilly, than whom no cricketer developed a deeper contempt for Jardine in 1932–33, found him friendly and agreeable, not only at a dinner he gave in the Masters' rooms at Trinity College, Oxford in 1953 but also in the Press box — long, angular, red-faced (O'Reilly called him Hiawatha) and forbidding yet human, even shyish. "I was thunderstruck. Surely this was not the same bloke?" said the old Tiger. "I liked him, and I told him so."[24] They sat beside each other at a dinner at London's Savoy Hotel when Sir Robert Menzies was holding forth: "I'm certain that there are very many Australians who think I'm the greatest bastard that ever stood in their country…" At that point Jardine leaned across to O'Reilly and remarked: "Bill, the honourable gentleman is misinformed. He could never possibly be more than number two."[25]

Having become a director of the Scottish Australian Company, with interests in sheep farming, Jardine faced a business trip to Australia with some trepidation — before receiving assurances from Jack Fingleton, as had

Larwood a few years earlier. So, against all probability, D.R. Jardine returned to Australia and had a most pleasant time of it. Prime Minister Menzies was quick to arrange a reunion lunch at the Pickwick Club, attended also by Charlie Macartney, Warren Bardsley, Johnny Taylor, Arthur Mailey, Bert Oldfield and Harold Larwood. Macartney predictably told Larwood he would have belted Bodyline, and Taylor said he could have played it with a broomstick.[26]

What stretched credulity for anyone who had been around at the time of the Bodyline summer was an invitation by an *Australian* radio station to *Douglas Jardine* to feature in a programme called *Guest of Honour*. He told somebody during that visit: "Though they may not hail me [in Australia] as Uncle Doug, I am no longer the bogeyman — just an old so-and-so who got away with it."[27]

In 1951 he had written (from 1 Hyde Park Place) to commentator John Arlott thanking him for two tickets to the Lord's Taverners Ball: "I will put on a dinner jacket and come and should the Duke of Edinburgh wish me to be introduced to him I shall gladly be introduced. Good luck with your new role in 'Twenty Questions'. You must be one of the busiest men in the country today."[28] It might have been that evening that Jardine confided to Arlott: "You know, we nearly didn't do it. The little man was bloody good."[29]

This strange man, who could shed tears of laughter at *The Goon Show*, who would buy a handful of shares in a company just so that he could attend the annual meeting, who umpired Amersham's centenary cricket match in a trilby hat and smoking a pipe, could just as easily revert to the petulant oyster of 1933, as when a reporter from Sydney was given a 40-minute interview with him in London shortly before his death. Who, in his opinion, was the greatest batsman? "Oh, Jack Hobbs," he said, smoking away placidly. Hobbs, he emphasised, was so good on bad wickets. "Is that why you put him above Bradman?" the writer followed up. Jardine gazed out of the office window and said absently: "Hobbs, yes" — leaving the interviewer to conclude that for the former England captain, Don Bradman did not exist.[30] Perhaps any temptation to speak kindly of the Australian had been stubbed out by an incident in 1948. Some of the younger Australians on tour were invited by Jardine for drinks. As a matter of courtesy they sought clearance from their captain. Bradman withheld it.

Probably the last recording of Jardine's voice was made during a BBC television interview in 1957. Standing at the front of his house, wearing a dark suit and looking more genial than of old because his face was fuller, he recalled how Larwood would subconsciously rub his knuckles on his shirt-front to clean off the dust which attached as his hand scraped the ground in the followthrough. "It was then," said his proud captain, "that I knew that everything was going just as it should and that 'the machine' was in perfect working order."

In 1957 Jardine went to Rhodesia (now Zimbabwe) on business. He took his second daughter with him. The trip was her 21st birthday present. There he contracted tick fever, and upon his return to London he was found to have lung cancer. Seeking relief from breathing difficulties, he went to a clinic in Montreux, Switzerland, and there he died on June 18, 1958, at the age of 57.

The England v New Zealand Test match at Lord's began next day, and MCC made sure that the flags were lowered to half-mast, a proper gesture that still bore a certain emotional complexity for those who knew their history or had actually been part of it.

Jardine's ashes were scattered on the heights of Cross Craigs, Perthshire.

Bill Woodfull generously said: "Australian sportsmen will mourn the loss of a great cricketer and captain." Sir Pelham Warner wrote a warm obituary, and at the memorial service Sir Hubert Ashton spoke of Jardine's unusual air and marked him as someone who was many things: provocative, austere, brusque, shy, humble, thoughtful, kindly, proud, sensitive, single-minded, and possessed of immense moral and physical courage. These characteristics are easily substantiated and surely demand a reassessment of one of cricket history's most extraordinary figures. In his elegant reworking of the Bodyline story in 1982, Ronald Mason coupled Jardine's name with that of A.W. Carr in a lament: "These two gifted players, who had each given great pleasure of varying kinds in their characteristically individual fashions, disappeared with small thanks from the sight of a public that owed them more than they cared to remember."[31]

When asked for his reaction to the news of Jardine's death, Sir Donald Bradman offered no comment.[32]

Douglas Jardine's widow later lived in Malta, then Guernsey. She burned his clothes and cricket gear — including the moth-eaten Harlequin cap.

It has long fascinated people passing through the Long Room at Lord's to see the stern oil portraits of Bradman and Jardine in close proximity to each other. That mischievous juxtaposition seems about to end. In 2002, the new MCC president, Ted Dexter, set out to remove Jardine's portrait and have it hung elsewhere. It seems he thought that the sight of it upset Australian visitors — some of whom, no doubt, wished that the subject himself had dangled from a cord in 1933. Not everybody concurs.

The shockwaves and repercussions of Bodyline bowling in 1932–33 should have prompted strict and immediate amendments to cricket's laws to safeguard it against intimidatory bowling for ever more. There were enough cricket-loving lawyers in London and around the world at that time for this to have been undertaken successfully. Instead, following the period of restraint which was the immediate legacy of the events of '32–33, far greater outrages of sustained hostility have been inflicted on international cricket since the Second World War. The aesthetics of batsmanship have been more severely damaged in recent years than during '32–33, when the hostile bursts were intermittent and drives, late cuts and glances were still to be seen for much of the day's play.

It took over a quarter of a century for the limitation on the number of leg-side fieldsmen to be adopted, and then it was introduced as a counter to negative rather than over-aggressive cricket at a time when offbreak bowlers and inswing merchants proliferated. Five on-side fieldsmen would be the maximum allowed, with no more than two behind the popping-crease, a restriction later amended — Law 41.5 The Fielder — to embrace only the two behind square.

The 2000 code of the Laws of Cricket introduced a preamble, clause 6 of which states: "There is no place for any act of violence on the field of play." We shall never know whether the embattled umpires of the 1980s — or Borwick and Hele during the hellfire days of '32–33 — would have used this sanction to curb underpitched fast bowling.

It is a long time since it was first suggested (in the hope that the game might be cleansed of intimidation) that a severe runs penalty be imposed against bowlers who overdid the bouncer. This would have made life easier for umpires, the majority of whom have been far too chicken-hearted to intervene. Nor have they always been certain of resolute backing from the authorities — in respect of stamping out either chucking or intimidation.

In certain parts of the world umpires have not even been sure of their own personal safety.

In an era of widespread shortage of self-control on the cricket field, the more businesslike ICC of today has worked hard at eradicating on-field misbehaviour by international cricketers, drafting an elaborate Players' Code of Conduct which empowers umpires and referees as never before and seemingly backs them without any equivocation. The officials are even given some legal training now to help them deal with behavioural problems.

While the limitation of the number of bouncers per over has gone some way towards restoring the game's health at long last, it can only be regretted that it took so long for the wit and resolve to do this to be found. The control has come too late for the legion of batsmen who have had their innings or careers terminated — through dismissal or injury — by muggers posing as fast bowlers.

And yet ... if the likes of Bill O'Reilly, who wholly detested D.R. Jardine during the tempestuous Bodyline series, were later capable of forgiving his violation of the spirit of cricket, and if we accept Jack Fingleton's considered remark in later life — "I think, looking back, the Australians perhaps made too much fuss about it"[33] — might we not find it in our hearts to be as charitable, particularly since, after all, the game has been saved by the renascence of spin bowling in the 1990s? Perhaps it's worth a try. So long as there is no recurrence.

ENDNOTES

PREFACE

1 Letter to the author, May 11, 1993
2 Letter to the author, May 17, 1986
3 *Daily Telegraph*, July 31, 1995
4 *Sunday Telegraph*, May 28, 2000

CHAPTER I ORIGINS

1 "Leg Theory" (Columbia DB 1140) (1933)
2 *Cricket, Lovely Cricket*, Frank Lee (Stanley Paul, 1960), p. 47
3 Alf Gover, in *Surrey CCC Yearbook*
4 *Wisden Cricket Monthly*, February 2002
5 *Sydney Morning Herald* article, Philip Derriman, 1998
6 *Fabulous Furphies*, Edward Docker and Lynette Silver (Milner, 1997)
7 *Test Tussles On and Off the Field*, D.K. Darling (Private, 1969), p. 37
8 *Cricket and I*, Learie Constantine (Allen, 1933), p. 186
9 *Cricket in the Sun*, Learie Constantine (Stanley Paul, 1946), p. 55
10 *Cricket and I*, Constantine, pp. 192, 195
11 *Letting Rip*, Simon Wilde (Witherby, 1994), pp. 212–14

CHAPTER 2 THE TARGET — THE SNIPERS

1 *My Cricketing Life*, Don Bradman (Stanley Paul, 1938), p.102
2 *Between Wickets*, Ray Robinson (Collins, 1949), p. 73
3 Harry Gordon's essay on Buggy in *The Makers of Australia's Sporting History*, ed. Michael McKernan (Melbourne University Press, 1993)
4 *Cricketers' Tales*, presented by Tim Bowden (Australian Broadcasting Commission, 1975)
5 *Farewell to Cricket*, Don Bradman (Hodder & Stoughton, 1950), p. 75
6 Letter to the author, September 13, 1989
7 *Cricket Crisis*, Jack Fingleton (Cassell, 1946), p. 40
8 *The Badminton Library: Cricket*, P.F. Warner (Longmans, Green, 1920), p. 149
9 *Long Innings*, Sir Pelham Warner (Harrap, 1951), p. 140
10 *Cricket, Lovely Cricket*, Lee, p. 49
11 *Cricket With the Lid Off*, A.W. Carr (Hutchinson, 1935), p. 49
12 *Never a Cross Bat*, Tom Reddick (Nelson, 1979), p. 68
13 *Basingstoke Boy*, John Arlott (CollinsWillow, 1990), p. 63
14 *Dai Davies Not Out . . . 78* (Dyfed, 1975), p. 27
15 *Cricket, Lovely Cricket*, Lee, p. 24

16 *Sort of a Cricket Person*, E.W.Swanton (Collins, 1972), p. 67
17 *Cricket Crisis*, Fingleton, pp. 42–43
18 *Follow On*, E.W.Swanton (Collins, 1977), p. 147
19 Related to the author by Jardine's daughter Fianach, February 2002

CHAPTER 3 SOUTHWARD HO

1   *Plum Warner*, Gerald Howat (Unwin Hyman, 1987), p. 109
2   *Wisden Cricket Monthly*, January 1996, p. 8: *The Duleep Papers* (Sussex County Record Office,Chichester)
3   *My Cricketing Reminiscences*, Maurice Tate (Stanley Paul, 1934), p. 176
4   *Express Deliveries*, Bill Bowes (Stanley Paul, 1949), p. 96
5   *Cricket and Empire*, Ric Sissons and Brian Stoddart (Allen & Unwin, 1984), p. 50
6   *A Cuckoo in the Bodyline Nest*, Gilbert Mant (Kangaroo Press, 1992), p. 95
7   *Sort of a Cricket Person*, Swanton, p. 17
8   ibid., p. 19
9   *Some of It Was Cricket*, Frank Browne (Murray, 1965), p. 35
10 Author's collection
11 Letter to the author, October 27, 1958
12 *Hedley Verity: A Portrait of a Cricketer*, Alan Hill (Kingswood, 1986), p. 47
13 Verity's diary entries, quoted in Hill's biography
14 *Cricket All the Way*, Eddie Paynter (A. Richardson, 1962), p. 21
15 *Cricket My Destiny*, Walter R.Hammond (Stanley Paul, 1946), p. 85
16 *Defending the Ashes 1932–1933*, R.W.E. Wilmot (Robertson & Mullens, 1933) p. 31
17 *Hedley Verity*, Hill pp. 134–38
18 *Defending the Ashes 1932–1933*, Wilmot, p. 38
19 *R.E.S. Wyatt – Fighting Cricketer*, Gerald Pawle (Allen & Unwin, 1985) p. 94
20 *Express Deliveries*, Bowes, p. 113
21 *R.E.S. Wyatt – Fighting Cricketer*, Pawle, p. 93
22 ibid., p. 94
23 *The Larwood Story*, Harold Larwood with Kevin Perkins (W.H. Allen, 1965), p. 83
24 *Bradman*, Charles Williams (Little, Brown, 1996), p. 90

CHAPTER 4 THE MAN IN THE HARLEQUIN CAP

1   *The WACA: An Australian Cricket Success Story*, Anthony J. Barker (Allen & Unwin, 1998), p. 99
2   *Cricket Crisis*, Fingleton, p. 99
3   *Cricket and Empire*, Sissons and Stoddart, p. 58
4   *The Larwood Story*, Larwood, p. 84
5   *Cricket My Desiny*, Hammond, p. 86
6   *Memorable Cricket Matches*, Sir Geoffrey Tomkinson (G.T.Cheshire, 1958), p. 62
7   *With the 15th Australian XI*, Sydney Smith Jr (E.T.Kibblewhite, 1922), p. 65
8   Hendry, in conversation with the author, 1975
9   *94 Declared: Cricket Reminiscences*, Ben Travers (Elm Tree, 1981), p. 38
10 ibid., p. 43
11 *100 Not Out: A Century of Cricket on the Adelaide Oval*, Sidney Downer (Rigby, 1972), p. 151
12 *For England and Yorkshire*, Herbert Sutcliffe (Edward Arnold, 1935), p. 117
13 *McGilvray: Captains of the Game*, as told to Norman Tasker (ABC Books, 1992), p. 72
14 *10 for 66 and All That*, Arthur Mailey (Phoenix, 1958), p. 127
15 Reproduced in Knight's Sporting Memorabilia Auctions' catalogue February 3, 4, 2001
16 Article in *The Australian*, 1995

CHAPTER 5 ACROSS THE WIDE BROWN LAND

[1] *Cricket Crisis,* Fingleton, p. 28
[2] *The WACA,* Barber, p. 101
[3] *Cricket Crisis,* Fingleton, p. 48
[4] ibid., p. 49
[5] *Sir Donald Bradman: A Biography,* Irving Rosenwater (Batsford, 1978), p. 175
[6] ibid., p. 177
[7] *Batting from Memory,* Jack Fingleton (Collins, 1981), p. 113
[8] *The Vic Richardson Story,* V.Y. Richardson (Angus & Robertson, 1968), p. 59
[9] *Cricket My Destiny,* Hammond, p. 88
[10] *The History of the South Australian Cricket Assocation,* Chris Harte (Sports Marketing, 1990), p. 268
[11] *The Australian Cricketer Autumn Annual 1932–33,* p. 9
[12] *The Vic Richardson Story,* Richardson, p. 123
[13] *Three Straight Sticks,* R.E.S. Wyatt (Stanley Paul, 1951), p. 86
[14] *Express Deliveries,* Bowes, p. 100
[15] *R.E.S. Wyatt – Fighting Cricketer,* Pawle, p. 215
[16] *Time of the Tiger: The Bill O'Reilly Story,* R.S. Whitington (Stanley Paul, 1970), pp. 179–80
[17] *The Larwood Story,* Larwood, p. 84
[18] *Plum Warner,* Howat, p. 112–13
[19] *Bodyline,* Philip Derriman (Collins, 1984), p. 54
[20] *Cricket Crisis,* Fingleton, p. 89
[21] *Three Straight Sticks,* Wyatt, p. 88
[22] *The Fight for the Ashes 1932–33,* J.B.Hobbs (Harrap, 1933), p. 43
[23] *Some of It Was Cricket,* Browne, p. 36
[24] *Seasons in the Sun: The Story of the Victorian Cricket Association,* Robert Coleman (Hargreen, 1993), p. 396
[25] ibid., p. 398
[26] *"Tiger" – 60 Years in Cricket,* Bill O'Reilly (Collins, 1985), p. 81
[27] Letter to the author from Percy Taylor, an *Argus* sportswriter (1923–57), December 2, 1990
[28] *Never a Dull Moment,* Trevor Wignall (Hutchinson, 1940), p. 129
[29] *True to the Blue: A History of the New South Wales Cricket Association,* Philip Derriman (Richard Smart, 1985), p. 154
[30] *Cricket Crisis,* Fingleton, p. 61
[31] *McGilvray: Captains of the Game,* Tasker, p. 73
[32] *Douglas Jardine: Spartan Cricketer,* Christopher Douglas (Allen & Unwin, 1984), p. 59
[33] *Cricket Crisis,* Fingleton, p. 63
[34] *Bradman and the Bodyline Series,* Edward Wybergh Docker (Angus & Robertson, 1978), p. 98
[35] *P.G.H. Fender: A Biography,* Richard Streeton (Faber, 1981), p. 148
[36] Quoted in *Plum Warner,* Howat, p. 110
[37] *Plum Warner,* Howat, p. 113
[38] From a letter written by Lady Game, quoted in *Bodyline,* Derriman, p. 74

CHAPTER 6 THE MAGIC OF McCABE

[1] *Australian Cricket Anecdotes,* ed. Gideon Haigh (Oxford University Press, 1996), p. 95
[2] John Arlott article in *Test Match Special,* ed. Peter Baxter (Queen Anne, 1981), p. 11
[3] Letter to the author, April 27, 1991
[4] *Bodyline Umpire,* R.S. Whitington and George Hele (Rigby, 1974), p. 18
[5] ibid., p. 54
[6] *The Oxford Companion to Australian Cricket,* ed. Richard Cashman, Warwick Franks, Jim Maxwell, Brian Stoddart, Amanda Weaver, Ray Webster (Oxford University Press, 1996), p. 71
[7] BBC Radio interview (John Dunn) in 1982, marking Allen's 80th birthday
[8] *The Game Goes On,* Denzil Batchelor (Eyre & Spottiswoode, 1947), p. 56

9   *Bodyline Umpire,* Whitington and Hele, p. 103
10 *The Game Goes On,* Batchelor, p. 54
11 *Between Wickets,* Robinson, p. 38
12 *"Tiger"– 60 Years in Cricket,* O'Reilly, p. 85
13 *Ray Lindwall: Cricket Legend,* John Ringwood (Kangaroo Press, 1995), p. 14
14 *80 Not Out: A Celebration of Test Cricket at the Sydney Cricket Ground,* Philip Derriman (Playbill, 1994), p. 70
15 ibid., p. 70 (McCabe interview with Alan Trengrove, 1965)
16 *Bodyline,* Derriman, p. 19
17 *'Ave a Go, Yer Mug!,* Richard Cashman (Collins, 1984), p. 76
18 *Bradman and the Bodyline Series,* Docker, p. 100
19 *Bodyline Umpire,* Whitington and Hele, p. 105
20 *The Game Goes On,* Batchelor, p. 61
21 *Time of the Tiger,* Whitington, p. 175
22 *Bodyline Umpire,* Whitington and Hele, p. 107
23 *The Larwood Story,* Larwood, p. 106
24 *Cricket Crisis,* Fingleton, p. 80
25 *True to the Blue,* Derriman, p. 156
26 *Bodyline,* Derriman, p. 107
27 *Plum Warner,* Howat, p. 114
28 *Body-Line?,* Harold Larwood (Elkin Mathews & Marrot, 1933), p. 72

CHAPTER 7 DON'S ODD DOUBLE

1   *Bradman,* A.G. Moyes (Harrap, 1948), p. 49
2   *Between Wickets,* Robinson, p. 91
3   *Bradman: the Illustrated Biography,* Michael Page (Macmillan, 1983), p. 179
4   Conversation with the author, December 2002
5   *Plum Warner,* Howat, p. 115
6   *46 Not Out,* R.C. Robertson-Glasgow (Hollis & Carter, 1948), p. 108
7   *"My Dear Victorious Stod",* David Frith (Lutterworth, 1977), p. 160
8   *Bodyline Umpire,* Whitington and Hele, pp. 109–10
9   *A History of Australian Cricket,* Chris Harte (Deutsche, 1993), p. 346
10 *Island Summers: a History of Tasmanian Representative Cricket,* Ric Finlay (St David's Park, 1992), p. 83
11 Mitchell interview by Stephen Brenkley, *Independent on Sunday,* December 18, 1994
12 *Bodyline Umpire,* Whitington and Hele, p. 115
13 *The Paddock That Grew: The Story of the Melbourne Cricket Club,* Keith Dunstan (Cassell, 1974), p. 141
14 Interview in *Bodyline,* a television programme aired in *Sports Arena,* April 12, 1970, presented by Ian Wooldridge
15 *And Then Came Larwood: An Account of the Test Matches 1932–33,* Arthur Mailey (Bodley Head, 1933), p. 63
16 *In Quest of the Ashes,* D.R. Jardine (Hutchinson, 1933), p. 111
17 *My Cricketing Life,* Bradman, p. 96
18 *Express Deliveries,* Bowes, p. 107
19 *Extra Cover* – interviews by Jack Egan (Pan, 1989), p. 133
20 *Batting from Memory,* Fingleton, p. 122
21 *Sir Donald Bradman,* Rosenwater, p. 187
22 *The Paddock That Grew: The Story of the Melbourne Cricket Club,* Dunstan, p. 157
23 O'Brien interview by the author, *Wisden Cricket Monthly,* April 1983
24 Wyatt in *Bodyline (Forty Minutes,* BBC Television, produced by Alan Patient, 1983)
25 *Defending the Ashes 1932–1933,* Wilmot, p. 104
26 *Afternoon Light,* Sir Robert Menzies (Cassell, 1967), p. 353
27 *The Australian Cricketer Autumn Annual 1932–1933,* p. 150

[28] *Cricket My Destiny,* Hammond, p. 93

[29] *The Match I Remember,* Denzil Batchelor (Werner Laurie, 1950), p. 183

[30] *Cricket My World,* Walter R. Hammond (Stanley Paul, 1948), p. 164

[31] *Defending the Ashes 1932–1933,* Wilmot, p. 91

[32] *The Australian Cricketer Autumn Annual 1932–1933,* p. 79

[33] *Bodyline Umpire,* Whitington and Hele, p. 127

[34] *In Quest of the Ashes,* Jardine, p. 24

[35] *The Barracker at Bay: An Outspoken Reply to Bodyliners,* A Barracker (R.T. Corrie) (Keating-Wood, 1933), p. 30

CHAPTER 8 ADELAIDE EARTHQUAKE

[1] *Cricket Between Two Wars,* Sir Pelham Warner (Chatto & Windus, 1942), pp. 134–35

[2] *The Larwood Story,* Larwood, pp. 123–24

[3] *Bendigo District Cricket 1853–1990,* John Harris and Ken Wust (Crown Castleton, 1991), p. 22

[4] *In Quest of the Ashes,* Jardine, p. 127

[5] *SACA history,* Harte, p. 268

[6] *My Cricketing Reminiscences,* Tate, pp. 195–96

[7] *Adelaide Oval Test Cricket 1884–1984,* Bernard Whimpress and Nigel Hart (Wakefield/SACA, 1984), p. 89

[8] *SACA history,* Harte, p. 268

[9] *Our Don Bradman,* ed. Philip Derriman (ABC Books, 2001), p. 95

[10] *My Cricketing Life,* Bradman, p. 98

[11] *"Tiger" – 60 Years in Cricket,* O'Reilly, p. 91

[12] *R.E.S. Wyatt – Fighting Cricketer,* Pawle, p. 98

[13] *Three Straight Sticks,* Wyatt, p. 96

[14] *Defending the Ashes 1932–1933,* Wilmot, p. 95

[15] *Bodyline Umpire,* Whitington and Hele, p. 128

[16] *Bodyline,* BBC Television, 1983

[17] *Cricket All the Way,* Paynter, p. 33

[18] *The Larwood Story,* Larwood, p. 117

[19] *Ponsford and Woodfull: A Premier Partnership,* Marc Fiddian (Five Mile Press, 1988), p. 103

[20] *Mr Cricket: The Autobiography of W.H. Ferguson, BEM,* as told to David Jack (Nicholas Kaye, 1957), p. 39

[21] *Cricket Crisis,* Fingleton, p. 91

[22] *The Wildest Tests,* Ray Robinson (Pelham, 1972), p. 31

[23] ibid., p. 31

[24] *Cricket Between Two Wars,* Warner, p. 129

[25] *Cricket Crisis,* Fingleton, p. 18

[26] *Mr Cricket,* Ferguson, p. 39

[27] Interview in *Wisden Cricket Monthly,* April 1983

[28] *Cricket Crisis,* Fingleton, p. 70

[29] *Fingleton on Cricket,* Jack Fingleton (Collins, 1972), p. 207

[30] Mitchell Library, Sydney collection; quoted in *The Bulletin,* July 26, 1994

[31] *"Tiger" – 60 Years of Cricket,* O'Reilly, p. 114

[32] *The Immortal Victor Trumper,* J.H. Fingleton (Collins, 1978), p. 108

[33] *Bradman: The Illustrated Biography,* Michael Page (Macmillan, 1983), p. 185

[34] *R.E.S. Wyatt – Fighting Cricketer,* Pawle, p. 100

[35] *Anglo-Australian Attitudes,* Michael Davie (Secker & Warburg, 2000), p. 107

[36] *Plum Warner,* Howat, p. 132

[37] *Adelaide Oval Test Cricket 1884–1984,* Whimpress and Hart, p. 92

[38] *Cricket Between Two Wars,* Warner, p. 128

[39] *Bodyline Umpire,* Whitington and Hele, p. 130

[40] *My Cricketing Reminiscences,* Tate, p. 196

[41] *Behind the Wicket: My Cricketing Reminiscences,* W.A. "Bert" Oldfield (Hutchinson, 1938), p. 90

42 *Time of the Tiger,* Whitington, p. 175
43 *The Bradman Era,* recalled by Bill O'Reilly; compiled by Jack Egan (ABC Books/Collins, 1983), p. 65
44 *The Larwood Story,* Larwood, p. 11
45 80th birthday interview (with John Dunn), BBC Radio, 1982
46 Interview by Trent Bouts in *Herald–Sun,* January 22, 1993
47 *100 Not Out: A Century of Cricket on the Adelaide Oval,* Downer, p. 105
48 ibid., p. 106
49 *A Cuckoo in the Bodyline Nest,* Mant, p. 100
50 ibid., p. 106
51 *Between Wickets,* Robinson, pp. 84–85
52 In conversation with the author
53 *Seasons in the Sun,* Coleman, p. 396
54 *Body-Line?,* Larwood, p. 135
55 Quoted in *The Bodyline Controversy,* Laurence Le Quesne (Secker & Warburg, 1983), p. 38
56 *Body-Line?,* Larwood, p. 71
57 *Cricket With the Lid Off,* Carr, p. 65
58 *Bodyline,* Derriman, p. 39
59 *In Quest of the Ashes,* Jardine, pp. 151–52
60 *Walter Hammond: A Cricketing Great* (HTV Video, 1987)
61 *Bradman and the Bodyline Series,* Docker, p. 116
62 *Cricket Heroes,* ed. John Kay (Phoenix House, 1959), pp. 40–41
63 *The Larwood Story,* Larwood, p. 150
64 *Bradman and the Bodyline Series,* Docker, p. 111

CHAPTER 9 CABLES AND LABELS

1 *A Cuckoo in the Bodyline Nest,* Mant, p. 99
2 *Cricket My Destiny,* Hammond, p. 96
3 *The Vic Richardson Story,* Richardson, p. 60
4 *Bodyline,* BBC Television, 1983
5 *Plum Warner,* Howat, p. 120
6 *Bodyline,* Derriman, p. 147
7 *Cricket and Empire,* Sissons and Stoddart, p. 93
8 ibid., p. 59
9 ibid., p. 76
10 *True to the Blue,* Derriman, p. 157
11 ibid., p. 158
12 *Cricket and Empire,* Sissons and Stoddart, p. 102
13 *Bodyline,* Derriman, p. 21
14 *Cricket Crisis,* Fingleton, p. 104
15 *Follow On,* Swanton, p. 150
16 Letters quoted from *The Way to Lord's: Cricketing Letters to The Times,* selected by Marcus Williams (Willow, 1983)
17 *Cricket Crisis,* Fingleton, p. 79
18 *The King of Games,* Frank Woolley (Stanley Paul, 1936), p. 135
19 *The Biography of Colonel His Highness Shri Sir Ranjitsinhji Vibhaji, Maharaja Jam Saheb of Nawanagar, GCSI, GBE, KCIE,* Roland Wild (Rich & Cowan, 1934), p. 298
20 Christie's, Melbourne, June 27, 1999
21 *Alan McGilvray's Backpage of Cricket,* with Norman Tasker (Lester-Townsend, 1989), p. 16
22 *Anti Body-line,* Alan Kippax (Hurst & Blackett, 1933), p. 53
23 Fully reproduced in *The Bradman Albums: Volume I 1925–1934* (Queen Anne, 1987), p. 335

CHAPTER 10 SILENT MANOEUVRES

1 *Bodyline,* Derriman, p. 22
2 *Follow On,* Swanton, p. 142
3 *Plum Warner,* Howat, p. 116
4 *Dictionary of National Biography*
5 *The Larwood Story,* Larwood, pp. 201–202
6 *Anglo-Australian Relations,* Davie, pp. 40–47
7 *Plum Warner,* Howat, p. 122
8 *The Bodyline Controversy,* Le Quesne, p. 123
9 *Cricket Crisis,* Fingleton, p. 107
10 *Cricket and Empire,* Sissons and Stoddart, p. 105
11 Letter (January 26, 1933) in MCC Collection (ex Legh Winser)

CHAPTER 11 FROM A HOSPITAL BED

1 Quoted in *Plum Warner,* Howat, p. 128
2 *The Larwood Story,* Larwood, p. 125
3 *Ponsford and Woodfull: A Premier Partnership,* Fiddian, p. 105
4 ibid., p. 105
5 *Mr Cricket,* Ferguson, p. 42
6 *The Barracker at Bay,* Corrie, p. 13
7 *My Cricketing Reminiscences,* Tate, p. 198
8 *Green Hills to the Gabba,* Ian Diehm (Playright, 2000), p. 163
9 *A Cuckoo in the Bodyline Nest,* Mant, p. 117
10 *Retailed in Bodyline,* Derriman, p. 140
11 *Cricket All the Way,* Paynter, p. 40
12 *Afternoon Light,* Menzies, p. 355
13 *Fingleton on Cricket,* p. 209
14 *Cricket Crisis,* Fingleton, p. 65
15 *'Ave a Go, Yer Mug!,* Cashman, p. 75
16 ibid., p. 76
17 *Between Wickets,* Robinson, p. 87
18 *In Quest of the Ashes,* Jardine, p. 163
19 *On Top Down Under: Australia's Cricket Captains,* Ray Robinson (Cassell, 1975), p. 161
20 *Mr Cricket,* Ferguson, p. 43
21 *Bodyline Umpire,* Whitington and Hele, p. 170
22 Letter to the author, c 1977
23 *Long Innings,* Warner, p. 141
24 *Mr Cricket,* Ferguson, p. 45
25 *Bodyline Umpire,* Whitington and Hele, p. 173
26 *Jardine Justified: The Truth about the Ashes,* Bruce Harris (Chapman & Hall, 1933), p. 156
27 *A Superb Century: 100 Years of the Gabba 1895–1995,* Wayne Smith (Focus, 1995), p. 68
28 *"Tiger" – 60 Years in Cricket,* O'Reilly, p. 100
29 ibid., p. 101
30 *Archie Jackson: The Keats of Cricket,* David Frith (Pavilion, 1987), p. 105
31 *Sir Donald Bradman,* Rosenwater, p. 204
32 *The Larwood Story,* Larwood, pp. 162–63

CHAPTER 12 THE FINAL SHOOT-OUT

1 *Runs, Wickets and Reminiscence: The NDCA's First 100 Years,* George Piggford and John Hay (NDCA, 1989), p. 33
2 *Oxford Companion to Australian Cricket,* p. 452
3 *Three Straight Sticks,* Wyatt, p. 105

4   *Defending the Ashes 1932–1933*, Wilmot, p. 207
5   *46 Not Out*, Robertson-Glasgow, p. 168
6   *Body-Line?*, Larwood, p. 104
7   *The Poms Down Under*, BBC Radio 5, 1994
8   *The Larwood Story*, Larwood, p. 166
9   Letter to the author from Queensland cricket connoisseur and collector P.J. Mullins
10 *"Tiger" – 60 Years in Cricket*, O'Reilly, p. 84
11 *Between Wickets*, Robinson, p. 86
12 *Oxford Companion to Australian Cricket*, p. 304
13 *Body-Line?*, Larwood, p. 153
14 *The Larwood Story*, Larwood, p. 168
15 *In Quest of the Ashes*, Jardine, p. 188
16 *80 Not Out*, Derriman, p. 84
17 Quoted in *Plum Warner*, Howat, p. 131
18 ibid., p. 131
19 *Cricket Crisis*, Fingleton, p. 64
20 *The Larwood Story*, Larwood, p. 171
21 *Bat and Ball: A New Book of Cricket*, ed. Thomas Moult (Arthur Barker, 1935), p. 86
22 *Bodyline Umpire*, Whitington and Hele, p. 182
23 Interview with Alexander by Philip Derriman, *Sydney Morning Herald*, February 6, 1993
24 ibid.
25 *Bodyline Umpire*, Whitington and Hele, p. 189

CHAPTER 13   SACKCLOTH AND ASHES

1   *Body-Line?*, Larwood, pp. 89–90
2   *Mr Cricket*, Ferguson, p. 36
3   *Plum Warner*, Howat, p. 131
4   *Extra Cover*, Egan, p. 134
5   Miller interview by the author, *Wisden Cricket Monthly*, November 1993
6   *Some of It Was Cricket*, Browne, p. 39
7   Claimed in a letter from author Allen Synge to Rowland Ryder, who reproduced the remarks in his book *Cricket Calling*, (Faber, 1995), p. 55
8   *Men in White: The History of New Zealand International Cricket 1894–1985*, Don Neely and Richard King (Moa, 1986), p. 133
9   Letter to the author, 1983
10 *Maurice Tate: A Biography*, Gerald Brodribb (London Magazine, 1976), p. 159
11 *Jardine Justified*, Harris, p. 135
12 *A Cuckoo in the Bodyline Nest*, Mant, pp. 128–29
13 *Cricket All the Way*, Paynter, p. 44
14 *Plum Warner*, Howat, pp. 132–33
15 *Gubby Allen: Man of Cricket*, E.W. Swanton (Hutchinson, 1985), pp. 141–42
16 *True to the Blue*, Derriman, pp. 158–59
17 *Hedley Verity*, Hill, p. 62
18 *Bodyline*, Derriman, p. 24
19 *Cricket Crisis*, Fingleton, p. 107
20 Bodyline letters in Boundary Books' catalogue, Spring 1998
21 *The Larwood Story*, Larwood, pp. 179–82
22 ibid., pp. 183–86
23 ibid., pp. 186–89
24 *Gubby Allen*, Swanton, p. 144
25 *Cricketers' School*, Walter Hammond (Stanley Paul, 1950), p. 53
26 *Walter Hammond: A Biography*, Ronald Mason (Hollis & Carter, 1962), p. 152
27 *Douglas Jardine*, Douglas, p. 157
28 *46 Not Out*, Robertson-Glasgow, p. 169

29 *"Tiger" Smith of Warwickshire and England: The Autobiography of E.J. Smith,* as told to Patrick Murphy (Lutterworth, 1981), p. 81

30 *Jack Grant's Story,* Jack Grant (Lutterworth, 1980), p. 172

31 *Cricket in the Sun,* Constantine, p. 60

32 *Cricket and I,* Constantine, pp. 194–97

33 *Bodyline,* Derriman, p. 100

34 Bodyline letters in Boundary Books' catalogue, Spring 1998

35 *Double Century: 200 Years of Cricket in The Times,* ed. Marcus Williams (Willow, 1985), pp. 287–88

36 *Cricketers' School,* Hammond, p. 54

37 *Tours and Tests,* Kenneth Farnes (Lutterworth, 1940), p. 46

38 *Cricket With the Lid Off,* Carr, p. 44

39 Quoted in *Cricket: A Weekly Record of the Game,* September 12, 1901, p. 402

40 *Cricket and Empire,* Sissons and Stoddart, p. 116

41 *Body-line?,* Larwood, p. 48

42 *Sir Donald Bradman,* Rosenwater, p. 201

43 *Lord's,* John Marshall (Pelham, 1969), p. 98

44 Letter in MCC archives

45 *Between Wickets,* Robinson, pp. 92–93

46 ibid., p. 94

47 Quoted in *Cricket and Empire,* Sissons and Stoddart, p. 125

48 Revealed by his son in a 1995 interview by Charles Williams: *Bradman,* p. 117

49 Letter in MCC archives

CHAPTER 14 CONSEQUENCES

1 *Cricket My World,* Hammond, p. 101

2 Taped interview by the author, March 18, 1970

3 *Bodyline,* Derriman, p. 25

4 *Was It All Cricket?,* Daniel Reese (Allen & Unwin, 1948), p. 430

5 Quoted in *Cricket and Empire,* Sissons and Stoddart, p. 24

6 Quoted in *The Story of Cricket in Australia,* Jack Egan (Macmillan, 1987), p. 160

7 *Cricket My Destiny,* Hammond, pp. 96–98

8 Quoted in Bat & Pad: *Writings on Australian Cricket 1804–2001,* compiled by Philip Derriman and Pat Mullins (Choice, 2001), p. 69

9 *The Don: A Bibliographical & Referential Journey,* compiled by Stephen W. Gibbs (privately published, 2001)

10 *Wisden Cricketers' Almanack 1963,* ed. Norman Preston (Sporting Handbooks), p. 72

11 In conversation with the author, May 3, 1991

12 *An Outdoor Wallah,* E.H.D. Sewell (Stanley Paul, 1945), p. 108

13 Quoted in Knight's auction catalogue, February 23, 2002

14 *History of Indian Cricket,* Edward Docker (Macmillan India, 1976), pp. 73–74

15 Quoted in *Follow On,* Swanton, p. 146

16 *Bodyline,* Derriman, p. 24

17 Quoted in *Cricket and Empire,* Sissons and Stoddart, p. 128

CHAPTER 15 THE CORPSE TWITCHES

1 Conversation with the author, March 2002

2 *The Larwood Story,* Larwood, p. 197

3 *Bodyline,* BBC Television, 1983

4 Bodyline letters in Boundary Books' catalogue, Spring 1998

5 *The Larwood Story,* Larwood, pp. 198–99

6 *Cricket Between Two Wars,* Warner, p. 158

7 *"Tiger" Smith,* Murphy, pp. 80–81

8   *"Tiger" – 60 Years in Cricket*, O'Reilly, pp. 125–26
9   From unpublished documents once belonging to Bushby, uncovered in 1990s by Rick Smith
10 *Express Deliveries*, Bowes, p. 120 (he mistakenly places it during the MCC v Australians match, in which he did not play)
11 *Between Wickets*, Robinson, p. 95
12 Bushby documents
13 *Cricket and Empire*, Sissons and Stoddart, p. 107
14 *Cricket Crisis*, Fingleton, p. 114
15 ibid., p. 11
16 *A Cuckoo in the Bodyline Nest*, Mant, p. 145
17 *Eighty Not Out: The Story of Arthur Richardson*, as told to Les R. Hill (privately published, 1968) p. 31
18 *The Great Laurie Nash*, E.A."Ned"Wallish (Ryan, 1998), pp. 80–82
19 ibid., p. 150
20 *Australian Summer: The Test Matches of 1936–7*, Neville Cardus (Hart-Davis, 1949), p. 174
21 *10 for 66 and All That*, Mailey, p. 158
22 *From the Boundary*, Ray Robinson (Collins, 1951), p. 156
23 Letter in *Wisden Cricket Monthly*, July 1995
24 *"Tiger" – 60 Years in Cricket*, O'Reilly, p. 97
25 *Cricket Caravan*, Keith Miller and R.S. Whitington (Latimer House, 1951), pp. 36–37
26 ibid., p. 37
27 *Plum Warner*, Howat, pp. 161–62
28 Bodyline letters in Boundary Books' catalogue, Spring 1998

CHAPTER 16   GATHERING OF THE GHOSTS

1   *Between Wickets*, Robinson, p. 94
2   *Cricket Crossfire*, Keith Miller (Oldbourne, 1956), pp. 32–33
3   *Cricket – The Silver Lining*, Cyril Washbrook (Sportsguide, 1950), p. 133
4   *Farewell to Cricket*, Bradman, p. 88
5   *From the Boundary*, Robinson, p. 160
6   *Batting from Memory*, Fingleton, p. 118
7   *Howzat! Sixteen Australian Cricketers Talk to Keith Butler* (Collins, 1979), p. 54
8   *Wisden Cricketers' Almanack 2002*, ed. Graeme Wright (John Wisden), p. 20
9   *Cricketing Legends: Sir Donald Bradman*, Jack Egan (BBC Sports Video, 1990)
10 *The Man They Couldn't Gag*, Peter Wilson (Stanley Paul, 1977), p. 93
11 *Three Straight Sticks*, Wyatt, p. 100
12 Letter to the author, October 26, 1992
13 *Wisden Cricket Monthly*, November 1981
14 *Harold Larwood: Famous Cricketers Series*, Peter Wynne-Thomas (Association of Cricket Statisticians)
15 Quoted in *The Bulletin*, July 26, 1994
16 *Behind the Wicket*, Oldfield, p. 205
17 Author's collection
18 *Douglas Jardine*, Douglas, p. 185
19 *Hedley Verity*, Hill, p. 142
20 *Douglas Jardine*, Douglas, p. 187
21 *Wisden Cricket Monthly*, March 1983
22 *Bodyline*, Derriman, p. 25
23 *Thanks to Cricket*, J.M. Kilburn (Stanley Paul, 1972), p. 57
24 *"Tiger" – 60 Years in Cricket*, O'Reilly, pp. 101–102
25 *The Penguin Book of Australian Sporting Anecdotes*, ed. Richard Smart (Penguin, 1996), p. 145
26 *The Larwood Story*, Larwood, p. 222
27 Quoted in *The Wildest Tests*, Robinson, p. 37
28 Author's collection

29 *Bodyline*, Derriman, p. 24
30 Quoted in *Bodyline: The Day England Declared War on Australia*, Philip Derriman (Fontana/Kennedy Miller, 1984), p. 148
31 *Ashes in the Mouth: The Story of the Bodyline Tour 1932–33*, Ronald Mason (Hambledon Press, 1982), p. 222
32 *Bodyline – Sports Arena*, 1970
33 Transcript of interview for *Arlott and Trueman on Cricket* (BBC Television, 1977)

ACKNOWLEDGMENTS

Over 200 books have been written on Jack the Ripper and still we are no nearer to knowing for certain who he was. So the much smaller number of books on the 1932–33 Bodyline Test series and its preamble and aftermath — all now long out of print — constitute a collection which is not excessive. In this attempt to gather up all that matters concerning Bodyline and to interpret it I have consulted all the previous works on the subject, and a great many other books, magazines and newspapers besides. The range is reflected in the endnotes, but it would be remiss not to single out with particular gratitude the principal reference sources among the books. These have been the contemporary works by Jack Hobbs, Arthur Mailey, Harold Larwood, R.W.E. Wilmot, Douglas Jardine, Alan Kippax and Bruce Harris.

Additionally, books of major Bodyline significance published some years afterwards have been those by Jack Fingleton, Philip Derriman, Gerald Howat (Warner biography), Don Bradman, Walter Hammond, Bill O'Reilly, R.S. Whitington (Hele and O'Reilly biographies), Laurence Le Quesne, Arthur Carr, Vic Richardson, Christopher Douglas (Jardine biography), Bill Bowes, Jack Egan, Eddie Paynter, W.H. Ferguson, Alan Hill (Verity biography), Gilbert Mant, Maurice Tate, Bert Oldfield, Kevin Perkins (Larwood's 1965 literary collaborator), Ray Robinson, E.W. Swanton (including his Gubby Allen biography), Gerald Pawle and R.E.S. Wyatt, and Ric Sissons and Brian Stoddart.

Among the numerous other titles frequently dipped into have been various editions of *The Australian Cricketer*, *New South Wales Cricket Association Yearbook*, *Wisden Cricketers' Almanack*, *The Cricketer* and that indispensable volume *Who's Who of First-Class Cricketers* (Bailey, Thorn and

Wynne-Thomas). Also, for the purity of its statistical content, Ray Webster's *First-Class Cricket in Australia Volume 1, 1850–51 to 1941–42* has been a most useful aid.

Of the many books studied and drawn upon beyond the cricket scene, I would thank principally the authors and publishers of *Australia Through Time* (Mynah Books, 1996: edited by Margaret Olds) and *The Macquarie Book of Events* (Macquarie Library, 1983: edited by Bryce Fraser).

That ever-increasing sums continue to be paid for "Bodylineana" underscores the enduring significance and fascination of this extraordinary conflict. Anything at all concerning the 1932–33 series makes mighty prices at auction — recently a stump fetched $2000 in Adelaide and an SS *Orontes* souvenir brochure, with rusted staples, almost £400 in Leicester — so it was a relief to be able to rely on my own copies, acquired in the good old days, of such key publications as *The "Sporting" English?* and *The Barracker at Bay*, as well as several other tour souvenirs. It has also been helpful to have a wide-ranging collection of letters written by cricketers and cricket people over a period of many years, together with scrapbooks and a personal archive of film and video recordings — plus, of course, that 1933 Foster/Larwood gramophone record, though the crackles get no less irritating with the passing years.

For an undertaking of this dimension, having one's own extensive cricket library does not mean that one never needs to leave the house. A visit to Lord's was essential, and my thanks are extended to Stephen Green, Glenys Williams and Ken Daldry at the MCC Library for their unstinting assistance. Much was gleaned from the old files of correspondence and from the original 1932–33 tour scorebook, written in Bill Ferguson's fine hand, the first scoresheet of each Test match headed with a delectable artistic design. In *Bodyline Autopsy* are published, I believe for the first time, the fully detailed scorecards of these Tests, with minutes batted, balls faced, and boundaries hit. The balls faced, adopted from Jardine's tour book, may not always add up precisely. Some keen member of the Association of Cricket Statisticians may care to go to Lord's some day and reconstruct each innings. This author simply ran out of time as he aimed to catch the 70th anniversary of cricket's stormiest summer.

I was glad of the chance to talk with Mrs Fianach Lawry, daughter of D.R. Jardine, Mrs Enid Todd, daughter of Harold Larwood, and Claude Corbett's daughter Helen. Special thanks also go to Mrs Yvonne Mant, for tracking me down in order to hand over documents, thus honouring the wish of her late husband, the charming Gilbert. Gratitude is also extended to my old London-anchored Aussie mate Murray Hedgcock, for keeping me on my toes during this seemingly never-ending project and persuading me that at least some small mention should be made of the book by Egon Kisch.

Stephen Gibbs in Sydney steered me towards a couple of unfamiliar areas of information and made me aware of Tessa Wooldridge's survey on the subject for the Australian National Library. In Melbourne, Gideon Haigh continued to egg his old editor on in spite of having had his eye on this particular subject himself. I hope he feels there is now no further need for such a book. And another loyal friend, John Havercroft in Perth, came through at the last moment with some good material on the 1932 fixtures in his hometown. I am also grateful to Helen Corbett and Roger Mann for their assistance in providing photographs.

It would be remiss not to acknowledge the support of Stuart Neal and Brigitta Doyle at ABC Enterprises in Sydney. Stuart's expressed belief in this work, as any writer in preliminary discussions with a publisher will appreciate, was the ignition key.

To my daughter Julie, my loving thanks for sorting out Tate's crocodile and for keeping her dad at it by peppering him with emails from Queensland enquiring how the book was coming along.

Just over 30 years ago I first expressed my loving appreciation to my wife Debbie for backing me through the grind of authorship. I should never have doubted that she would once more, so many years and projects later, be there to listen to my musings and speculations, keep the tea and sustenance coming, smile at my excitement, sympathise during the periods of hesitancy. Perhaps her support was not without reward, for I know that she, like me, has found Douglas Jardine a fascinating challenge to one's powers of comprehension.

DAVID FRITH

Guildford, Surrey, July 2002

INDEX

Illustrations are shown in italics

Abel, R. 224
Aberdare, Lord 224
Achong, E.E. 357
Adams, A.C. 407, 408
Adams, E.W. 226
Adams, G.C.A. 244, 245
Adcock, N.A.T. 16, 420
Agate, James 359
Akenhead, Mr 232
Albert of Saxe-Coburg, Prince 384
Alexander, H.H. 10, 85, 108, 140, 169, 260,
  261, 307, 314–19, 321, 324–27, 333, 388,
  425, 426
Allen, Geoffrey 64
Allen, G.O.B. 10, 33, 52, 55, 56, *59*, 63, 64,
  82, 83, 93, 95, 96, 100, *106*, 107, *115*, 116, 118,
  120, 122–24, 129, 132, 141, 146, 149, 153, 155,
  157–60, 164, 165, 174, 177–85, 193–96, 199,
  200, 202, 204, 205, 210, 211, 219, 220, 236,
  242, 261, 271, 277, 278, 282–85, 287–89,
  293–95, 301, 304, 309, 312–15, 321, 322, 324,
  325, 333, 334, 341, 346, 349, 354, 386–88, 391,
  397, 412, 414, 416, 431, 432, 434, 437, 442
Allen, Patricia 64
Allen, Pearl 64
Allen, Walter 64
Allenby, General 222
Amarnath, L. 394
Amar Singh 390
Ambrose, C.E.L. 12, 420
Ames, L.E.G. 10, 52, 55, 83, 104, *115*, 118,
  123, 132, 135, 141–45, 150, 156, *157*, 164,
  174, 183, 195, 206, 207, 215, 264, 266, 267,
  272, 278–80, 284, 287, 289, 298, 299, 301,
  311, 313, 317, *319*, 320, 325, 336, 337, 341,
  348, 355, 356, 358, 386, 388, 391, 416, 434–36

Anderson, General 126
Andrews, T.J.E. 28
Andrews, W.C. 271
Andrews, W.H.R. 24
Archdale, Betty 388
Aristotle 27
Arlott, John 9, 46, 435, 438, 446
Armstrong, W.W. 25, 26, 30, 57, 70, 113, 114,
  116, 201, 204, 382
Ashton, H. 447
Aspinal, Dr 109
Aspinall, Cecil 252
Astaire, Fred 343
Atherton, M.A. 16
Atkinson, J.A. 144
Attila the Hun 395

Badcock, C.L. 142, 413, 414
Badcock, F.T. 341
Bailey, J.A. 11
Baillie, E.H.M. 113
Baker, A. 306
Bakewell, A.H. 392
Baldwin, Stanley 225, 250, 350
Ballantine, E.W. 113
Barbour, E.P. 106, 107, 309, 379
Bardsley, W. 23, 107, 446
Barlow, A.N. 270
Barnes, Julian 386
Barnes, S.F. 18, 20, 32, 149, 244, 349, 357
Barnett, B.A. 96, 274, 403
Barnett, C.J. 414, 442
Barrow, I. 355
Barrymore, John 77
Bastard (footballer) 383
Batchelor, Denzil 119, 123, 135, 160
Beames, P.J. 261
Bean, C.E.W. 252, 253, 379

Bean, E.E.   27, 351
Beatty, R.G.   305
Beck, Mo and Sid   77
Bedi, B.S.   198
Bedkober, Martin   180
Bedser, A.V.   101
Bell, A.J.   21, 40, 48
Belper, Lord   340, 349
Benaud, R.   14
Benjamin, K.C.G.   12
Bennett, L.   141
Best, W.L.   170
Bett, H.D.   113, 127, 213, 229
Bettington, R.H.B.   237
Beveridge, R.   405
Biggs, M.   266
Bill, O.W.   101, 102, 112, 113
Bishop, I.R.   12, 420
Blackham, J.M.   148, 204
Blackie, D.D.   85
Bligh, Captain   308
Blundell, R.W.   384
Blythe, C.   32
Bonney, Lores   77–78
Booker, C.   385
Borwick, E.G.   10, 114, 115, 128, 129, 174, *199*,
    205, 270, 316, 326, 329, 414, 416, 427, 448
Bosanquet, B.J.T.   231
Bowes, W.E.   10, 33, 45, 47–50, 54–56, 58, 59,
    61, 62, 79, 84, 87, 89, 95, 100, 107, *115*, 142,
    144–46, 148, 150–53, 159, 160, 170, 173,
    215, 237, 263, 268, 271, 306, 333, 334, 336,
    337, 341, 345, 349, 355, 362, 363, 376, 386,
    388, 398, 402, 403, 408, 432, 436, 443
Boycott, G.   13
Bradman, D.G.   7, 8, 10, 13, 25–27, 29, 33–35,
    37–44, 48, 50, 55, 58, 60, 66, 67, 70, 72–74,
    77–86, 92, 94–97, 99–101, 103–05, 107–12,
    114–16, 120, 122, 133, 135, 138–40, 145, 147,
    149–54, 156, 157, 159–65, 167, 172, 173, 175,
    177, 178, 180–82, 186–93, 195, 201, 206–11,
    213, 216, 221, 226, 231, 232, 239, 240, 246,
    262–64, 266, 269, 272, 274, 275, 280–83, 287,
    290, 293, 298–302, 304, 305, 307–10, 312,
    315, 317–26, 328, 329, 337, *338*, 341, 342,
    351, 352, 355, 358, 359, 368, 379, 384–87,
    389, 395, 397–99, 402, 403, 408, 411–16, 418,
    419, 422–31, 433, 435, 440, 442, 446–48
Bradman, Jessie   60, 79, 138, 163, 246, 387, 426
Branson, V.M.   384
Braund, L.C.   26
Brearley, J.M.   26
Brearley, W.   50
Bridge, Mr   126
Bridgeman, Viscount   223, 225, 246, 349

Brindley, W.T.   65
Brittle, L.   266
Bromley, E.H.   108, 274, 284, 286, 287, 291,
    294, *295*, 297, 298, 307, 328, 334, 425
Brook, Clive   168
Brown, F.R.   10, 52, 55, *59*, 63, 65, 80, 87, 88,
    90, 96, 105, *115*, 141, 169, 183, 184, 195,
    262–64, 266, 271, 272, 274, 283, 291, 319,
    341, 349, 388, 436, 439
Brown, G.   47
Brown, G.R.R.   45
Brown, H.A.   52
Brown, W.A.   10, 140, 188, 192, 263, 264, 276,
    398, 400, 403, 411, 425
Browne, Frank   36, 58, 338
Bruce, Nigel   346
Bruce, S.M.   256, 257, 283, 350, 417
Bruce, Wallace   245
Bryant, R.J.   80, 82, 84
Buccleuch, Duke of   225
Buckmaster, Viscount   231
Buggy, Hugh   36, *37*, 91, 113, 200, 282
Bull, W.C.   216, 226, 403–05
Burke, Frank   113
Burns, W.B.   33, 34, 41
Burrows, A.O.   142, 145
Bushby, C.H.   216, *217*, 402–04
Bushell, H.   *217*
Byrne, James   194

Caddick, A.R.   21
Cahn, Julien   253, 341, 399, 401
Caine, C.S.   358
Calthorpe, F.S.G.   32
Cameron, H.B.   39, 47, 196, 201
Campbell, Norman   381
Campbell, R.H.   32, 33, 183
Capone, Al   98
Cardus, Neville   51, 194, 231, 292, 302, 359,
    364, 414
Carr, A.W.   23, 35, 41, 43–45, 106, 214, 238, 339,
    363, 382, 399–401, 403, 405, 407, 435, 447
Carter, H. "Sammy"   107
Case, C.C.C.   42
Casey, R.G.   254
Castle, Dennis   381, 444
Catchlove, W.E.   90
Chalk, F.G.H.   363
Chamberlain, Neville   257
Chapman, A.P.F.   51, 71, 91, 224, 237, 340
Chappell, G.S.   424
Chappell, I.M.   11, 152, 424
Charles II, King   222
Chatfield, E.J.   15
Chaucer, Geoffrey   61

Chester, F.   114
Chifley, Ben   439
Chilvers, H.C.   263, 264
Chipperfield, A.G.   305, 403
Christopherson, S.   224
Churchill, Winston   224
Cicero   339
Clark, E.W.   357, 391–93, 398, 402, 403, 408, 442
Clark, Manning   151, 335
Clarke, S.T.   420
Clay, J.C.   362
Close, D.B.   47, 63
Clover-Brown, C.   65
Coleman, Richard   386
Collins, H.L.   240
Compton, D.C.S.   27, 419, 428
Conan Doyle, A.   41
Coningham, A.   365
Constantine, L.N.   31, 32, 35, 231, 355–59, 361, 364, 411
Contractor, N.J.   420, 421
Cook, Captain James   72
Cook, G.G.   271, 272
Corbett, Claude   69, 90, 91, 113, 188–92, 302
Corbett, Helen   192
Corbett, J.   113
Corbett, Mac   192
Coriolanus   217
Corless, J.H.   113
Corrie, R.T.   112, 167, 175, 265, 379, 380
Cotter, A.   16, 30, 50, 107, 231
Coward, Mike   15
Cowdrey, M.C.   434, 439
Crawley, L.G.   231
Crockett, R.M.   18, 114
Croft, C.E.H.   13, 420
Cromer, Lord   404, 409
Crossland, J.   29
Crudgington, Mr   326, 327
Crutchley, E.T.   254–256, 258, 335
Cummins, F.S.   105, 263
Curran, K.M.   14
Currie, Alan   168
Curtin, John   80
Curtin, P.W.E.   79, 80
Cush, F.M.   99, 216, *217*, 226

Dalglish, Admiral   262
Daniel, W.W.   420
Darling, J.   16, 25, 30, 32, 35, 108, 144, 249
Darling, L.S.   10, 92, 93, 274, 284, 287, 294, 295, 300, *307*, 311–13, 325, 333, 403, 425
Darling, W.M.   198
Dartmouth, Earl of   222

Davie, B.J.   113
Davies, D.   46, 47
Davis, J.C.   55, 113, 233
Davis, Joe   78
Davis, W.W.   420
Dawson, E.W.   363
Dawson, Geoffrey   248
Deamer, Syd   36
Deedes, William   13
de Groot, Captain   77
Dempsey, Dan   276
Dempster, C.S.   340, 341
Denison, Hugh   139
Denness, M.H.   27
Dennis, C.J.   111
Derriman, Philip   99, 112, 241
Devine, Frank   73
Dexter, E.R.   63, 448
Didrikson, Babe   78
Dietrich, Marlene   168, 346
Dilawar Hussain   391–93
Dolling, C.E.   110, 200
Donald, A.A.   16, 420
Donnelly, J.L.   304
Douglas, J.W.H.T.   28, 32, 175
Downer, Fred   246
Drew, A.D.   79
Ducat, A.   381
Duckworth, G.   42, 44, 52, 55, 58, 59, 62–64, 83, 93, 96, 97, *115*, 118, 141, 145, 149, 169, 264, 267, 272, 292, 305, 314, 336, 347, 349, 352, 401, 402, 436, 438
Dudley, Lord   243
Duleepsinhji, K.S.   52, 53, 131, 236, 442
Dumas, Lloyd   245, 248, 249
Duncan, Walter   245
Duncan Hughes, John   245, 246
Durston, F.J.   201, 353, 384
Dwyer, E.A.   110, 126, 413
Dyson, Will   219

Eade, Charles   351
Eady, C.J.   144
Ebeling, H.I.   333, 414, 415
Eckersley, P.T.   292, 401
Edinburgh, Duke of   430, 446
Edrich, W.J.   419, 428
Edward VIII, King   444
Egan, Jack   335
Elliott, H.   394
Embury, J.E.   198
Evatt, H.V.   102

Fairbanks, Douglas Jr   346
Fairfax, A.G.   112, 231

Falcon, M.   224, 409
Farfield, Ted   219
Farnes, K.   49, 362, 363, 398, 402, 412, 413, 416
Farquhar, Jack   277
Fender, P.G.H.   21, 40, 43, 57, 105, 106, 308, 360, 386
Ferguson, W.H.   55, 59, 85, *115*, 185, 262, 286, 293, 335, 346, 347, 431
Ferris, J.J.   235
Fields, Gracie   341
Findlay, W.   54, 142, 220, 221, 223–25, 228, 348, 349, 370, 396, 397
Fingleton, J.H.W.   10, 13, 14, 37, 40, 48, 68, 75, 81–84, 99, *101*, 102, 108, 110, 112, 113, 118, 119, 131, 132, 134, 139, 145, 148, 150–53, 155, 158, 159, 165, 176, 178, 181, 185–92, 206–08, 235, 262–64, 270, 274, 275, 311, 323, 335, 351, 393, 410–12, 419, 422, 423, 425, 438, 439, 441, 442, 445, 449
Fingleton, Wally   190
Fisher, I.A.   194
Fleetwood-Smith, L.O.   85, 92, 93, 140, 333, 412, 413, 424
Flintoff, A.   26
Foenander, S.P.   172
Foley, C.P.   34
Forbes, George   340
Ford, Len   111
Forster, H.W.   223
Foster, F.R.   18–21, 28, 32, 34, 189, 357
Foster, J.S.   26
Franklin, W.B.   361
Franks, Warwick   305
Freeman, G.   29
French, Gerald   384
Fry, C.B.   25, 365

Gable, Clark   77
Gamble, H.S.   272
Game, Lady   108, 126
Game, Philip   76, *103,* 108
Gandhi, Mahatma   93
Garbo, Greta   77
Gardiner, A.G.   233
Gardner, C.H.   113
Garner, J.   12, 420
Garnsey, G.L.   100, 301, 388
Garrett, T.W.   106, 379
Gascoigne, S.H.   *see* Yabba
Gatting, M.W.   175
Gauld, G.O.   403, 404, 406, 407
Gavaskar, S.M.   26
Geary, G.   71
Gee, Hec   276
Gemmell, Malcolm   189, 190

George V, King   168, 250, 300, 354, 355
Gibson, Robert   75
Giffen, G.   114, 243
Gilbert, E.   40, 119, 266, 269–72, 305, 326, 384, 416
Gilchrist, R.   420
Giles, A.F.   26
Gillespie, J.N.   21
Gilligan, A.E.R.   91, 201, 237, 238, 424
Gilligan, A.H.H.   238
Gilmore, Charles   231
Glendenning, Raymond   431
Glover, Tom   92, 113
Goodman, Tom   113, 207, 214
Gough, D.   439
Gough, F.J.   269, 270
Govan, J.M.   272
Gover, A.R.   197, 238
Gowrie, Lord *see* Hore-Ruthven
Grace, E.M.   22, 41
Grace, W.G.   11, 16, 29, 32, 41, 244, 365
Grant, G.C.   32, 358, 362, 411
Grant, R.S.   358, 364
Green, A.W.   99
Gregory, J.M.   26, 30–33, 47, 50, 107, 201, 204, 233, 234, 237, 238, 240, 352, 381
Gregory, Mrs J.M.   145
Gregory, R.G.   413
Gregory, S.E.   234
Greswell, W.T.   22
Griffith, C.C.   420
Griffith, H.C.   39, 358
Grimmett, C.V.   10, 28, 72, 88, 108, 110, 123, 127, 128, 132, 154–57, 161, 164, 174, 176–78, 195, 205, 207, 211, 274, 299, 336, 337, 411, 415, 416, 424, 442
Gun, L.T.   27–29
Gunasekera, C.H.   65
Gunn, G.   20, 28, 197, 237, 238
Gunn, W.   129

Hadlee, R.J.   420
Haig, N.E.   237
Hailsham, Lord   224, 249, 349, 350, 360, 370, 375, 378, 384, 398, 400
Halcombe, R.A.   79–81
Hall, Ross   387
Hall, W.W.   15, 420
Hammond, W.R.   29, 31, 32, 39, 42, 44, 47, 52, 55, 56, 58, 59, 64, 66, 70–72, 81–83, 87, 88, 92, 93, 96, 102–04, *115*, 122, 124, 128, 129, 131, 132, 146, 151–54, 156, 159–61, 163, 164, 167, 169, 173, 179, 180, 183, 195, 200, 205, 206, 215, 218, 233, 263, 264, 266, 272, *277*, 280, 287, 294–96, 298, 301, 304, 305,

311–13, 315–18, 322, 328, 333, 337, 338, 340–43, 349, 355–58, 388, 389, 391, *409*, 412, 414, 428, 431–33, 442

Hammill, S.   170

Hampden, Viscount   224, 409

Hankey, Lord   406

Harlow, Jean   77

Harris, Bruce   35, 57, 96, 113, 169, 206, 263, 279, 299, 322, 343, 344

Harris, Lord   58, 63, 202, 237, 386, 387

Harris, Max   77

Harrison, Councillor   261

Hartigan, M.J.   216, *217*, 240, 258, 366, 372, 373

Hassett, A.L.   145, 436

Hawke, Lord   52, 58, 63, 64, 98, 223, 254, 348, 349, 352, 354, 360, 370, 371, 374, 378, 381, 395, 400, 408, 409

Hawker, Walter   200, 249

Hayward, Dudley   204

Hayward, T.W.   19

Hazlitt, G.R.   243

Headley, G.A.   39, 354, 355, 357, 362

Hearne, J.T.   234

Hearne, J.W.   19, 31

Hedgcock, Murray   435

Heine, P.S.   16, 420

Hele, G.A.   10, 21, 72, 104, 114, 115, 127, 128, 129, 131, 163, 165, 173, 175, 184, 196, *199*, 284, 287, 329, 448

Hendren, E.H.   47, 71, *361*, 362

Hendry, H.S.T.L.   71, 97, 98

Hepburn, Katharine   346

Heseltine, C.   224

Heydon, H.   134

Hick, G.A.   140

Higson, T.A.   52, 401, 403, 433

Hill, C.   25, 80, 87, 113, 173, *217*, 226, 229, 234, 249

Hill, Horace   167

Hill-Smith, W.   80

Hindenburg, President von   226

Hinkler, Bert   77, 205, 266

Hird, S.F.   104, 105, 110, 262

Hirst, G.H.   18, 20, 25, *369*,

Hislop, Ian   385

Hitch, J.W.   20, 235

Hitler, Adolf   226, 422, 430

Hobbs, Ida   140

Hobbs, J.B.   21, 23, 25, 28, 29, 31, 39, 49, 50, 57, 58, 61, 83, 93, 95, 103, 107, 110, 113, 118, 131, 140, 146, 155, 165, 178, 206, 236, 262, 263, 265, 282, 283, 294, 301, 302, 304, 306, 308, 316, 321, 329, 336, 337, 352, 363, 391, 438, 440, 446

Hodgetts, H.W.   206, 216, *217*, 246, 374

Hogarth, R.G.   407

Hogg, R.M.   420

Holding, M.A.   12, 420

Holdsworth, J.H.   111

Holmes, E.R.T.   395, 411

Holmes, P.   57

Holmes, Sherlock   293

Holmes à Court, Dr   109

Holt, Jim   387

Hooker, J.E.H.   305

Hopman, Harry   60

Horace   259

Horan, T.P.   27

Hordern, H.V.   28

Hore-Ruthven, Alexander   91, 225, 242–49, 258, 349, 369, 373, 374, 376, 382, 389, 396, 417, 427–29

Hornby, A.N.   202

Howard, Leslie   346

Howat, Gerald   64, 107, 158, 193, 339

Howell, W.H.   264

Howitt, G.   29

Hughes, E.S.   133, 157, 181

Hughes, J.S.   382

Hughes, M.G.   420

Hulls, Alan   113

Hulme, J.H.A.   361

Hunt, G.E.   42

Hunte, C.C.   15

Hussain, N.   26

Hutcheon, J.S.   216, *217*, 226, 258, 272, *273*, 291, 300, 372, 373

Hutton, L.   27, 101, 152, 337, 419, 428, 431, 433

Hylton, L.G.   411

Ikin, J.T.   427

Imran Khan   420

Ingham, Jack   57, 113, 169, 207

Ingle, R.A.   364

Inman, Melbourne   306

Inniss, C.D.   31

Inskip, Thomas   246

Inverarity, M.   80–82

Inverarity, R.J.   80

Iremonger, J.   45

Ironmonger, H.   40, 85, 93, 108, 110, 128, 140, 145, 155, 161, 163–65, 174, 175, 178, 205, 207, 211, 233, 272, 277, 285, 287, 289, 290, 294, 296–98, *307*, 314, 316, 318, 321, 325, 327, 328, 333, 386, 425

Isaacs, Isaac   75, 102, 244, 335

Jackson, A.A.   27, 42, 104, 263, 297, 298, 300, 301

Jackson, F.S.   50, 223, 246, 349, 369, 370, 386, 398, 403–05, 409, 432

Jackson, G.R. 409
Jackson, John 29
Jahangir Khan 362
James, G.T.H. 142
Jaques, A. 22–23
Jardine, D.R. 7, 9, 11, 16–20, 24, 25, 26, 29, 31,
    32, 36, 40, 41, 43, 44, 47, 48, 50–53, 55–59,
    61, 63, 64, 66–73, 79–83, 85, 87–94, 97–103,
    105–08, 110, 115–18, 120, 124, 128–30, 132,
    133, 140–44, 146–49, 151–53, 156–58, 160,
    161, 163, 165, 167–71, 173, 175, 177, 180–82,
    184, 186, 188, 193, 195, 199–205, 207–09,
    211, 213–15, 217, 219, 220, 225, 227, 228,
    232, 233, 236, 237, 239, 241, 242, 245, 246,
    248, 252, 254, 255, 257, 258, 260–62, 267–72,
    274, 276–82, 284–90, 292–96, 299–302, 304,
    306–10, 313–15, 317, 319, 321, 324–29, 332,
    333, 335–337, 339, 340, 342, 343, 345–50,
    352–61, 363, 364, 370, 374, 376–83, 385–88,
    390–98, 405, 406, 409, 410, 412, 417, 421,
    424, 425, 429, 430, 432–38, 441–49
Jardine, Margaret 391, 443, 444, 447
Jardine, M.R. 51, 445
Javed Miandad 140
Jeanes, W.H. 87, 134, 145, 170–72, 184, 192,
    217, 256, 258, 272, 307, 370, 372, 438
Jenkins, V.G.J. 362
Jessop, G.L. 30, 161
Joginder Singh 24
John, G. 31
Johnson, Amy 78
Johnson, I.W.G. 110
Johnson, K.O.E. 217
Johnson, Samuel 232, 302
Johnson, W.J. 110, 181, 351, 413
Johnstone, C.P. 393
Jones, A.C. 129
Jones, E. 16, 30, 32, 106, 107, 112, 186, 390
Jones, Roderick 344
Joseph 267, 279
Jupp, V.W.C. 352, 364

Kaiser Wilhelm 369
Kann, E.W. 113
Keeton, W.W. 362
Kelleway, C. 28
Kelly, J.J. 35, 240
Kelly, Ned 13, 136
Kelly, W.L. 114, 216, 372, 373
Kent Hughes, W. 242
Kilburn, J.M. 445
King, J.B. 231
Kingsford Smith, Charles 36, 78
Kipling, Rudyard 300, 444
Kippax, A.F. 10, 18, 29, 40, 42, 44, 50, 84, 95,

97, 101, 105, 108, 112, 113, 119, 131, 132,
    145, 186, 229, 240, 262–64, 301, 305, 344,
    351, 379, 403, 419, 423, 424, 435
Kisch, E.E. 383, 384
Kitchener, Lord 243
Kneebone, Harry 113
Knox, N.A. 34
Kortright, C.J. 30, 359
Kotze, J.J. 30, 50

Lacey, F.E. 224, 225
Laker, J.C. 14
Lang, Andrew 441
Lang, Jack 75–77
Langer, J.L. 305
Langridge, James 356, 357, 391
Langridge, Tom 138
Larwood, H. 7, 8, 10, 12, 13, 17, 18, 20, 21,
    23–25, 27, 29, 31, 33–35, 37, 40–48, 50,
    52, 53, 55, 56, 58, 59, 61–63, 66, 71, 79–81,
    83, 88, 89, 94–98, 100, 106, 112, 114–19,
    121–26, 131, 132, 136, 138, 139, 144,
    146–50, 152–55, 157–61, 165, 167, 169,
    170, 172, 179–84, 187, 189, 194–202, 204,
    206–11, 213–15, 217, 221, 229, 232–35,
    238–40, 244, 248, 249, 251, 253, 261, 262,
    264–69, 271, 272, 274, 276–78, 280–85,
    287, 289, 293–95, 298, 300–02, 304, 306,
    308–19, 322–26, 328, 329, 332, 339, 340,
    344, 347–55, 357–59, 362, 363, 366, 373,
    374, 376, 379, 381–89, 391, 394, 395,
    398–402, 405–08, 410, 413, 417, 419, 420,
    423–25, 429, 434, 435, 437–42, 446, 447
Larwood, Enid 441
Larwood, June 52, 340
Larwood, Lois 52, 340, 387, 438, 439, 440, 441
Larwood's parents 352, 353, 399, 400
Laver, F.J. 243
Lawrence, D.V. 14
Lawson, G.F. 140
Lawton, T. 267, 268
Lee, B. 21, 420
Lee, F.S. 42, 46, 47
Lee, P.K. 96, 108, 275, 307, 313, 315, 316, 318,
    321, 325, 328, 426
Le Quesne, Laurence 241, 242
Le Roux, G.S. 420
Leslie, Mayor 81
Lever, P. 15
Leveson Gower, H.D.G. 51, 60, 224, 360
Levy, R.M. 271
Lewisham, Viscount 218, 221–23, 246, 300,
    348, 409
Leyland, M. 49, 53, 55, 56, 58, 59, 62, 64, 79,
    82, 83, 88, 115, 118, 130, 132, 144, 156, 163,

173–76, 201, 205–07, 210, 211, 215, 261, 263, 264, 268, 272, 277, 278, 287, 292, 293, 295–98, 318, 319, 328, 336, 337, 433
Lillee, D.K.   11, 26, 234, 337, 387, 420
Lilley, B.   *44*, 404
Lincoln, Abraham   218
Lindrum, Walter   78
Lindwall, Jack   125
Lindwall, R.R.   15, 26, 125, 419, 420, 428, 436
Lister, W.H.L.   401
Litster, J.L.   266, 271
Little, R.C.J.   305, 306
Lloyd, C.H.   12, 233
Lockwood, W.H.   15, 30, 236
Lonergan, A.R.   81
Love, H.S.B.   103, 104, 108, 264, 274, 284, 286, 290, 294, 295, 307, 426
Low, David   385
Lower, Lennie   384
Lowry, T.C.   340
Lucan, Earl of   224
Lumsdaine, Jack   78
Lush, J.G.   414, 416
Luttrell, Bert   146
Lyons, Enid   76
Lyons, J.A.   68, 76, 78, 254–56, 258, 300, 414

MacArthur, Gen. Douglas   36
Macartney, C.G.   23, 105, 113, 239, 301, 446
Macaulay, G.G.   50, 357
Macaulay, T.B.   389
MacDonald, Ramsay   76, 225, 250, 253, 300
Macdonald, Robbie   364–66, 369–73, 375, 395, 396, 404
Macdonell, A.G.   385
MacFlecknoe   251
MacLaren, A.C.   17, 25, 35, 237
Maegraith, Kerwin   389
Maguire, Mick   267, 268, 288, 296
Mahomed Nissar   392
Mailer, Ramsay   216, 372, 373
Mailey, A.A.   32, 35, 60, 64, 72, 94, 113, 122, 130, 145, 148, 158, 205, 206, 213, 237, 239, 262, 272, 290, 301, 308, 328, 334, 337, 338, 343, *344*, 351, 389, 414, 415, 446
Major, John   440
Makepeace, J.H.W.   32
Mallett, R.H.   224, 370, 410
Manjrekar, V.L.   420
Manning, L.V.   234
Mant, Gilbert   10, 56, 57, 113, 169, 190–92, 206, 207, 218, 267, 268, 342–44, 411
Marcon, W.   29
Marconi, Guglielmo   230
Marriott, C.S.   391

Marsh, F.E.   405
Marsh, R.W.   87
Marshall, Howard   238
Marshall, John   369
Marshall, M.D.   12, 420
Martin, E.J.   80, 84
Martin, Ray   190
Martindale, E.A.   356–58, 364, 411
Mason, Ronald   447
Massie, H.H.   240
Maugher, Frank   113, 329
McAlister, P.A.   113, 226
McBeath, Neil   78
McCabe, Bert   110
McCabe, Bill   110
McCabe, Les   110
McCabe, S.J.   10, 42, 81–84, *86*, 87, 97, 101, 102, 105, 108, 110, 112, 120–27, 130–34, 153, 154, 156, 160, 171, 175, 177, 178, 182, 184, 205, 208, 210, 221, 232, 262, 281, 287, 289, 290, 294, 295, 298, 299, 301, *307*, 310–12, 316, 318, 325, 328, 351, 385, 386, 398, 403, 411–13, 423, 425, 439
McCormick, E.L.   412–16
McCraith, Douglas   406, 407
McDermott, C.J.   420
McDonald, E.A.   26, 30–32, 47, 107, 204, 234, 235, 237, 238, 314, 352, 437, 438
McDonnell, P.S.   365
McGilvray, Alan   72, 100
McGrath, G.D.   420
McGregor, Rod   111
McInnes, Graham   383
McKee, Steve   111
McKell, W.J.   134
McKenzie, G.D.   15
McLachlan, Ian   193, 395
McMillan, Frank   276
Melba, Nellie   77
Melle, B.G.V.   22
Melville, A.   362
Menzies, R.G.   91, 157, 158, 180, 181, 196, 202, 216, 217, 270, 390, 445, 446
Merchant, V.M.   393
Middleton, R.F.   216, *217*, 226
Miller, K.R.   26, 27, 152, 165, 337, 419, 420, 428, 436
Miller, Syd   69
Milligan, Spike   251
Mills, J.E.   341
Milne, A.A.   232
Minnett, R.B.   32
Mitchell, A.   358, 392
Mitchell, B.   296
Mitchell, F.   235

Mitchell, T.B. 53, 55, 56, 58, *59*, 61, 62, 64, *83*, 86, 87, 93, *115*, 141, 142, 145, 169, 263, 267, 268, 274, 277, 281, 284, 290, 293–95, 305–08, 325, 334, 337, 342, 436, 437

Mold, A.W. 29

Monash, General 252

Monfries, E. 243

Monkhouse, Dennis 177

Montgomery, Field–Marshal 430

Montgomery, Robert 346

Morris, H.M. 236

Morris, Mel 111

Morton, A. 31

Morton, R.L. *217*

Moseley, E.A. 420

Moses, Charles 111

Mosley, Oswald 250

Moule, W.H. 265, 266

Moyes, A.G. 113, 138, 191

Muncer, B.L. 405

Murdoch, W.L. 27, 296

Murray, George 195, 225, 245–47

Mussolini, Benito 430

Mynn, A. 29

Nagel, L.E. 93, 96, 108, 110, 124, 127, 129, 131, 132, 140, 145, 307, 425

Nagel, V.G. 93, 425

Naoomal Jeoomal 392, 393

Napoleon Bonaparte 124

Nash, L.J. 96, 413, 414

Nayudu, C.K. 394

Newbolt, Henry 229

Newman, J. 341

Nichols, M.S. 364, 391, 393, 394, 398

Nicolson, Nigel 17

Niemeyer, Otto 75

Nitschke, H.C. 89, 337

Noble, Joe 384

Noble, M.A. 111, 113, 116, 135, 161, 204, 209, 234, 239, 240, 249, 262, 302, 366

Norman, Ernie 275

Nothling, O.E. 266

Nuffield, Lord 427

Oakes, Edwyn 113

Oakley, H.H. 93, 333

O'Brien, L.P.J. 10, 12–13, 92, 93, 95, 96, 108, 145, 149, 150, 153, 159, 164, 182, 185–87, 191, 192, 203, 307, 310, 311, 318, 321, 325, 326, 333, 334, 388, 420, 423

O'Connell, M.G. 198

O'Connor, J. 45

O'Connor, W. 113

Odgers, P.B. 113

Officer, Keith 254

O'Hagan, Jack 78

O'Hannan, Father 62

Oldfield, P.C. 362

Oldfield, Ruth 201, *202*

Oldfield, W.A.S. 10, 97, 103, 108, 123, 130, 132, 154–56, 161, 165, 172, 173, 176, 194–205, 210, 213, 240, 245, 262, 274, 301, 307, 312–15, 318, 320, 321, 325, 328, 386, 419, 424, 428, 439, 441, 446

O'Neill, N.C. 58

O'Reilly, Molly 296

O'Reilly, W.J. 10, 35, 43, 55, 97, 103, 104, 108, 110, 122, 124, 126, 127, 131–33, 147, 155–58, 161, 163–65, 173, 174, 176–78, 181, 187, 188, 191, 198, 199, 204, 207, 211, 217, 220, 262, 277, 285–87, 290, 291, 295, 296, 298–300, *307*, 311–18, 321, 324, 325, 327, 328, 336, 386–88, 402, 411, 413, 415, 418, 424, 425, 439, 445, 449

O'Sullevan, Captain 58

Oxenham, R.K. 96, 145, 271, 272

Oxlade, R.A. 216, *217*, 226, 346, 372, 376

Packer, Kerry 13, 15, 139, 388

Packer, R.C. 139

Page, Michael 189

Palairet, L.C.H. 52, 348

Palairet, R.C.N. 52, 55, 66, *115*, 168, 185, 186, 193, 225, 228, 245, 246, 255, 265, 285, 334, 335, 345, 346, 348, 431, 443

Palmer, A.R.B. 113

Palmer, J.S. 336

Pardon, Sydney 26

Parr, G. 22

Parry, C.N. 274

Parsons, J.H. 237

Pascoe, L.S. 420

Pataudi, Nawab of 52, 53, 55, 56, 65, 79, 82, 8, 90, 93, 102, 103, 115, 118, 120, 129–31, 142, 145, 150, 156, 163, 170, 173, 206, 209, 215, 261, 264, 270, 272, 278, 295, 306, 332, 349, 421, 433, 442

Pataudi, Nawab of, jnr 421

Patiala, Maharajah of 394

Patiala, Yuvrajah of 393, 394

Patient, Alan 388

Pawson, H.A. 387

Paynter, E. 10, 45, 53, 55, 58–61, 63, 65, 67, 82, 83, 93, 96, 104, *115*, 141–43, 146, 171, 173, 177, 178, 195, 207, 233, 252, 262, 268, 272, 283, 287–92, 298, 299, 301, 304, 311, 313, 314, 320, 321, 336–38, 340–43, 347, 349, 391, 431

Paynter, May 291

Peel, R. 59
Perkins, S. 113
Perrin, P.A. 52, 400, 403
Phillip, Captain Arthur 383
Phillips, E.G. 194
Pike, Jim 301
Plumer, Lord 224
Pollock, P.M. 420
Pollock, S.M. 16, 420
Pollock, William 351
Ponsford, W.H. 10, 32, 34, 39, 44, 85, 92, 95,
  108, 109, 117–19, 131, 140, 145, 152, 156,
  182–84, 186, 191, 194, 195, 208, 209, 213,
  221, 282–84, 291, 293, 294, 301, 307, 332,
  398, 408, *409*, 422, 423, 430
Poon, H.R.G. 266
Pope, D.F. 45, *46*
Porter, B. 113
Porter, R. 169
Portland, Duke of 407
Powell, William 326
Procter, M.J. 420
Puddicombe, F.S. 113
Putman, S.W.L. 142
Puttnam, David 388

Ramprakash, M.R. 21
Ranjitsinhji, K.S. 32, 36, 50, 52, 131, 236
Ransford, V.S. 243, 380
Ratten, R. 169
Raymond, R.C. 266
Read, H.D. 411
Reddick, T.B. 45
Redgrave, J.S. 291
Rhodes, W. 19, 20, 28, 59, 114, 176, 204, 284,
  347, 381
Richards, I.V.A. 12
Richardson, A.J. 28, 411
Richardson, D.J. 9
Richardson, T. 15, 30, 106, 231, 236, 302,
  359
Richardson, V.Y. 11, 21, 28, 35, 42, 81–84, *86*,
  88, 89, 108, 112, 121, 122, 130–32, 153–56,
  158, 160, 161, 175, 176, 178, 183, 184, 191,
  194, 203, 204, 207, 210, 215, 218, 219, 221,
  240, 270, 274, 276–80, 286, 290, 293, 300,
  301, *307*, 308, 315, 316, 319, 322, *327*, 329,
  333, 335–38, 351, 366, 389, 411, 416, 424
Ricketts, E.W.C. 391
Rigg, K.E. 112, 332, 334
Ritchard, Cyril 136
Roach, C.A. 31
Roberts, A.M.E. 12, 420
Roberts, Cecil 265
Roberts, Lord 292, 300

Robertson, A.W.D. 81, 87, 216, *217*, 220, 226,
  228, 256, 372, 373, 376, 414
Robertson-Glasgow, R.C. 352, 356, 441
Robins, R.W.V. 52, 53, 356, 357, 418, 419
Robinson, Ray 10, 36, 95, 109, 123, 139, 181,
  209, 312, 403, 422
Robinson, R.H. 305
Rogers, Ginger 343
Rogerson, Bert 261
Rommel, Field-Marshal 430, 444
Root, C.F. 23, 24, 236
Rorke, G.F. 420
Rowe, R.C. 263, 264
Rowe, S.H.D. 216, *217*
Rudd, G.B.F. 236
Runyon, Damon 36
Rushforth, A.W. 142
Russell, C.A.G. 114
Russell, J. 113
Ruth, Babe 60
Ruthven, Lord 243
Rutledge, W.M. 113, 142, 185
Ryan, A.J. 336
Ryder, J. 186, 239, 240
Ryder, R.V. 52
Rymill, Kathie 175

Sadlier, S. 141
Sandham, A. 31, 32, 238
Sarfraz Nawaz 420
Savonarola 91
Scipio 339
Scott, C.W.A. 77
Scott, J.D. 28, 29, 389, 414, 416
Scotton, W.H. 32, 296
Scrymgour, B.V. 87, 216, 226
Scullin, J.H. 76
Seeley, Hugo 385
Seely Whitby, H. 407
Sellers, A.B. 236, 362
Sewell, E.H.D. 35, 224, 235, 350, 351
Shakoor Rana 175
Shelton, A.W. 399, 400, 417
Sheridan, John 230, 232
Sherman, General 207
Sherring, H.W. 113
Shields, Douglas 426
Shore, N. 231
Shortridge, Harry 78
Shrewsbury, A. 19, 129
Sides, F.W. 266
Simons, C.G. 113
Sinatra, Frank 441
Sinfield, R.A. 47
Sissons, Ric 225, 241, 254

Slater, M.J.   140
Slessor, Kenneth   113
Sly, S.   141
Smith, C.A.   346
Smith, E.J.   24, 357, 401, 402
Smith, H.A.   363
Smith, H.D.   341
Smith, R.A.   16
Smith, Stanley   276
Smith, Syd jnr   70, 225, 226
Snow, J.A.   420
Somers, Lord   443
Southerton, Sydney   56, 213, 358, 410
Spofforth, F.R.   29, 32
Spooner, C.D.   364
Squire, J.C.   230, 360
Stalker, W.   260, 261
Statham, J.B.   15
Staton, W.R.   379
Steele, K.N.   201
Stevens, B.S.B.   99, 321
Stock, H.E.   113
Stoddart, A.E.   141, 143, 234, 365
Stoddart, Brian   225, 241, 254
Storer, W.   32
Street, Jim   47
Streeton, Richard   105
Strudwick, H.   23, 31, 238
Stuart, Bill   328
Studd, Kynaston   221, 224, 246, 348, 349, 409
Sutcliffe, B.   342
Sutcliffe, H.   10, 28, 29, 31, 49, 52, 55–57, 59,
    66, 72, 74, 79, 81–83, 87, 88, 96, 102–04,
    106, 111, 115, 126–30, 132, 142, 145, 150, 154,
    156, 163, 168, 169, 173, 176, 178, 180, 199,
    201, 203, 213, 214, 236, 261, 266, 277, 279,
    282, 286, 287, 291, 295, 304, 309, 312–17,
    325, 333, 335, 341, 349, 352, 358, 391, 432,
    434, 438
Swanton, E.W.   14, 49, 57, 64, 191, 229, 230, 429
Sweet, Gary   386

Tallon, D.   266
Tarrant, F.A.   393, 394
Tarrant, G.   29
Tarzan   77
Tate, Kath   54
Tate, M.W.   53–56, 71, 100–02, 115, 140, 169–71,
    197, 263, 264, 267, 280, 324, 333, 336, 341,
    343, 345, 347, 434
Tate, Michael   54, 140
Taylor, H.W.   48
Taylor, J.M.   446
Taylor, Percy   113
Taylor, Squizzy   36

Tendulkar, S.R.   26
Tennyson, L.H.   32, 47, 60, 236
Thatcher, G.L.   113
Thomas, A.H.   113
Thomas, J.H.   242, 245–47, 249–51, 253, 255,
    300, 399, 400
Thomas, Phyllis   298
Thompson, Graeme   66
Thomson, J.R.   11, 26, 180, 387, 420
Thurlow, H.M.   119, 161, 406
Tiernan, W.P.   113
Tierney, F.   113
Tobin, B.J.   173, 274, 275, 297, 336, 337
Toone, F.C.   374
Townsend, D.C.H.   362
Townsend, John   84
Townsend, L.F.   391, 392
Travers, Ben   71, 381
Trueman, F.S.   15, 420, 439
Trumble, H.   25, 234, 243
Trumble, J.W.   234, 235
Trumper, V.T.   16, 18, 25, 77, 106, 126, 162, 188,
    189, 209, 239, 297
Truscott, K.W. "Bluey"   152
Turnbull, M.J.L.   46, 47, 236, 362
Turner, C.T.B.   235, 240
Twining, R.H.   47, 410
Tyldesley, G.E.   29, 30, 44, 45, 201, 233
Tyldesley, J.T.   17, 25
Tyson, F.H.   420

Ullswater, Viscount   224, 225, 349
Ullyett, Roy   371
Ulm, Charles   36
Ulyett, G.   202

Valentine, B.H.   48, 393
Valentine, V.A.   356
Vanburgh, Violet   343
van der Bijl, P.G.V.   49
Verity, Douglas   72, 347
Verity, H.   50, 53, 55, 56, 59, 61, 62, 72, 83,
    86–90, 93, 94, 100, 102, 104, 115, 118, 122,
    124, 126, 130, 132, 145, 146, 169, 173, 174,
    177, 178, 180, 183, 194, 207, 209, 210, 263, 264,
    271, 272, 277, 280, 282, 284, 288–91, 293, 294,
    301, 304, 312–314, 317, 321, 323–25, 327, 328,
    336, 341, 347, 349, 355, 357, 358, 360, 391,
    400, 425, 433, 436, 444
Verity, Kathleen   433
Vernon, G.F.   140
Victoria, Queen   384
Voce, Elsie   406
Voce, W.   10, 13, 18, 24, 27, 31, 33, 36, 41–43,
    45, 46, 48, 52, 55, 59, 62–64, 66, 83, 84, 93, 95,

100, 102, 104–06, 112, *115,* 117–19, 121–24, 126, 131, 132, 134, 135, 138, 146, 148, 152, 153, 155, 157, 158, 161, 165, 178, 180, 183, 189, 194, 195, 200, 204, 207, 217, 244, 262, 265–68, 271, 274, 277, 288, 305–07, 309, 311, 313, 321–23, 325, 337, 341, 347, 348, 353, 354, 362, 382, 383, 386, 387, 391, 392, 398, 400–08, 412, 413, 416, 423, 425, 427, 435, 436, 440, 442
von Moltke, General   261

Waddy, E.L.   111, 226
Wagg, Alfred   360
Waite, M.G.   88, 203
Wales, Prince of   350
Walker, C.W.   88, 274, 336
Walker, R.D.   33
Wall, T.W.   10, 80, 88, 108, 124, 126, 130, 132, 155–57, 161, 163, 173–76, 178, 195, 200, 201, 205–07, 211, 233, 275, 277, 286, 287, 290, 291, 295, 297, 307, 335, 387, 403, 425
Walsh, C.A.   12, 14, 420
Walsh, J.M.   145
Walters, C.F.   358, 390
Warne, S.K.   14, 88
Warner, Agnes   64, 107, 193, 254, 346
Warner, Charles   359
Warner, John   135
Warner, P.F.   20, 21, 33, 40, 41, 50–53, 55, 56, 60, 63–68, 85, 87, 90, 91, 98, 107, 113, *115,* 135, 142, 158, 168, 171, 185–88, 192–94, 196, 208, 211, 218, 220, 225, 227–29, 231, 235, 238, 241, 242, 245, 246, 254–58, 260, 261, 268, 269, 299–302, 304, 306, 320, 321, 334, 335, 339, 342, 345, 346, 348, 349, 354, 356, 359, 360, 365, 370, 373, 374, 376, 380, 386, 391, 396, 397, 401, 409, 417, 428, 430, 433, 435, 443, 447
Washbrook, C.   419, 420
Wasim Akram   420
Waterman, L.W.   272
Watson, C.D.   420
Watson, F.B.   362
Watt, Lionel   111
Waugh, Alec   360
Wazir Ali   48
Weaving, Hugo   386
Webb, S.G.   226
Webbe, A.J.   349
Weir, G.L.   341
Weissel, Eric   276
Wellings, E.M.   387
Wellington, Duke of   380
Wheeler, Paul   388
White, C.   26

White, J.C.   347
Whitington, R.S.   10, 88, 90, 146, 165, 175, 181, 416
Wignall, Trevor   98
Wilcox, D.R.   363
Wilde, S.   33
Williams, Guy   87
Williams, R.G.   336, 337
Willis, R.G.D.   198, 420
Wilmot, Chester   61
Wilmot, R.W.E.   36, 61, 65, 66, 98, 102, 113, 175, 200, 203, 206, 337, 444
Wilson, C.E.M.   395
Wilson, E.R.   70, 395
Wilson, Leslie   258, 267, 272, *273,* 299, 300
Winser, C.L.   244–46, 248, 258, 300
Wood, G.M.   198
Woodcock, John   440
Woodfull, Gwen   180
Woodfull, W.M.   23, 29, 33, 34, 44, 70, 77, 92–97, 108, 112, 114, 117, 118, 128, 131, 134, 147–50, 152, 158, 160, 164, 165, 167, 172, 173, 177–89, 191–96, 198, *199,* 201, 202, 206, 209–11, 213, 214, 216–18, 220, 221, 228, 237, 239, 240, 242, 245, 248, 249, 253, 261, 274, 276–79, 281, 286, 287, 289–91, 293, 294, 299–302, *307,* 309, 314–16, 322–25, 329, 332, 333, *338,* 351, 366, 368, 373, 381, 383–85, 398, 403, *404,* 406–08, 413, 414, 422, 424, 438, 440, 441, 447
Woodhead, F.G.   24
Woolley, F.E.   20, 48, 235
Wooster, Bertie   386
Worrall, J.   36, 113, 154, 156, 162
Worrell, F.M.M.   420, 439
Wright, Alby   173
Wright, V.   306
Wyatt, R.E.S.   10, 31, 51, 52, 55, 56, 61–66, 71, 88, 89, 94, 97, 103, 111, *115,* 120, 126–28, 141, 144, 153–55, 164, 174–76, 201, 204, 205, 210, 211, 214, 263, 264, 269, 272, 284, 285, 287, 288, 304, 306, 308, 312, 317, 319, 321, 325–28, 333, 336, 342, 343, 349, 358, 387, 388, 391, 400, 403, 404, 408, 410, 411, 432–34, 442

Yabba (S.H. Gascoigne)   115, 120, 127, *128,* 308
Yates, Dr   234
Young, Walter   245, 246